T0215540

Mastering MySQL Administration

High Availability, Security, Performance, and Efficiency

Y V Ravi Kumar
Arun Kumar Samayam
Naresh Kumar Miryala

Foreword by Christopher G. Chelliah,
SVP Technology, Oracle Corporation

Apress®

Mastering MySQL Administration: High Availability, Security, Performance, and Efficiency

Y V Ravi Kumar
Irving, TX, USA

Arun Kumar Samayam
Dallas, TX, USA

Naresh Kumar Miryala
Tracy, CA, USA

ISBN-13 (pbk): 979-8-8688-0251-5
https://doi.org/10.1007/979-8-8688-0252-2

ISBN-13 (electronic): 979-8-8688-0252-2

Managing Director, Apress Media LLC: Welmoed Spahr
Acquisitions Editor: Shaul Elson
Development Editor: Laura Berendson
Project Manager: Gryffin Winkler

Cover image by TJ Fitzsimmons on Unsplash (https://unsplash.com)

Distributed to the book trade worldwide by Springer Science+Business Media LLC, 1 New York Plaza, Suite 4600, New York, NY 10004. Phone 1-800-SPRINGER, fax (201) 348-4505, e-mail orders-ny@springer-sbm. com, or visit www.springeronline.com. Apress Media, LLC is a California LLC and the sole member (owner) is Springer Science + Business Media Finance Inc (SSBM Finance Inc). SSBM Finance Inc is a **Delaware** corporation.

For information on translations, please e-mail booktranslations@springernature.com; for reprint, paperback, or audio rights, please e-mail bookpermissions@springernature.com.

Apress titles may be purchased in bulk for academic, corporate, or promotional use. eBook versions and licenses are also available for most titles. For more information, reference our Print and eBook Bulk Sales web page at http://www.apress.com/bulk-sales.

Any source code or other supplementary material referenced by the author in this book is available to readers on the Github repository. For more detailed information, please visit https://www.apress.com/gp/services/source-code.

Paper in this product is recyclable

Table of Contents

About the Authors

 **Y V Ravi Kumar** is an Extraordinary Ability (EB1-A) Einstein Visa recipient from the United States, an Oracle Certified Master, a co-author, a mentor, a technical blogger, a frequent speaker at international conferences, and a technical reviewer. He is TOGAF certified, has published 100+ technical articles, and is an Oracle Open/cloud speaker (x4). He is an IEEE Senior Member with 26+ years of multinational leadership experience in the United States, Seychelles, and India in banking, financial services, and insurance (BFSI) verticals.

Ravi Kumar has co-authored four books: *Oracle Database Upgrade and Migration Methods, Oracle High Availability, Disaster Recovery, and Cloud Services, Oracle GoldenGate with MicroServices,* and *Oracle Global Data Services for Mission-Critical Systems.* And he served as technical reviewer on five books: *Oracle 19c AutoUpgrade Best Practices, Oracle Autonomous Database in Enterprise Architecture, End-to-End Observability with Grafana, Maximum Availability Architecture (MAA) with Oracle GoldenGate MicroServices in HUB Architecture,* and *The Cloud Computing Journey: Design and Deploy Resilient and Secure Multi-cloud Systems with Practical Guidance.*

Ravi Kumar is an Oracle Certified Professional (OCP) in Oracle 8i, 9i, 10g, 11g, 12c, and 19c, and he is also an Oracle Certified Expert (OCE) in Oracle GoldenGate, RAC, Performance Tuning, Oracle Cloud Infrastructure, Terraform, and Oracle Engineered Systems (Exadata, ZDLRA, and ODA), as well as certified in Oracle Security and Maximum Availability Architecture (MAA). He is certified in PostgreSQL, MySQL, and MySQL Heatwave platforms as well. He is also multi-cloud Architect certified (OCI, AWS, and GCP).

Ravi Kumar has published over 100+ Oracle technology articles, including on Oracle Technology Network (OTN) in ORAWORLD Magazine, on UKOUG in OTech Magazine, and on Redgate. He has spoken four times at Oracle Cloud/OpenWorld (OOW) in Las Vegas/San Francisco, United States. And over the last decade, he has delivered technical sessions at Oracle user groups: IOUG, OCW, NYOUG, AUSOUG, AIOUG, UTOUG, SOUG, DOUG, and Quest Oracle Community.

Ravi Kumar has designed data centers and implemented mission-critical databases for core banking solutions for two major central banks in the world. He has also received the honor of being named "TOP Data Architecture voice" from LinkedIn. And Oracle Corporation has published his profile on their OCM list and in their Spotlight on Success stories.

Arun Kumar Samayam is an experienced technology architect and a seasoned database professional with a profound passion for innovation. He is a Principal Cloud Solutions Architect in the Cloud and Engineering platform team at a global airline company. He is part of the Cloud Center of Excellence (CCoE) team, where he drives the organization's cloud transformation journey through cloud governance practices.

Before this role, Arun worked as a Product Technical leader for the Enterprise Database services team, where he had the opportunity to develop and hone his technical proficiency through engineering, managing, and supporting multiple database platforms like Oracle, MySQL, PostgreSQL, SQL server, and MongoDB. In addition, Arun is a multi-cloud certified professional, and his industry knowledge and experience have made him a speaker at prestigious events like Oracle OpenWorld, where he shared his insights and expertise on database products.

Naresh Kumar Miryala is a highly experienced engineering leader with nearly 20 years of industry experience and a strong background in cloud, platform engineering, and artificial intelligence. He has been leading high-performing cloud data platform teams in his current role at Meta Platforms, Inc. He has a proven track record of cloud transformations, infrastructure implementation, database management, ERP solutions, and DevOps deployments.

His expertise spans multiple domains such as database systems, large-scale back-end infrastructure, security, multi-cloud deployments, cloud infrastructure, DevOps, and artificial intelligence.

Naresh has contributed to esteemed organizations such as the Oracle Corporation and Computer Sciences Corporation, where he played a pivotal role in migrating and implementing enterprise technologies for Fortune 500 companies across the globe. His impact spans various industries, including pharmaceuticals, retail, banking, and gold mining companies worldwide.

Naresh's experience in cloud migrations, particularly involving relational, open source, and NoSQL databases, middleware, and applications, has granted him a comprehensive understanding of multifaceted technical and business challenges in the modern world and developing innovative solutions across the industry to solve large-scale data transformation and security problems using artificial intelligence.

He is a frequent speaker at international conferences and an active member of IEEE, IOUG, OATUG, and AIM Leaders Council, and holds certifications as a professional in cloud, database, and artificial intelligence platforms.

About the Technical Reviewer

Sri Ram Phani Kiran Kadambari is a seasoned IT Professional with 14 Years of expertise in Diverse Domains, Database Management, and Cloud Solutions. He has a relentless passion for databases, extensive expertise in Oracle (including Engineered Systems), Postgres, MySQL with heatwave, and a deep understanding of cloud platforms like OCI and AWS. His technical expertise helped various clients migrate their existing databases and mission-critical applications to cloud environments.

Phani's career commenced as a Database trainer, with a commitment and passion to knowledge-sharing, he has trained and mentored countless individuals shape their career as database engineers.

He is a Certified Oracle GoldenGate implementation specialist (for data replication and integration), Certified associate - PostgreSQL 13, gained multiple certifications in Oracle Cloud Infrastructure and AI.

Acknowledgments

I am grateful to God who gave us all the strength, courage, perseverance, and patience in this sincere and honest attempt of knowledge sharing. This fifth book of mine as a co-author would not have been possible without the following people: Shri Yenugula Venkata Pathi and Smt. Yenugula Krishna Kumari, my parents who instilled in me good thoughts and values, and Shri B. Suresh Kamath (founder of LaserSoft and Patterns Cognitive), my mentor, my guru, my strength, and my guide, who has inspired me for the last 26 years.

B. Suresh Kamath is an immensely talented and technically sound individual. He taught me how to be well read with no compromises. He led by example in being content yet hungry of knowledge. He motivated me to go that extra mile in attempting and experimenting with newer technologies/environments and in being regularly out of my comfort zone.

Anitha Ravi Kumar, my wife, was immensely tolerant with me. "Behind every successful man, there is a good woman," as they say. I believe she is the embodiment of this well-known belief. Special thanks to my daughter, Sai Hansika, and my son, Sai Theeraz, for giving me time to write a fifth book in the last six years.

I would like to thank Phani Kadambari for accepting to be the technical reviewer for this book. Special thanks to Shaul Elson, Gryffin Winkler, Celestin Suresh John, and Laura Berendson at Apress for giving me the opportunity to write my fourth book for Apress. Thank you to the readers for picking up this book. We have attempted to be as simple and straightforward as possible when sharing this knowledge, and we truly believe that it will help you to steadily deep dive into various interesting concepts and procedures.

I would like to express my gratitude to the complete Oracle MySQL/MySQL Heatwave team – Nipun Agarwal, Sastry Vedantam, Nick Mader, Perside Foster, Selena Paola Sánchez Maldonado, Ravish Patel, Satish Senapathy (PMP), Runit Malik, Dale Dasker, and Catherine Sheng Schrimsher.

I would also like to thank the complete Infolob Global team – Vijay Cherukuri, Tim Fox, Josh Turnbull, Nivas Nadimpalli, Satyendra Pasalapudi, and Senthil Prabu.

ACKNOWLEDGMENTS

My heartfelt gratitude to Binay Rath, Mohit Singh (my RAC guru), Rohit Rahi, Mariami Kupatadze, Lucia Hustatyova, Bal Mukund Sharma, and all of my LaserSoft colleagues.

—Venkata Ravi Kumar Yenugula

To my loving parents, thank you for teaching me the importance of hard work and perseverance. Your guidance and encouragement have molded me into the person I am today. I am forever grateful for your love and support.

To my dear wife Aruna, thank you for being my partner in every sense of the word. You are my rock, my confidante, and my best friend. I am constantly amazed by your strength, your intelligence, and your unwavering dedication to our family.

To my children Yojith and Yuvan, you both bring so much joy and laughter into our lives. You are the reason I strive to be a better person every day. I hope that this book will inspire you to chase your dreams and never give up on what you believe in.

To my cherished friends, thank you for being there for me through thick and thin. Your friendship means the world to me, and I am honored to have such amazing people in my life.

I would like to express my deepest gratitude to my co-authors Venkata Ravi Kumar Yenugula and Arun Kumar Samayam and technical reviewer Phani Kadambari for all their constant support and guidance.

Thanks to the Apress team for continuous support in making this book a reality.

—Naresh Kumar Miryala

I am forever grateful for the love and support of those who have shaped my life's journey and made this book possible.

To my parents, Ram Kumar and Lakshmi Sarada, for nurturing me with unwavering love, kindness, and the freedom to pursue my passions. Your encouragement and support have fueled my determination to chase my dreams.

To my beloved wife, Ramya, and our daughter, Iraa, whose boundless love and unwavering support have been the bedrock of strength in my life. Your belief in me has propelled me forward, urging me to strive for excellence in all endeavors.

To my mentor, Venkata Ravi Kumar Yenugula, for recognizing my potential, guiding me through challenges, and opening doors to new opportunities. Your wisdom, dedication, and noble pursuit of knowledge have been a constant source of inspiration.

To my co-authors, Venkata Ravi Kumar Yenugula and Naresh Kumar Miryala, along with technical reviewer Phani Kadambari, your dedication, collaboration, and unwavering support throughout the writing process have enriched this book and made it truly special.

I extend heartfelt gratitude to my entire database team at American Airlines – Sravan Akinapally, Andrea Shovlain, Ankur Goel, Prantik Baruah, Aravind Dhakshanamoorthy, Deepak Mani, Mohan Anney, and Sarju Patel – for their assistance and technical mentorship.

To my esteemed leadership team at American Airlines – Rasika Vaidya, Echo Jiang, Vijay Premkumar, Kalyan Kalyanaraman, Kevin Wehde, and Arvind Thoothukuri – for their unwavering support and encouragement on this journey.

To my Apress publishing team – Shaul Elson, Gryffin Winkler, Celestin Suresh John, and Laura Berendson – thank you for entrusting me with the opportunity to pen my debut book. I am confident that this book will serve as a practical guide for many aspiring database technologists.

Thank you all for being integral parts of this incredible journey.

—Arun Kumar Samayam

Foreword

The rapid ascension from Predictive (classic) AI to Generative AI over the last 12 months has pivoted the conversation from just GPUs to creating the models underpinning the use cases. Data fuels this ascension – whether it's to build the model in the first place or fine tuning or inference or retrieval augmentation.

Data is the key to monetizing AI. MySQL is anchored as and has been the most popular, open source database management system for most of the 28 years since its inception. It underpins a large number of cloud-native and traditional enterprises and is a key ingredient in today's modern data platform frameworks.

Security, performance, and resilience of data have always been a key tenet across the 30 years I've been working in this business. This is even more important today as organizations scramble to feed the AI momentum.

This book is aimed at developers, database administrators, and engineers responsible to deliver a robust data platform for an organization. Congratulations to YV Ravi Kumar, Arun Kumar Samayam, and Naresh Kumar Miryala in putting together a soup-to-nuts coverage of topics from the start of installation to the internals of the engine and all aspects of partitioning, clustering, performance, scale, and resiliency.

Christopher G. Chelliah
SVP Technology, Oracle Corporation

CHAPTER 1

MySQL Installation and Upgrade

Introduction

MySQL is one of the most popular open source relational database management systems developed, distributed, and supported by Oracle Corporation.

So what is an open source relational database management system? To understand this better, let us focus on the keywords "open source," "relational," and "database management systems."

A structured collection of data is called a database. We need a system that provides computing capabilities to add, access, and process data stored in a database. That system is called a database management system.

Installing MySQL 8.0

Before installing MySQL, it is important to understand some of the key outliers mentioned here:

- Which platform to run MySQL on? Windows, Linux, macOS, etc.

- Which release to install? Development or General Availability (GA)

- Which distribution to install?

MySQL is supported on various platforms, including Oracle Linux/Red Hat/CentOS, Oracle Solaris, Canonical (Ubuntu), SUSE, Debian, Microsoft Windows server, Microsoft Windows, and Apple. New platform support is continuously being added, and you can always refer to the latest information by visiting the MySQL website (`www.mysql.com/support/supportedplatforms/database.html`).

1

© Y V Ravi Kumar, Arun Kumar Samayam, Naresh Kumar Miryala 2024
Y V Ravi Kumar et al., *Mastering MySQL Administration*, https://doi.org/10.1007/979-8-8688-0252-2_1

Once you determine the platform for your MySQL installation, you need to choose which distribution to install. There are many MySQL versions available, and they are in different distribution formats. Before choosing the distribution and the version to install, let us understand the naming convention, which is a key decision driver.

MySQL naming convention combines release names that consist of three numbers and an optional suffix. Since this book covers installing MySQL 8.0.34 on two platforms, Linux (binary and YUM) and Microsoft Windows, let us use this as an example:

- 8 = Major version number

- 0 = Minor version number

- 34 = Version number within the release series*

*Release series = Major version + Minor version

Similarly, for MySQL 5.7, the Major version number is 5, and the Minor version number is 7, which makes the release series 5.7.

The release series depicts a stable feature set. The release names can include an optional suffix that indicates the stability level of the release. Here are the possible suffixes:

- dmr = Development Milestone Release (DMR)

- rc = Release Candidate (RC)

So what is the difference between the two? MySQL development follows a milestone model where a subset of thoroughly tested features are included in each milestone. And there could be times when a few features may be removed based on community feedback and hence considered to be of pre-production quality and have more chances of encountering bugs. All of these constitute a DMR. Meanwhile, RC versions are considered stable as they go through all of MySQL's internal testing. The focus is more on fixing bugs to stabilize earlier features, although a few new features might be introduced.

There could be versions with no suffixes, indicating a General Availability (GA) or a production release. GA releases are expected to be reliable, stable, free of critical bugs, and suited for running mission-critical production workloads.

Table 1-1. *Oracle Premier Support Model*

Oracle Premier Support: 5 years of General Availability		
MySQL 5.5	Dec 2010	Dec 2015
MySQL 5.6	Feb 2013	Feb 2018
MySQL 5.7	Oct 2015	Oct 2020
MySQL 8.0	Apr 2018	Apr 2025

Table 1-2. *Oracle Extended Support Model*

Oracle Extended Support: 3 years after Premier Support (8 years after GA)		
MySQL 5.5	Dec 2015	Dec 2018
MySQL 5.6	Feb 2018	Feb 2021
MySQL 5.7	Oct 2020	Oct 2023
MySQL 8.0	Apr 2025	Apr 2026

Table 1-3. *Oracle Sustaining Support Model*

Oracle Sustaining Support
Lifetime

Please refer to Oracle Support for the latest updates as these dates are subject to change.

Installing MySQL 8.0 on Linux Using the YUM Repository

We have several different ways to install MySQL on Linux. For example, **yum install** for RPM-based systems like Oracle Linux, CentOS, RHEL, and Fedora and **apt-get** for APT-based systems like Ubuntu and Debian.

Let us install MySQL on Linux using the MySQL YUM repository.

1. Go to MySQL YUM repository page (https://dev.mysql.com/
   downloads/repo/yum/) to download the release package. For
   example, on Enterprise Linux 7 (EL7)–based systems:

```
[root@mysql-a mysql_binaries]# wget https://dev.mysql.com/get/
mysql80-community-release-el7-10.noarch.rpm
--2023-10-09 22:05:52--  https://dev.mysql.com/get/mysql80-
community-release-el7-10.noarch.rpm
Resolving dev.mysql.com (dev.mysql.com)... 23.4.59.106,
2600:1404:6400:1691::2e31, 2600:1404:6400:1697::2e31
Connecting to dev.mysql.com (dev.mysql.com)|23.4.59.106|:443...
connected.
HTTP request sent, awaiting response... 302 Moved Temporarily
Location: https://repo.mysql.com//mysql80-community-release-
el7-10.noarch.rpm [following]
--2023-10-09 22:05:53--  https://repo.mysql.com//mysql80-
community-release-el7-10.noarch.rpm
Resolving repo.mysql.com (repo.mysql.com)... 104.90.18.174,
2600:1404:6400:158b::1d68, 2600:1404:6400:1582::1d68
Connecting to repo.mysql.com (repo.mysql.com)|104.90.18.174|:443...
connected.
HTTP request sent, awaiting response... 200 OK
Length: 11472 (11K) [application/x-redhat-package-manager]
Saving to: 'mysql80-community-release-el7-10.noarch.rpm'

100%[================================>] 11,472      --.-K/s   in 0s

2023-10-09 22:05:53 (390 MB/s) - 'mysql80-community-release-
el7-10.noarch.rpm' saved [11472/11472]

[root@mysql-a mysql_binaries]# ls -ltr
total 12
-rw-r--r-- 1 root root 11472 Aug 23 12:38 mysql80-community-
release-el7-10.noarch.rpm

[root@mysql-a mysql_binaries]#
```

2. Install MySQL.

[root@mysql-s mysql_binaries]# sudo yum install mysql80-community-release-el7-9.noarch.rpm

```
Loaded plugins: fastestmirror
Examining mysql80-community-release-el7-9.noarch.rpm: mysql80-
community-release-el7-9.noarch
Marking mysql80-community-release-el7-9.noarch.rpm to be installed
Resolving Dependencies
--> Running transaction check
---> Package mysql80-community-release.noarch 0:el7-9 will be
installed
--> Finished Dependency Resolution
```

Dependencies Resolved

```
============================================================
Package                   Arch    Version
Repository                          Size
============================================================
Installing:
mysql80-community-release  noarch  el7-9
/mysql80-community-release-el7-9.noarch  12 k

Transaction Summary
============================================================
Install  1 Package

Total size: 12 k
Installed size: 12 k
Is this ok [y/d/N]: y
Downloading packages:
Running transaction check
Running transaction test
Transaction test succeeded
Running transaction
Warning: RPMDB altered outside of yum.
  Installing : mysql80-community-release-el7-9.noarch         1/1
  Verifying  : mysql80-community-release-el7-9.noarch         1/1
```

Installed:
  mysql80-community-release.noarch 0:el7-9

Complete!
[root@mysql-s mysql_binaries]# yum repolist enabled | grep
"mysql.*-community.*"
mysql-connectors-community/x86_64 MySQL Connectors Community   227
mysql-tools-community/x86_64   MySQL Tools Community   100
mysql80-community/x86_64   MySQL 8.0 Community Server   425
[root@mysql-s mysql_binaries]# sudo yum install mysql-
community-server
Loaded plugins: fastestmirror
Loading mirror speeds from cached hostfile
 * base: ohioix.mm.fcix.net
 * epel: veronanetworks.mm.fcix.net
 * extras: mirror.team-cymru.com
 * updates: veronanetworks.mm.fcix.net
Resolving Dependencies
--> Running transaction check
---> Package mysql-community-server.x86_64 0:8.0.34-1.el7 will be
installed
--> Processing Dependency: mysql-community-common(x86-64) =
8.0.34-1.el7 for package: mysql-community-server-8.0.34-1.
el7.x86_64
--> Processing Dependency: mysql-community-icu-data-files =
8.0.34-1.el7 for package: mysql-community-server-8.0.34-1.
el7.x86_64
--> Processing Dependency: mysql-community-client(x86-64) >=
8.0.11 for package: mysql-community-server-8.0.34-1.el7.x86_64
--> Processing Dependency: net-tools for package: mysql-community-
server-8.0.34-1.el7.x86_64
--> Running transaction check
---> Package mysql-community-client.x86_64 0:8.0.34-1.el7 will be
installed
--> Processing Dependency: mysql-community-client-plugins = 8.0.
34-1.el7 for package: mysql-community-client-8.0.34-1.el7.x86_64

```
--> Processing Dependency: mysql-community-libs(x86-64) >= 8.0.11
for package: mysql-community-client-8.0.34-1.el7.x86_64
---> Package mysql-community-common.x86_64 0:8.0.34-1.el7 will be
installed
---> Package mysql-community-icu-data-files.x86_64 0:8.0.34-1.el7
will be installed
---> Package net-tools.x86_64 0:2.0-0.25.20131004git.el7 will be
installed
--> Running transaction check
---> Package mariadb-libs.x86_64 1:5.5.65-1.el7 will be obsoleted
--> Processing Dependency: libmysqlclient.so.18()(64bit) for
package: 2:postfix-2.10.1-9.el7.x86_64
--> Processing Dependency: libmysqlclient.so.18(libmysqlclient_18)
(64bit) for package: 2:postfix-2.10.1-9.el7.x86_64
---> Package mysql-community-client-plugins.x86_64 0:8.0.34-1.el7
will be installed
---> Package mysql-community-libs.x86_64 0:8.0.34-1.el7 will be
obsoleting
--> Running transaction check
---> Package mysql-community-libs-compat.x86_64 0:8.0.34-1.el7
will be obsoleting
--> Finished Dependency Resolution
```

Dependencies Resolved

```
===========================================================
 Package                        Arch      Version
Repository          Size
===========================================================
Installing:
 mysql-community-libs             x86_64  8.0.34-1.el7
mysql80-community    1.5 M
     replacing  mariadb-libs.x86_64 1:5.5.65-1.el7
 mysql-community-libs-compat      x86_64   .0.34-1.el7
mysql80-community    669 k
     replacing  mariadb-libs.x86_64 1:5.5.65-1.el7
 mysql-community-server           x86_64  8.0.34-1.el7
mysql80-community      64 M
```

7

```
Installing for dependencies:
 mysql-community-client          x86_64  8.0.34-1.el7
mysql80-community       16 M
  mysql-community-client-plugins  x86_64  8.0.34-1.el7
mysql80-community      3.6 M
  mysql-community-common          x86_64  8.0.34-1.el7
mysql80-community      666 k
  mysql-community-icu-data-files  x86_64   8.0.34-1.el7
mysql80-community      2.2 M
  net-tools                       x86_64  2.0-0.25.20131004git.el7
base                    306 k

Transaction Summary
================================================================
Install  3 Packages (+5 Dependent packages)

Total download size: 89 M
Is this ok [y/d/N]: y
Downloading packages:
warning: /var/cache/yum/x86_64/7/mysql80-community/packages/mysql-
community-client-plugins-8.0.34-1.el7.x86_64.rpm: Header V4 RSA/
SHA256 Signature, key ID 3a79bd29: NOKEY
Public key for mysql-community-client-plugins-8.0.34-1.el7.x86_64.
rpm is not installed
(1/8): mysql-community-client-plugins-8.0.34-1.el7.x86_64.rpm
| 3.6 MB  00:00:01
(2/8): mysql-community-common-8.0.34-1.el7.x86_64.rpm
| 666 kB  00:00:00
(3/8): mysql-community-icu-data-files-8.0.34-1.el7.x86_64.rpm
| 2.2 MB  00:00:00
(4/8): mysql-community-libs-8.0.34-1.el7.x86_64.rpm
| 1.5 MB  00:00:00
(5/8): mysql-community-libs-compat-8.0.34-1.el7.x86_64.rpm
| 669 kB  00:00:00
(6/8): net-tools-2.0-0.25.20131004git.el7.x86_64.rpm
| 306 kB  00:00:01
```

(7/8): mysql-community-client-8.0.34-1.el7.x86_64.rpm
| 16 MB   00:00:07
(8/8): mysql-community-server-8.0.34-1.el7.x86_64.rpm
| 64 MB   00:00:17

Total
4.3 MB/s | 89 MB   00:00:20
Retrieving key from file:///etc/pki/rpm-gpg/RPM-GPG-KEY-mysql-2022
Importing GPG key 0x3A79BD29:
 Userid   : "MySQL Release Engineering <mysql-build@oss.
oracle.com>"
 Fingerprint: 859b e8d7 c586 f538 430b 19c2 467b 942d 3a79 bd29
 Package   : mysql80-community-release-el7-9.noarch (@/mysql80-
community-release-el7-9.noarch)
 From   : /etc/pki/rpm-gpg/RPM-GPG-KEY-mysql-2022
Is this ok [y/N]: y
Retrieving key from file:///etc/pki/rpm-gpg/RPM-GPG-KEY-mysql
Importing GPG key 0x5072E1F5:
 Userid   : "MySQL Release Engineering <mysql-build@oss.
oracle.com>"
 Fingerprint: a4a9 4068 76fc bd3c 4567 70c8 8c71 8d3b 5072 e1f5
 Package   : mysql80-community-release-el7-9.noarch (@/mysql80-
community-release-el7-9.noarch)
 From   : /etc/pki/rpm-gpg/RPM-GPG-KEY-mysql
Is this ok [y/N]: y
Running transaction check
Running transaction test
Transaction test succeeded
Running transaction
Installing : mysql-community-common-8.0.34-1.el7.x86_64   1/9
Installing : mysql-community-client-plugins-8.0.34-1.el7.x86_64 2/9
Installing : mysql-community-libs-8.0.34-1.el7.x86_64   3/9
Installing : mysql-community-client-8.0.34-1.el7.x86_64   4/9
Installing : net-tools-2.0-0.25.20131004git.el7.x86_64   5/9
Installing : mysql-community-icu-data-files-8.0.34-1.el7.x86_64 6/9
Installing : mysql-community-server-8.0.34-1.el7.x86_64   7/9

```
Installing : mysql-community-libs-compat-8.0.34-1.el7.x86_64    8/9
Erasing    : 1:mariadb-libs-5.5.65-1.el7.x86_64                  9/9
Verifying  : mysql-community-server-8.0.34-1.el7.x86_64         1/9
Verifying  : mysql-community-client-plugins-8.0.34-1.el7.x86_64 2/9
Verifying  : mysql-community-icu-data-files-8.0.34-1.el7.x86_64 3/9
Verifying  : net-tools-2.0-0.25.20131004git.el7.x86_64          4/9
Verifying  : mysql-community-common-8.0.34-1.el7.x86_64         5/9
Verifying  : mysql-community-libs-8.0.34-1.el7.x86_64           6/9
Verifying  : mysql-community-libs-compat-8.0.34-1.el7.x86_64    7/9
Verifying  : mysql-community-client-8.0.34-1.el7.x86_64         8/9
Verifying  : 1:mariadb-libs-5.5.65-1.el7.x86_64                 9/9
```

Installed:
  **mysql-community-libs.x86_64 0:8.0.34-1.el7   mysql-community-
  libs-compat.x86_64 0:8.0.34-1.el7**
  mysql-community-server.x86_64 0:8.0.34-1.el7

Dependency Installed:
  **mysql-community-client.x86_64 0:8.0.34-1.el7 mysql-community-
  client-plugins.x86_64 0:8.0.34-1.el7**
  **mysql-community-common.x86_64 0:8.0.34-1.el7 mysql-community-
  icu-data-files.x86_64 0:8.0.34-1.el7**
  net-tools.x86_64 0:2.0-0.25.20131004git.el7

Replaced:
  mariadb-libs.x86_64 1:5.5.65-1.el7

Complete!

The following are RPM packages for the MySQL community
edition that were installed.

- **mysql-community-client**: MySQL client applications
  and tools

- **mysql-community-client-plugins**: MySQL client
  application shared plug-ins

- **mysql-community-common**: Common files for server and
  client libraries

- **mysql-community-devel**: MySQL database client development header files and libraries

- **msyql-community-embedded-compat**: MySQL server as an embedded library for applications using version 18 of the library

- **mysql-community-icu-data-files**: ICU data files MySQL package for MySQL regular expressions

- **mysql-community-libs**: MySQL database client application shared libraries

- **mysql-community-libs-compat**: Previous MySQL installation shared compatibility libraries

- **mysql-community-server**: MySQL database server and related tools

- **mysql-community-server-debug**: MySQL debug server and plug-in libraries

- **mysql-community-test**: MySQL server test suite

- **mysql-community**: Source code RPM

3. Start the MySQL server and check status.

```
[root@mysql-s mysql_binaries]# systemctl start mysqld
[root@mysql-s mysql_binaries]# ps -ef|grep mysqld
mysql   1598      1  5 22:40 ?          00:00:01 /usr/sbin/mysqld
root    1643   1338  0 22:41 pts/0      00:00:00 grep --color=auto
                                                 mysqld
[root@mysql-s mysql_binaries]# systemctl status mysqld
```

When starting the MySQL server, the following happens:

- Server is initialized.

- Secure Sockets Layer (SSL) certificate and key files are generated in the data directory.

11

- The password validation component, validate_password, is installed and enabled.

- A superuser account 'root'@localhost is created with a temporary password set and stored in the error log file.

4. Get the temporary password generated and change it to a new password.

```
[root@mysql-s mysql_binaries]# sudo grep 'temporary password'
/var/log/mysqld.log
2023-07-29T03:40:53.483206Z 6 [Note] [MY-010454] [Server] A
temporary password is generated for root@localhost: bK,Pbr83sb)z

[root@mysql-s mysql_binaries]# mysql -uroot -p
Enter password:

mysql> ALTER USER 'root'@'localhost' IDENTIFIED BY
'WElcome_1234#';
Query OK, 0 rows affected (0.00 sec)
```

5. Verify the MySQL configuration file. The default file name is /etc/my.cnf.

```
[root@mysql-s mysql_binaries]# cat /etc/my.cnf
# For advice on how to change settings please see
# http://dev.mysql.com/doc/refman/8.0/en/server-configuration-
defaults.html
[mysqld]
-- output truncated for better visibility

datadir=/var/lib/mysql
socket=/var/lib/mysql/mysql.sock

log-error=/var/log/mysqld.log
pid-file=/var/run/mysqld/mysqld.pid

[root@mysql-s mysql_binaries]#
```

The default data directory is /var/lib/mysql.

6. The installation also creates a user named **mysql** and a group
    name **mysql** on the system. Switch the user to **mysql** and validate
    the version.

```
[root@mysql-s mysql]# su - mysql
-bash-4.2$ mysql -u root -p
Enter password:
mysql> exit

[root@mysql-s mysql]# mysqladmin -u root -p version
Enter password:
mysqladmin  Ver 8.0.34 for Linux on x86_64 (MySQL Community
Server - GPL)
Copyright (c) 2000, 2023, Oracle and/or its affiliates.

Oracle is a registered trademark of Oracle Corporation and/or its
affiliates. Other names may be trademarks of their respective
owners.

Server version          8.0.34
Protocol version        10
Connection              Localhost via UNIX socket
UNIX socket             /var/lib/mysql/mysql.sock
Uptime:                 32 min 55 sec

Threads: 2  Questions: 7  Slow queries: 0  Opens: 130   Flush
tables: 3  Open tables: 46  Queries per second avg: 0.003
```

7. Run **mysql_secure_installation** to improve the security of the
    MySQL installation. This step allows you to set a password for
    root accounts, removes anonymous users, disallows remote root
    logins, drops the default database **test**, removes privileges to it,
    and reloads privilege tables.

```
[root@mysql-s mysql]# mysql_secure_installation

Securing the MySQL server deployment.
Enter password for user root:
```

VALIDATE PASSWORD COMPONENT can be used to test passwords and improve security. It checks the strength of password and allows the users to set only those passwords which are secure enough. Would you like to setup VALIDATE PASSWORD component?

Press y|Y for Yes, any other key for No: y
The password validation component is not available. Proceeding with the further steps without the component.
Using existing password for root.
Change the password for root ? ((Press y|Y for Yes, any other key for No) : n

 ... skipping.
By default, a MySQL installation has an anonymous user, allowing anyone to log into MySQL without having to have a user account created for them. This is intended only for testing, and to make the installation go a bit smoother. You should remove them before moving into a production environment.

Remove anonymous users? (Press y|Y for Yes, any other key for No) : y
Success.

Normally, root should only be allowed to connect from 'localhost'. This ensures that someone cannot guess at the root password from the network.

Disallow root login remotely? (Press y|Y for Yes, any other key for No) : y
Success.

By default, MySQL comes with a database named 'test' that anyone can access. This is also intended only for testing, and should be removed before moving into a production environment.

```
Remove test database and access to it? (Press y|Y for Yes, any
other key for No) : y
 - Dropping test database...
Success.

 - Removing privileges on test database...
Success.

Reloading the privilege tables will ensure that all changes
made so far will take effect immediately.

Reload privilege tables now? (Press y|Y for Yes, any other key
for No) : y
Success.

All done!
[root@mysql-s mysql]#
```

Installing MySQL 8.0 on Linux Using Binary Distribution

1. Check the OS version and type.

   ```
   [root@mysql-a ~]# date
   Sat Aug 19 14:10:29 CDT 2023
   [root@mysql-a ~]# uname -a
   Linux mysql-a 3.10.0-1127.el7.x86_64 #1 SMP Tue Mar 31 23:36:51
   UTC 2020 x86_64 x86_64 x86_64 GNU/Linux
   [root@mysql-a ~]# cat /etc/redhat-release
   CentOS Linux release 7.8.2003 (Core)
   ```

   Notice that my Linux version is 7.x.

2. Create a **mysql** user and group.

   ```
   [root@mysql-a ~]# mkdir -p /home/mysql
   [root@mysql-a ~]# groupadd mysql
   [root@mysql-a ~]# useradd -r -g mysql -d /home/mysql -s /bin/
                     bash mysql
   ```

15

```
[root@mysql-a ~]# chown -R mysql /home/mysql/
[root@mysql-a ~]# chgrp -R mysql /home/mysql/
[root@mysql-a ~]# ls -ltr /home
total 0
drwx------. 2 admin admin 62 Sep 26  2022 admin
drwxr-xr-x  2 mysql mysql  6 Sep  1 10:30 mysql
```

3. Download MySQL for Red Hat Enterprise Linux version 7, x86, 64-bit by visiting https://dev.mysql.com/downloads/mysql/.

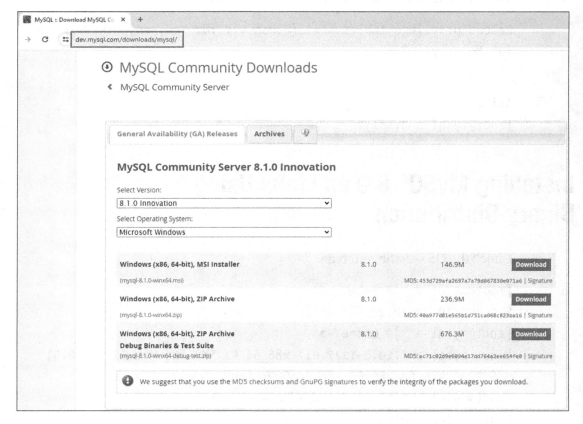

Figure 1-1. *MySQL Community Downloads page*

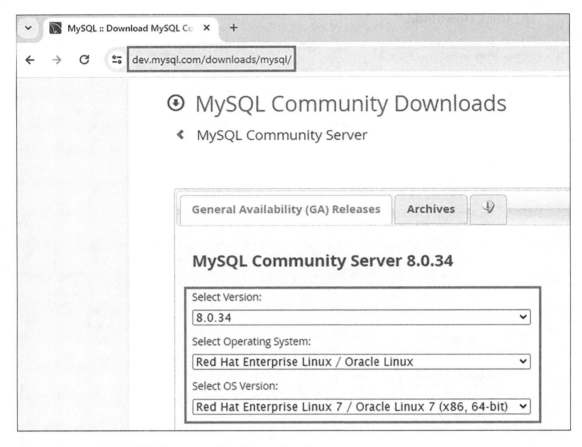

Figure 1-2. *MySQL Community Downloads page*

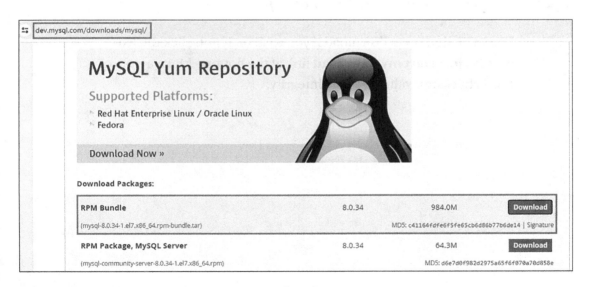

Figure 1-3. *MySQL Community Downloads page*

Click **Download**.

Figure 1-4. *MySQL Community Downloads page*

Log in or **sign up** to download if you wish to. If not, click the **No thanks, just start my download** link at the bottom. Make a note of MD5 checksum value to verify integrity.

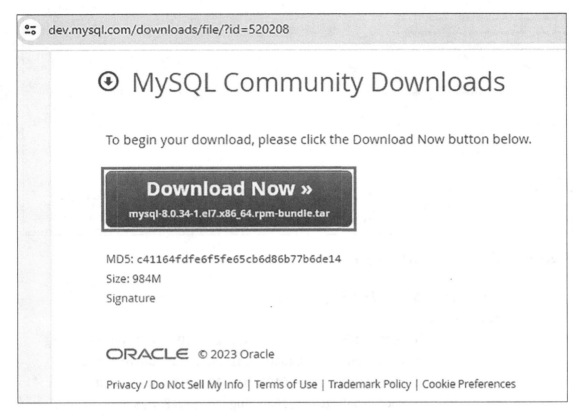

Figure 1-5. *MySQL Community Downloads page*

4. Copy the downloaded RPM bundle to the server using *WinSCP* or other file transfer methods or software.

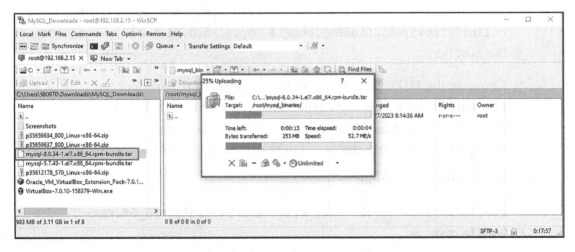

Figure 1-6. *WinSCP transfer page*

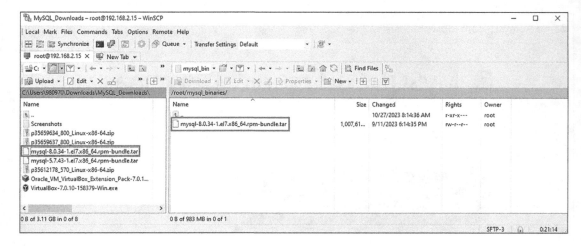

Figure 1-7. *WinSCP transfer page*

```
[root@mysql-a ~]# ls -ltr
total 1013568
-rw-------. 1 root root          1582 Sep 26   2022 anaconda-ks.cfg
-rw-r--r--  1 root root       3046107 Mar 20 09:18 download.1
-rw-r--r--  1 root root       3046107 Mar 20 09:18 download
-rw-r--r--  1 root root    1031792640 Aug 19 14:28 mysql-8.0.34-1.
el7.x86_64.rpm-bundle.tar
[root@mysql-a ~]#
```

5. Check file integrity using **MD5SUM**.

    ```
    [root@mysql-a ~]# md5sum mysql-8.0.34-1.el7.x86_64.rpm-bundle.tar
    c41164fdfe6f5fe65cb6d86b77b6de14  mysql-8.0.34-1.el7.x86_64.rpm-
    bundle.tar
    ```

    Compare the MD5SUM value with the one from step 3 to check file
    integrity. If we see a different value, there is a high chance that the
    file is either corrupted or not correctly downloaded. Download the
    file again and copy it to the server until the value matches.

6. Extract the RPM bundle.

    ```
    [root@mysql-a ~]# tar -xvf mysql-8.0.34-1.el7.x86_64.rpm-
    bundle.tar
    mysql-community-client-8.0.34-1.el7.x86_64.rpm
    ```

```
mysql-community-client-plugins-8.0.34-1.el7.x86_64.rpm
mysql-community-common-8.0.34-1.el7.x86_64.rpm
mysql-community-debuginfo-8.0.34-1.el7.x86_64.rpm
mysql-community-devel-8.0.34-1.el7.x86_64.rpm
mysql-community-embedded-compat-8.0.34-1.el7.x86_64.rpm
mysql-community-icu-data-files-8.0.34-1.el7.x86_64.rpm
mysql-community-libs-8.0.34-1.el7.x86_64.rpm
mysql-community-libs-compat-8.0.34-1.el7.x86_64.rpm
mysql-community-server-8.0.34-1.el7.x86_64.rpm
mysql-community-server-debug-8.0.34-1.el7.x86_64.rpm
mysql-community-test-8.0.34-1.el7.x86_64.rpm
[root@mysql-a ~]#
[root@mysql-a ~]# ls -ltr
total 2021192
-rw-------. 1 root root        1582 Sep 26  2022 anaconda-ks.cfg
-rw-r--r--  1 root root     3046107 Mar 20 09:18 download.1
-rw-r--r--  1 root root     3046107 Mar 20 09:18 download
-rw-r--r--  1 7155 31415  16755300 Jun 24 22:06 mysql-community-
client-8.0.34-1.el7.x86_64.rpm
-rw-r--r--  1 7155 31415   3745824 Jun 24 22:06 mysql-community-
client-plugins-8.0.34-1.el7.x86_64.rpm
-rw-r--r--  1 7155 31415    681724 Jun 24 22:06 mysql-community-
common-8.0.34-1.el7.x86_64.rpm
-rw-r--r--  1 7155 31415 528347988 Jun 24 22:07 mysql-community-
debuginfo-8.0.34-1.el7.x86_64.rpm
-rw-r--r--  1 7155 31415   1947800 Jun 24 22:07 mysql-community-
devel-8.0.34-1.el7.x86_64.rpm
-rw-r--r--  1 7155 31415   4217912 Jun 24 22:07 mysql-community-
embedded-compat-8.0.34-1.el7.x86_64.rpm
-rw-r--r--  1 7155 31415   2344364 Jun 24 22:07 mysql-community-
icu-data-files-8.0.34-1.el7.x86_64.rpm
-rw-r--r--  1 7155 31415   1563264 Jun 24 22:07 mysql-community-
libs-8.0.34-1.el7.x86_64.rpm
-rw-r--r--  1 7155 31415    685312 Jun 24 22:08 mysql-community-
libs-compat-8.0.34-1.el7.x86_64.rpm
```

```
-rw-r--r--  1 7155 31415   67410132 Jun 24 22:08 mysql-community-
server-8.0.34-1.el7.x86_64.rpm
-rw-r--r--  1 7155 31415   25637968 Jun 24 22:08 mysql-community-
server-debug-8.0.34-1.el7.x86_64.rpm
-rw-r--r--  1 7155 31415   378442676 Jun 24 22:10 mysql-community-
test-8.0.34-1.el7.x86_64.rpm
-rw-r--r--  1 root root   1031792640 Aug 19 14:28 mysql-8.0.34-1.
el7.x86_64.rpm-bundle.tar
[root@mysql-a ~]#
```

7. Install MySQL using **YUM**.

```
[root@mysql-a ~]# sudo yum install mysql-community-
{server,client,client-plugins,icu-data-files,common,libs}-*
Loaded plugins: fastestmirror
Examining mysql-community-server-8.0.34-1.el7.x86_64.rpm: mysql-
community-server-8.0.34-1.el7.x86_64
Marking mysql-community-server-8.0.34-1.el7.x86_64.rpm to be
installed
Examining mysql-community-server-debug-8.0.34-1.el7.x86_64.rpm:
mysql-community-server-debug-8.0.34-1.el7.x86_64
Marking mysql-community-server-debug-8.0.34-1.el7.x86_64.rpm to be
installed
Examining mysql-community-client-8.0.34-1.el7.x86_64.rpm: mysql-
community-client-8.0.34-1.el7.x86_64

  -- output truncated for better visibility

Installed:
  mysql-community-client.x86_64 0:8.0.34-1.el7
  mysql-community-client-plugins.x86_64 0:8.0.34-1.el7
  mysql-community-common.x86_64 0:8.0.34-1.el7
  mysql-community-icu-data-files.x86_64 0:8.0.34-1.el7
  mysql-community-libs.x86_64 0:8.0.34-1.el7
  mysql-community-libs-compat.x86_64 0:8.0.34-1.el7
  mysql-community-server.x86_64 0:8.0.34-1.el7
  mysql-community-server-debug.x86_64 0:8.0.34-1.el7
```

```
Dependency Installed:
  net-tools.x86_64 0:2.0-0.25.20131004git.el7
```

Complete!
```
[root@mysql-a ~]#
```

8. **Start** MySQL. Please note MySQL is NOT automatically started after the installation.

```
[root@mysql-a ~]# systemctl start mysqld
[root@mysql-a ~]# ps -ef|grep mysql
mysql      1442     1  7 15:03 ?        00:00:01 /usr/sbin/mysqld
root       1488  1235  0 15:03 pts/0    00:00:00 grep --color=
                                                 auto mysql
[root@mysql-a ~]# systemctl enable mysqld
```

9. Get the **temporary password** generated to be used as part of the MySQL secure install.

```
[root@mysql-a ~]# sudo grep 'temporary password' /var/log/
mysqld.log
2023-08-19T20:03:35.705456Z 6 [Note] [MY-010454] [Server] A
temporary password is generated for root@localhost: c>;?jG(Ps8LO
```

10. **Secure** the MySQL installation by running **mysql_secure_installation**. Enter the password from step 9 when asked for the password for the root user.

```
[root@mysql-a ~]# mysql_secure_installation

Securing the MySQL server deployment.
Enter password for user root: <Enter temporary password
from step 9>
The existing password for the user account root has expired.
Please set a new password.

New password:
Re-enter new password:

-- output truncated for better visibility
```

Reloading the privilege tables will ensure that all changes made so far will take effect immediately.

Reload privilege tables now? (Press y|Y for Yes, any other key for No) : Y
Success.

All done!
[root@mysql-a ~]#

11. **Switch** to **mysql** user and **log in** with the new root password to the MySQL instance, and validate.

```
[root@mysql-a ~]# su - mysql
Last login: Thu Aug 31 14:23:39 CDT 2023 on pts/0
-bash-4.2$ whoami
mysql
-bash-4.2$ mysql -u root -p
Enter password:
mysql> show databases;
+--------------------+
| Database           |
+--------------------+
| information_schema |
| mysql              |
| performance_schema |
| sys                |
+--------------------+
4 rows in set (0.00 sec)
```

12. Explore the MySQL configuration file located at **/etc/my.cnf**, which is the default location.

```
[root@mysql-a ~]# cat /etc/my.cnf
# For advice on how to change settings please see
# http://dev.mysql.com/doc/refman/8.0/en/server-configuration-
defaults.html
[mysqld]
```

-- output truncated for better visibility

```
datadir=/var/lib/mysql
socket=/var/lib/mysql/mysql.sock

log-error=/var/log/mysqld.log
pid-file=/var/run/mysqld/mysqld.pid
[root@mysql-a ~]#
```

13. Explore the default directories to understand the file locations, for example, **datadir**.

```
[root@mysql-a ~]# cd /var/lib/mysql
[root@mysql-a mysql]# ls -ltr
total 90568
-rw-r----- 1 mysql mysql         56 Aug 29 19:54 auto.cnf
-rw-r----- 1 mysql mysql    8585216 Aug 29 19:54 #ib_16384_1.dblwr
drwxr-x--- 2 mysql mysql       8192 Aug 29 19:54 performance_schema
-rw------- 1 mysql mysql       1680 Aug 29 19:54 ca-key.pem
-rw-r--r-- 1 mysql mysql       1112 Aug 29 19:54 ca.pem
-rw------- 1 mysql mysql       1676 Aug 29 19:54 server-key.pem
-rw-r--r-- 1 mysql mysql       1112 Aug 29 19:54 server-cert.pem
-rw------- 1 mysql mysql       1676 Aug 29 19:54 client-key.pem
-rw-r--r-- 1 mysql mysql       1112 Aug 29 19:54 client-cert.pem
-rw------- 1 mysql mysql       1676 Aug 29 19:54 private_key.pem
-rw-r--r-- 1 mysql mysql        452 Aug 29 19:54 public_key.pem
drwxr-x--- 2 mysql mysql        143 Aug 29 19:54 mysql
drwxr-x--- 2 mysql mysql         28 Aug 29 19:54 sys
-rw-r----- 1 mysql mysql       5959 Aug 29 19:54 ib_buffer_pool
drwxr-x--- 2 mysql mysql        187 Aug 29 19:54 #innodb_temp
-rw-r----- 1 mysql mysql         16 Aug 29 19:54 binlog.index
-rw------- 1 mysql mysql          5 Aug 29 19:54 mysql.sock.lock
srwxrwxrwx 1 mysql mysql          0 Aug 29 19:54 mysql.sock
drwxr-x--- 2 mysql mysql       4096 Aug 29 19:54 #innodb_redo
-rw-r----- 1 mysql mysql   12582912 Aug 29 19:54 ibtmp1
-rw-r----- 1 mysql mysql   25165824 Aug 29 19:56 mysql.ibd
-rw-r----- 1 mysql mysql   16777216 Aug 29 19:57 undo_001
```

```
-rw-r----- 1 mysql mysql 16777216 Aug 29 19:57 undo_002
-rw-r----- 1 mysql mysql   196608 Aug 29 19:57 #ib_16384_0.dblwr
-rw-r----- 1 mysql mysql 12582912 Aug 29 19:57 ibdata1
-rw-r----- 1 mysql mysql      825 Aug 29 19:57 binlog.000001
[root@mysql-a mysql]#
```

Here is the MySQL installation layout for your reference:

- **Client programs and scripts**: /usr/bin

- **mysqld server**: /usr/sbin

- **Configuration file**: /etc/my.cnf

- **Data directory**: /var/lib/mysql

- **Error log file**: /var/log/mysqld.log

- **Secure_file_priv**: /var/lib/mysql-files

- **System V init script**: /etc/init.d/mysql

- **Systemd service**: mysqld

- **Pid file**: /var/run/mysql/mysqld.pid

- **Socket**: /var/lib/mysql/mysql.sock

- **Keyring directory**: /vara/lib/mysql-keyring

- **Unix manual pages**: /usr/share/man

- **Include files**: /usr/include/mysql

- **Libraries**: /usr/lib/mysql

- **Miscellaneous support files**: /usr/share/mysql

14. Edit the **/etc/sudoers** file to include **mysql** user so we can run root commands using **sudo** without switching to root user.

```
[root@mysql-a ~]# passwd mysql
Changing password for user mysql.
New password:
Retype new password:
passwd: all authentication tokens updated successfully.
```

```
[root@mysql-a ~]# su - mysql
Last login: Thu Aug 31 14:31:57 CDT 2023 on pts/0

-bash-4.2$ sudo systemctl stop mysqld
```

We trust you have received the usual lecture from the local System
Administrator. It usually boils down to these three things:

```
    #1) Respect the privacy of others.
    #2) Think before you type.
    #3) With great power comes great responsibility.

[sudo] password for mysql:

-bash-4.2$ sudo systemctl start mysqld
```

The **/etc/sudoers** file should be like the one shown in Figure 1-8 with **mysql** user.

```
## Sudoers allows particular users to run various commands as
## the root user, without needing the root password.
##
## Examples are provided at the bottom of the file for collections
## of related commands, which can then be delegated out to particular
## users or groups.
##
## This file must be edited with the 'visudo' command.

## Host Aliases
## Groups of machines. You may prefer to use hostnames (perhaps using
## wildcards for entire domains) or IP addresses instead.
# Host_Alias     FILESERVERS = fs1, fs2
# Host_Alias     MAILSERVERS = smtp, smtp2

## User Aliases
## These aren't often necessary, as you can use regular groups
## (ie, from files, LDAP, NIS, etc) in this file - just use %groupname
## rather than USERALIAS
# User_Alias ADMINS = jsmith, mikem

mysql    ALL=(ALL)    ALL

## Command Aliases
## These are groups of related commands...
```

Figure 1-8. */etc/sudoers file*

Installing MySQL 8.0 on Linux Using Binary Distribution – Commercial Edition

1. Check OS version and type.

   ```
   [root@mysql-a ~]# date
   Sat Aug 19 14:10:29 CDT 2023
   ```

   ```
   [root@mysql-a ~]# uname -a
   Linux mysql-a 3.10.0-1127.el7.x86_64 #1 SMP Tue Mar 31 23:36:51
   UTC 2020 x86_64 x86_64 x86_64 GNU/Linux
   ```

   ```
   [root@mysql-a ~]# cat /etc/redhat-release
   CentOS Linux release 7.8.2003 (Core)
   ```

   Notice that the Linux version is *7.x*.

2. Create a **mysql** user and group.

   ```
   [root@mysql-a ~]# mkdir -p /home/mysql
   [root@mysql-a ~]# groupadd mysql
   [root@mysql-a ~]# useradd -r -g mysql -d /home/mysql -s /bin/
   bash mysql
   [root@mysql-a ~]# chown -R mysql /home/mysql/
   [root@mysql-a ~]# chgrp -R mysql /home/mysql/
   [root@mysql-a ~]# ls -ltr /home
   total 0
   drwx------. 2 admin admin 62 Sep 26  2022 admin
   drwxr-xr-x  2 mysql mysql  6 Sep  1 10:30 mysql
   ```

3. Log in to My Oracle Support by visiting https://support.oracle.
   com/portal/ and clicking **Login to My Oracle Support**. If you
   don't have an account, create one.

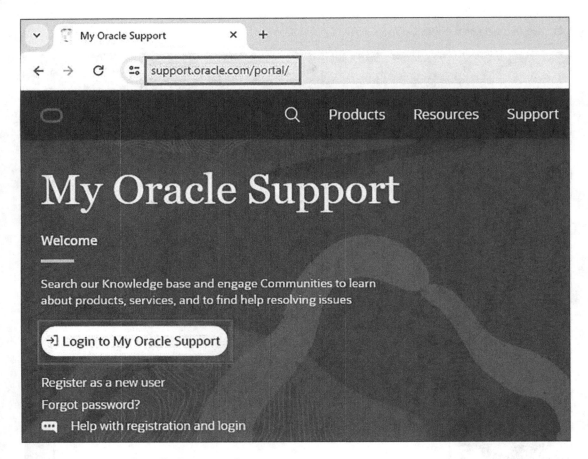

Figure 1-9. *My Oracle Support home page*

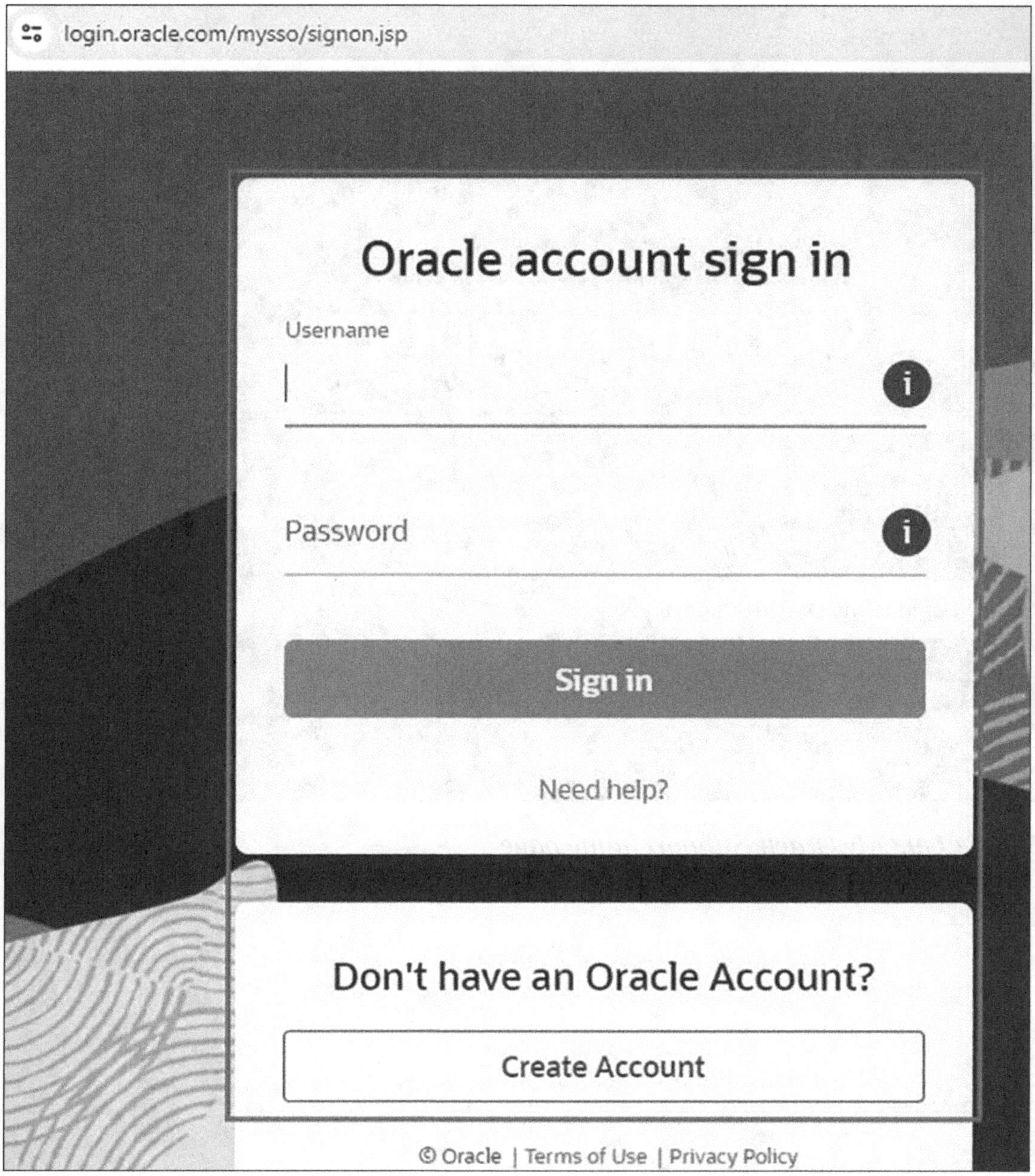

Figure 1-10. *My Oracle Support login page*

4. Go to **Patches & Updates**, select **Product or Family**, select
    Product as **MySQL Server**, and select **Release** as **MySQL Server
    5.7** and **Platform** as **Linux x86-64.** Click **Search.**

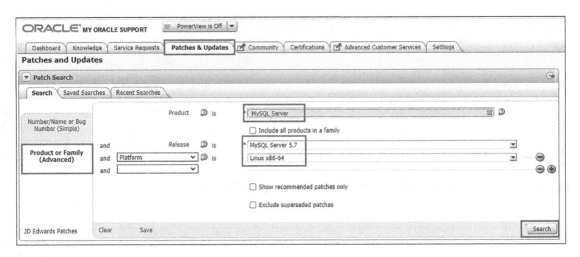

Figure 1-11. *My Oracle Support Patches and Updates page*

5. Select **Patch# 3562178**. Click on the patch and proceed with the
    download.

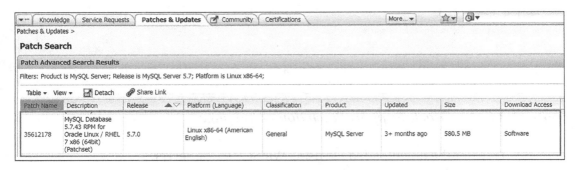

Figure 1-12. *My Oracle Support Patches download page*

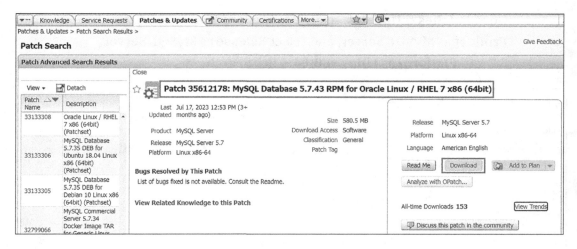

Figure 1-13. *My Oracle Support Patch download page*

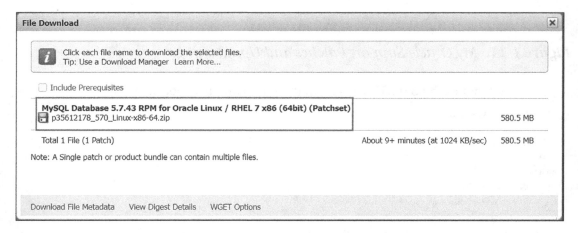

Figure 1-14. *My Oracle Support Patch download page*

6. Transfer the downloaded file using WinSCP to the server.

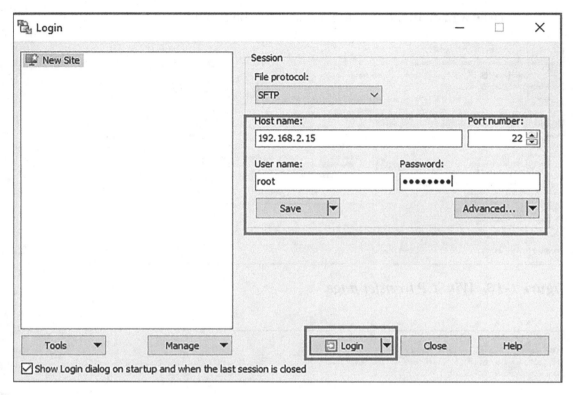

Figure 1-15. *WinSCP login page*

Create a directory named **/mysql_binaries** on the server to copy the
binaries like this one:

```
[root@mysql-a ~]# pwd
/root
[root@mysql-a ~]# mkdir -p mysql_binaries
[root@mysql-a ~]# chmod 775 mysql_binaries/
[root@mysql-a ~]# ls -ltr
total 5956
-rw-------. 1 root root    1582 Sep 26  2022
anaconda-ks.cfg
-rw-r--r--  1 root root 3046107 Mar 20 09:18 download.1
-rw-r--r--  1 root root 3046107 Mar 20 09:18 download
drwxrwxr-x  2 root root       6 Aug 30 21:30 mysql_binaries
```

Drag and drop the file onto the server to be copied.

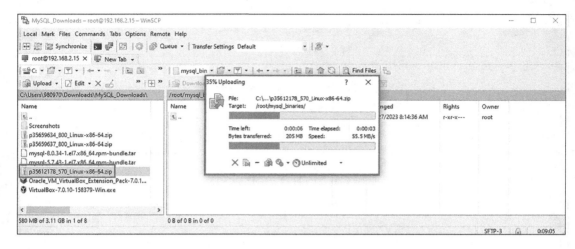

Figure 1-16. *WinSCP transfer page*

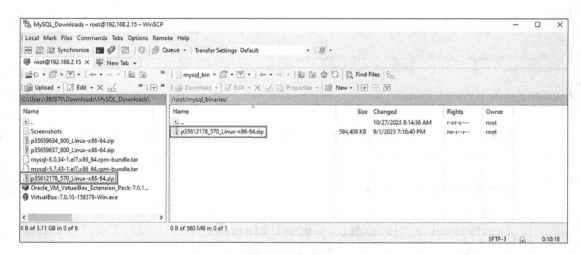

Figure 1-17. *WinSCP transfer page*

```
[root@mysql-a ~]# cd mysql_binaries/
[root@mysql-a mysql_binaries]# ls -ltr
total 594408
-rw-r--r-- 1 root root 608673108 Aug 30 20:52 p35612178_570_
Linux-x86-64.zip
[root@mysql-a mysql_binaries]#
```

7. **Unzip** the patch that was copied.

```
[root@mysql-a mysql_binaries]# unzip p35612178_570_
Linux-x86-64.zip
Archive:   p35612178_570_Linux-x86-64.zip
 extracting: mysql-commercial-client-5.7.43-1.1.el7.x86_64.rpm
 extracting: mysql-commercial-common-5.7.43-1.1.el7.x86_64.rpm
 extracting: mysql-commercial-devel-5.7.43-1.1.el7.x86_64.rpm
 extracting: mysql-commercial-embedded-5.7.43-1.1.el7.x86_64.rpm
 extracting: mysql-commercial-embedded-compat-5.7.43-1.1.el7.
 x86_64.rpm
 extracting: mysql-commercial-embedded-devel-5.7.43-1.1.el7.
 x86_64.rpm
 extracting: mysql-commercial-libs-5.7.43-1.1.el7.x86_64.rpm
 extracting: mysql-commercial-libs-compat-5.7.43-1.1.el7.
 x86_64.rpm
 extracting: mysql-commercial-server-5.7.43-1.1.el7.x86_64.rpm
 extracting: mysql-commercial-test-5.7.43-1.1.el7.x86_64.rpm
 extracting: README.txt

[root@mysql-a mysql_binaries]# ls -ltr
total 1188832
-rw-r--r-- 1 root root  32668404 Jun 22 15:26 mysql-commercial-
client-5.7.43-1.1.el7.x86_64.rpm
-rw-r--r-- 1 root root    322504 Jun 22 15:26 mysql-commercial-
common-5.7.43-1.1.el7.x86_64.rpm
-rw-r--r-- 1 root root   4972100 Jun 22 15:26 mysql-commercial-
devel-5.7.43-1.1.el7.x86_64.rpm
-rw-r--r-- 1 root root  48588980 Jun 22 15:26 mysql-commercial-
embedded-5.7.43-1.1.el7.x86_64.rpm
-rw-r--r-- 1 root root  23320452 Jun 22 15:26 mysql-commercial-
embedded-compat-5.7.43-1.1.el7.x86_64.rpm
-rw-r--r-- 1 root root 134430212 Jun 22 15:26 mysql-commercial-
embedded-devel-5.7.43-1.1.el7.x86_64.rpm
-rw-r--r-- 1 root root   1268576 Jun 22 15:26 mysql-commercial-
libs-compat-5.7.43-1.1.el7.x86_64.rpm
```

```
-rw-r--r-- 1 root root    3093632 Jun 22 15:26 mysql-commercial-
libs-5.7.43-1.1.el7.x86_64.rpm
-rw-r--r-- 1 root root 230784576 Jun 22 15:26 mysql-commercial-
server-5.7.43-1.1.el7.x86_64.rpm
-rw-r--r-- 1 root root 129217656 Jun 22 15:27 mysql-commercial-
test-5.7.43-1.1.el7.x86_64.rpm
-rw-r--r-- 1 root root       4120 Jul 13 08:32 README.txt
-rw-r--r-- 1 root root 608673108 Aug 30 20:52 p35612178_570_
Linux-x86-64.zip
[root@mysql-a mysql_binaries]#
```

8. Install MySQL using **YUM**.

```
[root@mysql-a mysql_binaries]# sudo yum install mysql-commercial-
{server,client,client-plugins,icu-data-files,common,libs}-*
Loaded plugins: fastestmirror
Examining mysql-commercial-server-5.7.43-1.1.el7.x86_64.rpm:
mysql-commercial-server-5.7.43-1.1.el7.x86_64
Marking mysql-commercial-server-5.7.43-1.1.el7.x86_64.rpm to be
installed
Examining mysql-commercial-client-5.7.43-1.1.el7.x86_64.rpm:
mysql-commercial-client-5.7.43-1.1.el7.x86_64
Marking mysql-commercial-client-5.7.43-1.1.el7.x86_64.rpm to be
installed
Loading mirror speeds from cached hostfile

  --output truncated for better visibility
Installed:
mysql-commercial-client.x86_64 0:5.7.43-1.1.el7
mysql-commercial-common.x86_64 0:5.7.43-1.1.el7
mysql-commercial-libs.x86_64 0:5.7.43-1.1.el7
mysql-commercial-libs-compat.x86_64 0:5.7.43-1.1.el7
mysql-commercial-server.x86_64 0:5.7.43-1.1.el7

Dependency Installed:
  net-tools.x86_64 0:2.0-0.25.20131004git.el7
```

```
Complete!
[root@mysql-a mysql_binaries]#
```

9. **Start** MySQL. Please note MySQL is NOT automatically started after the installation.

```
[root@mysql-a ~]# systemctl start mysqld
[root@mysql-a ~]# systemctl status mysqld
[root@mysql-a ~]# ps -ef|grep mysql
mysql       1532      1  0 21:57 ?          00:00:00 /usr/sbin/mysqld
--daemonize --pid-file=/var/run/mysqld/mysqld.pid
root        1563   1235  0 21:58 pts/0     00:00:00 grep --color=
                                                     auto mysql
[root@mysql-a ~]# systemctl enable mysqld
```

10. Get the **temporary password** generated to be used as part of the MySQL secure install.

```
[root@mysql-a ~]# sudo grep 'temporary password' /var/log/
mysqld.log
2023-08-31T02:57:37.294210Z 1 [Note] A temporary password is
generated for root@localhost: CUWfqjd593*S
```

11. **Secure** the MySQL installation by running **mysql_secure_installation**. Enter the password from step 10 when asked for the password for the root user.

```
[root@mysql-a ~]# mysql_secure_installation

Securing the MySQL server deployment.
Enter password for user root:

-- output truncated for better visibility

Reload privilege tables now? (Press y|Y for Yes, any other key
for No) : Y
Success.

All done!
[root@mysql-a ~]#
```

12. **Switch** to **mysql** user and **log in** with the new root password to the MySQL instance, and validate.

```
[root@mysql-a ~]# su - mysql
Last login: Thu Aug 31 14:23:39 CDT 2023 on pts/0
-bash-4.2$ whoami
mysql
-bash-4.2$ mysql -u root -p
Enter password:

mysql> show databases;
+--------------------+
| Database           |
+--------------------+
| information_schema |
| mysql              |
| performance_schema |
| sys                |
+--------------------+

4 rows in set (0.00 sec)
```

13. Explore the MySQL configuration file located at **/etc/my.cnf**, which is the default location.

```
[root@mysql-a ~]# cat /etc/my.cnf
# For advice on how to change settings please see
# http://dev.mysql.com/doc/refman/5.7/en/server-configuration-
defaults.html
[mysqld]

-- output truncated for better visibility

datadir=/var/lib/mysql
socket=/var/lib/mysql/mysql.sock

# Disabling symbolic-links is recommended to prevent assorted
security risks
symbolic-links=0
```

```
log-error=/var/log/mysqld.log
pid-file=/var/run/mysqld/mysqld.pid
[root@mysql-a ~]#
```

14. Explore the default directories to understand the file locations, for example, **datadir**.

```
[root@mysql-a ~]# cd /var/lib/mysql
[root@mysql-a mysql]# ls -ltr
total 122952
-rw-r----- 1 mysql mysql 50331648 Aug 30 21:57 ib_logfile1
-rw-r----- 1 mysql mysql       56 Aug 30 21:57 auto.cnf
-rw------- 1 mysql mysql     1680 Aug 30 21:57 ca-key.pem
-rw-r--r-- 1 mysql mysql     1112 Aug 30 21:57 ca.pem
-rw------- 1 mysql mysql     1676 Aug 30 21:57 server-key.pem
-rw-r--r-- 1 mysql mysql     1112 Aug 30 21:57 server-cert.pem
-rw------- 1 mysql mysql     1680 Aug 30 21:57 client-key.pem
-rw-r--r-- 1 mysql mysql     1112 Aug 30 21:57 client-cert.pem
-rw-r--r-- 1 mysql mysql      452 Aug 30 21:57 public_key.pem
-rw------- 1 mysql mysql     1676 Aug 30 21:57 private_key.pem
drwxr-x--- 2 mysql mysql     8192 Aug 30 21:57 performance_schema
drwxr-x--- 2 mysql mysql     4096 Aug 30 21:57 mysql
drwxr-x--- 2 mysql mysql     8192 Aug 30 21:57 sys
-rw-r----- 1 mysql mysql      436 Aug 30 21:57 ib_buffer_pool
-rw------- 1 mysql mysql        5 Aug 30 21:57 mysql.sock.lock
srwxrwxrwx 1 mysql mysql        0 Aug 30 21:57 mysql.sock
-rw-r----- 1 mysql mysql 12582912 Aug 30 21:57 ibtmp1
-rw-r----- 1 mysql mysql 12582912 Aug 30 21:57 ibdata1
-rw-r----- 1 mysql mysql 50331648 Aug 30 21:57 ib_logfile0
[root@mysql-a mysql]#
```

15. Edit the /**etc**/**sudoers** file to include **mysql** user so we can run root commands using **sudo** without switching to the root user.

```
[root@mysql-a ~]# vi /etc/sudoers
```

refer to the Figure 1.18 below on how the mysql user needs to be defined

39

```
[root@mysql-a ~]# passwd mysql
Changing password for user mysql.
New password:
Retype new password:
passwd: all authentication tokens updated successfully.
[root@mysql-a ~]#
[root@mysql-a ~]# su - mysql
Last login: Thu Aug 31 14:31:57 CDT 2023 on pts/0
-bash-4.2$
-bash-4.2$ sudo systemctl stop mysqld
```

We trust you have received the usual lecture from the local System Administrator. It usually boils down to these three things:

```
    #1) Respect the privacy of others.
    #2) Think before you type.
    #3) With great power comes great responsibility.
```

[sudo] password for mysql:

```
-bash-4.2$ sudo systemctl start mysqld
```

/etc/sudoers file should be like below with mysql user.

```
## Sudoers allows particular users to run various commands as
## the root user, without needing the root password.
##
## Examples are provided at the bottom of the file for collections
## of related commands, which can then be delegated out to particular
## users or groups.
##
## This file must be edited with the 'visudo' command.

## Host Aliases
## Groups of machines. You may prefer to use hostnames (perhaps using
## wildcards for entire domains) or IP addresses instead.
# Host_Alias     FILESERVERS = fs1, fs2
# Host_Alias     MAILSERVERS = smtp, smtp2

## User Aliases
## These aren't often necessary, as you can use regular groups
## (ie, from files, LDAP, NIS, etc) in this file - just use %groupname
## rather than USERALIAS
# User_Alias ADMINS = jsmith, mikem

mysql     ALL=(ALL)    ALL

## Command Aliases
## These are groups of related commands...
```

Figure 1-18. /etc/sudoers file

Installing MySQL 8.0 on Microsoft Windows

In this section, we will learn how to install MySQL 8.0 on the Microsoft Windows platform. MySQL is available for Windows 64-bit operating systems only and requires Microsoft Visual C++ 2019 redistributable package as a prerequisite. It can be downloaded from www.microsoft.com/en-us/download.

There are different ways to install MySQL on Windows:

- MySQL Installer

- MySQL no-install ZIP archives

- MySQL Docker images

The MySQL Installer method is the recommended way to install MySQL on Windows. In this section, let us install MySQL 8.0 using the installer method.

1. Download the MySQL Installer from https://dev.mysql.com/
   downloads/installer/.

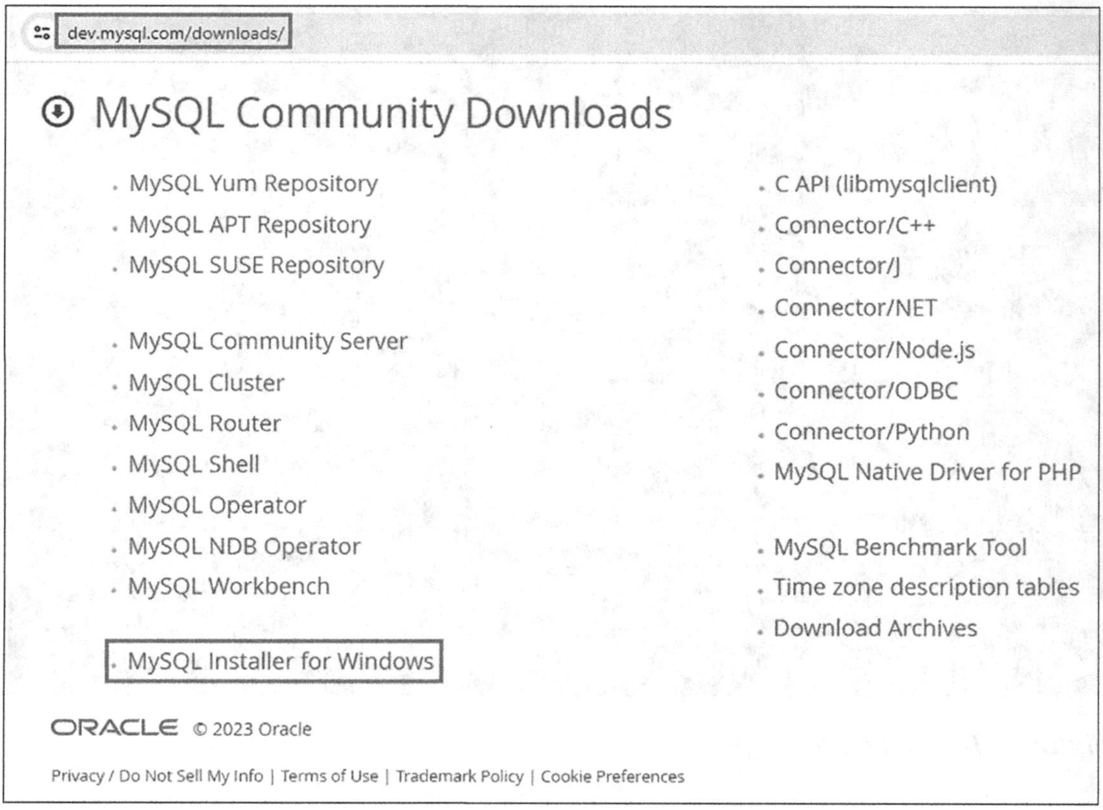

Figure 1-19. *MySQL Community Downloads page*

Figure 1-20. *MySQL Community Downloads page*

Figure 1-21. *MySQL Community Downloads page*

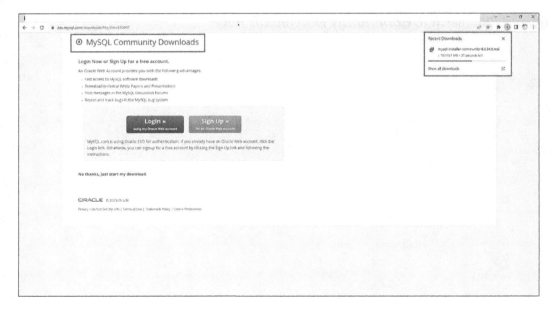

Figure 1-22. *MySQL Community Downloads page*

Launch the installer.

2. Choose the setup type based on your requirements.

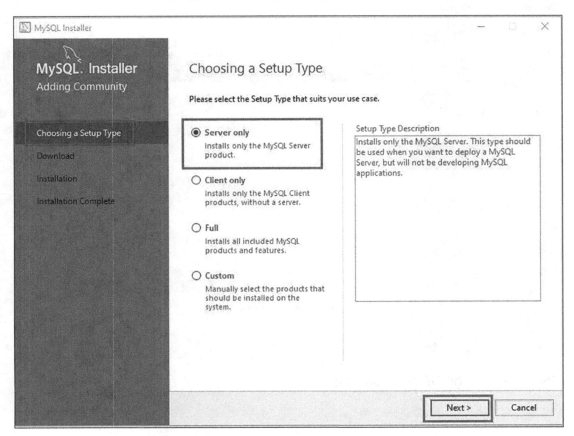

Figure 1-23. *MySQL Windows Installer*

In my example, I choose **Server only**. Click **Next**.

3. On the **Installation** tab, click **Execute** to install the packages.

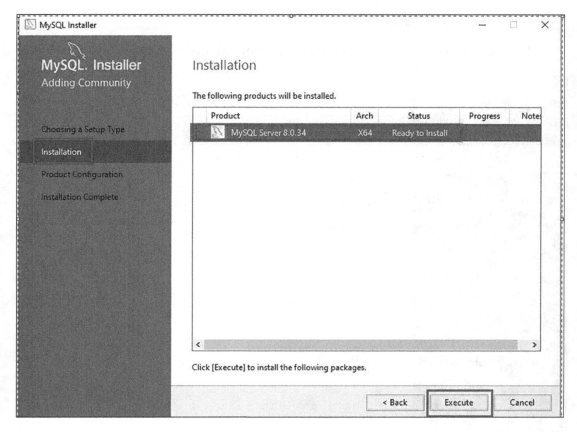

Figure 1-24. *MySQL Windows Installer*

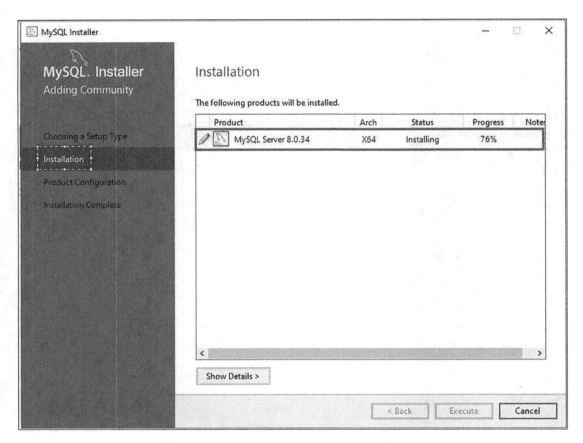

Figure 1-25. *MySQL Windows Installer*

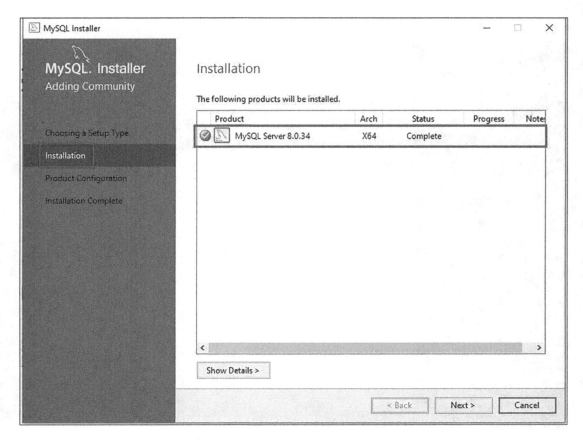

Figure 1-26. *MySQL Windows Installer*

4. On the **Product Configuration** tab, check the status and verify it is
    Ready to configure. Click **Next**.

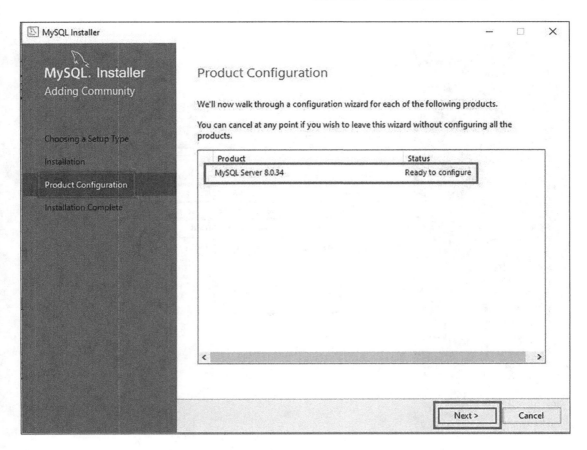

Figure 1-27. *MySQL Windows Installer*

5. On the **Type and Networking** tab, select the **Config Type**, and
    choose the **Connectivity** options like **Port** and **Named Pipe**.

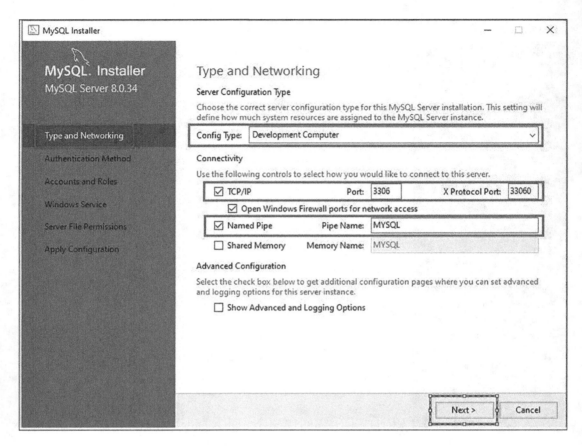

Figure 1-28. *MySQL Windows Installer*

Click **Next**.

6. On the **Named Pipe**, you can grant full or minimum access to all
    users. **Minimum access to all users** is recommended.

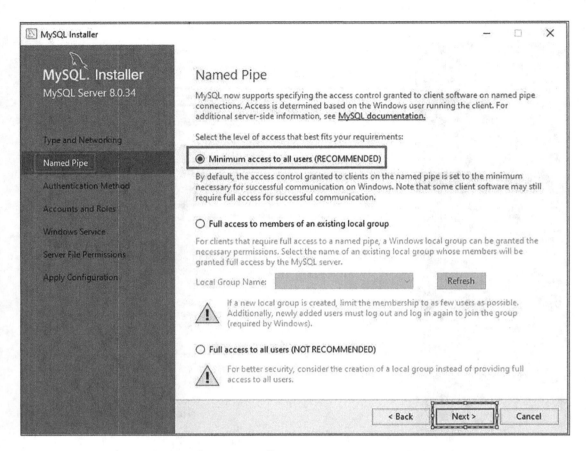

Figure 1-29. *MySQL Windows Installer*

Click **Next**.

7. On the **Authentication Method** tab, choose the method you want.

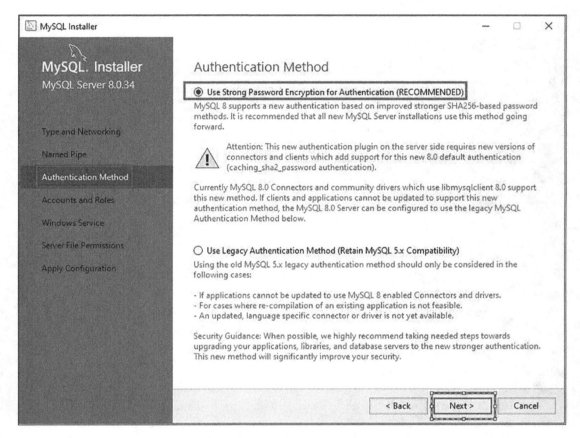

Figure 1-30. *MySQL Windows Installer*

Click **Next**.

8. On the **Accounts and Roles** tab, create the **MySQL Root Password** and add any additional MySQL user accounts needed, for example, **mysqladmin**.

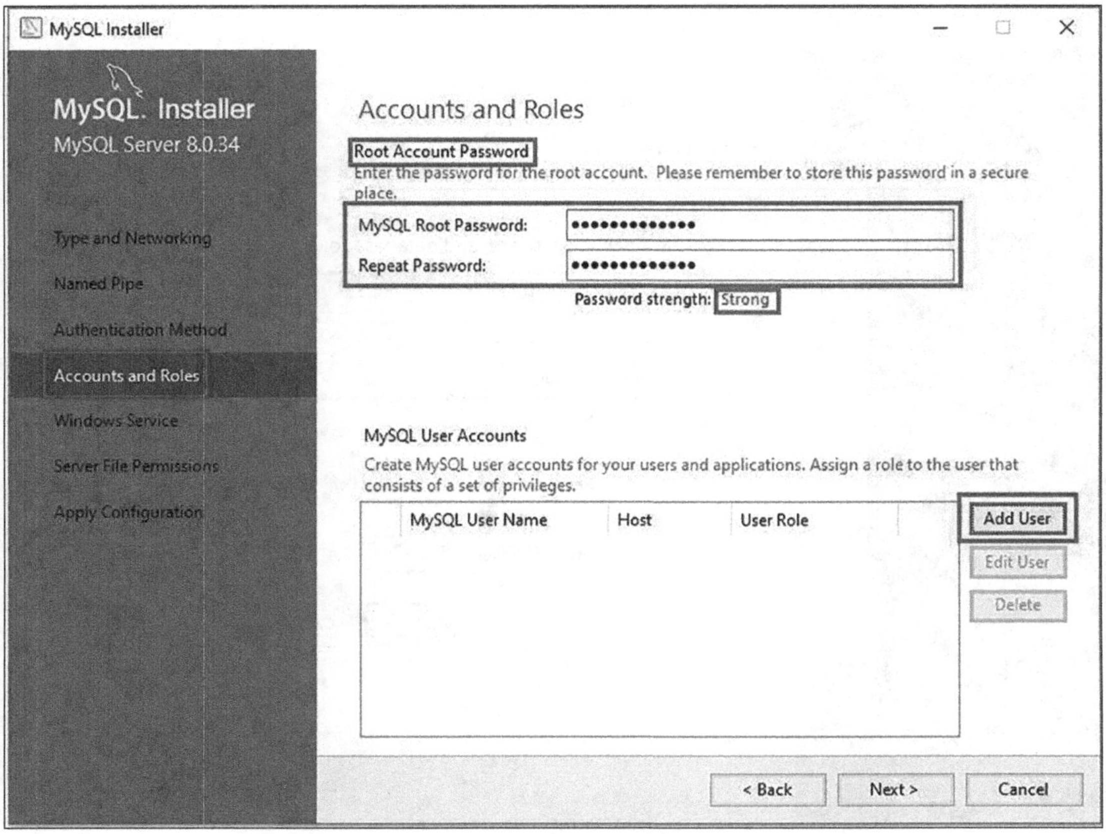

Figure 1-31. *MySQL Windows Installer*

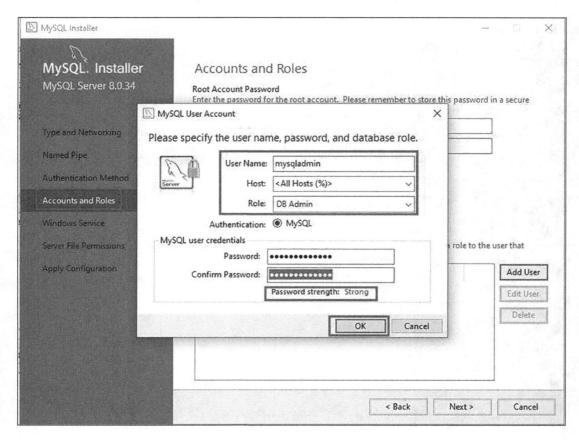

Figure 1-32. *MySQL Windows Installer*

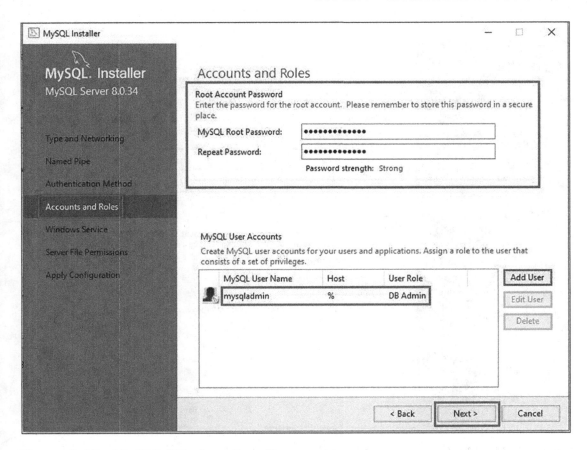

Figure 1-33. *MySQL Windows Installer*

Click **Next**.

9. On the **Windows Service** tab, choose **Configure MySQL Server as a Windows Service** and the **Windows Service Name**, and you can choose which user this Windows service you would like to run.

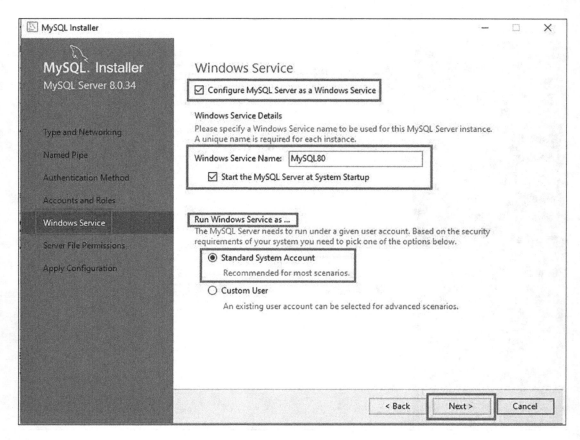

Figure 1-34. *MySQL Windows Installer*

10. On the **Server File Permissions** tab, we can choose the installer to update the permission of the files and folders located at the data directory.

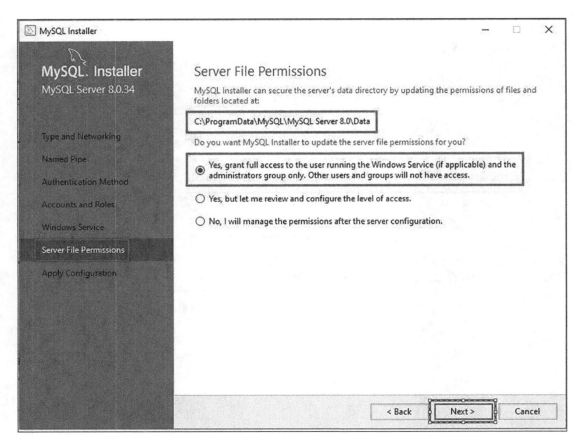

Figure 1-35. *MySQL Windows Installer*

Click **Next**.

11. On the **Apply Configuration** tab, click **Execute**.

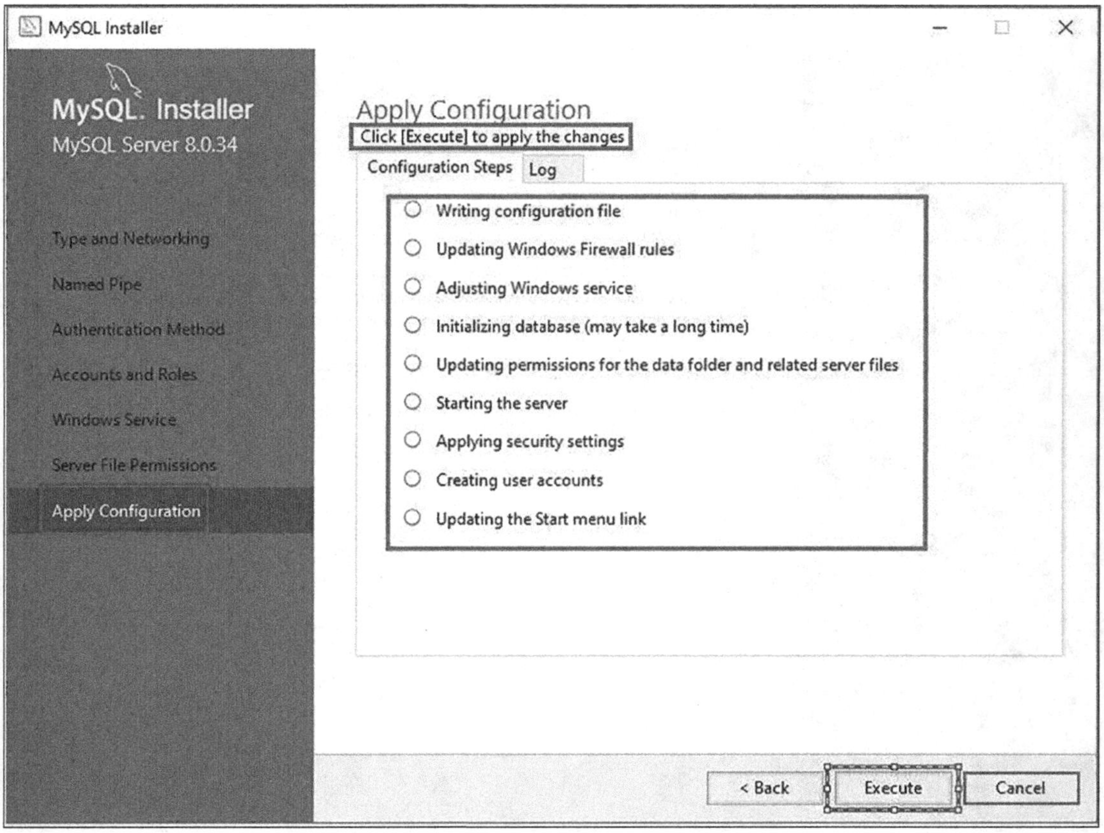

Figure 1-36. *MySQL Windows Installer*

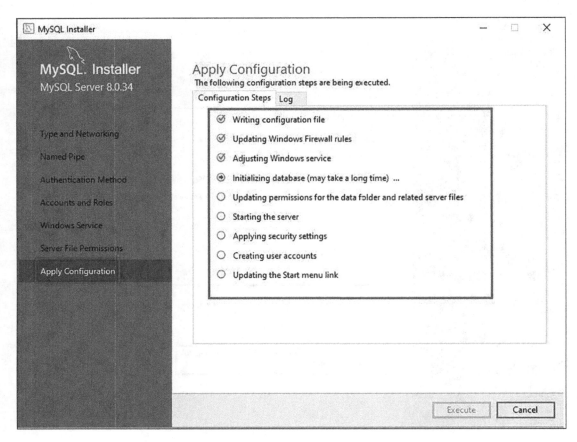

Figure 1-37. *MySQL Windows Installer*

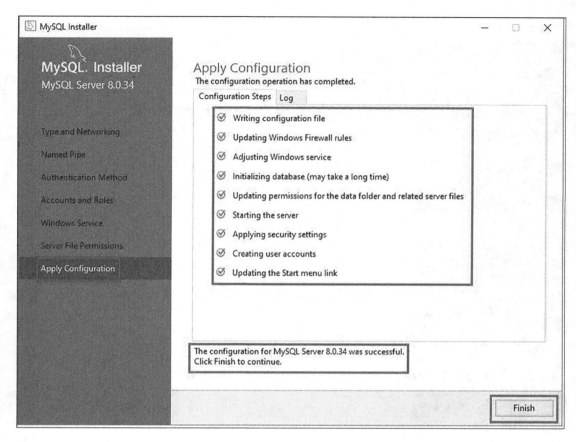

Figure 1-38. *MySQL Windows Installer*

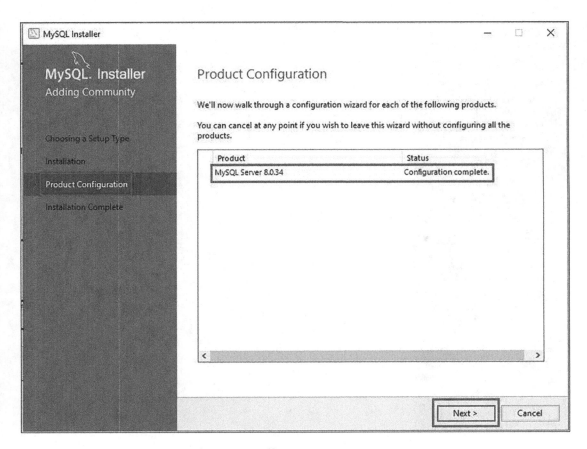

Figure 1-39. *MySQL Windows Installer*

This completes the **Product Configuration**. Click **Next.**

12. The installation is now complete, and you may choose to save the installation log if you wish. Click **Finish** to exit out of the installer.

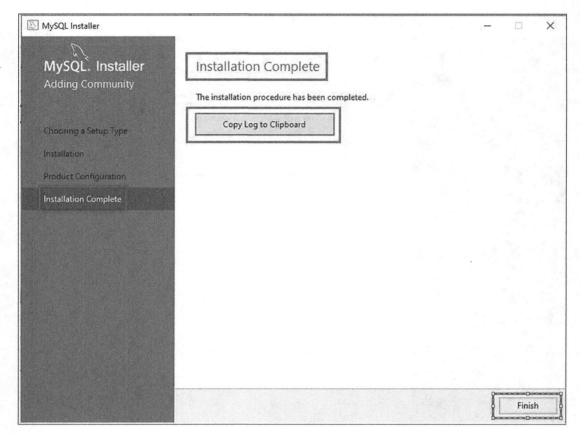

Figure 1-40. *MySQL Windows Installer*

13. Explore and validate the installation by referring to the MySQL
     installation layout for Microsoft Windows.

   - **mysqld server, client and utility programs**: bin

   - **Log files, databases**: %PROGRAMDATA%\MySQL\MySQL
     Server 8.0\

   - **Release documentation**: docs

   - **Include files**: include

   - **Libraries**: lib

   - **Miscellaneous files**: share

For example, see the following samples.

```
Command Prompt

C:\Program Files\MySQL\MySQL Server 8.0>dir
 Volume in drive C is WINDOWS
 Volume Serial Number is E85E-3596

 Directory of C:\Program Files\MySQL\MySQL Server 8.0

08/15/2023  09:17 PM    <DIR>          .
08/15/2023  09:17 PM    <DIR>          ..
08/15/2023  09:17 PM    <DIR>          bin
08/15/2023  09:17 PM    <DIR>          docs
08/15/2023  09:17 PM    <DIR>          etc
08/15/2023  09:17 PM    <DIR>          include
08/15/2023  09:17 PM    <DIR>          lib
06/22/2023  11:07 AM           279,815 LICENSE
06/22/2023  11:07 AM           114,697 LICENSE.router
06/22/2023  11:07 AM               666 README
06/22/2023  11:07 AM               679 README.router
08/15/2023  09:17 PM    <DIR>          share
               4 File(s)        395,857 bytes
               8 Dir(s)  297,360,752,640 bytes free

C:\Program Files\MySQL\MySQL Server 8.0>
```

Figure 1-41. *MySQL Windows Installation base directory*

```
Command Prompt

Directory of C:\Program Files\MySQL\MySQL Server 8.0\bin

08/15/2023  09:17 PM    <DIR>          .
08/15/2023  09:17 PM    <DIR>          ..
03/13/2023  11:32 AM            15,872 comerr64.dll
06/22/2023  12:09 PM           233,472 fido2.dll
06/22/2023  12:09 PM            54,418 fido2.lib
03/13/2023  11:32 AM           390,144 gssapi64.dll
06/22/2023  12:10 PM           797,184 harness-library.dll
06/22/2023  05:39 AM         6,422,600 ibd2sdi.exe
06/22/2023  05:39 AM         6,412,368 innochecksum.exe
12/08/2021  12:30 PM           269,312 jemalloc.dll
03/13/2023  11:32 AM            64,000 k5sprt64.dll
03/13/2023  11:32 AM         1,223,168 krb5_64.dll
03/13/2023  11:32 AM           112,128 krbcc64.dll
05/30/2023  02:31 PM         5,151,232 libcrypto-3-x64.dll
11/19/2021  08:03 PM         1,839,616 libmecab.dll
06/22/2023  11:49 AM         6,142,464 libprotobuf-debug.dll
06/22/2023  11:49 AM         1,390,592 libprotobuf-lite-debug.dll
06/22/2023  12:08 PM           598,528 libprotobuf-lite.dll
06/22/2023  12:08 PM           943,314 libprotobuf-lite.lib
06/22/2023  12:09 PM         2,844,672 libprotobuf.dll
06/22/2023  12:09 PM         3,976,168 libprotobuf.lib
06/02/2023  07:25 AM           110,592 libsasl.dll
05/30/2023  02:31 PM           777,728 libssl-3-x64.dll
06/22/2023  05:39 AM         6,353,488 lz4_decompress.exe
06/22/2023  05:39 AM         6,661,704 myisamchk.exe
06/22/2023  05:39 AM         6,504,520 myisamlog.exe
06/22/2023  05:39 AM         6,566,984 myisampack.exe
06/22/2023  05:39 AM         6,544,976 myisam_ftdump.exe
06/22/2023  05:40 AM         7,125,568 mysql.exe
06/22/2023  05:40 AM         7,012,432 mysqladmin.exe
06/22/2023  05:40 AM         7,394,384 mysqlbinlog.exe
06/22/2023  05:40 AM         7,018,064 mysqlcheck.exe
06/22/2023  05:40 AM        54,166,600 mysqld.exe
06/22/2023  05:40 AM         7,085,128 mysqldump.exe
06/22/2023  11:47 AM             7,881 mysqldumpslow.pl
06/22/2023  11:47 AM            28,776 mysqld_multi.pl
06/22/2023  05:40 AM            42,072 mysqlharness_stdx.dll
06/22/2023  05:40 AM            69,208 mysqlharness_tls.dll
06/22/2023  05:40 AM         7,005,264 mysqlimport.exe
06/22/2023  05:40 AM         7,520,840 mysqlpump.exe
06/22/2023  05:40 AM         7,529,040 mysqlrouter.exe
06/22/2023  05:40 AM            72,304 mysqlrouter_connection_pool.dll
06/22/2023  05:40 AM            97,904 mysqlrouter_destination_status.dll
06/22/2023  05:40 AM           272,472 mysqlrouter_http.dll
06/22/2023  05:40 AM           115,312 mysqlrouter_http_auth_backend.dll
06/22/2023  05:40 AM            38,512 mysqlrouter_http_auth_realm.dll
06/22/2023  05:40 AM         6,273,640 mysqlrouter_io_component.dll
06/22/2023  05:40 AM         6,313,568 mysqlrouter_keyring.exe
06/22/2023  05:40 AM         7,311,448 mysqlrouter_lib.dll
06/22/2023  05:40 AM         7,863,400 mysqlrouter_metadata_cache.dll
06/22/2023  05:40 AM         6,284,896 mysqlrouter_passwd.exe
06/22/2023  05:40 AM         6,269,032 mysqlrouter_plugin_info.exe
06/22/2023  05:40 AM         7,343,712 mysqlrouter_routing.dll
06/22/2023  05:40 AM         7,002,184 mysqlshow.exe
```

Figure 1-42. *MySQL Windows Installation base directory contents*

14. Login to MySQL and verify

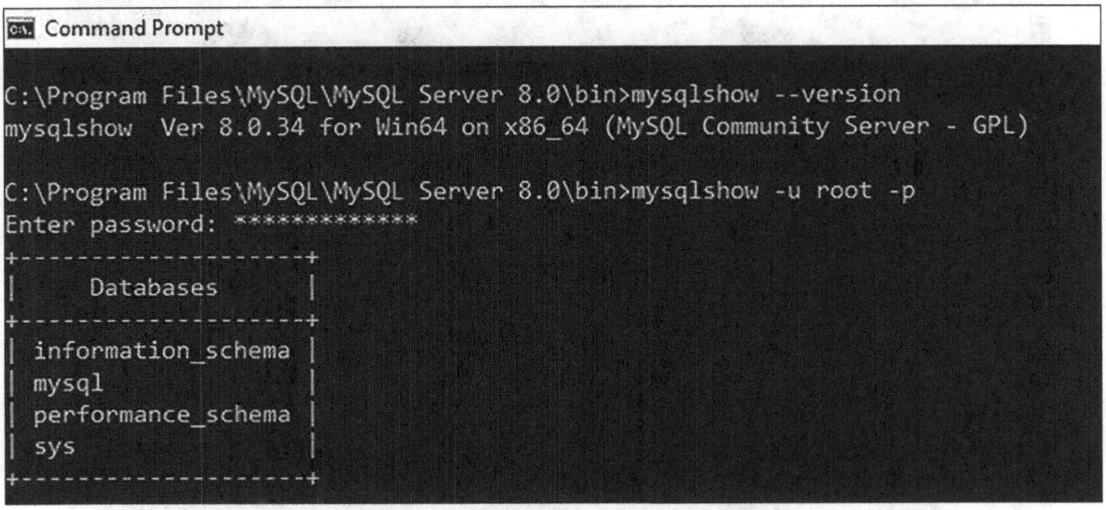

```
Command Prompt

C:\Program Files\MySQL\MySQL Server 8.0\bin>mysqlshow --version
mysqlshow  Ver 8.0.34 for Win64 on x86_64 (MySQL Community Server - GPL)

C:\Program Files\MySQL\MySQL Server 8.0\bin>mysqlshow -u root -p
Enter password: *************
+--------------------+
|     Databases      |
+--------------------+
| information_schema |
| mysql              |
| performance_schema |
| sys                |
+--------------------+
```

Figure 1-43. *MySQL Windows Installation login verification*

```
C:\Program Files\MySQL\MySQL Server 8.0\bin>mysqlshow -u root -p mysql
Enter password: *************
Database: mysql
+---------------------------------------------------------------+
|                            Tables                             |
+---------------------------------------------------------------+
| columns_priv                                                  |
| component                                                     |
| db                                                            |
| default_roles                                                 |
| engine_cost                                                   |
| func                                                          |
| general_log                                                   |
| global_grants                                                 |
| gtid_executed                                                 |
| help_category                                                 |
| help_keyword                                                  |
| help_relation                                                 |
| help_topic                                                    |
| innodb_index_stats                                            |
| innodb_table_stats                                            |
| ndb_binlog_index                                              |
| password_history                                              |
| plugin                                                        |
| procs_priv                                                    |
| proxies_priv                                                  |
| replication_asynchronous_connection_failover                 |
| replication_asynchronous_connection_failover_managed         |
| replication_group_configuration_version                      |
| replication_group_member_actions                             |
| role_edges                                                    |
| server_cost                                                   |
| servers                                                       |
| slave_master_info                                             |
| slave_relay_log_info                                          |
| slave_worker_info                                             |
| slow_log                                                      |
| tables_priv                                                   |
| time_zone                                                     |
| time_zone_leap_second                                         |
| time_zone_name                                                |
| time_zone_transition                                          |
| time_zone_transition_type                                     |
| user                                                          |
+---------------------------------------------------------------+

C:\Program Files\MySQL\MySQL Server 8.0\bin>
```

Figure 1-44. *MySQL Windows Installation login verification*

```
C:\Program Files\MySQL\MySQL Server 8.0\bin>mysql -e "SELECT User, Host, plugin FROM mysql.user" mysql -u root -p
Enter password: *************
+-------------------+-----------+----------------------+
| User              | Host      | plugin               |
+-------------------+-----------+----------------------+
| mysqladmin        | %         | caching_sha2_password |
| mysql.infoschema  | localhost | caching_sha2_password |
| mysql.session     | localhost | caching_sha2_password |
| mysql.sys         | localhost | caching_sha2_password |
| root              | localhost | caching_sha2_password |
+-------------------+-----------+----------------------+
```

Figure 1-45. *MySQL Windows Installation login verification*

15. Initialize MySQL server.

```
C:\Program Files\MySQL\MySQL Server 8.0\bin>mysqld --initialize --console
2023-08-16T03:13:41.371545Z 0 [System] [MY-013169] [Server] C:\Program Files\MySQL\MySQL Server 8.0\bin\mysqld.exe (mysqld 8.0.34) initializing of server in progress as process 1332
2023-08-16T03:13:41.408741Z 1 [System] [MY-013576] [InnoDB] InnoDB initialization has started.
2023-08-16T03:13:41.971642Z 1 [System] [MY-013577] [InnoDB] InnoDB initialization has ended.
2023-08-16T03:13:43.408214Z 6 [Note] [MY-010454] [Server] A temporary password is generated for root@localhost: NyCfHJhYB8/A
```

Figure 1-46. *MySQL Windows Installation Initialization*

Copy the temporary password generated and change it.

```
C:\Program Files\MySQL\MySQL Server 8.0\bin>mysql -u root -p
Enter password: *************
Welcome to the MySQL monitor.  Commands end with ; or \g.
Your MySQL connection id is 21
Server version: 8.0.34 MySQL Community Server - GPL

Copyright (c) 2000, 2023, Oracle and/or its affiliates.

Oracle is a registered trademark of Oracle Corporation and/or its
affiliates. Other names may be trademarks of their respective
owners.

Type 'help;' or '\h' for help. Type '\c' to clear the current input statement.

mysql> alter user 'root'@'localhost' identified by 'WElcome_1234#';
Query OK, 0 rows affected (0.01 sec)

mysql> \q
Bye

C:\Program Files\MySQL\MySQL Server 8.0\bin>
```

Figure 1-47. *MySQL Windows Installation password change*

16. Create a few sample databases and tables to test.

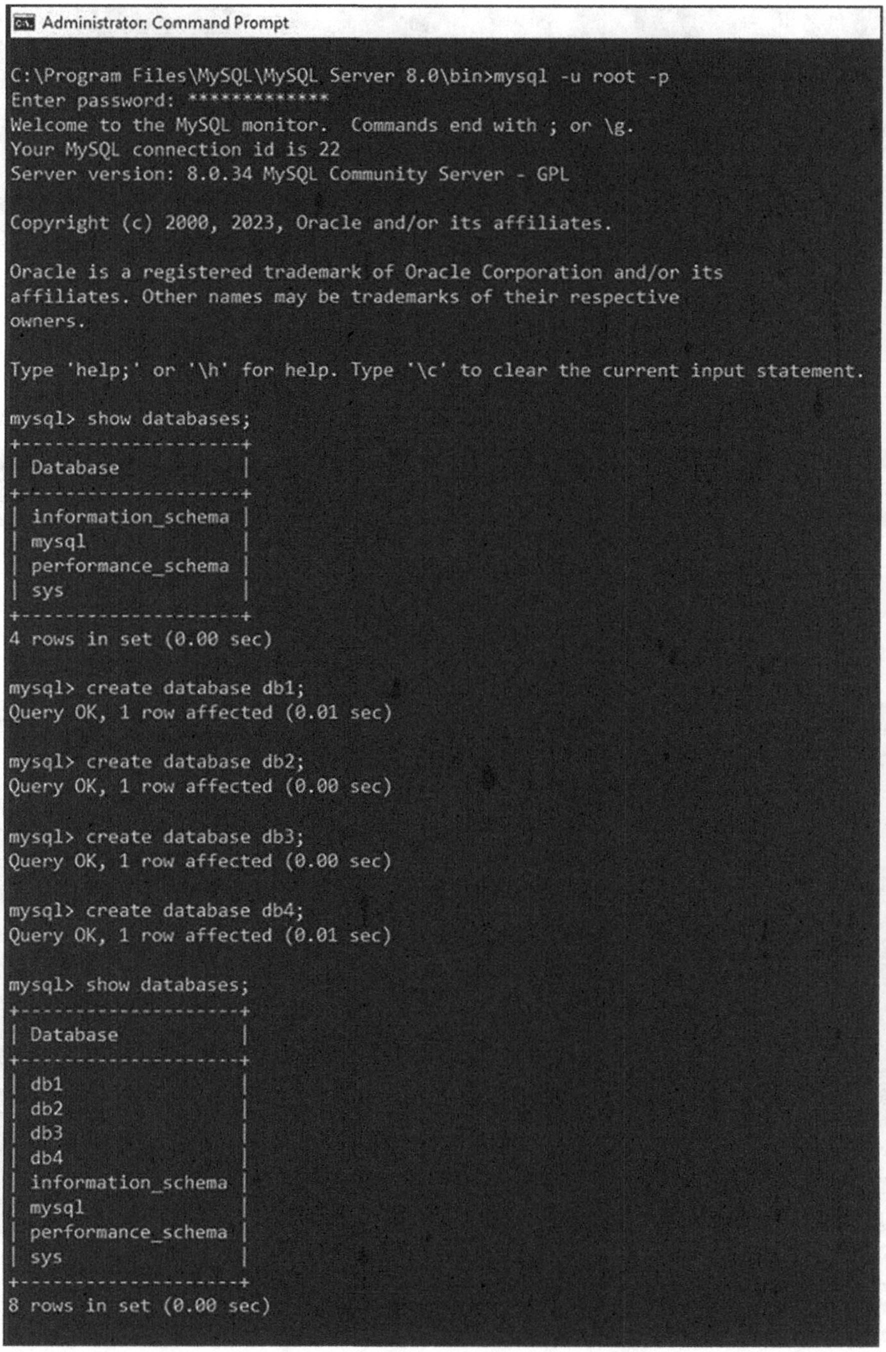
Administrator: Command Prompt
C:\Program Files\MySQL\MySQL Server 8.0\bin>mysql -u root -p
Enter password: *************
Welcome to the MySQL monitor. Commands end with ; or \g.
Your MySQL connection id is 22
Server version: 8.0.34 MySQL Community Server - GPL
Copyright (c) 2000, 2023, Oracle and/or its affiliates.
Oracle is a registered trademark of Oracle Corporation and/or its
affiliates. Other names may be trademarks of their respective
owners.
Type 'help;' or '\h' for help. Type '\c' to clear the current input statement.
mysql> show databases;
+--------------------+
| Database |
+--------------------+
| information_schema |
| mysql |
| performance_schema |
| sys |
+--------------------+
4 rows in set (0.00 sec)
mysql> create database db1;
Query OK, 1 row affected (0.01 sec)
mysql> create database db2;
Query OK, 1 row affected (0.00 sec)
mysql> create database db3;
Query OK, 1 row affected (0.00 sec)
mysql> create database db4;
Query OK, 1 row affected (0.01 sec)
mysql> show databases;
+--------------------+
| Database |
+--------------------+
| db1 |
| db2 |
| db3 |
| db4 |
| information_schema |
| mysql |
| performance_schema |
| sys |
+--------------------+
8 rows in set (0.00 sec)

Figure 1-48. *MySQL Windows Installation login verification*

```
mysql> use db1;
Database changed
mysql>
mysql> create table tab1 (no int);
Query OK, 0 rows affected (0.04 sec)

mysql> insert into tab1 values (1);
Query OK, 1 row affected (0.01 sec)

mysql> select * from tab1;
+------+
| no   |
+------+
|    1 |
+------+
1 row in set (0.00 sec)

mysql> exit
Bye

C:\Program Files\MySQL\MySQL Server 8.0\bin>
```

Figure 1-49. *MySQL Windows Installation login verification*

Installing MySQL 8.0 on Docker

1. Install Docker.

```
[root@mysql-a ~]# sudo yum install docker
Loaded plugins: fastestmirror
Determining fastest mirrors
epel/x86_64/metalink                              |  27 kB  00:00:00
 * base: mirror.lstn.net
 * epel: mirror.lstn.net
 * extras: mirror.dal.nexril.net
 * updates: mirror.steadfastnet.com
base                                              | 3.6 kB  00:00:00
epel                                              | 4.7 kB  00:00:00
extras                                            | 2.9 kB  00:00:00
updates                                           | 2.9 kB  00:00:00
(1/4): epel/x86_64/group_gz                       |  99 kB  00:00:00
(2/4): epel/x86_64/updateinfo                     | 1.0 MB  00:00:00
(3/4): epel/x86_64/primary_db                     | 7.0 MB  00:00:01
(4/4): updates/7/x86_64/primary_db                |  23 MB  00:00:20
Resolving Dependencies
--> Running transaction check
---> Package docker.x86_64 2:1.13.1-209.git7d71120.el7.centos will
be installed
--> Processing Dependency: docker-common = 2:1.13.1-209.
git7d71120.el7.centos for package:
```

--output truncated for better visibility

```
Installed:
  docker.x86_64 2:1.13.1-209.git7d71120.el7.centos

Dependency Installed:
  PyYAML.x86_64 0:3.10-11.el7
  atomic-registries.x86_64 1:1.22.1-33.gitb507039.el7_8
  audit-libs-python.x86_64 0:2.8.5-4.el7
  checkpolicy.x86_64 0:2.5-8.el7
```

```
container-selinux.noarch 2:2.119.2-1.911c772.el7_8
container-storage-setup.noarch 0:0.11.0-2.git5eaf76c.el7
containers-common.x86_64 1:0.1.40-11.el7_8
docker-client.x86_64 2:1.13.1-209.git7d71120.el7.centos
docker-common.x86_64 2:1.13.1-209.git7d71120.el7.centos
fuse-overlayfs.x86_64 0:0.7.2-6.el7_8
fuse3-libs.x86_64 0:3.6.1-4.el7
libcgroup.x86_64 0:0.41-21.el7
libnl.x86_64 0:1.1.4-3.el7
libseccomp.x86_64 0:2.3.1-4.el7
libsemanage-python.x86_64 0:2.5-14.el7
libyaml.x86_64 0:0.1.4-11.el7_0
oci-register-machine.x86_64 1:0-6.git2b44233.el7
oci-systemd-hook.x86_64 1:0.2.0-1.git05e6923.el7_6
oci-umount.x86_64 2:2.5-3.el7
policycoreutils-python.x86_64 0:2.5-34.el7
python-IPy.noarch 0:0.75-6.el7
python-backports.x86_64 0:1.0-8.el7
python-backports-ssl_match_hostname.noarch 0:3.5.0.1-1.el7
python-dateutil.noarch 0:1.5-7.el7
python-dmidecode.x86_64 0:3.12.2-4.el7
python-ethtool.x86_64 0:0.8-8.el7
python-inotify.noarch 0:0.9.4-4.el7
python-ipaddress.noarch 0:1.0.16-2.el7
python-pytoml.noarch 0:0.1.14-1.git7dea353.el7
python-setuptools.noarch 0:0.9.8-7.el7
python-syspurpose.x86_64 0:1.24.52-2.el7.centos
setools-libs.x86_64 0:3.3.8-4.el7
slirp4netns.x86_64 0:0.4.3-4.el7_8
subscription-manager.x86_64 0:1.24.52-2.el7.centos
subscription-manager-rhsm.x86_64 0:1.24.52-2.el7.centos
subscription-manager-rhsm-certificates.x86_64 0:1.24.52-2.el7.centos
usermode.x86_64 0:1.111-6.el7
yajl.x86_64 0:2.0.4-4.el7

Complete!
[root@mysql-a ~]#
```

2. Start Docker and check status.

```
[root@mysql-a ~]# systemctl start docker
[root@mysql-a ~]# systemctl status docker
● docker.service - Docker Application Container Engine
   Loaded: loaded (/usr/lib/systemd/system/docker.service;
   disabled; vendor preset: disabled)
   Active: active (running) since Tue 2023-10-17 21:21:30
   CDT; 5s ago
     Docs: http://docs.docker.com
 Main PID: 1492 (dockerd-current)
   CGroup: /system.slice/docker.service
├─1492 /usr/bin/dockerd-current --add-runtime docker-runc=/usr/
libexec/docker/docker-runc-current --default-runtime=docker-runc
--exec-opt native.cgrou...
            └─1497 /usr/bin/docker-containerd-current -l unix:///
            var/run/docker/libcontainerd/docker-containerd.sock
            --metrics-interval=0 --start-timeout 2m --stat...

Oct 17 21:21:30 mysql-a dockerd-current[1492]: time="2023-10-
17T21:21:30.609338431-05:00" level=warning msg="Docker could not
enable SELinux on the host system"
Oct 17 21:21:30 mysql-a dockerd-current[1492]: time="2023-10-1
7T21:21:30.674215163-05:00" level=info msg="Graph migration to
content-addressability took ... seconds"
Oct 17 21:21:30 mysql-a dockerd-current[1492]: time="2023-
10-17T21:21:30.675255889-05:00" level=info msg="Loading
containers: start."
Oct 17 21:21:30 mysql-a dockerd-current[1492]: time="2023-10-
17T21:21:30.744025480-05:00" level=info msg="Firewalld
running: false"
Oct 17 21:21:30 mysql-a dockerd-current[1492]: time="2023-10-
17T21:21:30.813890980-05:00" level=info msg="Default bridge
(docker0) is assigned with an IP... address"
Oct 17 21:21:30 mysql-a dockerd-current[1492]: time="2023-
10-17T21:21:30.844862458-05:00" level=info msg="Loading
containers: done."
```

```
Oct 17 21:21:30 mysql-a dockerd-current[1492]: time="2023-10-
17T21:21:30.873543369-05:00" level=info msg="Daemon has completed
initialization"
Oct 17 21:21:30 mysql-a dockerd-current[1492]: time="2023-10-
17T21:21:30.873558198-05:00" level=info msg="Docker daemon"
commit="7d71120/1.13.1" graphdri...on=1.13.1
Oct 17 21:21:30 mysql-a systemd[1]: Started Docker Application
Container Engine.
Oct 17 21:21:30 mysql-a dockerd-current[1492]: time="2023-10-
17T21:21:30.881584399-05:00" level=info msg="API listen on /var/
run/docker.sock"
Hint: Some lines were ellipsized, use -l to show in full.
[root@mysql-a ~]#
```

3. Pull the image from the Oracle container registry (https://
    container-registry.oracle.com/ords/f?p=113:10::::::) with
    tag=8.0.34-aarch64 to install MySQL 8.0.34.

    [root@mysql-a ~]# **docker pull container-registry.oracle.com/mysql/
    community-server:8.0.34-aarch64**
    ```
    Trying to pull repository container-registry.oracle.com/mysql/
    community-server ...
    8.0.34-aarch64: Pulling from container-registry.oracle.com/mysql/
    community-server
    48668e7fb41b: Pull complete
    f80f44da96ae: Pull complete
    25ed88bce03b: Pull complete
    058e05af9926: Pull complete
    ea31ac1af87f: Pull complete
    596b82002b8a: Pull complete
    626d85fe4081: Pull complete
    Digest: sha256:92d76ff849257c25fdb66585bb583647690a1cc770949a0c4
    3f20b4e430687a5
    Status: Downloaded newer image for container-registry.oracle.com/
    mysql/community-server:8.0.34-aarch64
    [root@mysql-a ~]#
    ```

4.   List the available Docker images using the "docker images" command.

```
[root@mysql-a ~]# docker images
REPOSITORY
TAG                    IMAGE ID           CREATED           SIZE
container-registry.oracle.com/mysql/community-server
8.0.34-aarch64    b8bf544a7906        2 months ago       588 MB
[root@mysql-a ~]#
```

5.   Start the MySQL server instance with the name "mysql1".

```
[root@mysql-a ~]# docker run --name=mysql1 --restart on-failure -d
container-registry.oracle.com/mysql/community-server:latest
Unable to find image 'container-registry.oracle.com/mysql/
community-server:latest' locally
Trying to pull repository container-registry.oracle.com/mysql/
community-server ...
latest: Pulling from container-registry.oracle.com/mysql/
community-server
9eb5239ad134: Pull complete
85cea793f1b7: Pull complete
ed8a58b8cd74: Pull complete
f31b34870daf: Pull complete
1737b693d5b9: Pull complete
16993fdacb44: Pull complete
f9191b7f0e57: Pull complete
Digest: sha256:6d5fe6463add652d081d6078fe9c3d2665e5383168130d7f6a9
7b5ca03ac7193
Status: Downloaded newer image for container-registry.oracle.com/
mysql/community-server:latest
4fcd9f288be6f66baa1be2d5150b1661006fa042ba05af20b7108f112148c271
[root@mysql-a ~]#
To check status of the container, issue:

[root@mysql-a ~]# docker ps
```

```
CONTAINER ID        IMAGE
                    COMMAND                    CREATED
STATUS              PORTS                      NAMES
4fcd9f288be6        container-registry.oracle.com/mysql/community-
server:latest   "/entrypoint.sh my..."   34 seconds ago
Up 33 seconds       3306/tcp, 33060-33061/tcp   mysql1
[root@mysql-a ~]#
```

6. To monitor the output of the logs, use the "docker logs" command.

```
[root@mysql-a ~]# docker logs mysql1
[Entrypoint] MySQL Docker Image 8.1.0-1.2.13-server
[Entrypoint] Initializing database
[Entrypoint] No password option specified for new database.
[Entrypoint]   A random onetime password will be generated.
2023-10-18T02:32:03.103937Z 0 [System] [MY-015017] [Server] MySQL
Server Initialization - start.

  --output truncated for better visibility

2023-10-18T02:32:12.925504Z 0 [System] [MY-010931] [Server] /usr/
sbin/mysqld: ready for connections. Version: '8.1.0'  socket:
'/var/lib/mysql/mysql.sock'  port: 3306  MySQL Community
Server - GPL.
2023-10-18T02:32:12.925609Z 0 [System] [MY-011323] [Server] X
Plugin ready for connections. Bind-address: '::' port: 33060,
socket: /var/run/mysqld/mysqlx.sock
[root@mysql-a ~]#
```

7. Get the temporary password generated upon MySQL
    initialization.

```
[root@mysql-a ~]# docker logs mysql1 2>&1 | grep GENERATED
[Entrypoint] GENERATED ROOT PASSWORD: =q892ft2e#T+9v6yz@
k3_%I&J6;NHakQ
[root@mysql-a ~]#
```

8. Connect to the MySQL server "mysql1" from within the server, log in with the temporary password generated, and reset the password.

```
[root@mysql-a ~]# docker exec -it mysql1 mysql -uroot -p
Enter password:
```

```
mysql> ALTER USER 'root'@'localhost' IDENTIFIED BY
'WElcome_1234#';
Query OK, 0 rows affected (0.02 sec)
```

```
mysql> exit
Bye
[root@mysql-a ~]# docker exec -it mysql1 mysql -uroot -p
Enter password:
```

```
mysql> show databases;
+--------------------+
| Database           |
+--------------------+
| information_schema |
| mysql              |
| performance_schema |
| sys                |
+--------------------+
4 rows in set (0.00 sec)
```

```
mysql> create database db1;
Query OK, 1 row affected (0.01 sec)
```

```
mysql> create database db2;
Query OK, 1 row affected (0.01 sec)
```

```
mysql> show databases;
+--------------------+
| Database           |
+--------------------+
| db1                |
| db2                |
```

```
| information_schema |
| mysql              |
| performance_schema |
| sys                |
+--------------------+
6 rows in set (0.00 sec)
```

9. For Shell access from within the container, issue the following
   command:

```
[root@mysql-a ~]# docker exec -it mysql1 bash
bash-4.4# ls -ltr /var/lib/mysql
total 96716
-rw-r----- 1 mysql mysql       56 Oct 18 02:32  auto.cnf
-rw-r----- 1 mysql mysql  8585216 Oct 18 02:32  '#ib_16384_1.dblwr'
drwxr-x--- 2 mysql mysql     8192 Oct 18 02:32  performance_schema
-rw------- 1 mysql mysql     1680 Oct 18 02:32  ca-key.pem
-rw-r--r-- 1 mysql mysql     1108 Oct 18 02:32  ca.pem
-rw------- 1 mysql mysql     1680 Oct 18 02:32  server-key.pem
-rw-r--r-- 1 mysql mysql     1108 Oct 18 02:32  server-cert.pem
-rw------- 1 mysql mysql     1680 Oct 18 02:32  client-key.pem
-rw-r--r-- 1 mysql mysql     1108 Oct 18 02:32  client-cert.pem
-rw------- 1 mysql mysql     1680 Oct 18 02:32  private_key.pem
-rw-r--r-- 1 mysql mysql      452 Oct 18 02:32  public_key.pem
drwxr-x--- 2 mysql mysql      143 Oct 18 02:32  mysql
drwxr-x--- 2 mysql mysql       28 Oct 18 02:32  sys
-rw-r----- 1 mysql mysql      180 Oct 18 02:32  binlog.000001
-rw-r----- 1 mysql mysql     5457 Oct 18 02:32  ib_buffer_pool
drwxr-x--- 2 mysql mysql      187 Oct 18 02:32  '#innodb_temp'
-rw-r----- 1 mysql mysql       32 Oct 18 02:32  binlog.index
-rw------- 1 mysql mysql        2 Oct 18 02:32  mysql.sock.lock
srwxrwxrwx 1 mysql mysql        0 Oct 18 02:32  mysql.sock
drwxr-x--- 2 mysql mysql     4096 Oct 18 02:32  '#innodb_redo'
-rw-r----- 1 mysql mysql 12582912 Oct 18 02:32  ibtmp1
-rw-r----- 1 mysql mysql 16777216 Oct 18 02:34  undo_001
-rw-r----- 1 mysql mysql      683 Oct 18 02:34  binlog.000002
-rw-r----- 1 mysql mysql 16777216 Oct 18 02:34  undo_002
```

```
-rw-r----- 1 mysql mysql   196608 Oct 18 02:34 '#ib_16384_0.dblwr'
-rw-r----- 1 mysql mysql 31457280 Oct 18 02:34   mysql.ibd
-rw-r----- 1 mysql mysql 12582912 Oct 18 02:34   ibdata1
bash-4.4#
bash-4.4# exit
exit
[root@mysql-a ~]# docker ps
CONTAINER ID          IMAGE
                      COMMAND                  CREATED
STATUS                PORTS                    NAMES
4fcd9f288be6          container-registry.oracle.com/mysql/community-
server:latest    "/entrypoint.sh my..."   3 minutes ago
Up 3 minutes          3306/tcp, 33060-33061/tcp   mysql1
[root@mysql-a ~]#
```

10. To stop the container, issue the following command:

```
[root@mysql-a ~]# docker stop mysql1
mysql1
[root@mysql-a ~]# docker ps
CONTAINER ID          IMAGE               COMMAND
CREATED               STATUS              PORTS                NAMES
[root@mysql-a ~]#
```

11. To start the container, issue the following command:

```
[root@mysql-a ~]# docker start mysql1
mysql1
[root@mysql-a ~]#
[root@mysql-a ~]# docker ps
CONTAINER ID          IMAGE
                      COMMAND                  CREATED
STATUS                PORTS                    NAMES
4fcd9f288be6          container-registry.oracle.com/mysql/community-
server:latest    "/entrypoint.sh my..."   4 minutes ago
Up 3 seconds          3306/tcp, 33060-33061/tcp   mysql1
[root@mysql-a ~]#
```

12. To restart the container, issue the following command:

```
[root@mysql-a ~]# docker restart mysql1
mysql1
[root@mysql-a ~]# docker ps
CONTAINER ID        IMAGE
                    COMMAND                     CREATED
STATUS              PORTS                       NAMES
4fcd9f288be6        container-registry.oracle.com/mysql/community-
server:latest   "/entrypoint.sh my..."    4 minutes ago
Up 2 seconds        3306/tcp, 33060-33061/tcp   mysql1
[root@mysql-a ~]#
```

13. To remove the Docker container, issue the following command:

```
[root@mysql-a ~]# docker rm mysql1
mysql1
[root@mysql-a ~]#
[root@mysql-a ~]# docker ps
CONTAINER ID        IMAGE               COMMAND
CREATED             STATUS              PORTS              NAMES
[root@mysql-a ~]#
```

Upgrading MySQL 5.7 to MySQL 8.0.34

There are two types of upgrades in MySQL: **in-place** and **logical** upgrades. In this
section, we perform an in-place upgrade from MySQL 5.7 to MySQL 8.0.34.

Overview

1. Back up the existing MySQL server configuration file and data.

2. Stop MySQL daemon.

3. Uninstall MySQL 5.7.

4. Download and install MySQL 8.0.

5. Start MySQL daemon.

6. Verify the upgrade.

Assumptions

- MySQL 5.7.x is installed and working as expected.

- MySQL 5.7.x has data.

Prerequisites

- Ensure backup is taken.

- Run **mysqlcheck** to ensure the following issues are not present and correct them if any issues are reported:

  - No tables present in the database with obsolete data types or functions.

  - No orphan **.frm** files.

  - Triggers must not have any missing or empty definer or an invalid creation context. Any triggers like those should be dumped, dropped, and recreated post upgrade.

- Ensure there are no partitioned tables that use a storage engine that does not have native partitioning support. Run the following query to identify such tables:

```
[root@mysql-a mysql]# ls -ltr *.frm
ls: cannot access *.frm: No such file or directory
[root@mysql-a mysql]#
[root@mysql-a mysql]# mysql -u root -p
Enter password:

mysql> SELECT TABLE_SCHEMA, TABLE_NAME
    -> FROM INFORMATION_SCHEMA.TABLES
    -> WHERE ENGINE NOT IN ('innodb', 'ndbcluster')
    -> AND CREATE_OPTIONS LIKE '%partitioned%';
Empty set (0.03 sec)
```

Any table reported here must be altered to use the **InnoDB**
storage engine. To convert a table storage engine to InnoDB, run

```
mysql> ALTER TABLE table_name ENGINE = INNODB;
```

To make a partitioned table nonpartitioned, run

```
mysql> ALTER TABLE table_name REMOVE PARTITIONING;
```

- Check the MySQL documentation to thoroughly review requirements
  to ensure no keywords that were not reserved previously are reserved
  in MySQL 8.x.

- There must be no tables in MySQL 5.7 **mysql** system database
  that have the same name as the table used in MySQL 8.0.34 data
  dictionary. To identify any tables that could conflict, run

```
mysql> use mysql;
Reading table information for completion of table and column names
You can turn off this feature to get a quicker startup with -A

Database changed
mysql>
mysql> SELECT TABLE_SCHEMA, TABLE_NAME
    -> FROM INFORMATION_SCHEMA.TABLES
    -> WHERE LOWER(TABLE_SCHEMA) = 'mysql'
    -> and LOWER(TABLE_NAME) IN
    -> (
    -> 'catalogs',
    -> 'character_sets',
    -> 'check_constraints',
    -> 'collations',
    -> 'column_statistics',
    -> 'column_type_elements',
    -> 'columns',
    -> 'dd_properties',
    -> 'events',
    -> 'foreign_key_column_usage',
    -> 'foreign_keys',
    -> 'index_column_usage',
```

```
    -> 'index_partitions',
    -> 'index_stats',
    -> 'indexes',
    -> 'parameter_type_elements',
    -> 'parameters',
    -> 'resource_groups',
    -> 'routines',
    -> 'schemata',
    -> 'st_spatial_reference_systems',
    -> 'table_partition_values',
    -> 'table_partitions',
    -> 'table_stats',
    -> 'tables',
    -> 'tablespace_files',
    -> 'tablespaces',
    -> 'triggers',
    -> 'view_routine_usage',
    -> 'view_table_usage'
    -> );
Empty set (0.00 sec)
```

- Ensure there are no tables that have foreign key constraints longer
  than 64 characters. To identify any constraints that are more than 64
  characters, run

```
mysql> use mysql;
Database changed
mysql> SELECT TABLE_SCHEMA, TABLE_NAME
    -> FROM INFORMATION_SCHEMA.TABLES
    -> WHERE TABLE_NAME IN
    ->   (SELECT LEFT(SUBSTR(ID,INSTR(ID,'/')+1),
    ->                INSTR(SUBSTR(ID,INSTR(ID,'/')+1),
    ->                '_ibfk_')-1)
    ->     FROM INFORMATION_SCHEMA.INNODB_SYS_FOREIGN
    ->     WHERE LENGTH(SUBSTR(ID,INSTR(ID,'/')+1))>64);
Empty set (0.01 sec)
```

Similarly, check for all databases.

- Ensure the *sql_mode* system variable defines no obsolete SQL modes. Verify the MySQL configuration file (/etc/my.cnf).

- Ensure there are no views with explicitly defined column names that exceed 64 characters. Use the *SHOW CREATE VIEW* statement or query the *information_schema.views* table.

- Ensure no tables or stored procedures with individual ENUM or SET column elements exceed 255 characters or 1020 bytes in length.

- Check the MySQL documentation to review changes on the server startup options and system variables and ensure there is no impact to the upgrade.

- Ensure schema and table names are in lowercase before the upgrade if you intend to change the *lower_case_table_names* value to 1 at upgrade time. This is usually not recommended.

Upgrade Steps

1. Ensure backup is taken before the upgrade. We can use either of the following methods to back up the MySQL server:

    a. MySQL Enterprise Backup

    b. Mysqldump

    c. Third-party backup tools

    For example, you can use MySQL **Enterprise Backup version 4.1** as this is the version for MySQL 5.7. I backed up using the following command:

    ```
    -bash-4.2$ /bin/mysqlbackup --user=mysqlbkpadmin --password
    --host=127.0.0.1 --backup-dir=/varlib/mysql/mysqlbackup --backup-
    image=mysql_preupgrade_bkp.mbi --with-timestamp backup-to-image
    ```

    ```
    -bash-4.2$ /bin/mysqldump -u root -p --all-databases > my_db_
    dump.sql
    ```

```
Enter password:
-bash-4.2$ ls -ltr
total 123820
-rw-r----- 1 mysql mysql 50331648 Sep  1 10:46 ib_logfile1
-rw-r----- 1 mysql mysql       56 Sep  1 10:46 auto.cnf
-rw------- 1 mysql mysql     1676 Sep  1 10:46 ca-key.pem
-rw-r--r-- 1 mysql mysql     1112 Sep  1 10:46 ca.pem
-rw------- 1 mysql mysql     1680 Sep  1 10:46 server-key.pem
-rw-r--r-- 1 mysql mysql     1112 Sep  1 10:46 server-cert.pem
-rw------- 1 mysql mysql     1680 Sep  1 10:46 client-key.pem
-rw-r--r-- 1 mysql mysql     1112 Sep  1 10:46 client-cert.pem
-rw-r--r-- 1 mysql mysql      452 Sep  1 10:46 public_key.pem
-rw------- 1 mysql mysql     1672 Sep  1 10:46 private_key.pem
drwxr-x--- 2 mysql mysql     8192 Sep  1 10:46 performance_schema
drwxr-x--- 2 mysql mysql     4096 Sep  1 10:46 mysql
drwxr-x--- 2 mysql mysql     8192 Sep  1 10:46 sys
-rw-r----- 1 mysql mysql      353 Sep  1 12:52 ib_buffer_pool
-rw------- 1 mysql mysql        5 Sep  1 12:52 mysql.sock.lock
srwxrwxrwx 1 mysql mysql        0 Sep  1 12:52 mysql.sock
-rw-r----- 1 mysql mysql 12582912 Sep  1 12:52 ibdata1
-rw-r----- 1 mysql mysql 50331648 Sep  1 12:52 ib_logfile0
-rw-rw-r-- 1 mysql mysql   887757 Sep  1 17:29 my_db_dump.sql
-rw-r----- 1 mysql mysql 12582912 Sep  1 17:29 ibtmp1
-bash-4.2$
```

The following are the options used for mysqlbackup client.

--user: Database server user name to connect

--password: Connection password

--host: Hostname to connect

--backup-dir: Directory to store data

--backup-image: Path name for the backup image

--with-timestamp: A subdirectory underneath backup directory
with a name formed from the timestamp of the backup operation

2. Check upgrade readiness using **mysqlcheck** as mysql user.

```
-bash-4.2$ /bin/mysqlcheck -u root -p --all-databases
--check-upgrade
Enter password:
db1.tab1                                        OK
db2.tab1                                        OK
db2.tab2                                        OK
db3.tab1                                        OK
db3.tab2                                        OK
db3.tab3                                        OK
mysql.columns_priv                             OK
mysql.db                                        OK
mysql.engine_cost                              OK
mysql.event                                     OK
mysql.func                                      OK
mysql.general_log                              OK
mysql.gtid_executed                            OK
mysql.help_category                            OK
mysql.help_keyword                             OK
mysql.help_relation                            OK
mysql.help_topic                               OK
mysql.innodb_index_stats                       OK
mysql.innodb_table_stats                       OK
mysql.ndb_binlog_index                         OK
mysql.plugin                                    OK
mysql.proc                                      OK
mysql.procs_priv                               OK
mysql.proxies_priv                             OK
mysql.server_cost                              OK
mysql.servers                                   OK
mysql.slave_master_info                        OK
mysql.slave_relay_log_info                     OK
mysql.slave_worker_info                        OK
mysql.slow_log                                  OK
mysql.tables_priv                              OK
```

```
mysql.time_zone                          OK
mysql.time_zone_leap_second              OK
mysql.time_zone_name                     OK
mysql.time_zone_transition               OK
mysql.time_zone_transition_type          OK
mysql.user                               OK
sys.sys_config                           OK
-bash-4.2$
```

3. As **root** user, download and install MySQL Shell using **wget** to run the upgrade utility.

```
[root@mysql-a ~]# wget https://dev.mysql.com/get/Downloads/MySQL-
Shell/mysql-shell-8.0.30-1.el7.x86_64.rpm
--2023-08-19 17:13:38--  https://dev.mysql.com/get/Downloads/
MySQL-Shell/mysql-shell-8.0.30-1.el7.x86_64.rpm
Resolving dev.mysql.com (dev.mysql.com)... 23.4.59.106,
2600:1404:6400:1697::2e31, 2600:1404:6400:1691::2e31
Connecting to dev.mysql.com (dev.mysql.com)|23.4.59.106|:443...
connected.
HTTP request sent, awaiting response... 302 Moved Temporarily
Location: https://cdn.mysql.com//archives/mysql-shell/mysql-
shell-8.0.30-1.el7.x86_64.rpm [following]
--2023-08-19 17:13:38--  https://cdn.mysql.com//archives/mysql-
shell/mysql-shell-8.0.30-1.el7.x86_64.rpm
Resolving cdn.mysql.com (cdn.mysql.com)... 173.222.252.243,
2600:1404:6400:1690::1d68, 2600:1404:6400:1682::1d68
Connecting to cdn.mysql.com (cdn.mysql.com)|173.222.252.243|:443...
connected.
HTTP request sent, awaiting response... 200 OK
Length: 36008988 (34M) [application/x-redhat-package-manager]
Saving to: 'mysql-shell-8.0.30-1.el7.x86_64.rpm'

100%[=============================>] 36,008,988  8.15MB/s   in 6.7s

2023-08-19 17:13:45 (5.13 MB/s) - 'mysql-shell-8.0.30-1.el7.
x86_64.rpm' saved [36008988/36008988]
```

```
[root@mysql-a ~]#

[root@mysql-a ~]# ls -ltr
total 1162656
-rw-r--r--  1 root  root    36008988 Jul 22  2022 mysql-
shell-8.0.30-1.el7.x86_64.rpm
-rw-r--r--  1 root  root     3624516 Sep 15  2022 meb-4.1.5-el7.
x86_64.rpm
-rw-------.  1 root  root        1582 Sep 26  2022 anaconda-ks.cfg
-rw-r--r--  1 root  root       14563 Oct 10  2022 README.txt
-rw-r--r--  1 root  root     3046107 Mar 20 09:18 download.1
-rw-r--r--  1 root  root     3046107 Mar 20 09:18 download
-rw-r--r--  1 7155 31415   32652444 Jun 22 08:27 mysql-community-
client-5.7.43-1.el7.x86_64.rpm
-rw-r--r--  1 7155 31415     320780 Jun 22 08:27 mysql-community-
common-5.7.43-1.el7.x86_64.rpm
-rw-r--r--  1 7155 31415    4969828 Jun 22 08:27 mysql-community-
devel-5.7.43-1.el7.x86_64.rpm
-rw-r--r--  1 7155 31415   48586584 Jun 22 08:27 mysql-community-
embedded-5.7.43-1.el7.x86_64.rpm
-rw-r--r--  1 7155 31415   23314208 Jun 22 08:27 mysql-community-
embedded-compat-5.7.43-1.el7.x86_64.rpm
-rw-r--r--  1 7155 31415  134413980 Jun 22 08:27 mysql-community-
embedded-devel-5.7.43-1.el7.x86_64.rpm
-rw-r--r--  1 7155 31415    3091092 Jun 22 08:27 mysql-community-
libs-5.7.43-1.el7.x86_64.rpm
-rw-r--r--  1 7155 31415    1266220 Jun 22 08:27 mysql-community-
libs-compat-5.7.43-1.el7.x86_64.rpm
-rw-r--r--  1 7155 31415  193030448 Jun 22 08:28 mysql-community-
server-5.7.43-1.el7.x86_64.rpm
-rw-r--r--  1 7155 31415  128921364 Jun 22 08:28 mysql-community-
test-5.7.43-1.el7.x86_64.rpm
-rw-r--r--  1 root  root   570583040 Aug 19 15:35 mysql-5.7.43-1.
el7.x86_64.rpm-bundle.tar
```

```
-rw-r--r--  1 root   root      3639321 Aug 19 16:35 p34688899_410_
Linux-x86-64.zip
drwxrwxr-x  2 mysql mysql          6 Aug 19 16:41 mysql_backup
[root@mysql-a ~]#

[root@mysql-a ~]# rpm -Uvh mysql-shell-8.0.30-1.el7.x86_64.rpm
warning: mysql-shell-8.0.30-1.el7.x86_64.rpm: Header V4 RSA/SHA256
Signature, key ID 3a79bd29: NOKEY
Preparing...                         ####################### [100%]
Updating / installing...
   1:mysql-shell-8.0.30-1.el7        ####################### [100%]
[root@mysql-a ~]# which mysqlsh
/usr/bin/mysqlsh

[root@mysql-a ~]#
```

4. Run the server upgrade utility as **mysql** user.

```
[root@mysql-a ~]# su - mysql
Last login: Sat Aug 19 17:15:49 CDT 2023 on pts/0
-bash-4.2$
-bash-4.2$ /bin/mysqlsh -uroot -p -h localhost -P3306 -e "util.
checkForServerUpgrade();"
Please provide the password for 'root@localhost:3306':
*************
Save password for 'root@localhost:3306'? [Y]es/[N]o/Ne[v]er
(default No): Y
The MySQL server at localhost:3306, version 5.7.43 - MySQL
Community Server
(GPL), will now be checked for compatibility issues for upgrade
to MySQL
8.0.30...

1) Usage of old temporal type
   No issues found

2) Usage of db objects with names conflicting with new reserved
keywords
   No issues found
```

-- output truncated for better visibility

```
Errors:    0
Warnings: 1
Notices:  1
```

NOTE: No fatal errors were found that would prevent an upgrade, but some potential issues were detected. Please ensure that the reported issues are not significant before upgrading.
-bash-4.2$

5. Download MySQL 8.0.34 binaries into a separate directory.

```
[root@mysql-a ~]# mkdir mysql8
```

```
[root@mysql-a ~]# ls -ltr
total 1162656
-rw-r--r--  1 root  root    36008988 Jul 22  2022 mysql-
shell-8.0.30-1.el7.x86_64.rpm
-rw-r--r--  1 root  root     3624516 Sep 15  2022 meb-4.1.5-el7.
x86_64.rpm
-rw-------. 1 root  root        1582 Sep 26  2022 anaconda-ks.cfg
-rw-r--r--  1 root  root       14563 Oct 10  2022 README.txt
-rw-r--r--  1 root  root     3046107 Mar 20 09:18 download.1
-rw-r--r--  1 root  root     3046107 Mar 20 09:18 download
-rw-r--r--  1 7155 31415   32652444 Jun 22 08:27 mysql-community-
client-5.7.43-1.el7.x86_64.rpm
-rw-r--r--  1 7155 31415     320780 Jun 22 08:27 mysql-community-
common-5.7.43-1.el7.x86_64.rpm
-rw-r--r--  1 7155 31415    4969828 Jun 22 08:27 mysql-community-
devel-5.7.43-1.el7.x86_64.rpm
-rw-r--r--  1 7155 31415   48586584 Jun 22 08:27 mysql-community-
embedded-5.7.43-1.el7.x86_64.rpm
-rw-r--r--  1 7155 31415   23314208 Jun 22 08:27 mysql-community-
embedded-compat-5.7.43-1.el7.x86_64.rpm
-rw-r--r--  1 7155 31415  134413980 Jun 22 08:27 mysql-community-
embedded-devel-5.7.43-1.el7.x86_64.rpm
```

```
-rw-r--r--   1  7155 31415    3091092 Jun 22 08:27 mysql-community-
libs-5.7.43-1.el7.x86_64.rpm
-rw-r--r--   1  7155 31415    1266220 Jun 22 08:27 mysql-community-
libs-compat-5.7.43-1.el7.x86_64.rpm
-rw-r--r--   1  7155 31415 193030448 Jun 22 08:28 mysql-community-
server-5.7.43-1.el7.x86_64.rpm
-rw-r--r--   1  7155 31415 128921364 Jun 22 08:28 mysql-community-
test-5.7.43-1.el7.x86_64.rpm
-rw-r--r--   1 root   root   570583040 Aug 19 15:35 mysql-5.7.43-1.
el7.x86_64.rpm-bundle.tar
-rw-r--r--   1 root   root     3639321 Aug 19 16:35 p34688899_410_
Linux-x86-64.zip
drwxrwxr-x  2 mysql mysql          6 Aug 19 16:41 mysql_backup
drwxr-xr-x  2 root   root          6 Aug 19 17:23 mysql8
```

```
[root@mysql-a ~]# cd mysql8
[root@mysql-a mysql8]# ls -ltr
total 0
[root@mysql-a mysql8]# wget https://dev.mysql.com/get/Downloads/
MySQL-8.0/mysql-8.0.34-1.el7.x86_64.rpm-bundle.tar
--2023-08-19 17:24:12--  https://dev.mysql.com/get/Downloads/
MySQL-8.0/mysql-8.0.34-1.el7.x86_64.rpm-bundle.tar
Resolving dev.mysql.com (dev.mysql.com)... 23.4.59.106,
2600:1404:6400:1691::2e31, 2600:1404:6400:1697::2e31
Connecting to dev.mysql.com (dev.mysql.com)|23.4.59.106|:443...
connected.
HTTP request sent, awaiting response... 302 Moved Temporarily
Location: https://cdn.mysql.com//Downloads/MySQL-8.0/
mysql-8.0.34-1.el7.x86_64.rpm-bundle.tar [following]
--2023-08-19 17:24:12--  https://cdn.mysql.com//Downloads/
MySQL-8.0/mysql-8.0.34-1.el7.x86_64.rpm-bundle.tar
Resolving cdn.mysql.com (cdn.mysql.com)... 173.222.252.243,
2600:1404:6400:1682::1d68, 2600:1404:6400:1690::1d68
Connecting to cdn.mysql.com (cdn.mysql.com)|173.222.252.243|:443...
connected.
HTTP request sent, awaiting response... 200 OK
```

Length: 1031792640 (984M) [application/x-tar]
Saving to: 'mysql-8.0.34-1.el7.x86_64.rpm-bundle.tar'

100%[======================>] 1,031,792,640 1.30MB/s   in 4m 19s

2023-08-19 17:28:33 (3.79 MB/s) - 'mysql-8.0.34-1.el7.x86_64.rpm-bundle.tar' saved [1031792640/1031792640]

[root@mysql-a mysql8]# **ls -ltr**
total 1007612
-rw-r--r-- 1 root root 1031792640 Jun 24 22:27 mysql-8.0.34-1.el7.x86_64.rpm-bundle.tar

[root@mysql-a mysql8]# **tar -xvf mysql-8.0.34-1.el7.x86_64.rpm-bundle.tar**
mysql-community-client-8.0.34-1.el7.x86_64.rpm
mysql-community-client-plugins-8.0.34-1.el7.x86_64.rpm
mysql-community-common-8.0.34-1.el7.x86_64.rpm
mysql-community-debuginfo-8.0.34-1.el7.x86_64.rpm
mysql-community-devel-8.0.34-1.el7.x86_64.rpm
mysql-community-embedded-compat-8.0.34-1.el7.x86_64.rpm
mysql-community-icu-data-files-8.0.34-1.el7.x86_64.rpm
mysql-community-libs-8.0.34-1.el7.x86_64.rpm
mysql-community-libs-compat-8.0.34-1.el7.x86_64.rpm
mysql-community-server-8.0.34-1.el7.x86_64.rpm
mysql-community-server-debug-8.0.34-1.el7.x86_64.rpm
mysql-community-test-8.0.34-1.el7.x86_64.rpm

[root@mysql-a mysql8]# **ls -ltr**
total 2015236
-rw-r--r-- 1 7155 31415   16755300 Jun 24 22:06 mysql-community-client-8.0.34-1.el7.x86_64.rpm
-rw-r--r-- 1 7155 31415   3745824 Jun 24 22:06 mysql-community-client-plugins-8.0.34-1.el7.x86_64.rpm
-rw-r--r-- 1 7155 31415   681724 Jun 24 22:06 mysql-community-common-8.0.34-1.el7.x86_64.rpm
-rw-r--r-- 1 7155 31415 528347988 Jun 24 22:07 mysql-community-debuginfo-8.0.34-1.el7.x86_64.rpm

91

```
-rw-r--r-- 1 7155 31415    1947800 Jun 24 22:07 mysql-community-
devel-8.0.34-1.el7.x86_64.rpm
-rw-r--r-- 1 7155 31415    4217912 Jun 24 22:07 mysql-community-
embedded-compat-8.0.34-1.el7.x86_64.rpm
-rw-r--r-- 1 7155 31415    2344364 Jun 24 22:07 mysql-community-
icu-data-files-8.0.34-1.el7.x86_64.rpm
-rw-r--r-- 1 7155 31415    1563264 Jun 24 22:07 mysql-community-
libs-8.0.34-1.el7.x86_64.rpm
-rw-r--r-- 1 7155 31415     685312 Jun 24 22:08 mysql-community-
libs-compat-8.0.34-1.el7.x86_64.rpm
-rw-r--r-- 1 7155 31415   67410132 Jun 24 22:08 mysql-community-
server-8.0.34-1.el7.x86_64.rpm
-rw-r--r-- 1 7155 31415   25637968 Jun 24 22:08 mysql-community-
server-debug-8.0.34-1.el7.x86_64.rpm
-rw-r--r-- 1 7155 31415  378442676 Jun 24 22:10 mysql-community-
test-8.0.34-1.el7.x86_64.rpm
-rw-r--r-- 1 root root  1031792640 Jun 24 22:27 mysql-8.0.34-1.
el7.x86_64.rpm-bundle.tar
[root@mysql-a mysql8]#
```

6. **Stop** MySQL daemon (mysqld).

```
[root@mysql-a ~]# systemctl stop mysqld
```

7. **Uninstall** MySQL 5.7.

```
[root@mysql-a ~]# rpm -qa |grep mysql
mysql-community-common-5.7.43-1.el7.x86_64
mysql-community-server-5.7.43-1.el7.x86_64
mysql-community-libs-5.7.43-1.el7.x86_64
mysql-community-libs-compat-5.7.43-1.el7.x86_64
mysql-shell-8.0.30-1.el7.x86_64
mysql-community-client-5.7.43-1.el7.x86_64

[root@mysql-a ~]# rpm -e mysql-community-common-5.7.43-1.el7.
x86_64 mysql-community-server-5.7.43-1.el7.x86_64 mysql-community-
libs-5.7.43-1.el7.x86_64 mysql-community-libs-compat-5.7.43-1.el7.
x86_64 mysql-community-client-5.7.43-1.el7.x86_64
```

```
[root@mysql-a ~]# rpm -qa |grep mysql
mysql-shell-8.0.30-1.el7.x86_64
[root@mysql-a ~]#
```

8. **Install** MySQL 8.0.

```
[root@mysql-a mysql8]# ls -ltr
total 2015236
-rw-r--r-- 1 7155 31415   16755300 Jun 24 22:06 mysql-community-
client-8.0.34-1.el7.x86_64.rpm
-rw-r--r-- 1 7155 31415    3745824 Jun 24 22:06 mysql-community-
client-plugins-8.0.34-1.el7.x86_64.rpm
-rw-r--r-- 1 7155 31415     681724 Jun 24 22:06 mysql-community-
common-8.0.34-1.el7.x86_64.rpm
-rw-r--r-- 1 7155 31415   528347988 Jun 24 22:07 mysql-community-
debuginfo-8.0.34-1.el7.x86_64.rpm
-rw-r--r-- 1 7155 31415    1947800 Jun 24 22:07 mysql-community-
devel-8.0.34-1.el7.x86_64.rpm
-rw-r--r-- 1 7155 31415    4217912 Jun 24 22:07 mysql-community-
embedded-compat-8.0.34-1.el7.x86_64.rpm
-rw-r--r-- 1 7155 31415    2344364 Jun 24 22:07 mysql-community-
icu-data-files-8.0.34-1.el7.x86_64.rpm
-rw-r--r-- 1 7155 31415    1563264 Jun 24 22:07 mysql-community-
libs-8.0.34-1.el7.x86_64.rpm
-rw-r--r-- 1 7155 31415     685312 Jun 24 22:08 mysql-community-
libs-compat-8.0.34-1.el7.x86_64.rpm
-rw-r--r-- 1 7155 31415   67410132 Jun 24 22:08 mysql-community-
server-8.0.34-1.el7.x86_64.rpm
-rw-r--r-- 1 7155 31415   25637968 Jun 24 22:08 mysql-community-
server-debug-8.0.34-1.el7.x86_64.rpm
-rw-r--r-- 1 7155 31415   378442676 Jun 24 22:10 mysql-community-
test-8.0.34-1.el7.x86_64.rpm
-rw-r--r-- 1 root root   1031792640 Jun 24 22:27 mysql-8.0.34-1.
el7.x86_64.rpm-bundle.tar
[root@mysql-a mysql8]#
[root@mysql-a mysql8]# rpm -ivh mysql-community-*.rpm
```

warning: mysql-community-client-8.0.34-1.el7.x86_64.rpm: Header V4
RSA/SHA256 Signature, key ID 3a79bd29: NOKEY
error: Failed dependencies:
        pkgconfig(openssl) is needed by mysql-community-
        devel-8.0.34-1.el7.x86_64
        perl(JSON) is needed by mysql-community-test-8.0.34-1.
        el7.x86_64
        perl(Test::More) is needed by mysql-community-
        test-8.0.34-1.el7.x86_64
[root@mysql-a mysql8]#

**Resolve failed dependencies by installing the missing packages
using the commands below**
yum install openssl*
yum install perl* --skip-broken

[root@mysql-a mysql8]# **rpm -ivh mysql-community-*.rpm**
warning: mysql-community-client-8.0.34-1.el7.x86_64.rpm: Header V4
RSA/SHA256 Signature, key ID 3a79bd29: NOKEY
Preparing...   ######################### [100%]
Updating / installing...
   1:mysql-community-common-8.0.34-1.e################# [8%]
   2:mysql-community-client-plugins-8.################# [17%]
   3:mysql-community-libs-8.0.34-1.el7################# [25%]
   4:mysql-community-client-8.0.34-1.e################# [33%]
   5:mysql-community-icu-data-files-8.################# [42%]
   6:mysql-community-server-8.0.34-1.e################# [50%]
   7:mysql-community-server-debug-8.0.################# [58%]
   8:mysql-community-test-8.0.34-1.el7################# [67%]
   9:mysql-community-devel-8.0.34-1.el################# [75%]
  10:mysql-community-libs-compat-8.0.3################# [83%]
  11:mysql-community-embedded-compat-8################# [92%]
  12:mysql-community-debuginfo-8.0.34################## [100%]
[root@mysql-a mysql8]#

9. **Start** MySQL daemon (mysqld).

    [root@mysql-a ~]# **systemctl start mysqld**

10. **Verify** installation.

[root@mysql-a ~]# **mysqladmin -u root -p --version**
mysqladmin Ver 8.0.34 for Linux on x86_64 (MySQL Community
Server - GPL)

[root@mysql-a ~]# **mysql -u root -p**
Enter password:

mysql> **show databases;**
```
+--------------------+
| Database           |
+--------------------+
| db1                |
| db2                |
| db3                |
| information_schema |
| mysql              |
| mysqlbackup        |
| performance_schema |
| sys                |
+--------------------+
```
8 rows in set (0.00 sec)

mysql> **use db1;**
Reading table information for completion of table and column names
You can turn off this feature to get a quicker startup with -A

Database changed

mysql> **select * from tab1;**
```
+------+
| no   |
+------+
|    1 |
+------+
```
1 row in set (0.00 sec)

mysql> **use db2;**

```
Reading table information for completion of table and column names
You can turn off this feature to get a quicker startup with -A

Database changed
```

mysql> **select * from tab1;**

```
+------+
| no   |
+------+
|    1 |
+------+
1 row in set (0.00 sec)
```

mysql> **select * from tab2;**

```
+------+
| no   |
+------+
|    1 |
+------+
1 row in set (0.00 sec)
```

The other option is to perform a **logical** upgrade, which involves exporting SQL from the MySQL 5.7 instance using a backup or an export utility such as **mysqldump**, installing the new MySQL server, and then applying the exported SQL to the new MySQL 8.0.34 instance. The following are the steps to perform a logical upgrade:

1. Check and verify that all upgrade prerequisites are met as described in the previous section.

2. Export existing data from MySQL 5.7 using the following command:

   [root@mysql-a ~]# **mysqldump -u root -p --add-drop-table -routines --events --all-databases --force > mydbdump.sql**

3. Shut down MySQL 5.7 server.

   [root@mysql-a ~]# **mysqladmin -u root -p shutdown**

4. Install MySQL 8.0 using any of the methods described previously.

5. Initialize the new data directory using

```
[root@mysql-a ~]# mysqld --initialize -datadir=<path_to_new_data_
directory>
```

A temporary password will be generated in the /var/log/mysqld.
log for use at first login.

6. Start MySQL 8.0 with the new data directory like the following:

```
[root@mysql-a ~]# msyqld_safe --user=msyql --datadir=<path_to_new_
data_directory> &
```

7. Reset the root password upon first logon.

```
[root@mysql-a ~]# mysql -u root -p
Enter password:                    <<<< enter temporary password from
                                   step 5 here
mysql> alter user user() identified by '<new_password>';
```

8. Load the data from the dump file created in step 2.

```
[root@mysql-a ~]# mysql -u root -p --force < mydbdump.sql
```

Please note that loading a dump file with GTIDs enabled is not
recommended.

9. Shut down the server and start it with --upgrade=FORCE to
ensure the server makes any changes required in the **mysql**
system schema between version 5.7 and version 8.0. In addition,
it updates the performance schema, information_schema, and
sys schema.

```
[root@mysql-a ~]# mysqladmin -u root -p shutdown
[root@mysql-a ~]# mysqld_safe --user=mysql -datadir=<path_to_new_
directory> --upgrade=FORCE &
```

10. Run **mysql_upgrade** to complete the remaining upgrade tasks.

```
[root@mysql-a ~]# msyql_upgrade -u root -p
```

11. Restart MySQL server to ensure all changes made are in effect.

```
[root@mysql-a ~]# mysqladmin -u root -p shutdown
[root@mysql-a ~]# mysqld_safe --user=mysql -datadir=<path_to_new_
directory> &
```

Downgrading MySQL

There is no downgrade utility to downgrade from MySQL 8.0 to MySQL 5.7 or a release before that. The only supported way is to restore from a backup you take before upgrading. Taking a backup before upgrading is always recommended to help in use cases like this.

MySQL 8.2

Through this book, we cover the MySQL version 8.0.36 and use this version in all the discussions and examples.

The latest version of MySQL is 8.2, which was released very recently. We will take a quick glance of the 8.2 version key features and enhancements.

What Is New in MySQL 8.2

1) Additional logging for server start/stop

   – Additional log messages are added for start/stop operations.

2) Enterprise audit

   – Added an uninstall script audit_log_filter_uninstall.sql to remove the enterprise audit installation

3) Authentication

   – MySQL supports authentication methods of FIDO and FIDO2 standards and supports smart cards, bio readers, and security keys.

4) Enterprise firewall

- MySQL allows memory caches to be reloaded frequently with the firewall info stored in the tables and added uninstall script to remove the enterprise firewall.

5) Privileges

- Added two new privileges: SET_ANY_DEFINER and ALLOW_NONEXISTENT_DEFINER

6) Explain plan for schema

- This version added a schema option to explain the statement.

What Is Deprecated in MySQL 8.2

1) Wildcard characters in database grants

- In this version, the use of the characters % and _ as wildcards in database grants is deprecated.

2) mysql_native_password

- The plug-in mysql_native_password, which was deprecated in the previous versions, can be disabled at server startup.

3) binlog_transaction_dependency_tracking

- Parameter binlog_transaction_dependency_tracking is deprecated in this version and will be removed in the future versions.

4) SET_USER_ID privilege

- This parameter is deprecated in this version and removed in the future versions; use newly introduced parameter SET_ANY_DEFINER for object creation.

Summary

MySQL is one of the most popular open source relational databases, with the latest version being 8.0.34. It is supported on several platforms and offers high availability, security, performance, and scalability. It's easy to install and to get started with MySQL.

The next chapter will discuss the available MySQL utilities and an overview of each utility in MySQL administration.

CHAPTER 2

MySQL Utilities

Introduction

MySQL installation comes with many utilities for working with databases. This chapter will discuss the tools available with MySQL and their usage. MySQL has all the tools that come with installation. Throughout this book, we will frequently use these tools, which are fundamental to working with MySQL databases.

The default location of the tools in MySQL with default installation is /usr/bin. All the utilities/tools are present in this location.

Note Some tools are available only in the Enterprise Edition. Here is an example from the Enterprise Edition installation.

```
[root@mysqlhost bin]# pwd
/usr/bin
[root@mysqlhost bin]# ls -lrt mysql*
-rwxr-xr-x 1 root root      6681 Jun 22 05:08 mysqldumpslow
-rwxr-xr-x 1 root root     29137 Jun 22 05:08 mysqld_safe
-rwxr-xr-x 1 root root      3380 Jun 22 05:08 mysqld_pre_systemd
-rwxr-xr-x 1 root root      4029 Jun 22 05:08 mysql_config-64
-rwxr-xr-x 1 root root       840 Jun 22 05:08 mysql_config
-rwxr-xr-x 1 root root   7510432 Jun 22 05:47 mysql_upgrade
-rwxr-xr-x 1 root root   6473592 Jun 22 05:47 mysqlrouter_plugin_info
-rwxr-xr-x 1 root root    662672 Jun 22 05:47 mysqlrouter
-rwxr-xr-x 1 root root   6650168 Jun 22 05:47 mysql_keyring_encryption_test
-rwxr-xr-x 1 root root   7485296 Jun 22 05:47 mysqldump
```

© Y V Ravi Kumar, Arun Kumar Samayam, Naresh Kumar Miryala 2024
Y V Ravi Kumar et al., *Mastering MySQL Administration*, https://doi.org/10.1007/979-8-8688-0252-2_2

```
-rwxr-xr-x 1 root root  7933752 Jun 22 05:47 mysql_client_test
-rwxr-xr-x 1 root root  9350520 Jun 22 05:47 mysqlxtest
-rwxr-xr-x 1 root root    17144 Jun 22 05:47 mysqltest_safe_process
-rwxr-xr-x 1 root root  7413952 Jun 22 05:47 mysqlslap
-rwxr-xr-x 1 root root   188680 Jun 22 05:47 mysqlrouter_keyring
-rwxr-xr-x 1 root root  7492336 Jun 22 05:47 mysql_migrate_keyring
-rwxr-xr-x 1 root root 14047128 Jun 22 05:47 mysqlbackup
-rwxr-xr-x 1 root root  7717912 Jun 22 05:47 mysql
-rwxr-xr-x 1 root root  7417176 Jun 22 05:47 mysqlcheck
-rwxr-xr-x 1 root root  7874304 Jun 22 05:47 mysqlbinlog
-rwxr-xr-x 1 root root  6431568 Jun 22 05:47 mysql_tzinfo_to_sql
-rwxr-xr-x 1 root root  6555808 Jun 22 05:47 mysql_ssl_rsa_setup
-rwxr-xr-x 1 root root  7394216 Jun 22 05:47 mysqlshow
-rwxr-xr-x 1 root root   151392 Jun 22 05:47 mysqlrouter_passwd
-rwxr-xr-x 1 root root  7400104 Jun 22 05:47 mysqlimport
-rwxr-xr-x 1 root root  6520432 Jun 22 05:47 mysql_config_editor
-rwxr-xr-x 1 root root  7403792 Jun 22 05:47 mysqladmin
-rwxr-xr-x 1 root root  8736128 Jun 22 05:47 mysqltest
-rwxr-xr-x 1 root root  7387664 Jun 22 05:47 mysql_secure_installation
-rwxr-xr-x 1 root root  8026184 Jun 22 05:47 mysqlpump
```

MySQL

MySQL is the most used and first command to manage MySQL databases, which helps connect to MySQL databases and do all the database operations. It is included with the standard installation. When we run the utility in the command prompt, it will ask for the user password we need to connect.

- Running SQL statements

- Managing users – create, delete, add roles, etc.

- Creating and deleting databases, tables, and indexes

- Troubleshooting and optimizing performance

Syntax:
```
# mysql -u<user> -p
```

Example:
```
root@mysqlhost01 ~]# mysql -uroot -p
Enter password:
```

Using the following example, we can pass the password in the command line and connect to MySQL database directly.

Note   Passing password over the command line is an insecure method and not recommended in production setup as this can expose the password.

```
root@mysqlhost01 ~]# mysql -uroot -pPassword@123
mysql: [Warning] Using a password on the command line interface can be insecure.
mysql>
```

MySQL Dump

MySQL Dump is a powerful and useful tool that helps us to take backup and restore when needed. This tool is included in standard installation and has various useful features for administrators to customize the backup process. We can take a single database backup or all databases with one command; mysqldump also helps us to transfer databases between servers.

Please find the example usage of the mysqldump command here:

Example:
```
[root@mysqlhost01 ~]# mysqldump -u [username] -p --databases [database_
name] > [dumpfile.sql]
```

Let's examine the command-line example and parameters to be passed to the mysqldump command.

[Username]: MySQL database user, which you would use to connect to the database.

[Databases]: The name or names of the database to be backed up.

[Dumpfile]: Dumpfile is the file where the backup will be written.

How to Back Up a Single Database

To back up a single database of MySQL, use the following command:

Syntax:
```
[root@mysqlhost01 ~]# mysqldump -u [username] -p --databases [database_
name] > [dumpfile.sql]
```

Example:
```
[root@mysqlhost01 ~]# mysqldump -u root -p --databases test1 > /backup/
databases_dumpfile.sql
```

How to Back Up Multiple Databases

We can back up multiple databases with the mysqldump command; the following command explains the syntax:

Syntax:
```
[root@mysqlhost01 ~]# mysqldump -u [username] -p --databases [database_
name] [database_name] > [dumpfile.sql]
```

Example:
```
[root@mysqlhost01 ~]# mysqldump -u root -p --databases test1 test2 >
/backup/databases_dumpfile.sql
```

How to Back Up All the Databases

Using the following command, we can back up all the databases in the MySQL servers. This command backs up the structure and data of all the databases in the MySQL instance.

Syntax:
```
[root@mysqlhost01 ~]# mysqldump -u [username] -p –all-databases >
[dumpfile.sql]
```

Example:
```
[root@mysqlhost01 ~]# mysqldump -u root -p --databases –all-databases >
/backup/all_databases_dumpfile.sql
```

Useful command line options with MySQL Dump

Table 2-1. Few more useful commands for mysqldump and their usage

`# mysqldump --help`	Use the help option to get all the options.
`# mysqldump --no-data`	Only backup structure, no data backup.
`# mysqldump --no-create-info`	Only backup data without structure.
`# mysqldump --login-path`	Database connects info shared in the file, instead of providing during the command line on the backup script.
`# mysqldump table1 database1`	To back up a single table name table1 from database database1.
`# mysqldump table1 table2 database1`	To back up multiple tables table1 and table2 from a database named database1.

How to Restore Single MySQL Database

To restore a database from the backup, please use the following commands to restore the test1 database from the backup dump.

Syntax:
```
[root@mysqlhost01 ~]# mysql -u [username] -p [database_name] <
[dumpfile.sql]
```

Example:
```
[root@mysqlhost01 ~]# mysql -u root -p  test1 < /backup/databases_
dumpfile.sql
```

How to Restore All MySQL Databases

Using the following command, we can back up all the databases in the MySQL servers; this command backs up the structure and data of all the databases in the MySQL instance.

Syntax:
```
[root@mysqlhost01 ~]# mysql -u [username] -p [database_name] <
[dumpfile.sql]
```

Example:
```
[root@mysqlhost01 ~]# mysql -u root -p  test1 < /backup/databases_
dumpfile.sql
```

MySQL Pump

mysqlpump is another powerful tool to take backups. It provides new features not available with mysqldump, such as parallel backups, support for streaming backups, and compression.

The following are the features:

- Multi-threaded
- Parallel schema backups
- Compression

It is highly recommended to use mysqldump if you are using MySQL 8.0. For lower versions, it is recommended to use mysqlpump because of the aforementioned advantages.

Syntax:
```
[root@mysqlhost01 ~]# mysqlpump -u [username] -p --all-databases >
[dumpfile.sql]
```

Example:
```
[root@mysqlhost01 ~]# mysqldump -u root -p --all-databases > /backup/all_
databases_dumpfile.sql
```

WARNING: mysqlpump is deprecated and will be removed in a future version. Use mysqldump instead.
Enter password:
Dump progress: 1/1 tables, 0/0 rows
Dump progress: 35/36 tables, 1539240/32639699 rows
Dump progress: 35/36 tables, 3209990/32639699 rows
Dump progress: 35/36 tables, 4867990/32639699 rows
Dump progress: 35/36 tables, 6511990/32639699 rows
Dump progress: 35/36 tables, 8161740/32639699 rows
Dump progress: 35/36 tables, 9811740/32639699 rows
Dump progress: 35/36 tables, 11462740/32639699 rows
Dump progress: 35/36 tables, 13117740/32639699 rows
Dump progress: 35/36 tables, 14773990/32639699 rows
Dump progress: 35/36 tables, 16270740/32639699 rows
Dump progress: 35/36 tables, 17909740/32639699 rows
Dump progress: 35/36 tables, 29220990/32639699 rows
Dump progress: 35/36 tables, 30875240/32639699 rows
Dump progress: 35/36 tables, 32538240/32639699 rows
Dump completed in 21765

MySQL Backup

mysqlbackup is a new tool with many more features than mysqldump and mysqlpump. It helps us to have backups compressed, encrypted, and easy to use. The following are the key features:

Note   mysqlbackup is available only in the Enterprise Edition; more details about this topic are discussed in detail in the enterprise backup Chapter 9.

- **Incremental backup**: This helps us to take incremental backup, which only backs up the data since the last full backup.

- **Encryption**: We can safeguard the backup using encryptions; it is a great security enhancement.

- **Parallel backups**: This helps to take backup of large databases and minimize the backup time.

- **Validation**: We can now validate the backups whether they are valid for restore or not.

Table 2-2. *Few backup parameter options and details around the options outlined*

Options	Description
--user	Backup username to connect to the database.
--password	Backup username password to connect to the database.
--with-timestamp	When the --with-timestamp option is used, a subdirectory under the --backup-dir location with timestamp is created and backup is written to this location.
--backup-dir	The directory location where to store the backup data and metadata.
--backup	Back up data to a directory.
--backup-and-apply	Back up data and apply logs into a directory.
--backup-to-image	Back up as single file to a directory (this is preferred).
--compress	Backup will be stored in compressed format.

Syntax:
```
mysqlbackup --user=[username] --password --host=[hostname]
--with-timestamp --backup-dir=[backup directory] backup
```

Example:
```
[root@mysqlhost01 ~]# mysqlbackup --user=root --password --host=mysqlhost01
--with-timestamp --backup-dir=/backup/mysql backup
Enter password:

231108 02:17:47 MAIN    INFO: Establishing connection to server.
231108 02:17:47 MAIN WARNING: --host option is specified. Ignoring the
                         option and using the localhost
```

WARNING: MYSQL_OPT_RECONNECT is deprecated and will be removed in a future version.
```
231108 02:17:47 MAIN      INFO: No SSL options specified.
231108 02:17:47 MAIN      INFO: MySQL server version is '8.0.34-commercial'
231108 02:17:47 MAIN      INFO: MySQL server compile os version is 'Linux'
231108 02:17:47 MAIN      INFO: Got some server configuration information
                          from running server.
231108 02:17:47 MAIN      INFO: Establishing connection to server for
                          locking.
231108 02:17:47 MAIN      WARNING: --host option is specified. Ignoring the
                          option and using the localhost
```
WARNING: MYSQL_OPT_RECONNECT is deprecated and will be removed in a future version.
```
231108 02:17:47 MAIN      INFO: No SSL options specified.
231108 02:17:47 MAIN      INFO: Backup directory exists:
```

--output truncated for better visibility

```
231108 02:17:51 MAIN      INFO: Full Image Backup operation completed
successfully.
231108 02:17:51 MAIN      INFO: Backup image created successfully.
231108 02:17:51 MAIN      INFO: Image Path = /backup/mysql/mysql_data.mbi
231108 02:17:51 MAIN      INFO: MySQL binlog position: filename
                          binlog.000051, position 157.


-------------------------------------------------------------
   Parameters Summary
-------------------------------------------------------------
   Start LSN              : 3857839616
   Last Checkpoint LSN    : 3857845904
   End LSN                : 3857846749
-------------------------------------------------------------
```
mysqlbackup completed OK! with 2 warnings

Note   In the preceding output, please ensure we get the message "**mysqlbackup completed OK!**".

Validate backups – It is a good practice that we must check for the integrity of the backups to ensure if the backup is available for restore; it will ensure reliability.

[root@mysqlhost01 ~]# mysqlbackup --backup-image=/backup/mysql/mysql_data. mbi validate

```
Starting with following command line ...
mysqlbackup
--backup-image=/tmp/mybkup/my.mbi
validate

IMPORTANT: Please check that mysqlbackup run completes successfully.
           At the end of a successful 'validate' run mysqlbackup
           prints "mysqlbackup completed OK!".

231108 02:23:54 MAIN      INFO: Backup Image MEB version string: 8.0.34
231108 02:23:54 MAIN      INFO: MySQL server version is '8.0.34'
231108 02:23:54 MAIN      INFO: The backup image has no keyring.
231108 02:23:54 MAIN      INFO: Creating 14 buffers each of size 16777216.
231108 02:23:54 MAIN      INFO: Validate operation starts with
                          following threads
231108 02:23:54 MAIN      INFO: Validating image ... /tmp/mybkup/my.mbi
231108 02:23:54 PCR1      INFO: Validate: [Dir]: meta
                RDR1      Progress in MB: 200 400 600 800 1000 1200 1400
                          1600 1800 2000 2200 2400 2600 2800 3000 3200 3400
                          3600 3800
231108 02:23:56 PCR6      INFO: Validate: [Dir]: datadir/mysql
231108 02:23:56 PCR4      INFO: Validate: [Dir]: datadir/performance_schema
```

--output truncate for better visibility

```
231108 02:23:56 MAIN      INFO: datadir/mysql/audit_log_user.ibd validated.
231108 02:23:56 MAIN      INFO: datadir/test/Companies.ibd validated.
231108 02:23:56 MAIN      INFO: datadir/test/TESTTABLE1.ibd validated.
validated.
231108 02:23:56 MAIN      INFO: Validate operation completed successfully.
```

```
231108 02:23:56 MAIN      INFO: Backup Image validation successful.
231108 02:23:56 MAIN      INFO: Source Image Path = /backup/mysql/mysql_
                          data.mbi
```

mysqlbackup completed OK!

MySQL Check

mysqlcheck helps check errors in MySQL databases and can be used to optimize and enhance the performance of MySQL databases. Periodically we must run mysqlcheck on our MySQL databases to detect any errors and repair them proactively. We can use mysqlcheck to check and repair individual tables.

mysqlcheck helps to perform many admin activities to validate database objects. Here are the frequent use cases.

Table 2-3. *Frequent use cases of mysqlcheck*

Activity	Details
Table corruption	It can happen due to various factors.
Missing or invalid indexes	It helps to run queries faster but needs extra care to maintain these indexes.
Unused indexes	It degrades performance by improper storage utilization.
Fragmented tables	It can cause MySQL queries to run slower.

Please find the following example and output for the mysqlcheck command; when the output shows as OK, the objects in the database test are showing as OK as they don't have any corruption or missing indexes or fragmentation issues.

Syntax:
 # /usr/bin/mysqlcheck --databases [databasename] -u[username] -p

Example:
[root@mysqlhost01 ~]# /usr/bin/mysqlcheck --databases test -uroot -p
```
Enter password:
test.Companies                                OK
test.EMPLOYEE                                 OK
```

```
test.EMPLOYEE1                                    OK
test.TESTTABLE1                                   OK
test.employee_table                               OK
```

MySQL Binlog

mysqlbinlog helps to read and process MySQL binary log files; it contains all changes made to a MySQL database; mysqlbinlog can be used to view the contents of binary log files, generate a report of the changes that have been made, or apply the changes in the binary log files to another MySQL database.

We can use mysqlbinlog for the following:

- Debugging database issues

- Restoring data from a backup

- Replicating data between MySQL database servers

- Performing point-in-time recovery

[root@mysqlhost01 ~]# mysqlbinlog /var/lib/mysql/binlog.000042

```
# The proper term is pseudo_replica_mode, but we use this
compatibility alias
# to make the statement usable on server versions 8.0.24 and older.
/*!50530 SET @@SESSION.PSEUDO_SLAVE_MODE=1*/;
/*!50003 SET @OLD_COMPLETION_TYPE=@@COMPLETION_TYPE,COMPLETION_TYPE=0*/;
DELIMITER /*!*/;
# at 4
#231020  9:21:16 server id 1  end_log_pos 126 CRC32 0x35bc63e6     Start:
binlog v 4, server v 8.0.34-commercial created 231020  9:21:16 at startup
ROLLBACK/*!*/;
BINLOG '
/KgyZQ8BAAAAAQAOC4wLjM0LWNvbW1lcmNpYWwAAAAAAAAAAAAAAAAAAAAAAAAAA
AAAAAAAAAAAAAAAAD8qDJlEwANAAgAAAAABAAEAAAAYgAEGggAAAAICAgCAAAACgoKK
'/*!*/;
# at 126
#231020  9:21:16 server id 1  end_log_pos **157** CRC32
```

```
0xa8340f6e        Previous-GTIDs
# [empty]
# at 157
#231020  9:24:34 server id 1   end_log_pos 180 CRC32 0x14069696         Stop
SET @@SESSION.GTID_NEXT= 'AUTOMATIC' /* added by mysqlbinlog */ /*!*/;
DELIMITER ;
# End of log file
/*!50003 SET COMPLETION_TYPE=@OLD_COMPLETION_TYPE*/;
/*!50530 SET @@SESSION.PSEUDO_SLAVE_MODE=0*/;
[root@mysqlhost01 ~]#
```

MySQL Safe

mysqld_safe is a standard recommended way to restart the mysqld server; most of the options in mysqld_safe are the same as those in mysqld. It reads all the options from mysqld, server, and mysqld_safe section in the config file.

mysqld_safe allows passing additional parameters to mysqld when restarting the MySQL server; the most critical and widely used one is the --skip-grant-tables option, which is used for resetting the root password without an old password.

Here are a few more useful commands for mysqld_safe and their usage.

Table 2-4. *msql_safe commands are listed and options*

`# mysql_safe --help`	Use the help option to get all the options.
`# mysql_safe --defaults-file=file_name`	Override the default file and point to a new default file.
`# mysql_safe --log-error=file_name`	Set where to write the error log into a file.
`# mysql_safe --port=number`	MySQL port number to run the TCP connections.
`# mysql_safe --no-defaults`	Override and set no default values to be set, so no option files are read.

MySQL Dump Slow

mysqldumpslow is a utility that is helpful in identifying the performance issue. MySQL has a feature through which we can write all the queries that are running more than a threshold defined (slow query log is discussed in further chapters) into a file for analysis.

Slow query log contains a format that is not easily readable; mysqldumpslow helps to summarize the information in the slow query log and present the output in a format that helps in debugging the issues with the information captured in the slow query log.

Here are a few more useful commands for mysqldumpslow and their usage.

Table 2-5. *mysqldumpslow log commands and options*

`# mysqldumpslow --help`	Uses the help option to get all the options.
`# mysqldumpslow /log/slow.log`	No options, provides output without any options.
`# mysqldumpslow -t 5 /log/slow.log`	Displays only the first five queries.
`# mysqldumpslow -s c /log/slow.log`	Displays output by sorting by count.
`# mysqldumpslow -r /log/slow.log`	Displays output by reversing the sort order.

MySQL Show

mysqlshow is another command-line utility that will show the details of the databases, tables, and columns; it will help us to check the details quickly.

Some examples are as follows.

Table 2-6. *mysqlshow commands and options*

Command	Details
`mysqlshow -uroot -p`	To display tables in all databases
`mysqlshow dbname -uroot -p`	To display tables in specific databases
`mysqlshow -t dbname tablename -uroot -p`	To describe a table in a specific database

Please find the following example command to list all the tables in the **test** database.

```
[root@mysqlhost01 ~]# mysqlshow test -uroot -p
Enter password:
Database: test
+----------------------------------------------------------+
|                         Tables                           |
+----------------------------------------------------------+
| employee                                                 |
| company                                                  |
| test                                                     |
| org                                                      |
| work                                                     |
| salary                                                   |
| salary_ex                                                |
       --output truncate for better visibility
| work_log                                                 |
| tables_priv                                              |
| time_zone                                                |
| time_zone_leap_second                                    |
| time_zone_name                                           |
| time_zone_transition                                     |
| time_zone_transition_type                                |
| user                                                     |
+----------------------------------------------------------+
```

Please find the following example where the database name **test** and table name **example**.

```
[root@mysqlhost01 ~]# mysqlshow -t test example -uroot -p
Enter password:
Database: test   Table: example
+-------+------+-----------+------+-
|Field | Type| Collation| Null| Key| Default| Extra| Privileges| Comment|
+------+------+--------+------+-----+--------+------+----------------
|Host|char(255)|ascii_general_ci|NO| PRI|||select,insert,update,references||
|Db |char(64)  | utf8mb3_bin     |NO| PRI|||select,insert,update,references||
|User| char(32)| utf8mb3_bin     |NO| PRI|||select,insert,update,references||
 --output truncate for better visibility

|Event_priv|       |utf8mb3_bin|NO|PRI|||select,insert,update,references ||
+----------------------+--------------+--------------------+------+
```

MySQL Secure Installation

Once database installation is completed, we can use the CLI to secure the database instead of the aforementioned manual methods. It will perform the following actions; these steps are optional, but they are necessary to secure databases in production environments.

- Reset the password of the root user.

- Delete anonymous user accounts.

- Remove the test database that was created by default during the installation.

- Disable remote root login.

- Enable password encryption.

- Reload privilege tables that will ensure that all the changes made so far will take effect immediately.

```
[root@mysqlhost ~]# /usr/bin/mysql_secure_installation
```

Securing the MySQL server deployment.

Enter password for user root:
The 'validate_password' component is installed on the server.
The subsequent steps will run with the existing configuration
of the component.
Using existing password for root.

Estimated strength of the password: 25
Change the password for root ? ((Press y|Y for Yes, any other key
for No) : Y

New password:

Re-enter new password:

Estimated strength of the password: 100
Do you wish to continue with the password provided?(Press y|Y for Yes, any
other key for No) : Y
By default, a MySQL installation has an anonymous user,
allowing anyone to log into MySQL without having to have
a user account created for them. This is intended only for
testing, and to make the installation go a bit smoother.
You should remove them before moving into a production
environment.

MySQL Import

mysqlimport is a CLI tool; it can be used to import data into a MySQL table from
different file formats, like TSV, CSV, and JSON; also we can import compressed files like
zip and GZ files.

Syntax:
[root@mysqlhost01 ~]# mysqlimport --local [schema] [localfile.txt]

Example:
[root@mysqlhost01 ~]# mysql -uroot -p
Enter password:

mysql> use test
Database changed

117

```
mysql> CREATE TABLE movies (id INT, Name VARCHAR(30));
Query OK, 0 rows affected (0.01 sec)

mysql> exit
Bye

[root@mysqlhost01 ~]# cat movies.txt
1    Avatar
2    Interstellar

[root@mysqlhost01 ~]# od -c movies.txt
0000000    1    \t   A   v   a   t   a   r       \n   2       \t   I   n
0000020    t   e   r   s   t   e   l   l   a   r   \n
0000033

[root@mysqlhost01 ~]# mysqlimport --local test movies.txt -uroot -p
Enter password:
mysqlimport: Error: 3948, Loading local data is disabled; this must be
enabled on both the client and server sides, when using table: movies
```

**Note: To fix the above error, please set the below line in /etc/my.cnf file
and restart mysql**
```
local_infile = 1

[root@mysqlhost01 ~]# mysqlimport --local test movies.txt -uroot -p
Enter password:
test.movies: Records: 2  Deleted: 0  Skipped: 0  Warnings: 2

[root@mysqlhost01 ~]# mysql -uroot -p -e 'select * from movies' test
Enter password:
+------+--------------+
| id   | Name         |
+------+--------------+
|    1 | Avatar       |
|    2 | Interstellar |
+------+--------------+
```

MySQL Config

mysql_config is a shell script that shows the details about the MySQL server and client libraries. It is used to compile and link MySQL client programs.

Note   This is a shell script, so this tool is only available on UNIX/Linux-based systems.

Compiler flags: The compiler flags that are needed to compile MySQL programs

Library paths: The paths to the MySQL client libraries

Version number: The version number of the MySQL server and client libraries

```
[root@mysqlhost1 ~]# mysql_config
Usage: /usr/bin/mysql_config-64 [OPTIONS]
Compiler: GNU 12.2.1
Options:
        --cflags        [-I/usr/include/mysql -m64 ]
        --cxxflags      [-I/usr/include/mysql -m64 ]
        --include       [-I/usr/include/mysql]
        --libs          [-L/usr/lib64/mysql -lmysqlclient -lpthread -ldl
                        -lssl -lcrypto -lresolv -lm -lrt]
        --libs_r        [-L/usr/lib64/mysql -lmysqlclient -lpthread -ldl
                        -lssl -lcrypto -lresolv -lm -lrt]
        --plugindir     [/usr/lib64/mysql/plugin]
        --socket        [/var/lib/mysql/mysql.sock]
        --port          [0]
        --version       [8.0.34]
        --variable=VAR   VAR is one of:
                pkgincludedir [/usr/include/mysql]
                pkglibdir     [/usr/lib64/mysql]
                plugindir     [/usr/lib64/mysql/plugin]
```

```
[root@mysqlhost1 ~]# mysql_config --cflags
-I/usr/include/mysql -m64

[root@mysqlhost1 ~]# gcc -c `mysql_config --cflags` example.c
Compilation completed
```

Note   In the preceding example, the mysql_config cflags output in the command is used to compile and build example.c

---

MySQL Config Editor

mysql_config_editor utility helps to store and manage MySQL credentials; we can make use of this to create, edit, and delete login paths, which helps in authentication. It helps us to have great security and a convenient way of managing the database credentials.

We should not hard-code the login credentials of the root user in any backup script; we can use mysql_config_editor to store it securely. This utility enhances security when automating scripts or applications that interact with MySQL without exposing plain text passwords.

Creating a login path in the MySQL login path file is a convenient way to store your connection information and avoid having to enter it every time you want to connect to the server. It is also a more secure way to store your password, as it is encrypted in the login path file.

```
[root@mysqlhost ~]# mysql_config_editor set --login-path=backupUser
--host=localhost --user=root --password

[root@mysqlhost ~]# file /root/.mylogin.cnf
/root/.mylogin.cnf: data

[root@mysqlhost ~]# mysql --login-path=backupUser
Welcome to the MySQL monitor.  Commands end with ; or \g.
Your MySQL connection id is 3699
Server version: 8.0.16 MySQL Community Server - GPL

Copyright (c) 2000, 2019, Oracle and/or its affiliates. All rights reserved.
```

```
Oracle is a registered trademark of Oracle Corporation and/or its
affiliates. Other names may be trademarks of their respective
owners.

Type 'help;' or '\h' for help. Type '\c' to clear the current input
statement.

mysql>
```

Now it will allow us to back up using mysqldump without prompting for password.

MySQL Slap

mysqlslap helps us to test the load for MySQL; it will be used to test the performance and scalability of MySQL database. It can be used for benchmarking; it also generates reports with all performance metrics like throughput and execution time.

Table 2-7. *MySQL Slap commands and options*

Options	Details
concurrency	How many connections it will hit at the same time.
iterations	How many times you want to run the test.
query	Provide the query that you want to test.
create-schema	Provide the schema name where the table resides.

Please find the following example of the mysqlslap execution for concurrency of 20 and 5 iterations.

```
[root@mysqlhost01 ~]# mysqlslap --concurrency=20 --iterations=5 --query=/
tmp/test.sql --create-schema=test -uroot -p
Enter password:
Benchmark
    Average number of seconds to run all queries: 0.001 seconds
    Minimum number of seconds to run all queries: 0.001 seconds
    Maximum number of seconds to run all queries: 0.003 seconds
    Number of clients running queries: 20
    Average number of queries per client: 1
```

MySQL Router

mysqlrouter is available in the Enterprise Edition of MySQL; router is a lightweight middleware software that can be installed as a container or a server. The router helps route the traffic in a clustered environment and provides high availability.

More detailed discussions on mysqlrouter and the usage of the router in a clustered environment are discussed in the InnoDB clustering Chapter 6.

[root@mysqlhost01 ~]# mysqlrouter --help

```
MySQL Router  Ver 8.0.34-commercial for Linux on x86_64 (MySQL
Enterprise - Commercial)
Copyright (c) 2015, 2023, Oracle and/or its affiliates.

Oracle is a registered trademark of Oracle Corporation and/or its
affiliates. Other names may be trademarks of their respective
owners.

Configuration read from the following files in the given order (enclosed
in parentheses means not available for reading):
  /etc/mysqlrouter/mysqlrouter.conf
  (/etc/mysqlrouter/mysqlrouter.ini)
  (/root/.mysqlrouter.conf)
  (/root/.mysqlrouter.ini)
Plugins Path:
  /usr/lib64/mysqlrouter
```

```
Default Log Directory:
  /var/log/mysqlrouter

Default Persistent Data Directory:
  /var/lib/mysqlrouter

Default Runtime State Directory:
  /run/mysqlrouter

# Usage

mysqlrouter (-?|--help)

mysqlrouter (-V|--version)

mysqlrouter [--account-host=<account-host>]
            (-B|--bootstrap=<server_url>)
            [--bootstrap-socket=<socket_name>]
            [--client-ssl-cert=<path>]
            [--client-ssl-cipher=<VALUE>]
            [--client-ssl-curves=<VALUE>]
```

MySQL Shell

mysqlshell is installed as client utility in client-side connections and is available for Linux and Windows platforms; mysqlshell enables the interactive client to directly connect and access the database objects using an interactive shell.

Download and install mysqlshell on a Linux platform.

```
[root@mysqlclient01 ~]# wget https://dev.mysql.com/get/Downloads/MySQL-
Shell/mysql-shell-8.0.34-1.el8.x86_64.rpm
--2023-10-22 15:57:12--  https://dev.mysql.com/get/Downloads/MySQL-Shell/
mysql-shell-8.0.34-1.el8.x86_64.rpm
Resolving dev.mysql.com (dev.mysql.com)... 2600:1408:7:1a1::2e31,
2600:1408:7:1a5::2e31, 104.108.116.193
Connecting to dev.mysql.com (dev.mysql.com)|2600:1408:7:1a1::2e31|:443...
connected.
HTTP request sent, awaiting response... 302 Moved Temporarily
```

```
Location: https://cdn.mysql.com//Downloads/MySQL-Shell/mysql-
shell-8.0.34-1.el8.x86_64.rpm [following]
--2023-10-22 15:57:12--  https://cdn.mysql.com//Downloads/MySQL-Shell/
mysql-shell-8.0.34-1.el8.x86_64.rpm
Resolving cdn.mysql.com (cdn.mysql.com)... 2600:1408:7:1bb::1d68,
2600:1408:7:1be::1d68, 23.204.255.142
Connecting to cdn.mysql.com (cdn.mysql.com)|2600:1408:7:1bb::1d68|:443...
connected.
HTTP request sent, awaiting response... 200 OK
Length: 28586732 (27M) [application/x-redhat-package-manager]
Saving to: 'mysql-shell-8.0.34-1.el8.x86_64.rpm'

mysql-shell-8.0.34-1.el8.x86_64.
rpm                        100%[=========================>]  27.26M
122MB/s      in 0.2s

2023-10-22 15:57:13 (122 MB/s) - 'mysql-shell-8.0.34-1.el8.x86_64.rpm'
saved [28586732/28586732]

[root@mysqlclient01 ~]# yum install mysql-shell-8.0.34-1.el8.x86_64.rpm
Updating Subscription Management repositories.
Unable to read consumer identity

This system is not registered with an entitlement server. You can use
subscription-manager to register.

FBIT-epel-x86_64                      114 kB/s | 4.7 kB     00:00
FBIT-fb-backports-x86_64               66 kB/s | 2.7 kB     00:00
FBIT-fb-runtime-x86_64                 29 kB/s | 1.5 kB     00:00
FBIT-fb-runtime-x86_64                4.8 MB/s | 9.8 MB     00:02
FBIT-fb-site-packages-x86_64           61 kB/s | 2.6 kB     00:00
FBIT-fbit-runtime-x86_64               18 kB/s | 1.5 kB     00:00
Dependencies resolved.
```

```
=======================================================================
 Package                Architecture Version      Repository   Size
=======================================================================
Installing:mysql-shell x86_64          8.0.34-1.el8  @commandline 27 M

Transaction Summary
=======================================================================
Install  1 Package

Total size: 27 M
Installed size: 195 M
Is this ok [y/N]: y
Downloading Packages:
Running transaction check
Transaction check succeeded.
Running transaction test
Transaction test succeeded.
Running transaction
  Preparing:  1/1
  Installing: mysql-shell-8.0.34-1.el8.x86_64       1/1
  Running scriptlet: mysql-shell-8.0.34-1.el8.x86_64      1/1
  Verifying: mysql-shell-8.0.34-1.el8.x86_64       1/1
Installed products updated.

Installed:
  mysql-shell-8.0.34-1.el8.x86_64

Complete!

[root@mysqlclient01 ~]# mysqlsh
MySQL Shell 8.0.34

Copyright (c) 2016, 2023, Oracle and/or its affiliates.
Oracle is a registered trademark of Oracle Corporation and/or its
affiliates.
Other names may be trademarks of their respective owners.

Type '\help' or '\?' for help; '\quit' to exit.
MySQL  JS >
```

MySQL Workbench

MySQL Workbench is a client-side GUI tool for admins/developers to connect to the database and query/update or analyze the database.

It is a GUI-based platform that allows users to design the database and develop the database queries with optimizations and a visualization platform to monitor the performance using the dashboards.

MySQL Workbench is downloaded on the client-side machine and installed, which connects to the database server to establish a connection and perform the design, development, and monitoring of the database operations.

Figure 2-1. *MySQL Workbench download page*

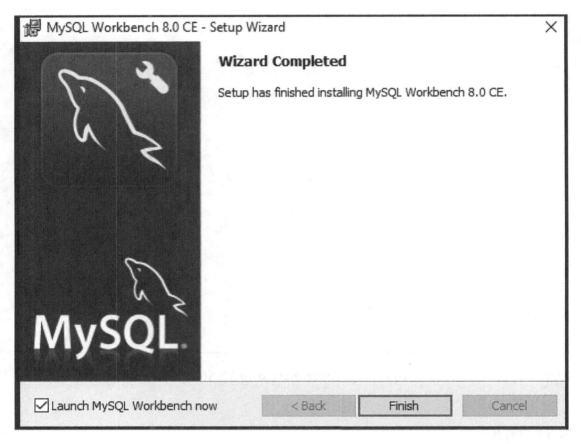

Figure 2-2. *Installation completion screen of MySQL Workbench*

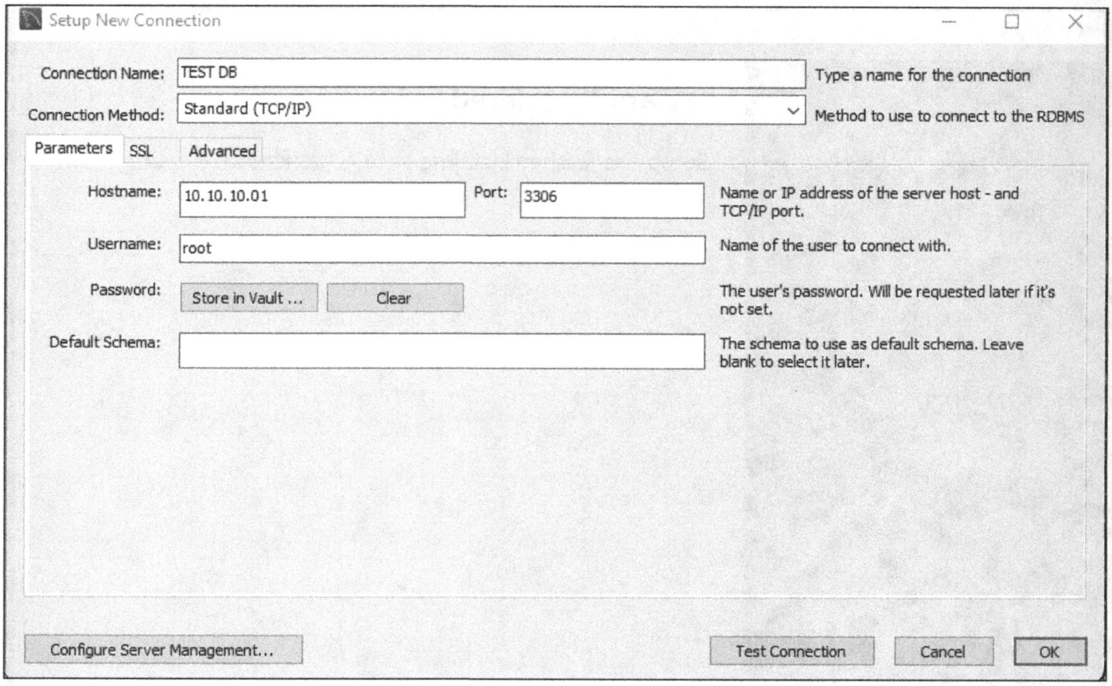

Figure 2-3. *Connecting to MySQL Instance using MySQL Workbench*

Summary

MySQL offers many rich tools to manage and administer the database; version 8.0 provides many new tools that are helpful in day-to-day operations to manage the database.

In this chapter, we have learned the tools available with MySQL installation and the usage of the tools for different use cases. In the next chapter, we will discuss MySQL general server administration concepts, configuration, and setup.

CHAPTER 3

MySQL Server Administration

Introduction

MySQL requires administrative knowledge and function to manage the database. In this chapter, we will discuss how to manage the MySQL database server.

This chapter overviews the MySQL server and covers general server administration functions like server configuration, data dictionary, server logs, connection management, components, plug-ins, loadable functions, storage engines, and running multiple MySQL instances on one host.

The main server program that performs most of the tasks in a MySQL installation is mysqld; this is a MySQL daemon that runs as an instance of MySQL database.

Configuring the MySQL Server

The MySQL server, **mysqld**, can be started with several configuration options and system variables. To get the values of the default variables, issue the following command:

```
[root@mysql-a ~]# mysqld --verbose --help
```

To check current system variables set, issue the following command:

```
[root@mysql-a ~]# su - mysql
Last login: Tue Aug  8 23:15:27 CDT 2023 on pts/0
-bash-4.2$
-bash-4.2$ mysql -uroot -p
```

© Y V Ravi Kumar, Arun Kumar Samayam, Naresh Kumar Miryala 2024
Y V Ravi Kumar et al., *Mastering MySQL Administration*, https://doi.org/10.1007/979-8-8688-0252-2_3

Enter password:
mysql> **show variables;**

We can also check using the following commands:

-bash-4.2$ **/bin/mysqladmin -uroot -p variables**
-bash-4.2$ **/bin/mysqladmin -uroot -p extended-status**

The system variables can be set at server startup using the command line or the MySQL configuration file, **/etc/my.cnf**, which is the default location. We can change these variables using the **SET** statement so we do not have to restart the MySQL server for it to take effect.

For example, see the following:

Command line

[root@mysql-a ~]# mysqld --data-dir=/my_data_dir --wait-timeout=10000

Configuration file
[mysqld]
datadir=/my_data_dir
wait_timeout=10000

Set global system variable
SET GLOBAL max_connections=500; or SET @@GLOBAL.max_connections=500;

To persist a global system variable to the mysqld-auto.cnf file and at runtime, use PERSIST
SET PERSIST max_connections=500; or SET @@PERSIST.max_connections=500;

To persist a global system variable to the mysql-auto.cnf file and NOT runtime, use PERSIST_ONLY
SET PERSIST_ONLY super_read_only=TRUE; or SET @@PERSIST_ONLY super_read_only=TRUE

To set a session system variable, use SESSION
SET SESSION sql_mode='ANSI'; or SET @@SESSION.sql_mode='ANSI';

We can even use expressions such as LIKE and operators when using SHOW or SET commands. See the following for examples.

To view process threads running on connections, issue the following command:

```
mysql> show processlist;
+----+-----------------+-----------+------+---------+------+-------+
| Id | User            | Host      | db   | Command | Time |
State                  | Info      |         |
+----+-----------------+-----------+------+---------+------+-------+
|  8 | event_scheduler | localhost | NULL | Daemon  | 1403 | Waiting on
empty queue | NULL          |           |
| 26 | root            | localhost | NULL | Query   |    0 | init
| show processlist |
+----+-----------------+-----------+------+---------+------+-------+
2 rows in set (0.01 sec)
```

To kill a process, use the **KILL id** command:

```
mysql> kill 26;
```

To limit user connectivity, set variable **max_user_connections** to a nonzero value. Other variables to limit resources for a single account are **max_queries_per_hour**, **max_updates_per_hour**, and **max_connections_per_hour.**

```
mysql> show variables like '%max_user%';
+----------------------+-------+
| Variable_name        | Value |
+----------------------+-------+
| max_user_connections | 0     |
+----------------------+-------+
1 row in set (0.10 sec)
```

To set resource limits, issue a command like this:

```
mysql> alter user 'test'@'localhost'
    -> with max_queries_per_hour 20
    -> max_updates_per_hour 20
    -> max_connections_per_hour 30
    -> max_user_connections 5;
```

To unset, just set the **max_connections_per_hour** to 0.

MySQL Data Directory

Now that we have looked at the server configuration and the variables, let us learn about the MySQL data directory that stores all the information related to the MySQL server. The following are the files usually found in the MySQL data directory:

- **mysql:** This is the system schema that contains all the data dictionary and system tables required to run the MySQL server.

- **performance_schema:** Provides all information collected during the execution of the server during runtime.

- **sys:** Contains a set of objects to interpret all the performance schema data easily.

- **ndbinfo:** Contains information specific to NDB cluster.

- **logfiles:** All log files of the MySQL server.

- **InnoDB tablespace and log files**

- **Autogenerated SSL and RSA key files**

- **Server process ID (PID) file**

- **mysqld-auto.cnf:** File that stores all the persistent global system variables and their values.

```
[root@mysql-a ~]# cat /etc/my.cnf
# For advice on how to change settings please see
# http://dev.mysql.com/doc/refman/8.0/en/server-configuration-defaults.html

[mysqld]
datadir=/mysqlbkup
socket=/mysqlbkup/mysql.sock

log-error=/var/log/mysqld.log
pid-file=/var/run/mysqld/mysqld.pid

[root@mysql-a ~]# cd /mysqlbkup
[root@mysql-a mysqlbkup]# pwd
/mysqlbkup
[root@mysql-a mysqlbkup]# ls -ltr
```

```
total 695788
-rw-r----- 1 mysql mysql          56 Aug  3 21:51 backup-auto.cnf
drwxr-x--- 2 mysql mysql          28 Aug  3 21:51 sys
drwxr-x--- 2 mysql mysql         196 Aug  3 21:51 mysql
-rw-r----- 1 mysql mysql         634 Aug  3 21:51 server-my.cnf
-rw-r----- 1 mysql mysql       19930 Aug  3 21:51 server-all.cnf
-rw-r--r-- 1 mysql mysql         711 Aug  3 21:51 backup_variables.txt
-rw-r----- 1 mysql mysql          56 Aug  3 21:57 auto.cnf
-rw-r----- 1 mysql mysql     8585216 Aug  3 21:57 #ib_16384_1.dblwr
-rw------- 1 mysql mysql        1680 Aug  3 21:57 ca-key.pem
-rw-r--r-- 1 mysql mysql        1112 Aug  3 21:57 ca.pem
-rw------- 1 mysql mysql        1680 Aug  3 21:57 server-key.pem
-rw-r--r-- 1 mysql mysql        1112 Aug  3 21:57 server-cert.pem
-rw------- 1 mysql mysql        1676 Aug  3 21:57 client-key.pem
-rw-r--r-- 1 mysql mysql        1112 Aug  3 21:57 client-cert.pem
-rw------- 1 mysql mysql        1680 Aug  3 21:57 private_key.pem
-rw-r--r-- 1 mysql mysql         452 Aug  3 21:57 public_key.pem
drwxr-x--- 3 mysql mysql          22 Aug  4 14:40 #ib_archive
drwxr-x--- 2 mysql mysql          86 Aug  8 23:16 db1
drwxr-x--- 2 mysql mysql          86 Aug  8 23:16 db2
drwxr-x--- 2 mysql mysql          86 Aug  8 23:17 db3
drwxr-x--- 2 mysql mysql          86 Aug  8 23:17 db4
drwxr-x--- 2 mysql mysql         243 Aug  9 21:00 mysql_innodb_cluster_
                                                  metadata
drwxr-x--- 2 mysql mysql           6 Aug 11 01:14 replication_test
-rw-r----- 1 mysql mysql        4500 Aug 11 02:10 ib_buffer_pool
-rw-r----- 1 mysql mysql      238286 Oct 26 17:39 binlog.000019
-rw-r----- 1 mysql mysql     1622194 Oct 26 21:28 binlog.000020
-rw-r----- 1 mysql mysql         382 Oct 26 21:28 mysql-a-relay-bin-group_
                                                  replication_applier.000014
-rw-r----- 1 mysql mysql         427 Oct 26 21:28 mysql-a-relay-bin-group_
                                                  replication_applier.000015
drwxr-x--- 2 mysql mysql        4096 Oct 26 22:29 #innodb_redo
drwxr-x--- 2 mysql mysql         187 Oct 26 22:29 #innodb_temp
-rw-r----- 1 mysql mysql    12582912 Oct 26 22:29 ibtmp1
```

```
drwxr-x--- 2 mysql mysql       8192 Oct 26 22:29 performance_schema
-rw-r----- 1 mysql mysql        389 Oct 26 22:29 binlog.000021
-rw-r----- 1 mysql mysql         64 Oct 26 22:29 binlog.index
-rw------- 1 mysql mysql          5 Oct 26 22:29 mysql.sock.lock
srwxrwxrwx 1 mysql mysql          0 Oct 26 22:29 mysql.sock
-rw-r----- 1 mysql mysql        382 Oct 26 22:29 mysql-a-relay-bin-group_
                                                 replication_applier.000016
-rw-r----- 1 mysql mysql        504 Oct 26 22:33 mysql-a-relay-bin-group_
                                                 replication_applier.000017
-rw-r----- 1 mysql mysql        265 Oct 26 22:33 mysql-a-relay-bin-group_
                                                 replication_applier.index
-rw-r----- 1 mysql mysql       2098 Oct 26 22:33 mysql-a-relay-bin-group_
                                                 replication_applier.000018
-rw-r----- 1 mysql mysql        157 Oct 26 22:34 mysql-a-relay-bin-group_
                                                 replication_recovery.000001
-rw-r----- 1 mysql mysql         54 Oct 26 22:34 mysql-a-relay-bin-group_
                                                 replication_recovery.index
-rw-r----- 1 mysql mysql       3874 Oct 26 22:34 mysqld-auto.cnf
-rw-r----- 1 mysql mysql    8538695 Oct 27 22:02 binlog.000022
-rw-r----- 1 mysql mysql   16777216 Oct 27 22:02 undo_002
-rw-r----- 1 mysql mysql   16777216 Oct 27 22:02 undo_001
-rw-r----- 1 mysql mysql   28311552 Oct 27 22:02 mysql.ibd
-rw-r----- 1 mysql mysql   12582912 Oct 27 22:02 ibdata1
-rw-r----- 1 mysql mysql     196608 Oct 27 22:02 #ib_16384_0.dblwr
-rw-r----- 1 mysql mysql  353511074 Oct 27 22:03 GCS_DEBUG_TRACE
[root@mysql-a mysqlbkup]#
```

Please note after every server shutdown, the current binlog file and the binlog.index file get reset and a new binlog file gets generated upon server startup. For example, see the following:

```
[root@mysql-a mysqlbkup]# ls -ltr *binlog*
-rw-r----- 1 mysql mysql    238286 Oct 26 17:39 binlog.000019
-rw-r----- 1 mysql mysql   1622194 Oct 26 21:28 binlog.000020
-rw-r----- 1 mysql mysql       389 Oct 26 22:29 binlog.000021
-rw-r----- 1 mysql mysql  10017263 Oct 28 00:29 binlog.000022
```

```
-rw-r----- 1 mysql mysql      6961 Oct 28 00:30 binlog.000023
-rw-r----- 1 mysql mysql     23341 Oct 28 00:32 binlog.000024
-rw-r----- 1 mysql mysql    386408 Oct 28 08:29 binlog.000025
-rw-r----- 1 mysql mysql       128 Oct 28 08:29 binlog.index
-rw-r----- 1 mysql mysql       389 Oct 28 08:29 binlog.000026
[root@mysql-a mysqlbkup]# systemctl stop mysqld
[root@mysql-a mysqlbkup]# systemctl start mysqld

[root@mysql-a mysqlbkup]# ls -ltr *binlog*
-rw-r----- 1 mysql mysql    238286 Oct 26 17:39 binlog.000019
-rw-r----- 1 mysql mysql   1622194 Oct 26 21:28 binlog.000020
-rw-r----- 1 mysql mysql       389 Oct 26 22:29 binlog.000021
-rw-r----- 1 mysql mysql  10017263 Oct 28 00:29 binlog.000022
-rw-r----- 1 mysql mysql      6961 Oct 28 00:30 binlog.000023
-rw-r----- 1 mysql mysql     23341 Oct 28 00:32 binlog.000024
-rw-r----- 1 mysql mysql    386408 Oct 28 08:29 binlog.000025
-rw-r----- 1 mysql mysql       412 Oct 28 10:49 binlog.000026
-rw-r----- 1 mysql mysql       144 Oct 28 10:49 binlog.index
-rw-r----- 1 mysql mysql       389 Oct 28 10:49 binlog.000027
[root@mysql-a mysqlbkup]#
```

Notice a new binlog file, binlog.000027, has been generated.

```
[root@mysql-a ~]# su - mysql
Last login: Thu Oct 26 21:34:35 CDT 2023 on pts/0

-bash-4.2$ mysql -uroot -p
Enter password:

mysql> show databases;
+-------------------------------+
| Database                      |
+-------------------------------+
| db1                           |
| db2                           |
| db3                           |
| db4                           |
| information_schema            |
```

```
| mysql                        |
| mysql_innodb_cluster_metadata |
| performance_schema            |
| replication_test              |
| sys                           |
+-------------------------------+
10 rows in set (0.09 sec)

mysql> use sys;
Reading table information for completion of table and column names
You can turn off this feature to get a quicker startup with -A

Database changed

mysql> show tables like '%use%';
+------------------------------------+
| Tables_in_sys (%use%)              |
+------------------------------------+
| memory_by_user_by_current_bytes    |
| schema_unused_indexes              |
| user_summary                       |
| user_summary_by_file_io            |
| user_summary_by_file_io_type       |
| user_summary_by_stages             |
| user_summary_by_statement_latency  |
| user_summary_by_statement_type     |
| waits_by_user_by_latency           |
| x$memory_by_user_by_current_bytes  |
| x$user_summary                     |
| x$user_summary_by_file_io          |
| x$user_summary_by_file_io_type     |
| x$user_summary_by_stages           |
| x$user_summary_by_statement_latency |
| x$user_summary_by_statement_type   |
| x$waits_by_user_by_latency         |
+------------------------------------+
```

```
17 rows in set (0.02 sec)

mysql> select * from user_summary\G
*************************** 1. row ***************************
                 user: mysql_innodb_cluster_3
           statements: 15
    statement_latency: 9.52 h
statement_avg_latency: 38.09 min
          table_scans: 0
             file_ios: 18
      file_io_latency: 1.86 ms
  current_connections: 1
    total_connections: 7
         unique_hosts: 1
       current_memory: 33.50 KiB
total_memory_allocated: 1.09 MiB

--output truncate for better visibility

*************************** 8. row ***************************
                 user: event_scheduler
           statements: 0
    statement_latency:    0 ps
statement_avg_latency:    0 ps
          table_scans: 0
             file_ios: 0
      file_io_latency:    0 ps
  current_connections: 1
    total_connections: 1
         unique_hosts: 1
       current_memory: 16.27 KiB
total_memory_allocated: 16.27 KiB
8 rows in set (0.13 sec)
```

As we have seen, the **mysql** system schema contains all the data dictionary and system tables required to run the MySQL server. It has the following tables to maintain operational information:

- **Data dictionary tables:** Contain metadata about all database objects

- **Grant system tables:** Contains information about grants on the user accounts and the privileges held by them

- **Object information system tables:** Contains information about components, loadable functions, and server-side plug-ins

- **Log system tables:** Contains the general query log table and slow query log table

- **Server-side help system tables:** Contains server-side help tables

- **Time zone system tables:** Contains time zone information

- **Replication system tables:** Contains system tables to support replication

- **Optimizer system tables:** Contains persistent optimizer statistics tables and cost estimate information tables

- **Miscellaneous system tables:** Contains system tables for audit, firewalls, etc.

The following are the different types of server logs:

- **Error log:** Contains **mysqld** startup and shutdown times including errors, warnings, and other notes during startup and shutdown and when the server is running, performance schema error log and stack traces

- **General query log:** Contains client logon and logoff information, every SQL statement received from clients

- **Binary log:** Contains events like table creation, changes to table data, and information of statements that could have made the data changes

- **Relay log:** Contains a set of files with events describing changes to the database

- **Slow query log:** Contains information about SQL statements that take longer time to execute

- **DDL log:** Contains information about metadata operations performed by DDL statements

As log files take space over time, it is a best practice to back up and remove log files and start logging to new log files. Flush the logs after backing up. Flushing of the logs generates new binary logs and closes and reopens the error log, general query log, and slow query log files. The current log files have to be renamed before flushing. You can always schedule a custom script or use the native **mysql-log-rotate** script that gets installed as part of the MySQL RPM install for a Red Hat Linux system. Please ensure all replicas process the binary logs before rotating the logs.

Here is an example on how to flush logs:

```
[root@mysql-a ~]#  cd /var/lib/mysql
[root@mysql-a ~]#  mv mysqld.log mysqld.log.old
[root@mysql-a ~]#  mv mysql-slow.log mysql-slow.log.old
[root@mysql-a ~]#  mysqladmin -uroot -p flush-logs
```

Startup and Shutdown of MySQL Server

The startup and shutdown of MySQL server can be performed using **systemctl**.

To shut down the MySQL server, use the following as an example:

```
[root@mysql-a ~]# systemctl stop mysqld
[root@mysql-a ~]# systemctl status mysqld
```

OR
```
[root@mysql-a ~]# mysqladmin -u root -p shutdown
Enter password:
```

To start the MySQL server, use the following:

```
[root@mysql-a ~]# systemctl start mysqld
[root@mysql-a ~]# systemctl status mysqld
```

Connection Management

MySQL 8.0 uses **caching_sha2_password** as the default authentication plug-in. To authenticate an account, MySQL uses the following:

- Username

- Password

- Client host

To connect to the local server using the **mysql** client, use the following syntax as an example:

```
$ mysql -u<username> -p<password>
```

```
-bash-4.2$ mysql -uroot -pWElcome_1234#
mysql: [Warning] Using a password on the command line interface can be
insecure.
mysql>
```

To connect to a remote server using the **mysql** client, use the following syntax as an example:

```
$ mysql -u<username> -p<password> -h <server_name>
```

```
-bash-4.2$ mysql -uroot -pWElcome_1234# -h mysql-b
mysql: [Warning] Using a password on the command line interface can be
insecure.
```

```
mysql> select @@hostname;
+------------+
| @@hostname |
+------------+
| mysql-b    |
+------------+
1 row in set (0.00 sec)
```

Let us understand this better using an example showcased here:

1. Create three users – mysql-1, mysql-3, and mysql-4 – as host-based users and mysql-2 as a localhost user.

```
mysql> create user 'mysql-1'@'192.168.2%' identified by 'Welcome@123';
Query OK, 0 rows affected (0.01 sec)

mysql> create user 'mysql-3'@'192.168.2%' identified by 'Welcome@123';
Query OK, 0 rows affected (0.01 sec)

mysql> create user 'mysql-4'@'192.168.2%' identified by 'Welcome@123';
Query OK, 0 rows affected (0.01 sec)

mysql> create user 'mysql-2'@'localhost' identified by 'Welcome@123';
Query OK, 0 rows affected (0.01 sec)

mysql> select user,host from mysql.user;
+-------------------------+------------+
| user                    | host       |
+-------------------------+------------+
| mysql_innodb_cluster_1  | %          |
| mysql_innodb_cluster_2  | %          |
| mysql_innodb_cluster_3  | %          |
| mysqlclusteradmin       | %          |
| routeradmin             | %          |
| mysql-1                 | 192.168.2% |
| mysql-3                 | 192.168.2% |
| mysql-4                 | 192.168.2% |
| mysql-2                 | localhost  |
| mysql.infoschema        | localhost  |
| mysql.session           | localhost  |
| mysql.sys               | localhost  |
| mysqlbkpadmin           | localhost  |
| root                    | localhost  |
| service_manager         | localhost  |
| test                    | localhost  |
| test_user               | localhost  |
+-------------------------+------------+
```

```
17 rows in set (0.00 sec)
```

2. Try modifying the password for mysql-2 as a remote host and we
    will get an error since it is a localhost user.

    ```
    mysql> alter user 'mysql-2'@'192.168.2%' identified by
    'Welcome@123';
    ERROR 1396 (HY000): Operation ALTER USER failed for
    'mysql-2'@'192.168.2%'
    mysql>
    ```

3. Create a few sample databases and tables within them. Grant
    permissions accordingly.

    ```
    mysql> show databases;
    +--------------------------------+
    | Database                       |
    +--------------------------------+
    | db1                            |
    | db2                            |
    | db3                            |
    | db4                            |
    | information_schema             |
    | mysql                          |
    | mysql_innodb_cluster_metadata  |
    | performance_schema             |
    | replication_test               |
    | sys                            |
    +--------------------------------+
    10 rows in set (0.00 sec)

    mysql> use db1;
    Reading table information for completion of table and column names
    You can turn off this feature to get a quicker startup with -A

    Database changed
    ```

142

```
mysql> show tables;
+---------------+
| Tables_in_db1 |
+---------------+
| dbusers1      |
| dbusers2      |
| dbusers3      |
| dbusers4      |
+---------------+
4 rows in set (0.00 sec)
```

<Repeat the same for rest of the databases db2, db3 and db4>

```
mysql> grant create,select,insert,delete,update,drop on *.* to
'mysql-1'@'192.168.2%';
Query OK, 0 rows affected (0.01 sec)

mysql> grant create,select,insert,delete,update,drop on *.* to
'mysql-3'@'192.168.2%';
Query OK, 0 rows affected (0.01 sec)

mysql> grant create,select,insert,delete,update,drop on *.* to
'mysql-4'@'192.168.2%';
Query OK, 0 rows affected (0.01 sec)
```

4. Let us try connecting remotely as mysql-2 user. In this, you will notice that we will be able to connect as a local user but not as a remote user.

   To connect locally, issue the following command:

   ```
   -bash-4.2$ mysql -u mysql-2 -pWelcome@123
   mysql: [Warning] Using a password on the command line interface
   can be insecure.
   mysql> exit
   ```

   <To connect remotely, issue the command below. You will notice this will fail as mysql-2 user was created with permissions on localhost only>

```
-bash-4.2$ mysql -u mysql-2 -pWelcome@123 -h 192.168.2.15
mysql: [Warning] Using a password on the command line interface
can be insecure.
ERROR 1045 (28000): Access denied for user 'mysql-2'@'mysql-a'
(using password: YES)
-bash-4.2$
```

5. Let us try connecting remotely as mysql-1, mysql-3, and mysql-4
    user remotely and verify:

```
-bash-4.2$ mysql -umysql-1 -pWelcome@123 -h 192.168.2.15 -D db2
mysql> exit
```

***<To connect locally, issue the command below. You will notice
this will fail as mysql-1 user was created with permissions on
192.168.2.%.>***

```
-bash-4.2$ mysql -umysql-1 -pWelcome@123 -h localhost -D db2
mysql: [Warning] Using a password on the command line interface
can be insecure.
ERROR 1045 (28000): Access denied for user 'mysql-1'@'localhost'
(using password: YES)
```

```
-bash-4.2$ mysql -umysql-1 -pWelcome@123 -h 192.168.2.15 -D db3
mysql> exit
```

```
-bash-4.2$ mysql -umysql-3 -pWelcome@123 -h 192.168.2.15 -D db1
mysql> exit
```

```
-bash-4.2$ mysql -umysql-3 -pWelcome@123 -h 192.168.2.15 -D db2
mysql> exit
```

```
-bash-4.2$ mysql -umysql-3 -pWelcome@123 -h 192.168.2.15 -D db3
mysql> exit
```

```
-bash-4.2$ mysql -umysql-4 -pWelcome@123 -h 192.168.2.15 -D db1
mysql> exit
```

```
-bash-4.2$ mysql -umysql-4 -pWelcome@123 -h 192.168.2.15 -D db2
mysql> exit
```

```
-bash-4.2$ mysql -umysql-4 -pWelcome@123 -h 192.168.2.15 -D db3
mysql> exit

-bash-4.2$ mysql -u mysql-1 -pWelcome@123 -h 192.168.2.15
mysql> exit
```

To create a user, use the following syntax as an example:

```
mysql> create user '<username>'@'<host_name>' identified by "<password">;

mysql> create user 'test'@'localhost' identified by "WElcome_1234#";
mysql> select user,host from mysql.user where user='test';
```

To grant permissions, it is a best practice to create a role that is a collection of privileges that makes adding, removing, and managing grants for a user easy.

Storage Engines

In MySQL, SQL operations for different table types are handled by the MySQL component called storage engines. **InnoDB** is the default storage engine for MySQL 5.5 and later. The default storage engine before MySQL 5.5 was MyISAM. We can enable storage engines to be loaded and unloaded from a running MySQL server using a pluggable storage engine architecture.

Issue the SHOW ENGINES statement to determine which storage engines are supported on the server. The **Support** column value of YES, NO, or DEFAULT indicates the engine availability or the current storage engine in use.

```
[root@mysql-a ~]# mysql -u root -p
Enter password:

mysql> show databases;
+--------------------+
| Database |
+--------------------+
| db1 |
| db2 |
| db3 |
| information_schema |
```

```
| mysql |
| mysqlbackup |
| performance_schema |
| sys |
+--------------------+
8 rows in set (0.01 sec)

mysql> show engines\G
************************** 1. row **************************
Engine: ndbcluster
Support: NO
Comment: Clustered, fault-tolerant tables
Transactions: NULL
XA: NULL
Savepoints: NULL
************************** 2. row **************************
Engine: FEDERATED
Support: NO
Comment: Federated MySQL storage engine
Transactions: NULL
XA: NULL
Savepoints: NULL
************************** 3. row **************************
Engine: MEMORY
Support: YES
Comment: Hash based, stored in memory, useful for temporary tables
Transactions: NO
XA: NO
Savepoints: NO
************************** 4. row **************************
Engine: InnoDB
Support: DEFAULT
Comment: Supports transactions, row-level locking, and foreign keys
Transactions: YES
XA: YES
Savepoints: YES
```

```
*************************** 5. row ***************************
Engine: PERFORMANCE_SCHEMA
Support: YES
Comment: Performance Schema
Transactions: NO
XA: NO
Savepoints: NO
*************************** 6. row ***************************
Engine: MyISAM
Support: YES
Comment: MyISAM storage engine
Transactions: NO
XA: NO
Savepoints: NO
*************************** 7. row ***************************
Engine: ndbinfo
Support: NO
Comment: MySQL Cluster system information storage engine
Transactions: NULL
XA: NULL
Savepoints: NULL
*************************** 8. row ***************************
Engine: MRG_MYISAM
Support: YES
Comment: Collection of identical MyISAM tables
Transactions: NO
XA: NO
Savepoints: NO
*************************** 9. row ***************************
Engine: BLACKHOLE
Support: YES
Comment: /dev/null storage engine (anything you write to it disappears)
Transactions: NO
XA: NO
Savepoints: NO
```

```
*************************** 10. row ***************************
Engine: CSV
Support: YES
Comment: CSV storage engine
Transactions: NO
XA: NO
Savepoints: NO
*************************** 11. row ***************************
Engine: ARCHIVE
Support: YES
Comment: Archive storage engine
Transactions: NO
XA: NO
Savepoints: NO
11 rows in set (0.00 sec)
```

There are two types of MySQL storage engines:

- Transactional (InnoDB)

- Nontransactional (MyISAM)

Transactional storage engines permit write operations to roll back if they fail providing the ability for original data to stay intact. Nontransactional storage engines commit the data on execution. Suppose a write operation fails at the end of a series of write operations. In that case, all the preceding operations have to be rolled back manually within the applications, making it challenging if a backup of previous values doesn't exist.

As MySQL storage engines follow a pluggable server architecture, it isolates the application programmer and database admins from all of the low-level implementation details at the storage level. Some of the key differentiating capabilities include the following:

- Concurrency

- Transaction support

- Referential integrity

- Physical storage

- Index support

- Memory caches

- Performance aids

- Table partitioning support

- Backup and recovery

- Full text search

- Spatial data support

Here is a quick overview of the MySQL storage engine architecture.

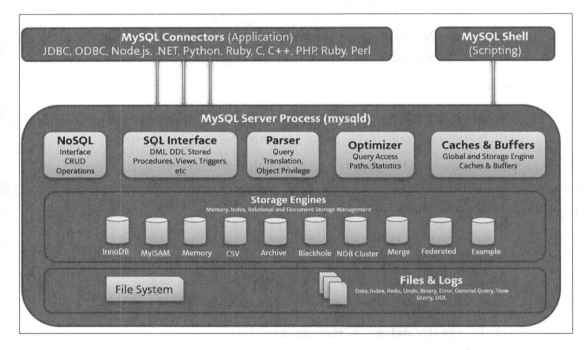

Figure 3-1. *MySQL storage engine architecture*

Each storage engine has a specific function, and the end user has the flexibility to choose between any of these storage engines based on the application need. The storage engines supported in MySQL 8.0 are as follows:

- **InnoDB**: Used when you need ACID compliance for transaction support.

- **MyISAM**: Used when you need read-only workloads.

- **Memory**: Used when you need fast access to noncritical data and stored in RAM.

- **CSV**: Used when you need export or import data in CSV format.

- **Archive**: Used when you have archival needs to store large amounts of frequently inaccessible data.

- **Blackhole**: Used in replication configurations where DML statements are sent to replica servers and source doesn't need to keep its own data.

- **NDB**: Used when your application has high uptime and availability requirements. It's a clustered database engine.

- **Merge**: Used when the end user wanted to group a series of identical MyISAM tables and reference them as one single object.

- **Federated**: Used when you need a distributed environment.

- **Example**: Used as an example storage engine for use by end users and it does not do anything as data cannot be stored on this one.

Now that we have seen the storage engine function and the different types of supported storage engines, let us explore them further to convert between storage engines and learn few considerations practically.

1. We will start with setting the storage engine using the **engine** keyword. For our example, let us create a sample database named **storage_engines** and tables tab1 to tab6 with different storage engines and explore the file structure and extensions.

```
mysql> create database storage_engines;
Query OK, 1 row affected (0.01 sec)
```

```
mysql> show databases;
+--------------------+
| Database           |
+--------------------+
| db1                |
| db2                |
```

```
| db3                |
| information_schema |
| mysql              |
| mysqlbackup        |
| performance_schema |
| storage_engines    |
| sys                |
+--------------------+
9 rows in set (0.00 sec)

mysql> use storage_engines;
Database changed

mysql> create table tab1 (no int);
Query OK, 0 rows affected (0.01 sec)

mysql> create table tab2 (no int) engine=CSV;
ERROR 1178 (42000): The storage engine for the table doesn't
support nullable columns

mysql> create table tab2 (no int NOT NULL) engine=CSV;
Query OK, 0 rows affected (0.01 sec)

mysql> create table tab3 (no int) engine=memory;
Query OK, 0 rows affected (0.00 sec)

mysql> create table tab4 (no int) engine=MyISAM;
Query OK, 0 rows affected (0.01 sec)

mysql> create table tab5 (no int) engine=blackhole;
Query OK, 0 rows affected (0.01 sec)

mysql> create table tab6 (no int) engine=archive;
Query OK, 0 rows affected (0.01 sec)
```

```
mysql> SELECT TABLE_NAME, ENGINE FROM INFORMATION_SCHEMA.TABLES
WHERE TABLE_SCHEMA = 'storage_engines';
+------------+-----------+
| TABLE_NAME | ENGINE    |
+------------+-----------+
| tab1       | InnoDB    |
| tab2       | CSV       |
| tab3       | MEMORY    |
| tab4       | MyISAM    |
| tab5       | BLACKHOLE |
| tab6       | ARCHIVE   |
+------------+-----------+
6 rows in set (0.01 sec)
mysql> exit

-bash-4.2$ pwd
/var/lib/mysql/storage_engines

-bash-4.2$ ls -ltr
total 144
-rw-r----- 1 mysql mysql 114688 Aug 20 16:42 tab1.ibd
-rw-r----- 1 mysql mysql 1645 Aug 20 16:44 tab2_575.sdi
-rw-r----- 1 mysql mysql 35 Aug 20 16:44 tab2.CSM
-rw-r----- 1 mysql mysql 0 Aug 20 16:44 tab2.CSV
-rw-r----- 1 mysql mysql 1639 Aug 20 16:45 tab3_576.sdi
-rw-r----- 1 mysql mysql 1639 Aug 20 16:47 tab4_577.sdi
-rw-r----- 1 mysql mysql 1024 Aug 20 16:47 tab4.MYI
-rw-r----- 1 mysql mysql 0 Aug 20 16:47 tab4.MYD
-rw-r----- 1 mysql mysql 1642 Aug 20 16:48 tab5_578.sdi
-rw-r----- 1 mysql mysql 1640 Aug 20 16:48 tab6_579.sdi
-rw-r----- 1 mysql mysql 88 Aug 20 16:48 tab6.ARZ
-bash-4.2$
```

Notice the different extensions depending on the type of storage engine we provide at the time of table creation.

2.   Now, let us convert all tables to the default InnoDB storage engine. To convert, issue an **ALTER TABLE** statement with the **engine** keyword.

```
mysql> alter table tab2 engine=InnoDB;
Query OK, 0 rows affected (0.04 sec)
Records: 0 Duplicates: 0 Warnings: 0

-bash-4.2$ ls -ltr
total 248
-rw-r----- 1 mysql mysql 114688 Aug 20 16:42 tab1.ibd
-rw-r----- 1 mysql mysql 1639 Aug 20 16:45 tab3_576.sdi
-rw-r----- 1 mysql mysql 1639 Aug 20 16:47 tab4_577.sdi
-rw-r----- 1 mysql mysql 1024 Aug 20 16:47 tab4.MYI
-rw-r----- 1 mysql mysql 0 Aug 20 16:47 tab4.MYD
-rw-r----- 1 mysql mysql 1642 Aug 20 16:48 tab5_578.sdi
-rw-r----- 1 mysql mysql 1640 Aug 20 16:48 tab6_579.sdi
-rw-r----- 1 mysql mysql 88 Aug 20 16:48 tab6.ARZ
-rw-r----- 1 mysql mysql 114688 Aug 20 16:54 tab2.ibd
-bash-4.2$
```

‹Notice the change in the extension for table tab2 to *.ibd›

```
mysql> alter table tab3 engine=InnoDB;
Query OK, 0 rows affected (0.02 sec)
Records: 0 Duplicates: 0 Warnings: 0

-bash-4.2$ ls -ltr
total 356
-rw-r----- 1 mysql mysql 114688 Aug 20 16:42 tab1.ibd
-rw-r----- 1 mysql mysql 1639 Aug 20 16:47 tab4_577.sdi
-rw-r----- 1 mysql mysql 1024 Aug 20 16:47 tab4.MYI
-rw-r----- 1 mysql mysql 0 Aug 20 16:47 tab4.MYD
-rw-r----- 1 mysql mysql 1642 Aug 20 16:48 tab5_578.sdi
-rw-r----- 1 mysql mysql 1640 Aug 20 16:48 tab6_579.sdi
-rw-r----- 1 mysql mysql 88 Aug 20 16:48 tab6.ARZ
-rw-r----- 1 mysql mysql 114688 Aug 20 16:54 tab2.ibd
-rw-r----- 1 mysql mysql 114688 Aug 20 16:56 tab3.ibd
-bash-4.2$
```

‹Notice the change in the extension for table tab3 to *.ibd›

```
mysql> alter table tab4 engine=InnoDB;
Query OK, 0 rows affected (0.04 sec)
Records: 0 Duplicates: 0 Warnings: 0

mysql> alter table tab5 engine=InnoDB;
Query OK, 0 rows affected (0.03 sec)
Records: 0 Duplicates: 0 Warnings: 0

mysql> alter table tab6 engine=InnoDB;
Query OK, 0 rows affected (0.03 sec)
Records: 0 Duplicates: 0 Warnings: 0

mysql> SELECT TABLE_NAME, ENGINE FROM INFORMATION_SCHEMA.TABLES
WHERE TABLE_SCHEMA = 'storage_engines';
+------------+--------+
| TABLE_NAME | ENGINE |
+------------+--------+
| tab1       | InnoDB |
| tab2       | InnoDB |
| tab3       | InnoDB |
| tab4       | InnoDB |
| tab5       | InnoDB |
| tab6       | InnoDB |
+------------+--------+
6 rows in set (0.00 sec)
mysql> exit

-bash-4.2$ ls -ltr
total 672
-rw-r----- 1 mysql mysql 114688 Aug 20 16:42 tab1.ibd
-rw-r----- 1 mysql mysql 114688 Aug 20 16:54 tab2.ibd
-rw-r----- 1 mysql mysql 114688 Aug 20 16:56 tab3.ibd
-rw-r----- 1 mysql mysql 114688 Aug 20 16:57 tab4.ibd
-rw-r----- 1 mysql mysql 114688 Aug 20 16:57 tab5.ibd
-rw-r----- 1 mysql mysql 114688 Aug 20 16:58 tab6.ibd
-bash-4.2$
```

3. Now convert all the respective tables to the original storage engine
they were created with.

tab2 -> CSV
tab3 -> Memory
tab4 -> MyISAM
tab5 -> Blackhole
tab6 -> Archive

```
mysql> alter table tab2 engine=CSV;
Query OK, 0 rows affected (0.03 sec)
Records: 0  Duplicates: 0  Warnings: 0

mysql> alter table tab3 engine=memory;
Query OK, 0 rows affected (0.02 sec)
Records: 0  Duplicates: 0  Warnings: 0

mysql> alter table tab4 engine=MyISAM;
Query OK, 0 rows affected (0.04 sec)
Records: 0  Duplicates: 0  Warnings: 0

mysql> alter table tab5 engine=Blackhole;
Query OK, 0 rows affected (0.02 sec)
Records: 0  Duplicates: 0  Warnings: 0

mysql> alter table tab6 engine=archive;
Query OK, 0 rows affected (0.03 sec)
Records: 0  Duplicates: 0  Warnings: 0

mysql> SELECT TABLE_NAME, ENGINE FROM INFORMATION_SCHEMA.TABLES
WHERE TABLE_SCHEMA = 'storage_engines';
+------------+-----------+
| TABLE_NAME | ENGINE    |
+------------+-----------+
| tab1       | InnoDB    |
| tab2       | CSV       |
| tab3       | MEMORY    |
| tab4       | MyISAM    |
| tab5       | BLACKHOLE |
```

```
| tab6         | ARCHIVE   |
+-------------+-----------+
6 rows in set (0.00 sec)

-bash-4.2$ ls -ltr
total 144
-rw-r----- 1 mysql mysql 114688 Aug 20 16:42 tab1.ibd
-rw-r----- 1 mysql mysql      0 Aug 20 17:01 tab2.CSV
-rw-r----- 1 mysql mysql     35 Aug 20 17:01 tab2.CSM
-rw-r----- 1 mysql mysql   1643 Aug 20 17:01 tab2_585.sdi
-rw-r----- 1 mysql mysql   1637 Aug 20 17:01 tab3_586.sdi
-rw-r----- 1 mysql mysql   1024 Aug 20 17:01 tab4.MYI
-rw-r----- 1 mysql mysql      0 Aug 20 17:01 tab4.MYD
-rw-r----- 1 mysql mysql   1637 Aug 20 17:01 tab4_587.sdi
-rw-r----- 1 mysql mysql   1640 Aug 20 17:02 tab5_588.sdi
-rw-r----- 1 mysql mysql     88 Aug 20 17:02 tab6.ARZ
-rw-r----- 1 mysql mysql   1638 Aug 20 17:02 tab6_589.sdi
-bash-4.2$
```

4. Everything works fine with tables with no data. Let us test when we have tables with data and find out if we experience any issues. To populate a database with sample data, follow these steps:

    Download a sample SQL file from `https://github.com/hhorak/mysql-sample-db/blob/master/mysqlsampledatabase.sql`.

    Create a SQL script with the name sampledb.sql.

    Log in as MySQL root user:

    ```
    [root@mysql-a ~]# mysql -u root -p
    Enter password:
    mysql>
    ```

    Run the sampledb.sql script to set up a sample database named **classicmodels** with data:

    ```
    mysql> source sampledb.sql;
    ```

5. Explore the **classicmodels** database and its tables.

```
mysql> show databases;
+--------------------+
| Database           |
+--------------------+
| classicmodels      |
| db1                |
| db2                |
| db3                |
| information_schema |
| mysql              |
| mysqlbackup        |
| performance_schema |
| storage_engines    |
| sys                |
+--------------------+
10 rows in set (0.00 sec)

mysql> use classicmodels;
Reading table information for completion of table and column names
You can turn off this feature to get a quicker startup with -A

Database changed

mysql> show tables;
+-------------------------+
| Tables_in_classicmodels |
+-------------------------+
| customers               |
| employees               |
| offices                 |
| orderdetails            |
| orders                  |
| payments                |
| productlines            |
| products                |
+-------------------------+
```

```
8 rows in set (0.00 sec)
```

mysql> **show engines\G;**
```
*************************** 1. row ***************************
        Engine: ndbcluster
       Support: NO
       Comment: Clustered, fault-tolerant tables
  Transactions: NULL
            XA: NULL
    Savepoints: NULL
*************************** 2. row ***************************
        Engine: FEDERATED
       Support: NO
       Comment: Federated MySQL storage engine
  Transactions: NULL
            XA: NULL
    Savepoints: NULL
*************************** 3. row ***************************
        Engine: MEMORY
       Support: YES
       Comment: Hash based, stored in memory, useful for
temporary tables
  Transactions: NO
            XA: NO
    Savepoints: NO
*************************** 4. row ***************************
        Engine: InnoDB
       Support: DEFAULT
       Comment: Supports transactions, row-level locking, and
        foreign keys
  Transactions: YES
            XA: YES
    Savepoints: YES
*************************** 5. row ***************************
        Engine: PERFORMANCE_SCHEMA
       Support: YES
```

```
      Comment: Performance Schema
 Transactions: NO
           XA: NO
   Savepoints: NO
*************************** 6. row ***************************
       Engine: MyISAM
      Support: YES
      Comment: MyISAM storage engine
 Transactions: NO
           XA: NO
   Savepoints: NO
*************************** 7. row ***************************
       Engine: ndbinfo
      Support: NO
      Comment: MySQL Cluster system information storage engine
 Transactions: NULL
           XA: NULL
   Savepoints: NULL
*************************** 8. row ***************************
       Engine: MRG_MYISAM
      Support: YES
      Comment: Collection of identical MyISAM tables
 Transactions: NO
           XA: NO
   Savepoints: NO
*************************** 9. row ***************************
       Engine: BLACKHOLE
      Support: YES
      Comment: /dev/null storage engine (anything you write to it
disappears)
 Transactions: NO
           XA: NO
   Savepoints: NO
```

```
*************************** 10. row ***************************
      Engine: CSV
     Support: YES
     Comment: CSV storage engine
Transactions: NO
          XA: NO
  Savepoints: NO
*************************** 11. row ***************************
      Engine: ARCHIVE
     Support: YES
     Comment: Archive storage engine
Transactions: NO
          XA: NO
  Savepoints: NO
11 rows in set (0.01 sec)
```

ERROR:
No query specified

mysql> **SELECT TABLE_NAME, ENGINE FROM INFORMATION_SCHEMA.TABLES WHERE TABLE_SCHEMA = 'classicmodels';**

```
+--------------+--------+
| TABLE_NAME   | ENGINE |
+--------------+--------+
| customers    | InnoDB |
| employees    | InnoDB |
| offices      | InnoDB |
| orderdetails | InnoDB |
| orders       | InnoDB |
| payments     | InnoDB |
| productlines | InnoDB |
| products     | InnoDB |
+--------------+--------+
8 rows in set (0.00 sec)
```

6. Let us try changing the storage engine for a few tables and explore
    what happens.

```
mysql> alter table customers engine='MyISAM';
ERROR 3776 (HY000): Cannot change table's storage engine because
the table participates in a foreign key constraint.
mysql>
```

*<Disable all foreign keys associated with the table 'customers'
and other tables referencing this table.>*

```
mysql> alter table customers disable keys;
Query OK, 0 rows affected, 1 warning (0.01 sec)
```

```
mysql> show warnings;
+-------+------+----------------------------------------------------+
| Level | Code |
Message                                                             |
+-------+------+----------------------------------------------------+
| Note  | 1031 | Table storage engine for 'customers' doesn't have
this option |
+-------+------+----------------------------------------------------+
1 row in set (0.00 sec)
```

```
mysql> alter table customers DROP FOREIGN KEY customers_ibfk_1;
Query OK, 0 rows affected (0.02 sec)
Records: 0  Duplicates: 0  Warnings: 0
```

```
mysql> alter table orders DROP FOREIGN KEY orders_ibfk_1;
Query OK, 0 rows affected (0.01 sec)
Records: 0  Duplicates: 0  Warnings: 0
```

```
mysql> alter table payments drop foreign key payments_ibfk_1;
Query OK, 0 rows affected (0.01 sec)
Records: 0  Duplicates: 0  Warnings: 0
```

```
mysql> alter table customers engine='MyISAM';
Query OK, 122 rows affected (0.03 sec)
Records: 122  Duplicates: 0  Warnings: 0
```

```
mysql> SELECT TABLE_NAME, ENGINE FROM INFORMATION_SCHEMA.TABLES
WHERE TABLE_SCHEMA = 'classicmodels';
+--------------+--------+
| TABLE_NAME   | ENGINE |
+--------------+--------+
| customers    | MyISAM |
| employees    | InnoDB |
| offices      | InnoDB |
| orderdetails | InnoDB |
| orders       | InnoDB |
| payments     | InnoDB |
| productlines | InnoDB |
| products     | InnoDB |
+--------------+--------+
8 rows in set (0.00 sec)

mysql> alter table customers ADD CONSTRAINT customers_
ibfk_1 FOREIGN KEY (salesRepEmployeeNumber) REFERENCES
employees(employeeNumber);
Query OK, 122 rows affected (0.02 sec)
Records: 122  Duplicates: 0  Warnings: 0
```

Note   This example showcases some of the limitations each storage engine could have. It is *not recommended* to disable/drop foreign key constraints as it will cause data integrity issues and should not be performed on a production system. This is purely for learning/exploration purposes only.

---

7. Let us explore a few more limitations with other storage engines.

```
mysql> SELECT TABLE_NAME, ENGINE FROM INFORMATION_SCHEMA.TABLES
WHERE TABLE_SCHEMA = 'classicmodels';
+--------------+-----------+
| TABLE_NAME   | ENGINE    |
+--------------+-----------+
| customers    | MyISAM    |
| employees    | MEMORY    |
| offices      | BLACKHOLE |
| orderdetails | MyISAM    |
| orders       | InnoDB    |
| payments     | InnoDB    |
| productlines | InnoDB    |
| products     | InnoDB    |
+--------------+-----------+
8 rows in set (0.00 sec)

mysql> alter table orders engine=CSV;
ERROR 1069 (42000): Too many keys specified; max 0 keys allowed

mysql> alter table orders engine=archive;
ERROR 1069 (42000): Too many keys specified; max 1 keys allowed

mysql> alter table orders engine=MyISAM;
Query OK, 326 rows affected (0.03 sec)
Records: 326  Duplicates: 0  Warnings: 0

mysql> alter table orders engine=InnoDB;
Query OK, 326 rows affected (0.05 sec)
Records: 326  Duplicates: 0  Warnings: 0

mysql> alter table orders engine=blackhole;
Query OK, 326 rows affected (0.04 sec)
Records: 326  Duplicates: 0  Warnings: 0

mysql> alter table orders engine=memory;
ERROR 1163 (42000): The used table type doesn't support
BLOB/TEXT columns
```

As we know that MySQL uses a pluggable storage engine architecture that enables storage engines to be loaded and unloaded from a running MySQL server, to load the storage engine, the storage engine plug-in shared library must be loaded into MySQL using the **INSTALL PLUGIN** statement. In the example here, let us install an EXAMPLE engine plug-in for an EXAMPLE storage engine with the shared library named ha_example.so. Let us create a new storage engine using the example plug-in described previously.

Step 1: Update .bash_profile with the following information:
"/usr/lib64/mysql/plugin"

```
[mysql@mysql-p ~]$ cat .bash_profile
# .bash_profile

# Get the aliases and functions
if [ -f ~/.bashrc ]; then
      . ~/.bashrc
fi

# User specific environment and startup programs

PATH=$PATH:$HOME/.local/bin:$HOME/bin:/usr/bin:/usr/lib64/mysql/plugin:
export PATH
[mysql@mysql-p ~]$
```

Step 2: Check the following directory:

```
[mysql@mysql-p ~]$ ls -lrth /usr/lib64/mysql/plugin
total 28M
-rwxr-xr-x 1 root root 107K Jun 22 07:51 validate_password.so
-rwxr-xr-x 1 root root  92K Jun 22 07:51 semisync_source.so
-rwxr-xr-x 1 root root  37K Jun 22 07:51 semisync_slave.so
-rwxr-xr-x 1 root root  37K Jun 22 07:51 semisync_replica.so
-rwxr-xr-x 1 root root  92K Jun 22 07:51 semisync_master.so
-rwxr-xr-x 1 root root 139K Jun 22 07:51 rewriter.so
-rwxr-xr-x 1 root root  16K Jun 22 07:51 rewrite_example.so
-rwxr-xr-x 1 root root  16K Jun 22 07:51 mysql_no_login.so
-rwxr-xr-x 1 root root 234K Jun 22 07:51 mysql_clone.so
```

```
-rwxr-xr-x 1 root root  16K Jun 22 07:51 mypluglib.so
-rwxr-xr-x 1 root root 1.3M Jun 22 07:51 libpluginmecab.so
-rwxr-xr-x 1 root root 235K Jun 22 07:51 libmemcached.so
-rwxr-xr-x 1 root root  24K Jun 22 07:51 keyring_udf.so
-rwxr-xr-x 1 root root 245K Jun 22 07:51 keyring_file.so
-rwxr-xr-x 1 root root 102K Jun 22 07:51 innodb_engine.so
-rwxr-xr-x 1 root root  57K Jun 22 07:51 ha_mock.so
-rwxr-xr-x 1 root root  46K Jun 22 07:51 ha_example.so
-rwxr-xr-x 1 root root 3.0M Jun 22 07:51 group_replication.so
-rwxr-xr-x 1 root root 228K Jun 22 07:51 ddl_rewriter.so
-rwxr-xr-x 1 root root  54K Jun 22 07:51 connection_control.so
-rwxr-xr-x 1 root root  16K Jun 22 07:51 auth_socket.so
-rwxr-xr-x 1 root root 6.5M Jun 22 07:51 authentication_oci_client.so
-rwxr-xr-x 1 root root 6.4M Jun 22 07:51 authentication_ldap_sasl_client.so
-rwxr-xr-x 1 root root 6.6M Jun 22 07:51 authentication_kerberos_client.so
-rwxr-xr-x 1 root root  33K Jun 22 07:51 authentication_fido_client.so
-rwxr-xr-x 1 root root  31K Jun 22 07:51 adt_null.so
-rwxr-xr-x 1 root root  49K Jun 22 07:51 version_token.so
-rwxr-xr-x 1 root root  15K Jun 22 07:51 locking_service.so
-rwxr-xr-x 1 root root 123K Jun 22 07:51 component_validate_password.so
-rwxr-xr-x 1 root root  42K Jun 22 07:51 component_reference_cache.so
-rwxr-xr-x 1 root root  16K Jun 22 07:51 component_query_attributes.so
-rwxr-xr-x 1 root root  41K Jun 22 07:51 component_mysqlbackup.so
-rwxr-xr-x 1 root root  20K Jun 22 07:51 component_log_sink_syseventlog.so
-rwxr-xr-x 1 root root  36K Jun 22 07:51 component_log_sink_json.so
-rwxr-xr-x 1 root root  28K Jun 22 07:51 component_log_filter_dragnet.so
-rwxr-xr-x 1 root root 1.9M Jun 22 07:51 component_keyring_file.so
-rwxr-xr-x 1 root root  25K Jun 22 07:51 component_audit_api_
message_emit.so
[mysql@mysql-p ~]$
```

Step 3: Log in to MySQL server as a "root" user.

```
mysql> install plugin EXAMPLE SONAME 'ha_example.so';
Query OK, 0 rows affected (0.01 sec)

mysql> show engines\G;
```

```
*************************** 1. row ***************************
     Engine: ndbcluster
    Support: NO
    Comment: Clustered, fault-tolerant tables
Transactions: NULL
         XA: NULL
 Savepoints: NULL
*************************** 2. row ***************************
     Engine: FEDERATED
    Support: NO
    Comment: Federated MySQL storage engine
Transactions: NULL
         XA: NULL
 Savepoints: NULL
*************************** 3. row ***************************
     Engine: MEMORY
    Support: YES
    Comment: Hash based, stored in memory, useful for temporary tables
Transactions: NO
         XA: NO
 Savepoints: NO
*************************** 4. row ***************************
     Engine: InnoDB
    Support: DEFAULT
    Comment: Supports transactions, row-level locking, and foreign keys
Transactions: YES
         XA: YES
 Savepoints: YES
*************************** 5. row ***************************
     Engine: PERFORMANCE_SCHEMA
    Support: YES
    Comment: Performance Schema
Transactions: NO
         XA: NO
 Savepoints: NO
```

```
*************************** 6. row ***************************
     Engine: MyISAM
    Support: YES
    Comment: MyISAM storage engine
Transactions: NO
         XA: NO
 Savepoints: NO
*************************** 7. row ***************************
     Engine: ndbinfo
    Support: NO
    Comment: MySQL Cluster system information storage engine
Transactions: NULL
         XA: NULL
 Savepoints: NULL
*************************** 8. row ***************************
     Engine: MRG_MYISAM
    Support: YES
    Comment: Collection of identical MyISAM tables
Transactions: NO
         XA: NO
 Savepoints: NO
*************************** 9. row ***************************
     Engine: BLACKHOLE
    Support: YES
    Comment: /dev/null storage engine (anything you write to it
             disappears)
Transactions: NO
         XA: NO
 Savepoints: NO
*************************** 10. row ***************************
     Engine: CSV
    Support: YES
    Comment: CSV storage engine
Transactions: NO
         XA: NO
 Savepoints: NO
```

```
*************************** 11. row ***************************
      Engine: ARCHIVE
     Support: YES
     Comment: Archive storage engine
Transactions: NO
          XA: NO
  Savepoints: NO
11 rows in set (0.01 sec)

ERROR:
No query specified
mysql>
```

Step 4: You can uninstall with the following command as a "root" user.

```
mysql> uninstall plugin EXAMPLE;
Query OK, 0 rows affected (0.00 sec)
```

```
mysql> show engines\G;
*************************** 1. row ***************************
      Engine: ndbcluster
     Support: NO
     Comment: Clustered, fault-tolerant tables
Transactions: NULL
          XA: NULL
  Savepoints: NULL
*************************** 2. row ***************************
      Engine: FEDERATED
     Support: NO
     Comment: Federated MySQL storage engine
Transactions: NULL
          XA: NULL
  Savepoints: NULL
```

```
*************************** 3. row ***************************
      Engine: MEMORY
     Support: YES
     Comment: Hash based, stored in memory, useful for temporary tables
Transactions: NO
          XA: NO
  Savepoints: NO
*************************** 4. row ***************************
      Engine: InnoDB
     Support: DEFAULT
     Comment: Supports transactions, row-level locking, and foreign keys
Transactions: YES
          XA: YES
  Savepoints: YES
*************************** 5. row ***************************
      Engine: PERFORMANCE_SCHEMA
     Support: YES
     Comment: Performance Schema
Transactions: NO
          XA: NO
  Savepoints: NO
*************************** 6. row ***************************
      Engine: MyISAM
     Support: YES
     Comment: MyISAM storage engine
Transactions: NO
          XA: NO
  Savepoints: NO
*************************** 7. row ***************************
      Engine: ndbinfo
     Support: NO
     Comment: MySQL Cluster system information storage engine
Transactions: NULL
          XA: NULL
  Savepoints: NULL
```

```
*************************** 8. row ***************************
      Engine: MRG_MYISAM
     Support: YES
     Comment: Collection of identical MyISAM tables
Transactions: NO
          XA: NO
  Savepoints: NO
*************************** 9. row ***************************
      Engine: BLACKHOLE
     Support: YES
     Comment: /dev/null storage engine (anything you write to it
disappears)
Transactions: NO
          XA: NO
  Savepoints: NO
*************************** 10. row ***************************
      Engine: CSV
     Support: YES
     Comment: CSV storage engine
Transactions: NO
          XA: NO
  Savepoints: NO
*************************** 11. row ***************************
      Engine: ARCHIVE
     Support: YES
     Comment: Archive storage engine
Transactions: NO
          XA: NO
  Savepoints: NO
11 rows in set (0.00 sec)

ERROR:
No query specified
```

Hence, it is very important to understand the application use case and requirements and verify documentation to ensure all requested features are supported before recommending a storage engine to the application team. All features are summarized and listed in https://dev.mysql.com/doc/refman/8.1/en/storage-engines.html to help us choose an appropriate storage engine.

As a best practice, please ensure you have consistent backups before making any changes to the storage engine, and always consider server crash behavior.

Multiple Instance Management

There can be use cases where there could be a need to run multiple instances of MySQL on a single host. For example, you can use this option to test a new release of MySQL without impacting the production environment. At the same time, we can use the same binary for multiple instances by creating separate data directories and a different port.

Let us look at this example that creates different directories and different ports – 3306, 3307, 3308:

1. Create a **mysql** OS user and install the binary for MySQL 8.0.34.

    ```
    [root@mysql-b ~]# systemctl status mysqld
    Unit mysqld.service could not be found.
    [root@mysql-b ~]# useradd -d /home/mysql -s /bin/bash mysql
    [root@mysql-b ~]# passwd mysql
    Changing password for user mysql.
    New password:
    Retype new password:
    passwd: all authentication tokens updated successfully.
    [root@mysql-b ~]#
    [root@mysql-b ~]# wget https://downloads.mysql.com/archives/
    get/p/23/file/mysql-8.0.34-el7-x86_64.tar.gz
    --2023-10-16 19:20:05--  https://downloads.mysql.com/archives/
    get/p/23/file/mysql-8.0.34-el7-x86_64.tar.gz
    Resolving downloads.mysql.com (downloads.mysql.com)...
    23.65.18.57, 2600:1404:1800:680::2e31, 2600:1404:1800:685::2e31
    Connecting to downloads.mysql.com (downloads.mysql.
    com)|23.65.18.57|:443... connected.
    HTTP request sent, awaiting response... 302 Moved Temporarily
    ```

Location: https://cdn.mysql.com/archives/mysql-8.0/mysql-8.0.34-el7-x86_64.tar.gz [following]
--2023-10-16 19:20:06-- https://cdn.mysql.com/archives/mysql-8.0/mysql-8.0.34-el7-x86_64.tar.gz
Resolving cdn.mysql.com (cdn.mysql.com)... 23.218.11.146, 2600:1404:1800:686::1d68, 2600:1404:1800:692::1d68
Connecting to cdn.mysql.com (cdn.mysql.com)|23.218.11.146|:443... connected.
HTTP request sent, awaiting response... 200 OK
Length: 492490461 (470M) [application/x-tar-gz]
Saving to: 'mysql-8.0.34-el7-x86_64.tar.gz'

100%[==============================>] 492,490,461 11.3MB/s   in 51s

2023-10-16 19:20:57 (9.13 MB/s) - 'mysql-8.0.34-el7-x86_64.tar.gz' saved [492490461/492490461]

[root@mysql-b ~]# **cd /usr/local**

[root@mysql-b local]# **tar xzvf /root/mysql-8.0.34-el7-x86_64.tar.gz**
mysql-8.0.34-el7-x86_64/bin/
mysql-8.0.34-el7-x86_64/bin/myisam_ftdump
mysql-8.0.34-el7-x86_64/bin/myisamchk
mysql-8.0.34-el7-x86_64/bin/myisamlog

--Output truncated for better visibility

mysql-8.0.34-el7-x86_64/lib/private/sasl2/libplain.so.3
mysql-8.0.34-el7-x86_64/lib/private/sasl2/libplain.so.3.0.0
mysql-8.0.34-el7-x86_64/lib/private/sasl2/libscram.so
mysql-8.0.34-el7-x86_64/lib/private/sasl2/libscram.so.3
mysql-8.0.34-el7-x86_64/lib/private/sasl2/libscram.so.3.0.0
mysql-8.0.34-el7-x86_64/share/
mysql-8.0.34-el7-x86_64/share/install_rewriter.sql
mysql-8.0.34-el7-x86_64/share/uninstall_rewriter.sql

[root@mysql-b local]# **ln -s /usr/local/mysql-8.0.34-el7-x86_64/ mysql**

```
[root@mysql-b local]# cd /usr/local/mysql/bin/
[root@mysql-b bin]# ll
total 645188
-rwxr-xr-x 1 7161 31415    838543 Jul  6  2022 ibd2sdi
-rwxr-xr-x 1 7161 31415    627297 Jul  6  2022 innochecksum
-rwxr-xr-x 1 7161 31415    423030 Jul  6  2022 lz4_decompress
-rwxr-xr-x 1 7161 31415   7457514 Jul  6  2022 myisamchk
-rwxr-xr-x 1 7161 31415   7190337 Jul  6  2022 myisam_ftdump
-rwxr-xr-x 1 7161 31415   7153603 Jul  6  2022 myisamlog
-rwxr-xr-x 1 7161 31415   7277060 Jul  6  2022 myisampack
-rwxr-xr-x 1 7161 31415    523164 Jul  6  2022 my_print_defaults
-rwxr-xr-x 1 7161 31415   8727346 Jul  6  2022 mysql
-rwxr-xr-x 1 7161 31415   8281507 Jul  6  2022 mysqladmin
-rwxr-xr-x 1 7161 31415   9136483 Jul  6  2022 mysqlbinlog
-rwxr-xr-x 1 7161 31415   8304186 Jul  6  2022 mysqlcheck
-rwxr-xr-x 1 7161 31415      5085 Jul  6  2022 mysql_config
-rwxr-xr-x 1 7161 31415    517722 Jul  6  2022 mysql_config_editor
-rwxr-xr-x 1 7161 31415 124663507 Jul  6  2022 mysqld
-rwxr-xr-x 1 7161 31415 398569041 Jul  6  2022 mysqld-debug
-rwxr-xr-x 1 7161 31415     27492 Jul  6  2022 mysqld_multi
-rwxr-xr-x 1 7161 31415     29183 Jul  6  2022 mysqld_safe
-rwxr-xr-x 1 7161 31415   8397779 Jul  6  2022 mysqldump
-rwxr-xr-x 1 7161 31415      7669 Jul  6  2022 mysqldumpslow
-rwxr-xr-x 1 7161 31415   8272892 Jul  6  2022 mysqlimport
-rwxr-xr-x 1 7161 31415   8546008 Jul  6  2022 mysql_migrate_keyring
-rwxr-xr-x 1 7161 31415   9621311 Jul  6  2022 mysqlpump
-rwxr-xr-x 1 7161 31415   8257156 Jul  6  2022 mysql_secure_
                                             installation
-rwxr-xr-x 1 7161 31415   8273197 Jul  6  2022 mysqlshow
-rwxr-xr-x 1 7161 31415   8296506 Jul  6  2022 mysqlslap
-rwxr-xr-x 1 7161 31415    607088 Jul  6  2022 mysql_ssl_rsa_setup
-rwxr-xr-x 1 7161 31415    371143 Jul  6  2022 mysql_tzinfo_to_sql
-rwxr-xr-x 1 7161 31415   8556891 Jul  6  2022 mysql_upgrade
-rwxr-xr-x 1 7161 31415   1268701 Jul  6  2022 perror
-rwxr-xr-x 1 7161 31415    387596 Jul  6  2022 zlib_decompress
[root@mysql-b bin]#
```

2. Create different directories and set up configuration files with the
    required parameters.

>>>> 3306 <<<<

```
[root@mysql-b data]# ls -ltrth
total 0
[root@mysql-b data]# cd ..
[root@mysql-b 3306]# ls -ltr
total 0
drwxr-xr-x 2 mysql mysql 6 Oct 16 19:22 data

[root@mysql-b 3306]# vi my.cnf
[root@mysql-b 3306]# cat my.cnf
[mysqld]
port=3306
basedir=/usr/local/mysql/
datadir=/mysql/3306/data
lower_case_table_names=1
innodb_buffer_pool_size=128M
socket=/tmp/mysql_3306.sock
log_error=/mysql/3306/data/mysql06.log
default-authentication-plugin=mysql_native_password
[root@mysql-b 3306]#
```

>>>> 3307 <<<<

```
[root@mysql-b 3306]# cd ../3307
[root@mysql-b 3307]# pwd
/mysql/3307
[root@mysql-b 3307]# ls -ltr
total 0
drwxr-xr-x 2 mysql mysql 6 Oct 16 19:22 data

[root@mysql-b 3307]# vi my.cnf
[root@mysql-b 3307]# cat my.cnf
[mysqld]
port=3307
```

```
basedir=/usr/local/mysql/
datadir=/mysql/3307/data
lower_case_table_names=1
innodb_buffer_pool_size=128M
socket=/tmp/mysql_3307.sock
log_error=/mysql/3307/data/mysql07.log
default-authentication-plugin=mysql_native_password
[root@mysql-b 3307]#
```

>>>> 3308 <<<<

```
[root@mysql-b 3307]# cd ../3308
[root@mysql-b 3308]# ls -ltr
total 0
drwxr-xr-x 2 mysql mysql 6 Oct 16 19:22 data
[root@mysql-b 3308]#
[root@mysql-b 3308]# vi my.cnf
[root@mysql-b 3308]# cat my.cnf
[mysqld]
port=3308
basedir=/usr/local/mysql/
datadir=/mysql/3308/data
lower_case_table_names=1
innodb_buffer_pool_size=128M
socket=/tmp/mysql_3308.sock
log_error=/mysql/3308/data/mysql08.log
default-authentication-plugin=mysql_native_password

[root@mysql-b 3308]# chown -R mysql:mysql /mysql
```

3. Initialize the data directories.

```
[root@mysql-b 3306]# /usr/local/mysql/bin/mysqld --defaults-
file=/mysql/3306/my.cnf --initialize --basedir=/usr/local/mysql/
--datadir=/mysql/3306/data
```

```
[root@mysql-b 3307]# /usr/local/mysql/bin/mysqld --defaults-
file=/mysql/3307/my.cnf --initialize --basedir=/usr/local/mysql/
--datadir=/mysql/3307/data
```

```
[root@mysql-b 3308]# /usr/local/mysql/bin/mysqld --defaults-
file=/mysql/3308/my.cnf --initialize --basedir=/usr/local/mysql/
--datadir=/mysql/3308/data

[root@mysql-b 3308]# ls -ltr /mysql/3306/data
total 78272
-rw-r----- 1 root root       56 Oct 16 19:28 auto.cnf
-rw-r----- 1 root root  8585216 Oct 16 19:28 #ib_16384_1.dblwr
drwxr-x--- 2 root root     8192 Oct 16 19:28 performance_schema
-rw------- 1 root root     1676 Oct 16 19:28 ca-key.pem
-rw-r--r-- 1 root root     1112 Oct 16 19:28 ca.pem
-rw------- 1 root root     1676 Oct 16 19:28 server-key.pem
-rw-r--r-- 1 root root     1112 Oct 16 19:28 server-cert.pem
-rw------- 1 root root     1680 Oct 16 19:28 client-key.pem
-rw-r--r-- 1 root root     1112 Oct 16 19:28 client-cert.pem
-rw-r--r-- 1 root root      452 Oct 16 19:28 public_key.pem
-rw------- 1 root root     1680 Oct 16 19:28 private_key.pem
-rw-r----- 1 root root      658 Oct 16 19:28 mysql06.log
drwxr-x--- 2 root root      143 Oct 16 19:28 mysql
drwxr-x--- 2 root root       28 Oct 16 19:28 sys
-rw-r----- 1 root root     5916 Oct 16 19:28 ib_buffer_pool
-rw-r----- 1 root root 16777216 Oct 16 19:28 undo_001
-rw-r----- 1 root root   196608 Oct 16 19:28 #ib_16384_0.dblwr
-rw-r----- 1 root root 16777216 Oct 16 19:28 undo_002
-rw-r----- 1 root root 25165824 Oct 16 19:28 mysql.ibd
drwxr-x--- 2 root root     4096 Oct 16 19:28 #innodb_redo
-rw-r----- 1 root root 12582912 Oct 16 19:28 ibdata1
drwxr-x--- 2 root root        6 Oct 16 19:28 #innodb_temp

[root@mysql-b 3307]# ls -ltr /mysql/3307/data
total 78272
-rw-r----- 1 root root       56 Oct 16 19:29 auto.cnf
-rw-r----- 1 root root  8585216 Oct 16 19:29 #ib_16384_1.dblwr
drwxr-x--- 2 root root     8192 Oct 16 19:29 performance_schema
-rw------- 1 root root     1676 Oct 16 19:29 ca-key.pem
-rw-r--r-- 1 root root     1112 Oct 16 19:29 ca.pem
-rw------- 1 root root     1680 Oct 16 19:29 server-key.pem
```

```
-rw-r--r-- 1 root root      1112 Oct 16 19:29 server-cert.pem
-rw------- 1 root root      1676 Oct 16 19:29 client-key.pem
-rw-r--r-- 1 root root      1112 Oct 16 19:29 client-cert.pem
-rw-r--r-- 1 root root       452 Oct 16 19:29 public_key.pem
-rw------- 1 root root      1676 Oct 16 19:29 private_key.pem
-rw-r----- 1 root root       658 Oct 16 19:29 mysql07.log
drwxr-x--- 2 root root       143 Oct 16 19:29 mysql
drwxr-x--- 2 root root        28 Oct 16 19:29 sys
-rw-r----- 1 root root      5960 Oct 16 19:29 ib_buffer_pool
-rw-r----- 1 root root  16777216 Oct 16 19:29 undo_002
-rw-r----- 1 root root  16777216 Oct 16 19:29 undo_001
-rw-r----- 1 root root    196608 Oct 16 19:29 #ib_16384_0.dblwr
-rw-r----- 1 root root  25165824 Oct 16 19:29 mysql.ibd
drwxr-x--- 2 root root      4096 Oct 16 19:29 #innodb_redo
-rw-r----- 1 root root  12582912 Oct 16 19:29 ibdata1
drwxr-x--- 2 root root         6 Oct 16 19:29 #innodb_temp

[root@mysql-b 3308]# ls -ltr /mysql/3308/data
total 78272
-rw-r----- 1 root root        56 Oct 16 19:29 auto.cnf
-rw-r----- 1 root root   8585216 Oct 16 19:29 #ib_16384_1.dblwr
drwxr-x--- 2 root root      8192 Oct 16 19:29 performance_schema
-rw------- 1 root root      1676 Oct 16 19:29 ca-key.pem
-rw-r--r-- 1 root root      1112 Oct 16 19:29 ca.pem
-rw------- 1 root root      1680 Oct 16 19:29 server-key.pem
-rw-r--r-- 1 root root      1112 Oct 16 19:29 server-cert.pem
-rw------- 1 root root      1680 Oct 16 19:29 client-key.pem
-rw-r--r-- 1 root root      1112 Oct 16 19:29 client-cert.pem
-rw-r--r-- 1 root root       452 Oct 16 19:29 public_key.pem
-rw------- 1 root root      1680 Oct 16 19:29 private_key.pem
-rw-r----- 1 root root       658 Oct 16 19:29 mysql08.log
drwxr-x--- 2 root root       143 Oct 16 19:29 mysql
drwxr-x--- 2 root root        28 Oct 16 19:29 sys
-rw-r----- 1 root root      5961 Oct 16 19:29 ib_buffer_pool
-rw-r----- 1 root root  16777216 Oct 16 19:29 undo_001
-rw-r----- 1 root root    196608 Oct 16 19:29 #ib_16384_0.dblwr
```

```
-rw-r----- 1 root root 16777216 Oct 16 19:29 undo_002
-rw-r----- 1 root root 25165824 Oct 16 19:29 mysql.ibd
drwxr-x--- 2 root root     4096 Oct 16 19:29 #innodb_redo
-rw-r----- 1 root root 12582912 Oct 16 19:29 ibdata1
drwxr-x--- 2 root root        6 Oct 16 19:29 #innodb_temp
[root@mysql-b 3308]#
```

4. Start the MySQL server using the **–defaults-file** option, which
    has the port information to run each instance on ports 3306,
    3307, 3308.

```
[root@mysql-b ~]# chown -R mysql:mysql /mysql

[root@mysql-b ~]# nohup /usr/local/mysql/bin/mysqld --defaults-
file=/mysql/3306/my.cnf --user=mysql &
[1] 1430
[root@mysql-b ~]# ps -ef |grep mysql
mysql     1430  1232 27 19:31 pts/0    00:00:01 /usr/local/mysql/
bin/mysqld --defaults-file=/mysql/3306/my.cnf --user=mysql
root      1475  1232  0 19:31 pts/0    00:00:00 grep --color=
                                                auto mysql
[root@mysql-b ~]# nohup /usr/local/mysql/bin/mysqld --defaults-
file=/mysql/3307/my.cnf --user=mysql &
[2] 1476
[root@mysql-b ~]# ps -ef |grep mysql
mysql     1430  1232  4 19:31 pts/0    00:00:01 /usr/local/mysql/
bin/mysqld --defaults-file=/mysql/3306/my.cnf --user=mysql
mysql     1476  1232 36 19:31 pts/0    00:00:01 /usr/local/mysql/
bin/mysqld --defaults-file=/mysql/3307/my.cnf --user=mysql
root      1519  1232  0 19:31 pts/0    00:00:00 grep --color=
                                                auto mysql
[root@mysql-b ~]# nohup /usr/local/mysql/bin/mysqld --defaults-
file=/mysql/3308/my.cnf --user=mysql &
[3] 1520
[root@mysql-b ~]# ps -ef |grep mysql
mysql     1430  1232  2 19:31 pts/0    00:00:01 /usr/local/mysql/
bin/mysqld --defaults-file=/mysql/3306/my.cnf --user=mysql
```

```
mysql     1476  1232  4 19:31 pts/0    00:00:01 /usr/local/mysql/
bin/mysqld --defaults-file=/mysql/3307/my.cnf --user=mysql
mysql     1520  1232 35 19:32 pts/0    00:00:01 /usr/local/mysql/
bin/mysqld --defaults-file=/mysql/3308/my.cnf --user=mysql
root      1563  1232  0 19:32 pts/0    00:00:00 grep --color=
                                                auto mysql
```

5. Verify the data directories and use the temporary password
   from the log file to log in to each of the instances and reset the
   passwords. Here is an example of doing it for one of the instances
   running on port 3306:

```
[root@mysql-b ~]# cd /mysql/3306/data/
[root@mysql-b data]# ls -ltr
total 90572
-rw-r----- 1 mysql mysql       56 Oct 16 19:28 auto.cnf
-rw-r----- 1 mysql mysql  8585216 Oct 16 19:28 #ib_16384_1.dblwr
drwxr-x--- 2 mysql mysql     8192 Oct 16 19:28 performance_schema
-rw------- 1 mysql mysql     1676 Oct 16 19:28 ca-key.pem
-rw-r--r-- 1 mysql mysql     1112 Oct 16 19:28 ca.pem
-rw------- 1 mysql mysql     1676 Oct 16 19:28 server-key.pem
-rw-r--r-- 1 mysql mysql     1112 Oct 16 19:28 server-cert.pem
-rw------- 1 mysql mysql     1680 Oct 16 19:28 client-key.pem
-rw-r--r-- 1 mysql mysql     1112 Oct 16 19:28 client-cert.pem
-rw-r--r-- 1 mysql mysql      452 Oct 16 19:28 public_key.pem
-rw------- 1 mysql mysql     1680 Oct 16 19:28 private_key.pem
drwxr-x--- 2 mysql mysql      143 Oct 16 19:28 mysql
drwxr-x--- 2 mysql mysql       28 Oct 16 19:28 sys
-rw-r----- 1 mysql mysql     5916 Oct 16 19:28 ib_buffer_pool
drwxr-x--- 2 mysql mysql      187 Oct 16 19:31 #innodb_temp
-rw-r----- 1 mysql mysql       16 Oct 16 19:31 binlog.index
-rw-r----- 1 mysql mysql      157 Oct 16 19:31 binlog.000001
-rw-r----- 1 mysql mysql        5 Oct 16 19:31 mysql-b.pid
-rw-r----- 1 mysql mysql     1782 Oct 16 19:31 mysql06.log
drwxr-x--- 2 mysql mysql     4096 Oct 16 19:31 #innodb_redo
-rw-r----- 1 mysql mysql 12582912 Oct 16 19:31 ibtmp1
```

```
-rw-r----- 1 mysql mysql 12582912 Oct 16 19:31 ibdata1
-rw-r----- 1 mysql mysql 16777216 Oct 16 19:31 undo_002
-rw-r----- 1 mysql mysql 16777216 Oct 16 19:31 undo_001
-rw-r----- 1 mysql mysql   196608 Oct 16 19:31 #ib_16384_0.dblwr
-rw-r----- 1 mysql mysql 25165824 Oct 16 19:31 mysql.ibd
```

[root@mysql-b data]# **tail -f mysql06.log**
2023-10-17T00:28:53.334323Z 0 [System] [MY-013169] [Server] /usr/
local/mysql/bin/mysqld (mysqld 8.0.34) initializing of server in
progress as process 1287
2023-10-17T00:28:53.342694Z 1 [System] [MY-013576] [InnoDB] InnoDB
initialization has started.
2023-10-17T00:28:54.461167Z 1 [System] [MY-013577] [InnoDB] InnoDB
initialization has ended.
2023-10-17T00:28:55.671637Z 6 [Note] [MY-010454] [Server] A
temporary password is generated for root@localhost: **isCeuwGxf4.X**
2023-10-17T00:31:23.236713Z 0 [Warning] [MY-010068] [Server] CA
certificate ca.pem is self signed.
2023-10-17T00:31:23.254696Z 0 [System] [MY-010931] [Server] /
usr/local/mysql/bin/mysqld: ready for connections. Version:
'8.0.34' socket: '/tmp/mysql_3306.sock' port: 3306 MySQL
Community Server - GPL.
2023-10-17T00:31:23.254741Z 0 [System] [MY-011323] [Server] X
Plugin ready for connections. Bind-address: '::' port: 33060,
socket: /tmp/mysqlx.sock
[root@mysql-b data]# **/usr/local/mysql/bin/mysqlshow -S /tmp/
mysql_3306.sock -p**
Enter password:
/usr/local/mysql/bin/mysqlshow: Your password has expired. To log in
you must change it using a client that supports expired passwords.
[root@mysql-b data]#
[root@mysql-b data]# **/usr/local/mysql/bin/mysqlshow -S /tmp/
mysql_3306.sock -p**
Enter password:
/usr/local/mysql/bin/mysqlshow: Your password has expired. To log in
you must change it using a client that supports expired passwords.

```
[root@mysql-b data]# cd

[root@mysql-b ~]#/usr/local/mysql/bin/mysql -S /tmp/mysql_3306.sock -p
Enter password:

mysql> alter user 'root'@'localhost' identified by 'Welcome@123';
Query OK, 0 rows affected (0.01 sec)

mysql> show databases;
+--------------------+
| Database           |
+--------------------+
| information_schema |
| mysql              |
| performance_schema |
| sys                |
+--------------------+
4 rows in set (0.01 sec)

mysql> exit
[root@mysql-b ~]#/usr/local/mysql/bin/mysql -S /tmp/mysql_3306.sock -p
Enter password:

mysql> show databases;
+--------------------+
| Database           |
+--------------------+
| information_schema |
| mysql              |
| performance_schema |
| sys                |
+--------------------+
4 rows in set (0.00 sec)
```

Repeat the same process for MySQL instances running on ports
3307 and 3308.

6. Verify the ports the MySQL servers are listening on for client
   connections.

```
[root@mysql-b ~]# ps -ef|grep mysql
mysql     1430  1232  0 19:31 pts/0    00:00:03 /usr/local/mysql/
bin/mysqld --defaults-file=/mysql/3306/my.cnf --user=mysql
mysql     1476  1232  0 19:31 pts/0    00:00:02 /usr/local/mysql/
bin/mysqld --defaults-file=/mysql/3307/my.cnf --user=mysql
mysql     1520  1232  0 19:32 pts/0    00:00:02 /usr/local/mysql/
bin/mysqld --defaults-file=/mysql/3308/my.cnf --user=mysql
root      1591  1232  0 19:40 pts/0    00:00:00 grep --color=
                                                auto mysql
[root@mysql-b ~]# which netstat
/usr/bin/which: no netstat in (/root/.cache/activestate/bin:/
root/.local/ActiveState/StateTool/release/bin:/usr/local/sbin:/
usr/local/bin:/usr/sbin:/usr/bin:/root/bin)
[root@mysql-b ~]#
[root@mysql-b ~]# sudo yum install net-tools
```

--Output truncated for better visibility

```
Installed:
  net-tools.x86_64 0:2.0-0.25.20131004git.el7
```

```
Complete!
[root@mysql-b ~]# netstat -ntl
Active Internet connections (only servers)
Proto Recv-Q Send-Q Local Address      Foreign Address      State
tcp       0      0 0.0.0.0:22         0.0.0.0:*            LISTEN
tcp6      0      0 :::3306                 :::*            LISTEN
tcp6      0      0 :::3307                 :::*            LISTEN
tcp6      0      0 :::3308                 :::*            LISTEN
tcp6      0      0 :::22                   :::*            LISTEN
tcp6      0      0 :::33060                :::*            LISTEN
[root@mysql-b ~]#
```

7. Check the status for each MySQL server instance by connecting
   using the port.

```
[root@mysql-b ~]# /usr/local/mysql/bin/mysqladmin -h127.0.0.1
-uroot -p -P3306 status
```

```
Enter password:
Uptime: 648  Threads: 2  Questions: 10  Slow queries: 0  Opens:
152  Flush tables: 3  Open tables: 68  Queries per second avg: 0.015
```

[root@mysql-b ~]# /usr/local/mysql/bin/mysqladmin -h127.0.0.1 -uroot -p -P3307 status

```
Enter password:
Uptime: 637  Threads: 2  Questions: 8  Slow queries: 0  Opens:
148  Flush tables: 3  Open tables: 64  Queries per second avg: 0.012
```

[root@mysql-b ~]# /usr/local/mysql/bin/mysqladmin -h127.0.0.1 -uroot -p -P3308 status

```
Enter password:
Uptime: 623  Threads: 2  Questions: 9  Slow queries: 0  Opens:
148  Flush tables: 3  Open tables: 64  Queries per second avg: 0.014
[root@mysql-b ~]#
```

In order to manage multiple instances at the same time, we can use **mysqld_multi** to start, reload, or stop any number of mysqld processes running on the same host. For this, we have to build a MySQL configuration file with all the parameters separated by **[mysqld#]** so they can be managed separately.

```
[root@mysql-b bin]# pwd
/usr/local/mysql/bin
[root@mysql-b bin]# cd /mysql/
[root@mysql-b mysql]# ls -ltr
total 0
drwxr-xr-x 3 mysql mysql 18 Oct 16 19:22 3309
drwxr-xr-x 3 mysql mysql 32 Oct 16 19:24 3306
drwxr-xr-x 3 mysql mysql 32 Oct 16 19:25 3307
drwxr-xr-x 3 mysql mysql 32 Oct 16 19:26 3308

[root@mysql-b mysql]# vi multi.cnf
[root@mysql-b mysql]# ls -ltr
total 0
drwxr-xr-x 3 mysql mysql 18 Oct 16 19:22 3309
drwxr-xr-x 3 mysql mysql 32 Oct 16 19:24 3306
drwxr-xr-x 3 mysql mysql 32 Oct 16 19:25 3307
drwxr-xr-x 3 mysql mysql 32 Oct 16 19:26 3308
```

```
-rw-r--r-- 1 root   root    0 Oct 16 21:30 multi.cnf

[root@mysql-b mysql]# cat 3306/my.cnf > multi.cnf
[root@mysql-b mysql]# cat multi.cnf
[mysqld]
port=3306
basedir=/usr/local/mysql/
datadir=/mysql/3306/data
lower_case_table_names=1
innodb_buffer_pool_size=128M
socket=/tmp/mysql_3306.sock
log_error=/mysql/3306/data/mysql06.log
default-authentication-plugin=mysql_native_password

[root@mysql-b mysql]# cat 3307/my.cnf >> multi.cnf
[root@mysql-b mysql]# cat multi.cnf
[mysqld]
port=3306
basedir=/usr/local/mysql/
datadir=/mysql/3306/data
lower_case_table_names=1
innodb_buffer_pool_size=128M
socket=/tmp/mysql_3306.sock
log_error=/mysql/3306/data/mysql06.log
default-authentication-plugin=mysql_native_password
[mysqld]
port=3307
basedir=/usr/local/mysql/
datadir=/mysql/3307/data
lower_case_table_names=1
innodb_buffer_pool_size=128M
socket=/tmp/mysql_3307.sock
log_error=/mysql/3307/data/mysql07.log
default-authentication-plugin=mysql_native_password

[root@mysql-b mysql]# cat 3308/my.cnf >> multi.cnf
[root@mysql-b mysql]# cat multi.cnf
```

```
[mysqld]
port=3306
basedir=/usr/local/mysql/
datadir=/mysql/3306/data
lower_case_table_names=1
innodb_buffer_pool_size=128M
socket=/tmp/mysql_3306.sock
log_error=/mysql/3306/data/mysql06.log
default-authentication-plugin=mysql_native_password
[mysqld]
port=3307
basedir=/usr/local/mysql/
datadir=/mysql/3307/data
lower_case_table_names=1
innodb_buffer_pool_size=128M
socket=/tmp/mysql_3307.sock
log_error=/mysql/3307/data/mysql07.log
default-authentication-plugin=mysql_native_password
[mysqld]
port=3308
basedir=/usr/local/mysql/
datadir=/mysql/3308/data
lower_case_table_names=1
innodb_buffer_pool_size=128M
socket=/tmp/mysql_3308.sock
log_error=/mysql/3308/data/mysql08.log
default-authentication-plugin=mysql_native_password
[root@mysql-b mysql]#
```

We also need to create a user that has the privileges to shut down each one of the servers. Do this on all MySQL servers you would like to manage using mysqld_multi.

```
[root@mysql-b mysql]# /usr/local/mysql/bin/mysql -S /tmp/mysql_3306.sock -p
Enter password:

mysql> create user 'multi_admin'@'localhost' identified by 'Welcome@123';
Query OK, 0 rows affected (0.01 sec)
```

```
mysql> grant shutdown on *.* to 'multi_admin'@'localhost';
Query OK, 0 rows affected (0.01 sec)

mysql> exit

[root@mysql-b mysql]# /usr/local/mysql/bin/mysql -S /tmp/mysql_3307.sock -p
Enter password:
ERROR 1045 (28000): Access denied for user 'root'@'localhost' (using
password: YES)

[root@mysql-b mysql]# /usr/local/mysql/bin/mysql -S /tmp/mysql_3307.sock -p
Enter password:

mysql> create user 'multi_admin'@'localhost' identified by 'Welcome@123';
Query OK, 0 rows affected (0.01 sec)

mysql> grant shutdown on *.* to 'multi_admin'@'localhost';
Query OK, 0 rows affected (0.01 sec)

mysql> exit
[root@mysql-b mysql]# /usr/local/mysql/bin/mysql -S /tmp/mysql_3308.sock -p
Enter password:

mysql> create user 'multi_admin'@'localhost' identified by 'Welcome@123';
Query OK, 0 rows affected (0.02 sec)

mysql> grant shutdown on *.* to 'multi_admin'@'localhost';
Query OK, 0 rows affected (0.01 sec)

mysql> exit

[root@mysql-b mysql]# vi multi.cnf
[root@mysql-b mysql]# ls -ltr
total 4
drwxr-xr-x 3 mysql mysql  18 Oct 16 19:22 3309
drwxr-xr-x 3 mysql mysql  32 Oct 16 19:24 3306
drwxr-xr-x 3 mysql mysql  32 Oct 16 19:25 3307
drwxr-xr-x 3 mysql mysql  32 Oct 16 19:26 3308
-rw-r--r-- 1 root  root  891 Oct 16 21:47 multi.cnf
[root@mysql-b mysql]#
```

```
[root@mysql-b mysql]# cat multi.cnf
[mysqld_multi]
mysqld      = /usr/local/mysql/bin/mysqld_safe
mysqladmin = /usr/local/mysql/bin/mysqladmin
user        = multi_admin
password    = Welcome@123

[mysqld1]
port=3306
basedir=/usr/local/mysql/
datadir=/mysql/3306/data
lower_case_table_names=1
innodb_buffer_pool_size=128M
socket=/tmp/mysql_3306.sock
log_error=/mysql/3306/data/mysql06.log
default-authentication-plugin=mysql_native_password

[mysqld2]
port=3307
basedir=/usr/local/mysql/
datadir=/mysql/3307/data
lower_case_table_names=1
innodb_buffer_pool_size=128M
socket=/tmp/mysql_3307.sock
log_error=/mysql/3307/data/mysql07.log
default-authentication-plugin=mysql_native_password

[mysqld3]
port=3308
basedir=/usr/local/mysql/
datadir=/mysql/3308/data
lower_case_table_names=1
innodb_buffer_pool_size=128M
socket=/tmp/mysql_3308.sock
log_error=/mysql/3308/data/mysql08.log
default-authentication-plugin=mysql_native_password
[root@mysql-b mysql]#
```

Once the configuration is in place, you can use the following commands to manage multiple MySQL servers:

```
[root@mysql-b ~]# /usr/local/mysql/bin/mysqld_multi stop
[root@mysql-b ~]# ps -ef |grep mysql
root       1428  1232  0 19:31 pts/0    00:00:00 grep --color=auto mysql
[root@mysql-b ~]# /usr/local/mysql/bin/mysqld_multi start
[root@mysql-b ~]# ps -ef |grep mysql
mysql      1430  1232  2 19:31 pts/0    00:00:01 /usr/local/mysql/bin/
mysqld --defaults-file=/mysql/3306/my.cnf --user=mysql
mysql      1476  1232  4 19:31 pts/0    00:00:01 /usr/local/mysql/bin/
mysqld --defaults-file=/mysql/3307/my.cnf --user=mysql
mysql      1520  1232 35 19:32 pts/0    00:00:01 /usr/local/mysql/bin/
mysqld --defaults-file=/mysql/3308/my.cnf --user=mysql
root       1563  1232  0 19:32 pts/0    00:00:00 grep --color=auto mysql
[root@mysql-b ~]#

[root@mysql-b ~]# /usr/local/mysql/bin/mysqld_multi stop 2
[root@mysql-b ~]# ps -ef |grep mysql
mysql      1430  1232  2 19:31 pts/0    00:00:01 /usr/local/mysql/bin/
mysqld --defaults-file=/mysql/3306/my.cnf --user=mysql
mysql      1520  1232 35 19:32 pts/0    00:00:01 /usr/local/mysql/bin/
mysqld --defaults-file=/mysql/3308/my.cnf --user=mysql
root       1563  1232  0 19:32 pts/0    00:00:00 grep --color=auto mysql
[root@mysql-b ~]#
```

Summary

In this chapter, we learned about configuring the MySQL server, its data dictionary, and startup and shutdown process, and we also looked at connection management and user management. In addition, we learned about MySQL's flexibility with a variety of different storage engines and how to maintain multiple MySQL instances on the same host. In the next chapter, we will discuss tablespace management in InnoDB and partitioning concepts and options in MySQL InnoDB.

CHAPTER 4

MySQL Tablespace Management and Partitioning

Introduction

In this chapter, we will discuss tablespace and partitioning. Partitioning divides a large dataset into smaller manageable subsets, usually called partitions. Partitions can be stored, managed, and accessed separately, improving the database's scalability, availability, and performance.

Before partitioning, there is guidance on physical data storage once we have the concept of tablespaces, which are logical representations of the data files within a database. In MySQL database, InnoDB storage engine supports tablespaces that store data in different physical directories and logically represent them using tablespaces within the database.

Let us learn the tablespaces available in MySQL 8.0 before learning about partitioning.

Tablespaces

A **tablespace** is a general storage area where database objects, such as tables and indexes, are stored. Tablespaces play an important role in managing the physical storage of data within a MySQL database.

The following are the different types of tablespaces in MySQL 8.0:

- **InnoDB system tablespace**: A storage area for the change buffer

- **InnoDB file-per-table tablespace**: A storage area of data and indexes of a single InnoDB table

- **General tablespace**: A shared storage area for data and indexes for multiple tables

- **UNDO tablespace**: A storage area for undo logs, which contains information to undo the last changes by a transaction

- **Temporary tablespace**: A temporary storage area for user-created and internal temporary tables

Tablespace Management – Resizing a System Tablespace

Resizing a tablespace includes increasing and decreasing the SYSTEM tablespace. The easiest way to increase the size of the system tablespace is to configure it to autoextend. Specify the **autoextend** attribute for the last data file in the **innodb_data_file_path** configuration parameter in the /**etc/my.cnf** file and restart the server.

The data file automatically increases in size by **8 MB** whenever there is a need to autoextend. The **innodb_autoextend_increment** configuration parameter can be configured to control the autoextend size.

We can also increase the system tablespace size by adding another data file. Here are the steps we perform to do so:

- Stop the MySQL server.

- Remove the autoextend attribute if the last data file in the **innodb_data_file_path** has it and add it to the current data file.

- Add a new data file to the **innodb_data_file_path** setting with the optional autoextend attribute.

Note   The autoextend attribute can only be added to the last data file in the innodb_data_file_path setting.

- Start the MySQL server.

In our example here, we will add another data file, **ibdata2**, with autoextend onto the SYSTEM tablespace.

1. Check status and verify the configuration file to determine default data directory.

```
[root@mysql-a ~]# systemctl status mysqld
[root@mysql-a ~]# vi /etc/my.cnf
[root@mysql-a ~]# cat /etc/my.cnf
[mysqld]
datadir=/var/lib/mysql
socket=/var/lib/mysql/mysql.sock
log-error=/var/log/mysqld.log
pid-file=/var/run/mysqld/mysqld.pid
```

2. Check current InnoDB variable settings like innodb_data_file_path, innodb_data_home_dir, innodb_autoextend_increment, and innodb_fast_shutdown.

```
[root@mysql-a ~]# su - mysql
Last login: Wed Sep 13 22:23:01 CDT 2023 on pts/0
-bash-4.2$
-bash-4.2$ mysql -u root -p
Enter password:

mysql> show global variables like 'innodb_data%';
+------------------------+------------------------+
| Variable_name          | Value                  |
+------------------------+------------------------+
| innodb_data_file_path  | ibdata1:12M:autoextend |
| innodb_data_home_dir   |                        |
+------------------------+------------------------+
2 rows in set (0.01 sec)

mysql> show variables like 'innodb_autoextend_increment';
```

```
+-----------------------------+-------+
| Variable_name               | Value |
+-----------------------------+-------+
| innodb_autoextend_increment | 64    |
+-----------------------------+-------+
1 row in set (0.01 sec)

mysql> show global variables like 'innodb_fast_shutdown';
+----------------------+-------+
| Variable_name        | Value |
+----------------------+-------+
| innodb_fast_shutdown | 1     |
+----------------------+-------+
1 row in set (0.00 sec)
```

3. It is recommended to set **innodb_fast_shutdown** to **slow shutdown (0)**. Slow shutdown ensures all the data files are fully prepared by doing a full purge and change buffer merge to ensure consistency and avoid the risk of data file corruption.

```
mysql> set global innodb_fast_shutdown=0;
Query OK, 0 rows affected (0.00 sec)

mysql> show global variables like 'innodb_fast_shutdown';
+----------------------+-------+
| Variable_name        | Value |
+----------------------+-------+
| innodb_fast_shutdown | 0     |
+----------------------+-------+
1 row in set (0.00 sec)
```

4. Stop the MySQL daemon.

```
-bash-4.2$ sudo systemctl stop mysqld
-bash-4.2$ sudo systemctl status mysqld
```

5. Create new data directories for the InnoDB system tablespace on
    a newer volume if you allocate more size and modify the MySQL
    configuration file (/etc/my.cnf) to reflect the new data directory.

```
-bash-4.2$ sudo mkdir /var/lib/mysql/innodb
-bash-4.2$ sudo mv /var/lib/mysql/ibdata1 /var/lib/mysql/innodb/
-bash-4.2$ sudo chown -R mysql:mysql /var/lib/mysql
-bash-4.2$ sudo vi /etc/my.cnf
[-bash-4.2$ cat /etc/my.cnf
[mysqld]
datadir=/var/lib/mysql
socket=/var/lib/mysql/mysql.sock
log-error=/var/log/mysqld.log
pid-file=/var/run/mysqld/mysqld.pid

# Innodb system tablespace
innodb-data-home-dir=/var/lib/mysql/innodb/
innodb-data-file-path=ibdata1:12M;ibdata2:12M:autoextend
```

6. Start the MySQL daemon and verify:

```
-bash-4.2$ sudo systemctl start mysqld
-bash-4.2$ sudo systemctl status mysqld
-bash-4.2$ ls -lrth /var/lib/mysql/innodb
total 36M
-rw-r----- 1 mysql mysql 12M Sep 16 20:59 ibdata2
-rw-r----- 1 mysql mysql 12M Sep 16 20:59 ibtmp1
-rw-r----- 1 mysql mysql 12M Sep 16 20:59 ibdata1
-bash-4.2$

-bash-4.2$ mysql -u root -p
Enter password:

mysql> show global variables like 'innodb_data%';
```

```
+----------------------+------------------------------------+
| Variable_name        | Value                              |
+----------------------+------------------------------------+
| innodb_data_file_path | ibdata1:12M;ibdata2:12M:autoextend |
| innodb_data_home_dir  | /var/lib/mysql/innodb/             |
+----------------------+------------------------------------+
2 rows in set (0.00 sec)

mysql> show variables like 'innodb_autoextend_increment';
+-----------------------------+-------+
| Variable_name               | Value |
+-----------------------------+-------+
| innodb_autoextend_increment | 64    |
+-----------------------------+-------+
1 row in set (0.00 sec)
```

Tablespace Management – Moving an Undo Tablespace

In this exercise, we will move an UNDO tablespace into another directory. Here are the steps to do so:

- Stop the MySQL server.

- Move the UNDO tablespace from the current data directory into the new directory.

- Add the **innodb-undo-directory** configuration parameter to the **/etc/my.cnf** file to point to the new directory where the UNDO tablespace will be moved to.

- Start the MySQL server and verify.

1. Identify the current undo file directory and files.

   ```
   -bash-4.2$ ls -lrth /var/lib/mysql/undo*
   -rw-r----- 1 mysql mysql 16M Sep 16 21:01 /var/lib/mysql/undo_001
   -rw-r----- 1 mysql mysql 16M Sep 16 21:01 /var/lib/mysql/undo_002
   ```

```
-bash-4.2$
-bash-4.2$ mysql -u root -p
Enter password:

mysql> show global variables like 'innodb_fast_shutdown';
+----------------------+-------+
| Variable_name        | Value |
+----------------------+-------+
| innodb_fast_shutdown | 1     |
+----------------------+-------+
1 row in set (0.00 sec)

mysql> set global innodb_fast_shutdown=0;
Query OK, 0 rows affected (0.00 sec)

mysql> show global variables like 'innodb_fast_shutdown';
+----------------------+-------+
| Variable_name        | Value |
+----------------------+-------+
| innodb_fast_shutdown | 0     |
+----------------------+-------+
1 row in set (0.00 sec)
```

2. Stop the MySQL daemon.

```
-bash-4.2$ sudo systemctl stop mysqld
-bash-4.2$ sudo systemctl status mysqld
```

Move the UNDO tablespace from the current data directory into the new directory and make MySQL configuration file changes

Current data directory: **/var/lib/mysql**

New UNDO directory: **/var/lib/mysql/innodb**

```
-bash-4.2$ sudo mv /var/lib/mysql/undo_* /var/lib/mysql/innodb/
-bash-4.2$ sudo chown -R mysql:mysql /var/lib/mysql
-bash-4.2$ sudo vi /etc/my.cnf
-bash-4.2$ cat /etc/my.cnf
[mysqld]
```

```
datadir=/var/lib/mysql
socket=/var/lib/mysql/mysql.sock
log-error=/var/log/mysqld.log
pid-file=/var/run/mysqld/mysqld.pid
# Innodb system tablespace
innodb-data-home-dir=/var/lib/mysql/innodb/
innodb-data-file-path=ibdata1:12M;ibdata2:12M:autoextend

# Innodb undo tablespace
innodb-undo-directory=/var/lib/mysql/innodb/
```

3. Start the MySQL daemon and verify.

```
-bash-4.2$ sudo systemctl start mysqld
-bash-4.2$ sudo systemctl status mysqld
-bash-4.2$ mysql -u root -p
Enter password:
mysql> select tablespace_name, file_name from information_schema.
files where file_type like 'undo log';
+-----------------+--------------------+
| TABLESPACE_NAME | FILE_NAME          |
+-----------------+--------------------+
| innodb_undo_001 | ./innodb/undo_001  |
| innodb_undo_002 | ./innodb/undo_002  |
+-----------------+--------------------+
2 rows in set (0.01 sec)
```

The undo files are now under **/var/lib/mysql/innodb**.

Tablespace Management – Dropping an Undo Tablespace

For this exercise, we will create a test UNDO tablespace and explore and drop it.

1. Verify the current UNDO file location.

```
-bash-4.2$ ls -lrth /var/lib/mysql/innodb/undo*
-rw-r----- 1 mysql mysql 16M Sep 16 21:48 /var/lib/mysql/innodb/
undo_001
-rw-r----- 1 mysql mysql 16M Sep 16 21:48 /var/lib/mysql/innodb/
undo_002
-bash-4.2$
-bash-4.2$ mysql -u root -p
Enter password:
```

```
mysql> select tablespace_name, file_name from information_schema.
files where file_type like 'undo log';
+-----------------+-------------------+
| TABLESPACE_NAME | FILE_NAME         |
+-----------------+-------------------+
| innodb_undo_001 | ./innodb/undo_001 |
| innodb_undo_002 | ./innodb/undo_002 |
+-----------------+-------------------+
2 rows in set (0.00 sec)
```

```
mysql> select name, state from information_schema.innodb_
tablespaces where name like '%_undo%';
+-----------------+--------+
| name            | state  |
+-----------------+--------+
| innodb_undo_001 | active |
| innodb_undo_002 | active |
+-----------------+--------+
2 rows in set (0.01 sec)
```

2. Create a test UNDO tablespace.

```
mysql> create undo tablespace tbs_undo_003 add datafile
'undo_003.ibu';
Query OK, 0 rows affected (0.60 sec)
```

```
mysql> select tablespace_name, file_name from information_schema.
files where file_type like 'undo log';
```

```
+-----------------+-------------------+
| TABLESPACE_NAME | FILE_NAME         |
+-----------------+-------------------+
| innodb_undo_001 | ./innodb/undo_001 |
| innodb_undo_002 | ./innodb/undo_002 |
| tbs_undo_003    | ./undo_003.ibu    |
+-----------------+-------------------+
3 rows in set (0.00 sec)
```

mysql> **select name, state from information_schema.innodb_ tablespaces where name like '%_undo%';**

```
+-----------------+--------+
| name            | state  |
+-----------------+--------+
| innodb_undo_001 | active |
| innodb_undo_002 | active |
| tbs_undo_003    | active |
+-----------------+--------+
3 rows in set (0.00 sec)
```

3. Ensure the UNDO tablespace is in **INACTIVE** state before dropping it.

   mysql> **alter undo tablespace tbs_undo_003 set inactive;**
   Query OK, 0 rows affected (0.01 sec)

   mysql> **drop undo tablespace tbs_undo_003;**
   Query OK, 0 rows affected (0.01 sec)

   mysql> **select tablespace_name, file_name from information_schema. files where file_type like 'undo log';**

```
+-----------------+-------------------+
| TABLESPACE_NAME | FILE_NAME         |
+-----------------+-------------------+
| innodb_undo_001 | ./innodb/undo_001 |
| innodb_undo_002 | ./innodb/undo_002 |
+-----------------+-------------------+
2 rows in set (0.01 sec)
```

```
mysql> select name, state from information_schema.innodb_
tablespaces where name like '%_undo%';
+-----------------+--------+
| name            | state  |
+-----------------+--------+
| innodb_undo_001 | active |
| innodb_undo_002 | active |
+-----------------+--------+
2 rows in set (0.00 sec)

mysql> exit
Bye
-bash-4.2$ ls -lrth /var/lib/mysql/innodb/undo*
-rw-r----- 1 mysql mysql 16M Sep 16 22:47 /var/lib/mysql/innodb/
undo_001
-rw-r----- 1 mysql mysql 16M Sep 16 22:47 /var/lib/mysql/innodb/
undo_002
```

Tablespace Management – Resizing a Temporary Tablespace

InnoDB has **two** types of temporary tablespaces:

- **Session** temporary tablespaces

- **Global** temporary tablespaces

Session temporary tablespaces store user-created temporary tables and internal temporary tables created by the optimizer when InnoDB is configured as the storage engine for on-disk internal temporary tables.

The global temporary tablespace (ibtmp1) stores rollback segments for changes made to user-created temporary tables.

In this section, we will explore temporary tablespace and resize it.

1. Check and verify current temporary tablespaces file locations.

```
-bash-4.2$ ls -lrth /var/lib/mysql/#innodb_temp/
total 800K
```

```
-rw-r----- 1 mysql mysql 80K Sep 16 21:46 temp_9.ibt
-rw-r----- 1 mysql mysql 80K Sep 16 21:46 temp_8.ibt
-rw-r----- 1 mysql mysql 80K Sep 16 21:46 temp_7.ibt
-rw-r----- 1 mysql mysql 80K Sep 16 21:46 temp_6.ibt
-rw-r----- 1 mysql mysql 80K Sep 16 21:46 temp_5.ibt
-rw-r----- 1 mysql mysql 80K Sep 16 21:46 temp_4.ibt
-rw-r----- 1 mysql mysql 80K Sep 16 21:46 temp_3.ibt
-rw-r----- 1 mysql mysql 80K Sep 16 21:46 temp_2.ibt
-rw-r----- 1 mysql mysql 80K Sep 16 21:46 temp_1.ibt
-rw-r----- 1 mysql mysql 80K Sep 16 21:46 temp_10.ibt
-bash-4.2$
-bash-4.2$ mysql -u root -p
Enter password:

mysql> select file_name, tablespace_name, engine, initial_size,
total_extents*extent_size as totalsizebytes, data_free, maximum_
size from information_schema.files where tablespace_name= 'innodb_
temporary'\G;
*************************** 1. row ***************************
      FILE_NAME: ./ibtmp1
TABLESPACE_NAME: innodb_temporary
         ENGINE: InnoDB
   INITIAL_SIZE: 12582912
 totalsizebytes: 12582912
      DATA_FREE: 6291456
   MAXIMUM_SIZE: 2147483648
1 row in set (0.00 sec)

ERROR:
No query specified

mysql> select @@innodb_temp_tablespaces_dir;
+-------------------------------+
| @@innodb_temp_tablespaces_dir |
+-------------------------------+
| ./#innodb_temp/               |
+-------------------------------+
1 row in set (0.00 sec)
```

```
mysql> select @@innodb_temp_data_file_path;
+------------------------------+
| @@innodb_temp_data_file_path |
+------------------------------+
| ibtmp1:12M:autoextend        |
+------------------------------+
1 row in set (0.00 sec)

mysql> show global variables like 'innodb_fast_shutdown';
+----------------------+-------+
| Variable_name        | Value |
+----------------------+-------+
| innodb_fast_shutdown | 1     |
+----------------------+-------+
1 row in set (0.01 sec)

mysql> set global innodb_fast_shutdown =0;
Query OK, 0 rows affected (0.00 sec)

mysql> show global variables like 'innodb_fast_shutdown';
+----------------------+-------+
| Variable_name        | Value |
+----------------------+-------+
| innodb_fast_shutdown | 0     |
+----------------------+-------+
1 row in set (0.01 sec)
```

2. Stop the MySQL daemon.

```
-bash-4.2$ sudo systemctl stop mysqld
-bash-4.2$ sudo systemctl status mysqld
```

3. Modify the MySQL configuration file to include InnoDB temp file location.

```
-bash-4.2$ sudo vi /etc/my.cnf
[sudo] password for mysql:
-bash-4.2$
-bash-4.2$ cat /etc/my.cnf
[mysqld]
```

```
datadir=/var/lib/mysql
socket=/var/lib/mysql/mysql.sock

log-error=/var/log/mysqld.log
pid-file=/var/run/mysqld/mysqld.pid

# Innodb system tablespace
innodb-data-home-dir=/var/lib/mysql/innodb/
innodb-data-file-path=ibdata1:12M;ibdata2:12M:autoextend

# Innodb undo tablespace
innodb-undo-directory=/var/lib/mysql/innodb/
```

#Innodb temp tablespace
innodb-temp-data-file-path=ibtmp1:12M:autoextend:max:2G

4. Start the MySQL daemon and verify the modified temporary tablespace size.

```
-bash-4.2$ sudo systemctl start mysqld
-bash-4.2$ sudo systemctl status mysqld
-bash-4.2$ mysql -u root -p
Enter password:
mysql> select file_name, tablespace_name, engine, initial_size,
total_extents*extent_size as totalsizebytes, data_free, maximum_
size from information_schema.files where tablespace_name =
'innodb_temporary'\G;
*************************** 1. row ***************************
      FILE_NAME: ./ibtmp1
TABLESPACE_NAME: innodb_temporary
         ENGINE: InnoDB
   INITIAL_SIZE: 12582912
 totalsizebytes: 12582912
      DATA_FREE: 6291456
   MAXIMUM_SIZE: 2147483648
1 row in set (0.00 sec)

ERROR:
No query specified
```

```
mysql> select @@innodb_temp_tablespaces_dir;
+-------------------------------+
| @@innodb_temp_tablespaces_dir |
+-------------------------------+
| ./#innodb_temp/               |
+-------------------------------+
1 row in set (0.00 sec)

mysql> select @@innodb_temp_data_file_path;
+------------------------------+
| @@innodb_temp_data_file_path |
+------------------------------+
| ibtmp1:12M:autoextend:max:2G |
+------------------------------+
1 row in set (0.00 sec)
```

Tablespace Management – File-per-Table Tablespaces

A **file-per-table tablespace** contains data and indexes for a single InnoDB table and is stored on the file system in a single data file.

1. Check and verify the current file location. Please note the file location should be outside of the data directory.

```
mysql> show variables like 'innodb_file_per_table';
+-----------------------+-------+
| Variable_name         | Value |
+-----------------------+-------+
| innodb_file_per_table | ON    |
+-----------------------+-------+
1 row in set (0.01 sec)

mysql> create tablespace db1_tbs add datafile '/var/lib/mysql/
innodb/db1_tbs.ibd';
ERROR 3121 (HY000): The DATAFILE location cannot be under the
datadir.
```

```
mysql> show variables like 'innodb_directories';
+--------------------+-------+
| Variable_name      | Value |
+--------------------+-------+
| innodb_directories |       |
+--------------------+-------+
1 row in set (0.00 sec)

mysql> show global variables like 'innodb_fast_shutdown';
+----------------------+-------+
| Variable_name        | Value |
+----------------------+-------+
| innodb_fast_shutdown | 1     |
+----------------------+-------+
1 row in set (0.00 sec)

mysql> set global innodb_fast_shutdown =0;
Query OK, 0 rows affected (0.00 sec)

mysql> show global variables like 'innodb_fast_shutdown';
+----------------------+-------+
| Variable_name        | Value |
+----------------------+-------+
| innodb_fast_shutdown | 0     |
+----------------------+-------+
1 row in set (0.00 sec)
```

2. Stop the MySQL daemon.

```
-bash-4.2$ sudo systemctl stop mysqld
-bash-4.2$ sudo systemctl status mysqld
```

3. Modify the MySQL configuration file to include the configuration
   parameter for the file-per-table directories.

```
-bash-4.2$ cat /etc/my.cnf
[mysqld]
datadir=/var/lib/mysql
socket=/var/lib/mysql/mysql.sock
```

```
log-error=/var/log/mysqld.log
pid-file=/var/run/mysqld/mysqld.pid

# Innodb system tablespace
innodb-data-home-dir=/var/lib/mysql/innodb/
innodb-data-file-path=ibdata1:12M;ibdata2:12M:autoextend

# Innodb undo tablespace
innodb-undo-directory=/var/lib/mysql/innodb/

#Innodb temp tablespace
innodb-temp-data-file-path=ibtmp1:12M:autoextend:max:2G
-bash-4.2$
-bash-4.2$ sudo vi /etc/my.cnf
-bash-4.2$ cat /etc/my.cnf
[mysqld]
datadir=/var/lib/mysql
socket=/var/lib/mysql/mysql.sock
log-error=/var/log/mysqld.log
pid-file=/var/run/mysqld/mysqld.pid

# Innodb system tablespace
innodb-data-home-dir=/var/lib/mysql/innodb/
innodb-data-file-path=ibdata1:12M;ibdata2:12M:autoextend

# Innodb undo tablespace
innodb-undo-directory=/var/lib/mysql/innodb/

#Innodb temp tablespace
innodb-temp-data-file-path=ibtmp1:12M:autoextend:max:2G

#Innodb directories
innodb-directories=/var/lib/tbs/
```

4. Start the MySQL daemon, create a new directory for the file-per-table tablespace, and verify.

```
-bash-4.2$ sudo systemctl start mysqld
-bash-4.2$ sudo systemctl status mysqld
-bash-4.2$ sudo mkdir /var/lib/tbs
```

```
-bash-4.2$ sudo chown -R mysql:mysql /var/lib/tbs
-bash-4.2$ mysql -uroot -p
Enter password:
mysql> show variables like 'innodb_directories';
+--------------------+---------------+
| Variable_name      | Value         |
+--------------------+---------------+
| innodb_directories | /var/lib/tbs/ |
+--------------------+---------------+
1 row in set (0.01 sec)
mysql> create tablespace db1_tbs add datafile '/var/lib/tbs/
db1_tbs.ibd';
Query OK, 0 rows affected (0.01 sec)

mysql> select name from information_schema.innodb_tablespaces;
+----------------------------+
| name                       |
+----------------------------+
| mysql                      |
| innodb_temporary           |
| innodb_undo_001            |
| innodb_undo_002            |
| sys/sys_config             |
| techsparks/emp_range#p#p0  |
| techsparks/emp_range#p#p1  |
| techsparks/emp_range#p#p2  |
| techsparks/emp_range#p#p3  |
| db1_tbs                    |
+----------------------------+
10 rows in set (0.00 sec)

mysql> select file_name,tablespace_name,extent_size,initial_
size,autoextend_size from information_schema.files where
tablespace_name in ('db1_tbs')\G;
*************************** 1. row ***************************
      FILE_NAME: /var/lib/tbs/db1_tbs.ibd
```

```
TABLESPACE_NAME: db1_tbs
     EXTENT_SIZE: 1048576
    INITIAL_SIZE: 114688
AUTOEXTEND_SIZE: 1048576
1 row in set (0.00 sec)

ERROR:
No query specified

mysql> use techsparks;
Reading table information for completion of table and column names
You can turn off this feature to get a quicker startup with -A

Database changed
mysql>
mysql> show tables;
+----------------------+
| Tables_in_techsparks |
+----------------------+
| emp_range            |
+----------------------+
1 row in set (0.00 sec)

mysql> alter table emp_range tablespace db1_tbs;
ERROR 1478 (HY000): InnoDB: A partitioned table is not allowed in
a shared tablespace.
mysql>
mysql> drop table emp_range;
Query OK, 0 rows affected (0.03 sec)

mysql> CREATE TABLE emp_range (
    -> id INT NOT NULL,
    -> fname VARCHAR(30),
    -> lname VARCHAR(30),
    -> hired DATE NOT NULL DEFAULT '2023-01-01',
    -> position INT NOT NULL,
    -> fired VARCHAR(5) NOT NULL DEFAULT 'No'
    -> );
```

```
Query OK, 0 rows affected (0.01 sec)

mysql> insert into emp_range values (10,'SACH','KAR','2020-10-10',
1,'NO');
Query OK, 1 row affected (0.00 sec)

mysql> insert into emp_range values (1,'RAV','GANY','2020-01-01',
2,'NO');
Query OK, 1 row affected (0.01 sec)

mysql> insert into emp_range values (12,'LAX','VVS','2020-11-11',
4,'NO');
Query OK, 1 row affected (0.00 sec)

mysql> insert into emp_range values (18,'MS','DNI','2020-12-12',
6,'NO');
Query OK, 1 row affected (0.01 sec)

mysql> alter table emp_range tablespace db1_tbs;
Query OK, 0 rows affected (0.03 sec)
Records: 0  Duplicates: 0  Warnings: 0

mysql> select count(*) from emp_range;
+----------+
| count(*) |
+----------+
|    4     |
+----------+
1 row in set (0.05 sec)

mysql> exit
Bye

-bash-4.2$ ls -lrt /var/lib/tbs/
total 112
-rw-r----- 1 mysql mysql 114688 Sep 17 00:07 db1_tbs.ibd
```

Now we have seen the different types of tablespaces and how to manage them. Let us learn about the types of partitioning and how each one works.

Types of Partitioning in MySQL

MySQL 8.0 offers several types of partitioning methods to cater to different data organization and access patterns.

Here are the main types of partitioning in MySQL 8.0:

- RANGE partitioning
- LIST partitioning
- COLUMNS partitioning
- HASH partitioning
- KEY partitioning
- SUBPARTITION

RANGE Partitioning

RANGE partitioning lets us use data falling within a given range, ranging from A to Z or from 0 to 9. A RANGE-partitioned table is partitioned so that each partition contains rows where the partitioning expression value lies within a given range. Ranges are usually defined by the **VALUES LESS THAN** operator.

To test RANGE partitioning, let us create a database named **techsparks**. Create a table **emp_range** with **PARTITION BY RANGE**. Insert some data and explore how RANGE partitioning works.

Please pay attention to the part where we try to insert a value for the RANGE partition for which a value is not mentioned and explore how to work around it in those cases.

>>>> Check MySQL daemon status

```
[root@mysql-a ~]# systemctl status mysqld

[root@mysql-a ~]# su - mysql
Last login: Wed Sep 13 22:23:01 CDT 2023 on pts/0
-bash-4.2$
-bash-4.2$ mysql -u root -p
Enter password:
```

```
mysql> show databases;
+--------------------+
| Database           |
+--------------------+
| information_schema |
| mysql              |
| performance_schema |
| sys                |
+--------------------+
4 rows in set (0.01 sec)

mysql> create database techsparks;
Query OK, 1 row affected (0.02 sec)

mysql> show databases;
+--------------------+
| Database           |
+--------------------+
| information_schema |
| mysql              |
| performance_schema |
| sys                |
| techsparks         |
+--------------------+
5 rows in set (0.00 sec)

mysql> use techsparks;
Database changed
mysql>
mysql> CREATE TABLE emp_range (
    -> id INT NOT NULL,
    -> fname VARCHAR(30),
    -> lname VARCHAR(30),
    -> hired DATE NOT NULL DEFAULT '2023-01-01',
    -> position INT NOT NULL,
```

```
    -> fired VARCHAR(5) NOT NULL DEFAULT 'No'
    -> )
    -> PARTITION BY RANGE (id) (
    -> PARTITION p0 VALUES LESS THAN (5),
    -> PARTITION p1 VALUES LESS THAN (10),
    -> PARTITION p2 VALUES LESS THAN (15),
    -> PARTITION p3 VALUES LESS THAN (20)
    -> );
Query OK, 0 rows affected (0.05 sec)

mysql> insert into emp_range values (10,'SAC','TEN','2020-10-10',1,'NO');
Query OK, 1 row affected (0.03 sec)

mysql> insert into emp_range values (1,'RAV','GAN','2020-01-01',2,'NO');
Query OK, 1 row affected (0.01 sec)

mysql> insert into emp_range values (12,'LAX','VVS','2020-11-11',4,'NO');
Query OK, 1 row affected (0.00 sec)

mysql> insert into emp_range values (18,'MS','DHO','2020-12-12',6,'NO');
Query OK, 1 row affected (0.01 sec)

mysql> select partition_name, table_rows from information_schema.partitions
where table_name='emp_range';
+----------------+------------+
| PARTITION_NAME | TABLE_ROWS |
+----------------+------------+
| p0             |          1 |
| p1             |          0 |
| p2             |          2 |
| p3             |          1 |
+----------------+------------+
4 rows in set (0.00 sec)
```

```
mysql> explain select * from emp_range;
+----+-------------+-----------+-------------+------+--
| id | select_type | table     | partitions  | type | possible_keys |
key  | key_len | ref  | rows | filtered | Extra |
+----+-------------+-----------+-------------+------+--
|  1 | SIMPLE      | emp_range | p0,p1,p2,p3 | ALL  | NULL          | NULL |
NULL | NULL    |    4 |   100.00 | NULL  |
+----+-------------+-----------+-------------+------+--
1 row in set, 1 warning (0.00 sec)
```

```
mysql> select * from emp_range;
+----+--------+-----------+------------+----------+-------+
| id | fname  | lname     | hired      | position | fired |
+----+--------+-----------+------------+----------+-------+
|  1 | RAV    | GAN       | 2020-01-01 |     2    | NO    |
| 10 | SAC    | TEN       | 2020-10-10 |     1    | NO    |
| 12 | LAX    | VVS       | 2020-11-11 |     4    | NO    |
| 18 | MS     | DHO       | 2020-12-12 |     6    | NO    |
+----+--------+-----------+------------+----------+-------+
4 rows in set (0.00 sec)
```

```
mysql> insert into emp_range values (23,'RAV','JAD','2020-12-12',6,'NO');
ERROR 1526 (HY000): Table has no partition for value 23
mysql>
mysql> alter table emp_range add partition (partition p4 VALUES LESS THAN
MAXVALUE);
Query OK, 0 rows affected (0.03 sec)
Records: 0  Duplicates: 0  Warnings: 0
```

```
mysql> select partition_name, table_rows from information_schema.partitions
where table_name='emp_range';
+----------------+------------+
| PARTITION_NAME | TABLE_ROWS |
+----------------+------------+
| p0             |          0 |
| p1             |          0 |
| p2             |          2 |
```

```
| p3             |        0 |
| p4             |        0 |
+----------------+----------+
5 rows in set (0.00 sec)
```

mysql> **explain select * from emp_range;**

```
+----+-------------+-----------+----------------+------+-
| id | select_type | table     | partitions     | type | possible_keys |
key | key_len | ref  | rows | filtered | Extra |
+----+-------------+-----------+----------------+------+-
|  1 | SIMPLE      | emp_range | p0,p1,p2,p3,p4 | ALL  | NULL          |
NULL | NULL    | NULL |    2 |   100.00 | NULL  |
+----+-------------+-----------+----------------+------+--
1 row in set, 1 warning (0.00 sec)
```

mysql> **select * from emp_range;**

```
+----+--------+----------+------------+----------+-------+
| id | fname  | lname    | hired      | position | fired |
+----+--------+----------+------------+----------+-------+
|  1 | RAV    | GAN      | 2020-01-01 |        2 | NO    |
| 10 | SAC    | TEN      | 2020-10-10 |        1 | NO    |
| 12 | LAX    | VVS      | 2020-11-11 |        4 | NO    |
| 18 | MS     | DHO      | 2020-12-12 |        6 | NO    |
+----+--------+----------+------------+----------+-------+
4 rows in set (0.00 sec)
```

mysql> **insert into emp_range values (23,'RAV','JAD','2020-12-12',6,'NO');**
Query OK, 1 row affected (0.00 sec)

mysql> **select * from emp_range;**

```
+----+--------+----------+------------+----------+-------+
| id | fname  | lname    | hired      | position | fired |
+----+--------+----------+------------+----------+-------+
|  1 | RAV    | GAN      | 2020-01-01 |        2 | NO    |
| 10 | SAC    | TEN      | 2020-10-10 |        1 | NO    |
| 12 | LAX    | VVS      | 2020-11-11 |        4 | NO    |
```

```
| 18 | MS       | DHO       | 2020-12-12 |    6     | NO   |
| 23 | RAV      | JAD       | 2020-12-12 |    6     | NO   |
+----+----------+-----------+------------+----------+------+
5 rows in set (0.00 sec)
```

mysql> **insert into emp_range values (28,'RIS','PAN','2020-12-12',6,'NO');**
Query OK, 1 row affected (0.01 sec)

mysql> **select * from emp_range;**

```
+----+----------+-----------+------------+----------+-------+
| id | fname    | lname     | hired      | position | fired |
+----+----------+-----------+------------+----------+-------+
|  1 | RAV      | GAN       | 2020-01-01 |    2     | NO    |
| 10 | SAC      | TEN       | 2020-10-10 |    1     | NO    |
| 12 | LAX      | VVS       | 2020-11-11 |    4     | NO    |
| 18 | MS       | DHO       | 2020-12-12 |    6     | NO    |
| 23 | RAV      | JAD       | 2020-12-12 |    6     | NO    |
| 28 | RIS      | PAN       | 2020-12-12 |    6     | NO    |
+----+----------+-----------+------------+----------+-------+
6 rows in set (0.00 sec)
```

mysql> **select partition_name, table_rows from information_schema.partitions
where table_name='emp_range';**

```
+----------------+------------+
| PARTITION_NAME | TABLE_ROWS |
+----------------+------------+
| p0             |     0      |
| p1             |     0      |
| p2             |     2      |
| p3             |     0      |
| p4             |     2      |
+----------------+------------+
5 rows in set (0.00 sec)
```

```
mysql> explain select * from emp_range;
+----+-------------+-----------+----------------+------+--
| id | select_type | table     | partitions     | type | possible_keys |
key | key_len | ref  | rows | filtered | Extra |
+----+-------------+-----------+----------------+------+--
|  1 | SIMPLE      | emp_range | p0,p1,p2,p3,p4 | ALL  | NULL          |
NULL | NULL    | NULL |    4 |  100.00  | NULL  |
+----+-------------+-----------+----------------+------+--
1 row in set, 1 warning (0.00 sec)
```

LIST Partitioning

LIST partitioning is like partitioning by RANGE, just that partitioning by LIST is completed by the user giving a specific list of values to partition the column with. This is done using **PARTITION BY LIST(expr)**. **expr** is a column value. We then define each partition using **VALUES IN (value_list)**. **value_list** is a comma-separated list of integers.

We create another table named emp_list within the techsparks database to test LIST partitioning. Insert some data and explore how LIST partitioning works. Please pay attention to the steps where we try to insert data within a department with dep_id not in the value list provided when creating the partitions.

```
mysql> CREATE TABLE emp_list (
    -> id INT NOT NULL,
    -> fname VARCHAR(30),
    -> lname VARCHAR(30),
    -> hired DATE NOT NULL DEFAULT '2023-01-01',
    -> position INT NOT NULL,
    -> fired VARCHAR(5) NOT NULL DEFAULT 'No',
    -> dep_id INT NOT NULL
    -> )
    -> PARTITION BY LIST(dep_id) (
    -> PARTITION first_dep VALUES IN (3,5,20),
    -> PARTITION second_dep VALUES IN (25,50,75),
    -> PARTITION third_dep VALUES IN (80,85,90,100,120,140,150,12,13,14,18)
    -> );
Query OK, 0 rows affected (0.04 sec)
```

```
mysql> insert into emp_list values (5678,'SHU','G','2023-01-01',2,'NO',5);
Query OK, 1 row affected (0.01 sec)

mysql> insert into emp_list values (2345,'SHR','I','2023-02-28',4,'NO',50);
Query OK, 1 row affected (0.01 sec)

mysql> insert into emp_list values (6540,'RAH','K','2023-03-11',5,'NO',80);
Query OK, 1 row affected (0.00 sec)

mysql> select partition_name, table_rows from information_schema.partitions
where table_name='emp_list';
+----------------+------------+
| PARTITION_NAME | TABLE_ROWS |
+----------------+------------+
| first_dep      |          1 |
| second_dep     |          1 |
| third_dep      |          1 |
+----------------+------------+
3 rows in set (0.00 sec)

mysql> explain select * from emp_list;
+----+-------------+----------+------------------------------+------+
| id | select_type | table    | partitions                   | type |
possible_keys | key  | key_len | ref  | rows | filtered | Extra |
+----+-------------+----------+------------------------------+------+
|  1 | SIMPLE      | emp_list | first_dep,second_dep,third_dep | ALL  |
NULL          | NULL | NULL    | NULL |    3 |   100.00 | NULL  |
+----+-------------+----------+------------------------------+------+
1 row in set, 1 warning (0.00 sec)

mysql> select * from emp_list;
+------+-------+-------+------------+----------+-------+--------+
| id   | fname | lname | hired      | position | fired | dep_id |
+------+-------+-------+------------+----------+-------+--------+
| 5678 | SHU   | G     | 2023-01-01 |        2 | NO    |      5 |
| 2345 | SHR   | I     | 2023-02-28 |        4 | NO    |     50 |
| 6540 | RAH   | K     | 2023-03-11 |        5 | NO    |     80 |
+------+-------+-------+------------+----------+-------+--------+
3 rows in set (0.00 sec)
```

```
mysql> insert into emp_list values (5678,'ISH','K','2023-01-01',2,'NO',15);
ERROR 1526 (HY000): Table has no partition for value 15
mysql>
mysql> insert into emp_list values (5678,'ISH','K','2023-01-01',2,'NO',75);
Query OK, 1 row affected (0.01 sec)

mysql> select * from emp_list;
+------+--------+--------+------------+----------+-------+--------+
| id   | fname  | lname  | hired      | position | fired | dep_id |
+------+--------+--------+------------+----------+-------+--------+
| 5678 | SHU    | G      | 2023-01-01 |    2     | NO    |      5 |
| 2345 | SHR    | I      | 2023-02-28 |    4     | NO    |     50 |
| 5678 | ISH    | K      | 2023-01-01 |    2     | NO    |     75 |
| 6540 | RAH    | K      | 2023-03-11 |    5     | NO    |     80 |
+------+--------+--------+------------+----------+-------+--------+
4 rows in set (0.00 sec)

mysql> select partition_name, table_rows from information_schema.partitions
where table_name='emp_list';
+----------------+------------+
| PARTITION_NAME | TABLE_ROWS |
+----------------+------------+
| first_dep      |          1 |
| second_dep     |          2 |
| third_dep      |          1 |
+----------------+------------+
3 rows in set (0.00 sec)

mysql> explain select * from emp_list;
+----+-------------+----------+-------------------------------+------+
| id | select_type | table    | partitions                    | type |
possible_keys | key  | key_len | ref  | rows | filtered | Extra |
+----+-------------+----------+-------------------------------+------+
|  1 | SIMPLE      | emp_list | first_dep,second_dep,third_dep | ALL  |
NULL       | NULL | NULL    | NULL |    4 |   100.00 | NULL  |
+----+-------------+----------+-------------------------------+------+
1 row in set, 1 warning (0.00 sec)
```

COLUMNS Partitioning

COLUMNS partitioning data by COLUMNS is a variant of partitioning by RANGE and partitioning by LIST. When data is partitioned by COLUMNS, columns are used as partitioning keys. We have two types of COLUMNS partitioning:

- **RANGE COLUMNS partitioning**

  - Uses **PARTITION BY RANGE COLUMNS (column_list)** and **value_list** which is the list of values provided for each partition definition.

  - Defines partitioning using ranges based on multiple column values.

  - **DATE** and **DATETIME** columns are also used as partitioning columns in addition to *integer* columns.

- **LIST COLUMNS partitioning**

  - Uses **PARTITION BY LIST COLUMNS (column_list)**.

  - Used when there is a need to use **non-integer** columns as partitioning columns.

  - **DATE** and **DATETIME** columns are also used as partitioning columns in addition to *string* type columns.

To test **RANGE COLUMNS** partitioning, we create another table named **emp_columns** within the **techsparks** database. Insert some data and explore how RANGE COLUMNS partitioning works.

```
mysql> CREATE TABLE emp_columns (
    -> id INT NOT NULL,
    -> fname VARCHAR(30),
    -> lname VARCHAR(30),
    -> hired DATE NOT NULL DEFAULT '2023-01-01',
    -> position INT NOT NULL,
    -> fired VARCHAR(5) NOT NULL DEFAULT 'No',
    -> dep_id INT NOT NULL
    -> )
```

```
    -> PARTITION BY RANGE COLUMNS(fname,lname,hired) (
    -> PARTITION p1 VALUES LESS THAN ('a','a','2023-02-02'),
    -> PARTITION p2 VALUES LESS THAN ('z','z','2099-12-31')
    -> );
Query OK, 0 rows affected (0.03 sec)

mysql> insert into emp_columns values (1505,'VIR','K','2023-06-11',1,
'NO',10);
Query OK, 1 row affected (0.01 sec)

mysql> insert into emp_columns values (1100,'YUV','S','2023-01-16',2,
'NO',20);
Query OK, 1 row affected (0.02 sec)

mysql> insert into emp_columns values (0010,'RAH','D','2021-09-15',1,
'NO',30);
Query OK, 1 row affected (0.01 sec)

mysql> select partition_name, table_rows from information_schema.partitions
where table_name='emp_columns';
+----------------+------------+
| PARTITION_NAME | TABLE_ROWS |
+----------------+------------+
| p1             |          0 |
| p2             |          3 |
+----------------+------------+
2 rows in set (0.00 sec)

mysql> explain select * from emp_columns;
+----+-------------+-------------+------------+------+---------------+
| id | select_type | table       | partitions | type | possible_keys |
key | key_len | ref | rows | filtered | Extra |
+----+-------------+-------------+------------+------+---------------+
|  1 | SIMPLE      | emp_columns | p1,p2      | ALL  | NULL          | NULL
| NULL    | NULL |    3 |   100.00 | NULL  |
+----+-------------+-------------+------------+------+---------------+
1 row in set, 1 warning (0.00 sec)
```

```
mysql> select * from emp_columns;
+------+--------+-------+------------+----------+-------+--------+
| id   | fname  | lname | hired      | position | fired | dep_id |
+------+--------+-------+------------+----------+-------+--------+
| 1505 | VIR    | K     | 2023-06-11 |     1    | NO    |     10 |
| 1100 | YUV    | S     | 2023-01-16 |     2    | NO    |     20 |
|   10 | RAH    | D     | 2021-09-15 |     1    | NO    |     30 |
+------+--------+-------+------------+----------+-------+--------+
3 rows in set (0.00 sec)
```

HASH Partitioning

HASH partitioning data by a HASH is useful when distributing data across partitions evenly. This is done using **PARTITION BY HASH(expr)**. **expr** is a column value. With HASH partitioning, we do not have to explicitly mention which partition a given column value or set of column values are to be stored in as the column value or set of column values are automatically hashed.

To test **HASH** partitioning, we create another table named **emp_hash** within the **techsparks** database. Insert some data and explore how HASH partitioning works. Notice the data when inserted is getting evenly distributed based on the HASH of the id column.

```
mysql> CREATE TABLE emp_hash (
    -> id INT NOT NULL,
    -> fname VARCHAR(30),
    -> lname VARCHAR(30),
    -> hired DATE NOT NULL DEFAULT '2023-01-01',
    -> position INT NOT NULL,
    -> fired VARCHAR(5) NOT NULL DEFAULT 'No',
    -> dep_id INT NOT NULL
    -> )
    -> PARTITION BY HASH(id)
    -> PARTITIONS 5;
Query OK, 0 rows affected (0.04 sec)

mysql> insert into emp_hash values(1234,'TIM','D','2023-03-18',2,'NO',30);
```

```
Query OK, 1 row affected (0.01 sec)
```

```
mysql> insert into emp_hash values(2345,'ROH','S','2023-04-21',4,'NO',20);
Query OK, 1 row affected (0.01 sec)
```

```
mysql> select partition_name, table_rows from information_schema.partitions
where table_name='emp_hash';
+----------------+------------+
| PARTITION_NAME | TABLE_ROWS |
+----------------+------------+
| p0             |          1 |
| p1             |          0 |
| p2             |          0 |
| p3             |          0 |
| p4             |          1 |
+----------------+------------+
5 rows in set (0.00 sec)
```

```
mysql> explain select * from emp_hash;
+----+-------------+----------+----------------+------+---------------+
| id | select_type | table    | partitions     | type | possible_keys |
key | key_len | ref  | rows | filtered | Extra |
+----+-------------+----------+----------------+------+---------------+
|  1 | SIMPLE      | emp_hash | p0,p1,p2,p3,p4 | ALL  | NULL          |
NULL | NULL    | NULL |    2 |   100.00 | NULL  |
+----+-------------+----------+----------------+------+---------------+
1 row in set, 1 warning (0.00 sec)
```

```
mysql> select * from emp_hash;
+------+-------+-------+------------+----------+-------+--------+
| id   | fname | lname | hired      | position | fired | dep_id |
+------+-------+-------+------------+----------+-------+--------+
| 2345 | ROH   | S     | 2023-04-21 |        4 | NO    |     20 |
| 1234 | TIM   | D     | 2023-03-18 |        2 | NO    |     30 |
+------+-------+-------+------------+----------+-------+--------+
2 rows in set (0.00 sec)
```

```
mysql> insert into emp_hash values(3456,'JAC','K','2022-03-27',4,'NO',40);
```

Query OK, 1 row affected (0.01 sec)

```
mysql> insert into emp_hash values(4567,'BRI','L','2020-11-27',4,'NO',20);
Query OK, 1 row affected (0.01 sec)

mysql> insert into emp_hash values(4567,'ADA','G','2021-12-25',4,'NO',50);
Query OK, 1 row affected (0.00 sec)

mysql> select partition_name, table_rows from information_schema.partitions
where table_name='emp_hash';
+----------------+------------+
| PARTITION_NAME | TABLE_ROWS |
+----------------+------------+
| p0             |          1 |
| p1             |          1 |
| p2             |          2 |
| p3             |          0 |
| p4             |          1 |
+----------------+------------+
5 rows in set (0.01 sec)

mysql> explain select * from emp_hash;
+----+-------------+----------+----------------+------+--
| id | select_type | table    | partitions     | type | possible_keys |
key  | key_len | ref  | rows | filtered | Extra |
+----+-------------+----------+----------------+------+---
|  1 | SIMPLE      | emp_hash | p0,p1,p2,p3,p4 | ALL  | NULL          |
NULL | NULL    | NULL |    5 |   100.00 | NULL  |
+----+-------------+----------+----------------+------+--
1 row in set, 1 warning (0.00 sec)

mysql> select * from emp_hash;
+------+--------+--------+------------+----------+-------+--------+
| id   | fname  | lname  | hired      | position | fired | dep_id |
+------+--------+--------+------------+----------+-------+--------+
| 2345 | ROH    | S      | 2023-04-21 |        4 | NO    |     20 |
| 3456 | JAC    | K      | 2022-03-27 |        4 | NO    |     40 |
| 4567 | BRI    | L      | 2020-11-27 |        4 | NO    |     20 |
```

```
| 4567 | ADA      | G       | 2021-12-25 |    4     | NO    |    50 |
| 1234 | TIM      | D       | 2023-03-18 |    2     | NO    |    30 |
+------+----------+---------+------------+----------+-------+-------+
5 rows in set (0.00 sec)
```

KEY Partitioning

With **KEY** partitioning, the hashing function for key partitioning is provided by the
MySQL server itself, whereas in HASH partitioning, the hashing function is provided by
a user-defined expression. This is done using **PARTITION BY KEY()**. KEY partitioning
type often takes zero column names into account and makes use of the primary key
on the table. If columns are specified, the primary key must be comprised of them. To
test **KEY** partitioning, we create another table named **emp_key** within the **techsparks**
database. Insert some data and explore how KEY partitioning works.

```
mysql> CREATE TABLE emp_key (
    -> id INT NOT NULL PRIMARY KEY,
    -> fname VARCHAR(30),
    -> lname VARCHAR(30),
    -> hired DATE NOT NULL DEFAULT '2023-01-01',
    -> position INT NOT NULL,
    -> fired VARCHAR(5) NOT NULL DEFAULT 'No',
    -> dep_id INT NOT NULL
    -> )
    -> PARTITION BY KEY()
    -> PARTITIONS 4;
Query OK, 0 rows affected (0.03 sec)

mysql> insert into emp_key values (7654,'SCO','L','2023-05-05',5,'NO',10);
Query OK, 1 row affected (0.01 sec)

mysql> insert into emp_key values (7766,'DAV','M','2023-07-24',3,'NO',30);
Query OK, 1 row affected (0.00 sec)

mysql> select partition_name, table_rows from information_schema.partitions
where table_name='emp_key';
```

```
+-----------------+------------+
| PARTITION_NAME  | TABLE_ROWS |
+-----------------+------------+
| p0              |          0 |
| p1              |          1 |
| p2              |          0 |
| p3              |          1 |
+-----------------+------------+
4 rows in set (0.00 sec)

mysql> explain select * from emp_key;
+----+-------------+---------+-------------+------+-----+
| id | select_type | table   | partitions  | type | possible_keys | key |
key_len | ref  | rows | filtered | Extra |
+----+-------------+---------+-------------+------+-----
|  1 | SIMPLE      | emp_key | p0,p1,p2,p3 | ALL  | NULL          | NULL |
NULL    | NULL |    2 |   100.00 | NULL  |
+----+-------------+---------+-------------+------+--------
1 row in set, 1 warning (0.00 sec)

mysql> select * from emp_key;
+------+--------+--------+------------+----------+-------+--------+
| id   | fname  | lname  | hired      | position | fired | dep_id |
+------+--------+--------+------------+----------+-------+--------+
| 7654 | SCO    | L      | 2023-05-05 |    5     | NO    |   10   |
| 7766 | DAV    | M      | 2023-07-24 |    3     | NO    |   30   |
+------+--------+--------+------------+----------+-------+--------+
2 rows in set (0.00 sec)
```

SUBPARTITION

SUBPARTITION refers to partitions within partitions. This is also referred to as **COMPOSITE** partitioning. This is done using **PARTITION BY RANGE** and then **SUBPARTITION BY HASH** or **SUBPARTITION BY KEY**. SUBPARTITION BY HASH and SUBPARTITION BY KEY use the same syntax rules as PARTITION BY HASH and

PARTITION BY KEY partitioning types. One key exception for SUBPARTITION BY KEY is that a column must be provided when using it even though the table has an explicit primary key. This is planned to be addressed in a future MySQL release.

To test SUBPARTITION, we create another table named **emp_subpart** within the **techsparks** database. Insert some data and explore how SUBPARTITION works.

```
mysql> CREATE TABLE emp_subpart (
    -> BILL_NO INT,
    -> sale_date DATE,
    -> cust_code VARCHAR(15),
    -> AMOUNT DECIMAL(8,2))
    -> PARTITION BY RANGE(YEAR(sale_date) )
    -> SUBPARTITION BY HASH(TO_DAYS(sale_date))
    -> SUBPARTITIONS 4 (
    -> PARTITION p0 VALUES LESS THAN (1990),
    -> PARTITION p1 VALUES LESS THAN (2000),
    -> PARTITION p2 VALUES LESS THAN (2010),
    -> PARTITION p3 VALUES LESS THAN MAXVALUE
    -> );
Query OK, 0 rows affected (0.14 sec)

mysql> insert into emp_subpart values (1214,'2023-09-12',0099120,231.8);
Query OK, 1 row affected (0.00 sec)

mysql> insert into emp_subpart values (2931,'2023-09-14',0053626,182.5);
Query OK, 1 row affected (0.01 sec)

mysql> select partition_name, table_rows from information_schema.partitions
where table_name='emp_subpart';
+----------------+------------+
| PARTITION_NAME | TABLE_ROWS |
+----------------+------------+
| p0             |          0 |
| p0             |          0 |
| p0             |          0 |
| p0             |          0 |
| p1             |          0 |
```

```
| p1              |          0 |
| p1              |          0 |
| p1              |          0 |
| p2              |          0 |
| p2              |          0 |
| p2              |          0 |
| p2              |          0 |
| p3              |          1 |
| p3              |          0 |
| p3              |          1 |
| p3              |          0 |
+-----------------+------------+
16 rows in set (0.00 sec)

mysql> explain select * from emp_subpart\G
*************************** 1. row ***************************
          id : 1
  select_type: SIMPLE
        table: emp_subpart
   partitions: p0_p0sp0,p0_p0sp1,p0_p0sp2,p0_p0sp3,p1_p1sp0,p1_p1sp1,p1_
p1sp2,p1_p1sp3,p2_p2sp0,
p2_p2sp1,p2_p2sp2,p2_p2sp3,
p3_p3sp0,p3_p3sp1,p3_p3sp2,p3_p3sp3
         type: ALL
possible_keys: NULL
          key: NULL
      key_len: NULL
          ref: NULL
         rows: 2
     filtered: 100.00
        Extra: NULL
1 row in set, 1 warning (0.00 sec)
```

Summary

In this chapter, we learned about tablespaces and managing the different types of tablespaces available within the MySQL database and how to logically represent them. Partitioning helps with managing large datasets efficiently, thereby increasing the scalability, availability, and performance of the database. In the next chapter, we will discuss the MySQL high availability, replication, and scalability concepts with examples.

CHAPTER 5

MySQL High Availability, Replication, and Scalability

Introduction

Replication is a technology to copy data from one MySQL database server to another asynchronously. Using MySQL replication options, you can replicate all databases, selected databases, or even selected tables, depending on your use case.

Some of the common use cases for replication are as follows:

- Scale-out solutions
- Data security
- Analytics and reporting
- Long-distance data distribution

MySQL 8.0 offers *two* methods of replication:

- Binlog position based
- Global transaction identifier (GTID) based

Binlog position based is considered more of a traditional method where we replicate events from the source's binary log and require the log files and positions to be synchronized between the source and the replica(s).

© Y V Ravi Kumar, Arun Kumar Samayam, Naresh Kumar Miryala 2024
Y V Ravi Kumar et al., *Mastering MySQL Administration*, https://doi.org/10.1007/979-8-8688-0252-2_5

GTID based is considered more of a transactional method and doesn't need to know the binary log and log file position to synchronize data between the source and the replica(s).

GTID-based replication is recommended as it guarantees consistency between the source and replica.

High-Level Overview

This chapter will replicate data from one source (mysql-a) to two replicas (mysql-b and mysql-c). We will start configuring binlog-based replication first and then set GTID-based replication.

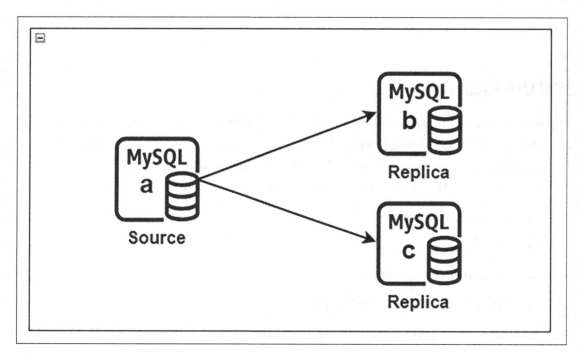

Figure 5-1. *Replication with one source and two replicas*

Binlog Replication

Here are some prerequisites you will need to follow to ensure binlog replication is set up correctly.

- Ensure binary logging is enabled on the source server.

- Ensure all servers within the replication configuration have a unique server ID.

- Ensure all servers within the replication configuration have a unique UUID.

- Create a separate user for replicas to authenticate against the source to read the binary log for replication.

1. Check the MySQL daemon status on the source (mysql-a) and all replicas (mysql-b/mysql-c).

   [root@mysql-a ~]# systemctl status mysqld

2. Make configuration file changes to include MySQL replication parameters required for binlog replication. Stop the MySQL daemon, edit the /etc/my.cnf file to include the parameters, and start the MySQL daemon.

Note   *server-id* should be different for each server in the replication configuration.

```
>>>>>>>>>>>>>>>>> mysql-a <<<<<<<<<<<<<<<<<
[root@mysql-a ~]# systemctl stop mysqld
[root@mysql-a ~]# cat /etc/my.cnf
[mysqld]
datadir=/var/lib/mysql
socket=/var/lib/mysql/mysql.sock
log-error=/var/log/mysqld.log
pid-file=/var/run/mysqld/mysqld.pid
[root@mysql-a ~]#
```

231

```
[root@mysql-a ~]# vi /etc/my.cnf
[root@mysql-a ~]# cat /etc/my.cnf
[mysqld]
# MySQL Replication parameters
log-bin=mysql-bin
log-bin-index=mysql-bin.index
server-id=1
binlog-format=ROW
innodb-flush-log-at-trx-commit=1
sync-binlog=1
datadir=/var/lib/mysql
socket=/var/lib/mysql/mysql.sock
log-error=/var/log/mysqld.log
pid-file=/var/run/mysqld/mysqld.pid
[root@mysql-a ~]#
[root@mysql-a ~]# systemctl start mysqld

>>>>>>>>>>>>>>>>>> mysql-b <<<<<<<<<<<<<<<<<<

[root@mysql-b ~]# systemctl stop mysqld
[root@mysql-b ~]# cat /etc/my.cnf
[mysqld]
datadir=/var/lib/mysql
socket=/var/lib/mysql/mysql.sock
log-error=/var/log/mysqld.log
pid-file=/var/run/mysqld/mysqld.pid
[root@mysql-b ~]#

[root@mysql-b ~]# vi /etc/my.cnf
[root@mysql-b ~]# cat /etc/my.cnf
[mysqld]
# MySQL Replication parameters
server-id=2
relay-log=relay-mysql-b
relay-log-index=relay-mysql-b.index
skip-slave-start
```

```
datadir=/var/lib/mysql
socket=/var/lib/mysql/mysql.sock
log-error=/var/log/mysqld.log
pid-file=/var/run/mysqld/mysqld.pid
[root@mysql-b ~]#
```

[root@mysql-b ~]# systemctl start mysqld

>>>>>>>>>>>>>>>> mysql-c <<<<<<<<<<<<<<<<

[root@mysql-c ~]# cat /etc/my.cnf
```
[mysqld]
datadir=/var/lib/mysql
socket=/var/lib/mysql/mysql.sock
log-error=/var/log/mysqld.log
pid-file=/var/run/mysqld/mysqld.pid
[root@mysql-c ~]#
```

[root@mysql-c ~]# systemctl stop mysqld
[root@mysql-c ~]# vi /etc/my.cnf
[root@mysql-c ~]# cat /etc/my.cnf
```
[mysqld]
```
server-id=3
relay-log=relay-mysql-c
relay-log-index=relay-mysql-c.index
skip-slave-start
```
datadir=/var/lib/mysql
socket=/var/lib/mysql/mysql.sock
log-error=/var/log/mysqld.log
pid-file=/var/run/mysqld/mysqld.pid
[root@mysql-c ~]#
```

[root@mysql-c ~]# systemctl start mysqld

3. Ensure the **SKIP_NETWORKING** variable is set to **OFF**. The
   replica cannot communicate with the source if this is set to
   ON. Set it on all three servers – mysql-a, mysql-b, and mysql-c –
   using the following sample reference:

```
>>>>>>>>>>>>>>>>> mysql-a <<<<<<<<<<<<<<<<<

[root@mysql-a ~]# su - mysql
Last login: Wed Sep 13 22:23:01 CDT 2023 on pts/0

-bash-4.2$ mysql -uroot -p
Enter password:

mysql> show variables like 'skip_networking';
+-----------------+-------+
| Variable_name   | Value |
+-----------------+-------+
| skip_networking | OFF   |
+-----------------+-------+
1 row in set (0.02 sec)
```

4. Create a user named **replication_user** for replication from source
   to each replica and grant **replication slave** privilege.

```
>>>>>>>>>>>>>>>>> mysql-a <<<<<<<<<<<<<<<<<

-bash-4.2$ mysql -uroot -p
Enter password:

mysql> create user 'replication_user'@'192.168.2.20' identified by
'WElcome_1234#';
Query OK, 0 rows affected (0.01 sec)

mysql> grant replication slave on *.* to 'replication_
user'@'192.168.2.20';
Query OK, 0 rows affected (0.00 sec)

mysql> create user 'replication_user'@'192.168.2.25' identified by
'WElcome_1234#';
Query OK, 0 rows affected (0.01 sec)
```

```
mysql> grant replication slave on *.* to 'replication_
user'@'192.168.2.25';
Query OK, 0 rows affected (0.01 sec)
```

```
mysql> flush privileges;
Query OK, 0 rows affected (0.00 sec)
```

```
mysql> select user,host from mysql.user;
+-------------------+--------------+
| user              | host         |
+-------------------+--------------+
| replication_user  | 192.168.2.20 |
| replication_user  | 192.168.2.25 |
| mysql.infoschema  | localhost    |
| mysql.session     | localhost    |
| mysql.sys         | localhost    |
| root              | localhost    |
+-------------------+--------------+
6 rows in set (0.00 sec)
```

5. Get binary log coordinates from the replication master. Get a read
    lock before doing so.

```
>>>>>>>>>>>>>>>>>> mysql-a <<<<<<<<<<<<<<<<<
```

```
mysql> flush tables with read lock;
Query OK, 0 rows affected (0.00 sec)
```

```
mysql> show master status;
+-------------------+----------+--------------+------------------+
|File               | Position | Binlog_Do_DB | Binlog_Ignore_DB |
Executed_Gtid_Set   |
+-------------------+----------+--------------+------------------+
| mysql-bin.000001  | 1482     |              |                  |
+-------------------+----------+--------------+------------------+
1 row in set (0.00 sec)
```

Make a note of the binlog file name and binlog position to use it
later when configuring replication source on the replicas.

6. Create a data snapshot depending on your use case. You can
    choose to replicate all existing data or a subset of data. In this
    case, we will replicate all existing data using the **--all-databases**
    parameter along with triggers, routines, and events. Unlock the
    tables once the logical backup is taken. To take logical backup,
    use mysqldump. The logical backup is named **replication_db_
    dump.db**.

>>>>>>>>>>>>>>>> mysql-a <<<<<<<<<<<<<<<

```
-bash-4.2$ mysqldump -uroot -p --all-databases --
triggers --routines --events --source-data --set-gtid-purged=OFF >
replication_db_dump.db
Enter password:
```

```
-bash-4.2$ ls -ltr
total 1256
-rw-rw-r-- 1 mysql mysql 1283914 Oct  6 10:46 replication_
db_dump.db
-bash-4.2$
```

```
-bash-4.2$ mysql -uroot -p
Enter password:
```

```
mysql> unlock tables;
Query OK, 0 rows affected (0.00 sec)
```

7. Copy the logical backup taken on source (mysql-a) and import
    it into replica servers (mysql-b and mysql-c). In the following
    example, we are copying the logical backup **replication_db_
    dump.db** to mysql-b and mysql-c.

>>>>>>>>>>>>>>>> mysql-a <<<<<<<<<<<<<<<

```
-bash-4.2$ ls -ltr
total 1256
-rw-rw-r-- 1 mysql mysql 1283914 Oct  6 10:46 replication_
db_dump.db
```

```
-bash-4.2$ scp -r replication_db_dump.db 192.168.2.20:/
home/mysql/.
The authenticity of host '192.168.2.20 (192.168.2.20)' can't be
established.
ECDSA key fingerprint is SHA256:YpDYEJtpp16FvKQ/
X2muJuFwkOiL9YG2fRJWnQLaxGE.
ECDSA key fingerprint is MD5:77:b3:32:b9:5f:74:27:6d:df:1c:0f:c9:7
6:16:7c:cb.
Are you sure you want to continue connecting (yes/no)? yes
Warning: Permanently added '192.168.2.20' (ECDSA) to the list of
known hosts.
mysql@192.168.2.20's password:
replication_db_dump.db                      100%
1254KB   73.0MB/s    00:00
-bash-4.2$
```

```
-bash-4.2$ scp -r replication_db_dump.db 192.168.2.25:/
home/mysql/.
The authenticity of host '192.168.2.25 (192.168.2.25)' can't be
established.
ECDSA key fingerprint is SHA256:YpDYEJtpp16FvKQ/
X2muJuFwkOiL9YG2fRJWnQLaxGE.
ECDSA key fingerprint is MD5:77:b3:32:b9:5f:74:27:6d:df:1c:0f:c9:7
6:16:7c:cb.
Are you sure you want to continue connecting (yes/no)? yes
Warning: Permanently added '192.168.2.25' (ECDSA) to the list of
known hosts.
mysql@192.168.2.25's password:
replication_db_dump.db                      100%
1254KB   73.0MB/s    00:00
-bash-4.2$
```

```
>>>>>>>>>>>>>>>>> mysql-b <<<<<<<<<<<<<<<<<
```

```
-bash-4.2$ ls -ltr
total 1256
```

```
-rw-r--r-- 1 mysql mysql 1283914 Oct  6 10:53 replication_
db_dump.db
-bash-4.2$
```

-bash-4.2$ mysql -uroot -p < replication_db_dump.db
```
Enter password:
-bash-4.2$
```

>>>>>>>>>>>>>>>> mysql-c <<<<<<<<<<<<<<<<

-bash-4.2$ ls -ltr
```
total 1256
-rw-r--r-- 1 mysql mysql 1283914 Oct  6 10:53 replication_
db_dump.db
-bash-4.2$
```

-bash-4.2$ mysql -uroot -p < replication_db_dump.db
```
Enter password:

-bash-4.2$
```

8. Verify the server ID is different for each server in the replication
    configuration (mysql-a, mysql-b, mysql-c) and ensure every
    server has a different UUID. If the server UUID is the same, please
    use the following steps to modify the server UUID:

>>>>>>>>>>>>>>>> mysql-a <<<<<<<<<<<<<<<<

-bash-4.2$ mysql -uroot -p
```
Enter password:
```

mysql> select @@server_id;
```
+-------------+
| @@server_id |
+-------------+
|           1 |
+-------------+
1 row in set (0.00 sec)
```

mysql> select @@server_uuid;

```
+----------------------------------------+
| @@server_uuid                          |
+----------------------------------------+
| d763ea33-52ad-11ee-84a8-080027cf69cc   |
+----------------------------------------+
1 row in set (0.00 sec)
```

>>>>>>>>>>>>>>>> mysql-b <<<<<<<<<<<<<<<<

-bash-4.2$ mysql -uroot -p
Enter password:

mysql> select @@server_id;
```
+-------------+
| @@server_id |
+-------------+
|           2 |
+-------------+
1 row in set (0.00 sec)
```

mysql> select @@server_uuid;
```
+----------------------------------------+
| @@server_uuid                          |
+----------------------------------------+
| d763ea33-52ad-11ee-84a8-080027cf69cc   |
+----------------------------------------+
1 row in set (0.00 sec)
```

```
mysql> exit
Bye
-bash-4.2$ exit
logout
```
[root@mysql-b ~]# systemctl stop mysqld
[root@mysql-b ~]# cd /var/lib/mysql

[root@mysql-b mysql]# ls -ltr *auto*
```
-rw-r----- 1 mysql mysql 56 Sep 13 22:21 auto.cnf
[root@mysql-b mysql]#
```

```
[root@mysql-b mysql]# mv auto.cnf /tmp/.
[root@mysql-b mysql]#

[root@mysql-b mysql]# ls -ltr *auto*
ls: cannot access *auto*: No such file or directory
[root@mysql-b mysql]#

[root@mysql-b mysql]# systemctl start mysqld
[root@mysql-b mysql]#

[root@mysql-b mysql]# ls -ltr *auto*
-rw-r----- 1 mysql mysql 56 Oct  6 11:04 auto.cnf
[root@mysql-b mysql]#

[root@mysql-b mysql]# cat auto.cnf
[auto]
server-uuid=1169b107-6462-11ee-b802-080027cf69cc
[root@mysql-b mysql]#
```

>>> Notice a new UUID is generated

>>>>>>>>>>>>>>>> mysql-c <<<<<<<<<<<<<<<<<

```
-bash-4.2$ mysql -uroot -p
Enter password:

mysql> select @@server_id;
+-------------+
| @@server_id |
+-------------+
|           3 |
+-------------+
1 row in set (0.00 sec)

mysql> select @@server_uuid;
+--------------------------------------+
| @@server_uuid                        |
+--------------------------------------+
| d763ea33-52ad-11ee-84a8-080027cf69cc |
+--------------------------------------+
```

```
1 row in set (0.00 sec)

mysql> exit
Bye
-bash-4.2$ exit
logout
[root@mysql-c ~]# systemctl stop mysqld
[root@mysql-c ~]# ls -ltr /var/lib/mysql/auto.cnf
-rw-r----- 1 mysql mysql 56 Sep 13 22:21 /var/lib/mysql/auto.cnf
[root@mysql-c ~]#

[root@mysql-c ~]# mv /var/lib/mysql/auto.cnf /tmp/.
[root@mysql-c ~]#

[root@mysql-c ~]# ls -ltr /var/lib/mysql/auto.cnf
ls: cannot access /var/lib/mysql/auto.cnf: No such file or
directory
[root@mysql-c ~]#

[root@mysql-c ~]# systemctl start mysqld

[root@mysql-c ~]# ls -ltr /var/lib/mysql/auto.cnf
-rw-r----- 1 mysql mysql 56 Oct  6 11:07 /var/lib/mysql/auto.cnf
[root@mysql-c ~]#

[root@mysql-c ~]# cat /var/lib/mysql/auto.cnf
[auto]
server-uuid=832d4368-6462-11ee-bcb2-080027cf69cc

[root@mysql-c ~]#
```

9. Configure the source on the replicas from which replication
   source it must replicate the data from and which binlog file and
   position it has to start replicating. Get the binlog file name and file
   position from step 5.

```
>>>>>>>>>>>>>>>>> mysql-b <<<<<<<<<<<<<<<<<

-bash-4.2$ mysql -uroot -p
Enter password:
```

```
mysql> CHANGE REPLICATION SOURCE TO
    -> SOURCE_HOST='192.168.2.15',
    -> SOURCE_USER='replication_user',
    -> SOURCE_PASSWORD='WElcome_1234#',
    -> SOURCE_LOG_FILE='mysql-bin.000001',
    -> SOURCE_LOG_POS=1482,
    -> GET_SOURCE_PUBLIC_KEY=1;
Query OK, O rows affected, 2 warnings (0.01 sec)

mysql> show replica status\G;
*************************** 1. row ***************************
             Replica_IO_State:
                  Source_Host: 192.168.2.15
                  Source_User: replication_user
                  Source_Port: 3306
                Connect_Retry: 60
              Source_Log_File: mysql-bin.000001
          Read_Source_Log_Pos: 1482
               Relay_Log_File: relay-mysql-b.000001
                Relay_Log_Pos: 4
        Relay_Source_Log_File: mysql-bin.000001
           Replica_IO_Running: No
          Replica_SQL_Running: No
              Replicate_Do_DB:
          Replicate_Ignore_DB:
           Replicate_Do_Table:
       Replicate_Ignore_Table:
      Replicate_Wild_Do_Table:
  Replicate_Wild_Ignore_Table:
                   Last_Errno: O
                   Last_Error:
                 Skip_Counter: O
          Exec_Source_Log_Pos: 1482
              Relay_Log_Space: 157
              Until_Condition: None
               Until_Log_File:
```

```
                Until_Log_Pos: 0
            Source_SSL_Allowed: No
            Source_SSL_CA_File:
            Source_SSL_CA_Path:
               Source_SSL_Cert:
             Source_SSL_Cipher:
                Source_SSL_Key:
          Seconds_Behind_Source: NULL
 Source_SSL_Verify_Server_Cert: No
                 Last_IO_Errno: 0
                 Last_IO_Error:
                Last_SQL_Errno: 0
                Last_SQL_Error:
    Replicate_Ignore_Server_Ids:
              Source_Server_Id: 0
                   Source_UUID:
              Source_Info_File: mysql.slave_master_info
                     SQL_Delay: 0
           SQL_Remaining_Delay: NULL
      Replica_SQL_Running_State:
             Source_Retry_Count: 86400
                   Source_Bind:
        Last_IO_Error_Timestamp:
       Last_SQL_Error_Timestamp:
                Source_SSL_Crl:
            Source_SSL_Crlpath:
             Retrieved_Gtid_Set:
              Executed_Gtid_Set:
                 Auto_Position: 0
           Replicate_Rewrite_DB:
                  Channel_Name:
            Source_TLS_Version:
         Source_public_key_path:
          Get_Source_public_key: 1
             Network_Namespace:
1 row in set (0.00 sec)
```

```
ERROR:
No query specified
```

>>>>>>>>>>>>>>>> mysql-c <<<<<<<<<<<<<<<<

-bash-4.2$ mysql -uroot -p
```
Enter password:
```

mysql> CHANGE REPLICATION SOURCE TO
**   -> SOURCE_HOST='192.168.2.15',**
**   -> SOURCE_USER='replication_user',**
**   -> SOURCE_PASSWORD='WElcome_1234#',**
**   -> SOURCE_LOG_FILE='mysql-bin.000001',**
**   -> SOURCE_LOG_POS=1482,**
**   -> GET_SOURCE_PUBLIC_KEY=1;**
```
Query OK, 0 rows affected, 2 warnings (0.01 sec)
```

mysql> show replica status\G;
```
*************************** 1. row ***************************
              Replica_IO_State:
                   Source_Host: 192.168.2.15
                   Source_User: replication_user
                   Source_Port: 3306
                 Connect_Retry: 60
               Source_Log_File: mysql-bin.000001
           Read_Source_Log_Pos: 1482
                Relay_Log_File: relay-mysql-c.000001
                 Relay_Log_Pos: 4
         Relay_Source_Log_File: mysql-bin.000001
            Replica_IO_Running: No
           Replica_SQL_Running: No
               Replicate_Do_DB:
           Replicate_Ignore_DB:
            Replicate_Do_Table:
        Replicate_Ignore_Table:
       Replicate_Wild_Do_Table:
   Replicate_Wild_Ignore_Table:
```

```
                     Last_Errno: 0
                     Last_Error:
                   Skip_Counter: 0
           Exec_Source_Log_Pos: 1482
               Relay_Log_Space: 157
               Until_Condition: None
                Until_Log_File:
                 Until_Log_Pos: 0
             Source_SSL_Allowed: No
             Source_SSL_CA_File:
             Source_SSL_CA_Path:
                Source_SSL_Cert:
              Source_SSL_Cipher:
                 Source_SSL_Key:
          Seconds_Behind_Source: NULL
  Source_SSL_Verify_Server_Cert: No
                  Last_IO_Errno: 0
                  Last_IO_Error:
                 Last_SQL_Errno: 0
                 Last_SQL_Error:
     Replicate_Ignore_Server_Ids:
               Source_Server_Id: 0
                    Source_UUID:
               Source_Info_File: mysql.slave_master_info
                      SQL_Delay: 0
            SQL_Remaining_Delay: NULL
      Replica_SQL_Running_State:
             Source_Retry_Count: 86400
                    Source_Bind:
       Last_IO_Error_Timestamp:
      Last_SQL_Error_Timestamp:
                 Source_SSL_Crl:
             Source_SSL_Crlpath:
             Retrieved_Gtid_Set:
              Executed_Gtid_Set:
                  Auto_Position: 0
```

245

```
                Replicate_Rewrite_DB:
                       Channel_Name:
                 Source_TLS_Version:
             Source_public_key_path:
              Get_Source_public_key: 1
                  Network_Namespace:
1 row in set (0.00 sec)
```

```
ERROR:
No query specified
```

10. Start replication by issuing the **start replica** statement on each
    replica server.

>>>>>>>>>>>>>>>> mysql-b <<<<<<<<<<<<<<<<

-bash-4.2$ hostname
```
mysql-b
```

-bash-4.2$ mysql -uroot -p
```
Enter password:
```
mysql> start replica;
```
Query OK, 0 rows affected (0.01 sec)
```

mysql> show replica status\G;
```
*************************** 1. row ***************************
             Replica_IO_State: Waiting for source to send event
                  Source_Host: 192.168.2.15
                  Source_User: replication_user
                  Source_Port: 3306
                Connect_Retry: 60
              Source_Log_File: mysql-bin.000001
          Read_Source_Log_Pos: 1482
               Relay_Log_File: relay-mysql-b.000002
                Relay_Log_Pos: 326
        Relay_Source_Log_File: mysql-bin.000001
           Replica_IO_Running: Yes
          Replica_SQL_Running: Yes
             Replicate_Do_DB:
```

```
                Replicate_Ignore_DB:
               Replicate_Do_Table:
           Replicate_Ignore_Table:
          Replicate_Wild_Do_Table:
      Replicate_Wild_Ignore_Table:
                        Last_Errno: 0
                        Last_Error:
                     Skip_Counter: 0
             Exec_Source_Log_Pos: 1482
                 Relay_Log_Space: 534
                Until_Condition: None
                 Until_Log_File:
                  Until_Log_Pos: 0
              Source_SSL_Allowed: No
              Source_SSL_CA_File:
              Source_SSL_CA_Path:
                Source_SSL_Cert:
              Source_SSL_Cipher:
                 Source_SSL_Key:
           Seconds_Behind_Source: 0
  Source_SSL_Verify_Server_Cert: No
                  Last_IO_Errno: 0
                  Last_IO_Error:
                 Last_SQL_Errno: 0
                 Last_SQL_Error:
      Replicate_Ignore_Server_Ids:
               Source_Server_Id: 1
                    Source_UUID: d763ea33-52ad-11ee-84a8-
                                 080027cf69cc
              Source_Info_File: mysql.slave_master_info
                      SQL_Delay: 0
            SQL_Remaining_Delay: NULL
     Replica_SQL_Running_State: Replica has read all relay log;
                                 waiting for more updates
             Source_Retry_Count: 86400
                    Source_Bind:
```

```
            Last_IO_Error_Timestamp:
           Last_SQL_Error_Timestamp:
                     Source_SSL_Crl:
                 Source_SSL_Crlpath:
                 Retrieved_Gtid_Set:
                  Executed_Gtid_Set:
                      Auto_Position: 0
              Replicate_Rewrite_DB:
                       Channel_Name:
                 Source_TLS_Version:
             Source_public_key_path:
              Get_Source_public_key: 1
                  Network_Namespace:
1 row in set (0.00 sec)

ERROR:
No query specified
```

>>>>>>>>>>>>>>>> mysql-c <<<<<<<<<<<<<<<<

-bash-4.2$ hostname
```
mysql-c
```

-bash-4.2$ mysql -u root -p
```
Enter password:
```

mysql> start replica;
```
Query OK, 0 rows affected (0.02 sec)
```

mysql> show replica status\G;
```
*************************** 1. row ***************************
            Replica_IO_State: Waiting for source to send event
                 Source_Host: 192.168.2.15
                 Source_User: replication_user
                 Source_Port: 3306
               Connect_Retry: 60
             Source_Log_File: mysql-bin.000001
          Read_Source_Log_Pos: 1482
```

```
            Relay_Log_File: relay-mysql-c.000002
             Relay_Log_Pos: 326
     Relay_Source_Log_File: mysql-bin.000001
         Replica_IO_Running: Yes
        Replica_SQL_Running: Yes
            Replicate_Do_DB:
        Replicate_Ignore_DB:
         Replicate_Do_Table:
     Replicate_Ignore_Table:
    Replicate_Wild_Do_Table:
Replicate_Wild_Ignore_Table:
                 Last_Errno: 0
                 Last_Error:
               Skip_Counter: 0
        Exec_Source_Log_Pos: 1482
            Relay_Log_Space: 534
            Until_Condition: None
             Until_Log_File:
              Until_Log_Pos: 0
          Source_SSL_Allowed: No
          Source_SSL_CA_File:
          Source_SSL_CA_Path:
             Source_SSL_Cert:
           Source_SSL_Cipher:
              Source_SSL_Key:
        Seconds_Behind_Source: 0
Source_SSL_Verify_Server_Cert: No
               Last_IO_Errno: 0
               Last_IO_Error:
              Last_SQL_Errno: 0
              Last_SQL_Error:
   Replicate_Ignore_Server_Ids:
             Source_Server_Id: 1
                 Source_UUID: d763ea33-52ad-11ee-
                              84a8-080027cf69cc
```

```
                Source_Info_File: mysql.slave_master_info
                       SQL_Delay: 0
             SQL_Remaining_Delay: NULL
       Replica_SQL_Running_State: Replica has read all relay log;
                                  waiting for more updates
              Source_Retry_Count: 86400
                     Source_Bind:
        Last_IO_Error_Timestamp:
       Last_SQL_Error_Timestamp:
                 Source_SSL_Crl:
             Source_SSL_Crlpath:
             Retrieved_Gtid_Set:
              Executed_Gtid_Set:
                  Auto_Position: 0
            Replicate_Rewrite_DB:
                    Channel_Name:
             Source_TLS_Version:
          Source_public_key_path:
           Get_Source_public_key: 1
               Network_Namespace:
1 row in set (0.00 sec)

ERROR:

No query specified
```

We can see based on the replica SQL running state, both the replicas are in sync with the source.

11. Create a few databases and tables in source mysql-a and verify if they are getting replicated to the replicas mysql-b and mysql-c.

>>>>>>>>>>>>>>>> mysql-a <<<<<<<<<<<<<<<<<

```
-bash-4.2$ hostname
mysql-a

-bash-4.2$ mysql -uroot -p
Enter password:
```

```
mysql> show databases;
+--------------------+
| Database           |
+--------------------+
| information_schema |
| mysql              |
| performance_schema |
| sys                |
+--------------------+
4 rows in set (0.00 sec)

mysql> create database db1;
Query OK, 1 row affected (0.01 sec)

mysql> create database db2;
Query OK, 1 row affected (0.01 sec)

mysql> create database db3;
Query OK, 1 row affected (0.00 sec)

mysql> use db1;
Database changed
mysql> create table tab1 (no int);
Query OK, 0 rows affected (0.02 sec)

mysql> create table tab2 (no int);
Query OK, 0 rows affected (0.01 sec)

mysql> create table tab3 (no int);
Query OK, 0 rows affected (0.02 sec)

mysql> show tables;
+---------------+
| Tables_in_db1 |
+---------------+
| tab1          |
| tab2          |
| tab3          |
+---------------+
3 rows in set (0.00 sec)
```

```
mysql> show databases;
+--------------------+
| Database           |
+--------------------+
| db1                |
| db2                |
| db3                |
| information_schema |
| mysql              |
| performance_schema |
| sys                |
+--------------------+
7 rows in set (0.00 sec)

>>>>>>>>>>>>>>>> mysql-b <<<<<<<<<<<<<<<<

-bash-4.2$ hostname
mysql-b

-bash-4.2$ mysql -uroot -p
Enter password:

mysql> show databases;
+--------------------+
| Database           |
+--------------------+
| db1                |
| db2                |
| db3                |
| information_schema |
| mysql              |
| performance_schema |
| sys                |
+--------------------+
7 rows in set (0.00 sec)
```

mysql> use db1;
Reading table information for completion of table and column names
You can turn off this feature to get a quicker startup with -A

Database changed

mysql> show tables;
```
+---------------+
| Tables_in_db1 |
+---------------+
| tab1          |
| tab2          |
| tab3          |
+---------------+
3 rows in set (0.00 sec)
```

>>>>>>>>>>>>>>>> mysql-c <<<<<<<<<<<<<<<<

-bash-4.2$ hostname
mysql-c

-bash-4.2$ mysql -uroot -p
Enter password:

mysql> show databases;
```
+--------------------+
| Database           |
+--------------------+
| db1                |
| db2                |
| db3                |
| information_schema |
| mysql              |
| performance_schema |
| sys                |
+--------------------+
7 rows in set (0.00 sec)
```

```
mysql> use db1;
Reading table information for completion of table and column names
You can turn off this feature to get a quicker startup with -A

Database changed

mysql> show tables;
+---------------+
| Tables_in_db1 |
+---------------+
| tab1          |
| tab2          |
| tab3          |
+---------------+
3 rows in set (0.00 sec)
```

GTID-Based Replication

A *global transaction identifier* (GTID) is a unique identifier created and associated with each transaction committed on the server of origin (source).

GTID = source_id:transaction_id

The *source_id* identifies the originating server. Normally, the source's *server_uuid* is used for this purpose. The *transaction_id* is a sequence number determined by the order in which the transaction was committed on the source.

The following are the high-level steps to set up GTID replication:

- Each server must be started with gtid_mode=ON and enforce_gtid_ consistency=ON.

- Configure replicas to use GTID-based auto-positioning by issuing a CHANGE MASTER TO statement with the MASTER_AUTO_ POSITION option.

- Validate and test.

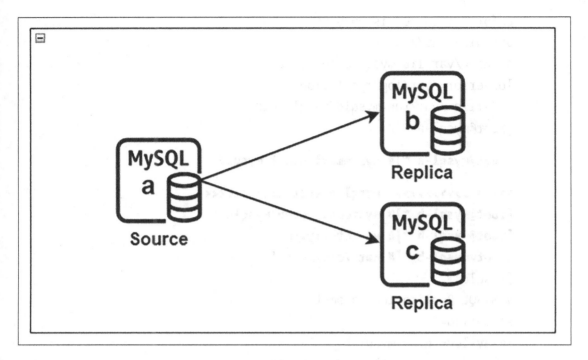

Figure 5-2.   *Replication with one source and two replicas*

1. Modify the MySQL configuration file for each server in the
   replication configuration to include the GTID replication
   parameters.

   >>>>>>>>>>>>>>>>> **mysql-a** <<<<<<<<<<<<<<<<<

   [root@mysql-a ~]# systemctl stop mysqld
   [root@mysql-a ~]# vi /etc/my.cnf
   [root@mysql-a ~]# cat /etc/my.cnf
   [mysqld]
   # MySQL Replication parameters
   log-bin=mysql-bin
   log-bin-index=mysql-bin.index
   server-id=1
   binlog-format=ROW
   innodb-flush-log-at-trx-commit=1
   sync-binlog=1
   gtid_mode=ON

```
enforce_gtid_consistency=ON
datadir=/var/lib/mysql
socket=/var/lib/mysql/mysql.sock
log-error=/var/log/mysqld.log
pid-file=/var/run/mysqld/mysqld.pid
[root@mysql-a ~]#
```

[root@mysql-a ~]# systemctl start mysqld

>>>>>>>>>>>>>>>>> mysql-b <<<<<<<<<<<<<<<<<
[root@mysql-b ~]# systemctl stop mysqld
[root@mysql-b ~]# vi /etc/my.cnf
[root@mysql-b ~]# cat /etc/my.cnf
```
[mysqld]
# MySQL Replication parameters
server-id=2
relay-log=relay-mysql-b
relay-log-index=relay-mysql-b.index
skip-slave-start
gtid_mode=ON
enforce_gtid_consistency=ON
datadir=/var/lib/mysql
socket=/var/lib/mysql/mysql.sock
log-error=/var/log/mysqld.log
pid-file=/var/run/mysqld/mysqld.pid

[root@mysql-b ~]#
```

[root@mysql-b ~]# systemctl start mysqld

>>>>>>>>>>>>>>>>> mysql-c <<<<<<<<<<<<<<<<<

[root@mysql-c ~]# systemctl stop mysqld
[root@mysql-c ~]# vi /etc/my.cnf
[root@mysql-c ~]# cat /etc/my.cnf
```
[mysqld]
server-id=3
relay-log=relay-mysql-c
relay-log-index=relay-mysql-c.index
```

```
skip-slave-start
gtid_mode=ON
enforce_gtid_consistency=ON
datadir=/var/lib/mysql
socket=/var/lib/mysql/mysql.sock
log-error=/var/log/mysqld.log
pid-file=/var/run/mysqld/mysqld.pid
[root@mysql-c ~]#
```

[root@mysql-c ~]# systemctl start mysqld

2. Configure the replicas mysql-b and mysql-c to use GTID-based replication.

>>>>>>>>>>>>>>>>> mysql-b <<<<<<<<<<<<<<<<<

-bash-4.2$ mysql -uroot -p
```
Enter password:
```

mysql> CHANGE REPLICATION SOURCE TO
**   -> SOURCE_HOST='192.168.2.15',**
**   -> SOURCE_USER='replication_user',**
**   -> SOURCE_PASSWORD='WElcome_1234#',**
**   -> SOURCE_AUTO_POSITION=1,**
**   -> GET_SOURCE_PUBLIC_KEY=1;**
```
Query OK, 0 rows affected, 2 warnings (0.02 sec)
```

mysql> start replica;
```
Query OK, 0 rows affected (0.01 sec)
```

mysql> show replica status\G;
```
*************************** 1. row ***************************
             Replica_IO_State: Waiting for source to send event
                  Source_Host: 192.168.2.15
                  Source_User: replication_user
                  Source_Port: 3306
                Connect_Retry: 60
              Source_Log_File: mysql-bin.000002
```

```
            Read_Source_Log_Pos: 157
                Relay_Log_File: relay-mysql-b.000002
                 Relay_Log_Pos: 373
         Relay_Source_Log_File: mysql-bin.000002
             Replica_IO_Running: Yes
            Replica_SQL_Running: Yes
               Replicate_Do_DB:
           Replicate_Ignore_DB:
             Replicate_Do_Table:
         Replicate_Ignore_Table:
        Replicate_Wild_Do_Table:
    Replicate_Wild_Ignore_Table:
                     Last_Errno: 0
                     Last_Error:
                   Skip_Counter: 0
            Exec_Source_Log_Pos: 157
                Relay_Log_Space: 581
                Until_Condition: None
                Until_Log_File:
                 Until_Log_Pos: 0
             Source_SSL_Allowed: No
             Source_SSL_CA_File:
             Source_SSL_CA_Path:
                Source_SSL_Cert:
              Source_SSL_Cipher:
                 Source_SSL_Key:
          Seconds_Behind_Source: 0
  Source_SSL_Verify_Server_Cert: No
                  Last_IO_Errno: 0
                  Last_IO_Error:
                 Last_SQL_Errno: 0
                 Last_SQL_Error:
     Replicate_Ignore_Server_Ids:
               Source_Server_Id: 1
                    Source_UUID: d763ea33-52ad-11ee-84a8-
                                 080027cf69cc
```

```
              Source_Info_File: mysql.slave_master_info
                     SQL_Delay: 0
           SQL_Remaining_Delay: NULL
     Replica_SQL_Running_State: Replica has read all relay log;
                                waiting for more updates
             Source_Retry_Count: 86400
                   Source_Bind:
       Last_IO_Error_Timestamp:
      Last_SQL_Error_Timestamp:
                Source_SSL_Crl:
            Source_SSL_Crlpath:
             Retrieved_Gtid_Set:
             Executed_Gtid_Set:
                 Auto_Position: 1
          Replicate_Rewrite_DB:
                  Channel_Name:
            Source_TLS_Version:
         Source_public_key_path:
          Get_Source_public_key: 1
             Network_Namespace:
1 row in set (0.00 sec)

ERROR:
No query specified
```

>>>>>>>>>>>>>>>>>> mysql-c <<<<<<<<<<<<<<<<<<

```
-bash-4.2$ mysql -uroot -p
Enter password:
```

mysql> CHANGE REPLICATION SOURCE TO
   -> SOURCE_HOST='192.168.2.15',
   -> SOURCE_USER='replication_user',
   -> SOURCE_PASSWORD='WElcome_1234#',
   -> SOURCE_AUTO_POSITION=1,
   -> GET_SOURCE_PUBLIC_KEY=1;
```
Query OK, 0 rows affected, 2 warnings (0.02 sec)
```

```
mysql> start replica;
Query OK, 0 rows affected (0.02 sec)

mysql> show replica status\G;
*************************** 1. row ***************************
             Replica_IO_State: Waiting for source to send event
                  Source_Host: 192.168.2.15
                  Source_User: replication_user
                  Source_Port: 3306
                Connect_Retry: 60
              Source_Log_File: mysql-bin.000002
          Read_Source_Log_Pos: 157
               Relay_Log_File: relay-mysql-c.000002
                Relay_Log_Pos: 373
        Relay_Source_Log_File: mysql-bin.000002
           Replica_IO_Running: Yes
          Replica_SQL_Running: Yes
              Replicate_Do_DB:
          Replicate_Ignore_DB:
           Replicate_Do_Table:
       Replicate_Ignore_Table:
      Replicate_Wild_Do_Table:
  Replicate_Wild_Ignore_Table:
                   Last_Errno: 0
                   Last_Error:
                 Skip_Counter: 0
          Exec_Source_Log_Pos: 157
              Relay_Log_Space: 581
              Until_Condition: None
               Until_Log_File:
                Until_Log_Pos: 0
           Source_SSL_Allowed: No
           Source_SSL_CA_File:
           Source_SSL_CA_Path:
             Source_SSL_Cert:
```

```
                   Source_SSL_Cipher:
                      Source_SSL_Key:
               Seconds_Behind_Source: 0
    Source_SSL_Verify_Server_Cert: No
                      Last_IO_Errno: 0
                      Last_IO_Error:
                     Last_SQL_Errno: 0
                     Last_SQL_Error:
       Replicate_Ignore_Server_Ids:
                   Source_Server_Id: 1
                        Source_UUID: d763ea33-52ad-11ee-84a8-
                                     080027cf69cc
                   Source_Info_File: mysql.slave_master_info
                          SQL_Delay: 0
                SQL_Remaining_Delay: NULL
         Replica_SQL_Running_State: Replica has read all relay log;
                                     waiting for more updates
                 Source_Retry_Count: 86400
                        Source_Bind:
           Last_IO_Error_Timestamp:
          Last_SQL_Error_Timestamp:
                     Source_SSL_Crl:
                 Source_SSL_Crlpath:
                 Retrieved_Gtid_Set:
                  Executed_Gtid_Set:
                      Auto_Position: 1
               Replicate_Rewrite_DB:
                       Channel_Name:
                 Source_TLS_Version:
             Source_public_key_path:
             Get_Source_public_key: 1
                  Network_Namespace:
1 row in set (0.00 sec)

ERROR:
No query specified
```

3. Test replication from source mysql-a to replicas mysql-b and
mysql-c. To test, create a few sample databases on source mysql-a
and verify if those are replicated to replicas mysql-b and mysql-c.

>>>>>>>>>>>>>>>>>> **mysql-a** <<<<<<<<<<<<<<<<<<

```
-bash-4.2$ mysql -uroot -p
Enter password:
```

mysql> show databases;
```
+---------------------+
| Database            |
+---------------------+
| db1                 |
| db2                 |
| db3                 |
| information_schema  |
| mysql               |
| performance_schema  |
| sys                 |
+---------------------+
7 rows in set (0.00 sec)
```

mysql> create database db4;
```
Query OK, 1 row affected (0.01 sec)
```

mysql> create database db5;
```
Query OK, 1 row affected (0.02 sec)
```

mysql> show databases;
```
+---------------------+
| Database            |
+---------------------+
| db1                 |
| db2                 |
| db3                 |
| db4                 |
| db5                 |
| information_schema  |
```

```
| mysql              |
| performance_schema |
| sys                |
+--------------------+
9 rows in set (0.00 sec)
```

>>>>>>>>>>>>>>>> mysql-b <<<<<<<<<<<<<<<<

mysql> select @@hostname;
```
+------------+
| @@hostname |
+------------+
| mysql-b    |
+------------+
1 row in set (0.00 sec)
```

mysql> show databases;
```
+--------------------+
| Database           |
+--------------------+
| db1                |
| db2                |
| db3                |
| db4                |
| db5                |
| information_schema |
| mysql              |
| performance_schema |
| sys                |
+--------------------+
9 rows in set (0.00 sec)
```

>>>>>>>>>>>>>>>> mysql-c <<<<<<<<<<<<<<<<

mysql> select @@hostname;
```
+------------+
| @@hostname |
+------------+
```

```
| mysql-c    |
+------------+
1 row in set (0.00 sec)
```

mysql> show databases;

```
+--------------------+
| Database           |
+--------------------+
| db1                |
| db2                |
| db3                |
| db4                |
| db5                |
| information_schema |
| mysql              |
| performance_schema |
| sys                |
+--------------------+
9 rows in set (0.00 sec)
```

MySQL Scalability

We can achieve scalability in MySQL in various replication configurations. MySQL provides scale-out solutions with various replication topologies like single-source replica, multi-source, chain topology, etc. In the following example, let us look at using the **clone plug-in** to remotely clone the data. The remote cloning operation removes the existing user-created objects and clones the data from the remote server and then performs a restart of the MySQL server.

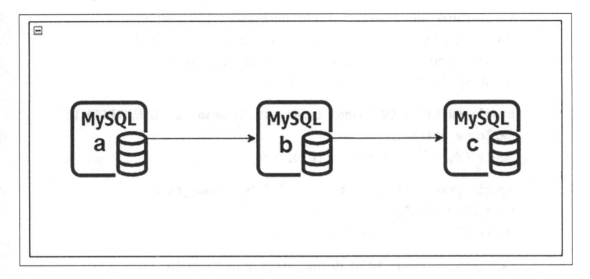

Figure 5-3. *MySQL chain replication topology*

In the preceding figure, we have GTID-based replication already set up between mysql-a and mysql-b. We will build mysql-c using remote cloning with source mysql-b.

1. Install the **clone** plug-in on both mysql-b and mysql-c.

```
[root@mysql-b ~]# su - mysql
Last login: Mon Nov  6 13:10:18 CST 2023 on pts/0
-bash-4.2$ mysql -uroot -p
Enter password:

mysql> install plugin clone soname 'mysql_clone.so';
Query OK, 0 rows affected (0.01 sec)

mysql> select plugin_name, plugin_status from information_schema.
plugins where plugin_name='clone';
+-------------+---------------+
| plugin_name | plugin_status |
+-------------+---------------+
| clone       | ACTIVE        |
+-------------+---------------+
1 row in set (0.01 sec)
```

Repeat the same on mysql-c.

2. Create the required users and grant necessary privileges on mysql-b and mysql-c. In the following example, we are creating a user named **donor_clone_user** for mysql-c and granting the privileges. Do the same on both servers.

```
mysql> CREATE USER 'donor_clone_user'@'mysql-c' IDENTIFIED BY 'WElcome_1234#';
Query OK, 0 rows affected (0.01 sec)
```

```
mysql> grant all privileges on *.* to 'donor_clone_user'@'mysql-c';
Query OK, 0 rows affected (0.00 sec)
```

3. Configure the **clone_valid_donor_list** parameter on the server from which we want to run the remote clone operation. In our case, it is mysql-c.

```
mysql> set global clone_valid_donor_list='mysql-b:3306';
Query OK, 0 rows affected (0.00 sec)
```

```
mysql> show variables like '%clone_valid%';
+------------------------+--------------+
| Variable_name          | Value        |
+------------------------+--------------+
| clone_valid_donor_list | mysql-b:3306 |
+------------------------+--------------+
1 row in set (0.01 sec)
```

4. Clone the data from mysql-b onto mysql-c.

```
mysql> clone instance from 'donor_clone_user'@'mysql-b':3306 identified by 'WElcome_1234#';

Query OK, 0 rows affected (1.69 sec)
```

5. On mysql-c, query the **performance_schema.clone_status** table to get the current binlog file name and position. Note this step is required only if you have statement-based replication instead of GTID-based replication.

```
mysql> select binlog_file, binlog_position from performance_
schema.clone_status;
ERROR 2013 (HY000): Lost connection to MySQL server during query
No connection. Trying to reconnect...
Connection id:    8
Current database: *** NONE ***

+---------------+-----------------+
| binlog_file   | binlog_position |
+---------------+-----------------+
| binlog.000019 |            2008 |
+---------------+-----------------+
1 row in set (0.02 sec)
```

6. On mysql-c, issue the CHANGE MASTER command to convert as the slave of mysql-b. Since GTID-based replication is already turned on, issue the following command without providing the binlog file coordinates.

```
mysql> change master to master_host='mysql-b', master_
port=3306, source_user='replication_user',source_
password='WElcome_1234#',source_auto_position=1,get_source_
public_key=1;
```

7. Start replica and check status.

```
mysql> start replica;
Query OK, 0 rows affected (0.02 sec)
```

```
mysql> show replica status\G;
*************************** 1. row ***************************
             Slave_IO_State: Waiting for source to send event
                Master_Host: mysql-b
                Master_User: replication_user
```

```
                  Master_Port: 3306
                Connect_Retry: 60
              Master_Log_File: binlog.000019
          Read_Master_Log_Pos: 2008
               Relay_Log_File: relay-mysql-c.000002
                Relay_Log_Pos: 411
        Relay_Master_Log_File: binlog.000019
             Slave_IO_Running: Yes
            Slave_SQL_Running: Yes
              Replicate_Do_DB:
          Replicate_Ignore_DB:
           Replicate_Do_Table:
       Replicate_Ignore_Table:
      Replicate_Wild_Do_Table:
  Replicate_Wild_Ignore_Table:
                   Last_Errno: 0
                   Last_Error:
                 Skip_Counter: 0
          Exec_Master_Log_Pos: 2008
              Relay_Log_Space: 619
              Until_Condition: None
               Until_Log_File:
                Until_Log_Pos: 0
            Master_SSL_Allowed: No
            Master_SSL_CA_File:
            Master_SSL_CA_Path:
               Master_SSL_Cert:
             Master_SSL_Cipher:
                Master_SSL_Key:
        Seconds_Behind_Master: 0
Master_SSL_Verify_Server_Cert: No
                Last_IO_Errno: 0
                Last_IO_Error:
               Last_SQL_Errno: 0
               Last_SQL_Error:
```

```
      Replicate_Ignore_Server_Ids:
                 Master_Server_Id: 2
                   Master_UUID: 7c17623b-397c-11ee-9a30-
                                 080027cf69cc
              Master_Info_File: mysql.slave_master_info
                     SQL_Delay: 0
           SQL_Remaining_Delay: NULL
       Slave_SQL_Running_State: Replica has read all relay log;
                                waiting for more updates
            Master_Retry_Count: 86400
                   Master_Bind:
        Last_IO_Error_Timestamp:
       Last_SQL_Error_Timestamp:
                 Master_SSL_Crl:
             Master_SSL_Crlpath:
             Retrieved_Gtid_Set:
              Executed_Gtid_Set: 7c17623b-397c-11ee-9a30-080027cf69
                                 cc:1-6,a52a1fb1-3272-11ee-9a0c-
                                 080027cf69cc:1-2
                  Auto_Position: 1
            Replicate_Rewrite_DB:
                   Channel_Name:
             Master_TLS_Version:
         Master_public_key_path:
          Get_master_public_key: 1
              Network_Namespace:
1 row in set, 1 warning (0.00 sec)

ERROR:
No query specified
```

269

8. Validate by creating a database in either mysql-a or mysql-b to verify. For example, a database named **db8** is created on mysql-a and it gets replicated to mysql-b and then to mysql-c.

>>>>>>>>> mysql-a <<<<<<<<<<<<<<<

mysql> select @@hostname;
```
+------------+
| @@hostname |
+------------+
| mysql-a|
+------------+
1 row in set (0.00 sec)
```

mysql> show databases;
```
+--------------------+
| Database           |
+--------------------+
| db1                |
| db2                |
| db3                |
| db4                |
| db5                |
| db6                |
| db7                |
| information_schema |
| mysql              |
| performance_schema |
| sys                |
+--------------------+
11 rows in set (0.00 sec)
```

mysql> create database db8;
```
Query OK, 1 row affected (0.01 sec)
```

```
mysql> show databases;
+--------------------+
| Database           |
+--------------------+
| db1                |
| db2                |
| db3                |
| db4                |
| db5                |
| db6                |
| db7                |
| db8                |
| information_schema |
| mysql              |
| performance_schema |
| sys                |
+--------------------+
12 rows in set (0.00 sec)

>>>>>>>>>> mysql-b <<<<<<<<<<<<<<

mysql> show databases;
+--------------------+
| Database           |
+--------------------+
| db1                |
| db2                |
| db3                |
| db4                |
| db5                |
| db6                |
| db7                |
| db8                |
| information_schema |
| mysql              |
```

```
| performance_schema |
| sys                |
+--------------------+
12 rows in set (0.00 sec)
```

>>>>>>>>>> mysql-c <<<<<<<<<<<<<<<<

mysql> show databases;

```
+--------------------+
| Database           |
+--------------------+
| db1                |
| db2                |
| db3                |
| db4                |
| db5                |
| db6                |
| db7                |
| db8                |
| information_schema |
| mysql              |
| performance_schema |
| sys                |
+--------------------+
12 rows in set (0.01 sec)
```

Summary

Overall, MySQL replication is used to distribute all or some parts of data closer to the
end user and can be used in scale-out architectures or to separate analytical or reporting
workloads. You can either use binlog or GTID-based replication. As an extension to this
capability, to achieve high availability and robust disaster recovery solutions, we use
InnoDB Cluster with Cluster Set and Replica Set configurations, which we will learn in
the next chapter.

## CHAPTER 6

MySQL InnoDB Cluster and ClusterSet

Introduction

MySQL InnoDB ClusterSet is primarily used for disaster recovery scenarios where it provides disaster recovery tolerance for a MySQL InnoDB Cluster by replicating data asynchronously using a dedicated replication channel between the primary InnoDB cluster and the secondary InnoDB cluster.

InnoDB cluster provides high availability within the region or data centers. InnoDB cluster requires a minimum of three MySQL server instances as part of the cluster and requires it to use MySQL Group Replication to replicate data within the cluster. It also has built-in failover.

High-Level Overview

In this chapter, we will create two InnoDB clusters, one as primary and the other as secondary with three MySQL servers in each InnoDB cluster. We will also set up MySQL Router to allow clients to connect transparently to the MySQL server in read-write mode.

© Y V Ravi Kumar, Arun Kumar Samayam, Naresh Kumar Miryala 2024
Y V Ravi Kumar et al., *Mastering MySQL Administration*, https://doi.org/10.1007/979-8-8688-0252-2_6

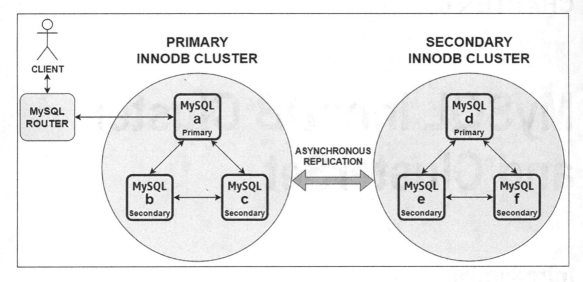

Figure 6-1. *InnoDB Clusterset*

The primary InnoDB cluster consists of three MySQL servers in the following configuration:

- mysql-a (R/W)

- mysql-b (R/O)

- mysql-c (R/O)

The secondary InnoDB cluster consists of three MySQL servers in the following configuration.

- mysql-d (R/W)

- mysql-e (R/O)

- mysql-f (R/O)

R/W = read-write R/O = read-only

Upon setting this environment, we will be testing a few real-time use cases to understand the concepts better and see the functionality in practice. Here are some of the use cases we will be testing in this chapter:

- Role switch of clusters

- Role switch of instances within the cluster

- Failure of an instance in secondary role within the cluster

- Failure of an instance in primary role within the secondary cluster

- Recovering the cluster or clusterset from a region-wide or multi-region outage

Configuring InnoDB Clusterset

The key components of an InnoDB cluster are as follows:

- **MySQL Shell:** Client and code editor for MySQL cluster administration

- **MySQL server with Group Replication:** Provides high availability

- **MySQL Router:** Provides transparent routing between your application and InnoDB cluster

As a prerequisite before configuring InnoDB Clusterset, we need to deploy InnoDB cluster. Here are some important configuration options to be set. Ensure

- Group replication is set up for all the servers, which are planned to be part of the cluster.

- All data must be stored on the InnoDB transactional storage engine, and all data stored in alternative storage engines need to be converted to the InnoDB storage engine prior to the cluster setup.

- No inbound replication channels on server instances.

- The **Group_replication_tls_source** variable must not be set to **mysql_admin**.

- Performance schema must be enabled on all instances within the cluster.

- MySQL Shell provisioning scripts are able to access Python.

- Every instance has a unique **server_id** within the cluster.

- Parallel replication applier is configured for every instance. Set the following system variables:

    - *binlog_transaction_dependency_tracking=WRITESET*

    - *slave_preserve_commit_order=ON*

    - *slave_parallel_type=LOGICAL_CLOCK*

    - *transaction_write_set_extraction=XXHASH64*

By default, **slave_parallel_workers** is set to 4.

1. Install MySQL Shell on all servers in the clusterset configuration.

```
[root@mysql-a ~]# sudo yum search mysql-shell
Loaded plugins: fastestmirror
Determining fastest mirrors
 * base: mirror.lstn.net
 * epel: d2lzkl7pfhq30w.cloudfront.net
 * extras: mirror.vacares.com
 * updates: mirrors.tripadvisor.com
==================== N/S matched: mysql-shell ====================
mysql-shell.x86_64 : Command line shell and scripting environment
for MySQL

  Name and summary matches only, use "search all" for everything.
```

```
[root@mysql-a ~]# sudo yum install mysql-shell
Loaded plugins: fastestmirror
Loading mirror speeds from cached hostfile

epel/x86_64/metalink                           |  20 kB  00:00:00
 * base: mirror.lstn.net
 * epel: d2lzkl7pfhq30w.cloudfront.net
 * extras: mirror.vacares.com
 * updates: mirrors.tripadvisor.com
base                                           | 3.6 kB  00:00:00
epel                                           | 4.7 kB  00:00:00
extras                                         | 2.9 kB  00:00:00
mysql-connectors-community                     | 2.6 kB  00:00:00
```

```
mysql-tools-community                          |  2.6 kB   00:00:00
mysql80-community                              |  2.6 kB   00:00:00
```

...output truncated for better visibility

```
 Installed:
   mysql-shell.x86_64 0:8.0.34-1.el7

Dependency Installed:
   libyaml.x86_64 0:0.1.4-11.el7_0
```

Complete!

If 'yum install' is not working as expected, go to `https://dev.mysql.com/downloads/shell/` and download **MySQL Shell 8.0.34** for RHEL 7. Use WinSCP to transfer the file downloaded to the server.

2. Transfer the file to the remaining servers in the clusterset and install.

[root@mysql-a ~]# cd mysql_binaries/
[root@mysql-a mysql_binaries]# scp mysql-shell-8.0.34-1.el7.
x86_64.rpm 192.168.2.20:/root/mysql_binaries/ .
```
root@192.168.2.20's password:
mysql-shell-8.0.34-1.el7.x86_64.
rpm      100%   38MB  71.5MB/s   00:00
```
[root@mysql-a mysql_binaries]# scp mysql-shell-8.0.34-1.el7.
x86_64.rpm 192.168.2.25:/root/mysql_binaries/ .
```
root@192.168.2.25's password:
mysql-shell-8.0.34-1.el7.x86_64.
rpm      100%   38MB  74.1MB/s   00:00
```

3. Install the **libyaml*** package, which is required for MySQL Shell.

[root@mysql-a mysql_binaries]# sudo yum install libyaml*
```
Loaded plugins: fastestmirror
Loading mirror speeds from cached hostfile
 * base: mirror.dal.nexril.net
 * epel: mirror.lstn.net
 * extras: forksystems.mm.fcix.net
```

```
 * updates: ix-denver.mm.fcix.net
Resolving Dependencies
--> Running transaction check
---> Package libyaml.x86_64 0:0.1.4-11.el7_0 will be installed
---> Package libyaml-devel.x86_64 0:0.1.4-11.el7_0 will be
installed
--> Finished Dependency Resolution
```

...output truncated for better visibility

```
Installed:
libyaml.x86_64 0:0.1.4-11.el7_0  libyaml-devel.x86_64
0:0.1.4-11.el7_0
```

```
Complete!
```
**[root@mysql-a mysql_binaries]# rpm -ivh mysql-shell-8.0.34-1.el7.
x86_64.rpm**
```
warning: mysql-shell-8.0.34-1.el7.x86_64.rpm: Header V4 RSA/SHA256
Signature, key ID 3a79bd29: NOKEY
Preparing...              ######################## [100%]
Updating / installing...
   1:mysql-shell-8.0.34-1.el7  ######################## [100%]
```
[root@mysql-a mysql_binaries]# rpm -qa |grep mysql-shell
```
mysql-shell-8.0.34-1.el7.x86_64
```

Repeat the same on the remaining servers participating in the clustersset.

4. Download **MySQL Router (MySQL Proxy)** [Patch *35611280* from Oracle Support] and transfer the file using WinSCP to mysql-a. We will be setting up our MySQL Router on mysql-a.

[root@mysql-a mysql_binaries]# sudo yum install libyaml*
```
Loaded plugins: fastestmirror
Loading mirror speeds from cached hostfile
 * base: mirror.dal.nexril.net
 * epel: mirror.lstn.net
 * extras: forksystems.mm.fcix.net
```

```
    * updates: ix-denver.mm.fcix.net
Resolving Dependencies
--> Running transaction check
---> Package libyaml.x86_64 0:0.1.4-11.el7_0 will be installed
---> Package libyaml-devel.x86_64 0:0.1.4-11.el7_0 will be
installed
--> Finished Dependency Resolution
```

...output truncated for better visibility

```
Installed:
libyaml.x86_64 0:0.1.4-11.el7_0  libyaml-devel.x86_64
0:0.1.4-11.el7_0

Complete!
```
[root@mysql-a mysql_binaries]# rpm -ivh mysql-shell-8.0.34-1.el7.
x86_64.rpm
```
warning: mysql-shell-8.0.34-1.el7.x86_64.rpm: Header V4 RSA/SHA256
Signature, key ID 3a79bd29: NOKEY
Preparing...                ######################### [100%]
Updating / installing...
   1:mysql-shell-8.0.34-1.el7  ######################### [100%]
[root@mysql-a mysql_binaries]#
```
[root@mysql-a mysql_binaries]# rpm -qa |grep mysql-shell
mysql-shell-8.0.34-1.el7.x86_64

5. Unzip MySQL Router and install on the server dedicated to run
   MySQL Router (MySQL Proxy).

[root@mysql-a mysql_binaries]# unzip p35611280_800_
Linux-x86-64.zip
```
Archive:  p35611280_800_Linux-x86-64.zip
 extracting: mysql-router-commercial-8.0.34-1.1.el7.x86_64.rpm
 extracting: README.txt
```
[root@mysql-a mysql_binaries]# ls -ltr
```
total 2080268
```

```
-rw-r--r-- 1 7155 31415    16755300 Jun 24 22:06 mysql-community-
client-8.0.34-1.el7.x86_64.rpm
-rw-r--r-- 1 7155 31415     3745824 Jun 24 22:06 mysql-community-
client-plugins-8.0.34-1.el7.x86_64.rpm
-rw-r--r-- 1 7155 31415      681724 Jun 24 22:06 mysql-community-
common-8.0.34-1.el7.x86_64.rpm
-rw-r--r-- 1 7155 31415   528347988 Jun 24 22:07 mysql-community-
debuginfo-8.0.34-1.el7.x86_64.rpm
-rw-r--r-- 1 7155 31415     1947800 Jun 24 22:07 mysql-community-
devel-8.0.34-1.el7.x86_64.rpm
-rw-r--r-- 1 7155 31415     4217912 Jun 24 22:07 mysql-community-
embedded-compat-8.0.34-1.el7.x86_64.rpm
-rw-r--r-- 1 7155 31415     2344364 Jun 24 22:07 mysql-community-
icu-data-files-8.0.34-1.el7.x86_64.rpm
-rw-r--r-- 1 7155 31415     1563264 Jun 24 22:07 mysql-community-
libs-8.0.34-1.el7.x86_64.rpm
-rw-r--r-- 1 7155 31415      685312 Jun 24 22:08 mysql-community-
libs-compat-8.0.34-1.el7.x86_64.rpm
-rw-r--r-- 1 7155 31415    67410132 Jun 24 22:08 mysql-community-
server-8.0.34-1.el7.x86_64.rpm
-rw-r--r-- 1 7155 31415    25637968 Jun 24 22:08 mysql-community-
server-debug-8.0.34-1.el7.x86_64.rpm
-rw-r--r-- 1 7155 31415   378442676 Jun 24 22:10 mysql-community-
test-8.0.34-1.el7.x86_64.rpm
-rw-r--r-- 1 root root     13137016 Jun 25 05:11 mysql-router-
commercial-8.0.34-1.1.el7.x86_64.rpm
-rw-r--r-- 1 root root         2589 Jul 16 01:25 README.txt
-rw-r--r-- 1 root root   1031792640 Sep 11 18:14 mysql-8.0.34-1.
el7.x86_64.rpm-bundle.tar
-rw-r--r-- 1 root root     40307744 Sep 30 12:12 mysql-
shell-8.0.34-1.el7.x86_64.rpm
-rw-r--r-- 1 root root     13139897 Sep 30 12:49 p35611280_800_
Linux-x86-64.zip
[root@mysql-a mysql_binaries]#
```

```
[root@mysql-a mysql_binaries]# rpm -ivh mysql-router-
commercial-8.0.34-1.1.el7.x86_64.rpm
warning: mysql-router-commercial-8.0.34-1.1.el7.x86_64.rpm: Header
V4 RSA/SHA256 Signature, key ID 3a79bd29: NOKEY
Preparing...                ######################### [100%]
Updating / installing...
   1:mysql-router-
commercial-8.0.34-1.######################## [100%]
```

6. Add additional logging settings to the MySQL configuration file to
    help with troubleshooting. Add parameters **log_error_verbosity**
    and **loose-group-replication-communication-debug-options**
    on all servers within the clusterset configuration, mysql-a,
    mysql-b, mysql-c, mysql-d, mysql-e, mysql-f.

```
[root@mysql-a ~]# cat /etc/my.cnf
[mysqld]
datadir=/mysqlbkup
socket=/mysqlbkup/mysql.sock
log-error=/var/log/mysqld.log
pid-file=/var/run/mysqld/mysqld.pid
[root@mysql-a ~]#

[root@mysql-a ~]# systemctl status mysqld
[root@mysql-a ~]# systemctl stop mysqld
[root@mysql-a ~]# vi /etc/my.cnf
[root@mysql-a ~]# systemctl start mysqld
[root@mysql-a ~]# cat /etc/my.cnf
[mysqld]
datadir=/var/lib/mysql
socket=/var/lib/mysql/mysql.sock
log-error=/var/log/mysqld.log
log_error_verbosity = 3
loose-group-replication-communication-debug-options = GCS_
DEBUG_ALL
pid-file=/var/run/mysqld/mysqld.pid
```

Repeat the same on remaining servers in the clusterset.

281

7. Unzip MySQL Router and install on the PRIMARY server (mysql-a).

```
[root@mysql-a ~]# rpm -qa |grep mysql-router
[root@mysql-a ~]# cd mysql_binaries/
[root@mysql-a mysql_binaries]# rpm -ivh mysql-router-
commercial-8.0.34-1.1.el7.x86_64.rpm
warning: mysql-router-commercial-8.0.34-1.1.el7.x86_64.rpm: Header
V4 RSA/SHA256 Signature, key ID 3a79bd29: NOKEY
Preparing...                ######################### [100%]
Updating / installing...
   1:mysql-router-commerci
al-8.0.34-1.####################### [100%]
[root@mysql-a mysql_binaries]#
```

```
[root@mysql-a mysql_binaries]# rpm -qa |grep mysql-router
```

```
mysql-router-commercial-8.0.34-1.1.el7.x86_64
```

8. Add MySQL Group Replication configuration settings on all three
    servers participating in the InnoDB cluster, mysql-a, mysql-b,
    mysql-c, mysql-d, mysql-e, mysql-f.

```
[root@mysql-a ~]# cat /etc/my.cnf
[mysqld]
datadir=/mysqlbkup
socket=/mysqlbkup/mysql.sock
log-error=/var/log/mysqld.log
log_error_verbosity = 3
loose-group-replication-communication-debug-options = GCS_
DEBUG_ALL
pid-file=/var/run/mysqld/mysqld.pid
[root@mysql-a ~]#
```

```
[root@mysql-a ~]# vi /etc/my.cnf
[root@mysql-a ~]# systemctl stop mysqld
[root@mysql-a ~]# systemctl start mysqld
[root@mysql-a mysql_binaries]# cat /etc/my.cnf
[mysqld]
datadir=/var/lib/mysql
```

```
socket=/var/lib/mysql/mysql.sock
#MySQL Group Replication parameters
disabled_storage_engines="MyISAM,BLACKHOLE,FEDERATED,ARCHI
VE,MEMORY"
server_id=1
gtid_mode=ON
enforce_gtid_consistency=ON
binlog_transaction_dependency_tracking=WRITESET
slave_preserve_commit_order=ON
slave_parallel_type=LOGICAL_CLOCK
transaction_write_set_extraction=XXHASH64
log-error=/var/log/mysqld.log
log_error_verbosity = 3
loose-group-replication-communication-debug-options = GCS_
DEBUG_ALL
pid-file=/var/run/mysqld/mysqld.pid
```

Repeat the same on the remaining servers within the cluster. Please note a different **server_id** has to be assigned for each one of the servers, mysql-a=1; mysql-b=2; mysql-c=3; mysql-d=4; mysql-e=5; mysql-f=6.

9. Update **/etc/hosts** to map all hosts with their identifiers on all servers in the clusterset.

[root@mysql-a ~]# vi /etc/hosts
[root@mysql-a ~]# cat /etc/hosts
```
127.0.0.1    localhost localhost.localdomain localhost4 localhost4.
localdomain4
::1          localhost localhost.localdomain localhost6 localhost6.
localdomain6
192.168.2.15 mysql-a mysql-a
192.168.2.20 mysql-b mysql-b
192.168.2.25 mysql-c mysql-c
192.168.2.30 mysql-d mysql-d
192.168.2.35 mysql-e mysql-e
192.168.2.40 mysql-f mysql-f
```

10. Start MySQL Shell connecting to NODE 1 (mysql-a) in the primary
     cluster.

```
[root@mysql-a ~]# mysqlsh -u root -p
Please provide the password for 'root@localhost': *************
Save password for 'root@localhost'? [Y]es/[N]o/Ne[v]er
(default No): Y
MySQL Shell 8.0.34
Creating a session to 'root@localhost'
MySQL  localhost:33060+ ssl  JS >
```

11. For each instance (mysql-a/mysql-b/mysql-c), verify it
     is configured correctly for InnoDB cluster using the **dba.
     checkInstanceConfiguration()** method. As part of this step,
     you will be asked to set up an admin account for InnoDB cluster.
     Name it as **mysqlclusteradmin**.

```
[root@mysql-a ~]# which mysqlsh
/usr/bin/mysqlsh
[root@mysql-a ~]# mysqlsh -u root -p
Please provide the password for 'root@localhost': *************
Save password for 'root@localhost'? [Y]es/[N]o/Ne[v]er
(default No): Y
MySQL Shell 8.0.34
Creating a session to 'root@localhost'
 MySQL  localhost:33060+ ssl  JS >
 MySQL  localhost:33060+ ssl  JS > dba.configureInstance("root@
localhost:3306")
Please provide the password for 'root@localhost:3306': *************
Save password for 'root@localhost:3306'? [Y]es/[N]o/Ne[v]er
(default No): Y
Configuring local MySQL instance listening at port 3306 for use in
an InnoDB cluster...

This instance reports its own address as mysql-a:3306
Clients and other cluster members will communicate with it through
this address by default. If this is not correct, the report_host
MySQL system variable should be changed.
```

ERROR: User 'root' can only connect from 'localhost'. New account(s) with proper source address specification to allow remote connection from all instances must be created to manage the cluster.

1) Create remotely usable account for 'root' with same grants and password
2) Create a new admin account for InnoDB cluster with minimal required grants
3) Ignore and continue
4) Cancel

Please select an option [1]: 2
Please provide an account name (e.g: icroot@%) to have it created with the necessary
privileges or leave empty and press Enter to cancel.
Account Name: mysqlclusteradmin
Password for new account: *************
Confirm password: ***********

applierWorkerThreads will be set to the default value of 4.

NOTE: Some configuration options need to be fixed:
+--+----------------+
----------------+
| Variable | Current Value |
 Required Value | Note |
+--+----------------+
----------------+
| binlog_transaction_dependency_tracking | COMMIT_ORDER |
 WRITESET | Update the server variable |
+--+----------------+
----------------+
Do you want to perform the required configuration changes?
[y/n]: y

Creating user mysqlclusteradmin@%.
Account mysqlclusteradmin@% was successfully created.

Configuring instance...
The instance 'mysql-a:3306' was configured to be used in an InnoDB cluster.

Repeat the same steps on all the servers in the cluster.

12. Ensure MySQL Group Replication prerequisites are met and set up a test bed accordingly. In this case, created databases (db1, db2, db3, db4), tables (dbuser1, dbuser2, dbuser3, dbuser4) with a primary key, and three users (dbuser01, dbuser02, dbuser03) in each database.

```
[root@mysql-a ~]# su - mysql
Last login: Mon Aug  7 22:10:43 CDT 2023 on pts/0
-bash-4.2$
-bash-4.2$ mysql -u root -p
Enter password:

mysql> show databases;
+--------------------+
| Database           |
+--------------------+
| db1                |
| db2                |
| db3                |
| db4                |
| information_schema |
| mysql              |
| performance_schema |
| sys                |
+--------------------+
8 rows in set (0.00 sec)

mysql> use db1;
Reading table information for completion of table and column names
You can turn off this feature to get a quicker startup with -A

Database changed
mysql> CREATE TABLE dbusers1(
```

```
    -> user_id INT AUTO_INCREMENT PRIMARY KEY,
    -> username VARCHAR(40)
    -> );
Query OK, 0 rows affected (0.01 sec)

mysql> insert into dbusers1 values (1, 'dbuser01');
Query OK, 1 row affected (0.00 sec)

mysql> insert into dbusers1 values (2, 'dbuser02');
Query OK, 1 row affected (0.00 sec)

mysql> insert into dbusers1 values (3, 'dbuser03');
Query OK, 1 row affected (0.00 sec)

mysql> CREATE TABLE dbusers2(
    -> user_id INT AUTO_INCREMENT PRIMARY KEY,
    -> username VARCHAR(40)
    -> );
Query OK, 0 rows affected (0.01 sec)

mysql> insert into dbusers2 values (1, 'dbuser01');
Query OK, 1 row affected (0.00 sec)

mysql> insert into dbusers2 values (2, 'dbuser02');
Query OK, 1 row affected (0.00 sec)

mysql> insert into dbusers2 values (3, 'dbuser03');
Query OK, 1 row affected (0.00 sec)

mysql> CREATE TABLE dbusers3(
    -> user_id INT AUTO_INCREMENT PRIMARY KEY,
    -> username VARCHAR(40)
    -> );
Query OK, 0 rows affected (0.00 sec)

mysql> insert into dbusers3 values (1, 'dbuser01');
Query OK, 1 row affected (0.01 sec)

mysql> insert into dbusers3 values (2, 'dbuser02');
Query OK, 1 row affected (0.00 sec)
```

```
mysql> insert into dbusers3 values (3, 'dbuser03');
Query OK, 1 row affected (0.00 sec)

mysql> CREATE TABLE dbusers4(
    -> user_id INT AUTO_INCREMENT PRIMARY KEY,
    -> username VARCHAR(40)
    -> );
Query OK, 0 rows affected (0.01 sec)

mysql> insert into dbusers4 values (1, 'dbuser01');
Query OK, 1 row affected (0.00 sec)

mysql> insert into dbusers4 values (2, 'dbuser02');
Query OK, 1 row affected (0.00 sec)

mysql> insert into dbusers4 values (3, 'dbuser03');
Query OK, 1 row affected (0.01 sec)

mysql> show tables;
+---------------+
| Tables_in_db1 |
+---------------+
| dbusers1      |
| dbusers2      |
| dbusers3      |
| dbusers4      |
| tab1          |
+---------------+
5 rows in set (0.00 sec)

mysql> show tables;
+---------------+
| Tables_in_db1 |
+---------------+
| dbusers1      |
| dbusers2      |
| dbusers3      |
| dbusers4      |
+---------------+
```

4 rows in set (0.00 sec)

mysql> use db2;
Reading table information for completion of table and column names
You can turn off this feature to get a quicker startup with -A

Database changed
mysql> CREATE TABLE dbusers1(
 -> user_id INT AUTO_INCREMENT PRIMARY KEY,
 -> username VARCHAR(40)
 ->);
Query OK, 0 rows affected (0.01 sec)

mysql> insert into dbusers1 values (1, 'dbuser01');
Query OK, 1 row affected (0.00 sec)

mysql> insert into dbusers1 values (2, 'dbuser02');
Query OK, 1 row affected (0.00 sec)

mysql> insert into dbusers1 values (3, 'dbuser03');
Query OK, 1 row affected (0.00 sec)

mysql> CREATE TABLE dbusers2(
 -> user_id INT AUTO_INCREMENT PRIMARY KEY,
 -> username VARCHAR(40)
 ->);
Query OK, 0 rows affected (0.00 sec)

mysql> insert into dbusers2 values (1, 'dbuser01');
Query OK, 1 row affected (0.00 sec)

mysql> insert into dbusers2 values (2, 'dbuser02');
Query OK, 1 row affected (0.01 sec)

mysql> insert into dbusers2 values (3, 'dbuser03');
Query OK, 1 row affected (0.00 sec)

mysql> CREATE TABLE dbusers3(
 -> user_id INT AUTO_INCREMENT PRIMARY KEY,
 -> username VARCHAR(40)

```
    -> );
Query OK, 0 rows affected (0.01 sec)

mysql> insert into dbusers3 values (1, 'dbuser01');
Query OK, 1 row affected (0.00 sec)

mysql> insert into dbusers3 values (2, 'dbuser02');
Query OK, 1 row affected (0.00 sec)

mysql> insert into dbusers3 values (3, 'dbuser03');
Query OK, 1 row affected (0.00 sec)

mysql> CREATE TABLE dbusers4(
    -> user_id INT AUTO_INCREMENT PRIMARY KEY,
    -> username VARCHAR(40)
    -> );
Query OK, 0 rows affected (0.01 sec)

mysql> insert into dbusers4 values (1, 'dbuser01');
Query OK, 1 row affected (0.00 sec)

mysql> insert into dbusers4 values (2, 'dbuser02');
Query OK, 1 row affected (0.00 sec)

mysql> insert into dbusers4 values (3, 'dbuser03');
Query OK, 1 row affected (0.00 sec)

mysql> show tables;
+---------------+
| Tables_in_db2 |
+---------------+
| dbusers1      |
| dbusers2      |
| dbusers3      |
| dbusers4      |
| tab2          |
+---------------+
5 rows in set (0.00 sec)

mysql> use db3;
```

Reading table information for completion of table and column names
You can turn off this feature to get a quicker startup with -A

Database changed

```
mysql> CREATE TABLE dbusers1(
    -> user_id INT AUTO_INCREMENT PRIMARY KEY,
    -> username VARCHAR(40)
    -> );
Query OK, 0 rows affected (0.01 sec)

mysql> insert into dbusers1 values (1, 'dbuser01');
Query OK, 1 row affected (0.00 sec)

mysql> insert into dbusers1 values (2, 'dbuser02');
Query OK, 1 row affected (0.00 sec)

mysql> insert into dbusers1 values (3, 'dbuser03');
Query OK, 1 row affected (0.01 sec)

mysql> CREATE TABLE dbusers2(
    -> user_id INT AUTO_INCREMENT PRIMARY KEY,
    -> username VARCHAR(40)
    -> );
Query OK, 0 rows affected (0.00 sec)

mysql> insert into dbusers2 values (1, 'dbuser01');
Query OK, 1 row affected (0.01 sec)

mysql> insert into dbusers2 values (2, 'dbuser02');
Query OK, 1 row affected (0.00 sec)

mysql> insert into dbusers2 values (3, 'dbuser03');
Query OK, 1 row affected (0.00 sec)

mysql> CREATE TABLE dbusers3(
    -> user_id INT AUTO_INCREMENT PRIMARY KEY,
    -> username VARCHAR(40)
    -> );
Query OK, 0 rows affected (0.01 sec)
```

```
mysql> insert into dbusers3 values (1, 'dbuser01');
Query OK, 1 row affected (0.00 sec)

mysql> insert into dbusers3 values (2, 'dbuser02');
Query OK, 1 row affected (0.00 sec)

mysql> insert into dbusers3 values (3, 'dbuser03');
Query OK, 1 row affected (0.00 sec)

mysql> CREATE TABLE dbusers4(
    -> user_id INT AUTO_INCREMENT PRIMARY KEY,
    -> username VARCHAR(40)
    -> );
Query OK, 0 rows affected (0.01 sec)

mysql> insert into dbusers4 values (1, 'dbuser01');
Query OK, 1 row affected (0.01 sec)

mysql> insert into dbusers4 values (2, 'dbuser02');
Query OK, 1 row affected (0.00 sec)

mysql> insert into dbusers4 values (3, 'dbuser03');
Query OK, 1 row affected (0.00 sec)

mysql> show tables;
+----------------+
| Tables_in_db3  |
+----------------+
| dbusers1       |
| dbusers2       |
| dbusers3       |
| dbusers4       |
| tab3           |
+----------------+
5 rows in set (0.00 sec)

mysql> use db4;
Reading table information for completion of table and column names
You can turn off this feature to get a quicker startup with -A
```

Database changed
mysql>

```
mysql> CREATE TABLE dbusers1(
    -> user_id INT AUTO_INCREMENT PRIMARY KEY,
    -> username VARCHAR(40)
    -> );
```
Query OK, 0 rows affected (0.01 sec)

```
mysql> insert into dbusers1 values (1, 'dbuser01');
```
Query OK, 1 row affected (0.01 sec)

```
mysql> insert into dbusers1 values (2, 'dbuser02');
```
Query OK, 1 row affected (0.00 sec)

```
mysql> insert into dbusers1 values (3, 'dbuser03');
```
Query OK, 1 row affected (0.00 sec)

```
mysql> CREATE TABLE dbusers2(
    -> user_id INT AUTO_INCREMENT PRIMARY KEY,
    -> username VARCHAR(40)
    -> );
```
Query OK, 0 rows affected (0.01 sec)

```
mysql> insert into dbusers2 values (1, 'dbuser01');
```
Query OK, 1 row affected (0.00 sec)

```
mysql> insert into dbusers2 values (2, 'dbuser02');
```
Query OK, 1 row affected (0.01 sec)

```
mysql> insert into dbusers2 values (3, 'dbuser03');
```
Query OK, 1 row affected (0.00 sec)

```
mysql> CREATE TABLE dbusers3(
    -> user_id INT AUTO_INCREMENT PRIMARY KEY,
    -> username VARCHAR(40)
    -> );
```
Query OK, 0 rows affected (0.01 sec)

```
mysql> insert into dbusers3 values (1, 'dbuser01');
```
Query OK, 1 row affected (0.00 sec)

```
mysql> insert into dbusers3 values (2, 'dbuser02');
Query OK, 1 row affected (0.00 sec)

mysql> insert into dbusers3 values (3, 'dbuser03');
Query OK, 1 row affected (0.00 sec)

mysql> CREATE TABLE dbusers4(
    -> user_id INT AUTO_INCREMENT PRIMARY KEY,
    -> username VARCHAR(40)
    -> );
Query OK, 0 rows affected (0.01 sec)

mysql> insert into dbusers4 values (1, 'dbuser01');
Query OK, 1 row affected (0.01 sec)

mysql> insert into dbusers4 values (2, 'dbuser02');
Query OK, 1 row affected (0.00 sec)

mysql> insert into dbusers4 values (3, 'dbuser03');
Query OK, 1 row affected (0.00 sec)

mysql> show tables;
+---------------+
| Tables_in_db4 |
+---------------+
| dbusers1      |
| dbusers2      |
| dbusers3      |
| dbusers4      |
| tab1          |
+---------------+
5 rows in set (0.00 sec)
```

Repeat the same on the rest of the servers in the clusterset.

13. Check instance configuration for each server using **dba.
checkInstanceConfiguration()**.

```
[root@mysql-a ~]# mysqlsh -u root -p
MySQL Shell 8.0.34
```

```
MySQL  localhost:33060+ ssl  JS > dba.checkInstanceConfiguration('
mysqlclusteradmin@localhost:3306')
```

Please provide the password for 'mysqlclusteradmin@
localhost:3306': *************

Save password for 'mysqlclusteradmin@localhost:3306'? [Y]es/[N]o/
Ne[v]er (default No): Y

Validating local MySQL instance listening at port 3306 for use in
an InnoDB cluster...

This instance reports its own address as mysql-a:3306
Clients and other cluster members will communicate with it through
this address by default. If this is not correct, the report_host
MySQL system variable should be changed.

Checking whether existing tables comply with Group Replication
requirements...
No incompatible tables detected

Checking instance configuration...
Instance configuration is compatible with InnoDB cluster

The instance 'mysql-a:3306' is valid to be used in an InnoDB
cluster.

```
{
    "status": "ok"
}
 MySQL  localhost:33060+ ssl  JS >
```

Repeat the same for all servers in the clusterset.

14. Log in as **mysqlclusteradmin** on the *primary* node (mysql-a) to
    create an InnoDB cluster named "**myPrimaryCluster**" using **dba.
    createCluster()**.

[root@mysql-a ~]# mysqlsh -u mysqlclusteradmin -p

Please provide the password for 'mysqlclusteradmin@localhost':
****

Save password for 'mysqlclusteradmin@localhost'? [Y]es/[N]o/
Ne[v]er (default No): Y

```
MySQL Shell 8.0.34
 MySQL  localhost:33060+ ssl  JS >
 MySQL  localhost:33060+ ssl  JS > dba.createCluster("myPrimary
Cluster");
A new InnoDB Cluster will be created on instance 'mysql-a:3306'.

Validating instance configuration at localhost:3306...

This instance reports its own address as mysql-a:3306

Instance configuration is suitable.
NOTE: Group Replication will communicate with other members using
'mysql-a:3306'. Use the localAddress option to override.

* Checking connectivity and SSL configuration...

Creating InnoDB Cluster 'myPrimaryCluster' on 'mysql-a:3306'...

Adding Seed Instance...
Cluster successfully created. Use Cluster.addInstance() to add
MySQL instances.
At least 3 instances are needed for the cluster to be able to
withstand up to one server failure.

<Cluster:myPrimaryCluster>
```

15. Create a variable "**cluster**" to work with the InnoDB cluster. In
    future, if we need to start mysqlsh session again, we can get the
    cluster instance option and also check cluster status using **cluster.
    status()**.

```
MySQL  localhost:33060+ ssl  JS > var cluster=dba.getCluster()
MySQL  localhost:33060+ ssl  JS > cluster.status()
{
    "clusterName": "myPrimaryCluster",
    "defaultReplicaSet": {
        "name": "default",
        "primary": "mysql-a:3306",
        "ssl": "REQUIRED",
        "status": "OK_NO_TOLERANCE",
```

```
      "statusText": "Cluster is NOT tolerant to any failures.",
      "topology": {
          "mysql-a:3306": {
              "address": "mysql-a:3306",
              "memberRole": "PRIMARY",
              "mode": "R/W",
              "readReplicas": {},
              "replicationLag": "applier_queue_applied",
              "role": "HA",
              "status": "ONLINE",
              "version": "8.0.34"
          }
      },
      "topologyMode": "Single-Primary"
  },
  "groupInformationSourceMember": "mysql-a:3306"
}
```

16. Add the other *two* instances (mysql-b/mysql-c) to the cluster
     using the cluster.addInstance() method and using the preferred
     recovery method. In this case, we use "clone". Run all the
     commands from the primary node, mysql-a.

>>>>>>>>>> Adding mysql-b to the cluster <<<<<<<<<<

MySQL localhost:33060+ ssl JS > **cluster.
addInstance('mysqlclusteradmin@mysql-b:3306')**

```
WARNING: A GTID set check of the MySQL instance at 'mysql-b:3306'
determined that it contains transactions that do not originate
from the cluster, which must be discarded before it can join the
cluster.

mysql-b:3306 has the following errant GTIDs that do not exist in
the cluster:
aaa6ecea-5fc2-11ee-bb4b-080027cf69cc:1-68
```

WARNING: Discarding these extra GTID events can either be done manually or by completely overwriting the state of mysql-b:3306 with a physical snapshot from an existing cluster member. To use this method by default, set the 'recoveryMethod' option to 'clone'.

Having extra GTID events is not expected, and it is recommended to investigate this further and ensure that the data can be removed prior to choosing the clone recovery method.

Please select a recovery method [C]lone/[A]bort (default Abort): C
Validating instance configuration at mysql-b:3306...

This instance reports its own address as mysql-b:3306

Instance configuration is suitable.
NOTE: Group Replication will communicate with other members using 'mysql-b:3306'. Use the localAddress option to override.

* Checking connectivity and SSL configuration...
A new instance will be added to the InnoDB Cluster. Depending on the amount of data on the cluster this might take from a few seconds to several hours.

Adding instance to the cluster...

Monitoring recovery process of the new cluster member. Press ^C to stop monitoring and let it continue in background.
Clone based state recovery is now in progress.

NOTE: A server restart is expected to happen as part of the clone process. If the server does not support the RESTART command or does not come back after a while, you may need to manually start it back.

* Waiting for clone to finish...
NOTE: mysql-b:3306 is being cloned from mysql-a:3306
** Stage DROP DATA: Completed
** Clone Transfer

```
FILE COPY   ################################  100%  Completed
PAGE COPY   ################################  100%  Completed
REDO COPY   ################################  100%  Completed
```

NOTE: mysql-b:3306 is shutting down...

* Waiting for server restart... ready
* mysql-b:3306 has restarted, waiting for clone to finish...
** Stage RESTART: Completed
* Clone process has finished: 75.50 MB transferred in about 1 second (~75.50 MB/s)

State recovery already finished for 'mysql-b:3306'

The instance 'mysql-b:3306' was successfully added to the cluster.

```
MySQL  localhost:33060+ ssl  JS > cluster.status();
{
    "clusterName": "myPrimaryCluster",
    "defaultReplicaSet": {
        "name": "default",
        "primary": "mysql-a:3306",
        "ssl": "REQUIRED",
        "status": "OK_NO_TOLERANCE",
        "statusText": "Cluster is NOT tolerant to any failures.",
        "topology": {
            "mysql-a:3306": {
                "address": "mysql-a:3306",
                "memberRole": "PRIMARY",
                "mode": "R/W",
                "readReplicas": {},
                "replicationLag": "applier_queue_applied",
                "role": "HA",
                "status": "ONLINE",
                "version": "8.0.34"
            },
            "mysql-b:3306": {
                "address": "mysql-b:3306",
```

```
                    "memberRole": "SECONDARY",
                    "mode": "R/O",
                    "readReplicas": {},
                    "replicationLag": "applier_queue_applied",
                    "role": "HA",
                    "status": "ONLINE",
                    "version": "8.0.34"
                }
            },
            "topologyMode": "Single-Primary"
        },
        "groupInformationSourceMember": "mysql-a:3306"
}
```

<<<<<<<<<<<<<<<<<<<<<<< Adding mysql-c >>>>>>>>>>>>>>>>>>>>>>>

**MySQL localhost:33060+ ssl JS > cluster.
addInstance('mysqlclusteradmin@mysql-c:3306',{recoveryMethod:'clo
ne'});**

WARNING: A GTID set check of the MySQL instance at 'mysql-c:3306'
determined that it contains transactions that do not originate
from the cluster, which must be discarded before it can join the
cluster.

mysql-c:3306 has the following errant GTIDs that do not exist in
the cluster:
f27350da-5fc2-11ee-baf0-080027cf69cc:1-68

WARNING: Discarding these extra GTID events can either be done
manually or by completely overwriting the state of mysql-c:3306
with a physical snapshot from an existing cluster member. To
use this method by default, set the 'recoveryMethod' option to
'clone'.

Having extra GTID events is not expected, and it is recommended to
investigate this further and ensure that the data can be removed
prior to choosing the clone recovery method.

Clone based recovery selected through the recoveryMethod option

Validating instance configuration at mysql-c:3306...

This instance reports its own address as mysql-c:3306

Instance configuration is suitable.
NOTE: Group Replication will communicate with other members using
'mysql-c:3306'. Use the localAddress option to override.

* Checking connectivity and SSL configuration...
A new instance will be added to the InnoDB Cluster. Depending
on the amount of data on the cluster this might take from a few
seconds to several hours.

Adding instance to the cluster...

Monitoring recovery process of the new cluster member. Press ^C to
stop monitoring and let it continue in background.
Clone based state recovery is now in progress.

NOTE: A server restart is expected to happen as part of the clone
process. If the server does not support the RESTART command or
does not come back after a while, you may need to manually start
it back.

* Waiting for clone to finish...
NOTE: mysql-c:3306 is being cloned from mysql-b:3306
** Stage DROP DATA: Completed
** Clone Transfer
    FILE COPY   ################################   100% Completed
    PAGE COPY   ################################   100% Completed
    REDO COPY   ################################   100% Completed

NOTE: mysql-c:3306 is shutting down...

* Waiting for server restart... ready
* mysql-c:3306 has restarted, waiting for clone to finish...
** Stage RESTART: Completed
* Clone process has finished: 75.49 MB transferred in about 1
second (~75.49 MB/s)

State recovery already finished for 'mysql-c:3306'

The instance 'mysql-c:3306' was successfully added to the cluster.

MySQL localhost:33060+ ssl JS > cluster.status()

```
{
    "clusterName": "myPrimaryCluster",
    "defaultReplicaSet": {
        "name": "default",
        "primary": "mysql-a:3306",
        "ssl": "REQUIRED",
        "status": "OK",
        "statusText": "Cluster is ONLINE and can tolerate up to
        ONE failure.",
        "topology": {
            "mysql-a:3306": {
                "address": "mysql-a:3306",
                "memberRole": "PRIMARY",
                "mode": "R/W",
                "readReplicas": {},
                "replicationLag": "applier_queue_applied",
                "role": "HA",
                "status": "ONLINE",
                "version": "8.0.34"
            },
            "mysql-b:3306": {
                "address": "mysql-b:3306",
                "memberRole": "SECONDARY",
                "mode": "R/O",
                "readReplicas": {},
                "replicationLag": "applier_queue_applied",
                "role": "HA",
                "status": "ONLINE",
                "version": "8.0.34"
            },
```

```
        "mysql-c:3306": {
            "address": "mysql-c:3306",
            "memberRole": "SECONDARY",
            "mode": "R/O",
            "readReplicas": {},
            "replicationLag": "applier_queue_applied",
            "role": "HA",
            "status": "ONLINE",
            "version": "8.0.34"
        }
    },
    "topologyMode": "Single-Primary"
    },
    "groupInformationSourceMember": "mysql-a:3306"
}
```

17. Create a clusterset named **"myClusterset"**.

**MySQL localhost:33060+ ssl JS > clusterset=cluster.createCluster
Set("myclusterset")**
A new ClusterSet will be created based on the Cluster
'myPrimaryCluster'.

* Validating Cluster 'myPrimaryCluster' for ClusterSet compliance.

* Creating InnoDB ClusterSet 'myclusterset' on
'myPrimaryCluster'...

* Updating metadata...

ClusterSet successfully created. Use ClusterSet.
createReplicaCluster() to add Replica Clusters to it.

<ClusterSet:myclusterset>

>>>> Check Cluster set status

```
 MySQL  localhost:33060+ ssl  JS > clusterset.status()
{
    "clusters": {
        "myPrimaryCluster": {
            "clusterRole": "PRIMARY",
            "globalStatus": "OK",
            "primary": "mysql-a:3306"
        }
    },
    "domainName": "myclusterset",
    "globalPrimaryInstance": "mysql-a:3306",
    "primaryCluster": "myPrimaryCluster",
    "status": "HEALTHY",
    "statusText": "All Clusters available."
}

 MySQL  localhost:33060+ ssl  JS > myclusterset=dba.
getClusterSet();
<ClusterSet:myclusterset>
 MySQL  localhost:33060+ ssl  JS > myclusterset.
status({extended:1})
{
    "clusters": {
        "myPrimaryCluster": {
            "clusterRole": "PRIMARY",
            "globalStatus": "OK",
            "primary": "mysql-a:3306",
            "status": "OK",
            "statusText": "Cluster is ONLINE and can tolerate up
            to ONE failure.",
            "topology": {
                "mysql-a:3306": {
                    "address": "mysql-a:3306",
                    "memberRole": "PRIMARY",
                    "mode": "R/W",
```

```
                    "status": "ONLINE",
                    "version": "8.0.34"
                },
                "mysql-b:3306": {
                    "address": "mysql-b:3306",
                    "memberRole": "SECONDARY",
                    "mode": "R/O",
                    "replicationLagFromImmediateSource": "",
                    "replicationLagFromOriginalSource": "",
                    "status": "ONLINE",
                    "version": "8.0.34"
                },
                "mysql-c:3306": {
                    "address": "mysql-c:3306",
                    "memberRole": "SECONDARY",
                    "mode": "R/O",
                    "replicationLagFromImmediateSource": "",
                    "replicationLagFromOriginalSource": "",
                    "status": "ONLINE",
                    "version": "8.0.34"
                }
            },
            "transactionSet": "861372a9-5fca-11ee-9711-08002
            7cf69cc:1-80,86138144-5fca-11ee-9711-080027cf6
            9cc:1-5,d763ea33-52ad-11ee-84a8-080027cf69cc:1-72"
        }
    },
    "domainName": "myclusterset",
    "globalPrimaryInstance": "mysql-a:3306",
    "metadataServer": "mysql-a:3306",
    "primaryCluster": "myPrimaryCluster",
    "status": "HEALTHY",
    "statusText": "All Clusters available."
}
```

18. Create the Replica cluster **"mydrcluster"** with **mysql-d** as the primary.

```
[root@mysql-a ~]# mysqlsh -u mysqlclusteradmin -p
MySQL Shell 8.0.34
MySQL  localhost:33060+ ssl  JS > mydrcluster=myclusterset.creat
eReplicaCluster("mysqlclusteradmin@mysql-d:3306", "mydrcluster",
{recoveryProgress:1, timeout:10})
Setting up replica 'mydrcluster' of cluster 'myPrimaryCluster' at
instance 'mysql-d:3306'.

A new InnoDB Cluster will be created on instance 'mysql-d:3306'.

Validating instance configuration at mysql-d:3306...

This instance reports its own address as mysql-d:3306

Instance configuration is suitable.
NOTE: Group Replication will communicate with other members using
'mysql-d:3306'. Use the localAddress option to override.

* Checking connectivity and SSL configuration...

* Checking transaction state of the instance...

WARNING: A GTID set check of the MySQL instance at 'mysql-d:3306'
determined that it contains transactions that do not originate
from the clusterset, which must be discarded before it can join
the clusterset.

mysql-d:3306 has the following errant GTIDs that do not exist in
the clusterset:
189570b3-5fc3-11ee-bb04-080027cf69cc:1-68

WARNING: Discarding these extra GTID events can either be done
manually or by completely overwriting the state of mysql-d:3306
with a physical snapshot from an existing clusterset member. To
use this method by default, set the 'recoveryMethod' option to
'clone'.
```

Having extra GTID events is not expected, and it is recommended to investigate this further and ensure that the data can be removed prior to choosing the clone recovery method.

Please select a recovery method [C]lone/[A]bort (default Abort): C
* Checking connectivity and SSL configuration to PRIMARY Cluster...

Waiting for clone process of the new member to complete. Press ^C to abort the operation.
* Waiting for clone to finish...
NOTE: mysql-d:3306 is being cloned from mysql-a:3306
** Stage DROP DATA: Completed
** Stage FILE COPY: Completed
** Stage PAGE COPY: Completed
** Stage REDO COPY: Completed
** Stage FILE SYNC: Completed
** Stage RESTART: Completed
* Clone process has finished: 75.49 MB transferred in about 1 second (~75.49 MB/s)

Creating InnoDB Cluster 'mydrcluster' on 'mysql-d:3306'...

Adding Seed Instance...
Cluster successfully created. Use Cluster.addInstance() to add MySQL instances.
At least 3 instances are needed for the cluster to be able to withstand up to
one server failure.

Cluster "memberAuthType" is set to 'PASSWORD' (inherited from the ClusterSet).
* Configuring ClusterSet managed replication channel...
** Changing replication source of mysql-d:3306 to mysql-a:3306

* Waiting for instance 'mysql-d:3306' to synchronize with PRIMARY Cluster...
** Transactions
replicated ################################### 100%

* Updating topology

* Waiting for the Cluster to synchronize with the PRIMARY
Cluster...
** Transactions
replicated ################################ 100%

Replica Cluster 'mydrcluster' successfully created on ClusterSet
'myclusterset'.

```
<Cluster:mydrcluster>
 MySQL  localhost:33060+ ssl  JS > myclusterset.status()
{
    "clusters": {
        "myPrimaryCluster": {
            "clusterRole": "PRIMARY",
            "globalStatus": "OK",
            "primary": "mysql-a:3306"
        },
        "mydrcluster": {
            "clusterRole": "REPLICA",
            "clusterSetReplicationStatus": "OK",
            "globalStatus": "OK"
        }
    },
    "domainName": "myclusterset",
    "globalPrimaryInstance": "mysql-a:3306",
    "primaryCluster": "myPrimaryCluster",
    "status": "HEALTHY",
    "statusText": "All Clusters available."
}
 MySQL  localhost:33060+ ssl  JS > myclusterset.
status({extended:1})
{
    "clusters": {
        "myPrimaryCluster": {
            "clusterRole": "PRIMARY",
```

```
"globalStatus": "OK",
"primary": "mysql-a:3306",
"status": "OK",
"statusText": "Cluster is ONLINE and can tolerate up
to ONE failure.",
"topology": {
    "mysql-a:3306": {
        "address": "mysql-a:3306",
        "memberRole": "PRIMARY",
        "mode": "R/W",
        "status": "ONLINE",
        "version": "8.0.34"
    },
    "mysql-b:3306": {
        "address": "mysql-b:3306",
        "memberRole": "SECONDARY",
        "mode": "R/O",
        "replicationLagFromImmediateSource": "",
        "replicationLagFromOriginalSource": "",
        "status": "ONLINE",
        "version": "8.0.34"
    },
    "mysql-c:3306": {
        "address": "mysql-c:3306",
        "memberRole": "SECONDARY",
        "mode": "R/O",
        "replicationLagFromImmediateSource": "",
        "replicationLagFromOriginalSource": "",
        "status": "ONLINE",
        "version": "8.0.34"
    }
},
"transactionSet": "861372a9-5fca-11ee-9711-08002
7cf69cc:1-98,86138144-5fca-11ee-9711-080027cf6
9cc:1-5,d763ea33-52ad-11ee-84a8-080027cf69cc:1-72"
```

```
        },
        "mydrcluster": {
            "clusterRole": "REPLICA",
            "clusterSetReplication": {
                "applierStatus": "APPLIED_ALL",
                "applierThreadState": "Waiting for an event from
                Coordinator",
                "applierWorkerThreads": 4,
                "receiver": "mysql-d:3306",
                "receiverStatus": "ON",
                "receiverThreadState": "Waiting for source to
                send event",
                "replicationSsl": null,
                "source": "mysql-a:3306"
            },
            "clusterSetReplicationStatus": "OK",
            "globalStatus": "OK",
            "status": "OK_NO_TOLERANCE",
            "statusText": "Cluster is NOT tolerant to any
            failures.",
            "topology": {
                "mysql-d:3306": {
                    "address": "mysql-d:3306",
                    "memberRole": "PRIMARY",
                    "mode": "R/O",
                    "replicationLagFromImmediateSource": "",
                    "replicationLagFromOriginalSource": "",
                    "status": "ONLINE",
                    "version": "8.0.34"
                }
            },
            "transactionSet": "3817f70d-5fd1-11ee-
            bb04-080027cf69cc:1,861372a9-5fca-11ee-9711-0800
            27cf69cc:1-98,86138144-5fca-11ee-9711-080027cf6
            9cc:1-5,d763ea33-52ad-11ee-84a8-080027cf69cc:1-72",
```

```
                "transactionSetConsistencyStatus": "OK",
                "transactionSetErrantGtidSet": "",
                "transactionSetMissingGtidSet": ""
            }
        },
        "domainName": "myclusterset",
        "globalPrimaryInstance": "mysql-a:3306",
        "metadataServer": "mysql-a:3306",
        "primaryCluster": "myPrimaryCluster",
        "status": "HEALTHY",
        "statusText": "All Clusters available."
    }
```

19. Add *mysql-e* to the Replica cluster **"mydrcluster"**.

[root@mysql-a ~]# mysqlsh -u mysqlclusteradmin -p
MySQL Shell 8.0.34
Creating a session to 'mysqlclusteradmin@localhost'
MySQL localhost:33060+ ssl JS > mydrcluster=myclusterset.creat
eReplicaCluster("mysqlclusteradmin@mysql-d:3306", "mydrcluster",
{recoveryProgress:1, timeout:10})
Setting up replica 'mydrcluster' of cluster 'myPrimaryCluster' at
instance 'mysql-d:3306'.

A new InnoDB Cluster will be created on instance 'mysql-d:3306'.

Validating instance configuration at mysql-d:3306...

This instance reports its own address as mysql-d:3306

Instance configuration is suitable.
NOTE: Group Replication will communicate with other members using
'mysql-d:3306'. Use the localAddress option to override.

* Checking connectivity and SSL configuration...

* Checking transaction state of the instance...

WARNING: A GTID set check of the MySQL instance at 'mysql-d:3306' determined that it contains transactions that do not originate from the clusterset, which must be discarded before it can join the clusterset.

mysql-d:3306 has the following errant GTIDs that do not exist in the clusterset:
189570b3-5fc3-11ee-bb04-080027cf69cc:1-68

WARNING: Discarding these extra GTID events can either be done manually or by completely overwriting the state of mysql-d:3306 with a physical snapshot from an existing clusterset member. To use this method by default, set the 'recoveryMethod' option to 'clone'.

Having extra GTID events is not expected, and it is recommended to investigate this further and ensure that the data can be removed prior to choosing the clone recovery method.

Please select a recovery method [C]lone/[A]bort (default Abort): C
* Checking connectivity and SSL configuration to PRIMARY Cluster...

Waiting for clone process of the new member to complete. Press ^C to abort the operation.
* Waiting for clone to finish...
NOTE: mysql-d:3306 is being cloned from mysql-a:3306
** Stage DROP DATA: Completed
** Stage FILE COPY: Completed
** Stage PAGE COPY: Completed
** Stage REDO COPY: Completed
** Stage FILE SYNC: Completed
** Stage RESTART: Completed
* Clone process has finished: 75.49 MB transferred in about 1 second (~75.49 MB/s)

Creating InnoDB Cluster 'mydrcluster' on 'mysql-d:3306'...

Adding Seed Instance...

```
Cluster successfully created. Use Cluster.addInstance() to add
MySQL instances.
At least 3 instances are needed for the cluster to be able to
withstand up to
one server failure.

Cluster "memberAuthType" is set to 'PASSWORD' (inherited from the
ClusterSet).
* Configuring ClusterSet managed replication channel...
** Changing replication source of mysql-d:3306 to mysql-a:3306

* Waiting for instance 'mysql-d:3306' to synchronize with PRIMARY
Cluster...
** Transactions
replicated  ################################  100%

* Updating topology

* Waiting for the Cluster to synchronize with the PRIMARY
Cluster...
** Transactions
replicated  ################################  100%

Replica Cluster 'mydrcluster' successfully created on ClusterSet
'myclusterset'.

<Cluster:mydrcluster>
 MySQL  localhost:33060+ ssl  JS >
 MySQL  localhost:33060+ ssl  JS > myclusterset.status()
{
    "clusters": {
        "myPrimaryCluster": {
            "clusterRole": "PRIMARY",
            "globalStatus": "OK",
            "primary": "mysql-a:3306"
        },
        "mydrcluster": {
            "clusterRole": "REPLICA",
            "clusterSetReplicationStatus": "OK",
```

```
                    "globalStatus": "OK"
            }
        },
        "domainName": "myclusterset",
        "globalPrimaryInstance": "mysql-a:3306",
        "primaryCluster": "myPrimaryCluster",
        "status": "HEALTHY",
        "statusText": "All Clusters available."
    }
 MySQL  localhost:33060+ ssl  JS > myclusterset.
status({extended:1})
    {
        "clusters": {
            "myPrimaryCluster": {
                "clusterRole": "PRIMARY",
                "globalStatus": "OK",
                "primary": "mysql-a:3306",
                "status": "OK",
                "statusText": "Cluster is ONLINE and can tolerate up
                to ONE failure.",
                "topology": {
                    "mysql-a:3306": {
                        "address": "mysql-a:3306",
                        "memberRole": "PRIMARY",
                        "mode": "R/W",
                        "status": "ONLINE",
                        "version": "8.0.34"
                    },
                    "mysql-b:3306": {
                        "address": "mysql-b:3306",
                        "memberRole": "SECONDARY",
                        "mode": "R/O",
                        "replicationLagFromImmediateSource": "",
                        "replicationLagFromOriginalSource": "",
                        "status": "ONLINE",
```

```
                    "version": "8.0.34"
                },
                "mysql-c:3306": {
                    "address": "mysql-c:3306",
                    "memberRole": "SECONDARY",
                    "mode": "R/O",
                    "replicationLagFromImmediateSource": "",
                    "replicationLagFromOriginalSource": "",
                    "status": "ONLINE",
                    "version": "8.0.34"
                }
            },
            "transactionSet": "861372a9-5fca-11ee-9711-08002
            7cf69cc:1-98,86138144-5fca-11ee-9711-080027cf6
            9cc:1-5,d763ea33-52ad-11ee-84a8-080027cf69cc:1-72"
        },
        "mydrcluster": {
            "clusterRole": "REPLICA",
            "clusterSetReplication": {
                "applierStatus": "APPLIED_ALL",
                "applierThreadState": "Waiting for an event from
                Coordinator",
                "applierWorkerThreads": 4,
                "receiver": "mysql-d:3306",
                "receiverStatus": "ON",
                "receiverThreadState": "Waiting for source to
                send event",
                "replicationSsl": null,
                "source": "mysql-a:3306"
            },
            "clusterSetReplicationStatus": "OK",
            "globalStatus": "OK",
            "status": "OK_NO_TOLERANCE",
            "statusText": "Cluster is NOT tolerant to any
            failures.",
```

```
                "topology": {
                    "mysql-d:3306": {
                        "address": "mysql-d:3306",
                        "memberRole": "PRIMARY",
                        "mode": "R/O",
                        "replicationLagFromImmediateSource": "",
                        "replicationLagFromOriginalSource": "",
                        "status": "ONLINE",
                        "version": "8.0.34"
                    }
                },
                "transactionSet": "3817f70d-5fd1-11ee-
                bb04-080027cf69cc:1,861372a9-5fca-11ee-9711-0800
                27cf69cc:1-98,86138144-5fca-11ee-9711-080027cf6
                9cc:1-5,d763ea33-52ad-11ee-84a8-080027cf69cc:1-72",
                "transactionSetConsistencyStatus": "OK",
                "transactionSetErrantGtidSet": "",
                "transactionSetMissingGtidSet": ""
            }
        },
        "domainName": "myclusterset",
        "globalPrimaryInstance": "mysql-a:3306",
        "metadataServer": "mysql-a:3306",
        "primaryCluster": "myPrimaryCluster",
        "status": "HEALTHY",
        "statusText": "All Clusters available."
    }
```

20. Add **mysql-f** to the Replica cluster **"mydrcluster"**.

**MySQL localhost:33060+ ssl JS > mydrcluster.
addInstance("mysqlclusteradmin@mysql-f:3306")**

WARNING: A GTID set check of the MySQL instance at 'mysql-f:3306'
determined that it contains transactions that do not originate
from the cluster, which must be discarded before it can join the
cluster.

mysql-f:3306 has the following errant GTIDs that do not exist in
the cluster:
51d07ec7-5fc3-11ee-bbcc-080027cf69cc:1-68

WARNING: Discarding these extra GTID events can either be done
manually or by completely overwriting the state of mysql-f:3306
with a physical snapshot from an existing cluster member. To
use this method by default, set the 'recoveryMethod' option to
'clone'.

Having extra GTID events is not expected, and it is recommended to
investigate this further and ensure that the data can be removed
prior to choosing the clone recovery method.

Please select a recovery method [C]lone/[A]bort (default Abort): C
Validating instance configuration at mysql-f:3306...

This instance reports its own address as mysql-f:3306

Instance configuration is suitable.
NOTE: Group Replication will communicate with other members using
'mysql-f:3306'. Use the localAddress option to override.

* Checking connectivity and SSL configuration...
A new instance will be added to the InnoDB Cluster. Depending
on the amount of data on the cluster this might take from a few
seconds to several hours.

Adding instance to the cluster...

* Waiting for the Cluster to synchronize with the PRIMARY
Cluster...
** Transactions
replicated ################################ 100%

* Configuring ClusterSet managed replication channel...
** Changing replication source of mysql-f:3306 to mysql-a:3306

Monitoring recovery process of the new cluster member. Press ^C to
stop monitoring and let it continue in background.

Clone based state recovery is now in progress.

NOTE: A server restart is expected to happen as part of the clone process. If the server does not support the RESTART command or does not come back after a while, you may need to manually start it back.

```
* Waiting for clone to finish...
NOTE: mysql-f:3306 is being cloned from mysql-e:3306
** Stage DROP DATA: Completed
** Clone Transfer
    FILE COPY  ###################################  100%  Completed
    PAGE COPY  ###################################  100%  Completed
    REDO COPY  ###################################  100%  Completed
```

NOTE: mysql-f:3306 is shutting down...

```
* Waiting for server restart... ready
* mysql-f:3306 has restarted, waiting for clone to finish...
** Stage RESTART: Completed
* Clone process has finished: 75.52 MB transferred in about 1
second (~75.52 MB/s)
```

State recovery already finished for 'mysql-f:3306'

The instance 'mysql-f:3306' was successfully added to the cluster.

21. Check clusterset status.

```
MySQL  localhost:33060+ ssl  JS > myclusterset.status()
{
    "clusters": {
        "myPrimaryCluster": {
            "clusterRole": "PRIMARY",
            "globalStatus": "OK",
            "primary": "mysql-a:3306"
        },
        "mydrcluster": {
            "clusterRole": "REPLICA",
```

```
            "clusterSetReplicationStatus": "OK",
            "globalStatus": "OK"
        }
    },
    "domainName": "myclusterset",
    "globalPrimaryInstance": "mysql-a:3306",
    "primaryCluster": "myPrimaryCluster",
    "status": "HEALTHY",
    "statusText": "All Clusters available."
}
```

**MySQL localhost:33060+ ssl JS > myclusterset.
status({extended:1})**

```
{
    "clusters": {
        "myPrimaryCluster": {
            "clusterRole": "PRIMARY",
            "globalStatus": "OK",
            "primary": "mysql-a:3306",
            "status": "OK",
            "statusText": "Cluster is ONLINE and can tolerate up
            to ONE failure.",
            "topology": {
                "mysql-a:3306": {
                    "address": "mysql-a:3306",
                    "memberRole": "PRIMARY",
                    "mode": "R/W",
                    "status": "ONLINE",
                    "version": "8.0.34"
                },
                "mysql-b:3306": {
                    "address": "mysql-b:3306",
                    "memberRole": "SECONDARY",
                    "mode": "R/O",
                    "replicationLagFromImmediateSource": "",
                    "replicationLagFromOriginalSource": "",
```

```
                    "status": "ONLINE",
                    "version": "8.0.34"
                },
                "mysql-c:3306": {
                    "address": "mysql-c:3306",
                    "memberRole": "SECONDARY",
                    "mode": "R/O",
                    "replicationLagFromImmediateSource": "",
                    "replicationLagFromOriginalSource": "",
                    "status": "ONLINE",
                    "version": "8.0.34"
                }
            },
            "transactionSet": "861372a9-5fca-11ee-9711-08002
            7cf69cc:1-118,86138144-5fca-11ee-9711-080027cf6
            9cc:1-5,d763ea33-52ad-11ee-84a8-080027cf69cc:1-72"
        },
        "mydrcluster": {
            "clusterRole": "REPLICA",
            "clusterSetReplication": {
                "applierStatus": "APPLIED_ALL",
                "applierThreadState": "Waiting for an event from
                Coordinator",
                "applierWorkerThreads": 4,
                "receiver": "mysql-d:3306",
                "receiverStatus": "ON",
                "receiverThreadState": "Waiting for source to
                send event",
                "replicationSsl": null,
                "source": "mysql-a:3306"
            },
            "clusterSetReplicationStatus": "OK",
            "globalStatus": "OK",
            "status": "OK",
            "statusText": "Cluster is ONLINE and can tolerate up
            to ONE failure.",
```

```
"topology": {
    "mysql-d:3306": {
        "address": "mysql-d:3306",
        "memberRole": "PRIMARY",
        "mode": "R/O",
        "replicationLagFromImmediateSource": "",
        "replicationLagFromOriginalSource": "",
        "status": "ONLINE",
        "version": "8.0.34"
    },
    "mysql-e:3306": {
        "address": "mysql-e:3306",
        "memberRole": "SECONDARY",
        "mode": "R/O",
        "replicationLagFromImmediateSource": "",
        "replicationLagFromOriginalSource": "",
        "status": "ONLINE",
        "version": "8.0.34"
    },
    "mysql-f:3306": {
        "address": "mysql-f:3306",
        "memberRole": "SECONDARY",
        "mode": "R/O",
        "replicationLagFromImmediateSource": "",
        "replicationLagFromOriginalSource": "",
        "status": "ONLINE",
        "version": "8.0.34"
    }
},
"transactionSet": "3817f70d-5fd1-11ee-
bb04-080027cf69cc:1-5,861372a9-5fca-11ee-9711-080
027cf69cc:1-118,86138144-5fca-11ee-9711-080027cf6
9cc:1-5,d763ea33-52ad-11ee-84a8-080027cf69cc:1-72",
"transactionSetConsistencyStatus": "OK",
"transactionSetErrantGtidSet": "",
```

```
                    "transactionSetMissingGtidSet": ""
        }
    },
    "domainName": "myclusterset",
    "globalPrimaryInstance": "mysql-a:3306",
    "metadataServer": "mysql-a:3306",
    "primaryCluster": "myPrimaryCluster",
    "status": "HEALTHY",
    "statusText": "All Clusters available."
}
```

22. Set up a MySQL Router account on primary (mysql-a).

[root@mysql-a ~]# mysqlsh -u mysqlclusteradmin -p
MySQL Shell 8.0.34
 **MySQL localhost:33060+ ssl JS > cluster.setupRouterAccount
("routeradmin")**

Missing the password for new account routeradmin@%. Please
provide one.
Password for new account: ************
Confirm password: ************

Creating user routeradmin@%.
Account routeradmin@% was successfully created.

23. Create an OS user to run and bootstrap MySQL Router. Verify
    the router configuration file once the bootstrapping process is
    complete.

[root@mysql-a ~]# useradd routeruser
[root@mysql-a ~]# mysqlrouter --bootstrap root@localhost:
3306 --directory /home/routeruser --conf-use-sockets --account
routeradmin --user=routeruser --force
Please enter MySQL password for root:
Bootstrapping MySQL Router instance at '/home/routeruser'...

Please enter MySQL password for routeradmin:
- Creating account(s) (only those that are needed, if any)
- Verifying account (using it to run SQL queries that would be run
  by Router)
- Storing account in keyring
- Adjusting permissions of generated files
- Creating configuration /home/routeruser/mysqlrouter.conf

MySQL Router configured for the ClusterSet 'myclusterset'

After this MySQL Router has been started with the generated
configuration

```
$ mysqlrouter -c /home/routeruser/mysqlrouter.conf
```

ClusterSet 'myclusterset' can be reached by connecting to:

MySQL Classic protocol

- Read/Write Connections: localhost:6446, /home/routeruser/
  mysql.sock
- Read/Only Connections: localhost:6447, /home/routeruser/
  mysqlro.sock

MySQL X protocol

- Read/Write Connections: localhost:6448, /home/routeruser/
  mysqlx.sock
- Read/Only Connections: localhost:6449, /home/routeruser/
  mysqlxro.sock

```
[root@mysql-a ~]#
```

[root@mysql-a ~]# ls -ltr /home/routeruser/
```
total 16
drwx------ 2 routeruser routeruser    6 Sep 30 15:58 run
-rw------- 1 routeruser routeruser   87 Sep 30 15:58
mysqlrouter.key
-rwx------ 1 routeruser routeruser  158 Sep 30 15:58 stop.sh
-rwx------ 1 routeruser routeruser  296 Sep 30 15:58 start.sh
```

```
-rw------- 1 routeruser routeruser 2033 Sep 30 15:58
mysqlrouter.conf
drwx------ 2 routeruser routeruser   29 Sep 30 15:58 log
drwx------ 2 routeruser routeruser  116 Sep 30 15:58 data
[root@mysql-a ~]#
```

[root@mysql-a ~]# cat /home/routeruser/mysqlrouter.conf
```
# File automatically generated during MySQL Router bootstrap
[DEFAULT]
user=routeruser
logging_folder=/home/routeruser/log
runtime_folder=/home/routeruser/run
data_folder=/home/routeruser/data
keyring_path=/home/routeruser/data/keyring
master_key_path=/home/routeruser/mysqlrouter.key
connect_timeout=5
read_timeout=30
dynamic_state=/home/routeruser/data/state.json
client_ssl_cert=/home/routeruser/data/router-cert.pem
client_ssl_key=/home/routeruser/data/router-key.pem
client_ssl_mode=PREFERRED
server_ssl_mode=AS_CLIENT
server_ssl_verify=DISABLED
unknown_config_option=error

[logger]
level=INFO

[metadata_cache:bootstrap]
cluster_type=gr
router_id=1
user=routeradmin
ttl=5
auth_cache_ttl=-1
auth_cache_refresh_interval=5
use_gr_notifications=1
```

```
[routing:bootstrap_rw]
bind_address=0.0.0.0
bind_port=6446
socket=/home/routeruser/mysql.sock
destinations=metadata-cache://myclusterset/?role=PRIMARY
routing_strategy=first-available
protocol=classic

[routing:bootstrap_ro]
bind_address=0.0.0.0
bind_port=6447
socket=/home/routeruser/mysqlro.sock
destinations=metadata-cache://myclusterset/?role=SECONDARY
routing_strategy=round-robin-with-fallback
protocol=classic

[routing:bootstrap_x_rw]
bind_address=0.0.0.0
bind_port=6448
socket=/home/routeruser/mysqlx.sock
destinations=metadata-cache://myclusterset/?role=PRIMARY
routing_strategy=first-available
protocol=x

[routing:bootstrap_x_ro]
bind_address=0.0.0.0
bind_port=6449
socket=/home/routeruser/mysqlxro.sock
destinations=metadata-cache://myclusterset/?role=SECONDARY
routing_strategy=round-robin-with-fallback
protocol=x

[http_server]
port=8443
ssl=1
ssl_cert=/home/routeruser/data/router-cert.pem
ssl_key=/home/routeruser/data/router-key.pem
```

```
[http_auth_realm:default_auth_realm]
backend=default_auth_backend
method=basic
name=default_realm

[rest_router]
require_realm=default_auth_realm

[rest_api]

[http_auth_backend:default_auth_backend]
backend=metadata_cache

[rest_routing]
require_realm=default_auth_realm

[rest_metadata_cache]
require_realm=default_auth_realm
```

24. Start MySQL Router and verify the MySQL Router log file.

```
[root@mysql-a ~]# cd /home/routeruser/
[root@mysql-a routeruser]# ls -ltr
total 16
drwx------ 2 routeruser routeruser    6 Sep 30 15:58 run
-rw------- 1 routeruser routeruser   87 Sep 30 15:58
mysqlrouter.key
-rwx------ 1 routeruser routeruser  158 Sep 30 15:58 stop.sh
-rwx------ 1 routeruser routeruser  296 Sep 30 15:58 start.sh
-rw------- 1 routeruser routeruser 2033 Sep 30 15:58
mysqlrouter.conf
drwx------ 2 routeruser routeruser   29 Sep 30 15:58 log
drwx------ 2 routeruser routeruser  116 Sep 30 15:58 data
[root@mysql-a routeruser]#
[root@mysql-a routeruser]# ./start.sh
[root@mysql-a routeruser]# PID 2480 written to '/home/routeruser/
mysqlrouter.pid'
stopping to log to the console. Continuing to log to filelog
```

[root@mysql-a routeruser]# cd log/
[root@mysql-a log]#
[root@mysql-a log]# pwd
/home/routeruser/log
[root@mysql-a log]# ls -ltr
total 8
-rw-r--r-- 1 routeruser routeruser 4356 Sep 30 16:01
mysqlrouter.log

[root@mysql-a log]# tail -20f mysqlrouter.log
 [routing:bootstrap_x_ro] started: listening using /home/
routeruser/mysqlxro.sock
2023-09-30 16:01:38 routing INFO [7fb3c77fe700] Start accepting
connections for routing routing:bootstrap_x_ro listening on 6449
and named socket /home/routeruser/mysqlxro.sock
2023-09-30 16:01:38 routing INFO [7fb3c6ffd700]
[routing:bootstrap_x_rw] started: routing strategy = first-
available
2023-09-30 16:01:38 routing INFO [7fb3c6ffd700]
[routing:bootstrap_x_rw] started: listening using /home/
routeruser/mysqlx.sock
2023-09-30 16:01:38 routing INFO [7fb3c6ffd700] Start accepting
connections for routing routing:bootstrap_x_rw listening on 6448
and named socket /home/routeruser/mysqlx.sock
2023-09-30 16:01:38 metadata_cache INFO [7fb3f02b7700] Connected
with metadata server running on mysql-b:3306
2023-09-30 16:01:38 metadata_cache INFO [7fb3f02b7700] Connected
with metadata server running on mysql-c:3306
2023-09-30 16:01:38 metadata_cache INFO [7fb3f02b7700] Connected
with metadata server running on mysql-d:3306
2023-09-30 16:01:38 metadata_cache INFO [7fb3f02b7700] Connected
with metadata server running on mysql-e:3306
2023-09-30 16:01:38 metadata_cache INFO [7fb3f02b7700] Connected
with metadata server running on mysql-f:3306
2023-09-30 16:01:38 metadata_cache INFO [7fb3f02b7700] Potential
changes detected in cluster after metadata refresh (view_id=2)

```
2023-09-30 16:01:38 metadata_cache INFO [7fb3f02b7700] Target
cluster(s) are part of a ClusterSet: accepting RW connections
2023-09-30 16:01:38 metadata_cache INFO [7fb3f02b7700] Cluster
'myPrimaryCluster': role of a cluster within a ClusterSet is
'primary';
2023-09-30 16:01:38 metadata_cache INFO [7fb3f02b7700] Metadata
for cluster 'myPrimaryCluster' has 3 member(s), single-primary:
2023-09-30 16:01:38 metadata_cache INFO
[7fb3f02b7700]    mysql-a:3306 / 33060 - mode=RW
2023-09-30 16:01:38 metadata_cache INFO
[7fb3f02b7700]    mysql-b:3306 / 33060 - mode=RO
2023-09-30 16:01:38 metadata_cache INFO
[7fb3f02b7700]    mysql-c:3306 / 33060 - mode=RO
2023-09-30 16:01:38 metadata_cache INFO [7fb3f02b7700] Enabling
GR notices for cluster 'myPrimaryCluster' changes on node
mysql-b:33060
[root@mysql-a log]#
```

Now that we got the InnoDB Clusterset working, let us go through a few scenarios to verify and validate our setup is working as expected.

InnoDB Cluster Connection Routing Using MySQL Router

MySQL Router provides transparent routing between your application and the back-end MySQL servers. MySQL Router is InnoDB cluster topology aware and knows which MySQL instance is primary at all times and transparently routes client connections to handle failover situations, providing the much needed high availability and scalability the application needs.

MySQL Router also provides proxy capabilities by not exposing the back-end MySQL servers and redirects all the client connections to the MySQL server, which is in primary role. Based on the configuration defined in the **mysqlrouter.conf**, the client connections can be configured to redirect based on their workload requirements. For example, you can choose to separate the read-write workload and read-only workload to separate MySQL servers for optimal performance. Starting with MySQL Router 8.2, which was released in October 2023, a new feature called **transparent read-write splitting** automatically redirects client connections without the clients having to make configuration changes to redirect their read-write or read-only workloads. In this section, let us learn about the InnoDB cluster connection routing based on your requirement. Here are the use cases summarized for your convenience.

Table 6-1. MySQL Router versions

MySQL Router versions used below	
Read-write workloads	MySQL Router 8.0
Read-only workloads	MySQL Router 8.0
Automatic read-write or read-only split	MySQL Router 8.2

For the MySQL Router 8.0 use cases, check the **mysqlrouter.conf** file to confirm the Read/Write and Read/Only connection ports. The default connection ports are as follows:

- **Read/Write connections:** Port 6446

- **Read/Only connections:** Port 6447

The following is the example of primary InnoDB cluster configuration:

```
mysql-a: primary
mysql-b: secondary
mysql-c: secondary
```

1. Check InnoDB cluster status.

```
[root@mysql-a ~]# mysqlsh -u mysqlclusteradmin -p
MySQL Shell 8.0.34
 MySQL  localhost:33060+ ssl  JS > var cluster=dba.getCluster()
 MySQL  localhost:33060+ ssl  JS >
 MySQL  localhost:33060+ ssl  JS > cluster.status()
{
    "clusterName": "myCluster",
    "defaultReplicaSet": {
        "name": "default",
```

```
    "primary": "mysql-a:3306",
    "ssl": "REQUIRED",
    "status": "OK",
    "statusText": "Cluster is ONLINE and can tolerate up to
ONE failure.",
    "topology": {
        "mysql-a:3306": {
            "address": "mysql-a:3306",
            "memberRole": "PRIMARY",
            "mode": "R/W",
            "readReplicas": {},
            "replicationLag": "applier_queue_applied",
            "role": "HA",
            "status": "ONLINE",
            "version": "8.0.34"
        },
        "mysql-b:3306": {
            "address": "mysql-b:3306",
            "memberRole": "SECONDARY",
            "mode": "R/O",
            "readReplicas": {},
            "replicationLag": "applier_queue_applied",
            "role": "HA",
            "status": "ONLINE",
            "version": "8.0.34"
        },
        "mysql-c:3306": {
            "address": "mysql-c:3306",
            "memberRole": "SECONDARY",
            "mode": "R/O",
            "readReplicas": {},
            "replicationLag": "applier_queue_applied",
            "role": "HA",
            "status": "ONLINE",
            "version": "8.0.34"
```

```
            }
        },
        "topologyMode": "Single-Primary"
    },
    "groupInformationSourceMember": "mysql-a:3306"
}
 MySQL  localhost:33060+ ssl  JS >
 MySQL  localhost:33060+ ssl  JS > \q
Bye!
```

2. Connect using read-write port 6446.

```
[root@mysql-a ~]# mysql -u mysqlclusteradmin -h mysql-a -P6446 -p
Enter password:

mysql> select @@hostname;
+------------+
| @@hostname |
+------------+
| mysql-a    |
+------------+
1 row in set (0.00 sec)
```

Notice that we have automatically connected to mysql-a which is in primary role and in read-write mode.

3. Connect using read-only port 6447 and verify:

```
[root@mysql-a ~]# mysql -u mysqlclusteradmin -h mysql-a -P6447 -p
Enter password:

mysql> select @@hostname;
+------------+
| @@hostname |
+------------+
| mysql-c    |
+------------+
1 row in set (0.00 sec)
```

>>>>>>>> Try connecting again...and this time it connects to mysql-b

```
[root@mysql-a ~]# mysql -u mysqlclusteradmin -h mysql-a -P6447 -p
Enter password:

mysql> select @@hostname;
+------------+
| @@hostname |
+------------+
| mysql-b    |
+------------+
1 row in set (0.01 sec)
```

Notice we are automatically connecting to the secondary instances.

Now, let us learn to use the new MySQL Router 8.2 transparent read-write splitting and see how it works.

4. Check the current MySQL Router version and status.

```
[root@mysql-a ~]# mysqlrouter --version
MySQL Router  Ver 8.0.34-commercial for Linux on x86_64 (MySQL
Enterprise - Commercial)
[root@mysql-a ~]# mysqlsh -u mysqlclusteradmin -p
MySQL Shell 8.0.34
Creating a session to 'mysqlclusteradmin@localhost'
 MySQL  localhost:33060+ ssl  JS >
 MySQL  localhost:33060+ ssl  JS > var cluster=dba.getCluster()
 MySQL  localhost:33060+ ssl  JS > cluster.listRouters({'onlyUpgra
deRequired':'true'})
{
    "clusterName": "myCluster",
    "routers": {}
}
 MySQL  localhost:33060+ ssl  JS > cluster.listRouters()
{
    "clusterName": "myCluster",
    "routers": {
```

```
        "mysql-a::": {
            "hostname": "mysql-a",
            "lastCheckIn": "2023-10-26 17:53:41",
            "roPort": "6447",
            "roXPort": "6449",
            "rwPort": "6446",
            "rwXPort": "6448",
            "version": "8.0.34"
        }
    }
}
```

5. Uninstall MySQL Router 8.0.

```
[root@mysql-a ~]# cd /tmp/router/
[root@mysql-a router]# ls -ltr
total 24
-rw------- 1 routeruser routeruser 82 Aug 11 00:46 mysqlrouter.key
drwx------ 2 routeruser routeruser 29 Aug 11 00:46 log
-rw-r--r-- 1 routeruser routeruser  6 Aug 11 00:58
mysqlrouter.pid.bk
-rw-r--r-- 1 routeruser routeruser  5 Oct 26 17:45 mysqlrouter.pid
srwxrwxrwx 1 routeruser routeruser  0 Oct 26 17:45 mysqlro.sock
srwxrwxrwx 1 routeruser routeruser  0 Oct 26 17:45 mysql.sock
srwxrwxrwx 1 routeruser routeruser  0 Oct 26 17:45 mysqlxro.sock
srwxrwxrwx 1 routeruser routeruser  0 Oct 26 17:45 mysqlx.sock
-rwx------ 1 routeruser routeruser 143 Oct 26 17:52 stop.sh
-rwx------ 1 routeruser routeruser 291 Oct 26 17:52 start.sh
-rw------- 1 routeruser routeruser 1980 Oct 26 17:52
mysqlrouter.conf
drwx------ 2 routeruser routeruser  84 Oct 26 17:52 data
[root@mysql-a router]#
[root@mysql-a router]# ./stop.sh
[root@mysql-a router]# ls -ltr
total 20
-rw------- 1 routeruser routeruser 82 Aug 11 00:46 mysqlrouter.key
```

```
drwx------ 2 routeruser routeruser 29 Aug 11 00:46 log
-rw-r--r-- 1 routeruser routeruser  6 Aug 11 00:58
mysqlrouter.pid.bk
-rwx------ 1 routeruser routeruser  143 Oct 26 17:52 stop.sh
-rwx------ 1 routeruser routeruser  291 Oct 26 17:52 start.sh
-rw------- 1 routeruser routeruser 1980 Oct 26 17:52
mysqlrouter.conf
drwx------ 2 routeruser routeruser   84 Oct 26 17:52 data
[root@mysql-a router]#
[root@mysql-a router]# rm -rf *
[root@mysql-a router]# ls -ltr
total 0
[root@mysql-a router]# cd
[root@mysql-a ~]#
[root@mysql-a ~]# yum remove mysql-router*
Loaded plugins: fastestmirror
Resolving Dependencies
--> Running transaction check
---> Package mysql-router-commercial.x86_64 0:8.0.34-1.1.el7 will
be erased
--> Finished Dependency Resolution

Dependencies Resolved

========================================================================
 Package                    Arch     Version          Repository  Size
========================================================================
Removing:
 mysql-router-commercial   x86_64   8.0.34-1.1.el7   installed    64 M

Transaction Summary
========================================================================
Remove  1 Package

Installed size: 64 M
Is this ok [y/N]: y
```

```
Downloading packages:
Running transaction check
Running transaction test
Transaction test succeeded
Running transaction
Warning: RPMDB altered outside of yum.
  Erasing    : mysql-router-commercial-8.0.34-1.1.el7.
x86_64       1/1
  Verifying  : mysql-router-commercial-8.0.34-1.1.el7.
x86_64       1/1
```

Removed:
  mysql-router-commercial.x86_64 0:8.0.34-1.1.el7

Complete!

6. Download and install MySQL Router 8.2 Innovation from
   https://dev.mysql.com/downloads/router.

```
[root@mysql-a ~]# cd mysql_binaries/
[root@mysql-a mysql_binaries]# rpm -ivh mysql-router-
community-8.2.0-1.el7.x86_64.rpm
Preparing...               ################################# [100%]
Updating / installing...
   1:mysql-router-community-8.2.0-1.el#################### [100%]
[root@mysql-a mysql_binaries]# rpm -qa |grep mysql-router
mysql-router-community-8.2.0-1.el7.x86_64
[root@mysql-a mysql_binaries]#
[root@mysql-a mysql_binaries]# cd
[root@mysql-a ~]# which mysqlrouter
/usr/bin/mysqlrouter
[root@mysql-a ~]# mysqlrouter --version
MySQL Router  Ver 8.2.0 for Linux on x86_64 (MySQL
Community - GPL)
```

7. Bootstrap MySQL Router 8.2.

```
[root@mysql-a ~]# mysqlrouter --bootstrap root@localhost:
3306 --directory /tmp/router --conf-use-sockets --account
routeradmin --user=routeruser --force
Please enter MySQL password for root:
# Bootstrapping MySQL Router 8.2.0 (MySQL Community - GPL)
instance at '/tmp/router'...

Please enter MySQL password for routeradmin:
- Creating account(s) (only those that are needed, if any)
- Verifying account (using it to run SQL queries that would be run
  by Router)
- Storing account in keyring
- Adjusting permissions of generated files
- Creating configuration /tmp/router/mysqlrouter.conf

# MySQL Router configured for the InnoDB Cluster 'myCluster'

After this MySQL Router has been started with the generated
configuration

    $ mysqlrouter -c /tmp/router/mysqlrouter.conf

InnoDB Cluster 'myCluster' can be reached by connecting to:

## MySQL Classic protocol

- Read/Write Connections: localhost:6446, /tmp/router/mysql.sock
- Read/Only Connections:  localhost:6447, /tmp/router/mysqlro.sock
- Read/Write Split Connections: localhost:6450, /tmp/router/
  mysqlsplit.sock

## MySQL X protocol

- Read/Write Connections: localhost:6448, /tmp/router/mysqlx.sock
- Read/Only Connections:  localhost:6449, /tmp/router/
  mysqlxro.sock
```

8. Check and verify the [routing:bootstrap_rw_split] section in the
    MySQL Router configuration file, /tmp/router/mysqlrouter.conf.

```
[root@mysql-a ~]# cat /tmp/router/mysqlrouter.conf
# File automatically generated during MySQL Router bootstrap
[DEFAULT]
user=routeruser
logging_folder=/tmp/router/log
runtime_folder=/tmp/router/run
data_folder=/tmp/router/data
keyring_path=/tmp/router/data/keyring
master_key_path=/tmp/router/mysqlrouter.key

    --Output truncated for better visibility

[routing:bootstrap_rw_split]
bind_address=0.0.0.0
bind_port=6450
socket=/tmp/router/mysqlsplit.sock
destinations=metadata-cache://myCluster/?role=PRIMARY_AND_
SECONDARY
routing_strategy=round-robin
protocol=classic
connection_sharing=1
client_ssl_mode=PREFERRED
server_ssl_mode=PREFERRED
access_mode=auto

[routing:bootstrap_x_rw]
bind_address=0.0.0.0
bind_port=6448
socket=/tmp/router/mysqlx.sock
destinations=metadata-cache://myCluster/?role=PRIMARY
routing_strategy=first-available
protocol=x

    --Output truncated for better visibility
```

9. Start MySQL Router 8.2.

```
[root@mysql-a ~]# cd /tmp/router/
[root@mysql-a router]# ls -ltr
total 16
drwx------ 2 routeruser routeruser     6 Oct 26 18:24 run
-rw------- 1 routeruser routeruser    82 Oct 26 18:24
mysqlrouter.key
-rwx------ 1 routeruser routeruser   143 Oct 26 18:24 stop.sh
-rwx------ 1 routeruser routeruser   291 Oct 26 18:24 start.sh
-rw------- 1 routeruser routeruser  2316 Oct 26 18:24
mysqlrouter.conf
drwx------ 2 routeruser routeruser    29 Oct 26 18:24 log
drwx------ 2 routeruser routeruser   116 Oct 26 18:24 data
[root@mysql-a router]# ./start.sh
[root@mysql-a router]# PID 5997 written to '/tmp/router/
mysqlrouter.pid'
stopping to log to the console. Continuing to log to filelog
[root@mysql-a router]# ls -ltr
total 20
drwx------ 2 routeruser routeruser     6 Oct 26 18:24 run
-rw------- 1 routeruser routeruser    82 Oct 26 18:24
mysqlrouter.key
-rwx------ 1 routeruser routeruser   143 Oct 26 18:24 stop.sh
-rwx------ 1 routeruser routeruser   291 Oct 26 18:24 start.sh
-rw------- 1 routeruser routeruser  2316 Oct 26 18:24
mysqlrouter.conf
drwx------ 2 routeruser routeruser    29 Oct 26 18:24 log
drwx------ 2 routeruser routeruser   116 Oct 26 18:24 data
-rw-r--r-- 1 routeruser routeruser     5 Oct 26 18:29
mysqlrouter.pid
srwxrwxrwx 1 routeruser routeruser     0 Oct 26 18:29 mysqlro.sock
srwxrwxrwx 1 routeruser routeruser     0 Oct 26 18:29 mysql.sock
srwxrwxrwx 1 routeruser routeruser     0 Oct 26 18:29
mysqlsplit.sock
```

```
srwxrwxrwx 1 routeruser routeruser    0 Oct 26 18:29 mysqlxro.sock
srwxrwxrwx 1 routeruser routeruser    0 Oct 26 18:29 mysqlx.sock
```

Notice a new process ID (PID) mysqlrouter.pid and socket files
(mysqlro.sock, mysql.sock) are generated upon starting the router.

10. Check cluster status.

```
[root@mysql-a ~]# mysqlsh -u mysqlclusteradmin -p
MySQL Shell 8.0.34
 MySQL  localhost:33060+ ssl  JS > var cluster=dba.getCluster()
 MySQL  localhost:33060+ ssl  JS > cluster.listRouters()
{
    "clusterName": "myCluster",
    "routers": {
        "mysql-a::": {
            "hostname": "mysql-a",
            "lastCheckIn": "2023-10-26 18:29:40",
            "roPort": "6447",
            "roXPort": "6449",
            "rwPort": "6446",
            "rwXPort": "6448",
            "version": "8.2.0"
        }
    }
}
 MySQL  localhost:33060+ ssl  JS > cluster.status()
{
    "clusterName": "myCluster",
    "defaultReplicaSet": {
        "name": "default",
        "primary": "mysql-a:3306",
        "ssl": "REQUIRED",
        "status": "OK",
        "statusText": "Cluster is ONLINE and can tolerate up to
        ONE failure.",
        "topology": {
```

```
            "mysql-a:3306": {
                "address": "mysql-a:3306",
                "memberRole": "PRIMARY",
                "mode": "R/W",
                "readReplicas": {},
                "replicationLag": "applier_queue_applied",
                "role": "HA",
                "status": "ONLINE",
                "version": "8.0.34"
            },
            "mysql-b:3306": {
                "address": "mysql-b:3306",
                "memberRole": "SECONDARY",
                "mode": "R/O",
                "readReplicas": {},
                "replicationLag": "applier_queue_applied",
                "role": "HA",
                "status": "ONLINE",
                "version": "8.0.34"
            },
            "mysql-c:3306": {
                "address": "mysql-c:3306",
                "memberRole": "SECONDARY",
                "mode": "R/O",
                "readReplicas": {},
                "replicationLag": "applier_queue_applied",
                "role": "HA",
                "status": "ONLINE",
                "version": "8.0.34"
            }
        },
        "topologyMode": "Single-Primary"
    },
    "groupInformationSourceMember": "mysql-a:3306"
}
```

```
MySQL  localhost:33060+ ssl  JS > cluster.status({extended:1})
{
    "clusterName": "myCluster",
    "defaultReplicaSet": {
        "GRProtocolVersion": "8.0.27",
        "communicationStack": "MYSQL",
        "groupName": "a810da47-3721-11ee-bdca-080027cf69cc",
        "groupViewChangeUuid": "a810e1ab-3721-11ee-
        bdca-080027cf69cc",
        "groupViewId": "16983604028537157:3",
        "name": "default",
        "paxosSingleLeader": "OFF",
        "primary": "mysql-a:3306",
        "ssl": "REQUIRED",
        "status": "OK",
        "statusText": "Cluster is ONLINE and can tolerate up to
        ONE failure.",
        "topology": {
            "mysql-a:3306": {
                "address": "mysql-a:3306",
                "applierWorkerThreads": 4,
                "fenceSysVars": [],
                "memberId": "a52a1fb1-3272-11ee-
                9a0c-080027cf69cc",
                "memberRole": "PRIMARY",
                "memberState": "ONLINE",
                "mode": "R/W",
                "readReplicas": {},
                "replicationLag": "applier_queue_applied",
                "role": "HA",
                "status": "ONLINE",
                "version": "8.0.34"
            },
            "mysql-b:3306": {
                "address": "mysql-b:3306",
                "applierWorkerThreads": 4,
```

```
                    "fenceSysVars": [
                        "read_only",
                        "super_read_only"
                    ],
                    "memberId": "c89e42ed-3723-11ee-
                    bfd3-080027cf69cc",
                    "memberRole": "SECONDARY",
                    "memberState": "ONLINE",
                    "mode": "R/O",
                    "readReplicas": {},
                    "replicationLag": "applier_queue_applied",
                    "role": "HA",
                    "status": "ONLINE",
                    "version": "8.0.34"
                },
                "mysql-c:3306": {
                    "address": "mysql-c:3306",
                    "applierWorkerThreads": 4,
                    "fenceSysVars": [
                        "read_only",
                        "super_read_only"
                    ],
                    "memberId": "f2d7c53a-3723-11ee-
                    bd72-080027cf69cc",
                    "memberRole": "SECONDARY",
                    "memberState": "ONLINE",
                    "mode": "R/O",
                    "readReplicas": {},
                    "replicationLag": "applier_queue_applied",
                    "role": "HA",
                    "status": "ONLINE",
                    "version": "8.0.34"
                }
            },
```

```
        "topologyMode": "Single-Primary"
    },
    "groupInformationSourceMember": "mysql-a:3306",
    "metadataVersion": "2.1.0"
}
 MySQL  localhost:33060+ ssl  JS > \q
```

11. Log in to any of the MySQL servers using port 6450 (Read/Write
    Split port). If you run a select query, it will be redirected to either
    mysql-b or mysql-c, which is in the R/O role automatically.

```
[root@mysql-a ~]# mysql -u mysqlclusteradmin -h mysql-a -P6450 -p
Enter password:

mysql> select @@hostname;
+------------+
| @@hostname |
+------------+
| mysql-b    |
+------------+
1 row in set (0.01 sec)
mysql> exit
[root@mysql-a ~]# mysql -u mysqlclusteradmin -h mysql-a -P6450 -p
Enter password:

mysql> select @@hostname;
+------------+
| @@hostname |
+------------+
| mysql-c    |
+------------+
1 row in set (0.01 sec)
```

12. Start a transaction in the same session and notice that the connection automatically gets redirected to mysql-a, which is in R/W mode.

```
[root@mysql-a ~]# mysql -u mysqlclusteradmin -h mysql-a -P6450 -p
Enter password:

mysql> select @@hostname, @@port;
+------------+--------+
| @@hostname | @@port |
+------------+--------+
| mysql-b    |   3306 |
+------------+--------+
1 row in set (0.01 sec)

mysql> start transaction;
Query OK, 0 rows affected (0.00 sec)

mysql> select @@hostname, @@port;
+------------+--------+
| @@hostname | @@port |
+------------+--------+
| mysql-a    |   3306 |
+------------+--------+
1 row in set (0.00 sec)

mysql> rollback;
Query OK, 0 rows affected (0.00 sec)

mysql> select @@hostname, @@port;
+------------+--------+
| @@hostname | @@port |
+------------+--------+
| mysql-b    |   3306 |
+------------+--------+
1 row in set (0.01 sec)

mysql> start transaction read only;
Query OK, 0 rows affected (0.01 sec)

mysql> select @@hostname, @@port;
```

```
+-------------+--------+
| @@hostname | @@port |
+-------------+--------+
| mysql-b    |   3306 |
+-------------+--------+
1 row in set (0.01 sec)

mysql> select @@hostname, @@port;
+-------------+--------+
| @@hostname | @@port |
+-------------+--------+
| mysql-b    |   3306 |
+-------------+--------+
1 row in set (0.00 sec)
```

Scenario 1: InnoDB Clusterset – Role Switch of Clusters

In this scenario, we will test the role switch of the clusters, where we will make the secondary cluster "mydrcluster" as primary and the primary cluster "myPrimaryCluster" as secondary.

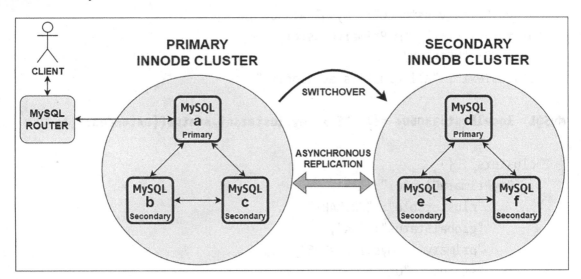

Figure 6-2. *InnoDB role switchover*

In order to perform the role switch, we use the **setPrimaryCluster()** method. You can even perform a dryrun of the switchover using **{dryrun:true}**.

```
[root@mysql-a ~]# mysqlsh -u mysqlclusteradmin -p
MySQL Shell 8.0.34
MySQL  localhost:33060+ ssl  JS > myclusterset=dba.getClusterSet();
<ClusterSet:myclusterset>
 MySQL  localhost:33060+ ssl  JS > myclusterset.status();
{
    "clusters": {
        "myPrimaryCluster": {
            "clusterRole": "PRIMARY",
            "globalStatus": "OK",
            "primary": "mysql-a:3306"
        },
        "mydrcluster": {
            "clusterRole": "REPLICA",
            "clusterSetReplicationStatus": "OK",
            "globalStatus": "OK"
        }
    },
    "domainName": "myclusterset",
    "globalPrimaryInstance": "mysql-a:3306",
    "primaryCluster": "myPrimaryCluster",
    "status": "HEALTHY",
    "statusText": "All Clusters available."
}
 MySQL  localhost:33060+ ssl  JS > myclusterset.status({extended:1});
{
    "clusters": {
        "myPrimaryCluster": {
            "clusterRole": "PRIMARY",
            "globalStatus": "OK",
            "primary": "mysql-a:3306",
            "status": "OK",
```

```json
    "statusText": "Cluster is ONLINE and can tolerate up to ONE
    failure.",
    "topology": {
        "mysql-a:3306": {
            "address": "mysql-a:3306",
            "memberRole": "PRIMARY",
            "mode": "R/W",
            "status": "ONLINE",
            "version": "8.0.34"
        },
        "mysql-b:3306": {
            "address": "mysql-b:3306",
            "memberRole": "SECONDARY",
            "mode": "R/O",
            "replicationLagFromImmediateSource": "",
            "replicationLagFromOriginalSource": "",
            "status": "ONLINE",
            "version": "8.0.34"
        },
        "mysql-c:3306": {
            "address": "mysql-c:3306",
            "memberRole": "SECONDARY",
            "mode": "R/O",
            "replicationLagFromImmediateSource": "",
            "replicationLagFromOriginalSource": "",
            "status": "ONLINE",
            "version": "8.0.34"
        }
    },
    "transactionSet": "861372a9-5fca-11ee-9711-08002
    7cf69cc:1-130,86138144-5fca-11ee-9711-080027cf69cc:1-5,
    d763ea33-52ad-11ee-84a8-080027cf69cc:1-72"
},
"mydrcluster": {
    "clusterRole": "REPLICA",
```

```
"clusterSetReplication": {
    "applierStatus": "APPLIED_ALL",
    "applierThreadState": "Waiting for an event from
    Coordinator",
    "applierWorkerThreads": 4,
    "receiver": "mysql-d:3306",
    "receiverStatus": "ON",
    "receiverThreadState": "Waiting for source to send event",
    "replicationSsl": null,
    "source": "mysql-a:3306"
},
"clusterSetReplicationStatus": "OK",
"globalStatus": "OK",
"status": "OK",
"statusText": "Cluster is ONLINE and can tolerate up to ONE
failure.",
"topology": {
    "mysql-d:3306": {
        "address": "mysql-d:3306",
        "memberRole": "PRIMARY",
        "mode": "R/O",
        "replicationLagFromImmediateSource": "",
        "replicationLagFromOriginalSource": "",
        "status": "ONLINE",
        "version": "8.0.34"
    },
    "mysql-e:3306": {
        "address": "mysql-e:3306",
        "memberRole": "SECONDARY",
        "mode": "R/O",
        "replicationLagFromImmediateSource": "",
        "replicationLagFromOriginalSource": "",
        "status": "ONLINE",
        "version": "8.0.34"
    },
```

```
            "mysql-f:3306": {
                "address": "mysql-f:3306",
                "memberRole": "SECONDARY",
                "mode": "R/O",
                "replicationLagFromImmediateSource": "",
                "replicationLagFromOriginalSource": "",
                "status": "ONLINE",
                "version": "8.0.34"
            }
        },
        "transactionSet": "3817f70d-5fd1-11ee-bb04-080027cf69cc:1-5,86
        1372a9-5fca-11ee-9711-080027cf69cc:1-130,86138144-5fca-11ee-97
        11-080027cf69cc:1-5,d763ea33-52ad-11ee-84a8-080027cf69cc:1-72",
        "transactionSetConsistencyStatus": "OK",
        "transactionSetErrantGtidSet": "",
        "transactionSetMissingGtidSet": ""
    }
},
"domainName": "myclusterset",
"globalPrimaryInstance": "mysql-a:3306",
"metadataServer": "mysql-a:3306",
"primaryCluster": "myPrimaryCluster",
"status": "HEALTHY",
"statusText": "All Clusters available."
}
 MySQL  localhost:33060+ ssl  JS > myclusterset.routingOptions();
{
    "domainName": "myclusterset",
    "global": {
        "invalidated_cluster_policy": "drop_all",
        "stats_updates_frequency": 0,
        "target_cluster": "primary",
        "use_replica_primary_as_rw": false
    },
```

```
    "routers": {
        "mysql-a::": {}
    }
}
```

**MySQL localhost:33060+ ssl JS > myclusterset.setPrimaryCluster('mydrclus
ter',{dryrun:true})**
Switching the primary cluster of the clusterset to 'mydrcluster'
NOTE: dryRun enabled, no changes will be made
* Verifying clusterset status
** Checking cluster mydrcluster
   Cluster 'mydrcluster' is available
** Checking cluster myPrimaryCluster
   Cluster 'myPrimaryCluster' is available

** Waiting for the promoted cluster to apply pending received
transactions...
* Reconciling 5 internally generated GTIDs

* Refreshing replication account of demoted cluster
* Synchronizing transaction backlog at mysql-d:3306

* Updating metadata

* Updating topology
** Changing replication source of mysql-b:3306 to mysql-d:3306
** Changing replication source of mysql-c:3306 to mysql-d:3306
** Changing replication source of mysql-a:3306 to mysql-d:3306
* Acquiring locks in replicaset instances
** Pre-synchronizing SECONDARIES
** Acquiring global lock at PRIMARY
** Acquiring global lock at SECONDARIES

* Synchronizing remaining transactions at promoted primary

* Updating replica clusters
Cluster 'mydrcluster' was promoted to PRIMARY of the clusterset. The
PRIMARY instance is 'mysql-d:3306'

dryRun finished.
```
```

```
MySQL  localhost:33060+ ssl  JS > myclusterset.setPrimaryCluster('myd
rcluster')
Switching the primary cluster of the clusterset to 'mydrcluster'
* Verifying clusterset status
** Checking cluster mydrcluster
  Cluster 'mydrcluster' is available
** Checking cluster myPrimaryCluster
  Cluster 'myPrimaryCluster' is available

** Waiting for the promoted cluster to apply pending received
transactions...
* Reconciling 5 internally generated GTIDs

* Refreshing replication account of demoted cluster
* Synchronizing transaction backlog at mysql-d:3306
** Transactions replicated  ################################  100%

* Updating metadata

* Updating topology
** Changing replication source of mysql-b:3306 to mysql-d:3306
** Changing replication source of mysql-c:3306 to mysql-d:3306
** Changing replication source of mysql-a:3306 to mysql-d:3306
* Acquiring locks in replicaset instances
** Pre-synchronizing SECONDARIES
** Acquiring global lock at PRIMARY
** Acquiring global lock at SECONDARIES

* Synchronizing remaining transactions at promoted primary
** Transactions replicated  ################################  100%

* Updating replica clusters
Cluster 'mydrcluster' was promoted to PRIMARY of the clusterset. The
PRIMARY instance is 'mysql-d:3306'

MySQL  localhost:33060+ ssl  JS > myclusterset.status();
{
    "clusters": {
        "myPrimaryCluster": {
```

```
            "clusterRole": "REPLICA",
            "clusterSetReplicationStatus": "OK",
            "globalStatus": "OK"
        },
        "mydrcluster": {
            "clusterRole": "PRIMARY",
            "globalStatus": "OK",
            "primary": "mysql-d:3306"
        }
    },
    "domainName": "myclusterset",
    "globalPrimaryInstance": "mysql-d:3306",
    "primaryCluster": "mydrcluster",
    "status": "HEALTHY",
    "statusText": "All Clusters available."
}
 MySQL  localhost:33060+ ssl  JS > myclusterset.status({extended:1});
{
    "clusters": {
        "myPrimaryCluster": {
            "clusterRole": "REPLICA",
            "clusterSetReplication": {
                "applierStatus": "APPLIED_ALL",
                "applierThreadState": "Waiting for an event from
                Coordinator",
                "applierWorkerThreads": 4,
                "receiver": "mysql-a:3306",
                "receiverStatus": "ON",
                "receiverThreadState": "Waiting for source to send event",
                "replicationSsl": null,
                "source": "mysql-d:3306"
            },
            "clusterSetReplicationStatus": "OK",
            "globalStatus": "OK",
            "status": "OK",
```

```
"statusText": "Cluster is ONLINE and can tolerate up to ONE
failure.",
"topology": {
    "mysql-a:3306": {
        "address": "mysql-a:3306",
        "memberRole": "PRIMARY",
        "mode": "R/O",
        "replicationLagFromImmediateSource": "",
        "replicationLagFromOriginalSource": "",
        "status": "ONLINE",
        "version": "8.0.34"
    },
    "mysql-b:3306": {
        "address": "mysql-b:3306",
        "memberRole": "SECONDARY",
        "mode": "R/O",
        "replicationLagFromImmediateSource": "",
        "replicationLagFromOriginalSource": "",
        "status": "ONLINE",
        "version": "8.0.34"
    },
    "mysql-c:3306": {
        "address": "mysql-c:3306",
        "memberRole": "SECONDARY",
        "mode": "R/O",
        "replicationLagFromImmediateSource": "",
        "replicationLagFromOriginalSource": "",
        "status": "ONLINE",
        "version": "8.0.34"
    }
},
"transactionSet": "3817f70d-5fd1-11ee-bb04-080027cf69cc:1-5,86
1372a9-5fca-11ee-9711-080027cf69cc:1-132,86138144-5fca-11ee-97
11-080027cf69cc:1-5,d763ea33-52ad-11ee-84a8-080027cf69cc:1-72",
"transactionSetConsistencyStatus": "OK",
```

```
            "transactionSetErrantGtidSet": "",
            "transactionSetMissingGtidSet": ""
        },
        "mydrcluster": {
            "clusterRole": "PRIMARY",
            "globalStatus": "OK",
            "primary": "mysql-d:3306",
            "status": "OK",
            "statusText": "Cluster is ONLINE and can tolerate up to ONE
            failure.",
            "topology": {
                "mysql-d:3306": {
                    "address": "mysql-d:3306",
                    "memberRole": "PRIMARY",
                    "mode": "R/W",
                    "status": "ONLINE",
                    "version": "8.0.34"
                },
                "mysql-e:3306": {
                    "address": "mysql-e:3306",
                    "memberRole": "SECONDARY",
                    "mode": "R/O",
                    "replicationLagFromImmediateSource": "",
                    "replicationLagFromOriginalSource": "",
                    "status": "ONLINE",
                    "version": "8.0.34"
                },
                "mysql-f:3306": {
                    "address": "mysql-f:3306",
                    "memberRole": "SECONDARY",
                    "mode": "R/O",
                    "replicationLagFromImmediateSource": "",
                    "replicationLagFromOriginalSource": "",
                    "status": "ONLINE",
                    "version": "8.0.34"
```

```
            }
        },
        "transactionSet": "3817f70d-5fd1-11ee-bb04-080027cf69cc:1-5,86
        1372a9-5fca-11ee-9711-080027cf69cc:1-132,86138144-5fca-11ee-97
        11-080027cf69cc:1-5,d763ea33-52ad-11ee-84a8-080027cf69cc:1-72"
    }
  },
  "domainName": "myclusterset",
  "globalPrimaryInstance": "mysql-d:3306",
  "metadataServer": "mysql-d:3306",
  "primaryCluster": "mydrcluster",
  "status": "HEALTHY",
  "statusText": "All Clusters available."
}
 MySQL  localhost:33060+ ssl  JS >
```

>>>>>>>>>> From /home/routeruser/log/mysqlrouter.log <<<<<<<<<<

```
2023-09-30 16:40:37 metadata_cache INFO [7fb3f02b7700] New target cluster
assigned in the metadata: 'mydrcluster'
2023-09-30 16:40:37 metadata_cache INFO [7fb3f02b7700] Potential changes
detected in cluster after metadata refresh (view_id=3)
2023-09-30 16:40:37 metadata_cache INFO [7fb3f02b7700] Target cluster(s)
are part of a ClusterSet: accepting RW connections
2023-09-30 16:40:37 metadata_cache INFO [7fb3f02b7700] Cluster
'mydrcluster': role of a cluster within a ClusterSet is 'primary';
2023-09-30 16:40:37 metadata_cache INFO [7fb3f02b7700] Metadata for cluster
'mydrcluster' has 3 member(s), single-primary:
2023-09-30 16:40:37 metadata_cache INFO [7fb3f02b7700]      mysql-d:3306 /
33060 - mode=RW
2023-09-30 16:40:37 metadata_cache INFO [7fb3f02b7700]      mysql-e:3306 /
33060 - mode=RO
2023-09-30 16:40:37 metadata_cache INFO [7fb3f02b7700]      mysql-f:3306 /
33060 - mode=RO
```

You can do another switchover to make the Primary cluster primary again by issuing the commands below:

```
[root@mysql-a ~]# mysqlsh -u mysqlclusteradmin -p
MySQL  localhost:33060+ ssl  JS > myclusterset=dba.getClusterSet();
MySQL  localhost:33060+ ssl  JS > myclusterset.status();
MySQL  localhost:33060+ ssl  JS > myclusterset.status({extended:1});
MySQL  localhost:33060+ ssl  JS > myclusterset.routingOptions();
MySQL  localhost:33060+ ssl  JS > myclusterset.setPrimaryCluster('myPrimary
cluster',{dryrun:true})
MySQL  localhost:33060+ ssl  JS > myclusterset.setPrimaryCluster('myPrimar
ycluster')
MySQL  localhost:33060+ ssl  JS > myclusterset.status({extended:1});
```

Scenario 2: Role Switch of Instances Within the Clusters

In this scenario, we will be switching the roles of instances within the primary cluster. In order to do this, we will use the **cluster.setPrimaryInstance()** method. We will be making mysql-b as the primary instance within the primary cluster **myPrimaryCluster**.

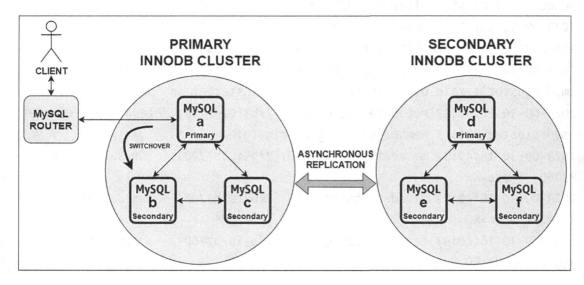

Figure 6-3. *InnoDB role switchover within the cluster*

```
MySQL  localhost:33060+ ssl  JS > dba.getCluster();
<Cluster:myPrimaryCluster>
MySQL  localhost:33060+ ssl  JS > var cluster=dba.getCluster();
MySQL  localhost:33060+ ssl  JS > cluster.status();
{
    "clusterName": "myPrimaryCluster",
    "clusterRole": "PRIMARY",
    "defaultReplicaSet": {
        "name": "default",
        "primary": "mysql-a:3306",
        "ssl": "REQUIRED",
        "status": "OK",
        "statusText": "Cluster is ONLINE and can tolerate up to ONE
        failure.",
        "topology": {
            "mysql-a:3306": {
                "address": "mysql-a:3306",
                "memberRole": "PRIMARY",
                "mode": "R/W",
                "readReplicas": {},
                "role": "HA",
                "status": "ONLINE",
                "version": "8.0.34"
            },
            "mysql-b:3306": {
                "address": "mysql-b:3306",
                "memberRole": "SECONDARY",
                "mode": "R/O",
                "readReplicas": {},
                "replicationLagFromImmediateSource": "",
                "replicationLagFromOriginalSource": "",
                "role": "HA",
                "status": "ONLINE",
                "version": "8.0.34"
            },
```

```
            "mysql-c:3306": {
                "address": "mysql-c:3306",
                "memberRole": "SECONDARY",
                "mode": "R/O",
                "readReplicas": {},
                "replicationLagFromImmediateSource": "",
                "replicationLagFromOriginalSource": "",
                "role": "HA",
                "status": "ONLINE",
                "version": "8.0.34"
            }
        },
        "topologyMode": "Single-Primary"
    },
    "domainName": "myclusterset",
    "groupInformationSourceMember": "mysql-a:3306"
}
 MySQL  localhost:33060+ ssl  JS >
 MySQL  localhost:33060+ ssl  JS > cluster.
setPrimaryInstance('mysql-b:3306')
Setting instance 'mysql-b:3306' as the primary instance of cluster
'myPrimaryCluster'...

Instance 'mysql-c:3306' remains SECONDARY.
Instance 'mysql-b:3306' was switched from SECONDARY to PRIMARY.
Instance 'mysql-a:3306' was switched from PRIMARY to SECONDARY.

The instance 'mysql-b:3306' was successfully elected as primary.
 MySQL  localhost:33060+ ssl  JS >
 MySQL  localhost:33060+ ssl  JS > cluster.status();
{
    "clusterName": "myPrimaryCluster",
    "clusterRole": "PRIMARY",
    "defaultReplicaSet": {
        "name": "default",
        "primary": "mysql-b:3306",
```

```
"ssl": "REQUIRED",
"status": "OK",
"statusText": "Cluster is ONLINE and can tolerate up to ONE
failure.",
"topology": {
    "mysql-a:3306": {
        "address": "mysql-a:3306",
        "memberRole": "SECONDARY",
        "mode": "R/O",
        "readReplicas": {},
        "replicationLagFromImmediateSource": "",
        "replicationLagFromOriginalSource": "",
        "role": "HA",
        "status": "ONLINE",
        "version": "8.0.34"
    },
    "mysql-b:3306": {
        "address": "mysql-b:3306",
        "memberRole": "PRIMARY",
        "mode": "R/W",
        "readReplicas": {},
        "role": "HA",
        "status": "ONLINE",
        "version": "8.0.34"
    },
    "mysql-c:3306": {
        "address": "mysql-c:3306",
        "memberRole": "SECONDARY",
        "mode": "R/O",
        "readReplicas": {},
        "replicationLagFromImmediateSource": "",
        "replicationLagFromOriginalSource": "",
        "role": "HA",
        "status": "ONLINE",
        "version": "8.0.34"
```

```
            }
        },
        "topologyMode": "Single-Primary"
    },
    "domainName": "myclusterset",
    "groupInformationSourceMember": "mysql-b:3306"
}
 MySQL  localhost:33060+ ssl  JS >
```

>>>>>>>>>> From /home/routeruser/log/mysqlrouter.log <<<<<<<<<<

```
2023-09-30 18:34:44 metadata_cache INFO [7fb3f02b7700] Potential changes
detected in cluster after metadata refresh (view_id=4)
2023-09-30 18:34:44 metadata_cache INFO [7fb3f02b7700] Target cluster(s)
are part of a ClusterSet: accepting RW connections
2023-09-30 18:34:44 metadata_cache INFO [7fb3f02b7700] Cluster
'myPrimaryCluster': role of a cluster within a ClusterSet is 'primary';
2023-09-30 18:34:44 metadata_cache INFO [7fb3f02b7700] Metadata for cluster
'myPrimaryCluster' has 3 member(s), single-primary:
2023-09-30 18:34:44 metadata_cache INFO [7fb3f02b7700]    mysql-a:3306 /
33060 - mode=RO
2023-09-30 18:34:44 metadata_cache INFO [7fb3f02b7700]    mysql-b:3306 /
33060 - mode=RW
2023-09-30 18:34:44 metadata_cache INFO [7fb3f02b7700]    mysql-c:3306 /
33060 - mode=RO
```

Scenario 3: Test Failure of an Instance in Secondary Role Within the Clusters

In this scenario, we shut down and restart one of the instances in a secondary role within the cluster and observe its impact on the clusterset configuration. For example, we will restart mysql-f first and will notice that there is no impact to the clusterset configuration as mysql-f automatically joins the cluster upon restart. Similarly, when we shut down mysql-f for a certain period of time simulating a failure scenario, the clusterset configuration reports that it is not able to connect to the server and reports the cluster is not tolerant to any failures. Once the server is back up and running, all of the data changes get replicated over to the server to keep the data in sync.

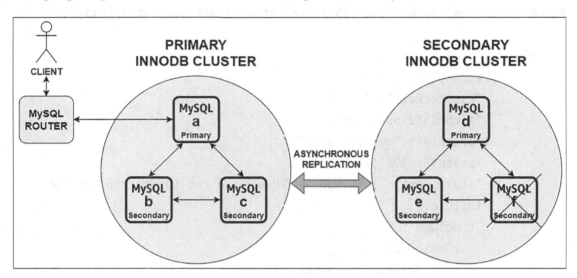

Figure 6-4. *Failure of an instance within the secondary cluster*

```
MySQL  localhost:33060+ ssl  JS > myclusterset.status();
{
    "clusters": {
        "myPrimaryCluster": {
            "clusterRole": "PRIMARY",
            "globalStatus": "OK",
            "primary": "mysql-b:3306"
        },
        "mydrcluster": {
            "clusterRole": "REPLICA",
            "clusterSetReplicationStatus": "OK",
            "globalStatus": "OK"
        }
    },
    "domainName": "myclusterset",
    "globalPrimaryInstance": "mysql-b:3306",
    "primaryCluster": "myPrimaryCluster",
```

```
    "status": "HEALTHY",
    "statusText": "All Clusters available."
}
 MySQL  localhost:33060+ ssl  JS > myclusterset.status({extended:1});
{
    "clusters": {
        "myPrimaryCluster": {
            "clusterRole": "PRIMARY",
            "globalStatus": "OK",
            "primary": "mysql-b:3306",
            "status": "OK",
            "statusText": "Cluster is ONLINE and can tolerate up to ONE
            failure.",
            "topology": {
                "mysql-a:3306": {
                    "address": "mysql-a:3306",
                    "memberRole": "SECONDARY",
                    "mode": "R/O",
                    "replicationLagFromImmediateSource": "",
                    "replicationLagFromOriginalSource": "",
                    "status": "ONLINE",
                    "version": "8.0.34"
                },
                "mysql-b:3306": {
                    "address": "mysql-b:3306",
                    "memberRole": "PRIMARY",
                    "mode": "R/W",
                    "status": "ONLINE",
                    "version": "8.0.34"
                },
                "mysql-c:3306": {
                    "address": "mysql-c:3306",
                    "memberRole": "SECONDARY",
                    "mode": "R/O",
                    "replicationLagFromImmediateSource": "",
```

```
                    "replicationLagFromOriginalSource": "",
                    "status": "ONLINE",
                    "version": "8.0.34"
                }
        },
        "transactionSet": "3817d5e7-5fd1-11ee-bb04-080027cf69cc:1-3,38
        17f70d-5fd1-11ee-bb04-080027cf69cc:1-5,861372a9-5fca-11ee-
        9711-080027cf69cc:1-132:1000071,86138144-5fca-11ee-9711-080027cf6
        9cc:1-5,d763ea33-52ad-11ee-84a8-080027cf69cc:1-72"
    },
    "mydrcluster": {
        "clusterRole": "REPLICA",
        "clusterSetReplication": {
            "applierStatus": "APPLYING",
            "applierThreadState": "Waiting for an event from
            Coordinator",
            "applierWorkerThreads": 4,
            "receiver": "mysql-d:3306",
            "receiverStatus": "ON",
            "receiverThreadState": "Waiting for source to send event",
            "replicationSsl": null,
            "source": "mysql-b:3306"
        },
        "clusterSetReplicationStatus": "OK",
        "globalStatus": "OK",
        "status": "OK",
        "statusText": "Cluster is ONLINE and can tolerate up to ONE
        failure.",
        "topology": {
            "mysql-d:3306": {
                "address": "mysql-d:3306",
                "memberRole": "PRIMARY",
                "mode": "R/O",
                "replicationLagFromImmediateSource": "",
                "replicationLagFromOriginalSource": "",
```

```
                        "status": "ONLINE",
                        "version": "8.0.34"
                },
                "mysql-e:3306": {
                        "address": "mysql-e:3306",
                        "memberRole": "SECONDARY",
                        "mode": "R/O",
                        "replicationLagFromImmediateSource": "",
                        "replicationLagFromOriginalSource": "",
                        "status": "ONLINE",
                        "version": "8.0.34"
                },
                "mysql-f:3306": {
                        "address": "mysql-f:3306",
                        "memberRole": "SECONDARY",
                        "mode": "R/O",
                        "replicationLagFromImmediateSource": "",
                        "replicationLagFromOriginalSource": "",
                        "status": "ONLINE",
                        "version": "8.0.34"
                }
        },
        "transactionSet": "3817d5e7-5fd1-11ee-bb04-080027cf69cc:1-3,38
        17f70d-5fd1-11ee-bb04-080027cf69cc:1-6,861372a9-5fca-11ee-
        9711-080027cf69cc:1-132:1000071,86138144-5fca-11ee-9711-080027cf6
        9cc:1-5,d763ea33-52ad-11ee-84a8-080027cf69cc:1-72",
        "transactionSetConsistencyStatus": "OK",
        "transactionSetErrantGtidSet": "",
        "transactionSetMissingGtidSet": ""
    }
},
"domainName": "myclusterset",
"globalPrimaryInstance": "mysql-b:3306",
"metadataServer": "mysql-b:3306",
"primaryCluster": "myPrimaryCluster",
```

```
    "status": "HEALTHY",
    "statusText": "All Clusters available."
}
```

>>>>>>>>>>>>>>>>>>>>>>>> Shutdown mysql-f: Status reports failed to connect to mysql-f. Reports DR cluster is not tolerant to any failures, 1 member is not active.

MySQL localhost:33060+ ssl JS > myclusterset.status({extended:1});
```
{
    "clusters": {
        "myPrimaryCluster": {
            "clusterRole": "PRIMARY",
            "globalStatus": "OK",
            "primary": "mysql-b:3306",
            "status": "OK",
            "statusText": "Cluster is ONLINE and can tolerate up to ONE
            failure.",
            "topology": {
                "mysql-a:3306": {
                    "address": "mysql-a:3306",
                    "memberRole": "SECONDARY",
                    "mode": "R/O",
                    "replicationLagFromImmediateSource": "",
                    "replicationLagFromOriginalSource": "",
                    "status": "ONLINE",
                    "version": "8.0.34"
                },
                "mysql-b:3306": {
                    "address": "mysql-b:3306",
                    "memberRole": "PRIMARY",
                    "mode": "R/W",
                    "status": "ONLINE",
                    "version": "8.0.34"
                },
                "mysql-c:3306": {
                    "address": "mysql-c:3306",
```

365

```
            "memberRole": "SECONDARY",
            "mode": "R/O",
            "replicationLagFromImmediateSource": "",
            "replicationLagFromOriginalSource": "",
            "status": "ONLINE",
            "version": "8.0.34"
        }
    },
    "transactionSet": "3817d5e7-5fd1-11ee-bb04-080027cf69cc:1-3,38
    17f70d-5fd1-11ee-bb04-080027cf69cc:1-5,861372a9-5fca-11ee-
    9711-080027cf69cc:1-132:1000071,86138144-5fca-11ee-9711-
    080027cf69cc:1-5,d763ea33-52ad-11ee-84a8-080027cf69cc:1-72"
},
"mydrcluster": {
    "clusterRole": "REPLICA",
    "clusterSetReplication": {
        "applierStatus": "APPLYING",
        "applierThreadState": "Waiting for an event from
        Coordinator",
        "applierWorkerThreads": 4,
        "receiver": "mysql-d:3306",
        "receiverStatus": "ON",
        "receiverThreadState": "Waiting for source to send event",
        "replicationSsl": null,
        "source": "mysql-b:3306"
    },
    "clusterSetReplicationStatus": "OK",
    "globalStatus": "OK",
    "status": "OK_NO_TOLERANCE_PARTIAL",
    "statusText": "Cluster is NOT tolerant to any failures. 1
    member is not active.",
    "topology": {
        "mysql-d:3306": {
            "address": "mysql-d:3306",
            "memberRole": "PRIMARY",
```

```
            "mode": "R/O",
            "replicationLagFromImmediateSource": "",
            "replicationLagFromOriginalSource": "",
            "status": "ONLINE",
            "version": "8.0.34"
        },
        "mysql-e:3306": {
            "address": "mysql-e:3306",
            "memberRole": "SECONDARY",
            "mode": "R/O",
            "replicationLagFromImmediateSource": "",
            "replicationLagFromOriginalSource": "",
            "status": "ONLINE",
            "version": "8.0.34"
        },
        "mysql-f:3306": {
            "address": "mysql-f:3306",
            "memberRole": "SECONDARY",
            "mode": "n/a",
            "shellConnectError": "MySQL Error 2003: Could not open
            connection to 'mysql-f:3306': Can't connect to MySQL
            server on 'mysql-f:3306' (110)",
            "status": "(MISSING)"
        }
    },
    "transactionSet": "3817d5e7-5fd1-11ee-bb04-080027cf69cc:1-3,
    3817f70d-5fd1-11ee-bb04-080027cf69cc:1-6,861372a9-5fca-11ee-
    9711-080027cf69cc:1-132:1000071,86138144-5fca-11ee-9711-080027cf6
    9cc:1-5,d763ea33-52ad-11ee-84a8-080027cf69cc:1-72",
    "transactionSetConsistencyStatus": "OK",
    "transactionSetErrantGtidSet": "",
    "transactionSetMissingGtidSet": ""
    }
},
```

```
    "domainName": "myclusterset",
    "globalPrimaryInstance": "mysql-b:3306",
    "metadataServer": "mysql-b:3306",
    "primaryCluster": "myPrimaryCluster",
    "status": "HEALTHY",
    "statusText": "All Clusters available."
}
```

Scenario 4: Test Failure of an Instance in Primary Role Within the DR Cluster

In this scenario, we simulate a failure of an instance that is in the primary role within the DR cluster and observe its impact on the clusterset configuration. For example, we will shut down mysql-d to simulate a failure scenario. As soon as the server is shut down, the DR cluster reports that it is not tolerant to any failures and one of the secondary servers will assume the primary role in the DR cluster. In my case, mysql-e assumed the primary role. Once mysql-d is back up and running, it joined the cluster as secondary in R/O mode and DR cluster reported that it can now tolerate failures.

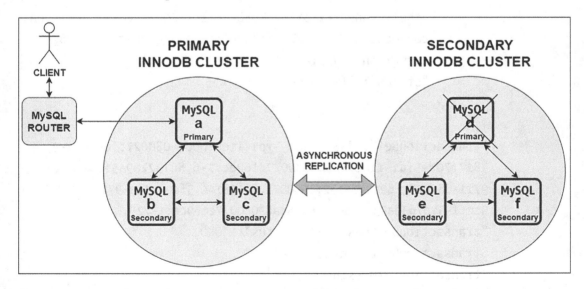

Figure 6-5. *Failure of a primary instance within the secondary cluster*

```
MySQL  localhost:33060+ ssl  JS > myclusterset.status();
{
    "clusters": {
        "myPrimaryCluster": {
            "clusterRole": "PRIMARY",
            "globalStatus": "OK",
            "primary": "mysql-b:3306"
        },
        "mydrcluster": {
            "clusterRole": "REPLICA",
            "clusterSetReplicationStatus": "OK",
            "globalStatus": "OK"
        }
    },
    "domainName": "myclusterset",
    "globalPrimaryInstance": "mysql-b:3306",
    "primaryCluster": "myPrimaryCluster",
    "status": "HEALTHY",
    "statusText": "All Clusters available."
}
MySQL  localhost:33060+ ssl  JS > myclusterset.status({extended:1});
{
    "clusters": {
        "myPrimaryCluster": {
            "clusterRole": "PRIMARY",
            "globalStatus": "OK",
            "primary": "mysql-b:3306",
            "status": "OK",
            "statusText": "Cluster is ONLINE and can tolerate up to ONE
            failure.",
            "topology": {
                "mysql-a:3306": {
                    "address": "mysql-a:3306",
                    "memberRole": "SECONDARY",
                    "mode": "R/O",
```

```
                    "replicationLagFromImmediateSource": "",
                    "replicationLagFromOriginalSource": "",
                    "status": "ONLINE",
                    "version": "8.0.34"
                },
                "mysql-b:3306": {
                    "address": "mysql-b:3306",
                    "memberRole": "PRIMARY",
                    "mode": "R/W",
                    "status": "ONLINE",
                    "version": "8.0.34"
                },
                "mysql-c:3306": {
                    "address": "mysql-c:3306",
                    "memberRole": "SECONDARY",
                    "mode": "R/O",
                    "replicationLagFromImmediateSource": "",
                    "replicationLagFromOriginalSource": "",
                    "status": "ONLINE",
                    "version": "8.0.34"
                }
            },
            "transactionSet": "3817d5e7-5fd1-11ee-bb04-080027cf69cc:1-3,38
            17f70d-5fd1-11ee-bb04-080027cf69cc:1-5,861372a9-5fca-11ee-
            9711-080027cf69cc:1-132:1000071-1000072,86138144-5fca-11ee-
            9711-080027cf69cc:1-5,d763ea33-52ad-11ee-84a8-080027cf69cc:1-72"
        },
        "mydrcluster": {
            "clusterRole": "REPLICA",
            "clusterSetReplication": {
                "applierStatus": "APPLIED_ALL",
                "applierThreadState": "Waiting for an event from
                Coordinator",
                "applierWorkerThreads": 4,
                "receiver": "mysql-e:3306",
```

```
        "receiverStatus": "ON",
        "receiverThreadState": "Waiting for source to send event",
        "replicationSsl": null,
        "source": "mysql-b:3306"
    },
    "clusterSetReplicationStatus": "OK",
    "globalStatus": "OK",
    "status": "OK_NO_TOLERANCE_PARTIAL",
    "statusText": "Cluster is NOT tolerant to any failures. 1
    member is not active.",
    "topology": {
        "mysql-d:3306": {
            "address": "mysql-d:3306",
            "memberRole": "SECONDARY",
            "mode": "n/a",
            "shellConnectError": "MySQL Error 2003: Could not open
            connection to 'mysql-d:3306': Can't connect to MySQL
            server on 'mysql-d:3306' (113)",
            "status": "(MISSING)"
        },
        "mysql-e:3306": {
            "address": "mysql-e:3306",
            "memberRole": "PRIMARY",
            "mode": "R/O",
            "replicationLagFromImmediateSource": "",
            "replicationLagFromOriginalSource": "",
            "status": "ONLINE",
            "version": "8.0.34"
        },
        "mysql-f:3306": {
            "address": "mysql-f:3306",
            "memberRole": "SECONDARY",
            "mode": "R/O",
            "replicationLagFromImmediateSource": "",
            "replicationLagFromOriginalSource": "",
```

```
                    "status": "ONLINE",
                    "version": "8.0.34"
                }
            },
            "transactionSet": "3817d5e7-5fd1-11ee-bb04-080027cf69cc:1-3,38
            17f70d-5fd1-11ee-bb04-080027cf69cc:1-7,861372a9-5fca-11ee-
            9711-080027cf69cc:1-132:1000071-1000072,86138144-5fca-11ee-
            9711-080027cf69cc:1-5,d763ea33-52ad-11ee-84a8-080027cf69cc:1-72",
            "transactionSetConsistencyStatus": "OK",
            "transactionSetErrantGtidSet": "",
            "transactionSetMissingGtidSet": ""
        }
    },
    "domainName": "myclusterset",
    "globalPrimaryInstance": "mysql-b:3306",
    "metadataServer": "mysql-b:3306",
    "primaryCluster": "myPrimaryCluster",
    "status": "HEALTHY",
    "statusText": "All Clusters available."
}
 MySQL  localhost:33060+ ssl  JS > myclusterset.status();
{
    "clusters": {
        "myPrimaryCluster": {
            "clusterRole": "PRIMARY",
            "globalStatus": "OK",
            "primary": "mysql-b:3306"
        },
        "mydrcluster": {
            "clusterRole": "REPLICA",
            "clusterSetReplicationStatus": "OK",
            "globalStatus": "OK"
        }
    },
    "domainName": "myclusterset",
    "globalPrimaryInstance": "mysql-b:3306",
```

372

```
    "primaryCluster": "myPrimaryCluster",
    "status": "HEALTHY",
    "statusText": "All Clusters available."
}
 MySQL  localhost:33060+ ssl  JS > myclusterset.status({extended:1});
{
    "clusters": {
        "myPrimaryCluster": {
            "clusterRole": "PRIMARY",
            "globalStatus": "OK",
            "primary": "mysql-b:3306",
            "status": "OK",
            "statusText": "Cluster is ONLINE and can tolerate up to ONE
            failure.",
            "topology": {
                "mysql-a:3306": {
                    "address": "mysql-a:3306",
                    "memberRole": "SECONDARY",
                    "mode": "R/O",
                    "replicationLagFromImmediateSource": "",
                    "replicationLagFromOriginalSource": "",
                    "status": "ONLINE",
                    "version": "8.0.34"
                },
                "mysql-b:3306": {
                    "address": "mysql-b:3306",
                    "memberRole": "PRIMARY",
                    "mode": "R/W",
                    "status": "ONLINE",
                    "version": "8.0.34"
                },
                "mysql-c:3306": {
                    "address": "mysql-c:3306",
                    "memberRole": "SECONDARY",
                    "mode": "R/O",
```

```
                "replicationLagFromImmediateSource": "",
                "replicationLagFromOriginalSource": "",
                "status": "ONLINE",
                "version": "8.0.34"
            }
        },
        "transactionSet": "3817d5e7-5fd1-11ee-bb04-080027cf69cc:1-3,38
        17f70d-5fd1-11ee-bb04-080027cf69cc:1-5,861372a9-5fca-11ee-
        9711-080027cf69cc:1-132:1000071-1000072,86138144-5fca-11ee-
        9711-080027cf69cc:1-5,d763ea33-52ad-11ee-84a8-080027cf69cc:1-72"
    },
    "mydrcluster": {
        "clusterRole": "REPLICA",
        "clusterSetReplication": {
            "applierStatus": "APPLIED_ALL",
            "applierThreadState": "Waiting for an event from
            Coordinator",
            "applierWorkerThreads": 4,
            "receiver": "mysql-e:3306",
            "receiverStatus": "ON",
            "receiverThreadState": "Waiting for source to send event",
            "replicationSsl": null,
            "source": "mysql-b:3306"
        },
        "clusterSetReplicationStatus": "OK",
        "globalStatus": "OK",
        "status": "OK",
        "statusText": "Cluster is ONLINE and can tolerate up to ONE
        failure.",
        "topology": {
            "mysql-d:3306": {
                "address": "mysql-d:3306",
                "memberRole": "SECONDARY",
                "mode": "R/O",
                "replicationLagFromImmediateSource": "",
```

```
                    "replicationLagFromOriginalSource": "",
                    "status": "ONLINE",
                    "version": "8.0.34"
                },
                "mysql-e:3306": {
                    "address": "mysql-e:3306",
                    "memberRole": "PRIMARY",
                    "mode": "R/O",
                    "replicationLagFromImmediateSource": "",
                    "replicationLagFromOriginalSource": "",
                    "status": "ONLINE",
                    "version": "8.0.34"
                },
                "mysql-f:3306": {
                    "address": "mysql-f:3306",
                    "memberRole": "SECONDARY",
                    "mode": "R/O",
                    "replicationLagFromImmediateSource": "",
                    "replicationLagFromOriginalSource": "",
                    "status": "ONLINE",
                    "version": "8.0.34"
                }
            },
            "transactionSet": "3817d5e7-5fd1-11ee-bb04-080027cf69cc:1-3,38
17f70d-5fd1-11ee-bb04-080027cf69cc:1-8,861372a9-5fca-11ee-
9711-080027cf69cc:1-132:1000071-1000072,86138144-5fca-11ee-
9711-080027cf69cc:1-5,d763ea33-52ad-11ee-84a8-080027cf69cc:1-72",
            "transactionSetConsistencyStatus": "OK",
            "transactionSetErrantGtidSet": "",
            "transactionSetMissingGtidSet": ""
        }
    },
    "domainName": "myclusterset",
    "globalPrimaryInstance": "mysql-b:3306",
    "metadataServer": "mysql-b:3306",
```

```
    "primaryCluster": "myPrimaryCluster",
    "status": "HEALTHY",
    "statusText": "All Clusters available."
}
```

InnoDB Clusterset Scenarios – Recover InnoDB Clusterset from a Major Outage

In this scenario, we simulate a very hypothetical situation of a multi-region outage where we shut down all six servers within the clusterset configuration. In order to recover the clusterset from the outage, we follow the high-level steps:

1. Start all six servers.

2. Issue **dba.rebootClusterFromCompleteOutage()** on one of the nodes (mysql-a/mysql-b/mysql-c) from the primary cluster.

3. Issue **dba.rebootClusterFromCompleteOutage()** on one of the nodes (mysql-d/mysql-e/mysql-f) from the DR cluster.

4. Verify clusterset status.

5. Recover and reconfigure MySQL Router.

>>>>>> After all servers are started. Status below:

```
[root@mysql-a ~]# mysqlsh -u mysqlclusteradmin -p
MySQL Shell 8.0.34
 MySQL  localhost:33060+ ssl  JS > myclusterset=dba.getClusterSet();
No PRIMARY member found for cluster 'myPrimaryCluster'
<ClusterSet:myclusterset>
 MySQL  localhost:33060+ ssl  JS > myclusterset.status();
{
    "clusters": {
        "myPrimaryCluster": {
            "clusterErrors": [
                "ERROR: Cluster members are reachable but they're all
                OFFLINE."
```

```
            ],
            "clusterRole": "PRIMARY",
            "globalStatus": "NOT_OK",
            "primary": null,
            "status": "OFFLINE",
            "statusText": "All members of the group are OFFLINE"
        },
        "mydrcluster": {
            "clusterErrors": [
                "ERROR: Cluster members are reachable but they're all
                OFFLINE.",
                "WARNING: Replication from the Primary Cluster not in
                expected state"
            ],
            "clusterRole": "REPLICA",
            "clusterSetReplicationStatus": "STOPPED",
            "globalStatus": "NOT_OK",
            "status": "OFFLINE",
            "statusText": "All members of the group are OFFLINE"
        }
    },
    "domainName": "myclusterset",
    "globalPrimaryInstance": null,
    "primaryCluster": "myPrimaryCluster",
    "status": "UNAVAILABLE",
    "statusText": "Primary Cluster is not available. ClusterSet
    availability may be restored by restoring the Primary Cluster or
    failover."
}
```

>>>>>>>>>>>> Issued dba.rebootClusterFromCompleteOutage();. Primary cluster came back up

MySQL localhost:33060+ ssl JS > var cluster = dba.
rebootClusterFromCompleteOutage();
```
No PRIMARY member found for cluster 'myPrimaryCluster'
Restoring the Cluster 'myPrimaryCluster' from complete outage...
```

Cluster instances: 'mysql-a:3306' (OFFLINE), 'mysql-b:3306' (OFFLINE),
'mysql-c:3306' (OFFLINE)
Waiting for instances to apply pending received transactions...
Validating instance configuration at localhost:3306...

This instance reports its own address as mysql-a:3306

Instance configuration is suitable.
* Waiting for seed instance to become ONLINE...
mysql-a:3306 was restored.
Validating instance configuration at mysql-b:3306...

This instance reports its own address as mysql-b:3306

Instance configuration is suitable.
Rejoining instance 'mysql-b:3306' to cluster 'myPrimaryCluster'...

Re-creating recovery account...
NOTE: User 'mysql_innodb_cluster_2'@'%' already existed at instance
'mysql-a:3306'. It will be deleted and created again with a new password.

* Waiting for the Cluster to synchronize with the PRIMARY Cluster...
** Transactions replicated ################################ 100%

The instance 'mysql-b:3306' was successfully rejoined to the cluster.

Validating instance configuration at mysql-c:3306...

This instance reports its own address as mysql-c:3306

Instance configuration is suitable.
Rejoining instance 'mysql-c:3306' to cluster 'myPrimaryCluster'...

Re-creating recovery account...
NOTE: User 'mysql_innodb_cluster_3'@'%' already existed at instance
'mysql-a:3306'. It will be deleted and created again with a new password.

* Waiting for the Cluster to synchronize with the PRIMARY Cluster...
** Transactions replicated ################################ 100%

The instance 'mysql-c:3306' was successfully rejoined to the cluster.

The Cluster was successfully rebooted.

```
 MySQL  localhost:33060+ ssl  JS > myclusterset.status();
{
    "clusters": {
        "myPrimaryCluster": {
            "clusterRole": "PRIMARY",
            "globalStatus": "OK",
            "primary": "mysql-a:3306"
        },
        "mydrcluster": {
            "clusterErrors": [
                "ERROR: Cluster members are reachable but they're all
                OFFLINE.",
                "WARNING: Replication from the Primary Cluster not in
                expected state",
                "WARNING: Replicating from wrong source. Expected
                mysql-a:3306 (d763ea33-52ad-11ee-84a8-080027cf69cc) but is
                mysql-b:3306 (aaa6ecea-5fc2-11ee-bb4b-080027cf69cc)"
            ],
            "clusterRole": "REPLICA",
            "clusterSetReplicationStatus": "STOPPED",
            "globalStatus": "NOT_OK",
            "status": "OFFLINE",
            "statusText": "All members of the group are OFFLINE"
        }
    },
    "domainName": "myclusterset",
    "globalPrimaryInstance": "mysql-a:3306",
    "primaryCluster": "myPrimaryCluster",
    "status": "AVAILABLE",
    "statusText": "Primary Cluster available, there are issues with a
    Replica cluster."
}
```

**>>>>>>>>>> To recover DR cluster. Issue dba.
rebootClusterFromCompleteOutage(); on any of the servers (mysql-d/mysql-e/
mysql-f) to recover the DR cluster mydrcluster**

```
[root@mysql-d ~]# mysqlsh -u mysqlclusteradmin -p
Please provide the password for 'mysqlclusteradmin@localhost':
*************
Save password for 'mysqlclusteradmin@localhost'? [Y]es/[N]o/Ne[v]er
(default No): Y
MySQL Shell 8.0.34
Creating a session to 'mysqlclusteradmin@localhost'
 MySQL  localhost:33060+ ssl  JS >
 MySQL  localhost:33060+ ssl  JS > var cluster = dba.
rebootClusterFromCompleteOutage();
Restoring the Cluster 'mydrcluster' from complete outage...

Cluster instances: 'mysql-d:3306' (OFFLINE), 'mysql-e:3306' (OFFLINE),
'mysql-f:3306' (OFFLINE)
Waiting for instances to apply pending received transactions...
Validating instance configuration at localhost:3306...

This instance reports its own address as mysql-d:3306

Instance configuration is suitable.
* Waiting for seed instance to become ONLINE...
mysql-d:3306 was restored.
Rejoining Cluster into its original ClusterSet...

Rejoining cluster 'mydrcluster' to the clusterset
* Reconciling 4 internally generated GTIDs

* Refreshing replication settings
** Changing replication source of mysql-d:3306 to mysql-a:3306

Cluster 'mydrcluster' was rejoined to the clusterset
Validating instance configuration at mysql-e:3306...

This instance reports its own address as mysql-e:3306

Instance configuration is suitable.
Rejoining instance 'mysql-e:3306' to cluster 'mydrcluster'...

* Waiting for the Cluster to synchronize with the PRIMARY Cluster...
** Transactions replicated  ################################  100%
```

```
* Configuring ClusterSet managed replication channel...
** Changing replication source of mysql-e:3306 to mysql-a:3306

Re-creating recovery account...
NOTE: User 'mysql_innodb_cluster_5'@'%' already existed at instance
'mysql-a:3306'. It will be deleted and created again with a new password.

* Waiting for the Cluster to synchronize with the PRIMARY Cluster...
** Transactions replicated  ################################  100%

The instance 'mysql-e:3306' was successfully rejoined to the cluster.

Validating instance configuration at mysql-f:3306...

This instance reports its own address as mysql-f:3306

Instance configuration is suitable.
Rejoining instance 'mysql-f:3306' to cluster 'mydrcluster'...

* Waiting for the Cluster to synchronize with the PRIMARY Cluster...
** Transactions replicated  ################################  100%

* Configuring ClusterSet managed replication channel...
** Changing replication source of mysql-f:3306 to mysql-a:3306

Re-creating recovery account...
NOTE: User 'mysql_innodb_cluster_6'@'%' already existed at instance
'mysql-a:3306'. It will be deleted and created again with a new password.

* Waiting for the Cluster to synchronize with the PRIMARY Cluster...
** Transactions replicated  ################################  100%

The instance 'mysql-f:3306' was successfully rejoined to the cluster.

The Cluster was successfully rebooted.
```

 MySQL localhost:33060+ ssl JS > cluster.status();
```
{
    "clusterName": "mydrcluster",
    "clusterRole": "REPLICA",
    "clusterSetReplicationStatus": "OK",
    "defaultReplicaSet": {
```

```
"name": "default",
"primary": "mysql-d:3306",
"ssl": "REQUIRED",
"status": "OK",
"statusText": "Cluster is ONLINE and can tolerate up to ONE
failure.",
"topology": {
    "mysql-d:3306": {
        "address": "mysql-d:3306",
        "memberRole": "PRIMARY",
        "mode": "R/O",
        "readReplicas": {},
        "replicationLagFromImmediateSource": "",
        "replicationLagFromOriginalSource": "",
        "role": "HA",
        "status": "ONLINE",
        "version": "8.0.34"
    },
    "mysql-e:3306": {
        "address": "mysql-e:3306",
        "memberRole": "SECONDARY",
        "mode": "R/O",
        "readReplicas": {},
        "replicationLagFromImmediateSource": "",
        "replicationLagFromOriginalSource": "",
        "role": "HA",
        "status": "ONLINE",
        "version": "8.0.34"
    },
    "mysql-f:3306": {
        "address": "mysql-f:3306",
        "memberRole": "SECONDARY",
        "mode": "R/O",
        "readReplicas": {},
        "replicationLagFromImmediateSource": "",
```

```
                    "replicationLagFromOriginalSource": "",
                    "role": "HA",
                    "status": "ONLINE",
                    "version": "8.0.34"
                }
            },
            "topologyMode": "Single-Primary"
        },
        "domainName": "myclusterset",
        "groupInformationSourceMember": "mysql-d:3306",
        "metadataServer": "mysql-a:3306"
}
```

>>>>>>>> Verify clusterset status

MySQL localhost:33060+ ssl JS > myclusterset.status();
```
{
    "clusters": {
        "myPrimaryCluster": {
            "clusterRole": "PRIMARY",
            "globalStatus": "OK",
            "primary": "mysql-a:3306"
        },
        "mydrcluster": {
            "clusterRole": "REPLICA",
            "clusterSetReplicationStatus": "OK",
            "globalStatus": "OK"
        }
    },
    "domainName": "myclusterset",
    "globalPrimaryInstance": "mysql-a:3306",
    "primaryCluster": "myPrimaryCluster",
    "status": "HEALTHY",
    "statusText": "All Clusters available."
}
```

```
MySQL  localhost:33060+ ssl  JS > myclusterset.status({extended:1});
{
    "clusters": {
        "myPrimaryCluster": {
            "clusterRole": "PRIMARY",
            "globalStatus": "OK",
            "primary": "mysql-a:3306",
            "status": "OK",
            "statusText": "Cluster is ONLINE and can tolerate up to ONE
            failure.",
            "topology": {
                "mysql-a:3306": {
                    "address": "mysql-a:3306",
                    "memberRole": "PRIMARY",
                    "mode": "R/W",
                    "status": "ONLINE",
                    "version": "8.0.34"
                },
                "mysql-b:3306": {
                    "address": "mysql-b:3306",
                    "memberRole": "SECONDARY",
                    "mode": "R/O",
                    "replicationLagFromImmediateSource": "",
                    "replicationLagFromOriginalSource": "",
                    "status": "ONLINE",
                    "version": "8.0.34"
                },
                "mysql-c:3306": {
                    "address": "mysql-c:3306",
                    "memberRole": "SECONDARY",
                    "mode": "R/O",
                    "replicationLagFromImmediateSource": "",
                    "replicationLagFromOriginalSource": "",
                    "status": "ONLINE",
                    "version": "8.0.34"
```

```
        }
    },
    "transactionSet": "3817d5e7-5fd1-11ee-bb04-080027cf69cc:1-3,38
    17f70d-5fd1-11ee-bb04-080027cf69cc:1-9,861372a9-5fca-11ee-
    9711-080027cf69cc:1-165:1000071-1000072,86138144-5fca-11ee-
    9711-080027cf69cc:1-8,d763ea33-52ad-11ee-84a8-080027cf69cc:1-72"
},
"mydrcluster": {
    "clusterRole": "REPLICA",
    "clusterSetReplication": {
        "applierStatus": "APPLIED_ALL",
        "applierThreadState": "Waiting for an event from
        Coordinator",
        "applierWorkerThreads": 4,
        "receiver": "mysql-d:3306",
        "receiverStatus": "ON",
        "receiverThreadState": "Waiting for source to send event",
        "replicationSsl": null,
        "source": "mysql-a:3306"
    },
    "clusterSetReplicationStatus": "OK",
    "globalStatus": "OK",
    "status": "OK",
    "statusText": "Cluster is ONLINE and can tolerate up to ONE
    failure.",
    "topology": {
        "mysql-d:3306": {
            "address": "mysql-d:3306",
            "memberRole": "PRIMARY",
            "mode": "R/O",
            "replicationLagFromImmediateSource": "",
            "replicationLagFromOriginalSource": "",
            "status": "ONLINE",
            "version": "8.0.34"
        },
```

```
                "mysql-e:3306": {
                    "address": "mysql-e:3306",
                    "memberRole": "SECONDARY",
                    "mode": "R/O",
                    "replicationLagFromImmediateSource": "",
                    "replicationLagFromOriginalSource": "",
                    "status": "ONLINE",
                    "version": "8.0.34"
                },
                "mysql-f:3306": {
                    "address": "mysql-f:3306",
                    "memberRole": "SECONDARY",
                    "mode": "R/O",
                    "replicationLagFromImmediateSource": "",
                    "replicationLagFromOriginalSource": "",
                    "status": "ONLINE",
                    "version": "8.0.34"
                }
            },
            "transactionSet": "3817d5e7-5fd1-11ee-bb04-080027cf69cc:1-3,38
            17f70d-5fd1-11ee-bb04-080027cf69cc:1-11,861372a9-5fca-11ee-
            9711-080027cf69cc:1-165:1000071-1000072,86138144-5fca-11ee-
            9711-080027cf69cc:1-8,d763ea33-52ad-11ee-84a8-080027cf69cc:1-72",
            "transactionSetConsistencyStatus": "OK",
            "transactionSetErrantGtidSet": "",
            "transactionSetMissingGtidSet": ""
        }
    },
    "domainName": "myclusterset",
    "globalPrimaryInstance": "mysql-a:3306",
    "metadataServer": "mysql-a:3306",
    "primaryCluster": "myPrimaryCluster",
    "status": "HEALTHY",
    "statusText": "All Clusters available."
}
```

>>>>> Recover and restart MySQL router configuration

[root@mysql-a ~]# cd /home/routeruser/
[root@mysql-a routeruser]# ls -ltr
total 20
drwx------ 2 routeruser routeruser   6 Sep 30 15:58 run
-rw------- 1 routeruser routeruser   87 Sep 30 15:58 mysqlrouter.key
-rwx------ 1 routeruser routeruser 158 Sep 30 15:58 stop.sh
-rwx------ 1 routeruser routeruser 296 Sep 30 15:58 start.sh
-rw------- 1 routeruser routeruser 2033 Sep 30 15:58 mysqlrouter.conf
drwx------ 2 routeruser routeruser   29 Sep 30 15:58 log
drwx------ 2 routeruser routeruser 116 Sep 30 15:58 data
-rw-r--r-- 1 routeruser routeruser   5 Sep 30 16:01 mysqlrouter.pid
srwxrwxrwx 1 routeruser routeruser   0 Sep 30 16:01 mysqlro.sock
srwxrwxrwx 1 routeruser routeruser   0 Sep 30 16:01 mysql.sock
srwxrwxrwx 1 routeruser routeruser   0 Sep 30 16:01 mysqlxro.sock
srwxrwxrwx 1 routeruser routeruser   0 Sep 30 16:01 mysqlx.sock
[root@mysql-a routeruser]#
[root@mysql-a routeruser]# ps -ef|grep routeruser
root   1470 1399 0 19:23 pts/1   00:00:00 grep --color=auto
routeruser
[root@mysql-a routeruser]#
[root@mysql-a routeruser]# ./start.sh
[root@mysql-a routeruser]# Error: PID file /home/routeruser/mysqlrouter.pid
found. Already running?

[root@mysql-a routeruser]# cat mysqlrouter.pid
2480
[root@mysql-a routeruser]# mv mysqlrouter.pid mysqlrouter.pid.bk
[root@mysql-a routeruser]# ls -ltr
total 20
drwx------ 2 routeruser routeruser   6 Sep 30 15:58 run
-rw------- 1 routeruser routeruser   87 Sep 30 15:58 mysqlrouter.key
-rwx------ 1 routeruser routeruser 158 Sep 30 15:58 stop.sh
-rwx------ 1 routeruser routeruser 296 Sep 30 15:58 start.sh
-rw------- 1 routeruser routeruser 2033 Sep 30 15:58 mysqlrouter.conf

```
drwx------ 2 routeruser routeruser   29 Sep 30 15:58 log
drwx------ 2 routeruser routeruser  116 Sep 30 15:58 data
-rw-r--r-- 1 routeruser routeruser    5 Sep 30 16:01 mysqlrouter.pid.bk
srwxrwxrwx 1 routeruser routeruser    0 Sep 30 16:01 mysqlro.sock
srwxrwxrwx 1 routeruser routeruser    0 Sep 30 16:01 mysql.sock
srwxrwxrwx 1 routeruser routeruser    0 Sep 30 16:01 mysqlxro.sock
srwxrwxrwx 1 routeruser routeruser    0 Sep 30 16:01 mysqlx.sock
[root@mysql-a routeruser]#
```

[root@mysql-a routeruser]# ./start.sh
```
[root@mysql-a routeruser]# PID 1483 written to '/home/routeruser/
mysqlrouter.pid'
stopping to log to the console. Continuing to log to filelog
```
[root@mysql-a routeruser]# ls -ltr
```
total 24
drwx------ 2 routeruser routeruser    6 Sep 30 15:58 run
-rw------- 1 routeruser routeruser   87 Sep 30 15:58 mysqlrouter.key
-rwx------ 1 routeruser routeruser  158 Sep 30 15:58 stop.sh
-rwx------ 1 routeruser routeruser  296 Sep 30 15:58 start.sh
-rw------- 1 routeruser routeruser 2033 Sep 30 15:58 mysqlrouter.conf
drwx------ 2 routeruser routeruser   29 Sep 30 15:58 log
drwx------ 2 routeruser routeruser  116 Sep 30 15:58 data
-rw-r--r-- 1 routeruser routeruser    5 Sep 30 16:01 mysqlrouter.pid.bk
-rw-r--r-- 1 routeruser routeruser    5 Sep 30 19:24 mysqlrouter.pid
srwxrwxrwx 1 routeruser routeruser    0 Sep 30 19:24 mysqlro.sock
srwxrwxrwx 1 routeruser routeruser    0 Sep 30 19:24 mysql.sock
srwxrwxrwx 1 routeruser routeruser    0 Sep 30 19:24 mysqlxro.sock
srwxrwxrwx 1 routeruser routeruser    0 Sep 30 19:24 mysqlx.sock
[root@mysql-a routeruser]#
```
[root@mysql-a routeruser]# cat mysqlrouter.pid
```
1483
```
[root@mysql-a routeruser]# cd log/
```
[root@mysql-a log]# ls -ltr
total 16
-rw-r--r-- 1 routeruser routeruser 13702 Sep 30 19:24 mysqlrouter.log
```
[root@mysql-a log]# tail -100f mysqlrouter.log

2023-09-30 16:01:38 routing INFO [7fb3c7fff700] [routing:bootstrap_rw]
started: routing strategy = first-available
2023-09-30 16:01:38 routing INFO [7fb3c7fff700] [routing:bootstrap_rw]
started: listening using /home/routeruser/mysql.sock
2023-09-30 16:01:38 routing INFO [7fb3c7fff700] Start accepting connections
for routing routing:bootstrap_rw listening on 6446 and named socket /home/
routeruser/mysql.sock
2023-09-30 16:01:38 routing INFO [7fb3c77fe700] [routing:bootstrap_x_ro]
started: routing strategy = round-robin-with-fallback
2023-09-30 16:01:38 routing INFO [7fb3c77fe700] [routing:bootstrap_x_ro]
started: listening using /home/routeruser/mysqlxro.sock
2023-09-30 16:01:38 routing INFO [7fb3c77fe700] Start accepting connections
for routing routing:bootstrap_x_ro listening on 6449 and named socket /
home/routeruser/mysqlxro.sock
2023-09-30 16:01:38 routing INFO [7fb3c6ffd700] [routing:bootstrap_x_rw]
started: routing strategy = first-available
2023-09-30 16:01:38 routing INFO [7fb3c6ffd700] [routing:bootstrap_x_rw]
started: listening using /home/routeruser/mysqlx.sock
2023-09-30 16:01:38 routing INFO [7fb3c6ffd700] Start accepting connections
for routing routing:bootstrap_x_rw listening on 6448 and named socket /
home/routeruser/mysqlx.sock
2023-09-30 16:01:38 metadata_cache INFO [7fb3f02b7700] Connected with
metadata server running on mysql-b:3306
2023-09-30 16:01:38 metadata_cache INFO [7fb3f02b7700] Connected with
metadata server running on mysql-c:3306
2023-09-30 16:01:38 metadata_cache INFO [7fb3f02b7700] Connected with
metadata server running on mysql-d:3306
2023-09-30 16:01:38 metadata_cache INFO [7fb3f02b7700] Connected with
metadata server running on mysql-e:3306
2023-09-30 16:01:38 metadata_cache INFO [7fb3f02b7700] Connected with
metadata server running on mysql-f:3306
2023-09-30 16:01:38 metadata_cache INFO [7fb3f02b7700] Potential changes
detected in cluster after metadata refresh (view_id=2)
2023-09-30 16:01:38 metadata_cache INFO [7fb3f02b7700] Target cluster(s)
are part of a ClusterSet: accepting RW connections

2023-09-30 16:01:38 metadata_cache INFO [7fb3f02b7700] Cluster
'myPrimaryCluster': role of a cluster within a ClusterSet is 'primary';
2023-09-30 16:01:38 metadata_cache INFO [7fb3f02b7700] Metadata for cluster
'myPrimaryCluster' has 3 member(s), single-primary:
2023-09-30 16:01:38 metadata_cache INFO [7fb3f02b7700]   mysql-a:3306 /
33060 - mode=RW
2023-09-30 16:01:38 metadata_cache INFO [7fb3f02b7700]   mysql-b:3306 /
33060 - mode=RO
2023-09-30 16:01:38 metadata_cache INFO [7fb3f02b7700]   mysql-c:3306 /
33060 - mode=RO
2023-09-30 16:01:38 metadata_cache INFO [7fb3f02b7700] Enabling GR notices
for cluster 'myPrimaryCluster' changes on node mysql-a:33060
2023-09-30 16:01:38 metadata_cache INFO [7fb3f02b7700] Enabling GR notices
for cluster 'myPrimaryCluster' changes on node mysql-b:33060
2023-09-30 16:01:38 metadata_cache INFO [7fb3f02b7700] Enabling GR notices
for cluster 'myPrimaryCluster' changes on node mysql-c:33060
2023-09-30 16:40:37 metadata_cache INFO [7fb3f02b7700] New target cluster
assigned in the metadata: 'mydrcluster'
2023-09-30 16:40:37 metadata_cache INFO [7fb3f02b7700] Potential changes
detected in cluster after metadata refresh (view_id=3)
2023-09-30 16:40:37 metadata_cache INFO [7fb3f02b7700] Target cluster(s)
are part of a ClusterSet: accepting RW connections
2023-09-30 16:40:37 metadata_cache INFO [7fb3f02b7700] Cluster
'mydrcluster': role of a cluster within a ClusterSet is 'primary';
2023-09-30 16:40:37 metadata_cache INFO [7fb3f02b7700] Metadata for cluster
'mydrcluster' has 3 member(s), single-primary:
2023-09-30 16:40:37 metadata_cache INFO [7fb3f02b7700]   mysql-d:3306 /
33060 - mode=RW
2023-09-30 16:40:37 metadata_cache INFO [7fb3f02b7700]   mysql-e:3306 /
33060 - mode=RO
2023-09-30 16:40:37 metadata_cache INFO [7fb3f02b7700]   mysql-f:3306 /
33060 - mode=RO
2023-09-30 16:40:37 metadata_cache INFO [7fb3f02b7700] Removing unused GR
notification session to 'mysql-a:33060'
2023-09-30 16:40:37 metadata_cache INFO [7fb3f02b7700] Removing unused GR

notification session to 'mysql-b:33060'

2023-09-30 16:40:37 metadata_cache INFO [7fb3f02b7700] Removing unused GR notification session to 'mysql-c:33060'

2023-09-30 16:40:37 metadata_cache INFO [7fb3f02b7700] Enabling GR notices for cluster 'mydrcluster' changes on node mysql-d:33060

2023-09-30 16:40:38 metadata_cache INFO [7fb3f02b7700] Enabling GR notices for cluster 'mydrcluster' changes on node mysql-e:33060

2023-09-30 16:40:38 metadata_cache INFO [7fb3f02b7700] Enabling GR notices for cluster 'mydrcluster' changes on node mysql-f:33060

2023-09-30 16:47:01 metadata_cache INFO [7fb3f02b7700] New target cluster assigned in the metadata: 'myPrimaryCluster'

2023-09-30 16:47:01 metadata_cache INFO [7fb3f02b7700] Potential changes detected in cluster after metadata refresh (view_id=4)

2023-09-30 16:47:01 metadata_cache INFO [7fb3f02b7700] Target cluster(s) are part of a ClusterSet: accepting RW connections

2023-09-30 16:47:01 metadata_cache INFO [7fb3f02b7700] Cluster 'myPrimaryCluster': role of a cluster within a ClusterSet is 'primary';

2023-09-30 16:47:01 metadata_cache INFO [7fb3f02b7700] Metadata for cluster 'myPrimaryCluster' has 3 member(s), single-primary:

2023-09-30 16:47:01 metadata_cache INFO [7fb3f02b7700]   mysql-a:3306 / 33060 - mode=RW

2023-09-30 16:47:01 metadata_cache INFO [7fb3f02b7700]   mysql-b:3306 / 33060 - mode=RO

2023-09-30 16:47:01 metadata_cache INFO [7fb3f02b7700]   mysql-c:3306 / 33060 - mode=RO

2023-09-30 16:47:01 metadata_cache INFO [7fb3f02b7700] Removing unused GR notification session to 'mysql-d:33060'

2023-09-30 16:47:01 metadata_cache INFO [7fb3f02b7700] Removing unused GR notification session to 'mysql-e:33060'

2023-09-30 16:47:01 metadata_cache INFO [7fb3f02b7700] Removing unused GR notification session to 'mysql-f:33060'

2023-09-30 16:47:01 metadata_cache INFO [7fb3f02b7700] Enabling GR notices for cluster 'myPrimaryCluster' changes on node mysql-a:33060

2023-09-30 16:47:02 metadata_cache INFO [7fb3f02b7700] Enabling GR notices for cluster 'myPrimaryCluster' changes on node mysql-b:33060

```
2023-09-30 16:47:02 metadata_cache INFO [7fb3f02b7700] Enabling GR notices
for cluster 'myPrimaryCluster' changes on node mysql-c:33060
2023-09-30 18:34:44 metadata_cache INFO [7fb3f02b7700] Potential changes
detected in cluster after metadata refresh (view_id=4)
2023-09-30 18:34:44 metadata_cache INFO [7fb3f02b7700] Target cluster(s)
are part of a ClusterSet: accepting RW connections
2023-09-30 18:34:44 metadata_cache INFO [7fb3f02b7700] Cluster
'myPrimaryCluster': role of a cluster within a ClusterSet is 'primary';
2023-09-30 18:34:44 metadata_cache INFO [7fb3f02b7700] Metadata for cluster
'myPrimaryCluster' has 3 member(s), single-primary:
2023-09-30 18:34:44 metadata_cache INFO [7fb3f02b7700]     mysql-a:3306 /
33060 - mode=RO
2023-09-30 18:34:44 metadata_cache INFO [7fb3f02b7700]     mysql-b:3306 /
33060 - mode=RW
2023-09-30 18:34:44 metadata_cache INFO [7fb3f02b7700]     mysql-c:3306 /
33060 - mode=RO
2023-09-30 18:51:49 metadata_cache WARNING [7fb3f02b7700] Failed connecting
with Metadata Server mysql-d:3306: Can't connect to MySQL server on
'mysql-d:3306' (110) (2003)
2023-09-30 18:56:29 metadata_cache INFO [7fb3f02b7700] Connected with
metadata server running on mysql-d:3306
2023-09-30 19:24:12 io INFO [7f7806b77880] starting 1 io-threads, using
backend 'linux_epoll'
2023-09-30 19:24:12 http_server INFO [7f7806b77880] listening on
0.0.0.0:8443
2023-09-30 19:24:12 routing INFO [7f77ed7f2700] [routing:bootstrap_ro]
started: routing strategy = round-robin-with-fallback
2023-09-30 19:24:12 routing WARNING [7f77ed7f2700] Socket file /home/
routeruser/mysqlro.sock already exists, but seems to be unused. Deleting
and retrying...
2023-09-30 19:24:12 routing INFO [7f77ed7f2700] [routing:bootstrap_ro]
started: listening using /home/routeruser/mysqlro.sock
2023-09-30 19:24:12 routing INFO [7f77ecff1700] [routing:bootstrap_rw]
started: routing strategy = first-available
2023-09-30 19:24:12 routing WARNING [7f77ecff1700] Socket file /home/
```

routeruser/mysql.sock already exists, but seems to be unused. Deleting and retrying...
2023-09-30 19:24:12 routing INFO [7f77ecff1700] [routing:bootstrap_rw] started: listening using /home/routeruser/mysql.sock
2023-09-30 19:24:12 routing INFO [7f77d7fff700] [routing:bootstrap_x_ro] started: routing strategy = round-robin-with-fallback
2023-09-30 19:24:12 routing WARNING [7f77d7fff700] Socket file /home/routeruser/mysqlxro.sock already exists, but seems to be unused. Deleting and retrying...
2023-09-30 19:24:12 routing INFO [7f77d7fff700] [routing:bootstrap_x_ro] started: listening using /home/routeruser/mysqlxro.sock
2023-09-30 19:24:12 metadata_cache_plugin INFO [7f77efff7700] Starting Metadata Cache
2023-09-30 19:24:12 metadata_cache INFO [7f77efff7700] Connections using ssl_mode 'PREFERRED'
2023-09-30 19:24:12 routing INFO [7f77d77fe700] [routing:bootstrap_x_rw] started: routing strategy = first-available
2023-09-30 19:24:12 routing WARNING [7f77d77fe700] Socket file /home/routeruser/mysqlx.sock already exists, but seems to be unused. Deleting and retrying...
2023-09-30 19:24:12 routing INFO [7f77d77fe700] [routing:bootstrap_x_rw] started: listening using /home/routeruser/mysqlx.sock
2023-09-30 19:24:12 routing INFO [7f77d77fe700] Start accepting connections for routing routing:bootstrap_x_rw listening on 6448 and named socket /home/routeruser/mysqlx.sock
2023-09-30 19:24:12 routing INFO [7f77d7fff700] Start accepting connections for routing routing:bootstrap_x_ro listening on 6449 and named socket /home/routeruser/mysqlxro.sock
2023-09-30 19:24:12 routing INFO [7f77ed7f2700] Start accepting connections for routing routing:bootstrap_ro listening on 6447 and named socket /home/routeruser/mysqlro.sock
2023-09-30 19:24:12 routing INFO [7f77ecff1700] Start accepting connections for routing routing:bootstrap_rw listening on 6446 and named socket /home/routeruser/mysql.sock
2023-09-30 19:24:12 metadata_cache INFO [7f7800454700] Starting metadata

```
cache refresh thread
2023-09-30 19:24:12 metadata_cache INFO [7f7800454700] Connected with
metadata server running on mysql-b:3306
2023-09-30 19:24:12 metadata_cache INFO [7f7800454700] New router options
read from the metadata '{"target_cluster": "primary", "stats_updates_
frequency": 0, "use_replica_primary_as_rw": false, "invalidated_cluster_
policy": "drop_all"}', was ''
2023-09-30 19:24:12 metadata_cache INFO [7f7800454700] New target cluster
assigned in the metadata: 'myPrimaryCluster'
2023-09-30 19:24:12 metadata_cache INFO [7f7800454700] Connected with
metadata server running on mysql-a:3306
2023-09-30 19:24:12 metadata_cache INFO [7f7800454700] Connected with
metadata server running on mysql-c:3306
2023-09-30 19:24:12 metadata_cache INFO [7f7800454700] Connected with
metadata server running on mysql-d:3306
2023-09-30 19:24:12 metadata_cache INFO [7f7800454700] Connected with
metadata server running on mysql-e:3306
2023-09-30 19:24:12 metadata_cache INFO [7f7800454700] Connected with
metadata server running on mysql-f:3306
2023-09-30 19:24:12 metadata_cache INFO [7f7800454700] Potential changes
detected in cluster after metadata refresh (view_id=4)
2023-09-30 19:24:12 metadata_cache INFO [7f7800454700] Target cluster(s)
are part of a ClusterSet: accepting RW connections
2023-09-30 19:24:12 metadata_cache INFO [7f7800454700] Cluster
'myPrimaryCluster': role of a cluster within a ClusterSet is 'primary';
2023-09-30 19:24:12 metadata_cache INFO [7f7800454700] Metadata for cluster
'myPrimaryCluster' has 3 member(s), single-primary:
2023-09-30 19:24:12 metadata_cache INFO [7f7800454700]      mysql-b:3306 /
33060 - mode=RO
2023-09-30 19:24:12 metadata_cache INFO [7f7800454700]      mysql-a:3306 /
33060 - mode=RW
2023-09-30 19:24:12 metadata_cache INFO [7f7800454700]      mysql-c:3306 /
33060 - mode=RO
[root@mysql-a log]#
```

Summary

Overall, InnoDB Clusterset offers a robust high availability and disaster recovery solution for MySQL. It uses a combination of key components, MySQL Shell, MySQL Group Replication, and MySQL Router to create an InnoDB cluster to provide high availability within the region or data center and then an InnoDB Clusterset to create a Replica Set in the disaster recovery region to provide disaster recovery capabilities. In the next chapter, we will discuss high availability clustering setup for MySQL NDB cluster.

CHAPTER 7

MySQL NDB Cluster

Introduction

MySQL offers different storage engines, that is, InnoDB, MyISAM, NDB, etc. NDB is one type of storage engine of MySQL offering that is not part of the standard MySQL Server software provided by Oracle.

NDB stands for Network Database, a powerful memory database providing low latency and high responsiveness with real-time performance features.

NDB is designed with shared-nothing architecture where clusters can handle any node failures with zero impact to data persistence. NDB is a highly distributed database that provides high performance and availability.

When to Use NDB

NDB is used in applications that are latency sensitive (high performance) and have low downtime requirements. Due to the nature of architecture, NDB performance is scalable and data is distributed across the nodes.

For those who would like to implement NDB, they need to understand the behavior of transaction, table limits, and other limitations with NDB as compared to InnoDB, which are due to the distributed nature of the architecture.

In summary, all the use cases can be addressed with InnoDB engine as a general-purpose transactional database; NDB needs to be considered in case of high performance and availability requirements.

Note There are limitations on the SQL statements and MySQL features when NDB is used; please check the MySQL documentation for the more details.

© Y V Ravi Kumar, Arun Kumar Samayam, Naresh Kumar Miryala 2024
Y V Ravi Kumar et al., *Mastering MySQL Administration*, https://doi.org/10.1007/979-8-8688-0252-2_7

NDB Cluster vs. InnoDB Cluster Comparison

The following comparison chart captures key feature comparison for InnoDB and NDB storage engines; it's very critical to choose the right storage engine meeting the business requirements for application performance and scalability.

Table 7-1. *NDB vs. InnoDB cluster comparison chart*

Features	InnoDB Engine	NDB Engine
High Availability	Yes	Yes
Replication	Yes	Yes
Real-Time Performance	No	Yes
In-Memory	No	Yes
MVCC	Yes	No
Compression	Yes	No

NDB Cluster Components

NDB cluster runs on a set of machines with different roles. As we dive into the NDB cluster setup, it's important to understand the key components in the NDB clusters.

Management Nodes

Management nodes are used for initial configuration and monitoring of the cluster status; they are required to manage the cluster, that is, start and stop. In a production environment, it's recommended to have multiple management servers.

Management node non-availability will not impact the database cluster availability; these nodes are used for managing the cluster services.

Data Nodes

Data nodes are the servers where actual data is stored in the NDB clusters; we can have multiple data nodes in a cluster, and data synchronization between the nodes is handled by the NDB cluster.

Any data node failures will not cause the data loss due to replicas and distributed nature of the NDB cluster.

SQL Nodes

SQL nodes are a set of machines where the MySQL process is started with an NDB storage engine; SQL nodes allow the access to the cluster data, and they are critical in case of replication setup between clusters in different data centers.

Fragmented Replicas

In order to meet the sharding and distributed database nature with high availability, fragmented replicas are used in the NDB cluster; during the NDB cluster configuration, we can specify the number of fragmented replicas; each node in the cluster will have at least one fragmented replica, so in case of any data node failure, the cluster still has all the replicas available to continue to serve the traffic without any impact.

Figure 7-1 outlines the replica setup in two data nodes; number replicas are configurable and scalable based on the data node setup.

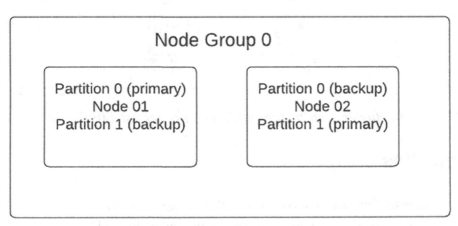

Figure 7-1. *Fragmented replicas in NDB cluster data nodes*

Node groups are not configurable; they are automatically calculated based on the number of partitions or replicas and data nodes:

Node groups = no. of data nodes/no of replicas

Cluster always checks if one partition is available to be marked as healthy; if all the partitions in a node group are not available, the cluster will be unhealthy.

The max number of node groups supported in a single NDB cluster instance is 48.

NDB Cluster Installation

High-Level Architecture

Figure 7-2 explains the high-level cluster architecture for NDB cluster. In this cluster installation, we have one management node, two data nodes, and two SQL nodes in each data center.

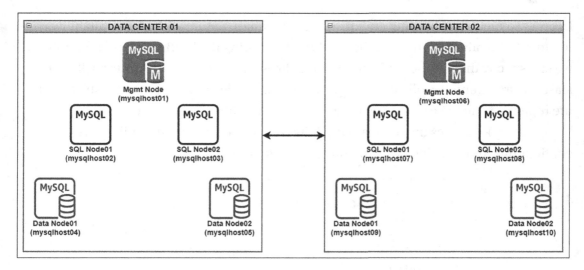

Figure 7-2. *NDB cluster architecture and node names used in this book*

Prerequisites

- Ensure all the cluster servers are in the same network zone; this is to avoid the network latency between the nodes due to FW or other network segregation.

- Ensure you have supported and latest operating systems across all the machines for installing NDB clusters.

- Ensure all the hardware and capacity requirements are met based on the requirements, that is, CPU, RAM, and Disk.

The following tables outline the server hostnames, roles, and node ID info used in this installation exercise.

Table 7-2. *Server hostnames and roles for primary data centers*

Data Center	Node	Hostname	IP Address	Node ID
DC1	Management Node	mysqlhost01	10.10.10.01	1
DC1	SQL Node 01	mysqlhost02	10.10.10.02	2
DC1	SQL Node 02	mysqlhost03	10.10.10.03	3
DC1	Data Node 01	mysqlhost04	10.10.10.04	4
DC1	Data Node 02	mysqlhost05	10.10.10.05	5

Table 7-3. *Server hostnames and roles for secondary data centers*

Data Center	Node	Hostname	IP Address	Node ID
DC2	Management Node	mysqlhost06	10.10.10.06	6
DC2	SQL Node 01	mysqlhost07	10.10.10.07	7
DC2	SQL Node 02	mysqlhost08	10.10.10.08	8
DC2	Data Node 01	mysqlhost09	10.10.10.09	9
DC2	Data Node 02	mysqlhost10	10.10.10.10	10

Download the Software

Go to `https://dev.mysql.com/downloads/` to download the required software; in this exercise, we are using NDB cluster 8.0.34 with Linux operating system as an example; you can download the software based on the operating system you plan to install. Figure 7-3 shows the download page.

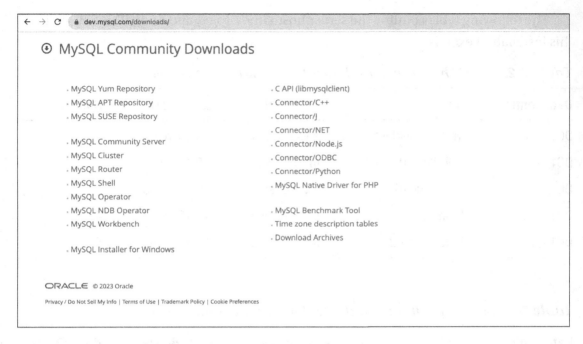

Figure 7-3. *Download page to go to MySQL cluster*

You will be directed to the MySQL cluster page and choose the MySQL version and operating system version in Figure 7-4.

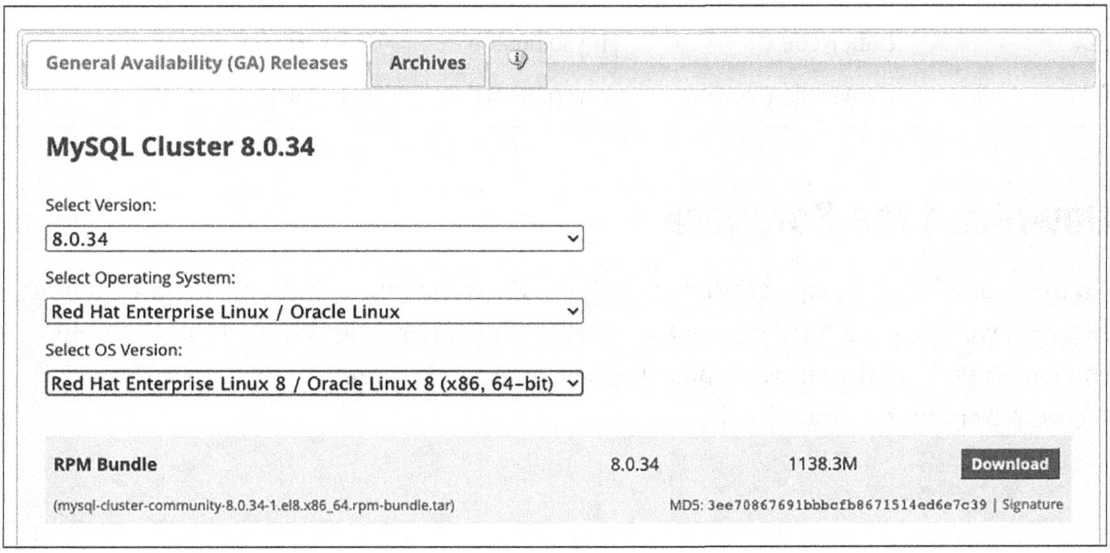

Figure 7-4. *Download page for the MySQL 8.0.34 with RHEL 8*

You have the option to log in if you have an account or sign up if you wish to create an account or simply click No thanks, just start my download as shown in Figure 7-5.

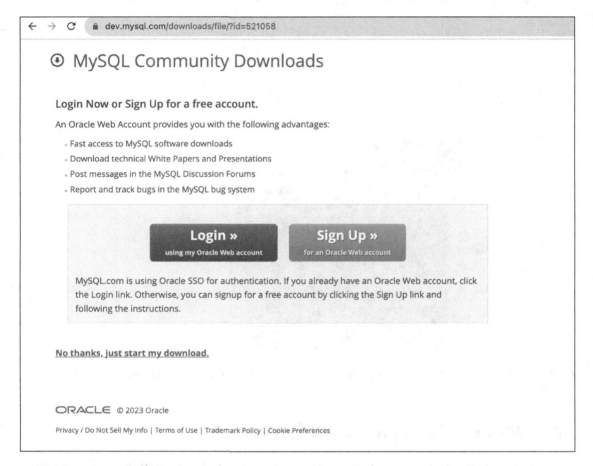

Figure 7-5. *Download page*

Downloading a desktop and transferring the software is a time-consuming process; the easiest option is get the direct download link as shown in Figure 7-6.

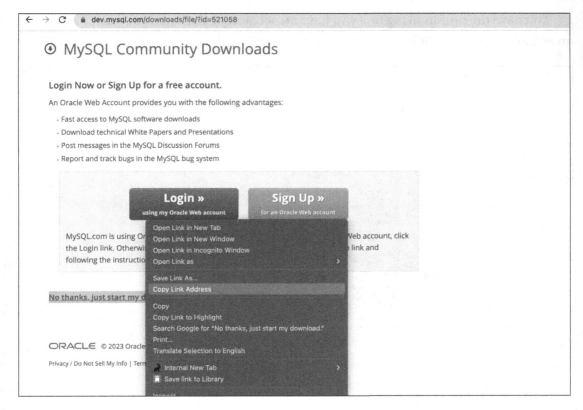

Figure 7-6. *Copy the direct software download link from the MySQL website*

Downloading the rpm to the Server

Log in to the server and download using the wget command as shown in the following; this downloads the rpm tar file in a location where you issue the wget command (please repeat this step in all the nodes).

```
root@mysqlhost01# > wget https://dev.mysql.com/get/Downloads/MySQL-
Cluster-8.0/mysql-cluster-community-8.0.34-1.el8.x86_64.rpm-bundle.tar
--2023-10-11 09:11:57--  https://dev.mysql.com/get/Downloads/MySQL-
Cluster-8.0/mysql-cluster-community-8.0.34-1.el8.x86_64.rpm-bundle.tar
Resolving dev.mysql.com (dev.mysql.com)... 2600:1408:c400:188c::2e31,
2600:1408:c400:1881::2e31, 104.108.116.193
Connecting to dev.mysql.com (dev.mysql.com)|2600:1408:c400:188c::
2e31|:443... connected.
```

```
HTTP request sent, awaiting response... 302 Moved Temporarily
Location: https://cdn.mysql.com//Downloads/MySQL-Cluster-8.0/mysql-cluster-
community-8.0.34-1.el8.x86_64.rpm-bundle.tar [following]
--2023-10-11 09:11:57--  https://cdn.mysql.com//Downloads/MySQL-
Cluster-8.0/mysql-cluster-community-8.0.34-1.el8.x86_64.rpm-
bundle.tar
Resolving cdn.mysql.com (cdn.mysql.com)... 2600:1408:c400:1884::1d68,
23.204.255.142
Connecting to cdn.mysql.com (cdn.mysql.com)|2600:1408:c400:1884::
1d68|:443... connected.
HTTP request sent, awaiting response... 200 OK
Length: 1193615360 (1.1G) [application/x-tar]
Saving to: 'mysql-cluster-community-8.0.34-1.el8.x86_64.rpm-bundle.tar'

mysql-cluster-community-8.0.34-1.el8.x
100%[================================>]   1.11G  7.96MB/s    in 2m 5s

2023-10-11 09:14:02 (9.12 MB/s) - 'mysql-cluster-community-8.0.34-1.el8.
x86_64.rpm-bundle.tar' saved [1193615360/1193615360]
```

Please check the downloaded tar bundle file in the current working directory.

root@mysqlhost01# > ls -ltr
```
total 1165640
-rw-r--r-- 1 root root 1193615360 Jun 23 21:12 mysql-cluster-
community-8.0.34-1.el8.x86_64.rpm-bundle.tar
```

You can extract the individual rpm file from the tar bundle or extract all the rpm files from the tar bundle as shown here (please repeat this step in all the nodes):

**root@mysqlhost01# > tar -xvf mysql-cluster-community-8.0.34-1.el8.x86_64.
rpm-bundle.tar**
```
mysql-cluster-community-client-8.0.34-1.el8.x86_64.rpm
mysql-cluster-community-client-debuginfo-8.0.34-1.el8.x86_64.rpm
mysql-cluster-community-client-plugins-8.0.34-1.el8.x86_64.rpm
mysql-cluster-community-client-plugins-debuginfo-8.0.34-1.el8.x86_64.rpm
mysql-cluster-community-common-8.0.34-1.el8.x86_64.rpm
```
  --output truncated for better visibility

```
mysql-cluster-community-server-debuginfo-8.0.34-1.el8.x86_64.rpm
mysql-cluster-community-test-8.0.34-1.el8.x86_64.rpm
mysql-cluster-community-test-debuginfo-8.0.34-1.el8.x86_64.rpm
```

We have three different components and servers that will be hosting these three different components.

The rpm required for the following three cluster components are different; you can choose to install only them by installing the required rpm from the bundle.

- Management node

- Data node

- SQL node

The alternate option is to install the rpm in all the nodes independent of the role; this makes installation easy, and switching the roles becomes easy in the future as all the required rpm are present in all the nodes.

Install the rpm Packages

Install all the rpm extracted from the tar bundle in all the nodes; use the wget command listed previously and download the rpm tar bundle in all the nodes and extract the rpm.

Once you have the rpm files on the server, please issue the following command (please repeat this step in all the nodes):

```
root@mysqlhost01# > yum install *.rpm
Updating Subscription Management repositories.
Unable to read consumer identity

This system is not registered with an entitlement server. You can use
subscription-manager to register.

Last metadata expiration check: 0:04:32 ago on Wed 11 Oct 2023
09:45:02 AM PDT.
Dependencies resolved.
======================================================================Package
Architecture                                    Version
Repository    Size
======================================================================Installing:
```

```
mysql-cluster-community-client                      x86_64 8.0.34-1.el8
@commandline   56 M
mysql-cluster-community-client-debuginfo            x86_64 8.0.34-1.el8
@commandline  110 M
mysql-cluster-community-client-plugins              x86_64 8.0.34-1.el8
@commandline  3.6 M
 mysql-cluster-community-client-plugins-debuginfo  x86_64 8.0.34-1.el8
@commandline  3.7 M
mysql-cluster-community-common                      x86_64 8.0.34-1.el8
@commandline  677 k
mysql-cluster-community-data-node                   x86_64 8.0.34-1.el8
```

--output truncated for better visibility

```
mysql-cluster-community-test-debuginfo              x86_64 8.0.34-1.el8
                  @commandline    26 M
Installing dependencies:
compat-openssl11  x86_64  1:1.1.1k-4.el9_0  fbit-rhel-appstream  1.5 M
openssl-devel     x86_64  1:3.0.7-17.el9_2  fbit-rhel-appstream  4.1 M
perl-JSON         noarch  4.03-5.el9        fbit-rhel-appstream   99 k

Transaction Summary
===========================================================Install   30 Packages

Total size: 1.1 G
Total download size: 5.7 M
Installed size: 4.6 G
Is this ok [y/N]: y
Downloading Packages:
(1/3):perl-JSON-4.03-5.el9.noarch.rpm            712 kB/s|  99 kB 00:00
(2/3):compat-openssl11-1.1.1k-4.el9_0.x86_64.rpm 9.3 MB/s|1.5 MB 00:00
(3/3):openssl-devel-3.0.7-17.el9_2.x86_64.rpm     12 MB/s|4.1 MB 00:00
-----------------------------------Total          16 MB/s|5.7 MB 00:00
Running transaction check
Transaction check succeeded.
Running transaction test
Transaction test succeeded.
Running transaction
```

```
Preparing   :                                               1/1
Installing  :mysql-cluster-community-debugsource-8.0.34-1.el8.x86_64
                                                            1/30
Installing:mysql-cluster-community-debuginfo-8.0.34-1.el8.x86_64   2/30
Installing:compat-openssl11-1:1.1.1k-4.el9_0.x86_64               3/30
Installing:mysql-cluster-community-client-plugins-8.0.34-1.el8.x86_64
                                                            4/30
```

   --output truncated for better visibility

```
Installed:
compat-openssl11-1:1.1.1k-4.el9_0.x86_64
mysql-cluster-community-client-8.0.34-1.el8.x86_64
mysql-cluster-community-client-debuginfo-8.0.34-1.el8.x86_64
mysql-cluster-community-client-plugins-8.0.34-1.el8.x86_64
mysql-cluster-community-client-plugins-debuginfo-8.0.34-1.el8.x86_64
mysql-cluster-community-common-8.0.34-1.el8.x86_64
mysql-cluster-community-data-node-8.0.34-1.el8.x86_64
mysql-cluster-community-test-debuginfo-8.0.34-1.el8.x86_64
  openssl-devel-1:3.0.7-17.el9_2.x86_64
perl-JSON-4.03-5.el9.noarch
```

```
Complete!
```

NDB Cluster Configuration

Configuring Management Nodes

We have installed the required packages (rpm) in all the cluster nodes; the first step is configuring the management nodes.

Create the following directories and manually edit the config.ini with the following configuration; this setup will configure the two replicas with two data nodes with one node group.

```
root@mysqlhost01# > mkdir /var/lib/mysql-cluster
root@mysqlhost01# > cd /var/lib/mysql-cluster
root@mysqlhost01# > vi config.ini
```

Edit the config.ini with the following content; the server details and roles are explained in Table 7-2.

```
[ndbd default]

# Options affecting ndbd processes on all data nodes:
NoOfReplicas=2 # Number of fragment replicas
DataMemory=98M # How much memory to allocate for data storage
[ndb_mgmd]

# Management process options:

HostName=10.10.10.01 # Hostname or IP address of management node
nodeid=1 # Node ID for this data node
DataDir=/var/lib/mysql-cluster # Directory for management node log files
[ndbd]

# Options for data node01:
# (one [ndbd] section per data node)

HostName=10.10.10.02 # Hostname or IP address
nodeid=2 # Node ID for this data node
DataDir=/usr/local/mysql/data # Directory for this data node's data files
[ndbd]

# Options for data node02:

HostName=10.10.10.03 # Hostname or IP address
nodeid=3 # Node ID for this data node
DataDir=/usr/local/mysql/data # Directory for this data node's data files

[mysqld]

# SQL node options for node01:

HostName=10.10.10.04 # Hostname or IP address
nodeid=4 # Node ID for this data node

[mysqld]

# SQL node options for node02:
```

```
HostName=10.10.10.05 # Hostname or IP address
nodeid=5 # Node ID for this data node
```

Configuring Data Nodes and SQL Nodes

In this section, we will discuss the steps to configure the data nodes; edit the /etc/my.cnf file in all the data and SQL nodes with the following parameters (please repeat these steps in all the data nodes):

```
[mysqld]
# Options for mysqld process:
ndbcluster # run NDB storage engine
[mysql_cluster]
# Options for NDB Cluster processes:
ndb-connectstring=10.10.10.01 # location of management server
```

   Create Data Directory in all the data nodes:

root@mysqlhost02# >mkdir -p /usr/local/mysql/data

root@mysqlhost03# >mkdir -p /usr/local/mysql/data

Configuring SQL API Nodes

In this section, we will discuss the steps to configure the SQL nodes; edit the /etc/my.cnf file in all the data and SQL nodes with the following parameters (please repeat this in all the SQL API nodes):

```
[mysqld]
user = root
# Options for mysqld process:
ndbcluster # run NDB storage engine
[mysql_cluster]
# Options for NDB Cluster processes:
ndb-connectstring=10.10.10.01 # location of management server
```

NDB Cluster Initiation

We have completed installation and configuration; in this section, we will discuss initiation of the cluster and starting the services.

Initiate the Management Node

With the config we saved in the config.ini, initiate the management node with the ndb_mgmd command.

```
root@mysqlhost01#ndb_mgmd --initial -f /var/lib/mysql-cluster/config.ini
MySQL Cluster Management Server mysql-8.0.34 ndb-8.0.34
2023-10-11 19:04:23 [MgmtSrvr] INFO     -- The default config directory
'/usr/mysql-cluster' does not exist. Trying to create it...
2023-10-11 19:04:23 [MgmtSrvr] INFO -- Sucessfully created config directory
root@mysqlhost01#
```

Initiate the Data Nodes

All the data nodes are initiated with the command ndbd; data nodes need to be initiated after the management node that was initiated in the previous step as the data node tries to make a connection to the management node.

Data Node 01

```
root@mysqlhost02# >ndbd
2023-10-11 16:18:33 [ndbd] INFO     -- Angel connected to '10.10.10.01:1186'
2023-10-11 16:18:33 [ndbd] INFO     -- Angel allocated nodeid: 2
root@mysqlhost02# >
```

Data Node 02

```
root@mysqlhost03# >ndbd
2023-10-11 16:19:10 [ndbd] INFO     -- Angel connected to '10.10.10.01:1186'
2023-10-11 16:19:10 [ndbd] INFO     -- Angel allocated nodeid: 3
root@mysqlhost03# >
```

Initiate the SQL API Nodes

Log in to all the SQL API nodes and start the mysqld; the steps to start SQL nodes are similar to regular MySQL steps.

SQL nodes run the mysqld process, and it can be managed with the systemctl.

SQL API Node 01

root@mysqlhost04# >systemctl start mysqld

SQL API Node 02

root@mysqlhost05# >systemctl start mysqld

Once SQL nodes are started, they will set up the random root password; please note the file location is different from the regular mysql.log as in this node, mysqld is running with NDB cluster.

Use the following steps and obtain a temporary root password and reset the password; each SQL API node will have a different temporary password and need to reset the password in all the SQL API nodes.

root@mysqlhost04# >cd /var/log
root@mysqlhost04# >grep -inr "temporary password"
```
messages:86262:Oct 11 16:26:57 mysqlhost04 mysqld_pre_systemd[331843]:
2023-10-11T23:26:57.003825Z 6 [Note] [MY-010454] [Server] A temporary
password is generated for root@localhost: Di/%oObC(yLj
```

root@mysqlhost04# >mysql -u root -p
```
Enter password:
```

mysql> ALTER USER 'root'@'localhost' IDENTIFIED BY 'xxxxx';
```
Query OK, 0 rows affected (0.00 sec)
```

Please repeat the preceding password reset steps in all the SQL API nodes.

Monitor the NDB Cluster from Management Node

We have successfully started all the nodes in the cluster; monitor the cluster status and health of all the nodes from the management node.

```
root@mysqlhost01# >ndb_mgm
-- NDB Cluster -- Management Client --
ndb_mgm> SHOW
Connected to Management Server at: localhost:1186
Cluster Configuration
---------------------
[ndbd(NDB)] 2 node(s)
id=2  @10.10.10.02   (mysql-8.0.34 ndb-8.0.34, Nodegroup: 0, *)
id=3  @10.10.10.03   (mysql-8.0.34 ndb-8.0.34, Nodegroup: 0)

[ndb_mgmd(MGM)] 1 node(s)
id=1  @10.10.10.01   (mysql-8.0.34 ndb-8.0.34)

[mysqld(API)] 2 node(s)
id=4  @10.10.10.04   (mysql-8.0.34 ndb-8.0.34)
id=5  @10.10.10.05   (mysql-8.0.34 ndb-8.0.34)
```

Shut down the cluster with ndb_mgm -e "SHUTDOWN"; this command will shut down all the nodes in the cluster.

```
root@mysqlhost01#ndb_mgm -e "SHUTDOWN"
Connected to Management Server at: localhost:1186
4 NDB Cluster node(s) have shutdown.
Disconnecting to allow management server to shutdown.
```

Check the status of the cluster.

```
root@mysqlhost01#ndb_mgm
-- NDB Cluster -- Management Client --
ndb_mgm> SHOW;
Connected to Management Server at: localhost:1186
Cluster Configuration
---------------------
[ndbd(NDB)] 2 node(s)
```

```
id=2 (not connected, accepting connect from 10.10.10.02)
id=3 (not connected, accepting connect from 10.10.10.03)

[ndb_mgmd(MGM)] 1 node(s)
id=1  @10.10.10.01  (mysql-8.0.34 ndb-8.0.34)

[mysqld(API)] 2 node(s)
id=4 (not connected, accepting connect from 10.10.10.04)
id=4 (not connected, accepting connect from 10.10.10.05)
```

Check status:

root@mysqlhost01#ndb_mgm
```
-- NDB Cluster -- Management Client --
```
ndb_mgm> SHOW
```
Connected to Management Server at: localhost:1186
Cluster Configuration
---------------------
[ndbd(NDB)] 2 node(s)
id=2  @10.10.10.02  (mysql-8.0.34 ndb-8.0.34, Nodegroup: 0, *)
id=3  @10.10.10.03  (mysql-8.0.34 ndb-8.0.34, Nodegroup: 0)

[ndb_mgmd(MGM)] 1 node(s)
id=1  @10.10.10.01    (mysql-8.0.34 ndb-8.0.34)

[mysqld(API)] 2 node(s)
id=4  @10.10.10.04    (mysql-8.0.34 ndb-8.0.34)
id=5  @10.10.10.05    (mysql-8.0.34 ndb-8.0.34)
```

Restart Node 02

Restart Node 02 services.

ndb_mgm> 2 RESTART
```
Node 2: Node shutdown initiated
Node 2: Node shutdown completed, restarting, no start.
Node 2 is being restarted

ndb_mgm> Node 2: Start initiated (version 8.0.34)
Node 2: Started (version 8.0.34)
```

414

```
ndb_mgm> 2 status
Node 2: started (mysql-8.0.34 ndb-8.0.34)
```

Restart all the nodes in the cluster:

ndb_mgm> ALL RESTART
```
Executing RESTART on all nodes.
Starting shutdown. This may take a while. Please wait...
Node 2: Cluster shutdown initiated
Node 3: Cluster shutdown initiated
Node 4: Cluster shutdown initiated
Node 2: Node shutdown completed, restarting, no start.
Node 3: Node shutdown completed, restarting, no start.
Node 4: Node shutdown completed, restarting, no start.

All DB nodes are being restarted.

ndb_mgm> Node 2: Start initiated (version 8.0.34)
Node 3: Start initiated (version 8.0.34)
Node 2: Started (version 8.0.34)
Node 3: Started (version 8.0.34)
Node 4: Started (version 8.0.34)
```

NDB Cluster Validation

We have successfully installed and tested the NDB cluster health check; in this section, we will perform the sample transactions to see the cluster behavior.

Create Sample Tables and Data

In order to communicate with a cluster database, initiate the transactions from the SQL API node, which communicates with cluster data nodes.

Create a sample database using the following syntax and insert sample records from SQL API node 01.

root@mysqlhost04# >mysql -u root -p
Enter password:

mysql> create database ndb_test_db;
Query OK, 1 row affected (0.08 sec)

mysql> use ndb_test_db;
Database changed
mysql> CREATE TABLE EMPLOYEE
    -> (
    -> ID int(10) NOT NULL AUTO_INCREMENT,
    -> NAME char(50) NOT NULL DEFAULT '',
    -> SALARY int(20) NOT NULL DEFAULT '10000',
    -> PRIMARY KEY (ID)
    ->) ENGINE=NDBCLUSTER;
Query OK, 0 rows affected, 2 warnings (0.15 sec)

mysql> show tables;
```
+-----------------------+
| Tables_in_ndb_test_db |
+-----------------------+
| EMPLOYEE              |
+-----------------------+
```
1 row in set (0.00 sec)

mysql> show databases;
```
+--------------------+
| Database           |
+--------------------+
| information_schema |
| mysql              |
| ndb_test_db        |
| ndbinfo            |
| performance_schema |
| sys                |
+--------------------+
```
6 rows in set (0.01 sec)

```
mysql> INSERT INTO EMPLOYEE VALUES (1,'Employee1',100000);
Query OK, 1 row affected (0.00 sec)

mysql> INSERT INTO EMPLOYEE VALUES (2,'Employee2',200000);
Query OK, 1 row affected (0.00 sec)
```

The data created from SQL API node 01 can be directly accessed from SQL API node 02.

```
root@mysqlhost05# >mysql -u root -p
Enter password:

mysql> show databases;
+--------------------+
| Database           |
+--------------------+
| information_schema |
| mysql              |
| ndb_test_db        |
| ndbinfo            |
| performance_schema |
| sys                |
+--------------------+
6 rows in set (0.01 sec)

mysql> use ndb_test_db
Reading table information for completion of table and column names
You can turn off this feature to get a quicker startup with -A

Database changed
mysql> select * from EMPLOYEE;
+----+-----------+--------+
| ID | NAME      | SALARY |
+----+-----------+--------+
|  1 | Employee1 | 100000 |
|  2 | Employee2 | 200000 |
+----+-----------+--------+
2 rows in set (0.01 sec)
```

417

NDB Cluster Restart

NDB Cluster Graceful Restart

In case we need to restart a complete NDB cluster, we can perform the restart operation from the management node.

root@mysqlhost01#ndb_mgm

```
-- NDB Cluster -- Management Client --
```

ndb_mgm> SHOW

```
Connected to Management Server at: 10.10.10.01:1186
Cluster Configuration
---------------------
[ndbd(NDB)] 2 node(s)
id=2  @10.10.10.02  (mysql-8.0.34 ndb-8.0.34, Nodegroup: 0, *)
id=3  @10.10.10.03  (mysql-8.0.34 ndb-8.0.34, Nodegroup: 0)

[ndb_mgmd(MGM)] 1 node(s)
id=1  @10.10.10.01   (mysql-8.0.34 ndb-8.0.34)

[mysqld(API)] 2 node(s)
id=4  @10.10.10.04   (mysql-8.0.34 ndb-8.0.34)
id=5  @10.10.10.05   (mysql-8.0.34 ndb-8.0.34)
```

ndb_mgm> ALL RESTART

```
Executing RESTART on all nodes.
Starting shutdown. This may take a while. Please wait...
Node 2: Cluster shutdown initiated
Node 3: Cluster shutdown initiated
Node 4: Cluster shutdown initiated
Node 2: Node shutdown completed, restarting, no start.
Node 3: Node shutdown completed, restarting, no start.
Node 4: Node shutdown completed, restarting, no start.

All DB nodes are being restarted.
```

NDB Cluster Force Restart

In this section, we will perform shutdown of all the cluster nodes first and start all the cluster nodes to bring up the full cluster to a healthy state.

root@mysqlhost01# ndb_mgm -e "SHUTDOWN"
```
Connected to Management Server at: 10.10.10.01:1186
5 NDB Cluster node(s) have shutdown.
Disconnecting to allow management server to shutdown.
[root@mysqlhost01 ~]#
```

1. **Management node**

   Try connecting to management node; it will fail with the following error as it could not connect as mgmd service it did not start.

   ```
   [root@mysqlhost01 ~]# ndb_mgmd
   MySQL Cluster Management Server mysql-8.0.34 ndb-8.0.34
   2023-11-12 11:00:51 [MgmtSrvr] WARNING  -- --ndb-connectstring is
   ignored when mgmd is started from binary config.
   [root@mysqlhost01 ~]#
   ```

   To start management service, use the following command:

   [root@mysqlhost01 ~]# ndb_mgmd --initial -f /var/lib/mysql-cluster/config.ini
   ```
   MySQL Cluster Management Server mysql-8.0.34 ndb-8.0.34
   WARNING: --ndb-connectstring is ignored when mgmd is started
   with -f or config-file.
   ```

   ```
   [root@mysqlhost01 ~]# ndb_mgm
   -- NDB Cluster -- Management Client --
   ```

   ndb_mgm> SHOW
   ```
   Connected to Management Server at: 10.10.10.01:1186
   Cluster Configuration
   ---------------------
   [ndbd(NDB)] 2 node(s)
   id=2 (not connected, accepting connect from 10.10.10.02)
   id=3 (not connected, accepting connect from 10.10.10.03)
   ```

```
[ndb_mgmd(MGM)] 1 node(s)
id=1  @10.10.10.01   (mysql-8.0.34 ndb-8.0.34)

[mysqld(API)] 2 node(s)
id=4 (not connected, accepting connect from 10.10.10.04)
id=5 (not connected, accepting connect from 10.10.10.05)
```

2. **Data nodes**

   From the output, we can understand only management node
   services have started now and all the services are still down. Start
   data nodes using the following commands:

[root@mysqlhost02 ~]# ndbd
```
2023-11-12 10:07:48 [ndbd] INFO      -- Angel connected to
                                        10.10.10.1:1186'

2023-11-12 10:07:48 [ndbd] INFO      -- Angel allocated nodeid: 2
[root@mysqlhost02 ~]#
```

[root@mysqlhost03 ~]# ndbd
```
2023-11-12 10:08:22 [ndbd] INFO      -- Angel connected to
                                        '10.10.10.1:1186'

2023-11-12 10:08:22 [ndbd] INFO      -- Angel allocated nodeid: 3
[root@mysqlhost03 ~]#
```

Check status of the data nodes

root@mysqlhost01#ndb_mgm
```
-- NDB Cluster -- Management Client --
```
ndb_mgm> SHOW
```
Connected to Management Server at: 10.10.10.01:1186
Cluster Configuration
---------------------
[ndbd(NDB)] 2 node(s)
id=2  @10.10.10.02  (mysql-8.0.34 ndb-8.0.34, Nodegroup: 0, *)
id=3  @10.10.10.03  (mysql-8.0.34 ndb-8.0.34, Nodegroup: 0)

[ndb_mgmd(MGM)] 1 node(s)
id=1  @10.10.10.01   (mysql-8.0.34 ndb-8.0.34)
```

```
[mysqld(API)] 2 node(s)
id=4 (not connected, accepting connect from 10.10.10.04)
id=5 (not connected, accepting connect from 10.10.10.05)
```

3. **SQL API nodes**

   We have started management and data nodes; to start MySQL API nodes, we just mysqld service similar to regular MySQL service.

   [root@mysqlhost03 ~]# systemctl start mysqld
   [root@mysqlhost04 ~]# systemctl start mysqld

   root@mysqlhost01#ndb_mgm
   ```
   -- NDB Cluster -- Management Client --
   ```
   ndb_mgm> SHOW
   ```
   Connected to Management Server at: 10.10.10.01:1186
   Cluster Configuration
   ---------------------
   [ndbd(NDB)] 2 node(s)
   id=2  @10.10.10.02  (mysql-8.0.34 ndb-8.0.34, Nodegroup: 0, *)
   id=3  @10.10.10.03  (mysql-8.0.34 ndb-8.0.34, Nodegroup: 0)

   [ndb_mgmd(MGM)] 1 node(s)
   id=1  @10.10.10.01   (mysql-8.0.34 ndb-8.0.34)

   [mysqld(API)] 2 node(s)
   id=4  @10.10.10.04   (mysql-8.0.34 ndb-8.0.34)
   id=5  @10.10.10.05   (mysql-8.0.34 ndb-8.0.34)
   ```

NDB Cluster Data Node Crash

In an NDB cluster, when we have multiple data nodes, if one of the nodes is crashed in the node group, the cluster will handle the data consistency with other data nodes in the node groups; if multiple data nodes are crashed in a cluster, which impacts node groups, the cluster will go to unhealthy state.

We are performing a crash scenario by killing the NDB process on one of the data nodes, and once the process is killed, NDB detects if the node is evicted or not available in the cluster.

421

```
[root@mysqlhost03 ~]# ps -ef|grep ndb
root       1373011        1  0 11:41 ?        00:00:00 ndbd
root       1373012 1373011  0 11:41 ?        00:00:01 ndbd
root       1379662 1331608  0 11:49 pts/0    00:00:00 grep --color=auto ndb
[root@mysqlhost03 ~]# kill -9 1373011 1373012
[root@mysqlhost03 ~]#
```

root@mysqlhost01#ndb_mgm
```
-- NDB Cluster -- Management Client --
```
ndb_mgm> SHOW
```
Connected to Management Server at: 10.10.10.01:1186
Cluster Configuration
---------------------
[ndbd(NDB)] 2 node(s)
id=2  (not connected, accepting connect from 10.10.10.02)
id=3  @10.10.10.03  (mysql-8.0.34 ndb-8.0.34, Nodegroup: 0)

[ndb_mgmd(MGM)] 1 node(s)
id=1  @10.10.10.01    (mysql-8.0.34 ndb-8.0.34)

[mysqld(API)] 2 node(s)
id=4  @10.10.10.04    (mysql-8.0.34 ndb-8.0.34)
id=5  @10.10.10.05    (mysql-8.0.34 ndb-8.0.34)
```

Now we have only one data node in the cluster, but when we query the tables, we can see the data is served without any failures as node 02 of the data node is serving the traffic.

root@mysqlhost05# >mysql -u root -p
```
Enter password:
```

mysql> show databases;
```
+--------------------+
| Database           |
+--------------------+
| information_schema |
| mysql              |
| ndb_test_db        |
```

```
| ndbinfo            |
| performance_schema |
| sys                |
+--------------------+
6 rows in set (0.01 sec)
```

mysql> use ndb_test_db
```
Reading table information for completion of table and column names
You can turn off this feature to get a quicker startup with -A
```

```
Database changed
```
mysql> select * from EMPLOYEE;
```
+----+-----------+--------+
| ID | NAME      | SALARY |
+----+-----------+--------+
|  1 | Employee1 | 100000 |
|  2 | Employee2 | 200000 |
+----+-----------+--------+
2 rows in set (0.01 sec)
```

mysql> exit
```
Bye
```

NDB Cluster Replication

Replication process is capturing all the transactions in the source database logged into the bin logs and shipped to the target database cluster to replicate them. NDB clusters with the nature of being highly available will be able to handle the fault tolerance in case of server issues in the same region or data centers.

In case of complete data center outage or unexpected natural disasters, replication across the data centers is a key requirement.

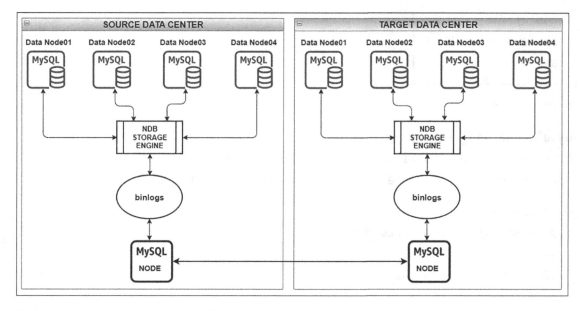

Figure 7-7. *NDB cluster to cluster replication outline*

Requirements for NDB Cluster Replication

- Versions of the MySQL binaries and OS versions should be the same across the cluster; minor version differences might work, but generally it's highly recommended to match the versions in the cluster for smooth replication.

- Bin log format should be ROW or MIXED (the default value for the binlog format is MIXED).

- If statement-based replication is used, restrictions are applied for cluster replication.

- Node ID should not be the same in source and replica cluster; this is a hard requirement; plan well in advance to ensure the ID does not match between the clusters.

Preparing the NDB Cluster for Replication

NDB cluster replication is done via mysqld, which is installed on the SQL API servers; all the steps performed on the source and target need to be executed on the SQL API servers.

Prepare Source and Create Replica User

Replication user is required to replicate data from data center A to data center B; in this replication process, binlogs are transmitted over the network using the replication user created in the source.

Please use a separate account for replication users; do not use the employee or other accounts for security and reliability purposes.

Please perform this action on the source SQL API node.

```
root@mysqlhost04# >mysql -u root -p
Enter password:

mysql> CREATE USER 'replica_user'@'10.10.10.04' IDENTIFIED BY 'xxxxxxx';
Query OK, 0 rows affected (0.01 sec)
mysql> GRANT REPLICATION SLAVE ON *.* TO 'replica_user'@'10.10.10.04';
Query OK, 0 rows affected (0.00 sec)
```

Check the users created:

```
mysql> select user,host from mysql.user;
+------------------+----------------+
| user             | host           |
+------------------+----------------+
| replica_user     | 10.10.10.04    |
| mysql.infoschema | localhost      |
| mysql.session    | localhost      |
| mysql.sys        | localhost      |
| root             | localhost      |
```

Check the master/source status:

```
mysql> show master status;
+----------------------+----------+--------------+------------------+-------------------+
| File                 | Position | Binlog_Do_DB | Binlog_Ignore_DB | Executed_Gtid_Set |
+----------------------+----------+--------------+------------------+-------------------+
| mysqlhost04-bin.000001 |    565 |              |                  |                   |
+----------------------+----------+--------------+------------------+-------------------+
1 row in set (0.00 sec)
```

Stop existing MySQL instance and start with replication mode:

[root@mysqlhost04 ~]# systemctl stop mysqld

Start the NDB replication on SQL API node.

[root@mysqlhost04 ~]# mysqld --ndbcluster --server-id=
4 --log-bin --ndb-log-bin

```
2023-10-12T03:09:37.995907Z 0 [System] [MY-010116] [Server] /usr/sbin/
mysqld (mysqld 8.0.34-cluster) starting as process 362117
2023-10-12T03:09:38.001681Z 1 [System] [MY-013576] [InnoDB] InnoDB
initialization has started.
2023-10-12T03:09:38.096149Z 1 [System] [MY-013577] [InnoDB] InnoDB
initialization has ended.
2023-10-12T03:09:38.166525Z 0 [System] [MY-010866] [NDB] Metadata:
Initialization
2023-10-12T03:09:38.913512Z 0 [System] [MY-010865] [NDB] connection[0],
NodeID: 4, all storage nodes connected
2023-10-12T03:09:38.913683Z 0 [System] [MY-010866] [NDB] Binlog: Starting...
2023-10-12T03:09:38.913770Z 2 [System] [MY-010866] [NDB] Binlog: Started
2023-10-12T03:09:38.913782Z 2 [System] [MY-010866] [NDB] Binlog: Setting up
2023-10-12T03:09:38.913814Z 0 [System] [MY-010866] [NDB] Index Stat: Starting...
2023-10-12T03:09:38.913858Z 0 [System] [MY-010866] [NDB] Index Stat: Wait
for server start
2023-10-12T03:09:38.913862Z 0 [System] [MY-010866] [NDB] Metadata: Starting...
  --output truncated for better visibility

first event
2023-10-12T03:09:39.267051Z 2 [System] [MY-010866] [NDB] Binlog: NDB tables
writable
2023-10-12T03:09:39.267268Z 2 [System] [MY-010866] [NDB] Binlog: Startup
and setup completed
2023-10-12T03:09:39.277346Z 2 [System] [MY-010865] [NDB] Data node 2
reports subscribe from node 5
2023-10-12T03:09:39.277364Z 2 [System] [MY-010865] [NDB] Data node 3
reports subscribe from node 5
2023-10-12T03:09:39.277498Z 2 [System] [MY-010866] [NDB] Binlog: Reloaded
metadata cache
```

Prepare Target and Create Replication User

Create replication user in replica/target env; this will be helpful for switching the roles of master and slave replication.

```
root@mysqlhost09# >mysql -u root -p
Enter password:

mysql> CREATE USER 'replica_user'@'10.10.10.09' IDENTIFIED BY 'xxxxxxx';
Query OK, 0 rows affected (0.01 sec)
mysql> GRANT REPLICATION SLAVE ON *.* TO 'replica_user'@'10.10.10.09';
Query OK, 0 rows affected (0.00 sec)
```

Enable replication on the target:

```
root@mysqlhost09# >mysql -u root -p
Enter password:

mysql> CHANGE REPLICATION SOURCE TO SOURCE_HOST='10.10.10.04', SOURCE_
PORT=3306, SOURCE_USER='replica_user', SOURCE_PASSWORD='xxxxx';
Query OK, 0 rows affected, 2 warnings (0.01 sec)
```

Position the replication to the point we need to sync the data from.

```
mysql> STOP REPLICA;
Query OK, 0 rows affected (0.01 sec)

mysql> CHANGE REPLICATION SOURCE TO SOURCE_LOG_FILE='mysqlhost04-
bin.000001', SOURCE_LOG_POS=4;
Query OK, 0 rows affected (0.01 sec)

mysql> START REPLICA;
Query OK, 0 rows affected (0.01 sec)
```

Check slave status. If there are any issues, it will be reported in the output.

```
mysql> SHOW  SLAVE STATUS;
```

Query the database and check the data from the source are replicated to the target database.

From primary cluster database node:

root@mysqlhost05# >mysql -u root -p
Enter password:

mysql> show databases;
```
+--------------------+
| Database           |
+--------------------+
| information_schema |
| mysql              |
| ndb_test_db        |
| ndbinfo            |
| performance_schema |
| sys                |
+--------------------+
6 rows in set (0.01 sec)
```

mysql> use ndb_test_db
```
Reading table information for completion of table and column names
You can turn off this feature to get a quicker startup with -A
```

Database changed
mysql> select * from EMPLOYEE;
```
+----+-----------+--------+
| ID | NAME      | SALARY |
+----+-----------+--------+
|  1 | Employee1 | 100000 |
|  2 | Employee2 | 200000 |
+----+-----------+--------+
2 rows in set (0.01 sec)
```

From secondary database cluster node:

root@mysqlhost09# >mysql -u root -p
Enter password:

```
mysql> show databases;
+--------------------+
| Database           |
+--------------------+
| information_schema |
| mysql              |
| ndb_test_db        |
| ndbinfo            |
| performance_schema |
| sys                |
+--------------------+
6 rows in set (0.01 sec)

mysql> use ndb_test_db
Reading table information for completion of table and column names
You can turn off this feature to get a quicker startup with -A

Database changed
mysql> select * from EMPLOYEE;
+----+-----------+--------+
| ID | NAME      | SALARY |
+----+-----------+--------+
|  1 | Employee1 | 100000 |
|  2 | Employee2 | 200000 |
+----+-----------+--------+
2 rows in set (0.01 sec)
```

Summary

NDB (Network Database) storage engine is a highly distributed and highly available database that provides low latency. NDB is not used as a general-purpose database; it is specifically designed and used for the low-latency transaction requirements.

NDB provides a lot of benefits with high availability and performance requirements. Along with rich features, NDB has a set of limitations on the SQL statements syntax and database features as this is directly not part of the MySQL bundle and many custom libraries are used, though analysis of business requirements and feature parity need to be done before deciding on the NDB engine.

The next chapter discusses the MySQL logical backup options available with the open-source MySQL version.

CHAPTER 8

MySQL Logical Backup

Introduction

In most enterprises using open source versions of MySQL, MySQL Enterprise Backup might not be an option to perform backup and restore operations. In such cases, we have a few logical backup options that we showcase here in this chapter. In addition, there are several third-party licensed backup softwares in the market that can help meet your backup and restore needs:

- mysqldump
- mydumper and myloader
- Percona XtraBackup

Using mysqldump

This is a client utility that performs logical backups of a MySQL database. The mysqldump utility provides a series of SQL statements that can be executed to restore the backed database objects and data.

1. Perform a single database backup. In the following example, we will back up the employees database, and the backup file is named **single_db_bk_employees.sql**.

```
-bash-4.2$ pwd
/home/mysql/mysql_backup
-bash-4.2$
-bash-4.2$ mkdir -p single_database
-bash-4.2$ cd single_database/
```

© Y V Ravi Kumar, Arun Kumar Samayam, Naresh Kumar Miryala 2024
Y V Ravi Kumar et al., *Mastering MySQL Administration*, https://doi.org/10.1007/979-8-8688-0252-2_8

```
-bash-4.2$ ls -ltr
total 0
-bash-4.2$ pwd
/home/mysql/mysql_backup/single_database
-bash-4.2$
-bash-4.2$ mysql -uroot -p
Enter password:

mysql> show databases;
+--------------------+
| Database           |
+--------------------+
| db1                |
| db2                |
| db3                |
| db4                |
| db5                |
| employees          |
| information_schema |
| mysql              |
| performance_schema |
| sys                |
+--------------------+
10 rows in set (0.00 sec)

mysql> use employees;
Reading table information for completion of table and column names
You can turn off this feature to get a quicker startup with -A

Database changed
mysql> show tables;
+----------------------+
| Tables_in_employees  |
+----------------------+
| current_dept_emp     |
| departments          |
| dept_emp             |
```

```
| dept_emp_latest_date |
| dept_manager         |
| employees            |
| salaries             |
| titles               |
+----------------------+
8 rows in set (0.00 sec)

mysql> exit
Bye
-bash-4.2$ pwd
/home/mysql/mysql_backup/single_database
-bash-4.2$
-bash-4.2$ mysqldump -u root -p employees >
single_db_bk_employees.sql
Enter password:
-bash-4.2$ ls -ltr
total 262080
-rw-rw-r-- 1 mysql mysql 168378509 Oct  6 14:47
single_db_bk_employees.sql
```

2. Perform a multiple database backup. In the following example,
    we will back up databases **db2** and **db3** to a backup file named
    multiple_db_bk.sql.

```
-bash-4.2$ pwd
/home/mysql/mysql_backup/single_database
-bash-4.2$
-bash-4.2$ cd ..
-bash-4.2$ ls -ltr
total 0
drwxrwxr-x 2 mysql mysql 40 Oct  6 14:47 single_database
-bash-4.2$
-bash-4.2$ mysqldump --databases -u root -p db2 db3 employees >
multiple_db_bk.sql
```

433

```
Enter password:
-bash-4.2$ ls -ltr
total 164436
drwxrwxr-x 2 mysql mysql           40 Oct  6 14:47 single_database
-rw-rw-r-- 1 mysql mysql    168379268 Oct  6 14:53 multiple_db_bk.sql
```

3. Perform a backup of all databases. In the following example, use
    the **--all-databases** parameter to a backup file named **alldbs.sql**.

```
-bash-4.2$ pwd
/home/mysql/mysql_backup
-bash-4.2$
-bash-4.2$ mysqldump --all-databases -u root -p > alldbs.sql
Enter password:
-bash-4.2$ ls -ltr
total 330148
drwxrwxr-x 2 mysql mysql           40 Oct  6 14:47 single_database
-rw-rw-r-- 1 mysql mysql  168379268 Oct  6 14:53 multiple_db_bk.sql
-rw-rw-r-- 1 mysql mysql  169688666 Oct  6 14:56 alldbs.sql
```

4. Perform metadata backup of a database. In the following example,
    use **--no-data parameter** with the **employees** database to a
    backup file named **employees_metadata.sql**.

```
-bash-4.2$ pwd
/home/mysql/mysql_backup
-bash-4.2$
-bash-4.2$ mysqldump -u root -p --no-data employees > employees_
metadata.sql
Enter password:
-bash-4.2$ ls -ltr
total 330160
drwxrwxr-x 2 mysql mysql         40 Oct  6 14:47 single_database
-rw-rw-r-- 1 mysql mysql 168379268 Oct  6 14:53 multiple_db_bk.sql
-rw-rw-r-- 1 mysql mysql 169688666 Oct  6 14:56 alldbs.sql
-rw-rw-r-- 1 mysql mysql      10517 Oct  6 14:58 employees_
                                                 metadata.sql
```

5. Perform a table backup. In the following example, let us back up table **tab1** within the **db1** database to a backup file named **db1_tab1_table.sql**.

```
-bash-4.2$ pwd
/home/mysql/mysql_backup
-bash-4.2$
-bash-4.2$ ls -ltr
total 330160
drwxrwxr-x 2 mysql mysql         40 Oct  6 14:47 single_database
-rw-rw-r-- 1 mysql mysql 168379268 Oct  6 14:53 multiple_db_bk.sql
-rw-rw-r-- 1 mysql mysql 169688666 Oct  6 14:56 alldbs.sql
-rw-rw-r-- 1 mysql mysql      10517 Oct  6 14:58 employees_
metadata.sql
-bash-4.2$
-bash-4.2$ mysqldump -u root -p db1 tab1 > db1_tab1_table.sql
Enter password:
-bash-4.2$ ls -ltr
total 347184
drwxrwxr-x 2 mysql mysql         40 Oct  6 14:47 single_database
-rw-rw-r-- 1 mysql mysql 168379268 Oct  6 14:53 multiple_db_bk.sql
-rw-rw-r-- 1 mysql mysql 169688666 Oct  6 14:56 alldbs.sql
-rw-rw-r-- 1 mysql mysql      10517 Oct  6 14:58 employees_
metadata.sql
-rw-rw-r-- 1 mysql mysql   17425108 Oct  6 15:02 employees_emp_
table.sql
-rw-rw-r-- 1 mysql mysql       2049 Oct  6 15:03 db1_tab1_table.sql
```

6. Perform a table metadata backup. In the following example, use the **--no-data** parameter to take the backup of table **tab1** within the **db1** database to a backup file named **db1_emp_table_metadata.sql**.

```
-bash-4.2$ pwd
/home/mysql/mysql_backup
-bash-4.2$
-bash-4.2$ ls -ltr
```

```
total 330160
drwxrwxr-x 2 mysql mysql          40 Oct  6 14:47 single_database
-rw-rw-r-- 1 mysql mysql 168379268 Oct  6 14:53 multiple_db_bk.sql
-rw-rw-r-- 1 mysql mysql 169688666 Oct  6 14:56 alldbs.sql
-rw-rw-r-- 1 mysql mysql      10517 Oct  6 14:58
employees_metadata.sql
-bash-4.2$
-bash-4.2$ mysqldump -u root -p --no-data db1 tab1 > db1_emp_
table_metadata.sql
Enter password:
```

7. Table backup with data only. In the example, use the **--no-create-info** parameter to take backup of table **tab1** within **db1** to a backup file named **db1_emp_data.sql**. The parameter **--no-create-info** removes the CREATE statements from the output and will just include the data.

```
-bash-4.2$ mysqldump -u root -p --no-create-info db1 tab1 > db1_
emp_data.sql
Enter password:
```

8. Restore db1 database from backup **db1.sql**.

```
[mysql@mysql-p mysql_backup]$ ls -ltr
total 4195812
-rw-rw-r-- 1 mysql mysql 1946232849 Oct  1 21:00 db1.sql
-rw-rw-r-- 1 mysql mysql      10768 Oct  1 21:04 db2_db3.sql
-rw-rw-r-- 1 mysql mysql 1947578333 Oct  1 21:13 alldbs.sql
-rw-rw-r-- 1 mysql mysql      11194 Oct  1 21:16 db1_
                                                metadata.sql
-rw-rw-r-- 1 mysql mysql  201334658  Oct  1 21:19 db1_emp_
                                                table.sql
-rw-rw-r-- 1 mysql mysql       1633 Oct  1 21:20 db1_emp_table_
                                                metadata.sql
-rw-rw-r-- 1 mysql mysql  201334272 Oct  1 21:24 db1_emp_
                                                data.sql

[mysql@mysql-p mysql_backup]$
```

```
[mysql@mysql-p mysql_backup]$ mysql db1<db1.sql>db1_restore.log
[mysql@mysql-p mysql_backup]$
[mysql@mysql-p mysql_backup]$ ls -ltr
total 4195812
-rw-rw-r-- 1 mysql mysql   1946232849 Oct  1 21:00 db1.sql
-rw-rw-r-- 1 mysql mysql        10768 Oct  1 21:04 db2_db3.sql
-rw-rw-r-- 1 mysql mysql   1947578333 Oct  1 21:13 alldbs.sql
-rw-rw-r-- 1 mysql mysql        11194 Oct  1 21:16 db1_
                                                    metadata.sql
-rw-rw-r-- 1 mysql mysql    201334658 Oct  1 21:19 db1_emp_
                                                    table.sql
-rw-rw-r-- 1 mysql mysql         1633 Oct  1 21:20 db1_emp_table_
                                                    metadata.sql
-rw-rw-r-- 1 mysql mysql    201334272 Oct  1 21:24 db1_emp_
                                                    data.sql
-rw-rw-r-- 1 mysql mysql            0 Oct  1 21:26 db1_restore.log
[mysql@mysql-p mysql_backup]$
[mysql@mysql-p mysql_backup]$ mysql -u root -p
Enter password:

mysql> show databases;
+--------------------+
| Database           |
+--------------------+
| db1                |
| db2                |
| db3                |
| db4                |
| db5                |
| information_schema |
| mysql              |
| performance_schema |
| sys                |
+--------------------+
9 rows in set (0.02 sec)
```

```
mysql> use db1;
Reading table information for completion of table and column names
You can turn off this feature to get a quicker startup with -A

Database changed
mysql> show tables;
+-----------------+
| Tables_in_db1   |
+-----------------+
| country         |
| dept            |
| emp             |
| emp1            |
| emp_columns     |
| emp_hash        |
| emp_key         |
| emp_list        |
| emp_pruning     |
| emp_range       |
| emp_reorg       |
| emp_subpart     |
| mgr             |
| person          |
| subpart_second  |
| tests           |
+-----------------+
16 rows in set (0.00 sec)
```

9. Perform a backup of the database excluding a table. In the
    following example, use the parameter **--ignore-table** to exclude
    db1.emp table from the backup to a backup file named **db1_wo_
    emp_table.sql.**

```
[mysql@mysql-p mysql_backup]$ mysqldump -u root -p db1 --ignore-
table=db1.emp > db1_wo_emp_table.sql
Enter password:
[mysql@mysql-p mysql_backup]$ ls -ltr
```

```
total 6358440
-rw-rw-r-- 1 mysql mysql  1946232849 Oct  1 21:00 db1.sql
-rw-rw-r-- 1 mysql mysql       10768 Oct  1 21:04 db2_db3.sql
-rw-rw-r-- 1 mysql mysql  1947578333 Oct  1 21:13 alldbs.sql
-rw-rw-r-- 1 mysql mysql       11194 Oct  1 21:16 db1_metadata.sql
-rw-rw-r-- 1 mysql mysql   201334658 Oct  1 21:19 db1_emp_table.sql
-rw-rw-r-- 1 mysql mysql        1633 Oct  1 21:20 db1_emp_table_
                                                  metadata.sql
-rw-rw-r-- 1 mysql mysql   201334272 Oct  1 21:24 db1_emp_data.sql
-rw-rw-r-- 1 mysql mysql           0 Oct  1 21:26 db1_restore.log
-rw-rw-r-- 1 mysql mysql    67112792 Oct  1 21:46 db1_emp_record.sql
-rw-rw-r-- 1 mysql mysql  1744899438 Oct  1 21:57 db1_wo_emp_table.sql
```

10. Perform a backup of database **db1** and compress it during runtime
    using **gzip** to a backup file named **db1_gzip_compressed.sql.gz**.

```
[mysql@mysql-p mysql_backup]$ mysqldump -u root -p db1 | gzip  >
db1_gzip_compressed.sql.gz
Enter password:
[mysql@mysql-p mysql_backup]$ ls -ltr
total 7675008
-rw-rw-r-- 1 mysql mysql 1946232849 Oct  1 21:00 db1.sql
-rw-rw-r-- 1 mysql mysql      10768 Oct  1 21:04 db2_db3.sql
-rw-rw-r-- 1 mysql mysql 1947578333 Oct  1 21:13 alldbs.sql
-rw-rw-r-- 1 mysql mysql      11194 Oct  1 21:16 db1_metadata.sql
-rw-rw-r-- 1 mysql mysql  201334658 Oct  1 21:19 db1_emp_table.sql
-rw-rw-r-- 1 mysql mysql       1633 Oct  1 21:20 db1_emp_table_
                                                 metadata.sql
-rw-rw-r-- 1 mysql mysql  201334272 Oct  1 21:24 db1_emp_data.sql
-rw-rw-r-- 1 mysql mysql          0 Oct  1 21:26 db1_restore.log
-rw-rw-r-- 1 mysql mysql   67112792 Oct  1 21:46 db1_emp_record.sql
-rw-rw-r-- 1 mysql mysql 1744899438 Oct  1 21:57 db1_wo_emp_
                                                 table.sql
-rw-rw-r-- 1 mysql mysql 1744898912 Oct  1 22:01 db1_wo_emp_emp1_
                                                 table.sql
-rw-rw-r-- 1 mysql mysql    5782613 Oct  1 22:10 db1_gzip_
                                                 compressed.sql.gz
```

11. Perform a backup of database **db1** with timestamp to a backup file
    named **db1-$(date +%Y%m%d).sql**.

```
[mysql@mysql-p mysql_backup]$ mysqldump -u root -p db1  > db1-
$(date +%Y%m%d).sql
Enter password:
[mysql@mysql-p mysql_backup]$
[mysql@mysql-p mysql_backup]$ ls -ltr
total 9575628
-rw-rw-r-- 1 mysql mysql 1946232849 Oct  1 21:00 db1.sql
-rw-rw-r-- 1 mysql mysql      10768 Oct  1 21:04 db2_db3.sql
-rw-rw-r-- 1 mysql mysql 1947578333 Oct  1 21:13 alldbs.sql
-rw-rw-r-- 1 mysql mysql      11194 Oct  1 21:16 db1_metadata.sql
-rw-rw-r-- 1 mysql mysql  201334658 Oct  1 21:19 db1_emp_table.sql
-rw-rw-r-- 1 mysql mysql       1633 Oct  1 21:20 db1_emp_table_
                                                 metadata.sql
-rw-rw-r-- 1 mysql mysql  201334272 Oct  1 21:24 db1_emp_data.sql
-rw-rw-r-- 1 mysql mysql          0 Oct  1 21:26 db1_restore.log
-rw-rw-r-- 1 mysql mysql   67112792 Oct  1 21:46 db1_emp_record.sql
-rw-rw-r-- 1 mysql mysql 1744899438 Oct  1 21:57 db1_wo_emp_
                                                 table.sql
-rw-rw-r-- 1 mysql mysql 1744898912 Oct  1 22:01 db1_wo_emp_emp1_
                                                 table.sql
-rw-rw-r-- 1 mysql mysql    5782613 Oct  1 22:10 db1_gzip_
                                                 compressed.sql.gz
-rw-rw-r-- 1 mysql mysql 1946232849 Oct  1 22:19 db1-20231001.sql
```

12. Perform a backup of database **db1** with global read lock to a
    backup file named **db1_global_readlock.sql**.

```
[mysql@mysql-p mysql_backup]$ mysqldump -u root -p --lock-all-
tables db1  > db1_global_readlock.sql
Enter password:
[mysql@mysql-p mysql_backup]$
[mysql@mysql-p mysql_backup]$ ls -ltr
total 9575628
```

```
-rw-rw-r-- 1 mysql mysql 1946232849 Oct  1 21:00 db1.sql
-rw-rw-r-- 1 mysql mysql      10768 Oct  1 21:04 db2_db3.sql
-rw-rw-r-- 1 mysql mysql 1947578333 Oct  1 21:13 alldbs.sql
-rw-rw-r-- 1 mysql mysql      11194 Oct  1 21:16 db1_metadata.sql
-rw-rw-r-- 1 mysql mysql  201334658 Oct  1 21:19 db1_emp_table.sql
-rw-rw-r-- 1 mysql mysql       1633 Oct  1 21:20 db1_emp_table_
                                                 metadata.sql
-rw-rw-r-- 1 mysql mysql  201334272 Oct  1 21:24 db1_emp_data.sql
-rw-rw-r-- 1 mysql mysql          0 Oct  1 21:26 db1_restore.log
-rw-rw-r-- 1 mysql mysql   67112792 Oct  1 21:46 db1_emp_record.sql
-rw-rw-r-- 1 mysql mysql 1744899438 Oct  1 21:57 db1_wo_emp_
                                                 table.sql
-rw-rw-r-- 1 mysql mysql 1744898912 Oct  1 22:01 db1_wo_emp_emp1_
                                                 table.sql
-rw-rw-r-- 1 mysql mysql    5782613 Oct  1 22:10 db1_gzip_
                                                 compressed.sql.gz
-rw-rw-r-- 1 mysql mysql 1946232849 Oct  1 22:19 db1-20231001.sql
-rw-rw-r-- 1 mysql mysql 1946432849 Oct  1 22:25 db1_global_
readlock.sql
```

13. Perform a backup of database **db1** with binary log file name and
    position to a backup file named **db1_master_data.sql** using the
    parameter **--master-data.**

    ```
    [mysql@mysql-p mysql_backup]$ mysqldump -u root -p --master-data
    db1  > db1_master_data.sql
    Enter password:
    [mysql@mysql-p mysql_backup]$
    [mysql@mysql-p mysql_backup]$ ls -ltr
    total 9575628
    -rw-rw-r-- 1 mysql mysql 1946232849 Oct  1 21:00 db1.sql
    -rw-rw-r-- 1 mysql mysql      10768 Oct  1 21:04 db2_db3.sql
    -rw-rw-r-- 1 mysql mysql 1947578333 Oct  1 21:13 alldbs.sql
    -rw-rw-r-- 1 mysql mysql      11194 Oct  1 21:16 db1_metadata.sql
    -rw-rw-r-- 1 mysql mysql  201334658 Oct  1 21:19 db1_emp_table.sql
    ```

```
-rw-rw-r-- 1 mysql mysql       1633 Oct  1 21:20 db1_emp_table_
                                                 metadata.sql
-rw-rw-r-- 1 mysql mysql  201334272 Oct  1 21:24 db1_emp_data.sql
-rw-rw-r-- 1 mysql mysql          0 Oct  1 21:26 db1_restore.log
-rw-rw-r-- 1 mysql mysql   67112792 Oct  1 21:46 db1_emp_record.sql
-rw-rw-r-- 1 mysql mysql 1744899438 Oct  1 21:57 db1_wo_emp_
                                                 table.sql
-rw-rw-r-- 1 mysql mysql 1744898912 Oct  1 22:01 db1_wo_emp_emp1_
                                                 table.sql
-rw-rw-r-- 1 mysql mysql    5782613 Oct  1 22:10 db1_gzip_
                                                 compressed.sql.gz
-rw-rw-r-- 1 mysql mysql 1946232849 Oct  1 22:19 db1-20231001.sql
-rw-rw-r-- 1 mysql mysql 1946432849 Oct  1 22:25 db1_global_
                                                 readlock.sql
-rw-rw-r-- 1 mysql mysql 1946849219 Oct  1 22:29 db1_master_
                                                 data.sql
```

Using MyDumper

MyDumper is a logical backup tool for MySQL with multithreading capabilities. It has two tools:

- mydumper

- myloader

mydumper is used to take a consistent backup of a MySQL database. **myloader** reads the backup taken from mydumper, connects to the target database, and imports it.

To use MyDumper:

1. Download and install mydumper from https://github.com/mydumper/mydumper.

   [root@mysql-a ~]# release=$(curl -Ls -o /dev/null -w %{url_effective} https://github.com/mydumper/mydumper/releases/latest | cut -d'/' -f8)
   stall https://github.com/mydumper/mydumper/releases/download/${release}/mydumper-${release:1}.el7.x86_64.rpm

```
yum install https://github.com/mydumper/mydumper/releases/
download/${release}/mydumper-${release:1}.el8.x86_64.rpm
[root@mysql-a~]# yum install https://github.com/mydumper/mydumper/
releases/download/${release}/mydumper-${release:1}.el7.x86_64.rpm
Loaded plugins: fastestmirror
mydumper-0.15.1-3.el7.x86_64.rpm                        | 1.6 MB  00:00:00
Examining /var/tmp/yum-root-zzGc3D/mydumper-0.15.1-3.el7.x86_64.
rpm: mydumper-0.15.1-3.x86_64
Marking /var/tmp/yum-root-zzGc3D/mydumper-0.15.1-3.el7.x86_64.rpm
to be installed
Resolving Dependencies
--> Running transaction check
---> Package mydumper.x86_64 0:0.15.1-3 will be installed
--> Finished Dependency Resolution

Dependencies Resolved

=====================================================================
 Package  Arch    Version   Repository                      Size
=====================================================================
Installing:
Mydumper  x86_64  0.15.1-3  /mydumper-0.15.1-3.el7.x86_64   8.0 M

Transaction Summary
=====================================================================
Install  1 Package

Total size: 8.0 M
Installed size: 8.0 M
Is this ok [y/d/N]: y
Is this ok [y/d/N]: y
Downloading packages:
Running transaction check
Running transaction test
Transaction test succeeded
Running transaction
Installing : mydumper-0.15.1-3.x86_64                             1/1
Verifying  : mydumper-0.15.1-3.x86_64                             1/1
```

```
Installed:
  mydumper.x86_64 0:0.15.1-3

Complete!
[root@mysql-a ~]# ls -ltr
total 7216
-rw-------. 1 root root    1582 Sep 26 2022 anaconda-ks.cfg
-rw-r--r--  1 root root 3046107 Mar 20 2023 download.1
-rw-r--r--  1 root root 3046107 Mar 20 2023 download
drwxr-xr-x  2 root root    4096 Sep 13 22:20 mysql_binaries
-rw-r--r--  1 root root 1283914 Oct  6 10:46 replication_db_dump.db
[root@mysql-a ~]#
[root@mysql-a ~]# which mydumper
/usr/bin/mydumper
[root@mysql-a ~]# which myloader
/usr/bin/myloader
```

2. Perform a backup of database **db1** using mydumper.

```
-bash-4.2$ mydumper --database=db1 --host=localhost --user=
root --password=WElcome_1234# --outputdir=mysql_
backup/  -G -E -R  --threads=4 --rows=10
-bash-4.2$ ls -ltr
total 0
drwxr-x--- 2 mysql mysql 163 Oct  6 15:33 mysql_backup
-bash-4.2$ cd mysql_backup/
-bash-4.2$ ls -ltr
total 20
-rw-rw-r-- 1 mysql mysql 216 Oct  6 15:33 db1.tab2-schema.sql
-rw-rw-r-- 1 mysql mysql 216 Oct  6 15:33 db1.tab1-schema.sql
-rw-rw-r-- 1 mysql mysql 152 Oct  6 15:33 db1-schema-create.sql
-rw-rw-r-- 1 mysql mysql 404 Oct  6 15:33 metadata
-rw-rw-r-- 1 mysql mysql 216 Oct  6 15:33 db1.tab3-schema.sql
-rw-rw-r-- 1 mysql mysql   0 Oct  6 15:33 db1-schema-triggers.sql
```

- - database = Database to dump

- - host = The hostname to connect to

- - user = The username with the correct privileges to take the dump

- - password= password of the user

- - outputdir = directory to output files to

- G = - - triggers = Dump triggers. By default, do not dump triggers

- E = - - events = Dump events. By default, do not dump events

- R = - - routines = Dump stored procedures and functions. By
default, do not dump stored procedures and functions

3. Restore database **db1** using myloader.

```
-bash-4.2$ pwd
/home/mysql/mysql_backup/mysql_backup
-bash-4.2$
-bash-4.2$ ls -ltr
total 20
-rw-rw-r-- 1 mysql mysql 216 Oct  6 15:33 db1.tab2-schema.sql
-rw-rw-r-- 1 mysql mysql 216 Oct  6 15:33 db1.tab1-schema.sql
-rw-rw-r-- 1 mysql mysql 152 Oct  6 15:33 db1-schema-create.sql
-rw-rw-r-- 1 mysql mysql 404 Oct  6 15:33 metadata
-rw-rw-r-- 1 mysql mysql 216 Oct  6 15:33 db1.tab3-schema.sql
-rw-rw-r-- 1 mysql mysql   0 Oct  6 15:33 db1-schema-triggers.sql
-bash-4.2$
-bash-4.2$ mysql -u root -p
Enter password:

mysql> show databases;
+----------------------+
| Database             |
+----------------------+
| db1                  |
| db2                  |
| db3                  |
| db4                  |
| db5                  |
| information_schema   |
```

```
| mysql              |
| performance_schema |
| sys                |
+--------------------+
9 rows in set (0.01 sec)
```

mysql> **drop database db1;**
Query OK, 3 rows affected (0.02 sec)

mysql> **exit**
Bye
-bash-4.2**$ myloader --host=localhost --user=
root --password=WElcome_1234# --database=db1 --directory=/home/
mysql/mysql_backup/mysql_backup --queries-
per-transaction=10 --threads=4 --verbose=3**
** Message: 15:38:08.643: Connection via default library settings
using password:
        Host: localhost
        User: root
** Message: 15:38:08.658: Initializing initialize_worker_schema

** Message: 15:38:08.664: S-Thread 6: Starting import
** Message: 15:38:08.666: Intermediate thread: SHUTDOWN
** Message: 15:38:08.666: Thread 7: restoring table `db1`.`tab1`
from /home/mysql/mysql_backup/mysql_backup/db1.tab1-schema.sql
** Message: 15:38:08.666: Thread 7: Creating table `db1`.`tab1`
from content in /home/mysql/mysql_backup/mysql_backup/db1.tab1-
schema.sql.
** Message: 15:38:08.666: Thread 8: restoring table `db1`.`tab2`
from /home/mysql/mysql_backup/mysql_backup/db1.tab2-schema.sql
** Message: 15:38:08.666: Thread 8: Creating table `db1`.`tab2`
from content in /home/mysql/mysql_backup/mysql_backup/db1.tab2-
schema.sql.
** Message: 15:38:08.667: Thread 6: restoring table `db1`.`tab3`
from /home/mysql/mysql_backup/mysql_backup/db1.tab3-schema.sql
** Message: 15:38:08.667: Thread 6: Creating table `db1`.`tab3` from
content in /home/mysql/mysql_backup/mysql_backup/db1.tab3-schema.sql.

** Message: 15:38:08.678: S-Thread 5: Import completed
** Message: 15:38:08.692: Thread 8: Table `db1`.`tab2` created.
Tables 0 of 3 completed
** Message: 15:38:08.692: S-Thread 8: Import completed
** Message: 15:38:08.696: Thread 7: Table `db1`.`tab1` created.
Tables 0 of 3 completed
** Message: 15:38:08.696: S-Thread 7: Import completed
** Message: 15:38:08.699: Thread 6: Table `db1`.`tab3` created.
Tables 0 of 3 completed
** Message: 15:38:08.699: S-Thread 6: Import completed
** Message: 15:38:08.700: SHUTDOWN last_wait_control_job_to_shutdown
** Message: 15:38:08.700: Sending start_innodb_optimize_keys_
all_tables
** Message: 15:38:08.703: Thread 16: Starting post import task
over table
** Message: 15:38:08.703: Thread 16: restoring trigger on `db1`
from db1-
schema-triggers.sql. Tables 0 of 3 completed
** Message: 15:38:08.703: Thread 15: Starting post import task
over table
** Message: 15:38:08.705: Errors found:
- Tablespace: 0
- Schema: 0
- Data: 0
- View: 0
- Sequence: 0
- Index: 0
- Trigger: 0
- Constraint: 0
- Post: 0
Retries: 0
-bash-4.2$
-bash-4.2$ **mysql -u root -p**
Enter password:

```
mysql> show databases;
+--------------------+
| Database           |
+--------------------+
| db1                |
| db2                |
| db3                |
| db4                |
| db5                |
| information_schema |
| mysql              |
| performance_schema |
| sys                |
+--------------------+
9 rows in set (0.00 sec)

mysql> use db1;
Reading table information for completion of table and column names
You can turn off this feature to get a quicker startup with -A

Database changed
mysql> show tables;
+----------------+
| Tables_in_db1  |
+----------------+
| tab1           |
| tab2           |
| tab3           |
+----------------+
3 rows in set (0.00 sec)
```

4. Multiple database backup. Back up databases **db3** and **db4**.

```
[mysql@mysql-p mysql_backup]$ mydumper --host=
localhost --user=root --password=Welcome@123 --outputdir=/home/
mysql/mysql_backup/mysql_backup --rows=50000 -G -E -R --threads=
4 --regex '^(db3\.|db4\.)' -L /tmp/mydumper-logs.txt
```

```
[mysql@mysql-p mysql_backup]$
[mysql@mysql-p mysql_backup]$ ls -ltr
total 12
-rw-rw-r-- 1 mysql mysql 127 Oct  3 22:50 db3-schema-create.sql
-rw-rw-r-- 1 mysql mysql 127 Oct  3 22:50 db4-schema-create.sql
-rw-rw-r-- 1 mysql mysql 133 Oct  3 22:50 metadata
```

- - regex = Regular expression for matching

- L = logfile

5. Perform a selective table backup. Backing up tables **emp** and **country** from **db1** database.

```
[mysql@mysql-p mysql_backup]$ mydumper --host=localhost --user
=root --password=Welcome@123 --outputdir=/home/mysql/mysql_backup/
mysql_backup --rows=50000 -G -E -R --threads=8 --regex '^(db1\.
emp$|db1\.country$)' -L /tmp/mydumper-logs.txt
[mysql@mysql-p mysql_backup]$
[mysql@mysql-p mysql_backup]$ ls -ltr
total 1999020
-rw-rw-r-- 1 mysql mysql         127 Oct  3 22:56 db1-schema-
                                                  create.sql
-rw-rw-r-- 1 mysql mysql         169 Oct  3 22:56 db1.country.sql
-rw-rw-r-- 1 mysql mysql         276 Oct  3 22:56 db1.emp_columns.sql
-rw-rw-r-- 1 mysql mysql         225 Oct  3 22:56 db1.emp_hash.sql
-rw-rw-r-- 1 mysql mysql         225 Oct  3 22:56 db1.emp_key.sql
-rw-rw-r-- 1 mysql mysql         271 Oct  3 22:56 db1.emp_list.sql
-rw-rw-r-- 1 mysql mysql         397 Oct  3 22:56 db1.emp_pruning.sql
-rw-rw-r-- 1 mysql mysql         314 Oct  3 22:56 db1.emp_reorg.sql
-rw-rw-r-- 1 mysql mysql         207 Oct  3 22:56 db1.emp_subpart.sql
-rw-rw-r-- 1 mysql mysql   109054756 Oct  3 22:57 db1.mgr.sql
-rw-rw-r-- 1 mysql mysql         344 Oct  3 22:57 db1.country-
                                                  schema.sql
-rw-rw-r-- 1 mysql mysql         221 Oct  3 22:57 db1.dept-schema.sql
-rw-rw-r-- 1 mysql mysql         250 Oct  3 22:57 db1.emp-schema.sql
-rw-rw-r-- 1 mysql mysql         217 Oct  3 22:57 db1.emp1-schema.sql
```

```
-rw-rw-r-- 1 mysql mysql        635 Oct  3 22:57 db1.emp_columns-
                                                 schema.sql

-rw-rw-r-- 1 mysql mysql        481 Oct  3 22:57 db1.emp_hash-
                                                 schema.sql

-rw-rw-r-- 1 mysql mysql        497 Oct  3 22:57 db1.emp_key-
                                                 schema.sql

-rw-rw-r-- 1 mysql mysql        676 Oct  3 22:57 db1.emp_list-
                                                 schema.sql

-rw-rw-r-- 1 mysql mysql        594 Oct  3 22:57 db1.emp_pruning-
                                                 schema.sql

-rw-rw-r-- 1 mysql mysql        656 Oct  3 22:57 db1.emp_range-
                                                 schema.sql

-rw-rw-r-- 1 mysql mysql        807 Oct  3 22:57 db1.emp_reorg-
                                                 schema.sql

-rw-rw-r-- 1 mysql mysql        257 Oct  3 22:57 db1.mgr-schema.sql
-rw-rw-r-- 1 mysql mysql        673 Oct  3 22:57 db1.emp_subpart-
                                                 schema.sql

-rw-rw-r-- 1 mysql mysql        676 Oct  3 22:57 db1.subpart_second-
                                                 schema.sql

-rw-rw-r-- 1 mysql mysql        326 Oct  3 22:57 db1.person-
                                                 schema.sql

-rw-rw-r-- 1 mysql mysql        317 Oct  3 22:57 db1.tests-
                                                 schema.sql

-rw-rw-r-- 1 mysql mysql  218110495 Oct  3 22:57 db1.tests.sql
-rw-rw-r-- 1 mysql mysql  251664642 Oct  3 22:59 db1.emp.sql
-rw-rw-r-- 1 mysql mysql        133 Oct  3 22:59 metadata
-rw-rw-r-- 1 mysql mysql 1468052041 Oct  3 22:59 db1.emp_range.sql
```

6. Perform a single table **db1.mgr** backup with compression.

```
[mysql@mysql-p mysql_backup]$ mydumper --host=localhost --user
=root --password=Welcome@123 --outputdir=/home/mysql/mysql_backup/
mysql_backup --rows=50000 -G -E -R --threads=4 --regex '^(db1\.
mgr$)' --compress --verbose 3 -L /tmp/mydumper-logs.txt
[mysql@mysql-p mysql_backup]$
[mysql@mysql-p mysql_backup]$ ls -ltr
```

```
total 672296
-rw-rw-r-- 1 mysql mysql       127 Oct   4 07:10 db1-schema-create.sql
-rw-rw-r-- 1 mysql mysql       276 Oct   4 07:10 db1.emp_columns.sql
-rw-rw-r-- 1 mysql mysql       225 Oct   4 07:10 db1.emp_hash.sql
-rw-rw-r-- 1 mysql mysql       225 Oct   4 07:10 db1.emp_key.sql
-rw-rw-r-- 1 mysql mysql       169 Oct   4 07:10 db1.country.sql
-rw-rw-r-- 1 mysql mysql       271 Oct   4 07:10 db1.emp_list.sql
-rw-rw-r-- 1 mysql mysql       397 Oct   4 07:10 db1.emp_pruning.sql
-rw-rw-r-- 1 mysql mysql       314 Oct   4 07:10 db1.emp_reorg.sql
-rw-rw-r-- 1 mysql mysql       207 Oct   4 07:10 db1.emp_subpart.sql
-rw-rw-r-- 1 mysql mysql       344 Oct   4 07:10 db1.country-
                                                  schema.sql
-rw-rw-r-- 1 mysql mysql   221 Oct   4 07:10 db1.dept-schema.sql
-rw-rw-r-- 1 mysql mysql       250 Oct   4 07:10 db1.emp-schema.sql
-rw-rw-r-- 1 mysql mysql       217 Oct   4 07:10 db1.emp1-schema.sql
-rw-rw-r-- 1 mysql mysql       481 Oct   4 07:10 db1.emp_hash-
                                                  schema.sql
-rw-rw-r-- 1 mysql mysql       635 Oct   4 07:10 db1.emp_columns-
                                                  schema.sql
-rw-rw-r-- 1 mysql mysql       497 Oct   4 07:10 db1.emp_key-
                                                  schema.sql
-rw-rw-r-- 1 mysql mysql       676 Oct   4 07:10 db1.emp_list-
                                                  schema.sql
-rw-rw-r-- 1 mysql mysql       594 Oct   4 07:10 db1.emp_pruning-
                                                  schema.sql
-rw-rw-r-- 1 mysql mysql       807 Oct   4 07:10 db1.emp_reorg-
                                                  schema.sql
-rw-rw-r-- 1 mysql mysql       656 Oct   4 07:10 db1.emp_range-
                                                  schema.sql
-rw-rw-r-- 1 mysql mysql       673 Oct   4 07:10 db1.emp_subpart-
                                                  schema.sql
-rw-rw-r-- 1 mysql mysql       676 Oct   4 07:10 db1.subpart_second-
                                                  schema.sql
-rw-rw-r-- 1 mysql mysql       326 Oct   4 07:10 db1.person-schema.sql
```

```
-rw-rw-r-- 1 mysql mysql        317 Oct  4 07:10 db1.tests-schema.sql
-rw-rw-r-- 1 mysql mysql 218110495 Oct  4 07:10 db1.tests.sql
-rw-rw-r-- 1 mysql mysql 251664642 Oct  4 07:12 db1.emp.sql
-rw-rw-r-- 1 mysql mysql        257 Oct  4 07:25 db1.mgr-schema.sql
-rw-rw-r-- 1 mysql mysql 218109385 Oct  4 07:25 db1.mgr.sql
-rw-rw-r-- 1 mysql mysql        211 Oct  4 07:27 db1.mgr-schema.sql.gz
-rw-rw-r-- 1 mysql mysql        133 Oct  4 07:28 metadata
-rw-rw-r-- 1 mysql mysql     428946 Oct  4 07:28 db1.mgr.sql.gz
```

7. Restore single table **db1.mgr** from compressed backup.

```
[mysql@mysql-p mysql_backup]$ mysql -u root -p
Enter password:

mysql> show databases;
+--------------------+
| Database           |
+--------------------+
| db1                |
| db2                |
| db3                |
| db4                |
| db5                |
| information_schema |
| mysql              |
| performance_schema |
| sys                |
+--------------------+
9 rows in set (0.00 sec)

mysql> use db1;
Reading table information for completion of table and column names
You can turn off this feature to get a quicker startup with -A

Database changed
mysql>
mysql> show tables;
```

```
+-----------------+
| Tables_in_db1   |
+-----------------+
| country         |
| dept            |
| emp             |
| emp1            |
| emp_columns     |
| emp_hash        |
| emp_key         |
| emp_list        |
| emp_pruning     |
| emp_range       |
| emp_reorg       |
| emp_subpart     |
| mgr             |
| person          |
| subpart_second  |
| tests           |
+-----------------+
16 rows in set (0.00 sec)

mysql> drop table mgr;
Query OK, 0 rows affected (0.09 sec)

mysql> show tables;
+-----------------+
| Tables_in_db1   |
+-----------------+
| country         |
| dept            |
| emp             |
| emp1            |
| emp_columns     |
| emp_hash        |
| emp_key         |
```

```
| emp_list       |
| emp_pruning    |
| emp_range      |
| emp_reorg      |
| emp_subpart    |
| person         |
| subpart_second |
| tests          |
+----------------+
15 rows in set (0.00 sec)

mysql> exit
Bye
[mysql@mysql-p mysql_backup]$
[mysql@mysql-p mysql_backup]$ myloader --host=localhost --user
=root --password=Welcome@123 -B db1 --directory=/home/mysql/mysql_
backup/mysql_backup --queries-per-transaction=
50000 --threads=4 --verbose=3 --overwrite-tables
** Message: 07:50:58.564: 4 threads created
** Message: 07:50:58.680: Dropping table or view (if exists)
`db1`.`country`
** Message: 07:51:00.382: Creating table `db1`.`country`
** Message: 07:51:01.289: Dropping table or view (if exists)
`db1`.`dept`
  --output truncated for better visibility

** Message: 07:52:39.378: Creating table `db1`.`emp_columns`
** Message: 07:52:39.436: Dropping table or view (if exists)
`db1`.`emp_hash`
** Message: 07:52:39.468: Creating table `db1`.`emp_hash`
** Message: 07:52:39.539: Dropping table or view (if exists)
`db1`.`emp_key`
** Message: 07:52:39.573: Creating table `db1`.`emp_key`
** Message: 07:52:39.625: Dropping table or view (if exists)
`db1`.`emp_list`
** Message: 07:52:39.656: Creating table `db1`.`emp_list`
```

--output truncated for better visibility

```
** Message: 07:52:40.386: Creating table `db1`.`tests`
** Message: 07:52:40.399: Dropping table or view (if exists)
`db1`.`mgr`
** Message: 07:52:40.404: Creating table `db1`.`mgr`
** Message: 07:52:40.413: Thread 1 restoring
`db1`.`country` part 0
** Message: 07:52:40.414: Thread 2 restoring `db1`.`emp` part 0
** Message: 07:52:40.414: Thread 3 restoring `db1`.`emp_
columns` part 0
```

--output truncated for better visibility

```
** Message: 07:52:40.625: Thread 3 restoring `db1`.`mgr` part 0
** Message: 07:56:52.297: Thread 4 shutting down
** Message: 07:59:36.057: Thread 1 shutting down
** Message: 07:59:40.302: Thread 3 shutting down
** Message: 08:01:45.229: Thread 2 shutting down
[mysql@mysql-p mysql_backup]$
[mysql@mysql-p mysql_backup]$ mysql -u root -p
Enter password:

mysql> show databases;
+--------------------+
| Database           |
+--------------------+
| db1                |
| db2                |
| db3                |
| db4                |
| db5                |
| information_schema |
| mysql              |
| performance_schema |
| sys                |
+--------------------+
9 rows in set (0.06 sec)
```

```
mysql> use db1;
Reading table information for completion of table and column names
You can turn off this feature to get a quicker startup with -A

Database changed
mysql>
mysql> show tables;
+----------------+
| Tables_in_db1  |
+----------------+
| country        |
| dept           |
| emp            |
| emp1           |
| emp_columns    |
| emp_hash       |
| emp_key        |
| emp_list       |
| emp_pruning    |
| emp_range      |
| emp_reorg      |
| emp_subpart    |
| mgr            |
| person         |
| subpart_second |
| tests          |
+----------------+
16 rows in set (0.00 sec)
```

Using Percona Xtrabackup

Percona Xtrabackup is an open source backup utility for MySQL servers. It can perform hot backups and can keep the database available fully. Percona Xtrabackup supports both InnoDB and MyISAM storage engines. Please note Percona Xtrabackup 8.0 should be used for MySQL 8.0 and it doesn't support versions less than MySQL 8.0. For versions less than MySQL 8.0, use Percona Xtrabackup 2.4.

1. Install Percona Xtrabackup.

```
[root@mysql-p yum.repos.d]# pwd
/etc/yum.repos.d
[root@mysql-p yum.repos.d]# sudo yum install -y https://repo.
percona.com/yum/percona-release-latest.noarch.rpm
Loaded plugins: fastestmirror
percona-release-latest.noarch.rpm                |  20 kB  00:00:00
Examining /var/tmp/yum-root-IxJkSO/percona-release-latest.noarch.
rpm: percona-release-1.0-27.noarch
Marking /var/tmp/yum-root-IxJkSO/percona-release-latest.noarch.rpm
to be installed
Resolving Dependencies
--> Running transaction check
---> Package percona-release.noarch 0:1.0-27 will be installed
--> Finished Dependency Resolution

Dependencies Resolved

========================================================================
 Package          Arch    Version Repository                    Size
========================================================================
Installing:
percona-release  noarch  1.0-27  /percona-release-latest.noarch 32 k

Transaction Summary
========================================================================
Install  1 Package

Total size: 32 k
Installed size: 32 k
Downloading packages:
Running transaction check
Running transaction test
Transaction test succeeded
Running transaction
  Installing : percona-release-1.0-27.noarch                     1/1
* Enabling the Percona Original repository
```

```
<*> All done!
* Enabling the Percona Release repository
<*> All done!
```

The percona-release package now contains a percona-release script that can enable additional repositories for our newer products.

For example, to enable the Percona Server 8.0 repository use:

```
percona-release setup ps80
```

Note: To avoid conflicts with older product versions, the percona-release setup command may disable our original repository for some products.

For more information, please visit:
  https://www.percona.com/doc/percona-repo-config/percona-release.html

```
  Verifying  : percona-release-1.0-27.noarch                         1/1
```

Installed:
  percona-release.noarch 0:1.0-27

Complete!
```
[root@mysql-p yum.repos.d]# ls -ltr
total 80
-rw-r--r-- 1 root root   616 Nov 23  2020 CentOS-x86_64-
                                          kernel.repo
-rw-r--r-- 1 root root  8515 Nov 23  2020 CentOS-Vault.repo
-rw-r--r-- 1 root root  1331 Nov 23  2020 CentOS-Sources.repo
-rw-r--r-- 1 root root   630 Nov 23  2020 CentOS-Media.repo
-rw-r--r-- 1 root root   314 Nov 23  2020 CentOS-fasttrack.repo
-rw-r--r-- 1 root root   649 Nov 23  2020 CentOS-Debuginfo.repo
-rw-r--r-- 1 root root  1309 Nov 23  2020 CentOS-CR.repo
-rw-r--r-- 1 root root  1664 Nov 23  2020 CentOS-Base.repo
-rw-r--r-- 1 root root  1457 Sep  4  2021 epel-testing.repo
-rw-r--r-- 1 root root  1358 Sep  4  2021 epel.repo
-rw-r--r-- 1 root root  2132 Aug 26  2022 mysql-community-
                                          source.repo
```

```
-rw-r--r--  1 root root  1147 Aug 26  2022 mysql-community-
                                              debuginfo.repo
-rw-r--r--. 1 root root 11335 Nov 23  2022 pgdg-redhat-all.repo
-rw-r--r--  1 root root  2062 Aug 30 15:46 mysql-community.repo
-rw-r--r--  1 root root   780 Oct  5 23:15 percona-original-
                                              release.repo
-rw-r--r--  1 root root   301 Oct  5 23:15 percona-prel-
                                              release.repo
[root@mysql-p yum.repos.d]#
```

>>>>>>>>>>>>>>>>>>>>> Check the repo <<<<<<<<<<<<<<<<<<<<<<<<<

```
[root@mysql-p ~]# cd /etc/yum.repos.d

[root@mysql-p yum.repos.d]# ls -lrth perc*
-rw-r--r-- 1 root root 20K Aug 17  2021 percona-release-latest.
noarch.rpm
[root@mysql-p yum.repos.d]#

[root@mysql-p yum.repos.d]# percona-release setup ps80
* Disabling all Percona Repositories
* Enabling the Percona Server 8.0 repository
* Enabling the Percona Tools repository
<*> All done!
[root@mysql-p yum.repos.d]#
```

>>>>>>>>>>>>>>>>>>>>>>>>>> Xtrabackup installation

```
[root@mysql-p yum.repos.d]# yum install percona-xtrabackup-80
Loaded plugins: fastestmirror
Determining fastest mirrors
epel/x86_64/metalink                      | 9.8 kB  00:00:00
 * base: tx-mirror.tier.net
 * epel: reflector.westga.edu
 * extras: nc-centos-mirror.iwebfusion.net
 * updates: mirror.atl.genesisadaptive.com
base
```

  --output truncated for better visibility

Installed:

percona-xtrabackup-80.x86_64 0:8.0.34-29.1.el7

Dependency Installed:

```
  libev.x86_64 0:4.15-7.el7                perl-Compress-Raw-Bzip2.
  x86_64 0:2.061-3.el7 perl-Compress-Raw-Zlib.x86_64 1:2.061-4.el7
  perl-DBD-MySQL.x86_64 0:4.023-6.el7
  perl-DBI.x86_64 0:1.627-4.el7            perl-Digest.noarch
  0:1.17-245.el7                perl-Digest-MD5.x86_64 0:2.52-3.el7
  perl-IO-Compress.noarch 0:2.061-2.el7
  perl-Net-Daemon.noarch 0:0.48-5.el7 perl-PlRPC.noarch
  0:0.2020-14.el7                zstd.x86_64 0:1.5.5-1.el7
```

Complete!

2. Check the version.

```
[root@mysql-p yum.repos.d]# rpm -qa|grep percona-xtra
percona-xtrabackup-80-8.0.34-29.1.el7.x86_64
[root@mysql-p yum.repos.d]#
[root@mysql-p yum.repos.d]# xtrabackup --version
2023-10-05T23:26:21.289623-05:00 0 [Note] [MY-011825] [Xtrabackup]
recognized server arguments: --log_bin=/var/lib/mysql/
binlog --datadir=/var/lib/mysql --innodb_data_home_dir=/var/lib/
mysql/innodb/ --innodb_data_file_path=ibdata1:12M;ibdata2:12M:aut
oextend --innodb_undo_directory=/var/lib/mysql/innodb/ --innodb_
directories=/var/lib/tbs/
xtrabackup version 8.0.34-29 based on MySQL server 8.0.34 Linux
(x86_64) (revision id: 5ba706ee)
[root@mysql-p yum.repos.d]#
```

3. Perform a backup of the MySQL server.

```
[root@mysql-a ~]# mkdir -p /var/lib/backup
[root@mysql-a ~]# chown -R mysql:mysql /var/lib/backup/
[root@mysql-a ~]#
[root@mysql-a ~]# ls -ltr /var/lib/backup/
total 0
```

[root@mysql-a ~]# **su - mysql**
-bash-4.2$ **xtrabackup -uroot -pWElcome_1234# --backup --target-dir=/var/lib/backup/**
2023-10-20T13:34:31.781136-05:00 0 [Note] [MY-011825] [Xtrabackup]
recognized server arguments: --datadir=/var/lib/mysql
2023-10-20T13:34:31.781419-05:00 0 [Note] [MY-011825] [Xtrabackup]
recognized client arguments: --user=root --password=* --backup=
1 --target-dir=/var/lib/backup/
xtrabackup version 8.0.34-29 based on MySQL server 8.0.34 Linux
(x86_64) (revision id: 5ba706ee)

  --output truncated for better visibility

2023-10-20T13:34:33.797670-05:00 0 [Note] [MY-011825] [Xtrabackup]
Executing UNLOCK INSTANCE
2023-10-20T13:34:33.797924-05:00 0 [Note] [MY-011825] [Xtrabackup]
All tables unlocked
2023-10-20T13:34:33.798029-05:00 0 [Note] [MY-011825] [Xtrabackup]
Copying ib_buffer_pool to /var/lib/backup/ib_buffer_pool
2023-10-20T13:34:33.798085-05:00 0 [Note] [MY-011825] [Xtrabackup]
Done: Copying ib_buffer_pool to /var/lib/backup/ib_buffer_pool
2023-10-20T13:34:33.799551-05:00 0 [Note] [MY-011825] [Xtrabackup]
Backup created in directory '/var/lib/backup/'
2023-10-20T13:34:33.799572-05:00 0 [Note] [MY-011825] [Xtrabackup]
MySQL binlog position: filename 'binlog.000012', position '157'
2023-10-20T13:34:33.799697-05:00 0 [Note] [MY-011825] [Xtrabackup]
Writing /var/lib/backup/backup-my.cnf
2023-10-20T13:34:33.799764-05:00 0 [Note] [MY-011825] [Xtrabackup]
Done: Writing file /var/lib/backup/backup-my.cnf
2023-10-20T13:34:33.801844-05:00 0 [Note] [MY-011825] [Xtrabackup]
Writing /var/lib/backup/xtrabackup_info
2023-10-20T13:34:33.801958-05:00 0 [Note] [MY-011825] [Xtrabackup]
Done: Writing file /var/lib/backup/xtrabackup_info
2023-10-20T13:34:34.806096-05:00 0 [Note] [MY-011825] [Xtrabackup]
Transaction log of lsn (2429716240) to (2429716240) was copied.
2023-10-20T13:34:35.016501-05:00 0 [Note] [MY-011825] **[Xtrabackup]
completed OK!**

4. Verify backup.

```
-bash-4.2$ cd /var/lib/backup/
-bash-4.2$ ls -ltr
total 119856
-rw-r----- 1 mysql mysql 12582912 Oct 20 13:34 ibdata1
drwxr-x--- 2 mysql mysql       28 Oct 20 13:34 sys
-rw-r----- 1 mysql mysql 26214400 Oct 20 13:34 mysql.ibd
drwxr-x--- 2 mysql mysql      132 Oct 20 13:34 employees
-rw-r----- 1 mysql mysql 67108864 Oct 20 13:34 undo_002
-rw-r----- 1 mysql mysql 16777216 Oct 20 13:34 undo_001
drwxr-x--- 2 mysql mysql      143 Oct 20 13:34 mysql
drwxr-x--- 2 mysql mysql     8192 Oct 20 13:34 performance_schema
-rw-r----- 1 mysql mysql      157 Oct 20 13:34 binlog.000012
-rw-r----- 1 mysql mysql       16 Oct 20 13:34 binlog.index
-rw-r----- 1 mysql mysql       18 Oct 20 13:34 xtrabackup_
                                               binlog_info
-rw-r----- 1 mysql mysql     2560 Oct 20 13:34 xtrabackup_logfile
-rw-r----- 1 mysql mysql      140 Oct 20 13:34 xtrabackup_
                                               checkpoints
-rw-r----- 1 mysql mysql     3631 Oct 20 13:34 ib_buffer_pool
-rw-r----- 1 mysql mysql      447 Oct 20 13:34 backup-my.cnf
-rw-r----- 1 mysql mysql      471 Oct 20 13:34 xtrabackup_info
-rw-r----- 1 mysql mysql       39 Oct 20 13:34 xtrabackup_
                                               tablespaces
-bash-4.2$
-bash-4.2$ cat xtrabackup_info
uuid = 50891026-6f77-11ee-a96d-080027cf69cc
name =
tool_name = xtrabackup
tool_command = -uroot -p=... --backup --target-dir=/var/
lib/backup/
tool_version = 8.0.34-29
ibbackup_version = 8.0.34-29
server_version = 8.0.34
start_time = 2023-10-20 13:34:31
```

```
end_time = 2023-10-20 13:34:33
lock_time = 0
binlog_pos = filename 'binlog.000012', position '157'
innodb_from_lsn = 0
innodb_to_lsn = 2429716240
partial = N
incremental = N
format = file
compressed = N
encrypted = N
```

5. Before creating an incremental backup, create a few tables
    since the initial full backup is already taken so we can validate
    incremental backup. The target directory --target-dir contains the
    delta backup files from the full backup, and the --incremental-
    basedir contains the base backup files from a full backup.

```
-bash-4.2$ mysql -uroot -p
Enter password:

mysql> show databases;
+--------------------+
| Database           |
+--------------------+
| employees          |
| information_schema |
| mysql              |
| performance_schema |
| sys                |
+--------------------+
5 rows in set (0.00 sec)

mysql> use employees;
Reading table information for completion of table and column names
You can turn off this feature to get a quicker startup with -A

Database changed
mysql> show tables;
```

```
+-----------------------+
| Tables_in_employees   |
+-----------------------+
| current_dept_emp      |
| departments           |
| dept_emp              |
| dept_emp_latest_date  |
| dept_manager          |
| employees             |
| salaries              |
| titles                |
+-----------------------+
8 rows in set (0.00 sec)
```

mysql> **create table dept as select * from employees;**
Query OK, 300024 rows affected (2.01 sec)
Records: 300024 Duplicates: 0 Warnings: 0

mysql> **create table hr as select * from employees;**
Query OK, 300024 rows affected (2.01 sec)
Records: 300024 Duplicates: 0 Warnings: 0

mysql> **show tables;**

```
+-----------------------+
| Tables_in_employees   |
+-----------------------+
| current_dept_emp      |
| departments           |
| dept                  |
| dept_emp              |
| dept_emp_latest_date  |
| dept_manager          |
| employees             |
| hr                    |
| salaries              |
| titles                |
+-----------------------+
```

```
10 rows in set (0.00 sec)

mysql> exit
Bye
-bash-4.2$ exit
logout
[root@mysql-a ~]# mkdir -p /var/lib/incremental_backup
[root@mysql-a ~]# chown -R mysql:mysql /var/lib/
incremental_backup/
[root@mysql-a ~]# su - mysql
Last login: Fri Oct 20 13:33:57 CDT 2023 on pts/0
-bash-4.2$
```

```
-bash-4.2$ xtrabackup --backup --user=root --password=WElcome_1234#
--target-dir=/var/lib/incremental_backup/ --incremental-basedir=/
var/lib/backup/
```

```
2023-10-20T13:44:10.895110-05:00 0 [Note] [MY-011825] [Xtrabackup]
recognized server arguments: --datadir=/var/lib/mysql
2023-10-20T13:44:10.895255-05:00 0 [Note] [MY-011825] [Xtrabackup]
recognized client arguments: --backup=1 --user=root --password=*
--target-dir=/var/lib/incremental_backup/ --incremental-basedir=/
var/lib/backup/
xtrabackup version 8.0.34-29 based on MySQL server 8.0.34 Linux
(x86_64) (revision id: 5ba706ee)
```

   --output truncated for better visibility

```
2023-10-20T13:44:13.010080-05:00 0 [Note] [MY-011825] [Xtrabackup]
Executing UNLOCK INSTANCE
2023-10-20T13:44:13.010458-05:00 0 [Note] [MY-011825] [Xtrabackup]
All tables unlocked
2023-10-20T13:44:13.010542-05:00 0 [Note] [MY-011825] [Xtrabackup]
Copying ib_buffer_pool to /var/lib/incremental_backup/ib_
buffer_pool
2023-10-20T13:44:13.010935-05:00 0 [Note] [MY-011825] [Xtrabackup]
Done: Copying ib_buffer_pool to /var/lib/incremental_backup/ib_
buffer_pool
```

```
2023-10-20T13:44:13.012040-05:00 0 [Note] [MY-011825] [Xtrabackup]
Backup created in directory '/var/lib/incremental_backup/'
2023-10-20T13:44:13.012067-05:00 0 [Note] [MY-011825] [Xtrabackup]
MySQL binlog position: filename 'binlog.000013', position '157'
2023-10-20T13:44:13.012154-05:00 0 [Note] [MY-011825] [Xtrabackup]
Writing /var/lib/incremental_backup/backup-my.cnf
2023-10-20T13:44:13.012237-05:00 0 [Note] [MY-011825] [Xtrabackup]
Done: Writing file /var/lib/incremental_backup/backup-my.cnf
2023-10-20T13:44:13.017660-05:00 0 [Note] [MY-011825] [Xtrabackup]
Writing /var/lib/incremental_backup/xtrabackup_info
2023-10-20T13:44:13.017760-05:00 0 [Note] [MY-011825] [Xtrabackup]
Done: Writing file /var/lib/incremental_backup/xtrabackup_info
2023-10-20T13:44:14.021264-05:00 0 [Note] [MY-011825] [Xtrabackup]
Transaction log of lsn (2494511882) to (2494511882) was copied.
2023-10-20T13:44:14.232876-05:00 0 [Note] [MY-011825] [Xtrabackup]
completed OK!
```

6. Verify incremental backup taken in the previous step.

```
-bash-4.2$ cd /var/lib/incremental_backup/
-bash-4.2$ ls -ltr
total 11428
-rw-r----- 1 mysql mysql      64 Oct 20 13:44 ibdata1.meta
-rw-r----- 1 mysql mysql   49152 Oct 20 13:44 ibdata1.delta
drwxr-x--- 2 mysql mysql      61 Oct 20 13:44 sys
-rw-r----- 1 mysql mysql      73 Oct 20 13:44 mysql.ibd.meta
-rw-r----- 1 mysql mysql  622592 Oct 20 13:44 mysql.ibd.delta
drwxr-x--- 2 mysql mysql    4096 Oct 20 13:44 employees
-rw-r----- 1 mysql mysql      69 Oct 20 13:44 undo_002.meta
-rw-r----- 1 mysql mysql 5488640 Oct 20 13:44 undo_002.delta
-rw-r----- 1 mysql mysql      69 Oct 20 13:44 undo_001.meta
-rw-r----- 1 mysql mysql 5472256 Oct 20 13:44 undo_001.delta
drwxr-x--- 2 mysql mysql     143 Oct 20 13:44 mysql
drwxr-x--- 2 mysql mysql    8192 Oct 20 13:44 performance_schema
```

```
-rw-r----- 1 mysql mysql      157 Oct 20 13:44 binlog.000013
-rw-r----- 1 mysql mysql       16 Oct 20 13:44 binlog.index
-rw-r----- 1 mysql mysql       18 Oct 20 13:44 xtrabackup_
                                               binlog_info
-rw-r----- 1 mysql mysql     2560 Oct 20 13:44 xtrabackup_logfile
-rw-r----- 1 mysql mysql      147 Oct 20 13:44 xtrabackup_
                                               checkpoints
-rw-r----- 1 mysql mysql     3631 Oct 20 13:44 ib_buffer_pool
-rw-r----- 1 mysql mysql      447 Oct 20 13:44 backup-my.cnf
-rw-r----- 1 mysql mysql      544 Oct 20 13:44 xtrabackup_info
-rw-r----- 1 mysql mysql       39 Oct 20 13:44 xtrabackup_
                                               tablespaces
-bash-4.2$
-bash-4.2$ cat xtrabackup_info
uuid = a9c5b9f8-6f78-11ee-a96d-080027cf69cc
name =
tool_name = xtrabackup
tool_command = --backup --user=root --password=... --target-dir=/
var/lib/incremental_backup/ --incremental-basedir=/var/lib/backup/
tool_version = 8.0.34-29
ibbackup_version = 8.0.34-29
server_version = 8.0.34
start_time = 2023-10-20 13:44:10
end_time = 2023-10-20 13:44:13
lock_time = 1
binlog_pos = filename 'binlog.000013', position '157'
innodb_from_lsn = 2429716240
innodb_to_lsn = 2494511882
partial = N
incremental = Y
format = file
compressed = N
encrypted = N
```

7. To simulate a data loss scenario, let us drop tables **dept** and **hr**.

```
-bash-4.2$ mysql -uroot -p
Enter password:

mysql> show databases;
+--------------------+
| Database           |
+--------------------+
| employees          |
| information_schema |
| mysql              |
| performance_schema |
| sys                |
+--------------------+
5 rows in set (0.00 sec)

mysql> use employees;
Reading table information for completion of table and column names
You can turn off this feature to get a quicker startup with -A

Database changed
mysql> show tables;
+----------------------+
| Tables_in_employees  |
+----------------------+
| current_dept_emp     |
| departments          |
| dept                 |
| dept_emp             |
| dept_emp_latest_date |
| dept_manager         |
| employees            |
| hr                   |
| salaries             |
| titles               |
+----------------------+
10 rows in set (0.00 sec)
```

```
mysql> drop table dept;
Query OK, 0 rows affected (0.03 sec)

mysql> drop table hr;
Query OK, 0 rows affected (0.04 sec)

mysql> show tables;
+----------------------+
| Tables_in_employees  |
+----------------------+
| current_dept_emp     |
| departments          |
| dept_emp             |
| dept_emp_latest_date |
| dept_manager         |
| employees            |
| salaries             |
| titles               |
+----------------------+
8 rows in set (0.00 sec)
```

8. Before performing a restore, the backup taken using xtrabackup
    needs to be prepared as the backup is not consistent due to
    pending transactions in memory. To restore to the latest state, we
    will need to first restore a full backup and then the incremental
    backup to get the database to the latest state so we can restore the
    dept and **hr** tables that were dropped earlier.

```
-bash-4.2$ xtrabackup --prepare=TRUE --apply-log-only=
TRUE --target-dir=/var/lib/backup/
2023-10-20T07:32:12.357650-05:00 0 [Note] [MY-011825]
[Xtrabackup] recognized server arguments: --innodb_checksum_
algorithm=crc32 --innodb_log_checksums=1 --innodb_data_file_
path=ibdata1:12M:autoextend --innodb_log_file_size=50331648 --
innodb_page_size=16384 --innodb_undo_directory=./ --innodb_undo_
tablespaces=2 --server-id=0 --innodb_log_checksums=ON --innodb_
redo_log_encrypt=0 --innodb_undo_log_encrypt=0
```

2023-10-20T07:32:12.357864-05:00 0 [Note] [MY-011825] [Xtrabackup]
recognized client arguments: --prepare=1 --apply-log-only=
1 --target-dir=/var/lib/backup/
xtrabackup version 8.0.34-29 based on MySQL server 8.0.34 Linux
(x86_64) (revision id: 5ba706ee)
2023-10-20T07:32:12.357907-05:00 0 [Note] [MY-011825] [Xtrabackup]
cd to /var/lib/backup/
2023-10-20T07:32:12.359336-05:00 0 [Note] [MY-011825] [Xtrabackup]
This target seems to be not prepared yet.
2023-10-20T07:32:12.378678-05:00 0 [Note] [MY-011825] [Xtrabackup]
xtrabackup_logfile detected: size=8388608, start_lsn=(2429716240)
2023-10-20T07:32:12.381865-05:00 0 [Note] [MY-011825] [Xtrabackup]
using the following InnoDB configuration for recovery:
2023-10-20T07:32:12.381910-05:00 0 [Note] [MY-011825] [Xtrabackup]
innodb_data_home_dir = .
2023-10-20T07:32:12.381923-05:00 0 [Note] [MY-011825] [Xtrabackup]
innodb_data_file_path = ibdata1:12M:autoextend
2023-10-20T07:32:12.381971-05:00 0 [Note] [MY-011825] [Xtrabackup]
innodb_log_group_home_dir = .
2023-10-20T07:32:12.381984-05:00 0 [Note] [MY-011825] [Xtrabackup]
innodb_log_files_in_group = 1
2023-10-20T07:32:12.382001-05:00 0 [Note] [MY-011825] [Xtrabackup]
innodb_log_file_size = 8388608
2023-10-20T07:32:12.382569-05:00 0 [Note] [MY-011825] [Xtrabackup]
inititialize_service_handles suceeded
2023-10-20T07:32:12.383680-05:00 0 [Note] [MY-011825] [Xtrabackup]
using the following InnoDB configuration for recovery:
2023-10-20T07:32:12.383708-05:00 0 [Note] [MY-011825] [Xtrabackup]
innodb_data_home_dir = .
2023-10-20T07:32:12.383720-05:00 0 [Note] [MY-011825] [Xtrabackup]
innodb_data_file_path = ibdata1:12M:autoextend
2023-10-20T07:32:12.383741-05:00 0 [Note] [MY-011825] [Xtrabackup]
innodb_log_group_home_dir = .
2023-10-20T07:32:12.383757-05:00 0 [Note] [MY-011825] [Xtrabackup]
innodb_log_files_in_group = 1

2023-10-20T07:32:12.383773-05:00 0 [Note] [MY-011825] [Xtrabackup] innodb_log_file_size = 8388608
2023-10-20T07:32:12.383797-05:00 0 [Note] [MY-011825] [Xtrabackup] Starting InnoDB instance for recovery.
2023-10-20T07:32:12.383948-05:00 0 [Note] [MY-011825] [Xtrabackup] Using 104857600 bytes for buffer pool (set by --use-memory parameter)
2023-10-20T07:32:12.384046-05:00 0 [Note] [MY-012932] [InnoDB] PUNCH HOLE support available
2023-10-20T07:32:12.384100-05:00 0 [Note] [MY-012944] [InnoDB] Uses event mutexes
2023-10-20T07:32:12.384122-05:00 0 [Note] [MY-012945] [InnoDB] GCC builtin __atomic_thread_fence() is used for memory barrier
2023-10-20T07:32:12.384154-05:00 0 [Note] [MY-012948] [InnoDB] Compressed tables use zlib 1.2.13
2023-10-20T07:32:12.384560-05:00 0 [Note] [MY-012951] [InnoDB] Using hardware accelerated crc32 and polynomial multiplication.
2023-10-20T07:32:12.384938-05:00 0 [Note] [MY-012203] [InnoDB] Directories to scan './'
2023-10-20T07:32:12.384990-05:00 0 [Note] [MY-012204] [InnoDB] Scanning './'
2023-10-20T07:32:12.445057-05:00 0 [Note] [MY-012208] [InnoDB] Completed space ID check of 10 files.
2023-10-20T07:32:12.446341-05:00 0 [Note] [MY-012955] [InnoDB] Initializing buffer pool, total size = 128.000000M, instances = 1, chunk size =128.000000M
2023-10-20T07:32:12.467838-05:00 0 [Note] [MY-012957] [InnoDB] Completed initialization of buffer pool
2023-10-20T07:32:12.583942-05:00 0 [Note] [MY-011952] [InnoDB] If the mysqld execution user is authorized, page cleaner thread priority can be changed. See the man page of setpriority().
2023-10-20T07:32:12.786137-05:00 0 [Note] [MY-013883] [InnoDB] The latest found checkpoint is at lsn = 2429716240 in redo log file ./#innodb_redo/#ib_redo0.
2023-10-20T07:32:12.786250-05:00 0 [Note] [MY-012560] [InnoDB] The log sequence number 2084509636 in the system tablespace does not match the log sequence number 2429716240 in the redo log files!

```
2023-10-20T07:32:12.786278-05:00 0 [Note] [MY-012551] [InnoDB]
Database was not shutdown normally!
2023-10-20T07:32:12.786294-05:00 0 [Note] [MY-012552] [InnoDB]
Starting crash recovery.
2023-10-20T07:32:12.805431-05:00 0 [Note] [MY-013086] [InnoDB]
Starting to parse redo log at lsn = 2429716002, whereas
checkpoint_lsn = 2429716240 and start_lsn = 2429715968
2023-10-20T07:32:12.805491-05:00 0 [Note] [MY-012550] [InnoDB]
Doing recovery: scanned up to log sequence number 2429716240
2023-10-20T07:32:12.833385-05:00 0 [Note] [MY-013083] [InnoDB] Log
background threads are being started...
```

--output truncated for better visibility

```
2023-10-20T07:32:13.675389-05:00 0 [Note] [MY-011825] [Xtrabackup]
starting shutdown with innodb_fast_shutdown = 1
2023-10-20T07:32:13.675608-05:00 0 [Note] [MY-012330] [InnoDB] FTS
optimize thread exiting.
2023-10-20T07:32:14.654402-05:00 0 [Note] [MY-013072] [InnoDB]
Starting shutdown...
2023-10-20T07:32:14.760810-05:00 0 [Note] [MY-013084] [InnoDB] Log
background threads are being closed...
2023-10-20T07:32:14.812041-05:00 0 [Note] [MY-012980] [InnoDB]
Shutdown completed; log sequence number 2429716250
2023-10-20T07:32:14.814999-05:00 0 [Note] [MY-011825] [Xtrabackup]
completed OK!
-bash-4.2$
```

>>>>>>>>>>> Preparing Incremental backup <<<<<<<<<<<<<<<<<<

```
-bash-4.2$ xtrabackup --prepare=TRUE --target-dir=/var/lib/
backup/ --incremental-dir=/var/lib/incremental_backup/
2023-10-20T07:33:40.345095-05:00 0 [Note] [MY-011825]
[Xtrabackup] recognized server arguments: --innodb_checksum_
algorithm=crc32 --innodb_log_checksums=1 --innodb_data_file_
path=ibdata1:12M:autoextend --innodb_log_file_size=50331648 --innodb_
page_size=16384 --innodb_undo_directory=./ --innodb_undo_
```

tablespaces=2 --server-id=0 --innodb_log_checksums=ON --innodb_
redo_log_encrypt=0 --innodb_undo_log_encrypt=0
2023-10-20T07:33:40.345325-05:00 0 [Note] [MY-011825] [Xtrabackup]
recognized client arguments: --prepare=1 --target-dir=/var/lib/
backup/ --incremental-dir=/var/lib/incremental_backup/
xtrabackup version 8.0.34-29 based on MySQL server 8.0.34 Linux
(x86_64) (revision id: 5ba706ee)
2023-10-20T07:33:40.346606-05:00 0 [Note] [MY-011825] [Xtrabackup]
incremental backup from 2429716240 is enabled.
2023-10-20T07:33:40.346657-05:00 0 [Note] [MY-011825] [Xtrabackup]
cd to /var/lib/backup/
2023-10-20T07:33:40.346767-05:00 0 [Note] [MY-011825] [Xtrabackup]
This target seems to be already prepared with --apply-log-only.
2023-10-20T07:33:40.355168-05:00 0 [Note] [MY-011825] [Xtrabackup]
xtrabackup_logfile detected: size=8388608, start_lsn=(2494511882)
2023-10-20T07:33:40.356132-05:00 0 [Note] [MY-011825] [Xtrabackup]
using the following InnoDB configuration for recovery:
2023-10-20T07:33:40.356172-05:00 0 [Note] [MY-011825] [Xtrabackup]
innodb_data_home_dir = .
2023-10-20T07:33:40.356192-05:00 0 [Note] [MY-011825] [Xtrabackup]
innodb_data_file_path = ibdata1:12M:autoextend

  --Output truncated for better visibility

2023-10-20T07:33:45.161112-05:00 0 [Note] [MY-011825] [Xtrabackup]
Done: Copying /var/lib/incremental_backup//performance_schema/
tls_channel_stat_190.sdi to ./performance_schema/tls_channel_
stat_190.sdi
2023-10-20T07:33:45.162869-05:00 0 [Note] [MY-011825] [Xtrabackup]
Copying /var/lib/incremental_backup//performance_schema/keyring_
componen_191.sdi to ./performance_schema/keyring_componen_191.sdi
2023-10-20T07:33:45.163615-05:00 0 [Note] [MY-011825] [Xtrabackup]
Done: Copying /var/lib/incremental_backup//performance_schema/
keyring_componen_191.sdi to ./performance_schema/keyring_
componen_191.sdi

```
2023-10-20T07:33:45.165738-05:00 0 [Note] [MY-011825] [Xtrabackup]
Copying /var/lib/incremental_backup//xtrabackup_binlog_info to ./
xtrabackup_binlog_info
2023-10-20T07:33:45.166623-05:00 0 [Note] [MY-011825] [Xtrabackup]
Done: Copying /var/lib/incremental_backup//xtrabackup_binlog_info
to ./xtrabackup_binlog_info
2023-10-20T07:33:45.169198-05:00 0 [Note] [MY-011825] [Xtrabackup]
Copying /var/lib/incremental_backup//xtrabackup_info to ./
xtrabackup_info
2023-10-20T07:33:45.169929-05:00 0 [Note] [MY-011825] [Xtrabackup]
Done: Copying /var/lib/incremental_backup//xtrabackup_info to ./
xtrabackup_info
2023-10-20T07:33:45.172566-05:00 0 [Note] [MY-011825] [Xtrabackup]
Copying /var/lib/incremental_backup//xtrabackup_tablespaces to ./
xtrabackup_tablespaces
2023-10-20T07:33:45.172696-05:00 0 [Note] [MY-011825] [Xtrabackup]
Done: Copying /var/lib/incremental_backup//xtrabackup_tablespaces
to ./xtrabackup_tablespaces
2023-10-20T07:33:45.177401-05:00 0 [Note] [MY-011825] [Xtrabackup]
Copying /var/lib/incremental_backup/binlog.000013 to ./
binlog.000013
2023-10-20T07:33:45.178057-05:00 0 [Note] [MY-011825] [Xtrabackup]
Done: Copying /var/lib/incremental_backup/binlog.000013 to ./
binlog.000013
2023-10-20T07:33:45.180641-05:00 0 [Note] [MY-011825] [Xtrabackup]
Copying /var/lib/incremental_backup/binlog.index to ./binlog.index
2023-10-20T07:33:45.180822-05:00 0 [Note] [MY-011825] [Xtrabackup]
Done: Copying /var/lib/incremental_backup/binlog.index to ./
binlog.index
2023-10-20T07:33:45.183626-05:00 0 [Note] [MY-011825] [Xtrabackup]
completed OK!
-bash-4.2$
```

9. Stop the MySQL daemon before restoring the backup.

   ```
   [root@mysql-a ~]# systemctl stop mysqld
   ```

10. Create a new directory to restore the backup.

```
[root@mysql-a ~]# cd /var/lib/
[root@mysql-a lib]#
[root@mysql-a lib]# mv mysql mysql_old
[root@mysql-a lib]# mkdir mysql
[root@mysql-a lib]# chown -R mysql:mysql /var/lib/mysql
[root@mysql-a lib]#
[root@mysql-a lib]# su - mysql
Last login: Fri Oct 20 07:31:34 CDT 2023 on pts/0
-bash-4.2$ cd /var/lib/mysql
-bash-4.2$ ls -ltr
total 0
-bash-4.2$ ls -al
total 4
drwxr-xr-x   2 mysql mysql      6 Oct 20 07:40 .
drwxr-xr-x. 32 root  root    4096 Oct 20 07:40 ..
```

11. Perform a restore using the backup. To restore the backup,
     use the - - **copy-back** option.

```
-bash-4.2$ xtrabackup --copy-back --target-dir=/var/lib/backup/
2023-10-20T07:42:22.743375-05:00 0 [Note] [MY-011825] [Xtrabackup]
recognized server arguments: --datadir=/var/lib/mysql
2023-10-20T07:42:22.743777-05:00 0 [Note] [MY-011825] [Xtrabackup]
recognized client arguments: --copy-back=1 --target-dir=/var/
lib/backup/
xtrabackup version 8.0.34-29 based on MySQL server 8.0.34 Linux
(x86_64) (revision id: 5ba706ee)
2023-10-20T07:42:22.743876-05:00 0 [Note] [MY-011825] [Xtrabackup]
cd to /var/lib/backup/
2023-10-20T07:42:22.745659-05:00 0 [Note] [MY-011825] [Xtrabackup]
Copying undo_001 to /var/lib/mysql/undo_001
2023-10-20T07:42:22.781976-05:00 0 [Note] [MY-011825] [Xtrabackup]
Done: Copying undo_001 to /var/lib/mysql/undo_001
2023-10-20T07:42:22.820127-05:00 0 [Note] [MY-011825] [Xtrabackup]
Copying undo_002 to /var/lib/mysql/undo_002
```

2023-10-20T07:42:22.997549-05:00 0 [Note] [MY-011825] [Xtrabackup]
Done: Copying undo_002 to /var/lib/mysql/undo_002
2023-10-20T07:42:23.036000-05:00 0 [Note] [MY-011825] [Xtrabackup]
Copying ibdata1 to /var/lib/mysql/ibdata1
2023-10-20T07:42:23.061039-05:00 0 [Note] [MY-011825] [Xtrabackup]
Done: Copying ibdata1 to /var/lib/mysql/ibdata1
2023-10-20T07:42:23.089785-05:00 0 [Note] [MY-011825] [Xtrabackup]
Copying binlog.000013 to /var/lib/mysql/binlog.000013
2023-10-20T07:42:23.090078-05:00 0 [Note] [MY-011825] [Xtrabackup]
Done: Copying binlog.000013 to /var/lib/mysql/binlog.000013
2023-10-20T07:42:23.092019-05:00 0 [Note] [MY-011825] [Xtrabackup]
Copying binlog.index to /var/lib/mysql/binlog.index
2023-10-20T07:42:23.092179-05:00 0 [Note] [MY-011825] [Xtrabackup]
Done: Copying binlog.index to /var/lib/mysql/binlog.index
2023-10-20T07:42:23.105612-05:00 1 [Note] [MY-011825] [Xtrabackup]
Copying ./sys/sys_config.ibd to /var/lib/mysql/sys/sys_config.ibd

--Output truncated for better visibility

2023-10-20T07:42:24.527528-05:00 1 [Note] [MY-011825] [Xtrabackup]
Done: Copying ./performance_schema/persisted_variab_187.sdi to /
var/lib/mysql/performance_schema/persisted_variab_187.sdi
2023-10-20T07:42:24.529833-05:00 1 [Note] [MY-011825] [Xtrabackup]
Copying ./performance_schema/user_defined_fun_188.sdi to
2023-10-20T07:42:24.539101-05:00 1 [Note] [MY-011825] [Xtrabackup]
Copying ./ib_buffer_pool to /var/lib/mysql/ib_buffer_pool
2023-10-20T07:42:24.539646-05:00 1 [Note] [MY-011825] [Xtrabackup]
Done: Copying ./ib_buffer_pool to /var/lib/mysql/ib_buffer_pool
2023-10-20T07:42:24.541151-05:00 1 [Note] [MY-011825] [Xtrabackup]
Creating directory ./#innodb_redo
2023-10-20T07:42:24.541306-05:00 1 [Note] [MY-011825] [Xtrabackup]
Done: creating directory ./#innodb_redo
2023-10-20T07:42:24.541408-05:00 1 [Note] [MY-011825] [Xtrabackup]
Copying ./ibtmp1 to /var/lib/mysql/ibtmp1
2023-10-20T07:42:24.561168-05:00 1 [Note] [MY-011825] [Xtrabackup]
Done: Copying ./ibtmp1 to /var/lib/mysql/ibtmp1

```
2023-10-20T07:42:24.593293-05:00 1 [Note] [MY-011825] [Xtrabackup]
Copying ./xtrabackup_info to /var/lib/mysql/xtrabackup_info
2023-10-20T07:42:24.593449-05:00 1 [Note] [MY-011825] [Xtrabackup]
Done: Copying ./xtrabackup_info to /var/lib/mysql/xtrabackup_info
2023-10-20T07:42:24.636757-05:00 0 [Note] [MY-011825] [Xtrabackup]
completed OK!
```

12. Verify that the backup files are copied back to the new backup
    directory.

```
-bash-4.2$ pwd
/var/lib/mysql
-bash-4.2$ ls -ltr
total 132124
-rw-r----- 1 mysql mysql 16777216 Oct 20 07:42 undo_001
-rw-r----- 1 mysql mysql 67108864 Oct 20 07:42 undo_002
drwxr-x--- 2 mysql mysql        6 Oct 20 07:42 #innodb_redo
-rw-r----- 1 mysql mysql 12582912 Oct 20 07:42 ibdata1
-rw-r----- 1 mysql mysql      157 Oct 20 07:42 binlog.000013
-rw-r----- 1 mysql mysql       14 Oct 20 07:42 binlog.index
drwxr-x--- 2 mysql mysql       28 Oct 20 07:42 sys
drwxr-x--- 2 mysql mysql      162 Oct 20 07:42 employees
-rw-r----- 1 mysql mysql 26214400 Oct 20 07:42 mysql.ibd
drwxr-x--- 2 mysql mysql      143 Oct 20 07:42 mysql
drwxr-x--- 2 mysql mysql     8192 Oct 20 07:42 performance_schema
-rw-r----- 1 mysql mysql     3631 Oct 20 07:42 ib_buffer_pool
-rw-r----- 1 mysql mysql 12582912 Oct 20 07:42 ibtmp1
-rw-r----- 1 mysql mysql      544 Oct 20 07:42 xtrabackup_info
```

13. Start the MySQL daemon and verify tables **dept** and **hr** are
    restored successfully.

```
[root@mysql-a lib]# systemctl start mysqld
[root@mysql-a lib]# systemctl status mysqld
[root@mysql-a lib]# su - mysql
Last login: Fri Oct 20 07:40:36 CDT 2023 on pts/0
```

```
-bash-4.2$ mysql -uroot -p
Enter password:

mysql> show databases;
+--------------------+
| Database           |
+--------------------+
| employees          |
| information_schema |
| mysql              |
| performance_schema |
| sys                |
+--------------------+
5 rows in set (0.00 sec)

mysql> use employees;
Reading table information for completion of table and column names
You can turn off this feature to get a quicker startup with -A

Database changed
mysql>
mysql> show tables;
+----------------------+
| Tables_in_employees  |
+----------------------+
| current_dept_emp     |
| departments          |
| dept                 |
| dept_emp             |
| dept_emp_latest_date |
| dept_manager         |
| employees            |
| hr                   |
| salaries             |
| titles               |
+----------------------+
10 rows in set (0.00 sec)
```

14. Perform a backup with compression. Xtrabackup needs **qpress** utility to perform compression. Upon installing the utility, perform a compress using the parameter --**compress**.

```
[root@mysql-p yum.repos.d]# rpm -qa |grep qpress
[root@mysql-p yum.repos.d]# yum install qpress
Loaded plugins: fastestmirror
Loading mirror speeds from cached hostfile
 * base: tx-mirror.tier.net
 * epel: reflector.westga.edu
 * extras: nc-centos-mirror.iwebfusion.net
 * updates: mirror.atl.genesisadaptive.com
Resolving Dependencies
--> Running transaction check
---> Package qpress.x86_64 0:11-3.el7 will be installed
--> Finished Dependency Resolution

Dependencies Resolved

=======================================================================
 Package        Arch      Version    Repository              Size
=======================================================================
Installing:
 qpress         x86_64    11-3.el7   tools-release-x86_64    32 k

Transaction Summary
=======================================================================
Total download size: 32 k
Installed size: 32 k
Is this ok [y/d/N]: y
Downloading packages:
qpress-11-3.el7.x86_64.rpm                            |  32 kB  00:00:00
Running transaction check
Running transaction test
Transaction test succeeded
Running transaction
  Installing : qpress-11-3.el7.x86_64                             1/1
  Verifying  : qpress-11-3.el7.x86_64                             1/1
```

Installed:

  qpress.x86_64 0:11-3.el7

Complete!
[root@mysql-p yum.repos.d]#

[root@mysql-p ~]# **percona-release enable tools**
* Enabling the Percona Tools repository
<*> **All done!**
[root@mysql-p ~]#
[root@mysql-p ~]# **su - mysql**
Last login: Wed Oct 4 10:25:12 CDT 2023 on pts/0
[mysql@mysql-p ~]$
[mysql@mysql-p mysql_backup]$ **ls -ltr**
total 4555832
-rw-r----- 1 mysql mysql   12582912 Oct 5 23:29 ibdata1
-rw-r----- 1 mysql mysql   12582912 Oct 5 23:29 ibdata2
drwxr-x--- 2 mysql mysql   28 Oct 5 23:29 sys
-rw-r----- 1 mysql mysql 3003121664 Oct 5 23:29 db1_tbs.ibd
drwxr-x--- 2 mysql mysql   4096 Oct 5 23:29 db1
-rw-r----- 1 mysql mysql   26214400 Oct 5 23:29 mysql.ibd
drwxr-x--- 2 mysql mysql   4096 Oct 5 23:29 db2
-rw-r----- 1 mysql mysql 671088640 Oct 5 23:30 undo_003.ibu
-rw-r----- 1 mysql mysql 687865856 Oct 5 23:30 undo_002
-rw-r----- 1 mysql mysql 251658240 Oct 5 23:30 undo_001
drwxr-x--- 2 mysql mysql   143 Oct 5 23:30 mysql
drwxr-x--- 2 mysql mysql   8192 Oct 5 23:30 performance_schema
drwxr-x--- 2 mysql mysql   20 Oct 5 23:30 db3
drwxr-x--- 2 mysql mysql   20 Oct 5 23:30 innodb1
drwxr-x--- 2 mysql mysql   20 Oct 5 23:30 db4
drwxr-x--- 2 mysql mysql   20 Oct 5 23:30 db5
-rw-r----- 1 mysql mysql   157 Oct 5 23:30 binlog.000077
-rw-r----- 1 mysql mysql   29 Oct 5 23:30 binlog.index
-rw-r----- 1 mysql mysql   18 Oct 5 23:30 xtrabackup_
                                                 binlog_info
-rw-r----- 1 mysql mysql   2560 Oct 5 23:30 xtrabackup_logfile

```
-rw-r----- 1 mysql mysql        143 Oct  5 23:30 xtrabackup_
                                                 checkpoints
-rw-r----- 1 mysql mysql       4031 Oct  5 23:30 ib_buffer_pool
-rw-r----- 1 mysql mysql        479 Oct  5 23:30 backup-my.cnf
-rw-r----- 1 mysql mysql        480 Oct  5 23:30 xtrabackup_info
-rw-r----- 1 mysql mysql        138 Oct  5 23:30 xtrabackup_
                                                 tablespaces
[mysql@mysql-p mysql_backup]$
```

```
-bash-4.2$ xtrabackup -uroot -pWElcome_1234# --backup --
compress --target-dir=/var/lib/backup
2023-10-20T09:19:58.426396-05:00 0 [Note] [MY-011825] [Xtrabackup]
recognized server arguments: --datadir=/var/lib/mysql
2023-10-20T09:19:58.426648-05:00 0 [Note] [MY-011825] [Xtrabackup]
recognized client arguments: --user=root --password=* --backup=
1 --compress --target-dir=/var/lib/backup
xtrabackup version 8.0.34-29 based on MySQL server 8.0.34 Linux
(x86_64) (revision id: 5ba706ee)

   --output truncated for better visibility

2023-10-20T09:20:01.407952-05:00 0 [Note] [MY-011825] [Xtrabackup]
Executing UNLOCK INSTANCE
2023-10-20T09:20:01.408165-05:00 0 [Note] [MY-011825] [Xtrabackup]
All tables unlocked
2023-10-20T09:20:01.408260-05:00 0 [Note] [MY-011825] [Xtrabackup]
Compressing ib_buffer_pool to /var/lib/backup/ib_buffer_pool.zst
2023-10-20T09:20:01.408320-05:00 0 [Note] [MY-011825] [Xtrabackup]
Done: Compressing ib_buffer_pool to /var/lib/backup/ib_buffer_
pool.zst
2023-10-20T09:20:01.409255-05:00 0 [Note] [MY-011825] [Xtrabackup]
Backup created in directory '/var/lib/backup/'
2023-10-20T09:20:01.409272-05:00 0 [Note] [MY-011825] [Xtrabackup]
MySQL binlog position: filename 'binlog.000016', position '157'
2023-10-20T09:20:01.409364-05:00 0 [Note] [MY-011825] [Xtrabackup]
Compressing /var/lib/backup/backup-my.cnf.zst
```

481

```
2023-10-20T09:20:01.409388-05:00 0 [Note] [MY-011825] [Xtrabackup]
Done: Compressing file /var/lib/backup/backup-my.cnf.zst
2023-10-20T09:20:01.410645-05:00 0 [Note] [MY-011825] [Xtrabackup]
Compressing /var/lib/backup/xtrabackup_info.zst
2023-10-20T09:20:01.410695-05:00 0 [Note] [MY-011825] [Xtrabackup]
Done: Compressing file /var/lib/backup/xtrabackup_info.zst
2023-10-20T09:20:02.412868-05:00 0 [Note] [MY-011825] [Xtrabackup]
Transaction log of lsn (2494560019) to (2494560019) was copied.
2023-10-20T09:20:02.636287-05:00 0 [Note] [MY-011825] [Xtrabackup]
completed OK!
```

15. Similar to the full database restore process, the following series
of commands will help with restore of the compressed backup.
We prepare the backup using - - prepare parameter, decompress
using - - decompress parameter and - - copy-back parameter to
restore the backup.

```
$ xtrabackup --prepare=TRUE --target-dir=/var/lib/backup/
$ xtrabackup --decompress --target-dir=/var/lib/backup/
$ xtrabackup --copy-back --target-dir=/var/lib/backup/
```

Summary

mysqldump, mydumper, and Percona Xtrabackup provide the logical backup options
for open source MySQL platforms. It is important to review updated documentation or
release notes for any changes to ensure consistent backups are taken for a successful
restore in case of a data loss scenario. In the next chapter, we will discuss the MySQL
Enterprise Backup (MEB) features and functionalities on how to utilize the Enterprise
Backup and its capabilities.

CHAPTER 9

MySQL Enterprise Backup and Recovery

Introduction

MySQL Enterprise Backup (MEB) is a multiplatform, high-performance backup utility for MySQL databases. MEB can perform a variety of backup and restore operations including hot, incremental, differential, selective backup and restore, encrypted, and compressed and even supports backing up to a cloud storage.

MEB supports all types of storage engines supported by MySQL while it is optimized for use with InnoDB tables. It provides great performance with its read-write process and block-level parallelism. MEB uses the **mysqlbackup** client and is included in the MySQL Enterprise Edition only.

It is important to efficiently design your backup strategy. Here are some few considerations:

- How quickly can I complete my backup?

- What is the impact on my database server CPU performance?

- How big is my backup size?

- Is my backup easily portable between different systems in case a need arises?

- What is the impact to the application when backups are being performed?

- Do I need to perform a full backup or incremental or differential backup?

- Will my backup strategy help me recover at this point in time?

- How quickly can I recover based on the backup format?

Based on the level of disruption the backup can cause to the application, the backups are classified as follows:

- **Hot**: A backup that can be performed while the database is running

- **Warm**: A backup that can be performed with the database in read-only mode

- **Cold**: A backup performed when the database is stopped

Please note MySQL Enterprise Backup 8.0 does not support cold backups anymore. Here is a quick summary of the level of disruption that each backup could cause.

Table 9-1. *Summary of the backup types and levels of disruption*

Backup type	Level of disruption
Hot	Low
Warm	Medium
Cold	High

Depending on the type of backup you would like to perform, here are the types of backups:

- **Full**: A complete database backup

- **Differential**: A backup that includes all changes to the data since the last full backup

- **Incremental**: A backup that includes all the changes since the last backup

Here are the files generated by the **mysqlbackup** client.

- **meta/backup_create.xml**: List of command-line arguments and environments in which the backup was created

- **meta/backup_content.xml**: Metadata for the files and database definitions of the backup data

- **backup-my.cnf**: Contains the important configuration parameters that apply to the backup

- **server-my.cnf**: Contains the values of the backed-up server's global variables that are set to nondefault values

- **server-all.cnf**: Contains values of all the global variables of the backed-up server

Before proceeding with performing the backups, let us understand what happens when we perform a backup using the **mysqlbackup** client.

1. During the backup, the following files are being copied while the database server is running:

   a. InnoDB data files

   b. Redo log files

   c. Binary log files

   d. Relay log files

2. A backup lock is applied on the server instance that blocks the DDL operations. DML operations are performed as usual.

3. A FLUSH TABLES <table_name1> [,<table_name2>]... WITH READ LOCK is applied on all non-InnoDB tables.

4. A logging activity block is applied on the server for the backup client to collect logging related information like the current InnoDB Log Sequence Number (LSN), binary log position, GTID, replication source or replica status, etc.

5. Read lock on the non-InnoDB tables is released.

6. Based on the information from step 4, the useful portion of the binary log or relay log file currently in use is copied to ensure a consistent recovery.

7. Backup lock on the server is released.

8. Redo log files that are not yet copied are copied or created.

9. Backup operation is completed, and the backup client **mysqlbackup** returns success.

Installing MySQL Enterprise Backup

MySQL Enterprise Backup (MEB) must be installed on every database server we need to back up. Please use the following steps to install MEB:

1. Check MySQL daemon status.

   [root@mysql-a ~]# systemctl status mysqld

2. Download MEB software from My Oracle Support by visiting https://support.oracle.com/portal/, patch number **35611240**.

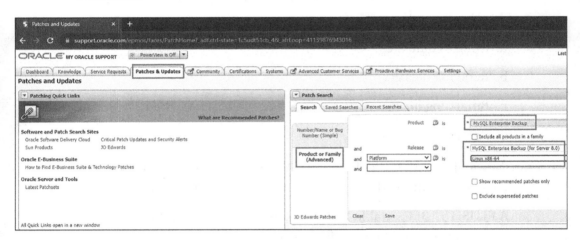

Figure 9-1. *Oracle Support Patch number*

3. Transfer the downloaded file to the MySQL server using WinSCP or any other file transfer utility. Verify if the file has transferred successfully.

```
[root@mysql-a mysql_binaries]# pwd
/root/mysql_binaries
[root@mysql-a mysql_binaries]# ls -ltr
total 1014904
-rw-r--r-- 1 root root 1031792640 Sep 11 18:14 mysql-8.0.34-1.el7.
x86_64.rpm-bundle.tar
-rw-r--r--  1 root root    7466095 Sep 26 21:53
p35611240_800_Linux-
x86-64.zip
```

4.   Unzip the downloaded file.

```
[root@mysql-a mysql_binaries]# ls -ltr
total 1014904
-rw-r--r-- 1 root root 1031792640 Sep 11 18:14 mysql-8.0.34-1.el7.
x86_64.rpm-bundle.tar
-rw-r--r-- 1 root root    7466095 Sep 26 21:53
p35611240_800_Linux-
x86-64.zip
[root@mysql-a mysql_binaries]#
[root@mysql-a mysql_binaries]# unzip p35611240_800_
Linux-x86-64.zip
Archive:   p35611240_800_Linux-x86-64.zip
 extracting: mysql-commercial-backup-8.0.34-1.1.el7.x86_64.rpm
 extracting: README.txt
[root@mysql-a mysql_binaries]# ls -ltr
total 1022200
-rw-r--r-- 1 root root    7463784 Jun 25 05:00 mysql-commercial-
backup-8.0.34-1.1.el7.x86_64.rpm
-rw-r--r-- 1 root root       2019 Jul 14 08:56 README.txt
-rw-r--r-- 1 root root 1031792640 Sep 11 18:14 mysql-8.0.34-1.el7.
x86_64.rpm-bundle.tar
-rw-r--r-- 1 root root    7466095 Sep 26 21:53
p35611240_800_Linux-
x86-64.zip
```

5.   Install and verify MySQL Enterprise Backup.

```
[root@mysql-a mysql_binaries]# ls -ltr
total 1022200
-rw-r--r-- 1 root root    7463784 Jun 25 05:00 mysql-commercial-
backup-8.0.34-1.1.el7.x86_64.rpm
-rw-r--r-- 1 root root       2019 Jul 14 08:56 README.txt
-rw-r--r-- 1 root root 1031792640 Sep 11 18:14 mysql-8.0.34-1.el7.
x86_64.rpm-bundle.tar
-rw-r--r-- 1 root root    7466095 Sep 26 21:53 p35611240_800_
                                  Linux-x86-64.zip
```

```
[root@mysql-a mysql_binaries]#
[root@mysql-a mysql_binaries]# rpm -qa|grep mysqlbackup
[root@mysql-a mysql_binaries]#
[root@mysql-a mysql_binaries]# rpm -ivh mysql-commercial-
backup-8.0.34-1.1.el7.x86_64.rpm
warning: mysql-commercial-backup-8.0.34-1.1.el7.x86_64.rpm: Header
V4 RSA/SHA256 Signature, key ID 3a79bd29: NOKEY
Preparing...                 ########################### [100%]
Updating / installing...
   1:mysql-commercial-backup-8.0.34-1.################### [100%]
[root@mysql-a mysql_binaries]# which mysqlbackup
/usr/bin/mysqlbackup
```

Configuring MySQL Enterprise Backup

Before performing a backup, please ensure we gather basic information like MySQL configuration file, port, path to MySQL data directory, ID and password of the privileged user, path to store backup, etc.

1. Gather MySQL configuration file (*/etc/my.cnf*) data.

   ```
   [root@mysql-a mysql_binaries]# cat /etc/my.cnf
   [mysqld]
   datadir=/var/lib/mysql
   socket=/var/lib/mysql/mysql.sock
   log-error=/var/log/mysqld.log
   pid-file=/var/run/mysqld/mysqld.pid
   ```

2. Check PID.

   ```
   [root@mysql-a mysql_binaries]# ps -ef|grep mysql
   mysql    1097     1  0 21:16 ?        00:00:25 /usr/sbin/mysqld
   root     1371  1307  0 22:16 pts/0    00:00:00
                                         grep --color=auto mysql
   ```

3. Gather port information.

```
[root@mysql-a mysql_binaries]# su - mysql
Last login: Wed Sep 13 22:23:01 CDT 2023 on pts/0
-bash-4.2$
-bash-4.2$ mysql -uroot -p
Enter password:
mysql> show global variables like 'PORT';
+---------------+-------+
| Variable_name | Value |
+---------------+-------+
| port          | 3306  |
+---------------+-------+
1 row in set (0.01 sec)
```

4. Create a user to perform backup and grant the required privileges.

```
-bash-4.2$ mysql -uroot -p
Enter password:
mysql> CREATE USER 'mysqlbkpadmin'@'localhost' IDENTIFIED BY
'WElcome_1234#';
Query OK, 0 rows affected (0.02 sec)

mysql> GRANT SELECT, BACKUP_ADMIN, RELOAD, PROCESS, SUPER,
REPLICATION CLIENT ON *.* TO 'mysqlbkpadmin'@'localhost';
Query OK, 0 rows affected, 1 warning (0.02 sec)

mysql> GRANT CREATE, INSERT, DROP, UPDATE ON mysql.backup_progress
TO 'mysqlbkpadmin'@'localhost';
Query OK, 0 rows affected (0.00 sec)

mysql> GRANT CREATE, INSERT, DROP, UPDATE, SELECT, ALTER ON mysql.
backup_history TO 'mysqlbkpadmin'@'localhost';
Query OK, 0 rows affected (0.01 sec)

mysql> GRANT LOCK TABLES, CREATE, DROP, FILE, INSERT, ALTER ON *.*
TO 'mysqlbkpadmin'@'localhost';
Query OK, 0 rows affected (0.01 sec)
```

```
mysql> GRANT CREATE, DROP, UPDATE ON mysql.backup_sbt_history TO
'mysqlbkpadmin'@'localhost';
Query OK, 0 rows affected (0.01 sec)

mysql> GRANT ENCRYPTION_KEY_ADMIN ON *.* TO
'mysqlbkpadmin'@'localhost';
Query OK, 0 rows affected (0.01 sec)

mysql> GRANT INNODB_REDO_LOG_ARCHIVE ON *.* TO
'mysqlbkpadmin'@'localhost';
Query OK, 0 rows affected (0.01 sec)

mysql> GRANT CREATE, INSERT, DROP ON mysql.backup_progress_old TO
'mysqlbkpadmin'@'localhost';
Query OK, 0 rows affected (0.01 sec)

mysql> GRANT CREATE, INSERT, DROP, ALTER ON mysql.backup_progress_
new TO 'mysqlbkpadmin'@'localhost';
Query OK, 0 rows affected (0.00 sec)

mysql> GRANT CREATE, INSERT, DROP ON mysql.backup_sbt_history_old
TO 'mysqlbkpadmin'@'localhost';
Query OK, 0 rows affected (0.01 sec)

mysql> GRANT CREATE, INSERT, DROP, ALTER ON mysql.backup_sbt_
history_new TO 'mysqlbkpadmin'@'localhost';
Query OK, 0 rows affected (0.01 sec)

mysql> show grants for 'mysqlbkpadmin'@'localhost';
+-------------------------------------------------------+
| Grants for mysqlbkpadmin@
localhost                                              |
+-------------------------------------------------------+
| GRANT SELECT, INSERT, CREATE, DROP, RELOAD, PROCESS, FILE,
ALTER, SUPER, LOCK TABLES, REPLICATION CLIENT ON *.* TO
`mysqlbkpadmin`@`localhost` |
| GRANT BACKUP_ADMIN,ENCRYPTION_KEY_ADMIN,INNODB_REDO_LOG_ARCHIVE
ON *.* TO `mysqlbkpadmin`@`localhost`                   |
```

```
| GRANT SELECT, INSERT, UPDATE, CREATE, DROP, ALTER
ON `mysql`.`backup_history` TO `mysqlbkpadmin`@`localhost`              |
| GRANT INSERT, CREATE, DROP, ALTER ON `mysql`.`backup_progress_
new` TO `mysqlbkpadmin`@`localhost`                                      |
| GRANT INSERT, CREATE, DROP ON `mysql`.`backup_progress_old` TO
`mysqlbkpadmin`@`localhost`                                             |
| GRANT INSERT, UPDATE, CREATE, DROP ON `mysql`.`backup_progress`
TO `mysqlbkpadmin`@`localhost`                                          |
| GRANT INSERT, CREATE, DROP, ALTER ON `mysql`.`backup_sbt_
history_new` TO `mysqlbkpadmin`@`localhost`                             |
| GRANT INSERT, CREATE, DROP ON `mysql`.`backup_sbt_history_old` TO
`mysqlbkpadmin`@`localhost`                                             |
| GRANT UPDATE, CREATE, DROP ON `mysql`.`backup_sbt_history` TO
`mysqlbkpadmin`@`localhost`                                             |
+-----------------------------------------------------------+
9 rows in set (0.00 sec)
```

Perform a Full Instance Backup

1. Perform a full instance backup using --backup-to-image with the
   format *.mbi.

   ```
   -bash-4.2$ /bin/mysqlbackup --user=mysqlbkpadmin --password --host
   =127.0.0.1 --backup-dir=/var/lib/mysql-files --backup-image=my_
   first_mysql_bkp.mbi --with-timestamp backup-to-image

   Starting with following command line ...
   /bin/mysqlbackup
   --user=mysqlbkpadmin
   --password
   --host=127.0.0.1
   --backup-dir=/var/lib/mysql-files
   --backup-image=my_first_mysql_bkp.mbi
   --with-timestamp
   backup-to-image

     --Output truncated for better visibility
   ```

```
230926 22:42:58 MAIN     INFO: Full Image Backup operation
completed successfully.
230926 22:42:58 MAIN     INFO: Backup image created successfully.
230926 22:42:58 MAIN     INFO: Image Path = /var/lib/mysql-
files/2023-09-26_22-42-57/my_first_mysql_bkp.mbi
230926 22:42:58 MAIN     INFO: MySQL binlog position: filename
binlog.000002, position 3442.
---------------------------------------------------------------
    Parameters Summary
---------------------------------------------------------------
    Start LSN              : 19724800
    Last Checkpoint LSN    : 19724997
    End LSN                : 19731869
---------------------------------------------------------------
mysqlbackup completed OK!
```

2. Verify backup and check backup files created in the backup
   directory.

```
-bash-4.2$ cd /var/lib/mysql-files/
-bash-4.2$ ls -ltr
total 0
drwxr-x--- 4 mysql mysql 127 Sep 26 22:42 2023-09-26_22-42-57
-bash-4.2$ cd 2023-09-26_22-42-57/
-bash-4.2$ ls -ltr
total 71664
-rw-rw-r-- 1 mysql mysql      255 Sep 26 22:42 backup-my.cnf
-rw-r----- 1 mysql mysql      634 Sep 26 22:42 server-my.cnf
-rw-r----- 1 mysql mysql    19930 Sep 26 22:42 server-all.cnf
drwxr-x--- 2 mysql mysql      159 Sep 26 22:42 meta
-rw-rw---- 1 mysql mysql 73351235 Sep 26 22:42 my_first_
mysql_bkp.mbi
drwxr-x--- 2 mysql mysql        6 Sep 26 22:42 datadir
```

3. Validate the backup taken.

```
[root@mysql-a ~]# su - mysql
Last login: Tue Sep 26 22:40:27 CDT 2023 on pts/0
-bash-4.2$ cd /var/lib/mysql-files/
-bash-4.2$ ls -ltr
total 0
drwxr-x--- 4 mysql mysql 127 Sep 26 22:42 2023-09-26_22-42-57
-bash-4.2$
-bash-4.2$ cd 2023-09-26_22-42-57/
-bash-4.2$ ls -ltr
total 71664
-rw-rw-r-- 1 mysql mysql      255 Sep 26 22:42 backup-my.cnf
-rw-r----- 1 mysql mysql      634 Sep 26 22:42 server-my.cnf
-rw-r----- 1 mysql mysql    19930 Sep 26 22:42 server-all.cnf
drwxr-x--- 2 mysql mysql      159 Sep 26 22:42 meta
-rw-rw---- 1 mysql mysql 73351235 Sep 26 22:42 my_first_
mysql_bkp.mbi
drwxr-x--- 2 mysql mysql        6 Sep 26 22:42 datadir
-bash-4.2$ pwd
/var/lib/mysql-files/2023-09-26_22-42-57
-bash-4.2$
-bash-4.2$ /bin/mysqlbackup --backup-image=my_first_mysql_bkp.mbi
validate

Starting with following command line ...
/bin/mysqlbackup
--backup-image=my_first_mysql_bkp.mbi
validate

230927 21:58:51 MAIN     INFO: Backup Image MEB version
                               string: 8.0.34
230927 21:58:51 MAIN     INFO: MySQL server version is '8.0.34'
230927 21:58:51 MAIN     INFO: The backup image has no keyring.
230927 21:58:51 MAIN     INFO: Creating 14 buffers each of size
                               16777216.
```

```
230927 21:58:51 MAIN        INFO: Validate operation starts with
                            following threads
                                    1 read-threads    6 process-threads
230927 21:58:51 MAIN        INFO: Validating image ... /var/lib/
                            mysql-files/2023-09-26_22-42-57/my_first_
                            mysql_bkp.mbi
230927 21:58:51 PCR4        INFO: Validate: [Dir]: meta
230927 21:58:51 PCR3        INFO: Validate: [Dir]: datadir/mysql
230927 21:58:51 PCR3        INFO: Validate: [Dir]: datadir/
                            performance_schema
230927 21:58:51 PCR3        INFO: Validate: [Dir]: datadir/sys
230927 21:58:51 MAIN        INFO: datadir/mysql.ibd validated.
230927 21:58:51 MAIN        INFO: datadir/mysql/backup_history.ibd
                            validated.
230927 21:58:51 MAIN        INFO: datadir/mysql/backup_progress.ibd
                            validated.
230927 21:58:51 MAIN        INFO: datadir/ibdata1 validated.
230927 21:58:51 MAIN        INFO: datadir/undo_002 validated.
230927 21:58:51 MAIN        INFO: datadir/undo_001 validated.
230927 21:58:51 MAIN        INFO: datadir/sys/sys_config.ibd
                            validated.
230927 21:58:51 MAIN        INFO: Validate operation completed
                            successfully.
230927 21:58:51 MAIN        INFO: Backup Image validation successful.
230927 21:58:51 MAIN        INFO: Source Image Path = /var/lib/mysql-
                            files/2023-09-26_22-42-57/my_first_
                            mysql_bkp.mbi
mysqlbackup completed OK!
```

Perform an Incremental Backup

1. Perform an incremental backup using the backup
    parameters --*incremental* and --*incremental-base*. Please note
    that the directory to save temporary backup files needs to be
    always empty before running a new backup.

```
-bash-4.2$ rm -rf /mysqlbkuptmp/*
-bash-4.2$ ls -ltr /mysqlbkuptmp/
total 0
-bash-4.2$ /bin/mysqlbackup --user=mysqlbkpadmin --password --host
=127.0.0.1 --incremental --incremental-base=history:last_
backup --backup-dir=/mysqlbkuptmp --backup-image=/mysql_backup/
test_incremental_backup.mbi backup-to-image
```

Starting with following command line ...
/bin/mysqlbackup
--user=mysqlbkpadmin
--password
--host=127.0.0.1
--incremental
--incremental-base=history:last_backup
--backup-dir=/mysqlbkuptmp
--backup-image=/mysql_backup/test_incremental_backup.mbi
backup-to-image

Enter password:
230927 22:46:14 MAIN   INFO: Establishing connection to server.
WARNING: MYSQL_OPT_RECONNECT is deprecated and will be removed in
a future version.
230927 22:46:14 MAIN   INFO: No SSL options specified.
230927 22:46:14 MAIN   INFO: MySQL server version is '8.0.34'
230927 22:46:14 MAIN   INFO: MySQL server compile os version
                          is 'Linux'
230927 22:46:14 MAIN   INFO: SSL/TLS version used for connection
                          is TLSv1.2
230927 22:46:14 MAIN   INFO: Got some server configuration
                          information from running server.
230927 22:46:14 MAIN   INFO: Establishing connection to server
                          for locking.
WARNING: MYSQL_OPT_RECONNECT is deprecated and will be removed in
a future version.
230927 22:46:14 MAIN   INFO: No SSL options specified.
```
```

```
230927 22:46:14 MAIN        INFO: Backup directory exists:
                            '/mysqlbkuptmp'
230927 22:46:14 MAIN        INFO: MySQL server version_comment is
                            'MySQL Community Server - GPL'
230927 22:46:14 MAIN        INFO: Mysqlbackup component not installed.
WARNING: MYSQL_OPT_RECONNECT is deprecated and will be removed in
a future version.
230927 22:46:14 MAIN        INFO: Location of last successful backup:
                            /mysqlbkuptmp/2023-09-27_22-34-56.
230927 22:46:14 MAIN        INFO: End time of last successful backup:
                            2023-09-27 22:34:56.
230927 22:46:14 MAIN        INFO: Last backup type: FULL.
230927 22:46:14 MAIN        INFO: Using start_lsn=19818740,
                            calculated from backup_history table of
                            MySQL server.
230927 22:46:14 MAIN        INFO: Using "full-scan" algorithm for
                            this incremental backup.
```

--Output truncated for better visibility

```
230927 22:46:14 MAIN        INFO: Incremental Image Backup operation
                            completed successfully.
230927 22:46:14 MAIN        INFO: Backup image created successfully.
230927 22:46:14 MAIN        INFO: Image Path = /mysql_backup/test_
                            incremental_backup.mbi
230927 22:46:14 MAIN        INFO: Backup contains changes from lsn
                            19818741 to lsn 19831397.
230927 22:46:14 MAIN        INFO: MySQL binlog position: filename
                            binlog.000003, position 157.
-----------------------------------------------------------------
    Parameters Summary
-----------------------------------------------------------------
    Start LSN              : 19818741
    Last Checkpoint LSN    : 19825643
    End LSN                : 19831397
-----------------------------------------------------------------
mysqlbackup completed OK!
```

Perform an Encrypted Backup

MySQL Enterprise Backup provides encryption for single-file backups to enhance security for the backed-up data. We use the ***--encrypt*** parameter and ***--key*** or ***--key-file*** options to perform encrypted backups. The encryption uses AES 256 block cipher in CBC mode, which generates a key string of 64 hexadecimal digits. The decryption is performed using the same key and the parameter ***--decrypt*** along with ***--key*** or ***--key-file*** options. The cipher can either be passed during the backup and restore operations directly as a key or as part of a key file. To generate a random key, we can use open source tools like **OpenSSL**. Please note the backup image will be with the ***.enc** format.

```
-bash-4.2$ openssl rand -hex 32
56392a9158cc09b64a59fdaf07af0b0806437bc79a841af9e1b786040e4a52cf
-bash-4.2$
-bash-4.2$ /bin/mysqlbackup --user=mysqlbkpadmin --password --host
=127.0.0.1 --backup-dir=/var/lib/mysql-files --backup-image=my_first_mysql_
bkp.enc --encrypt --key=56392a9158cc09b64a59fdaf07af0b0806437bc79a841af9e1
b786040e4a52cf --with-timestamp backup-to-image

Starting with following command line ...
/bin/mysqlbackup
--user=mysqlbkpadmin
--password
--host=127.0.0.1
--backup-dir=/var/lib/mysql-files
--backup-image=my_first_mysql_bkp.enc
--encrypt
--key=xxxxxxxxxxxxxxxxxxxxxxxxxxxxxxxxxxxxxxxxxxxxxxxxxxxxxxxxxxxxxxxxxx
--with-timestamp
backup-to-image

Enter password:
231107 22:10:00 MAIN     INFO: Establishing connection to server.
WARNING: MYSQL_OPT_RECONNECT is deprecated and will be removed in a future
version.
231107 22:10:00 MAIN     INFO: No SSL options specified.
231107 22:10:00 MAIN     INFO: MySQL server version is '8.0.34'
```

```
231107 22:10:00 MAIN      INFO: MySQL server compile os version is 'Linux'
231107 22:10:00 MAIN      INFO: SSL/TLS version used for connection
                          is TLSv1.2
231107 22:10:00 MAIN      INFO: Got some server configuration information
                          from running server.
```

--Output truncated for better visibility

```
231107 22:10:04 MAIN      INFO: Backup image created successfully.
231107 22:10:04 MAIN      INFO: Image Path = /var/lib/mysql-
                          files/2023-11-07_22-10-00/my_first_mysql_bkp.enc
231107 22:10:04 MAIN      INFO: MySQL binlog position: filename
                          binlog.000004, position 197.
231107 22:10:04 MAIN      INFO: GTID_EXECUTED is 7c17623b-397c-11ee-9a30-08
                          0027cf69cc:1-6,a52a1fb1-3272-11ee-9a0c-080027c
                          f69cc:1-3.

-----------------------------------------------------------------
   Parameters Summary
-----------------------------------------------------------------
   Start LSN               : 24981504
   Last Checkpoint LSN     : 24981830
   End LSN                 : 24984451
-----------------------------------------------------------------
```

mysqlbackup completed OK!
```
-bash-4.2$
-bash-4.2$ cd /var/lib/mysql-files/2023-11-07_22-10-00
-bash-4.2$ ls -ltr
total 73688
-rw-r--r-- 1 mysql mysql      255 Nov  7 22:10 backup-my.cnf
-rw-r----- 1 mysql mysql      748 Nov  7 22:10 server-my.cnf
-rw-r----- 1 mysql mysql    20447 Nov  7 22:10 server-all.cnf
drwxr-x--- 2 mysql mysql      191 Nov  7 22:10 meta
-rw-r----- 1 mysql mysql 75425683 Nov  7 22:10 my_first_mysql_bkp.enc
drwxr-x--- 2 mysql mysql        6 Nov  7 22:10 datadir
```

Perform a Backup of a Replica Server

1. Perform a backup of a replica server using the *--replica-info* parameter as part of the mysqlbackup command.

2. The option *--replica-info* creates a file named *meta/ ibbackup_replica_info* inside the backup directory that has all the information related to source and includes the *CHANGE REPLICATION SOURCE TO* statement with the binlog position saved in the *ibbackup_replica_info* file.

3. Before we issue the backup command to back up the replica server, ensure *replica_open_temp_tables* is 0 to ensure the replication state is consistent.

    ```
    -bash-4.2$ mysql -u root -p
    Enter password:

    mysql> show variables like '%replica_open_temp_tables%';
    Empty set (0.07 sec)

    mysql> exit
    Bye
    -bash-4.2$ /bin/mysqlbackup --user=mysqlbkpadmin --password --host
    =127.0.0.1 --backup-dir=/var/lib/mysql-files --backup-
    image=my_first_mysql_bkp.mbi --with-timestamp backup-to-
    image --replica-info

    Starting with following command line ...
    /bin/mysqlbackup
    --user=mysqlbkpadmin
    --password
    --host=127.0.0.1
    --backup-dir=/var/lib/mysql-files
    --backup-image=my_first_mysql_bkp.mbi
    --with-timestamp
    backup-to-image
    --replica-info
    ```

```
Enter password:
231107 21:33:10 MAIN      INFO: Establishing connection to server.
WARNING: MYSQL_OPT_RECONNECT is deprecated and will be removed in
a future version.
231107 21:33:10 MAIN      INFO: No SSL options specified.
231107 21:33:10 MAIN      INFO: MySQL server version is '8.0.34'
231107 21:33:10 MAIN      INFO: MySQL server compile os version
                          is 'Linux'
231107 21:33:10 MAIN      INFO: SSL/TLS version used for connection
                          is TLSv1.2
231107 21:33:10 MAIN      INFO: Got some server configuration
                          information from running server.

231107 21:33:10 MAIN      INFO: Establishing connection to server
                          for locking.
WARNING: MYSQL_OPT_RECONNECT is deprecated and will be removed in
a future version.
231107 21:33:10 MAIN      INFO: No SSL options specified.
231107 21:33:10 MAIN      INFO: Backup directory created: '/var/
                          lib/mysql-files/2023-11-07_21-33-10'
231107 21:33:10 MAIN      INFO: MySQL server version_comment is
                          'MySQL Community Server - GPL'
231107 21:33:10 MAIN      INFO: Mysqlbackup component version
                          : 8.0.34
231107 21:33:10 MAIN      INFO: [page-track] Unable to get page
                          track startlsn:0.
231107 21:33:10 MAIN      INFO: [page-track] Pagetrack service
                          could not be initialized
231107 21:33:10 MAIN      INFO: MEB logfile created at /var/lib/
                          mysql-files/2023-11-07_21-33-10/meta/
                          MEB_2023-11-07.21-33-10_backup-to-
                          image.log
```

--Output truncated for better visibility

```
231107 21:33:11 RDR1      INFO: Writing '/var/lib/mysql-files/
                          2023-11-07_21-33-10/meta/ibbackup_
                          replica_info'.
231107 21:33:11 RDR1      INFO: Copying meta file /var/lib/mysql-
                          files/2023-11-07_21-33-10/meta/backup_
                          variables.txt.
231107 21:33:11 RDR1      INFO: Copying meta file /var/lib/mysql-
                          files/2023-11-07_21-33-10/datadir/
                          ibbackup_logfile.
231107 21:33:11 RDR1      INFO: Copying meta file /var/lib/mysql-
                          files/2023-11-07_21-33-10/server-all.cnf.
231107 21:33:11 RDR1      INFO: Copying meta file /var/lib/mysql-
                          files/2023-11-07_21-33-10/server-my.cnf.
231107 21:33:11 RDR1      INFO: Copying meta file /var/lib/mysql-
                          files/2023-11-07_21-33-10/meta/ibbackup_
                          replica_info.
231107 21:33:11 RDR1      INFO: Copying meta file /var/lib/mysql-
                          files/2023-11-07_21-33-10/meta/backup_
                          gtid_executed.sql.
231107 21:33:11 RDR1      INFO: Copying meta file /var/lib/mysql-
                          files/2023-11-07_21-33-10/meta/backup_
                          content.xml.
231107 21:33:11 RDR1      INFO: Copying meta file /var/lib/mysql-
                          files/2023-11-07_21-33-10/meta/image_
                          files.xml.
231107 21:33:11 MAIN      INFO: Reset the backup id.
231107 21:33:11 MAIN      INFO: Full Image Backup operation
                          completed successfully.
231107 21:33:11 MAIN      INFO: Backup image created successfully.
231107 21:33:11 MAIN      INFO: Image Path = /var/lib/mysql-
                          files/2023-11-07_21-33-10/my_first_
                          mysql_bkp.mbi
231107 21:33:11 MAIN      INFO: MySQL binlog position: filename
                          binlog.000004, position 197.
```

```
231107 21:33:11 MAIN        INFO: MySQL replica binlog position:
                            source host mysql-e, source port
                            3306, source user replication_user,
                            filename binlog.000019, position
                            2197,  channel name .
231107 21:33:11 MAIN        INFO: GTID_EXECUTED is 7c17623b-397c-
                            11ee-9a30-080027cf69cc:1-6,a52a1fb1-3272-
                            11ee-9a0c-080027cf69cc:1-3.

-------------------------------------------------------------
    Parameters Summary
-------------------------------------------------------------
    Start LSN                : 24972288
    Last Checkpoint LSN      : 24972391
    End LSN                  : 24974799
-------------------------------------------------------------
```

mysqlbackup completed OK!
-bash-4.2$

-bash-4.2$ **cd /var/lib/mysql-files/2023-11-07_21-33-10/meta**
-bash-4.2$ ls -ltr
total 80
-rw-r----- 1 mysql mysql 4850 Nov 7 21:33 backup_create.xml
-rw-r----- 1 mysql mysql   171 Nov 7 21:33 **ibbackup_replica_info**
-rw-r--r-- 1 mysql mysql   315 Nov 7 21:33 backup_gtid_
executed.sql
-rw-r--r-- 1 mysql mysql   967 Nov 7 21:33 backup_variables.txt
-rw-r----- 1 mysql mysql 8351 Nov 7 21:33 image_files.xml
-rw-r----- 1 mysql mysql 31769 Nov 7 21:33 backup_content.xml
-rw-r--r-- 1 mysql mysql 13884 Nov 7 21:33
MEB_2023-11-07.21-33-10_backup-
to-image.log
-bash-4.2$ **cat ibbackup_replica_info**
CHANGE REPLICATION SOURCE TO SOURCE_LOG_FILE='binlog.000019',
SOURCE_LOG_POS=2197, SOURCE_HOST='mysql-e', SOURCE_PORT=3306,
SOURCE_USER='replication_user' FOR CHANNEL '';

Perform a Restore of Complete MySQL Server from Backup

1. Before restoring the backup, ensure the following prerequisites are met:

   a. Ensure MySQL server is shut down.

   b. Ensure there are no files in the data directory and other innodb directories (innodb_data_home_dir, innodb_log_group_home_dir, innodb_undo_directory).

   ```
   [root@mysql-a ~]# systemctl status mysqld
   [root@mysql-a ~]# systemctl stop mysqld
   [root@mysql-a ~]# systemctl status mysqld
   ```

2. Create the directories required. */mysqldata* as the new data directory. */mysqlbkuptmp* as the directory to store temporary files generated during restore. It is important to create these directories outside of the current file location.

   ```
   [root@mysql-a ~]# pwd
   /root
   [root@mysql-a ~]# cd ..
   [root@mysql-a /]# mkdir -p mysqldata
   [root@mysql-a /]# chown -R mysql:mysql mysqldata
   [root@mysql-a /]# ls -ltr
   total 16
   drwxr-xr-x.   2 root   root      6 Apr 10  2018 srv
   drwxr-xr-x.   2 root   root      6 Apr 10  2018 opt
   drwxr-xr-x.   2 root   root      6 Apr 10  2018 mnt
   drwxr-xr-x.   2 root   root      6 Apr 10  2018 media
   lrwxrwxrwx.   1 root   root      7 Sep 26  2022 bin -> usr/bin
   lrwxrwxrwx.   1 root   root      8 Sep 26  2022 sbin -> usr/sbin
   lrwxrwxrwx.   1 root   root      9 Sep 26  2022 lib64 -> usr/lib64
   lrwxrwxrwx.   1 root   root      7 Sep 26  2022 lib -> usr/lib
   drwxr-xr-x.  19 root   root    267 Sep 26  2022 var
   dr-xr-xr-x.   5 root   root   4096 Sep 26  2022 boot
   ```

503

```
drwxr-xr-x.  13 root   root    155 Jul 28 21:10 usr
drwxr-xr-x.   4 root   root     32 Sep 13 22:17 home
dr-xr-x---.   7 root   root    246 Sep 27 22:16 root
drwxr-xr-x    6 mysql mysql    151 Sep 28 17:26 mysqlbkuptmp
drwxr-xr-x    5 mysql mysql    232 Sep 28 17:29 mysql_backup
drwxr-xr-x   20 root   root   3100 Sep 28 21:15 dev
drwxr-xr-x.  82 root   root   8192 Sep 28 21:15 etc
drwxr-xr-x   25 root   root    700 Sep 28 21:15 run
dr-xr-xr-x  113 root   root      0 Sep 28 21:15 proc
drwxrwxrwt.   7 root   root     93 Sep 28 21:15 tmp
drwxr-xr-x    2 mysql mysql      6 Sep 28 21:20 mysqldata
dr-xr-xr-x   13 root   root      0 Sep 28 21:20 sys
```

3. Remove all files from the current data directory **/var/lib/mysql** to simulate a data loss scenario.

```
[root@mysql-a /]# cd /var/lib/mysql
[root@mysql-a mysql]# ls -ltr
total 79312
-rw-r----- 1 mysql mysql        56 Sep 13 22:21 auto.cnf
-rw-r----- 1 mysql mysql   8585216 Sep 13 22:21 #ib_16384_1.dblwr
drwxr-x--- 2 mysql mysql      8192 Sep 13 22:21 performance_schema
-rw------- 1 mysql mysql      1676 Sep 13 22:21 ca-key.pem
-rw-r--r-- 1 mysql mysql      1112 Sep 13 22:21 ca.pem
-rw------- 1 mysql mysql      1680 Sep 13 22:21 server-key.pem
-rw-r--r-- 1 mysql mysql      1112 Sep 13 22:21 server-cert.pem
-rw------- 1 mysql mysql      1676 Sep 13 22:21 client-key.pem
-rw-r--r-- 1 mysql mysql      1112 Sep 13 22:21 client-cert.pem
-rw------- 1 mysql mysql      1676 Sep 13 22:21 private_key.pem
-rw-r--r-- 1 mysql mysql       452 Sep 13 22:21 public_key.pem
drwxr-x--- 2 mysql mysql        28 Sep 13 22:21 sys
-rw-r----- 1 mysql mysql       826 Sep 26 21:16 binlog.000001
drwxr-x--- 2 mysql mysql       196 Sep 26 22:39 mysql
-rw-r----- 1 mysql mysql      3442 Sep 27 21:45 binlog.000002
-rw-r----- 1 mysql mysql       157 Sep 28 16:43 binlog.000003
drwxr-x--- 2 mysql mysql        54 Sep 28 16:52 db1
```

```
drwxr-x--- 2 mysql mysql       54 Sep 28 16:52 db2
drwxr-x--- 2 mysql mysql       54 Sep 28 16:52 db3
drwxr-x--- 2 mysql mysql       54 Sep 28 16:53 db4
drwxr-x--- 2 mysql mysql     4096 Sep 28 21:15 #innodb_redo
-rw-r----- 1 mysql mysql     3519 Sep 28 21:15 binlog.000004
-rw-r----- 1 mysql mysql       80 Sep 28 21:15 binlog.index
-rw-r----- 1 mysql mysql 26214400 Sep 28 21:15 mysql.ibd
-rw-r----- 1 mysql mysql      180 Sep 28 21:15 binlog.000005
-rw-r----- 1 mysql mysql     3836 Sep 28 21:15 ib_buffer_pool
-rw-r----- 1 mysql mysql 16777216 Sep 28 21:15 undo_001
-rw-r----- 1 mysql mysql   196608 Sep 28 21:15 #ib_16384_0.dblwr
-rw-r----- 1 mysql mysql 16777216 Sep 28 21:15 undo_002
-rw-r----- 1 mysql mysql 12582912 Sep 28 21:15 ibdata1
drwxr-x--- 2 mysql mysql        6 Sep 28 21:15 #innodb_temp
[root@mysql-a mysql]#
[root@mysql-a mysql]# rm -rf *
[root@mysql-a mysql]# ls -ltr
total 0
[root@mysql-a mysql]#
```

4. Choose which backup to restore from and perform a restore of the MySQL server. In the following example, we are restoring from a **2023-09-28_17-29-14** backup.

```
[root@mysql-a mysql]# cd /mysql_backup/
[root@mysql-a mysql_backup]# ls -ltr
total 149068
-rw-rw---- 1 mysql mysql 73347718 Sep 27 22:20 test_single_file_
backup.mbi
-rw-rw---- 1 mysql mysql 4286000 Sep 27 22:34 test_compressed_
mysql_bkp.img
-rw-rw---- 1 mysql mysql 2121901 Sep 27 22:46 test_incremental_
backup.mbi
-rw-rw---- 1 mysql mysql 72879768 Sep 28 16:54 test_include_
tables_backup.mbi
drwxr-x--- 4 mysql mysql      127 Sep 28 17:29 2023-09-28_17-29-00
```

```
drwxr-x--- 4 mysql mysql       127 Sep 28 17:29 2023-09-28_17-29-07
drwxr-x--- 4 mysql mysql       127 Sep 28 17:29 2023-09-28_17-29-14
[root@mysql-a mysql_backup]#
[root@mysql-a mysql_backup]# cd 2023-09-28_17-29-14/
[root@mysql-a 2023-09-28_17-29-14]# ls -ltr
total 74072
-rw-rw-r-- 1 mysql mysql       255 Sep 28 17:29 backup-my.cnf
-rw-r----- 1 mysql mysql       634 Sep 28 17:29 server-my.cnf
-rw-r----- 1 mysql mysql     19930 Sep 28 17:29 server-all.cnf
drwxr-x--- 2 mysql mysql       159 Sep 28 17:29 meta
-rw-rw---- 1 mysql mysql  75818683 Sep 28 17:29 my_first_
mysql_bkp.mbi
drwxr-x--- 2 mysql mysql         6 Sep 28 17:29 datadir
[root@mysql-a 2023-09-28_17-29-14]#
[root@mysql-a 2023-09-28_17-29-14]# pwd
/mysql_backup/2023-09-28_17-29-14
[root@mysql-a 2023-09-28_17-29-14]# su - mysql
Last login: Thu Sep 28 17:08:02 CDT 2023 on pts/0
-bash-4.2$ /bin/mysqlbackup --datadir=/mysqldata --backup-image=/
mysql_backup/2023-09-28_17-29-14/my_first_mysql_bkp.mbi --backup-
dir=/mysqlbkuptmp copy-back-and-apply-log
```

Starting with following command line ...
/bin/mysqlbackup
--datadir=/mysqldata
--backup-image=/mysql_backup/2023-09-28_17-29-14/my_first_
mysql_bkp.mbi
--backup-dir=/mysqlbkuptmp
copy-back-and-apply-log

   --Output truncated for better visibility

230928 21:30:23 PCR1   INFO: Starting to apply a batch of log
records to the database....
InnoDB: Progress in percent: 8 16 25 33
230928 21:30:23 PCR1   INFO: Create redo log files. target
start_lsn 0 last_checkpoint 0 end_lsn 0

```
230928 21:30:23 PCR1        INFO: Create redo log files. source
                            start_lsn 20147712 last_checkpoint
                            20148086 end_lsn 20150445
230928 21:30:23 PCR1        INFO: Updating last checkpoint to
                            20148086 in redo log
230928 21:30:23 PCR1        INFO: We were able to parse ibbackup_
                            logfile up to lsn 20150445.
230928 21:30:23 PCR1        INFO: Last MySQL binlog file position 0
                            3519, file name binlog.000004
230928 21:30:23 PCR1        INFO: The first data file is '/mysqldata/
                            ibdata1' and the new created log files
                            are at '/mysqldata'
230928 21:30:23 MAIN        INFO: Apply-log operation completed
                            successfully.
230928 21:30:23 MAIN        INFO: Full Backup has been restored
                            successfully.
```

mysqlbackup completed OK! with 1 warnings

5. Verify restored files in the new data directory */mysqldata*.

```
-bash-4.2$ ls -ltr /mysqldata/
total 70724
-rw-rw---- 1 mysql mysql       56 Sep 28 21:30 backup-auto.cnf
drwxr-x--- 2 mysql mysql       28 Sep 28 21:30 sys
drwxr-x--- 2 mysql mysql       54 Sep 28 21:30 db2
drwxr-x--- 2 mysql mysql       54 Sep 28 21:30 db1
drwxr-x--- 2 mysql mysql       54 Sep 28 21:30 db3
drwxr-x--- 2 mysql mysql       54 Sep 28 21:30 db4
-rw-rw---- 1 mysql mysql 26214400 Sep 28 21:30 mysql.ibd
-rw-rw---- 1 mysql mysql     3437 Sep 28 21:30 ib_buffer_pool
-rw-rw---- 1 mysql mysql      157 Sep 28 21:30 binlog.000003
-rw-rw---- 1 mysql mysql     3442 Sep 28 21:30 binlog.000002
-rw-rw---- 1 mysql mysql      826 Sep 28 21:30 binlog.000001
drwxr-x--- 2 mysql mysql      196 Sep 28 21:30 mysql
drwxr-x--- 2 mysql mysql     8192 Sep 28 21:30 performance_schema
-rw-rw---- 1 mysql mysql     3519 Sep 28 21:30 binlog.000004
```

```
-rw-r----- 1 mysql mysql      634 Sep 28 21:30 server-my.cnf
-rw-r----- 1 mysql mysql    19930 Sep 28 21:30 server-all.cnf
-rw-rw---- 1 mysql mysql       64 Sep 28 21:30 binlog.index
-rw-rw---- 1 mysql mysql 16777216 Sep 28 21:30 undo_002
-rw-rw---- 1 mysql mysql 16777216 Sep 28 21:30 undo_001
-rw-rw---- 1 mysql mysql 12582912 Sep 28 21:30 ibdata1
drwxrwx--- 2 mysql mysql       23 Sep 28 21:30 #innodb_redo
-rw-rw-r-- 1 mysql mysql      711 Sep 28 21:30 backup_
                                                variables.txt
```

6. Modify MySQL configuration file /etc/my.cnf to reflect new data
   directory /mysqldata and location of the sock file.

   ```
   [root@mysql-a ~]# cat /etc/my.cnf
   [mysqld]
   datadir=/var/lib/mysql
   socket=/var/lib/mysql/mysql.sock

   log-error=/var/log/mysqld.log
   pid-file=/var/run/mysqld/mysqld.pid
   [root@mysql-a ~]#
   [root@mysql-a ~]# vi /etc/my.cnf
   [root@mysql-a ~]# cat /etc/my.cnf
   [mysqld]
   datadir=/mysqldata
   socket=/mysqldata/mysql.sock

   log-error=/var/log/mysqld.log
   pid-file=/var/run/mysqld/mysqld.pid
   ```

7. Create a symbolic link to ensure the sock file is in the default
   location.

   ```
   [root@mysql-a ~]# ln -s /mysqldata/mysql.sock /var/lib/mysql/
   mysql.sock
   [root@mysql-a ~]# ls -ltr /var/lib/mysql/mysql.sock
   lrwxrwxrwx 1 root root 21 Sep 28 21:45 /var/lib/mysql/
   mysql.sock -> /mysqldata/mysql.sock
   ```

8. Start MySQL server with the modified MySQL configuration file
   /etc/my.cnf.

```
[root@mysql-a ~]# systemctl status mysqld
[root@mysql-a ~]# systemctl start mysqld
[root@mysql-a ~]# systemctl status mysqld
```

9. Log in to the MySQL server and verify if all databases and
   their objects are restored successfully. You can see that all the
   databases and corresponding tables have been restored from
   the backup.

```
[root@mysql-a ~]# su - mysql
Last login: Thu Sep 28 21:28:23 CDT 2023 on pts/0
-bash-4.2$ mysql -uroot -p
Enter password:

mysql> show databases;
+---------------------+
| Database            |
+---------------------+
| db1                 |
| db2                 |
| db3                 |
| db4                 |
| information_schema  |
| mysql               |
| performance_schema  |
| sys                 |
+---------------------+
8 rows in set (0.02 sec)

mysql> use db1;
Reading table information for completion of table and column names
You can turn off this feature to get a quicker startup with -A

Database changed
mysql>
```

```
mysql> show tables;
+---------------+
| Tables_in_db1 |
+---------------+
| tab1          |
| tab2          |
| tab3          |
+---------------+
3 rows in set (0.00 sec)
```

Perform a Restore of an Incremental Backup

Restore an incremental backup using **--incremental** option with **copy-back-and-apply-log**. Before restoring an incremental backup, a restore from a full backup needs to be performed.

Ensure you shut down the server, perform the restore operation, modify the configuration file to point to the new data directory, and create a symbolic link to the sock file, and then start the MySQL server with the new configuration file.

In the following example, we will take a full backup of the MySQL server that has databases *db1*, *db2*, *db3*, *db4*, and *db5*. Then we are going to add another database named *db6*. Perform an incremental backup and then delete all the files in the data directory simulating a data loss scenario and perform the restore using both the full backup and the incremental backup to get to the current state.

1. Check the current status of the MySQL server and the databases it hosts.

    ```
    [root@mysql-a ~]# su - mysql
    Last login: Thu Sep 28 22:50:12 CDT 2023 on pts/0
    -bash-4.2$
    -bash-4.2$ mysql -uroot -p
    Enter password:
    ```

```
mysql> show databases;
+--------------------+
| Database           |
+--------------------+
| db1                |
| db2                |
| db3                |
| db4                |
| db5                |
| information_schema |
| mysql              |
| performance_schema |
| sys                |
+--------------------+
9 rows in set (0.00 sec)
```

2. Perform a full backup.

```
-bash-4.2$ /bin/mysqlbackup --user=mysqlbkpadmin --password --host
=127.0.0.1 --backup-dir=/mysql_backup --backup-image=full_mysql_
bkp_0929.mbi --with-timestamp backup-to-image

Starting with following command line ...
/bin/mysqlbackup
--user=mysqlbkpadmin
--password
--host=127.0.0.1
--backup-dir=/mysql_backup
--backup-image=full_mysql_bkp_0929.mbi
--with-timestamp
backup-to-image

Enter password:
230929 08:56:23 MAIN    INFO: Establishing connection to server.
WARNING: MYSQL_OPT_RECONNECT is deprecated and will be removed in
a future version.
230929 08:56:23 MAIN    INFO: No SSL options specified.
```

```
230929 08:56:23 MAIN        INFO: MySQL server version is '8.0.34'
230929 08:56:23 MAIN        INFO: MySQL server compile os version
                            is 'Linux'
230929 08:56:23 MAIN        INFO: SSL/TLS version used for connection
                            is TLSv1.2
230929 08:56:23 MAIN        INFO: Got some server configuration
                            information from running server.

230929 08:56:23 MAIN        INFO: Establishing connection to server
                            for locking.
WARNING: MYSQL_OPT_RECONNECT is deprecated and will be removed in
a future version.
230929 08:56:23 MAIN        INFO: No SSL options specified.
230929 08:56:23 MAIN        INFO: Backup directory created: '/mysql_
                            backup/2023-09-29_08-56-23'
230929 08:56:23 MAIN        INFO: MySQL server version_comment is
                            'MySQL Community Server - GPL'
230929 08:56:23 MAIN        INFO: Mysqlbackup component not
                            installed.
230929 08:56:23 MAIN        INFO: MEB logfile created at /mysql_
                            backup/2023-09-29_08-56-23/meta/
                            MEB_2023-09-29.08-56-23_backup-to-
                            image.log
```

--Output truncated for better visibility

```
230929 08:56:23 RDR1        INFO: Writing server defaults files
                            'server-my.cnf' and 'server-all.
                            cnf' for server '8.0.34' in '/mysql_
                            backup/2023-09-29_08-56-23'.
230929 08:56:23 RDR1        INFO: Copying meta file /mysql_backup/
                            2023-09-29_08-56-23/meta/backup_
                            variables.txt.
230929 08:56:23 RDR1        INFO: Copying meta file /mysql_backup/
                            2023-09-29_08-56-23/datadir/ibbackup_
                            logfile.
```

```
230929 08:56:23 RDR1      INFO: Copying meta file /mysql_
                          backup/2023-09-29_08-56-23/
                          server-all.cnf.
230929 08:56:23 RDR1      INFO: Copying meta file /mysql_
                          backup/2023-09-29_08-56-23/server-my.cnf.
230929 08:56:23 RDR1      INFO: Copying meta file /mysql_
                          backup/2023-09-29_08-56-23/meta/backup_
                          content.xml.
230929 08:56:23 RDR1      INFO: Copying meta file /mysql_
                          backup/2023-09-29_08-56-23/meta/image_
                          files.xml.
230929 08:56:23 MAIN      INFO: Full Image Backup operation
                          completed successfully.
230929 08:56:23 MAIN      INFO: Backup image created successfully.
230929 08:56:23 MAIN      INFO: Image Path = /mysql_
                          backup/2023-09-29_08-56-23/full_mysql_
                          bkp_0929.mbi
230929 08:56:23 MAIN      INFO: MySQL binlog position: filename
                          binlog.000006, position 157.

-------------------------------------------------------------
   Parameters Summary
-------------------------------------------------------------
    Start LSN              : 20300800
    Last Checkpoint LSN    : 20300844
    End LSN                : 20303004
-------------------------------------------------------------
```

mysqlbackup completed OK!

3. Create another database named **db6** so it will be included in the incremental backup.

```
-bash-4.2$ mysql -uroot -p
Enter password:
```

```
mysql> show databases;
+---------------------+
| Database            |
+---------------------+
| db1                 |
| db2                 |
| db3                 |
| db4                 |
| db5                 |
| information_schema  |
| mysql               |
| performance_schema  |
| sys                 |
+---------------------+
9 rows in set (0.00 sec)

mysql> create database db6;
Query OK, 1 row affected (0.01 sec)

mysql> use db6;
Database changed
mysql>
mysql> create table tab1 (no int);
Query OK, 0 rows affected (0.01 sec)

mysql> create table tab2 (no int);
Query OK, 0 rows affected (0.02 sec)

mysql> create table tab3 (no int);
Query OK, 0 rows affected (0.02 sec)

mysql> show tables;
+---------------+
| Tables_in_db6 |
+---------------+
| tab1          |
| tab2          |
```

```
| tab3            |
+---------------+
3 rows in set (0.00 sec)
```

4. Perform an incremental backup using the **--incremental**
    and **--incremental-base** parameters.

-bash-4.2$ **/bin/mysqlbackup --user=mysqlbkpadmin --password --host**
=127.0.0.1 --incremental --incremental-base=history:last_
backup --backup-dir=/mysqlbkuptmp --backup-image=/mysql_backup/
incremental_backup_0929.mbi backup-to-image

```
Starting with following command line ...
/bin/mysqlbackup
--user=mysqlbkpadmin
--password
--host=127.0.0.1
--incremental
--incremental-base=history:last_backup
--backup-dir=/mysqlbkuptmp
--backup-image=/mysql_backup/incremental_backup_0929.mbi
backup-to-image

Enter password:
230929 08:58:40 MAIN     INFO: Establishing connection to server.
WARNING: MYSQL_OPT_RECONNECT is deprecated and will be removed in
a future version.
230929 08:58:40 MAIN     INFO: No SSL options specified.
230929 08:58:40 MAIN     INFO: MySQL server version is '8.0.34'
230929 08:58:40 MAIN     INFO: MySQL server compile os version
is 'Linux'
230929 08:58:40 MAIN     INFO: SSL/TLS version used for connection
                         is TLSv1.2
230929 08:58:40 MAIN     INFO: Got some server configuration
                         information from running server.

230929 08:58:40 MAIN     INFO: Establishing connection to server
                         for locking.
```

```
WARNING: MYSQL_OPT_RECONNECT is deprecated and will be removed in
a future version.
230929 08:58:40 MAIN      INFO: No SSL options specified.
230929 08:58:40 MAIN      INFO: Backup directory exists: '/
                          mysqlbkuptmp'
```

--Output truncated for better visibility

```
230929 08:58:40 RDR1      INFO: Copying meta file /mysqlbkuptmp/
                          meta/image_files.xml.
230929 08:58:40 MAIN      INFO: Incremental Image Backup operation
                          completed successfully.
230929 08:58:40 MAIN      INFO: Backup image created successfully.
230929 08:58:40 MAIN      INFO: Image Path = /mysql_backup/
                          incremental_backup_0929.mbi
230929 08:58:40 MAIN      INFO: Backup contains changes from lsn
                          20303005 to lsn 20357671.
230929 08:58:40 MAIN      INFO: MySQL binlog position: filename
                          binlog.000006, position 906.
-------------------------------------------------------------
    Parameters Summary
-------------------------------------------------------------
    Start LSN               : 20303005
    Last Checkpoint LSN     : 20351917
    End LSN                 : 20357671
-------------------------------------------------------------
```

mysqlbackup completed OK!

5. Verify incremental backup files.

```
-bash-4.2$ ls -ltr /mysql_backup/
total 154168
-rw-rw---- 1 mysql mysql 73347718 Sep 27 22:20 test_single_file_
backup.mbi
-rw-rw---- 1 mysql mysql  4286000 Sep 27 22:34 test_compressed_
mysql_bkp.img
-rw-rw---- 1 mysql mysql  2121901 Sep 27 22:46 test_incremental_
backup.mbi
```

```
-rw-rw---- 1 mysql mysql 72879768 Sep 28 16:54 test_include_
tables_backup.mbi
drwxr-x--- 4 mysql mysql      127 Sep 28 17:29 2023-09-28_17-29-00
drwxr-x--- 4 mysql mysql      127 Sep 28 17:29 2023-09-28_17-29-07
drwxr-x--- 4 mysql mysql      127 Sep 28 17:29 2023-09-28_17-29-14
drwxr-x--- 4 mysql mysql      123 Sep 28 22:44 2023-09-28_22-44-38
-rw-rw---- 1 mysql mysql  1927454 Sep 28 22:45 new_incremental_
backup.mbi
drwxr-x--- 4 mysql mysql      128 Sep 29 08:56 2023-09-29_08-56-23
-rw-rw---- 1 mysql mysql  3292772 Sep 29 08:58 incremental_
backup_0929.mbi
-bash-4.2$
```

6. Create a data loss scenario by removing all the files in the directory.

```
-bash-4.2$ ls -ltr /mysqldata/
total 91640
drwxr-x--- 2 mysql mysql         28 Sep 28 22:57 sys
drwxr-x--- 2 mysql mysql         54 Sep 28 22:57 db1
drwxr-x--- 2 mysql mysql         54 Sep 28 22:57 db3
drwxr-x--- 2 mysql mysql         54 Sep 28 22:57 db2
drwxr-x--- 2 mysql mysql         54 Sep 28 22:57 db5
drwxr-x--- 2 mysql mysql         54 Sep 28 22:57 db4
-rw-rw---- 1 mysql mysql       3519 Sep 28 22:57 binlog.000004
-rw-rw---- 1 mysql mysql        157 Sep 28 22:57 binlog.000003
-rw-rw---- 1 mysql mysql       3442 Sep 28 22:57 binlog.000002
-rw-rw---- 1 mysql mysql        826 Sep 28 22:57 binlog.000001
-rw-rw---- 1 mysql mysql         56 Sep 28 22:57 backup-auto.cnf
drwxr-x--- 2 mysql mysql        196 Sep 28 22:57 mysql
drwxr-x--- 2 mysql mysql       8192 Sep 28 22:57 performance_schema
-rw-r----- 1 mysql mysql        618 Sep 28 22:57 server-my.cnf
-rw-r----- 1 mysql mysql      19898 Sep 28 22:57 server-all.cnf
-rw-rw-r-- 1 mysql mysql        735 Sep 28 22:57 backup_
variables.txt
-rw-r----- 1 mysql mysql         56 Sep 29 08:45 auto.cnf
-rw-r----- 1 mysql mysql    8585216 Sep 29 08:45 #ib_16384_1.dblwr
drwxrwx--- 2 mysql mysql       4096 Sep 29 08:45 #innodb_redo
```

```
drwxr-x--- 2 mysql mysql        187 Sep 29 08:45 #innodb_temp
-rw-rw---- 1 mysql mysql        906 Sep 29 08:45 binlog.000005
-rw-r----- 1 mysql mysql         96 Sep 29 08:45 binlog.index
-rw------- 1 mysql mysql       1680 Sep 29 08:45 ca-key.pem
-rw-r--r-- 1 mysql mysql       1112 Sep 29 08:45 ca.pem
-rw------- 1 mysql mysql       1676 Sep 29 08:45 server-key.pem
-rw-r--r-- 1 mysql mysql       1112 Sep 29 08:45 server-cert.pem
-rw-r----- 1 mysql mysql   12582912 Sep 29 08:45 ibtmp1
-rw------- 1 mysql mysql       1680 Sep 29 08:45 client-key.pem
-rw-r--r-- 1 mysql mysql       1112 Sep 29 08:45 client-cert.pem
-rw------- 1 mysql mysql       1680 Sep 29 08:45 private_key.pem
-rw-r--r-- 1 mysql mysql        452 Sep 29 08:45 public_key.pem
-rw------- 1 mysql mysql          5 Sep 29 08:45 mysql.sock.lock
srwxrwxrwx 1 mysql mysql          0 Sep 29 08:45 mysql.sock
drwxr-x--- 2 mysql mysql         54 Sep 29 08:57 db6
-rw-r----- 1 mysql mysql        906 Sep 29 08:57 binlog.000006
-rw-r----- 1 mysql mysql       3573 Sep 29 08:58 ib_buffer_pool
-rw-rw---- 1 mysql mysql   12582912 Sep 29 08:58 ibdata1
-rw-rw---- 1 mysql mysql   26214400 Sep 29 08:58 mysql.ibd
-rw-rw---- 1 mysql mysql   16777216 Sep 29 08:59 undo_001
-rw-r----- 1 mysql mysql     196608 Sep 29 08:59 #ib_16384_0.dblwr
-rw-rw---- 1 mysql mysql   16777216 Sep 29 08:59 undo_002
-bash-4.2$
-bash-4.2$ rm -rf /mysqldata/*
-bash-4.2$ ls -ltr /mysqldata/
total 0
-bash-4.2$
```

7. Perform a restore operation. In order to get the database to a
   consistent state, we need to restore to the last full backup first and
   then apply the incremental backup.

```
-bash-4.2$ ls -ltr /mysql_backup/
total 154168
-rw-rw---- 1 mysql mysql 73347718 Sep 27 22:20 test_single_file_
backup.mbi
```

```
-rw-rw----  1 mysql mysql  4286000 Sep 27 22:34 test_compressed_
                                                 mysql_bkp.img
-rw-rw----  1 mysql mysql  2121901 Sep 27 22:46 test_incremental_
                                                 backup.mbi
-rw-rw----  1 mysql mysql 72879768 Sep 28 16:54 test_include_
                                                 tables_backup.mbi
drwxr-x---  4 mysql mysql      127 Sep 28 17:29
                                                 2023-09-28_17-29-00
drwxr-x---  4 mysql mysql      127 Sep 28 17:29
                                                 2023-09-28_17-29-07
drwxr-x---  4 mysql mysql      127 Sep 28 17:29
                                                 2023-09-28_17-29-14
drwxr-x---  4 mysql mysql      123 Sep 28 22:44
                                                 2023-09-28_22-44-38
-rw-rw----  1 mysql mysql  1927454 Sep 28 22:45 new_incremental_
                                                 backup.mbi
drwxr-x---  4 mysql mysql      128 Sep 29 08:56
                                                 2023-09-29_08-56-23
-rw-rw----  1 mysql mysql  3292772 Sep 29 08:58 incremental_
                                                 backup_0929.mbi
-bash-4.2$
-bash-4.2$ cd /mysql_backup/2023-09-29_08-56-23
-bash-4.2$ ls -ltr
total 74412
-rw-rw-r--  1 mysql mysql      255 Sep 29 08:56 backup-my.cnf
-rw-r-----  1 mysql mysql      491 Sep 29 08:56 server-my.cnf
-rw-r-----  1 mysql mysql    19898 Sep 29 08:56 server-all.cnf
drwxr-x---  2 mysql mysql      159 Sep 29 08:56 meta
-rw-rw----  1 mysql mysql 76166692 Sep 29 08:56 full_mysql_
                                                 bkp_0929.mbi
drwxr-x---  2 mysql mysql        6 Sep 29 08:56 datadir
-bash-4.2$
-bash-4.2$ /bin/mysqlbackup --datadir=/mysqldata --backup-image=/
mysql_backup/2023-09-29_08-56-23/full_mysql_bkp_0929.mbi --backup-
dir=/mysqlbkuptmp copy-back-and-apply-log
```

```
Starting with following command line ...
/bin/mysqlbackup
--datadir=/mysqldata
--backup-image=/mysql_backup/2023-09-29_08-56-23/full_mysql_
bkp_0929.mbi
--backup-dir=/mysqlbkuptmp
copy-back-and-apply-log
```

```
230929 09:19:23 MAIN     INFO: Backup Image MEB version
                         string: 8.0.34
230929 09:19:23 MAIN     INFO: MySQL server version is '8.0.34'
230929 09:19:23 MAIN     INFO: Backup directory exists:
                         '/mysqlbkuptmp'
230929 09:19:23 MAIN  WARNING: If you restore to a server of a
different version, the innodb_data_file_path parameter might
have a different default. In that case you need to add 'innodb_
data_file_path=ibdata1:12M:autoextend' to the target server
configuration.
230929 09:19:23 MAIN     INFO: MEB logfile created at
                         /mysqlbkuptmp/meta/
                         MEB_2023-09-29.09-19-23_copy-back-and-
                         apply-log.log
```

   --Output truncated for better visibility

```
230929 09:19:23 MAIN     INFO: Loading the space id 1 name
                         '/mysqldata/sys/sys_config.ibd'.
230929 09:19:23 MAIN     INFO: Loading the space id 4294967294
                         name '/mysqldata/mysql.ibd'.
230929 09:19:23 MAIN     INFO: Loading the space id 4294967279
                         name '/mysqldata/undo_001'.
230929 09:19:23 MAIN     INFO: Loading the space id 4294967278
                         name '/mysqldata/undo_002'.
230929 09:19:23 PCR1     INFO: Starting to parse redo log at
                         lsn = 20300844, whereas checkpoint_lsn =
                         20300844 and start_lsn = 20300800.
```

```
230929 09:19:23 PCR1      INFO: Doing recovery: scanned up to log
                          sequence number 20303004.
230929 09:19:23 PCR1      INFO: Starting to apply a batch of log
                          records to the database....
InnoDB: Progress in percent: 12 25 37 50
230929 09:19:23 PCR1      INFO: Create redo log files. target
                          start_lsn 0 last_checkpoint 0 end_lsn 0
230929 09:19:23 PCR1      INFO: Create redo log files. source
                          start_lsn 20300800 last_checkpoint
                          20300844 end_lsn 20303004
230929 09:19:23 PCR1      INFO: Updating last checkpoint to 20300844 in
                          redo log
230929 09:19:23 PCR1      INFO: We were able to parse ibbackup_
                          logfile up to lsn 20303004.
230929 09:19:23 PCR1      INFO: Last MySQL binlog file position 0
                          157, file name binlog.000006
230929 09:19:23 PCR1      INFO: The first data file is '/mysqldata/
                          ibdata1' and the new created log files
                          are at '/mysqldata'
230929 09:19:23 MAIN      INFO: Apply-log operation completed
                          successfully.
230929 09:19:23 MAIN      INFO: Full Backup has been restored
                          successfully.
```

mysqlbackup completed OK! with 1 warnings

8.   Now apply the incremental backup.

```
-bash-4.2$ /bin/mysqlbackup --backup-image=/mysql_backup/
incremental_backup_0929.mbi --backup-dir=/mysqlbkuptmp --datadir=/
mysqldata --incremental copy-back-and-apply-log

Starting with following command line ...
/bin/mysqlbackup
--backup-image=/mysql_backup/incremental_backup_0929.mbi
--backup-dir=/mysqlbkuptmp
--datadir=/mysqldata
```

```
--incremental
copy-back-and-apply-log
```

```
230929 09:21:59 MAIN        INFO: Backup Image MEB version
                            string: 8.0.34
230929 09:21:59 MAIN        INFO: The input backup image contains
                            incremental backup.
230929 09:21:59 MAIN        INFO: MySQL server version is '8.0.34'
230929 09:21:59 MAIN        INFO: Backup directory exists:
                            '/mysqlbkuptmp'
```

--Output truncated for better visibility

```
230929 09:21:59 MAIN        INFO: Loading the space id 17 name
                            '/mysqldata/db5/tab2.ibd'.
230929 09:21:59 MAIN        INFO: Loading the space id 18 name
                            '/mysqldata/db5/tab3.ibd'.
230929 09:21:59 MAIN        INFO: Loading the space id 19 name
                            '/mysqldata/db6/tab1.ibd'.
230929 09:21:59 MAIN        INFO: Loading the space id 20 name
                            '/mysqldata/db6/tab2.ibd'.
230929 09:21:59 MAIN        INFO: Loading the space id 21 name
                            '/mysqldata/db6/tab3.ibd'.
230929 09:21:59 MAIN        INFO: Loading the space id 3 name
                            '/mysqldata/mysql/backup_history.ibd'.
230929 09:21:59 MAIN        INFO: Loading the space id 2 name
                            '/mysqldata/mysql/backup_progress.ibd'.
230929 09:21:59 MAIN        INFO: Loading the space id 1 name
                            '/mysqldata/sys/sys_config.ibd'.
230929 09:21:59 MAIN        INFO: Loading the space id 4294967294
                            name '/mysqldata/mysql.ibd'.
230929 09:21:59 MAIN        INFO: Loading the space id 4294967279
                            name '/mysqldata/undo_001'.
230929 09:21:59 MAIN        INFO: Loading the space id 4294967278
                            name '/mysqldata/undo_002'.
```

230929 09:21:59 PCR1   INFO: Starting to parse redo log at
                        lsn = 20351795, whereas checkpoint_lsn =
                        20351917 and start_lsn = 20351488.

230929 09:21:59 PCR1   **INFO: Doing recovery: scanned up to log
                        sequence number 20357671.**

230929 09:21:59 PCR1   **INFO: Starting to apply a batch of log
                        records to the database....**

InnoDB: Progress in percent: 7 14 21 28 35

230929 09:21:59 PCR1   INFO: Create redo log files. target
                        start_lsn 20300800 last_checkpoint
                        20300844 end_lsn 20303004

230929 09:21:59 PCR1   INFO: Create redo log files. source
                        start_lsn 20303005 last_checkpoint
                        20351917 end_lsn 20357671

230929 09:21:59 PCR1   INFO: Updating last checkpoint to
                        20351917 in redo log

230929 09:21:59 PCR1   INFO: We were able to parse ibbackup_
                        logfile up to lsn 20357671.

230929 09:21:59 PCR1   INFO: Last MySQL binlog file position 0
                        906, file name binlog.000006

230929 09:21:59 PCR1   INFO: The first data file is '/mysqldata/
                        ibdata1' and the new created log files
                        are at '/mysqldata'

230929 09:21:59 MAIN   **INFO: Apply-log operation completed
                        successfully.**

230929 09:21:59 MAIN   **INFO: Incremental backup applied
                        successfully.**

mysqlbackup completed OK! with 1 warnings
-bash-4.2$

9. Verify the backup directory to see all the files are copied back.

```
-bash-4.2$ ls -ltr /mysqldata/
total 70732
drwxr-x--- 2 mysql mysql      28 Sep 29 09:19 sys
drwxr-x--- 2 mysql mysql      54 Sep 29 09:19 db3
```

```
drwxr-x--- 2 mysql mysql          54 Sep 29 09:19 db2
drwxr-x--- 2 mysql mysql          54 Sep 29 09:19 db1
drwxr-x--- 2 mysql mysql          54 Sep 29 09:19 db5
drwxr-x--- 2 mysql mysql          54 Sep 29 09:19 db4
-rw-rw---- 1 mysql mysql         906 Sep 29 09:19 binlog.000005
-rw-rw---- 1 mysql mysql        3519 Sep 29 09:19 binlog.000004
-rw-rw---- 1 mysql mysql         157 Sep 29 09:19 binlog.000003
-rw-rw---- 1 mysql mysql        3442 Sep 29 09:19 binlog.000002
-rw-rw---- 1 mysql mysql         826 Sep 29 09:19 binlog.000001
-rw-rw---- 1 mysql mysql          56 Sep 29 09:21 backup-auto.cnf
drwxr-x--- 2 mysql mysql          54 Sep 29 09:21 db6
drwxr-x--- 2 mysql mysql         196 Sep 29 09:21 mysql
-rw-rw---- 1 mysql mysql        3573 Sep 29 09:21 ib_buffer_pool
drwxr-x--- 2 mysql mysql        8192 Sep 29 09:21 performance_schema
-rw-rw---- 1 mysql mysql         906 Sep 29 09:21 binlog.000006
-rw-r----- 1 mysql mysql         618 Sep 29 09:21 server-my.cnf
-rw-r----- 1 mysql mysql       19898 Sep 29 09:21 server-all.cnf
-rw-rw---- 1 mysql mysql          96 Sep 29 09:21 binlog.index
-rw-rw---- 1 mysql mysql    16777216 Sep 29 09:21 undo_002
-rw-rw---- 1 mysql mysql    16777216 Sep 29 09:21 undo_001
-rw-rw---- 1 mysql mysql    26214400 Sep 29 09:21 mysql.ibd
-rw-rw---- 1 mysql mysql    12582912 Sep 29 09:21 ibdata1
drwxrwx--- 2 mysql mysql          23 Sep 29 09:21 #innodb_redo
-rw-rw-r-- 1 mysql mysql         735 Sep 29 09:21 backup_
                                                  variables.txt
```

10. Start the MySQL daemon and verify all databases including
    db6 are restored, which confirms we have restored from an
    incremental backup.

```
[root@mysql-a ~]# systemctl start mysqld
[root@mysql-a ~]# su - mysql
Last login: Fri Sep 29 08:55:23 CDT 2023 on pts/0
-bash-4.2$
-bash-4.2$ mysql -uroot -p
```

```
Enter password:

mysql> show databases;
+---------------------+
| Database            |
+---------------------+
| db1                 |
| db2                 |
| db3                 |
| db4                 |
| db5                 |
| db6                 |
| information_schema  |
| mysql               |
| performance_schema  |
| sys                 |
+---------------------+
10 rows in set (0.01 sec)
```

Perform a Backup to a Cloud Storage

In this section, we are going to perform a backup to an object storage in Oracle Cloud Infrastructure (OCI). In order to back up to cloud storage, you will need **MySQL Shell 8.1** and an object storage bucket with pre-authenticated request setup.

1. Download MySQL Shell 8.1 by visiting https://dev.mysql.com/ downloads/shell/ and by choosing the corresponding OS and version.

Figure 9-2. MySQL Community download page

2. Transfer the downloaded file to the server using a file transfer
    utility like WinSCP.

3. Install MySQL Shell 8.1.

```
[root@mysql-a mysql_binaries]# rpm -ivh mysql-shell-8.1.1-1.el7.
x86_64.rpm
warning: mysql-shell-8.1.1-1.el7.x86_64.rpm: Header V4 RSA/SHA256
Signature, key ID 3a79bd29: NOKEY
Preparing...                          ######################### [100%]
Updating / installing...
   1:mysql-shell-8.1.1-1.el7          ######################### [100%]
[root@mysql-a mysql_binaries]#
```

4.   Create a bucket in OCI.

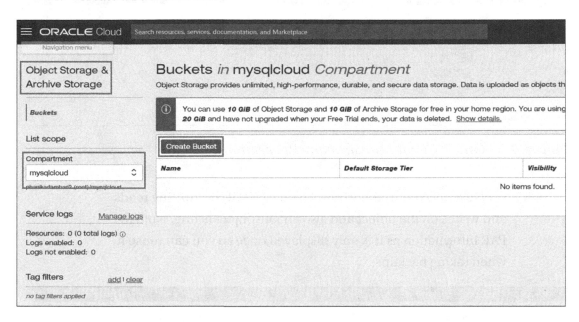

Figure 9-3.   *Oracle Cloud Infrastructure Object Storage & Archive Storage*

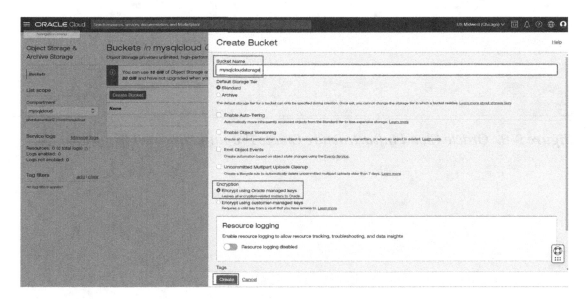

Figure 9-4.   *Oracle Cloud Infrastructure Create Bucket page*

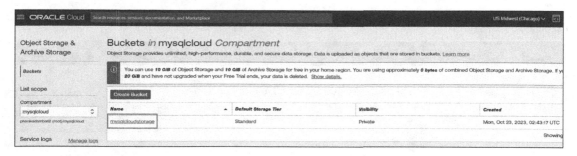

Figure 9-5. *Oracle Cloud Infrastructure Bucket name*

5. Create a new pre-authenticated request (PAR) permitting reads and writes on the object and also enable object listing. Note the PAR information as it is only displayed once so you can reuse it when taking backups.

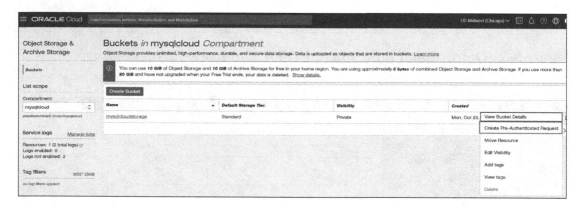

Figure 9-6. *Oracle Cloud Infrastructure Create Pre-authenticated Request*

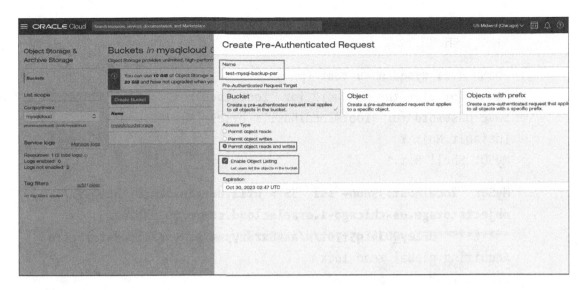

Figure 9-7. *Oracle Cloud Infrastructure Create Pre-authenticated Request information*

Pre-Authenticated Request Details

Name *Read-only*

test-mysql-backup-par

Pre-Authenticated Request URL *Read-only*

https://objectstorage.us-chicago-1.oraclecloud.com/p/zu_aXu   ,IDF14Dyqut

⊙ Copy this URL for your records. It will not be shown again.

⊙ The current URL is deprecated and will no longer be supported in a future release of the console. A new URL will be used as shown below. Learn more

https://axu8xzdzypmm.objectstorage.us-chicago-1.oci.customer-oci.com/p/zu_aXu7Aq-
cJL   budstorage/o/

Close

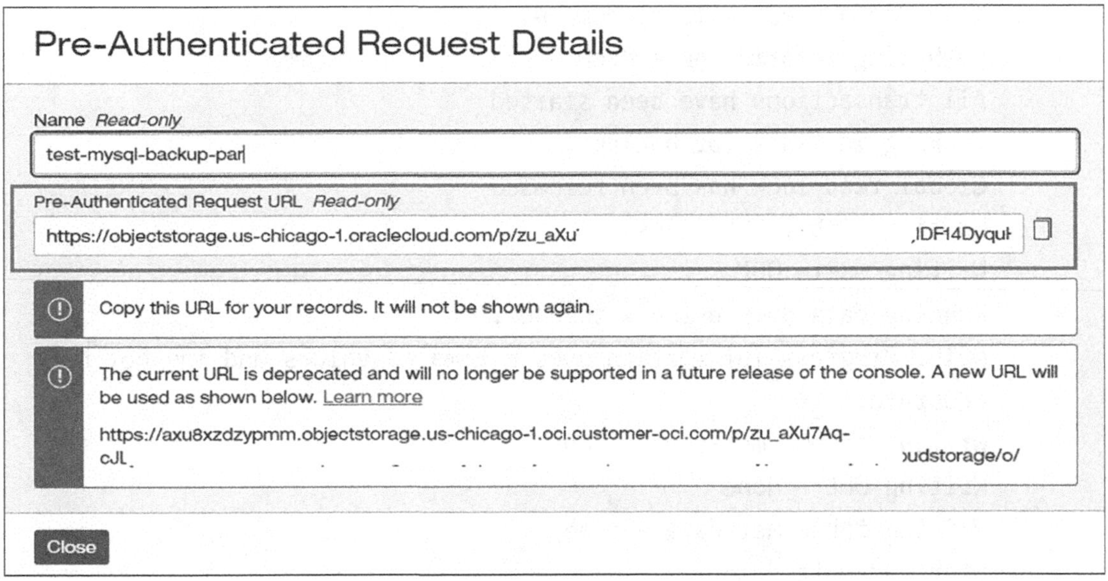

Figure 9-8. *Oracle Cloud Infrastructure Create Pre-authenticated Request information*

6. Create a backup using the dumpInstance() method from
    MySQL Shell.

```
-bash-4.2$ mysqlsh -u root -p
Please provide the password for 'root@localhost': *************
Save password for 'root@localhost'? [Y]es/[N]o/Ne[v]er
(default No): Y
MySQL Shell 8.1.1

MySQL  localhost:33060+ ssl  JS > util.dumpInstance("https://
objectstorage.us-chicago-1.oraclecloud.com/p/zu_aXu7Aq-
**********HFIeyQDJALq5f70t/n/axu8xzdzypmm/b/mysqlcloudstorage/o/")
Acquiring global read lock
Global read lock acquired
Initializing - done
1 out of 5 schemas will be dumped and within them 6 tables,
2 views.
1 out of 4 users will be dumped.
Gathering information - done
All transactions have been started
Locking instance for backup
Global read lock has been released
Writing global DDL files
Writing users DDL
Running data dump using 4 threads.
NOTE: Progress information uses estimated values and may not be
accurate.
Writing schema metadata - done
Writing DDL - done
Writing table metadata - done
Starting data dump
100% (3.92M rows / ~3.92M rows), 546.78K rows/s, 19.13 MB/s
uncompressed, 5.00 MB/s compressed
Dump duration: 00:00:08s
Total duration: 00:00:09s
Schemas dumped: 1
```

```
Tables dumped: 6
Uncompressed data size: 141.50 MB
Compressed data size: 36.99 MB
Compression ratio: 3.8
Rows written: 3919015
Bytes written: 36.99 MB
Average uncompressed throughput: 17.31 MB/s
Average compressed throughput: 4.52 MB/s
```

7. Verify backup files on object storage bucket in OCI.

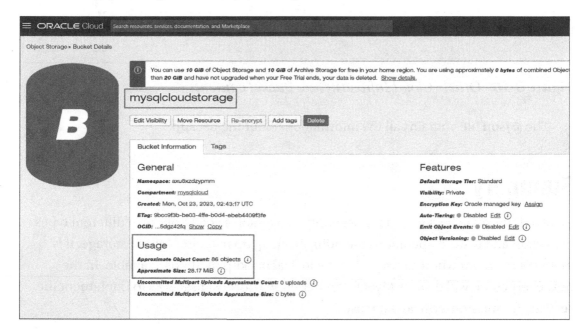

Figure 9-9. *Oracle Cloud Infrastructure Bucket overview page*

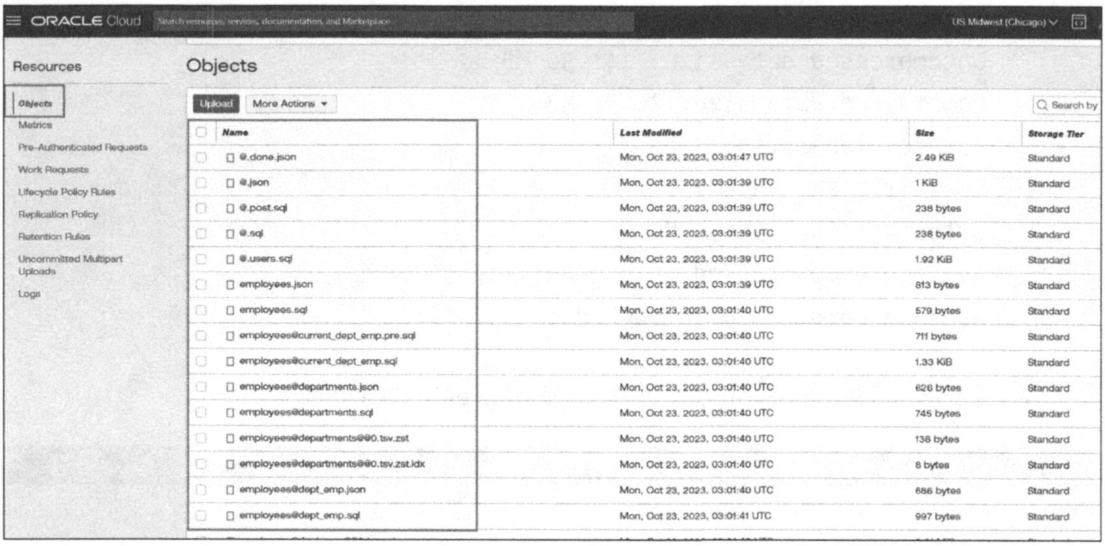

Figure 9-10. *Oracle Cloud Infrastructure Bucket contents*

The **@json** file contains all the information about the backup.

Summary

MySQL Enterprise Backup is a robust utility that enables you to perform different types of backup and restore operations including backing up to a direct cloud storage. It is highly performant when compared to the logical backup methods available. In the next chapter, we will discuss MySQL database security best practices to implement the security for mission-critical databases.

CHAPTER 10

MySQL Security

Introduction

In this chapter, we will discuss MySQL database security best practices and how to protect your database once you install/set up the database.

Database security is critical and essential to protect any organization's data. With increased cyber threats, it's essential to secure data and databases, and it's very critical to implement security measures to limit unauthorized data access, modification, and destruction.

Securing organizational databases brings many compliance and security benefits in protecting the mission-critical data in the organization. Implementing the best practices for database security helps to improve the trust of the partners and customers using the database and feel secure data is protected.

Securing the database and building the auditing capabilities are compliance requirements for PCI, GDPR, HIPAA, SOX, and other regulatory requirements.

There are various benefits of implementing best practices on security that are summarized as follows:

- Reducing the risk of data breaches and various security attacks

- Protecting organizational resources and assets

- Restricting unauthorized access to the data and limiting access to required personnel

- Improving trust and confidence of the customers and partners

- Meeting compliance and regulatory requirements

- Organizational efficiency and smooth business function

© Y V Ravi Kumar, Arun Kumar Samayam, Naresh Kumar Miryala 2024
Y V Ravi Kumar et al., *Mastering MySQL Administration*, https://doi.org/10.1007/979-8-8688-0252-2_10

Best Practices for Securing MySQL Database

We will discuss the best practices for the security of MySQL databases; by implementing the following methods, you will be able to secure your database to meet security and compliance requirements.

Use of Strong Passwords

Passwords help to prevent unauthorized access; hence, we must use strong passwords for root users. We also have to make sure to set password complexity and length of password as a standard, and all users should have strong passwords and should be changed regularly. Also, avoid hard-coding credentials in configuration files or any code. We should track failed sign-in random password generations to enhance security.

MySQL provides many built-in password features like password complexity, minimum password length, and banned passwords. Password validation helps to ensure all the passwords on our databases are complex and challenging to crack, which eventually helps to protect our database from unauthorized access.

Upgrade MySQL Software to the Latest Version

One of the best ways to secure MySQL databases is by upgrading to the latest version as MySQL releases security updates frequently; this also helps us to get regular security updates, which ensures robust protection.

Role-Based Access Control (RBAC)

RBAC helps us to manage user privileges and ensure that users only have the privileges that are needed, as RBAC allows us to create and manage roles, then assign users to those roles.

Operating System Hardening

Always run your databases on supported and latest OS versions. Legacy OS contains many OS vulnerabilities, which weaken the security of the databases running on them.

534

Audit Logging

Enabling audit logging helps to log all activity on the MySQL database, which helps us to identify attackers and their suspicious activity. Database auditing is a compliance requirement along with security best practices.

Robust Monitoring

We must have good monitoring capabilities that help us to identify and respond quickly to security threats to detect any suspicious activity.

Secure Data Through Encryption

As part of data security, encrypting data at rest and in transit is critical. Encryption at rest helps to protect data that is stored on any device, such as hard drives or the cloud. Encryption in transit helps to protect the data that is being transmitted between two devices.

Secure Backup and Recovery Strategy

Backup security is not widely recognized as a critical element in securing databases. Compromised backup data can leak all the information in the database. Encryption on backup is critical to avoid internal data leaks from the backups or backup storage media.

Firewall Configuration

We must configure a firewall that should allow incoming requests to MySQL port (use the nondefault port as best practice) and block others, which helps to prevent unauthorized access.

Securing MySQL Installation

Once you complete the installation of MySQL standalone to cluster, please perform the following steps to secure your installed MySQL databases.

If you have already installed and run the database in production, please follow the steps to modify your config to implement security and compliance requirements.

Change Default Root Password

MySQL sets a default root password when you install the database; please reset the password to a strong password (using password complexity discussed in the following).

Search the installation log file and get the default password.

[root@mysqlhost01~]# grep 'temporary password' /var/log/mysqld.log
```
2023-10-05T21:39:36.785108Z 6 [Note] [MY-010454] [Server] A temporary
password is generated for root@localhost: g#BB*cmch_3?a
```

Log in to MySQL database using the default password.

[root@mysqlhost01~]# mysql -u root -p
```
Enter password:
```

Reset the root password to a strong password using the password policy described previously.

mysql> ALTER USER 'root'@'localhost' IDENTIFIED BY 'xxxxxxxxxxxx';
```
Query OK, 0 rows affected (0.01 sec)
```

Remove Anonymous Users

By default, with every installation of MySQL, there is an anonymous user created; this user allows the login to MySQL without any user created; this is a security risk, and this should not exist in the production database.

[root@mysqlhost01~]# mysql -u root -p
```
Enter password:
```

mysql> DELETE FROM mysql.user WHERE User = '';
```
Query OK, 0 rows affected (0.00 sec)
```

Remove the Test Database

MySQL by default creates a database named "test"; this database can be accessed by anyone, and it's created for testing purposes; we should drop this database in the production database.

```
mysql> USE mysql;
Reading table information for completion of table and column names
You can turn off this feature to get a quicker startup with -A

Database changed
mysql>
mysql> DROP DATABASE IF EXISTS test;
Query OK, 0 rows affected, 1 warning (0.01 sec)
```

Set Password Complexity

Password complexity is a critical element for database security; it's required from security and compliance requirements.

From compliance requirements, a password is considered strong when it meets the minimum requirements:

- At least 12 characters long

- Combination of uppercase letters, lowercase letters, and special characters:

    ```
    mysql> SET GLOBAL validate_password.policy = 'STRONG';
    Query OK, 0 rows affected (0.00 sec)
    ```

    ```
    mysql> SET GLOBAL validate_password.length = 12;
    Query OK, 0 rows affected (0.00 sec)
    ```

Restricting Privileges of User Accounts

Privilege escalation is one of the security and audit compliance concerns where users have more than required access to perform their job function. It's a requirement to review the users and privileges granted and take necessary actions to adjust the privileges based on the user roles.

In general, use the least privilege principle, that is, grant only the minimum necessary privileges to each user account to perform their intended tasks. The following are some commonly used privileges.

Table 10-1. *Commonly used privileges*

SELECT	Select privilege provides access to query table data.
INSERT	Insert allows you to manipulate data by inserting new table rows.
UPDATE	Update allows users to update/change an existing table row.
DELETE	Delete allows users to delete the rows from the tables.
CREATE	Create allows users to create a new database, table, or index.
DROP	Drop allows users to drop/delete tables or indexes.
ALTER	Alter allows users to alter/modify the structure of the table.

Create a user and grant privileges as shown here:

```
mysql> CREATE USER 'mysqluser'@'localhost' IDENTIFIED BY 'xxxxx!';
Query OK, 1 rows affected (0.01 sec)

mysql> GRANT SELECT, INSERT ON suppliers.inventory
to  'mysqluser'@'localhost';
Query OK, 1 rows affected (0.01 sec)
```

Check existing user privileges as shown here:

```
mysql> SHOW GRANTS FOR 'mysqluser'@'localhost';
+---------------------------------------------------------------------------+
| Grants for mysqluser@localhost                                            |
+---------------------------------------------------------------------------+
| GRANT USAGE ON *.* TO `mysqluser`@`localhost`                             |
| GRANT SELECT, INSERT ON `suppliers`.`inventory` TO `mysqluser`@`localhost` |
+---------------------------------------------------------------------------+
```

Disable Remote Access for Root User

Root is a super user that allows access to the database as a super user; securing root user is a critical requirement.

By default, root logins are allowed from remote machines; in general, there is no need for a root user to log in from remote machines; allowing this exposes the risk of anyone guessing the root password and trying to exploit the login.

It's best practice to disable the remote login for root users.

```
mysql> DELETE FROM mysql.user WHERE User='root' AND Host NOT IN
('localhost', '127.0.0.1', '::1');
Query OK, 0 rows affected (0.01 sec)

mysql> flush privileges;
Query OK, 0 rows affected (0.00 sec)
```

Securing Using CLI

Once database installation is completed, we can use the CLI to secure the database instead of manual methods outlined previously; it will perform the following actions; these steps are optional, but they are necessary to secure databases in production environments.

- Reset the password of the root user.

- Delete anonymous user accounts.

- Remove the test database, which was created by default during the installation.

- Disable remote root login.

- Enable password encryption.

- Reload privilege tables to ensure that all the changes made so far will take effect immediately.

Reset the password of the root user as shown here:

[root@mysqlhost01~]# /usr/bin/mysql_secure_installation

Securing the MySQL server deployment.

Enter password for user root:
The 'validate_password' component is installed on the server.
The subsequent steps will run with the existing configuration
of the component.
Using existing password for root.

Estimated strength of the password: 25
Change the password for root ? ((Press y|Y for Yes, any other key
for No) : **Y**

New password:
Re-enter new password:

Estimated strength of the password: 100
Do you wish to continue with the password provided?(Press y|Y for Yes, any
other key for No) : Y
By default, a MySQL installation has an anonymous user,
allowing anyone to log into MySQL without having to have
a user account created for them. This is intended only for
testing, and to make the installation go a bit smoother.
You should remove them before moving into a production
environment.

Delete anonymous user accounts as shown below.

By default, a MySQL installation has an anonymous user,
allowing anyone to log into MySQL without having to have
a user account created for them. This is intended only for
testing, and to make the installation go a bit smoother.
You should remove them before moving into a production
environment.

Remove anonymous users? (Press y|Y for Yes, any other key for No) : Y
Success.

Disable remote root login as shown here:

```
Normally, root should only be allowed to connect from
'localhost'. This ensures that someone cannot guess at
the root password from the network.
```

Disallow root login remotely? (Press y|Y for Yes, any other key for No) : Y
```
Success.
```

Remove the test database that was created by default during the installation:

```
By default, MySQL comes with a database named 'test' that
anyone can access. This is also intended only for testing,
and should be removed before moving into a production
environment.
```

Remove test database and access to it? (Press y|Y for Yes, any other key for No) : Y
```
 - Dropping test database...
Success.
```

```
 - Removing privileges on test database...
Success.
```

```
Reloading the privilege tables will ensure that all changes
made so far will take effect immediately.
```

Reload privilege tables now? (Press y|Y for Yes, any other key for No) : Y
```
Success.
```

```
All done!
```

Changing the Default Port in MySQL

Changing the default port in MySQL is very important for various reasons:

- **Security**: We can make it more difficult for attackers to find and exploit vulnerabilities in our MySQL server by changing the default port 3306 to some other port.

- **Compliance:** As a standard practice, we can implement compliance requirements that certain ports are not allowed to be open.

- **Reliability:** It helps us to reduce the port contention when we run multiple MySQL servers on the same machine.

How to Change the Ports

We can change the default port in the MySQL configuration file (/etc/my.cnf on Linux machines).

$ ls -ltr /etc/my.cnf
```
-rw-r--r-- 1 root root 1243 Jun 21 02:13 /etc/my.cnf
```

Check what port the database is running:

[root@mysqlhost01~]# netstat -alnp|grep mysql |grep tcp
```
tcp6     0     0      :::3306      :::*      LISTEN      1109150/mysqld
```

Changing the Port Numbers

1. Update /etc/my.cnf with port parameter, and use the port number as you require (add this value if it doesn't exist).

   [root@mysqlhost01~]# cat /etc/my.cnf |grep port
   ```
   # Remove leading # and set to the amount of RAM for the
   most important data
   # Remove leading # to set options mainly useful for
   reporting servers.
   port=8306
   ```

2. Restart the MySQL server to take effect.

   [root@mysqlhost01~]# systemctl restart mysqld

3. Validate port.

   [root@mysqlhost01~]# netstat -alnp|grep mysql |grep tcp
   ```
   tcp6     0     0      :::8306      :::*      LISTEN      2271642/mysqld
   ```

How to Run MySQL As a Non-root User

To enhance the security of MySQL database server, it is highly recommended to run MySQL as a non-root user, and it helps to protect the database from attacks and potential vulnerabilities.

Note   If the installation is done using the repository or rpm, mysqld should be run by the root user.

You can mysqld non-root user in case installation is done by the *.tar packages; there is a prerequisite for changing the user; datadir needs to be changed to non-root user so database OS users can write to the data files.

Change Default datadir and Run As Non-root User

It is preferred to move the non-root partition as MySQL data should not be kept in the root mount. This is because the root mount is typically the smallest partition on a system, and it is also the partition that contains the most critical system files. If the MySQL data directory is located on the root mount, it can fill up quickly, which can lead to performance problems or even system failure.

First, stop the MySQL server.

```
[root@mysqlhost01~]# systemctl stop mysql
```

Copy existing data (it's preferred to move the non-root partition).

```
[root@mysqlhost01~]# mkdir -p /opt/app/mysql
[root@mysqlhost01~]# chown mysql:mysql /opt/app/mysql
[root@mysqlhost01~]# cp -pr /var/lib/mysql/* /opt/app/mysql
[root@mysqlhost01~]# chmod -R 755 /opt/app/mysql
```

Update Config to Change the User

Update the MySQL configuration file /etc/my.cnf.

```
[mysqld]
datadir=/opt/app/mysql
user=mysql
```

Start MySQL server.

[root@mysqlhost01~]# systemctl start mysql

Validate user process.

[root@mysqlhost01~] # ps -ef|grep mysql
```
mysql    2271642      1  0 12:19 ?           00:00:06 /usr/sbin/mysqld
```

Data-at-Rest Encryption (DARE/TDE)

Data-at-rest encryption is supported by the default MySQL storage engine InnoDB, and it is essential to secure the data in MySQL databases; it was first introduced in MySQL 5.7.11. InnoDB provides data-at-rest encryption for file-per-table tablespaces, general tablespaces, MySQL system tablespaces, redo logs, and undo logs.

Database encryption at rest, also called TDE (Transparent Data Encryption), protects data stored in the operating files and disks. Data files stored in the disk or tape media can be directly accessed by unauthorized users, and it can cause data exfiltration.

DARE helps to secure data in the files or media from unauthorized access. MySQL offers the transparent nature of access to users by loading the modules during the startup, which allows the transparent encryption/decryption on the database using the keyring.

InnoDB uses a two-tier encryption key architecture:

- **Master encryption key:** Used to encrypt and decrypt tablespace keys

- **Tablespace key:** An encrypted key that is stored in the tablespace header

Applications/users request to access encrypted tablespace data. InnoDB uses a master encryption key to decrypt the tablespace key. The master encryption key is created upon enabling tablespace encryption and is maintained outside the database. The tablespace key, once decrypted, remains constant, while the master encryption key can be modified as needed.

Note   It supports only the Advanced Encryption Standard (AES) encryption algorithm.

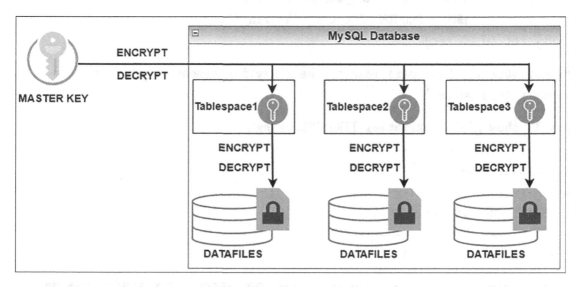

Figure 10-1. *Encryption of database files on the disk with tablespace and master key*

Prerequisites of Encryption

At startup, the installation and configuration of a keyring component or plug-in are required. This early setup ensures that the component or plug-in is ready for use before the InnoDB storage engine initialization begins.

We should enable only one keyring component or plug-in at a time. Enabling multiple keyring components or plug-ins is not supported and may lead to unexpected results.

Starting from MySQL 8.0.16, the default_table_encryption variable determines encryption settings for schemas and general tablespaces; it applies only at the time we use CREATE TABLESPACE and CREATE SCHEMA but does not apply for ALTER SCHEMA and ALTER TABLESPACE.

Pre-checks for Enabling Encryption

Before enabling encryption:

```
[root@mysqlhost01~]# mysql -u root -p
Enter password:

mysql> SELECT PLUGIN_NAME, PLUGIN_STATUS
    ->          FROM INFORMATION_SCHEMA.PLUGINS
    ->          WHERE PLUGIN_NAME LIKE 'keyring%';
Empty set (0.00 sec)

mysql> SELECT * FROM performance_schema.keyring_component_status;
Empty set (0.00 sec)

mysql> show global variables like '%keyring%';
+---------------------+-------+
| Variable_name       | Value |
+---------------------+-------+
| keyring_operations  | ON    |
+---------------------+-------+
1 row in set (0.00 sec)

mysql> select plugin_name, plugin_status FROM INFORMATION_SCHEMA.PLUGINS
WHERE plugin_name LIKE '%keyring%';
+-----------------------------+---------------+
| plugin_name                 | plugin_status |
+-----------------------------+---------------+
| daemon_keyring_proxy_plugin | ACTIVE        |
+-----------------------------+---------------+
1 row in set (0.00 sec)

mysql> show global variables like 'default_table_encryption';
+--------------------------+-------+
| Variable_name            | Value |
+--------------------------+-------+
| default_table_encryption | OFF   |
+--------------------------+-------+
```

Enable Encryption

For enabling the encryption, the following variables are to be addedin the /etc/my.cnf file to log in the plug-in and restart MySQL services or load the plug-in globally.

```
[mysqld] early-plugin-load=keyring_file.so
```

We can use the following syntax to enable encryption globally:

```
mysql> SET GLOBAL default_table_encryption=ON;
Query OK, 0 rows affected (0.00 sec)
```

Post Enable Encryption

```
[root@mysqlhost01~]# mysql -u root -p
Enter password:
```

```
mysql> show global variables like '%keyring%';
+--------------------+-------------------------------+
| Variable_name      | Value                         |
+--------------------+-------------------------------+
| keyring_file_data  | /var/lib/mysql-keyring/keyring |
| keyring_operations | ON                            |
+--------------------+-------------------------------+
2 rows in set (0.00 sec)
```

```
mysql> show global variables like 'default_table_encryption';
+--------------------------+-------+
| Variable_name            | Value |
+--------------------------+-------+
| default_table_encryption | ON    |
+--------------------------+-------+
1 row in set (0.00 sec)
```

General Tablespace Encryption

```
mysql> create tablespace test01 add datafile 'test01.ibd' ENCRYPTION ='Y'
Engine=InnoDB;
Query OK, 0 rows affected (0.01 sec)
```

Verify Encrypted Tablespaces

```
mysql> select space,name, space_type, encryption from
information_schema.innodb_tablespaces where encryption='Y';
+--------+-----------------+------------+------------+
| space  | name            | space_type | encryption |
+--------+-----------------+------------+------------+
|      2 | test01          | General    | Y          |
+--------+-----------------+------------+------------+
```

File-per-Table Tablespace Encryption

It adopts the default encryption of the schema in which the table is created, unless an ENCRYPTION clause is explicitly specified.

```
[root@mysqlhost01~]# mysql -u root -p
Enter password:

mysql> CREATE TABLE ITEMS (
    ->      item_id INT AUTO_INCREMENT PRIMARY KEY,
    ->      item_name VARCHAR(255) NOT NULL,
    ->      item_description TEXT,
    ->      item_price DECIMAL(10, 2),
    ->      quantity_in_stock INT
    -> )  ENCRYPTION = 'Y';
Query OK, 0 rows affected (0.02 sec)

mysql> select table_schema, table_name, create_options from information_
schema.tables where table_schema ='inventory';
```

```
+--------------+------------+-----------------+
| TABLE_SCHEMA | TABLE_NAME | CREATE_OPTIONS  |
+--------------+------------+-----------------+
| inventory    | ITEMS      | ENCRYPTION='Y'  |
+--------------+------------+-----------------+
1 row in set (0.00 sec)
```

Redo Log Encryption

Redo log encryption is disabled by default; however, we can enable using the innodb_redo_log_encrypt configuration option.

When "innodb_redo_log_encrypt" is enabled, existing unencrypted redo log pages on disk will remain unencrypted, while new redo log pages are written in an encrypted format. Conversely, when "innodb_redo_log_encrypt" is disabled, existing encrypted redo log pages on disk will remain encrypted, and newly written redo log pages will be stored in an unencrypted format.

Undo Log Encryption

Undo log encryption is disabled by default; however, we can enable using the innodb_undo_log_encrypt.

If "innodb_undo_log_encrypt" is enabled, existing undo log pages on an unencrypted disk will stay unencrypted, and any new undo log pages will be written to disk in an encrypted format. Conversely, when "innodb_undo_log_encrypt" is disabled, existing encrypted undo log pages on disk will remain encrypted, and new undo log pages will be stored in an unencrypted form.

Master Key Rotation

The master encryption key should undergo regular rotation and should also be rotated whenever there is suspicion that the key may have been compromised.

```
[root@mysqlhost01~]# mysql -u root -p
Enter password:
```

```
mysql> ALTER INSTANCE ROTATE INNODB MASTER KEY;
Query OK, 0 rows affected (0.00 sec)

mysql> select * from performance_schema.keyring_keys;
+-------------------------------------------------+-----------+----------------+
| KEY_ID                                          | KEY_OWNER | BACKEND_KEY_ID |
+-------------------------------------------------+-----------+----------------+
| INNODBKey-ad86c716-63c7-11ee-adf5-005056892298-1 |           |                |
| INNODBKey-ad86c716-63c7-11ee-adf5-005056892298-2 |           |                |
+-------------------------------------------------+-----------+----------------+
2 rows in set (0.00 sec)
```

Database Encryption in Transit (SSL/TLS)

Enabling encryption in transit using SSL/TLS in MySQL is a crucial security practice to protect data as it travels between the MySQL client and server. MySQL supports multiple TLS protocols and ciphers and enables configuring which protocols and ciphers to permit for encrypted connections.

When we set require_secure_transport to ON, MySQL will only allow connections established over SSL/TLS (Secure Sockets Layer/Transport Layer Security) encrypted connections.

To enhance the security of your MySQL connections, follow these best practices:

- Make sure to use strong encryption algorithms and key lengths for our SSL certificates.

- Keep updating and patching MySQL databases to get the latest security fixes and improvements.

- Implement firewall and ACLs to restrict access to MySQL server.

- Monitor server logs and SSL connections to identify any unusual activity.

- Ensure to renew SSL certificates as and when needed.

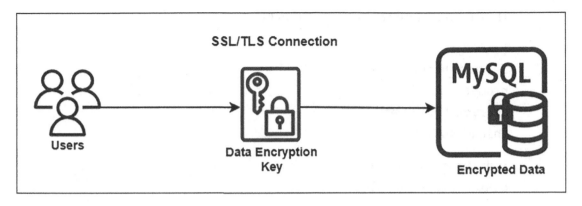

Figure 10-2. *Encryption with SSL/TLS certificates*

1. **How to generate certificates.**

    MySQL with installation provides the cert files, but these
    are default certificates that are not recommended for
    enterprise deployments as these are not issued by a certificate
    authority (CA).

    ```
    [root@mysqlhost01 ~]# ls -lhtr /var/lib/mysql  |grep pem
    -rw------- 1 mysql mysql 1.7K Oct 12 00:53 ca-key.pem
    -rw-r--r-- 1 mysql mysql 1.1K Oct 12 00:53 ca.pem
    -rw------- 1 mysql mysql 1.7K Oct 12 00:53 server-key.pem
    -rw-r--r-- 1 mysql mysql 1.1K Oct 12 00:53 server-cert.pem
    -rw------- 1 mysql mysql 1.7K Oct 12 00:53 client-key.pem
    -rw-r--r-- 1 mysql mysql 1.1K Oct 12 00:53 client-cert.pem
    -rw------- 1 mysql mysql 1.7K Oct 12 00:53 private_key.pem
    -rw-r--r-- 1 mysql mysql  452 Oct 12 00:53 public_key.pem
    ```

    It's recommended to use your organization's SSL files using
    trusted CA. Use the below methods to generate certificates.

    a. Generate a private key and CSR file. You can use OpenSSL to
        do this.

    b. You will need to create a configuration file to generate a CSR
        file using OpenSSL req -batch -config. The configuration file
        specifies the information included in the CSR file, such as the
        common name, organization name, and country.

Here is an example of a configuration file:

```
[ req ]
default_bits = 2048
prompt = no
encrypt_key = yes
unique_subject = yes

[ distinguished_name ]
commonName = example.com
organizationName = Example Company
countryName = the US
```

Once you have created the configuration file, you can generate the CSR file using the following command:

[root@mysqlhost01~]# openssl req -batch -config config.txt -out hostname.com.csr

This will create a CSR file called hostname.com.csr.

We can also use the mysql_ssl_rsa_setup utility that is included with MySQL, and it can be used to create the SSL certificate and private key files required to enable TLS encryption for MySQL connections.

Submit the CSR file to a certificate authority (CA) for an SSL certificate. There are many CAs available, like in-house CAs, commercial CAs, and open source CAs; we can choose one of them based on our requirements.

Install/copy the SSL (cert and key) certificates issued by the CA on your MySQL server.

2. **Configure the MySQL server for SSL connections in /etc/my.cnf.**

```
[mysqld]

# Path to the server certificates and key files
ssl_ca=/opt/app/certs/ca-cert.pem
```

```
ssl_cert=/opt/app/certs/hostname-cert.pem
ssl_key=/opt/app/certs/hostname-key.pem
require_secure_transport=ON
```

3. **Restart mysqld daemon.**

   [root@mysqlhost01~]# systemctl restart mysqld

4. **Create a user and test the connection from the client.**

   Create a user using the X509 authentication method.

   [mysql@mysqlhost01~]$ mysql -uroot -p
   Enter password:

   mysql> alter user 'mysqluser'@'10.10.10.100%' identified by 'Password@123' REQUIRE X509;
   Query OK, 0 rows affected (0.01 sec)

   mysql> flush privileges;
   Query OK, 0 rows affected (0.00 sec)

   Copy the client certs from MySQL server to the client machine.

   [mysql@mysqlhost01~]$ cd /var/lib/mysql/

   [mysql@mysqlhost01~]$ scp -i /var/lib/mysql/client* mysql@10.10.10.100

   Test the connection from the client machine.

   [mysql@mysqlclient01 ~]$ mysql -umysqluser -p --ssl-cert=client-cert.pem --ssl-key=client-key.pem -h mysqlhost01
   Enter password:

5. **Log in to MySQL and check the TLS versions supported.**

   [root@mysqlhost01~]# mysql -u root -p
   Enter password:

   mysql> SHOW GLOBAL VARIABLES LIKE 'tls_version';

```
+---------------+-----------------+
| Variable_name | Value           |
+---------------+-----------------+
| tls_version   | TLSv1.2,TLSv1.3 |
+---------------+-----------------+
1 row in set (0.00 sec)
```

Please use the following table to understand the supported TLS versions with MySQL database versions.

Table 10-2. *MySQL versions and TLS support matrix*

MySQL Versions	TLS Support
>8.0.28	TLSv1.2 and TLSv1.3
8.0.18 to 8.0.25	TLSv1, TLSv1.1, TLSv1.2, TLSv1.3
8.0.16 to 8.0.17	TLSv1, TLSv1.1, TLSv1.2, TLSv1.3 (No Group Replication)
<=8.0.15	TLSv1, TLSv1.1, TLSv1.2

Secure MySQL Backups

Securing database backup files is one of the critical security items as backups are stored for a longer time. They are moved between servers and storage media.

Implement secure methods for backup to secure overall backup files by enabling encryption on the backups and not hard-coding the login credentials of the root user in any backup script.

To store the credentials, we can use mysql_config_editor to store them securely. This utility enhances security when automating scripts or applications that interact with MySQL without exposing plain text passwords.

Creating a login path in the MySQL login path file is a convenient way to store your connection information and avoid having to enter it every time you want to connect to the server. It is also a more secure way to store your password, as it is encrypted in the login path file.

```
[root@mysqlhost01~]#mysql_config_editor set --login-path=backupUser
--host=localhost --user=root --password
```

```
[root@mysqlhost01~]# file /root/.mylogin.cnf
/root/.mylogin.cnf: data
```

Now it will allow us to back up using mysqldump without prompting for password.

```
[root@mysqlhost01~]#mysqldump --login-path=backupUser  --lock-all-tables
--set-gtid-purged=OFF --all-databases --triggers --routines --events >
/opt/app/Allbackup-${date}.sql
[root@mysqlhost01~]
```

Use Encryption Along with mysqldump

1. Generate an encryption key.

   [root@mysqlhost01~]#openssl rand -base64 32

2. Encrypt the backup using the preceding encryption key.

   [root@mysqlhost01~]#mysqldump --all-databases --single-transaction --triggers --routines | gzip | openssl enc -aes-256-cbc <encryption_key> > /opt/app/Allbackup-${date}.enc
   ```
   file Allbackup-20230214-18-1697331601.sql
   Allbackup-20230214-18-1697331601.enc: openssl enc'd data
   with salted password
   ```

   - Use a strong encryption key. The encryption key is used to encrypt and decrypt the backup, so it is important to use a strong key.

   - Keep the encryption key secret. Do not share the encryption key with anyone you do not trust.

   - Store the encryption key in a secure location. You should store the encryption key securely, such as a password manager or a hardware security module (HSM).

   - Test your backups regularly to make sure that they are restorable.

mysqldump-secure is a third-party tool, and it is a very powerful tool that helps to have secure backups of our MySQL databases; it does the following:

- It can encrypt backups using OpenSSL and compress backups using gzip, bzip2, xz, lzma, pigz, or pbzip2.

- It can back up multiple databases at once; also it helps to exclude certain tables from being backed up.

- We can control the number of backups it can keep, and it can automatically rotate backups.

Enterprise Firewall

Firewall is a set of rules rendered in runtime to decide on accepting or rejecting a client SQL statement.

Enterprise Firewall is a plug-in available in the Enterprise Edition of MySQL that is useful in setting up and guarding the database against SQL injections and other attacks.

Firewall can be interpreted as a set of rules stored in the buffer and checked against every SQL statement being executed; in order to optimize the performance, they are grouped and executed at runtime.

All the profile rules are custom defined, and users have flexibility to adjust and define an action for the statement matching.

Installing the Firewall Plug-in

```
mysql> SHOW GLOBAL VARIABLES LIKE 'mysql_firewall_mode';
Empty set (0.01 sec)

[root@mysqlhost01~]# mysql -u root -p <
/usr/share/mysql-8.0/linux_install_firewall.sql
Enter password:
```

Configuring the Firewall Plug-in

Create a user and enable the recording mode; all the queries executed by the user are captured and loaded into the database.

```
mysql> CREATE USER 'mysqluser'@'localhost' IDENTIFIED BY 'password';

mysql> GRANT ALL ON test TO 'mysqluser'@'localhost'

mysql> CALL mysql.sp_set_firewall_mode('mysqluser'@localhost',
'RECORDING');;
+------------------------------------------------+
| read_firewall_whitelist(arg_userhost,FW.rule)  |
+------------------------------------------------+
| Imported users: 0 Imported rules: 0            |
+------------------------------------------------+
1 row in set (0.00 sec)

Query OK, 0 rows affected (0.00 sec)

mysql> SELECT MODE FROM INFORMATION_SCHEMA.MYSQL_FIREWALL_USERS
    ->         WHERE USERHOST = 'mysqluser'@localhost';
+-----------+
| MODE      |
+-----------+
| RECORDING |
+-----------+
1 row in set (0.00 sec)
```

Understanding Different Operational Modes

In the preceding example, we have enabled firewall for a user (mysqluser) in the recording mode; we will examine different modes firewall operates.

```
mysql> SELECT RULE FROM INFORMATION_SCHEMA.MYSQL_FIREWALL_WHITELIST WHERE
USERHOST = 'mysqluser@localhost';
```

```
+-----------------------------------------------------------------------------+
| RULE                                                                        |
+-----------------------------------------------------------------------------+
| SELECT * FROM `employee_table`                                              |
| SHOW SCHEMAS                                                                 |
| SELECT * FROM `Companies`                                                    |
| SHOW TABLES                                                                  |
| SELECT SCHEMA ( )                                                           |
| SELECT `RULE` FROM `INFORMATION_SCHEMA` . `MYSQL_FIREWALL_WHITELIST` WHERE `USERHOST` = ? |
| SELECT @@`version_comment` LIMIT ?                                          |
+-----------------------------------------------------------------------------+
7 rows in set (0.00 sec)
```

OFF	This is the default option, or we can turn off the firewall when we need to disable the firewall functionality.
RECORDING	In this mode, the firewall records all the queries executed by the user against the database.
PROTECTING	When protection is set, the queries in the profile are being protected; that is, they will be rejected and the user would not be able to run against the database.
DETECTING	When detection is set, the firewall will not block the statements from execution. In this mode, the firewall writes the suspected statement to the log file and continues to execute them.

Enable Protection Mode

mysql> CALL mysql.sp_set_firewall_group_mode('mysqluser@localhost', 'PROTECTING');

Now queries captured in the recording mode will be blocked as we have enabled the protection mode on the mysqluser.

mysql> SELECT * FROM `Companies` ;
```
ERROR 1045 (28000): Statement was blocked by Firewall
```

Enterprise Audit

Restricting access alone will not help secure access from the outside world; we must audit regularly within our organization. We need to audit users' activity, admins, and also overall application.

Database auditing is vital to every organization's compliance with governmental, financial, and ISO regulations. It helps to track users' actions like selecting and modifying the data and user privilege grants in the database.

MySQL Audit capabilities are available only in the Enterprise Edition, and use the following steps to enable auditing:

1. **Install the MySQL plug-in.**

   /usr/share/mysql-8.0/audit_log_filter_linux_install.sql, which is installed along with MySQL Enterprise Edition installation, and load the plug-in.

   Before MySQL 8.0.34:

   ```
   [root@mysqlhost01~]# mysql -u root -p <
   /usr/share/mysql-8.0/audit_log_filter_linux_install.sql
   Enter password:
   Result
   OK
   ```

   MySQL 8.0.34 and higher:

   ```
   [root@mysqlhost01~]# mysql -u root -p -D mysql <
   /usr/share/mysql-8.0/audit_log_filter_linux_install.sql
   Enter password:
   Result
   OK
   ```

2. **Validate the plug-in status.**

   ```
   [root@mysqlhost01~]# mysql -u root -p
   Enter password:

   mysql> SELECT PLUGIN_NAME, PLUGIN_STATUS
       -> FROM INFORMATION_SCHEMA.PLUGINS
       -> WHERE PLUGIN_NAME LIKE 'audit%';
   ```

```
+--------------+----------------+
| PLUGIN_NAME  | PLUGIN_STATUS  |
+--------------+----------------+
| audit_log    | ACTIVE         |
+--------------+----------------+
1 row in set (0.00 sec)

mysql> SELECT VARIABLE_NAME, VARIABLE_VALUE
    -> FROM performance_schema.global_variables
    -> WHERE VARIABLE_NAME LIKE 'audit_log_encryption' ;
+-----------------------+----------------+
| VARIABLE_NAME         | VARIABLE_VALUE |
+-----------------------+----------------+
| audit_log_encryption  | NONE           |
+-----------------------+----------------+
1 row in set (0.00 sec)

mysql> select @@datadir, @@audit_log_file;
+-----------------+-------------------+
| @@datadir       | @@audit_log_file  |
+-----------------+-------------------+
| /var/lib/mysql/ | audit.log         |
+-----------------+-------------------+
1 row in set (0.00 sec)
```

Make Plug-in Persistent

Once you install/enable MySQL Audit log, use --audit-log to load the audit plug-in during the subsequent restarts. Edit the /etc/my.cnf, add the following lines, and restart the mysqld.

```
[mysqld]
audit-log=FORCE_PLUS_PERMANENT
```

[root@mysqlhost01~]# systemctl restart mysqld

[root@mysqlhost01~]# mysql -uroot -p
```
Enter password:
```

```
mysql> SELECT PLUGIN_NAME, PLUGIN_STATUS
    -> FROM INFORMATION_SCHEMA.PLUGINS
    -> WHERE PLUGIN_NAME LIKE 'audit%';
+-------------+---------------+
| PLUGIN_NAME | PLUGIN_STATUS |
+-------------+---------------+
| audit_log   | ACTIVE        |
+-------------+---------------+
1 row in set (0.00 sec)

mysql> SELECT VARIABLE_NAME, VARIABLE_VALUE
    -> FROM performance_schema.global_variables
    -> WHERE VARIABLE_NAME LIKE 'audit_log_encryption' ;
+----------------------+----------------+
| VARIABLE_NAME        | VARIABLE_VALUE |
+----------------------+----------------+
| audit_log_encryption | NONE           |
+----------------------+----------------+
1 row in set (0.01 sec)

mysql> select @@datadir, @@audit_log_file;
+----------------+------------------+
| @@datadir      | @@audit_log_file |
+----------------+------------------+
| /var/lib/mysql/ | audit.log       |
+----------------+------------------+
1 row in set (0.00 sec)
```

Enable Auditing for All the Users

In the latest version of MySQL, auditing is by default not enabled for any users (this is different from legacy behavior) even with the plug-in active. Rule-based filters are needed to enable the auditing. The following is an example filter that logs all the user activity in the audit log:

```
mysql> SELECT audit_log_filter_set_filter('log_all', '{ "filter":
{ "log": true } }');
```

```
+----------------------------------------------------------------------+
| audit_log_filter_set_filter('log_all', '{ "filter": { "log": true } }') |
+----------------------------------------------------------------------+
| OK                                                                   |
+----------------------------------------------------------------------+
1 row in set (0.01 sec)

mysql> SELECT audit_log_filter_set_user('%', 'log_all');
+-------------------------------------------+
| audit_log_filter_set_user('%', 'log_all') |
+-------------------------------------------+
| OK                                        |
+-------------------------------------------+
1 row in set (0.00 sec)
```

Validate Audit Logs

We have enabled the audit logging and created the rule to capture the audit logs; now examine the audit log behavior and content in the audit log. Get the audit log location from the database.

```
mysql> select @@datadir, @@audit_log_file;
+-----------------+------------------+
| @@datadir       | @@audit_log_file |
+-----------------+------------------+
| /var/lib/mysql/ | audit.log        |
+-----------------+------------------+
1 row in set (0.00 sec)
```

Check the location on the OS:

```
[root@mysqlhost01~]# ls  /var/lib/mysql/audit.log
/var/lib/mysql/audit.log
```

Create example table in the database:

```
mysql> CREATE TABLE test.Companies (
    ->    id int,
    ->    name varchar(50),
```

```
    ->    address text,
    ->    email varchar(50),
    ->    phone varchar(10)
    -> );
```
Query OK, 0 rows affected (0.01 sec)

Examine the content in the audit log:

[root@mysqlhost01~]# tail 100   /var/lib/mysql/audit.log

```
 </AUDIT_RECORD>
 <AUDIT_RECORD>
  <TIMESTAMP>2023-10-14T16:51:51 UTC</TIMESTAMP>
  <RECORD_ID>4_2023-10-14T16:47:18</RECORD_ID>
  <NAME>Query</NAME>
  <CONNECTION_ID>12</CONNECTION_ID>
  <STATUS>0</STATUS>
  <STATUS_CODE>0</STATUS_CODE>
  <USER>root[root] @ localhost []</USER>
  <OS_LOGIN/>
  <HOST>localhost</HOST>
  <IP/>
  <COMMAND_CLASS>create_table</COMMAND_CLASS>
  <SQLTEXT>CREATE TABLE test.Companies (
 id int,
 name varchar(50),
 address text,
 email varchar(50),
 phone varchar(10)
)</SQLTEXT>
 </AUDIT_RECORD>
 <AUDIT_RECORD>
  <TIMESTAMP>2023-10-14T16:52:07 UTC</TIMESTAMP>
  <RECORD_ID>5_2023-10-14T16:47:18</RECORD_ID>
```

Role-Based Access Control

Role-based access control is a powerful security model that can help us to enhance the security of MySQL databases.

- It allows us to define roles and assign users to those roles.

- It helps in improving auditability; it will let us know who has access to what resources in our MySQL database.

- RBAC will allow us to view and manage the permissions at the role level rather than individual level.

- It helps us to comply with data protection regulations like GDPR (General Data Protection Regulation).

How Can We Implement RBAC in MySQL ?

1. Create a role in the database.

   ```
   [root@mysqlhost01~]# mysql -u root -p
   Enter password:
   ```

   ```
   mysql>CREATE ROLE SALESADMIN;
   ```

2. Grant permissions to the roles.

   ```
   mysql>GRANT SELECT, INSERT, UPDATE, DELETE ON INVENTORY.
   ITEMS TO SALESADMIN;
   ```

3. Assign users to the roles.

   ```
   mysql>GRANT SALESADMIN TO CHARLES;
   ```

Authentication with MySQL

MySQL database comes with different authentication options; with MySQL 8.0 and later, the support for different methods increased. In this section, we will discuss different authentication methods available in MySQL and supported versions.

Native Authentication

MySQL comes with three authentication plug-ins for native authentication using username/password.

From MySQL 8.0, caching_sha2_password is the default authentication plug-in. Before 8.0, mysql_native_password was an authentication plug-in used for basic authentication, and it's on the path to being deprecated.

sha256_password and caching_sha2_password implement the SHA-2 authentication plug-in, and caching_sha2_password uses server-side caching for better performance.

```
mysql> show plugins;
+---------------------------------+----------+----------------+---------+-------------+
| Name                            | Status   | Type           | Library | License     |
+---------------------------------+----------+----------------+---------+-------------+
|mysql_native_password            | ACTIVE   | AUTHENTICATION | NULL    | PROPRIETARY |
|sha256_password                  | ACTIVE   | AUTHENTICATION | NULL    | PROPRIETARY |
|caching_sha2_password            | ACTIVE   | AUTHENTICATION | NULL    | PROPRIETARY |
+---------------------------------+----------+----------------+---------+-------------+
```

Using sha256_password for authentication:

```
mysql> CREATE USER 'mysqluser'@'localhost'
    -> IDENTIFIED WITH sha256_password BY 'xxxxxx';
Query OK, 0 rows affected (0.01 sec)
```

To start the server with the default plug-in as sha256_password, edit /etc/my.cnf and update as follows:

```
[mysqld]
default_authentication_plugin=sha256_password
```

Now we can create a user without specifying the plug-in type explicitly.

```
mysql> CREATE USER 'mysqluser'@'localhost'
    -> IDENTIFIED BY 'xxxxxx';
Query OK, 0 rows affected (0.01 sec)
```

Using caching_sha2_password for authentication, the default authentication plug-in in MySQL 8.0 is caching_sha2_password.

```
mysql> CREATE USER 'mysqluser'@'localhost'
    -> IDENTIFIED WITH caching_sha2_password BY 'xxxxxxx';
Query OK, 0 rows affected (0.01 sec)
```

LDAP Authentication

LDAP (Lightweight Directory Access Protocol) authentication allows users to authenticate against organization LDAP servers. MySQL will delegate the authentication to the LDAP directory (Active Directory) instead of using local authentication.

Prerequisite for LDAP Authentication

To enable LDAP authentication, we need an LDAP server that is reachable from the MySQL database servers in the network.

LDAP should support the LDAP simple bind and SSL SASL on the LDAP server side.

Note   To use server-side authentication_ldap_sasl or authentication_ldap_simple plug-in, your LDAP server should support them.

Enable LDAP with Simple Bind

Plug-in authentication_ldap_simple allows users to connect to the LDAP server in cleartext password from MySQL to LDAP, but most organizations do not allow the simple bind. Ensuring your LDAP supports the simple bind on the LDAP port is important.

```
[root@mysqlhost01~]# cat /etc/my.cnf
# For advice on how to change settings please see
# http://dev.mysql.com/doc/refman/8.0/en/server-configuration-defaults.html

[mysqld]

plugin-load-add=authentication_ldap_simple.so
authentication_ldap_simple_server_host="ldap://myldap.company.com:389"
```

authentication_ldap_simple_bind_base_dn="dc=company,dc=com"

[root@mysqlhost01~]# systemctl restart mysqld

Validate the plug-in and create a user.

mysql> SELECT PLUGIN_NAME, PLUGIN_STATUS FROM INFORMATION_SCHEMA.PLUGINS WHERE PLUGIN_NAME LIKE '%ldap%';

```
+---------------------------+---------------+
| PLUGIN_NAME               | PLUGIN_STATUS |
+---------------------------+---------------+
| authentication_ldap_simple | ACTIVE       |
+---------------------------+---------------+
1 row in set (0.00 sec)
```

mysql> CREATE USER 'mysqluser'@'localhost'
** ->   IDENTIFIED WITH authentication_ldap_simple**
** ->   AS 'mysqluser,ou=People,dc=company,dc=com';**
```
Query OK, 0 rows affected (0.00 sec)
```

Connect to the database using LDAP authentication.

[root@mysqlhost01~]# mysql --user=mysqluser --password --enable-cleartext-plugin
```
Enter password: <enter your LDAP password>
```

Enable LDAP with SASL Plug-in

The major concern with LDAP simple bind is it connects to LDAP and sends the password in plain text; this is a security concern to most organizations and usually simple binds are disabled. We can use the SASL plug-in to address this, which sends the password in encrypted format.

Note This plug-in only supports the SCRAM-SHA-1 authentication method, and make sure your AD and LDAP support this authentication method.

```
[root@mysqlhost01~]# cat /etc/my.cnf
# For advice on how to change settings please see
# http://dev.mysql.com/doc/refman/8.0/en/server-configuration-defaults.html

[mysqld]

plugin-load-add=authentication_ldap_simple.so
authentication_ldap_simple_server_host="ldap://myldap.company.com:389"
authentication_ldap_simple_bind_base_dn="dc=company,dc=com"
plugin-load-add=authentication_ldap_sasl.so
authentication_ldap_sasl_server_host="ldaps://myldap.company.com:686"
authentication_ldap_sasl_bind_base_dn="dc=company,dc=com"
```

[root@mysqlhost01~]# systemctl restart mysqld

```
mysql> SELECT PLUGIN_NAME, PLUGIN_STATUS
       FROM INFORMATION_SCHEMA.PLUGINS
       WHERE PLUGIN_NAME LIKE '%ldap%';
+-----------------------------+---------------+
| PLUGIN_NAME                 | PLUGIN_STATUS |
+-----------------------------+---------------+
| authentication_ldap_sasl    | ACTIVE        |
| authentication_ldap_simple  | ACTIVE        |
+-----------------------------+---------------+

mysql> CREATE USER 'mysqluser'@'localhost'
    ->     IDENTIFIED WITH authentication_ldap_sasl
    ->     AS 'umysqluser,ou=People,dc=company,dc=com';
Query OK, 0 rows affected (0.00 sec)

mysql> exit
Bye
```

[root@mysqlhost01~]# mysql --user=mysqluser --password
```
Enter password: <enter your LDAP password>
```

PAM Authentication

PAM authentication addresses the limitation with LDAP plug-in with simple and SASL-based authentication. PAM (Pluggable Authentication Modules) enables the servers to use various authentication methods like Unix passwords or LDAP, etc.

The prerequisite for enabling the PAM authentication is that the server needs to be part of the LDAP, and ensure ldap.conf is configured and connected to LDAP servers. Contact your server admin or network team for help in setting up the LDAP on the server.

```
[root@mysqlhost01~]#  cat  /etc/ldap.conf
# Generated by Chef.
# Local modifications will be overwritten.
#
base dc=company,dc=com
ldap_version 3
nss_base_passwd dc=company,dc=com?sub
nss_base_shadow dc=company,dc=com?sub
nss_base_group OU=Unix Groups,OU=CompanySecurityGrp,DC=Company,DC=com
nss_map_objectclass posixAccount user
nss_map_objectclass shadowAccount user
nss_map_objectclass posixGroup group
nss_map_attribute gecos name
nss_map_attribute homeDirectory unixHomeDirectory
nss_map_attribute uniqueMember memberOf
nss_map_attribute loginShell loginShell
pam_filter objectClass=User
referrals no
scope sub
tls_cacertfile /etc/pem/tls-ca-cert.pem
tls_reqcert allow
uri ldaps://myldap.company.com/
```

Validate If Any LDAP Settings Are Used

```
mysql> SELECT PLUGIN_NAME, PLUGIN_STATUS
    ->         FROM INFORMATION_SCHEMA.PLUGINS
    ->         WHERE PLUGIN_NAME LIKE '%ldap%';
Empty set (0.00 sec)
```

Configure PAM to Use LDAP

Add the following entries in the PAM bridge file to LDAP:

```
[root@mysqlhost01~]#  cat /etc/pam.d/mysql-unix
#%PAM-1.0
auth            include         password-auth
account         include         password-auth
```

Restart the server to enable PAM and load into the database.

```
[root@mysqlhost01~]#  systemctl restart mysqld
```

Install auth_pam Plug-in

```
mysql> INSTALL PLUGIN auth_pam SONAME 'auth_pam.so';
Query OK, 0 rows affected (0.08 sec)

mysql> INSTALL PLUGIN auth_pam_compat SONAME 'auth_pam_compat.so';
Query OK, 0 rows affected (0.05 sec)

mysql> SELECT PLUGIN_NAME, PLUGIN_STATUS          FROM INFORMATION_SCHEMA.
PLUGINS         WHERE PLUGIN_NAME LIKE '%pam%';
+---------------------+---------------+
| PLUGIN_NAME         | PLUGIN_STATUS |
+---------------------+---------------+
| authentication_pam  | ACTIVE        |
+---------------------+---------------+
1 row in set (0.00 sec)
```

Create a user with PAM authentication:

```
mysql> CREATE USER mysqluser
  IDENTIFIED WITH authentication_pam
  AS 'mysql-unix';
```

Validate Login

We need to use --enable-cleartext-plugin to log in with PAM; this raises question on password in plain text; this is required because MySQL needs to capture the password in plain text and send it to PAM to validate against LDAP; PAM uses encryption when it connects with LDAP, but MySQL needs to provide it in plain text.

```
[root@mysqlhost01 ~]# mysql --user=mysqluser --password --enable-
cleartext-plugin
```

Sending a password in cleartext might raise concerns with the security. To address this, we can use TCP encryption from client to server so the password is unavailable in cleartext over the network.

It's security best practice to enable SSL for the client to the server, but this can be disabled by passing an argument --ssl-mode=DISABLED when trying to log in; we need to disable this, which allows the user to disable the SSL encryption.

Please follow these steps and enable require_secure_transport so users do not have the option to disable the SSL mode:

```
mysql> SELECT @@require_secure_transport;
+----------------------------+
| @@require_secure_transport |
+----------------------------+
|                          0 |
+----------------------------+
1 row in set (0.00 sec)

mysql> SET GLOBAL require_secure_transport = ON;
Query OK, 0 rows affected (0.00 sec)

mysql> SELECT @@require_secure_transport;
```

```
+-----------------------------+
| @@require_secure_transport |
+-----------------------------+
|                           1 |
+-----------------------------+
1 row in set (0.00 sec)
```

Windows Authentication

We can enable windows authentication for MySQL login; perform the following steps to enable windows authentication:

[mysqld]
plugin-load-add=authentication_windows.dll

Install windows authentication plugin.

mysql> INSTALL PLUGIN authentication_windows SONAME 'authentication_windows.dll';

mysql> SELECT PLUGIN_NAME, PLUGIN_STATUS
        FROM INFORMATION_SCHEMA.PLUGINS
        WHERE PLUGIN_NAME LIKE '%windows%';

```
+-------------------------+---------------+
| PLUGIN_NAME             | PLUGIN_STATUS |
+-------------------------+---------------+
| authentication_windows  | ACTIVE        |
+-------------------------+---------------+
```

Create mysqluser with windows authentication.

mysql> CREATE USER mysqluser
  IDENTIFIED WITH authentication_windows;

Log in with the mysqluser.

C:\> mysql --user=mysqluser

Summary

Securing the MySQL database is critical to protecting organizational data and meeting compliance requirements.

MySQL provides many features to enable and configure databases to the highest security standards, which helps improve the overall security posture of the databases.

Most tools for securing databases are available in the community version, and some require an enterprise edition of MySQL database. Implementing the security best practices when implementing the database helps to secure the database from known vulnerabilities and continue to focus on security as a key element to run secure database systems.

The next chapter will explore the MySQL performance tuning considerations, best practices on designing, architecting, and scaling MySQL database for optimum performance, and addressing the performance challenges in large-scale MySQL deployments.

CHAPTER 11

MySQL Performance Tuning

Introduction

Performance is one of the key areas where organizations focus as this directly impacts end users of the systems.

Performance tuning starts with good system architecture design and data based on the application type and user expectations. Performance is directly associated with organizations' revenue in highly transactional OLTP systems like shopping carts. System timeouts or bad user experience during checkout will lead to customers choosing a competitor to purchase the products. In contrast, in a batch-processing financial systems business, the customer controls the re-processing or waits for the system to complete the transactions.

Fundamental aspects of designing systems for performance start with baseline expectations of the performance of the database and additional tuning efforts to improve the system's overall performance.

Performance tuning has always been seen as a science. Still, it involves identifying the bottlenecks and understanding what good performance looks like and what areas must be focused on to improve the user experience.

Performance tuning has been projected as a cult skill and requires very advanced skills to solve them.

Tuning starts with understanding the fundamental aspects of the system, to be precise, asking questions about where the **time is spent**. Understanding and identifying where the time is spent by the query or applications will lead to many clues to solve them. This is the first step to understanding and tuning the system for better performance.

© Y V Ravi Kumar, Arun Kumar Samayam, Naresh Kumar Miryala 2024
Y V Ravi Kumar et al., *Mastering MySQL Administration*, https://doi.org/10.1007/979-8-8688-0252-2_11

There is a general tendency to tune the database aggressively, that is, identifying any top SQL and trying to tune or improve it. This approach might not sometimes lead to the expected results. Tuning needs to have the objective of addressing specific or general problems. Only some queries that run longer are problems in the database, and not every query runs longer.

An objective approach to performance tuning starts with ensuring identifying the benchmarking or understanding the capacity allocated and expected performance. This chapter will discuss the approach to performance tuning from the benchmark, design, deployment, and database tuning based on the applications/business requirements.

Design Database for Optimum Performance

Database performance depends on the hardware resources and database parameters, its combination of available system resources, and how they are adjusted to get optimum performance from the system.

Careful consideration of the application load, database size, and expected performance helps to design the system from hardware resources to database parameters.

It's good practice to perform the design and plan for the future growth of the database to avoid the performance issues at a later stage, which would require more effort to solve.

Server Requirements

System hardware resources play a critical role in the performance. Careful performance considerations are needed when choosing server resources to meet the performance requirements.

Three major resources impact the performance of the database.

CPU

CPU processing power makes a significant difference in the performance of the database. Number of CPU and the speed of the processor help to improve the overall performance. CPU cores anywhere from 16 to 96 can be chosen based on the performance requirements.

Memory

Server memory is directly related to database size and buffer size, based on the database size needed to get the RAM. This helps to have a higher buffer cache to improve the performance.

Disk Storage

Disk is an important consideration for a high IO-bound system with a high amount of data modifications. SSDs are preferred over spinning disks; high-performance SSDs provide IO throughput, which helps for better performance.

Database Settings

When you set up or install a database using default parameters, it's designed for small or medium-sized databases.

innodb_dedicated_server

This parameter was introduced in 8.0.30; when innodb_dedicated_server is set, InnoDB will configure the innodb_buffer_pool_size and innodb_redo_log_capacity automatically. Use innodb_dedicated_server only on dedicated servers where all the resources can be used for MySQL. This is recommended in Docker and dedicated server setup.

By default, this innodb_dedicated_server is disabled on the server, and innodb_buffer_pool_size and innodb_redo_log_capacity are enabled.

```
mysql> SHOW VARIABLES LIKE 'innodb_version';
+----------------+--------+
| Variable_name  | Value  |
+----------------+--------+
| innodb_version | 8.0.34 |
+----------------+--------+
1 row in set (0.00 sec)
```

```
mysql> SHOW VARIABLES LIKE 'innodb_dedicated_server';
+-------------------------+-------+
| Variable_name           | Value |
+-------------------------+-------+
| innodb_dedicated_server | OFF   |
+-------------------------+-------+
1 row in set (0.01 sec)

[mysqld]
innodb_dedicated_server=ON
mysql> SHOW VARIABLES LIKE 'innodb_dedicated_server';
+-------------------------+-------+
| Variable_name           | Value |
+-------------------------+-------+
| innodb_dedicated_server | ON    |
+-------------------------+-------+
1 row in set (0.00 sec)
```

Innodb_buffer_pool_size

Innodb_buffer_pool_size is a key performance parameter in setting the right memory allocation for the database that impacts overall performance. It's suggested to keep 70% of available memory on the server.

```
[mysqld]
innodb_buffer_pool_size=10G
```

```
mysql> SHOW VARIABLES LIKE 'Innodb_buffer_pool_size';
+-------------------------+-------------+
| Variable_name           | Value       |
+-------------------------+-------------+
| innodb_buffer_pool_size | 10737418240 |
+-------------------------+-------------+
1 row in set (0.00 sec)
```

Innodb_buffer_pool_instances

Innodb_buffer_pool_instances parameter helps to create multiple buffer pool instances to reduce contention in high transactional workload databases. It's suggested to start with 8, continue to monitor for performance optimization, and change the instances.

```
mysql> SHOW VARIABLES LIKE 'Innodb_buffer_pool_instances';
+-----------------------------+-------+
| Variable_name               | Value |
+-----------------------------+-------+
| innodb_buffer_pool_instances | 8    |
+-----------------------------+-------+
1 row in set (0.00 sec)
```

Innodb_log_file_size

Innodb_log_file_size parameter determines the size of the log file; for medium to large databases, 512M to 1G is considered a good size; setting too large would negatively impact the time taken for recovery.

Note   This parameter is deprecated from the 8.0.30 version.

```
mysql> SHOW VARIABLES LIKE 'Innodb_log_file_size';
+----------------------+----------+
| Variable_name        | Value    |
+----------------------+----------+
| innodb_log_file_size | 50331648 |
+----------------------+----------+
1 row in set (0.00 sec)
```

innodb_log_files_in_group

innodb_log_files_in_group controls the number of log files in the logfile group; the database writes in a circle to the log files; the default is 2, and it can be increased to 4 in a highly transactional database.

Note   This parameter is deprecated from the 8.0.30 version.

```
[mysqld]
innodb_log_files_in_group=ON
```

```
mysql> SHOW VARIABLES LIKE 'innodb_log_files_in_group';
+---------------------------+-------+
| Variable_name             | Value |
+---------------------------+-------+
| innodb_log_files_in_group | 2     |
+---------------------------+-------+
1 row in set (0.00 sec)
```

Innodb_redo_log_capacity

Innodb_redo_log_capacity parameter was introduced in 8.0.30; when innodb_redo_log_capacity is set, innodb_log_files_in_group and innodb_log_file_size settings are ignored. The minimum default value is 100M, and max is 128GB.

```
mysql> SHOW VARIABLES LIKE 'Innodb_redo_log_capacity';
+---------------------------+-----------+
| Variable_name             | Value     |
+---------------------------+-----------+
| innodb_redo_log_capacity  | 104857600 |
+---------------------------+-----------+
1 row in set (0.00 sec)
```

innodb_log_buffer_size

innodb_log_buffer_size defines the size of the database transaction log in the memory; the default size is 16MB, and it is suggested to have a larger buffer size in a large transaction processing system, which reduces the need to write the logs to the disk frequently.

```
mysql> SHOW VARIABLES LIKE 'innodb_log_buffer_size';
+------------------------+----------+
| Variable_name          | Value    |
+------------------------+----------+
| innodb_log_buffer_size | 16777216 |
+------------------------+----------+
1 row in set (0.00 sec)
```

Innodb_flush_log_at_trx_commit

Innodb_flush_log_at_trx_commit controls the database commit transaction's consistency; the default value is 1, which allows the logs to be written to the disk per each transaction. This parameter can be adjusted from 0 to 2, but it's highly recommended to keep this to 1.

```
mysql> SHOW VARIABLES LIKE 'Innodb_flush_log_at_trx_commit';
+--------------------------------+-------+
| Variable_name                  | Value |
+--------------------------------+-------+
| innodb_flush_log_at_trx_commit | 1     |
+--------------------------------+-------+
1 row in set (0.00 sec)
```

innodb_flush_log_at_timeout

The innodb_flush_log_at_timeout default value is once per second; this parameter controls the flush from buffer to disk interval time.

```
mysql> SHOW VARIABLES LIKE 'innodb_flush_log_at_timeout';
+-----------------------------+-------+
| Variable_name               | Value |
+-----------------------------+-------+
| innodb_flush_log_at_timeout | 1     |
+-----------------------------+-------+
1 row in set (0.00 sec)
```

innodb_file_per_table

innodb_file_per_table is used with InnoDB; with this parameter, file-per-table tablespace contains data and index for every single table and is stored on the disk as a single data file.

```
[mysqld]
innodb_file_per_table=ON
```

mysql> SET GLOBAL innodb_file_per_table=ON;
Query OK, 0 rows affected (0.00 sec)

mysql> SHOW VARIABLES LIKE 'innodb_file_per_table';

```
+-----------------------+-------+
| Variable_name         | Value |
+-----------------------+-------+
| innodb_file_per_table | ON    |
+-----------------------+-------+
1 row in set (0.00 sec)
```

mysql> USE test;
Database changed

mysql> CREATE TABLE TESTTABLE1 (name VARCHAR(20));
Query OK, 0 rows affected (0.01 sec)

[root@mysqlhost01 test]# cd /var/lib/mysql/test
[root@mysqlhost01 test]# ls -ltr TEST*
-rw-r----- 1 mysql mysql 114688 Oct 20 06:38 TESTTABLE1.ibd

mysql> SHOW VARIABLES LIKE 'Innodb_log_files_in_group';

```
+---------------------------+-------+
| Variable_name             | Value |
+---------------------------+-------+
| innodb_log_files_in_group | 2     |
+---------------------------+-------+
1 row in set (0.01 sec)
```

Innodb_doublewrite

Innodb_doublewrite is enabled by default; this parameter specifies the doublewrite buffer in the InnoDB buffer storage area where pages are flushed from the buffer pool before writing these pages into the data files.

Though it looks like doublewrite is writing the buffer pool pages twice, the amount of the IP overhead is not twice, and enabling the Innodb_doublewrite provides additional protection for the crash recovery where the good copied will be used for the Innodb_doublewrite buffer in case of system crash situations and during the crash recovery of the mysqld process.

```
mysql> SHOW VARIABLES LIKE 'Innodb_doublewrite';
+--------------------+-------+
| Variable_name      | Value |
+--------------------+-------+
| innodb_doublewrite | ON    |
+--------------------+-------+
1 row in set (0.01 sec)
```

Innodb_flush_method

Innodb_flush_method determines the flushing from buffer to disk; the default value is fsync, which is used in Linux/Unix operating systems.

This parameter has a significant impact on the performance. It's suggested to use the default value in most cases, and in case of locally attached fast IP, O_DIRECT can be used. Using O_DIRECT will avoid the doublewrite buffer.

```
mysql> SHOW VARIABLES LIKE 'Innodb_flush_method';
+---------------------+-------+
| Variable_name       | Value |
+---------------------+-------+
| innodb_flush_method | fsync |
+---------------------+-------+
1 row in set (0.00 sec)
```

sort_buffer_size

sort_buffer_size determines the amount of memory for a buffer allocated for the sessions performing sort operations. This parameter is not specific to any storage engine.

This parameter has a significant impact on the performance; it needs to be adjusted to handle additional workload for the sort operations like order by and group by.

The max size allocated for this parameter is 4GB.

```
mysql> SHOW VARIABLES LIKE 'sort_buffer_size';
+------------------+--------+
| Variable_name    | Value  |
+------------------+--------+
| sort_buffer_size | 262144 |
+------------------+--------+
1 row in set (0.01 sec)
```

join_buffer_size

join_buffer_size determines the amount of buffer allocated for index scans and full table scans; increasing the value of this parameter helps improve performance when creating additional indexes is not possible.

The default allocated size is 256KB, and max value for this parameter is 4GB.

```
mysql> SHOW VARIABLES LIKE 'join_buffer_size';
+------------------+--------+
| Variable_name    | Value  |
+------------------+--------+
| join_buffer_size | 262144 |
+------------------+--------+
1 row in set (0.00 sec)
```

read_buffer_size

read_buffer_size is mainly used in the MyISAM storage engine; each request that performs a sequential scan of the table allocates a read buffer.

The value is multiple of 4 KB; this parameter is used for bulk insert into partitions and caching nested results.

```
mysql> SHOW VARIABLES LIKE 'read_buffer_size';
+------------------+--------+
| Variable_name    | Value  |
+------------------+--------+
| read_buffer_size | 131072 |
+------------------+--------+
1 row in set (0.00 sec)
```

log_queries_not_using_indexes

log_queries_not_using_indexes enables MySQL to log all the queries not using the indexes in a slow query log.

The general behavior is only the long_query_time that determines a query to be listed in the slow query log, when log_queries_not_using_indexes is enabled all the queries irrespective of the long_query_time parameter.

```
mysql> SHOW VARIABLES LIKE 'log_queries_not_using_indexes';
+-------------------------------+-------+
| Variable_name                 | Value |
+-------------------------------+-------+
| log_queries_not_using_indexes | OFF   |
+-------------------------------+-------+
1 row in set (0.00 sec)
```

Best Practices for Performance Optimization

For improved performance and utilizing the optimum database resources, please follow best practices in setting up the MySQL database.

Database Config Changes

As discussed in the "Database Settings" section, please set up the /etc/my.cnf with tuned parameter values to get the best results with the performance.

[root@mysqlhost01 ~]# free -gt

	total	used	free	shared	buff/cache	available
Mem:	15	9	0	0	5	5
Swap:	3	0	3			
Total:	19	9	4			

[root@mysqlhost01 ~]# lscpu

```
Architecture:            x86_64
  CPU op-mode(s):        32-bit, 64-bit
  Address sizes:         43 bits physical, 48 bits virtual
  Byte Order:            Little Endian
CPU(s):                  8
  On-line CPU(s) list:   0-7
```

Please use the following parameters for small/mid-sized database; edit the /etc/my.cnf with the following:

MySQL 8.0 with dedicated server parameters:

```
[mysqld]
innodb_dedicated_server = 1
innodb_buffer_pool_instances = 24
innodb_log_buffer_size = 48M
innodb_file_per_table = 1
max_connections = 500
slow-query-log = 1
slow_query_log_file = /var/log/slow_query.log
```

MySQL 8.0 without dedicated server parameters:

```
[mysqld]
innodb_buffer_pool_size = 10G
innodb_buffer_pool_instances = 24
Innodb_redo_log_capacity = 32G
innodb_log_buffer_size = 48M
innodb_file_per_table = 1
max_connections = 500
slow-query-log = 1
slow_query_log_file = /var/log/slow_query.log
```

Analyze Performance Bottlenecks

Performance issues are quite challenging and need full understanding and analysis of the bottlenecks across the system from OS, database, and application queries.

Monitor OS Resources

- **Check CPU resources.**

  Using TOP and other OS utilities, check the CPU consumption to avoid the latency on highly transactional systems, ensuring to have faster and sufficient CPU capacity.

  [root@mysqlhost01 ~]# top
  ```
  top - 13:33:50 up 13 days,  9:01,  1 user,  load average: 0.00, 0.00, 0.00
  Tasks: 180 total,   1 running, 179 sleeping,   0 stopped,   0 zombie
  %Cpu(s):  0.0 us,  0.0 sy,  0.0 ni, 99.9 id,  0.0 wa,  0.0 hi,  0.0 si,  0.0 st
  MiB Mem :  15726.3 total,    885.6 free,   9650.3 used,   5535.8 buff/cache
  MiB Swap:   4096.0 total,   4008.2 free,     87.8 used.   6076.1 avail Mem

  PID USER      PR  NI    VIRT    RES    SHR S  %CPU  %MEM     TIME+ COMMAND
  2844203 mysql    20   0   11.7g   8.2g  42744 S   0.3  53.7   8:45.03 mysqld
  1 root        20   0  170816  15028  10104 S   0.0   0.1   2:41.23 systemd
  ```

- **Check memory resources.**

  RAM (memory) bottlenecks lead to excess swapping and performance issues; allocation of required RAM and buffer cache is critical for the performance optimization in MySQL.

  [root@mysqlhost01 ~]# free -gt
  ```
                total      used      free    shared  buff/cache   available
  Mem:             15         9         0         0           5           5
  Swap:             3         0         3
  Total:           19         9         4
  ```

- **Check IO resources.**

  IO bottlenecks are very predominant in the long-running and high-volume database queries; optimizing IO and using the high throughput and latency disks are critical; SSDs are preferred over spinning disks to avoid disk IO issues.

```
[root@ash-mysqlhost01 ~]# iostat 2 3
Linux 5.14.0-284.30.1.el9_2.x86_64 (mysqlhost01)   10/22/2023  _x86_64_    (8 CPU)
avg-cpu:  %user   %nice %system %iowait  %steal    %idle
          0.40    0.01    0.11    0.00    0.00    99.48
Device      tps   kB_read/s  kB_wrtn/s  kB_dscd/s   kB_read   kB_wrtn  kB_dscd
dm-0       2.03      1.37      76.60       0.00    1587938  88542301        0
sda        1.83      1.58      76.68       0.00    1829931  88633210        0
sdb        0.03      0.60       0.00       0.00     692176         0        0
```

Slow Query Log

MySQL allows to capture the queries that are running slow in the database to capture in the real time to slow query log; by default, this is disabled, and the following parameters need to be set in the my.cnf to capture the slow-running query statements.

Use long_query_time to set the query execution time to capture the SQL; the default is 10 sec for a query to capture as a slow query in the log. In high latency-sensitive systems, this can be set to a much lower value; in the following example, it was set to 1 sec.

```
[mysqld]
slow-query-log = 1
slow_query_log_file = /var/log/slow_query.log
long_query_time = 1
```

All the queries logged in the slow query log are not really candidates for tuning or we can't classify all of them as bad queries; slow query gives indication of the queries that are running more than a threshold value that was set up in the config. Setting the value of long_query_time high will miss out the queries, and setting it too low will make the log file too noisy.

Slow query log is very useful for understanding the potential queries for tuning or indicating the database performance.

Performance Schema

Performance schema is enabled in MySQL by default and initialized during the startup; all the performance metrics are stored in this schema, which helps to troubleshoot, analyze, and understand the performance bottlenecks.

MySQL database engines write all the events, locks, bottlenecks, and metrics information for all the database activities into the performance schema tables for analysis. Most tools that work with monitoring or analyzing the performance are dependent on the information stored in this schema.

```
mysql> SHOW VARIABLES LIKE 'performance_schema';
+--------------------+-------+
| Variable_name      | Value |
+--------------------+-------+
| performance_schema | ON    |
+--------------------+-------+
1 row in set (0.00 sec)
```

We can examine all the objects in the performance schema, and some key objects are highlighted, which will be useful in performance tuning.

```
mysql> select TABLE_NAME,TABLE_ROWS FROM  INFORMATION_SCHEMA.TABLES WHERE
TABLE_SCHEMA = 'performance_schema';
+-------------------------------------------------------+------------+
| TABLE_NAME                                            | TABLE_ROWS |
+-------------------------------------------------------+------------+
| accounts                                              |        128 |
| binary_log_transaction_compression_stats              |          0 |
| cond_instances                                        |        256 |
| data_lock_waits                                       |      99999 |
| data_locks                                            |      99999 |
| error_log                                             |       2654 |
| events_errors_summary_by_account_by_error             |     209792 |
| events_errors_summary_by_host_by_error                |     209792 |
| events_errors_summary_by_thread_by_error              |     419584 |
| events_errors_summary_by_user_by_error                |     209792 |
| events_errors_summary_global_by_error                 |       5293 |
| events_stages_current                                 |        256 |
| events_stages_history                                 |       2560 |
| events_stages_history_long                            |      10000 |
| events_stages_summary_by_account_by_event_name        |      22400 |
| events_stages_summary_by_host_by_event_name           |      22400 |
```

events_stages_summary_by_thread_by_event_name	44800
events_stages_summary_by_user_by_event_name	22400
events_stages_summary_global_by_event_name	175
events_statements_current	2560
events_statements_histogram_by_digest	10000
events_statements_histogram_global	450
events_statements_history	2560
events_statements_history_long	10000
events_statements_summary_by_account_by_event_name	28032
events_statements_summary_by_digest	10000
events_statements_summary_by_host_by_event_name	28032
events_statements_summary_by_program	0
events_statements_summary_by_thread_by_event_name	56064
events_statements_summary_by_user_by_event_name	28032
events_statements_summary_global_by_event_name	219
events_transactions_current	256
events_transactions_history	2560
events_transactions_history_long	10000
events_transactions_summary_by_account_by_event_name	128
events_transactions_summary_by_host_by_event_name	128
events_transactions_summary_by_thread_by_event_name	256
events_transactions_summary_by_user_by_event_name	128
events_transactions_summary_global_by_event_name	1
events_waits_current	1536
events_waits_history	2560
events_waits_history_long	10000
events_waits_summary_by_account_by_event_name	83712
events_waits_summary_by_host_by_event_name	83712
events_waits_summary_by_instance	10752
events_waits_summary_by_thread_by_event_name	167424
events_waits_summary_by_user_by_event_name	83712
events_waits_summary_global_by_event_name	654
file_instances	4096
file_summary_by_event_name	80
file_summary_by_instance	4096

```
| firewall_group_allowlist                                      |        100 |
| firewall_groups                                               |        100 |
| firewall_membership                                           |        100 |
| global_status                                                 |        271 |
| global_variables                                              |        707 |
| host_cache                                                    |        628 |
| hosts                                                         |        128 |
| innodb_redo_log_files                                         |          1 |
| keyring_component_status                                      |         64 |
| keyring_keys                                                  |         96 |
| log_status                                                    |          1 |
| memory_summary_by_account_by_event_name                       |      57600 |
| memory_summary_by_host_by_event_name                          |      57600 |
| memory_summary_by_thread_by_event_name                        |     115200 |
| memory_summary_by_user_by_event_name                          |      57600 |
| memory_summary_global_by_event_name                           |        450 |
| metadata_locks                                                |       1024 |
| mutex_instances                                               |       4096 |
| objects_summary_global_by_type                                |       4096 |
| performance_timers                                            |          5 |
| persisted_variables                                           |          2 |
| prepared_statements_instances                                 |          0 |
| processlist                                                   |        256 |
| replication_applier_configuration                             |        256 |
| replication_applier_filters                                   |          0 |
| replication_applier_global_filters                            |          0 |
| replication_applier_status                                    |        256 |
| replication_applier_status_by_coordinator                     |        256 |
| replication_applier_status_by_worker                          |       8192 |
| replication_asynchronous_connection_failover                  |          0 |
| replication_asynchronous_connection_failover_managed |          0 |
| replication_connection_configuration                          |        256 |
| replication_connection_status                                 |        256 |
| replication_group_member_stats                                |          0 |
| replication_group_members                                     |          0 |
```

```
| rwlock_instances                          |       2048 |
| session_account_connect_attrs             |     131072 |
| session_connect_attrs                     |     131072 |
| session_status                            |        271 |
| session_variables                         |        707 |
| setup_actors                              |        128 |
| setup_consumers                           |         16 |
| setup_instruments                         |       1500 |
| setup_objects                             |        128 |
| setup_threads                             |        100 |
| socket_instances                          |        256 |
| socket_summary_by_event_name              |         10 |
| socket_summary_by_instance                |        256 |
| status_by_account                         |      34688 |
| status_by_host                            |      34688 |
| status_by_thread                          |      69376 |
| status_by_user                            |      34688 |
| table_handles                             |       1024 |
| table_io_waits_summary_by_index_usage     |       8192 |
| table_io_waits_summary_by_table           |       4096 |
| table_lock_waits_summary_by_table         |       4096 |
| threads                                   |        256 |
| tls_channel_status                        |         96 |
| user_defined_functions                    |         36 |
| user_variables_by_thread                  |       2560 |
| users                                     |        128 |
| variables_by_thread                       |     180992 |
| variables_info                            |        707 |
+-------------------------------------------+------------+
114 rows in set (0.01 sec)
```

Performance Tuning Tools

To improve performance, we have tools available in MySQL that can be used for periodic maintenance. These tools are effective when used to solve specific problems. All the database maintenance tools are suggested to run during the non-peak hours as some tools require locks on the table, which pauses all the write operations during the maintenance activities.

Analyze Table

MySQL uses stored key distributions; this analysis stores the information about tables and indexes and is used to identify the optimum path with database queries executed.

For better performance, it is suggested to perform Analyze on the tables where huge DML operations are performed.

Note   The table is locked with a read lock when you issue the Analyze command. Write statements and transactions would have to wait for the command to complete.

```
mysql> ANALYZE TABLE EMPLOYEE1;
+----------------+---------+----------+----------+
| Table          | Op      | Msg_type | Msg_text |
+----------------+---------+----------+----------+
| test.EMPLOYEE1 | analyze | status   | OK       |
+----------------+---------+----------+----------+
1 row in set (0.00 sec)

mysql> select count(*) from EMPLOYEE1;
+----------+
| count(*) |
+----------+
| 16384000 |
+----------+
1 row in set (0.29 sec)
```

```
mysql> SELECT @@explain_format;
+-------------------+
| @@explain_format  |
+-------------------+
| TRADITIONAL       |
+-------------------+
1 row in set (0.00 sec)

mysql> explain select *  from EMPLOYEE1 \G;
*************************** 1. row ***************************
           id: 1
  select_type: SIMPLE
        table: EMPLOYEE1
   partitions: NULL
         type: ALL
possible_keys: NULL
          key: NULL
      key_len: NULL
          ref: NULL
         rows: 32637074
     filtered: 100.00
        Extra: NULL
1 row in set, 1 warning (0.00 sec)
```

Optimize Table Statement

Optimize table re-organizes the physical storage of table and index data on the disk; this helps to reorg the objects to save the disk space and improve the performance. In highly transactional database (DML) systems, it's important to keep the objects re-organized for better storage and performance.

Optimize table uses an online DDL option for tables, which helps to reduce the downtime for the DMZ operations as optimize will place a table lock.

```
mysql> explain select *  from EMPLOYEE1 \G;
*************************** 1. row ***************************
           id: 1
  select_type: SIMPLE
        table: EMPLOYEE1
   partitions: NULL
         type: ALL
possible_keys: NULL
          key: NULL
      key_len: NULL
          ref: NULL
         rows: 32637074
     filtered: 100.00
        Extra: NULL
1 row in set, 1 warning (0.00 sec)

ERROR:
No query specified

mysql> OPTIMIZE TABLE EMPLOYEE1 \G;
*************************** 1. row ***************************
   Table: test.EMPLOYEE1
      Op: optimize
Msg_type: note
Msg_text: Table does not support optimize, doing recreate + analyze instead
*************************** 2. row ***************************
   Table: test.EMPLOYEE1
      Op: optimize
Msg_type: status
Msg_text: OK
2 rows in set (58.17 sec)
```

```
mysql> show table status like "EMPLOYEE1" \G
*************************** 1. row ***************************
           Name: EMPLOYEE1
         Engine: InnoDB
        Version: 10
     Row_format: Dynamic
           Rows: 32637074
 Avg_row_length: 75
    Data_length: 2476720128
Max_data_length: 0
   Index_length: 0
      Data_free: 3145728
 Auto_increment: NULL
    Create_time: 2023-10-21 16:44:36
    Update_time: NULL
     Check_time: NULL
      Collation: utf8mb4_0900_ai_ci
       Checksum: NULL
 Create_options:
        Comment:
1 row in set (0.00 sec)

mysql> select table_name,data_length,data_free from information_schema.
tables where table_name='EMPLOYEE1' order by data_free desc;
+------------+-------------+-----------+
| TABLE_NAME | DATA_LENGTH | DATA_FREE |
+------------+-------------+-----------+
| EMPLOYEE1  |  2476720128 |   3145728 |
+------------+-------------+-----------+
1 row in set (0.00 sec)
```

Information Schema Table Stats View

When performing analysis and querying the informational schema for the table info, we have different columns explaining different values; it's important to understand the significance of each.

```
mysql> select * from information_schema.INNODB_TABLESTATS  where
NAME='test/EMPLOYEE1'\G;
*************************** 1. row ***************************
        TABLE_ID: 1078
            NAME: test/EMPLOYEE1
STATS_INITIALIZED: Initialized
        NUM_ROWS: 32637074
 CLUST_INDEX_SIZE: 151167
 OTHER_INDEX_SIZE: 0
MODIFIED_COUNTER: 0
         AUTOINC: 0
       REF_COUNT: 5
1 row in set (0.00 sec)
```

Table 11-1. *Information schema table stats view*

TABLE ID	Each table has an identifier that represents the stats available.
NAME	Value is Initialized if stats are already collected; if stats are not collected, it will have a value Uninitialized.
STATS_INITIALIZED	Value explains the number of pages on the disk that stores the clustered index.
CLUST_INDEX_SIZE	Value explains the number of pages on the disk that stores the clustered index.
OTHER_INDEX_SIZE	Value represents other index size or secondary index size, that is, number of pages on the disk that stores the secondary index.
MODIFIED_COUNTER	Value represents the number of rows changed by DML statements in the database.
AUTOINC	Value represents how many auto-increment numbers requested and allocated.
REF_COUNT	When REF_COUNT reaches zero, metadata of the table will be evicted from the table cache.

Check Table Statement

Check table helps to check the integrity of the database objects tables and indexes. Check table checks version for version issues, data consistency issues, compatibility issues, and index issues.

```
mysql> check table EMPLOYEE1;
+----------------+-------+----------+----------+
| Table          | Op    | Msg_type | Msg_text |
+----------------+-------+----------+----------+
| test.EMPLOYEE1 | check | status   | OK       |
+----------------+-------+----------+----------+
1 row in set (5.95 sec)
```

Checksum Table Statement

The CHECKSUM TABLE command checks for the content before and after backup, rollback, or any other critical database maintenance operations; this command is used to check the state of the data after a major maintenance operation on the database.

```
mysql> checksum table EMPLOYEE1;
+----------------+-----------+
| Table          | Checksum  |
+----------------+-----------+
| test.EMPLOYEE1 | 513748992 |
+----------------+-----------+
1 row in set (8.49 sec)

mysql> insert into EMPLOYEE1 select * from EMPLOYEE1;
Query OK, 16384000 rows affected (1 min 21.58 sec)
Records: 16384000  Duplicates: 0  Warnings: 0

mysql> checksum table EMPLOYEE1;
+----------------+------------+
| Table          | Checksum   |
+----------------+------------+
| test.EMPLOYEE1 | 1027497984 |
+----------------+------------+
1 row in set (16.89 sec)
```

```
mysql> select count(*) from EMPLOYEE1;
+-----------+
| count(*)  |
+-----------+
| 32768000  |
+-----------+
1 row in set (0.59 sec)
```

MySQL Indexes

MySQL indexes are database objects created on selected table columns and are used to optimize the MySQL database performance by increasing the query efficiency to retrieve data from tables.

When created on a column, the index automatically stores a copy of column data in a sorted format along with references (pointers) to actual table rows, thus giving the optimizer an option to generate an optimal execution plan, avoiding full table scans.

Index Structures

Based on the type of storage engine, SQL query condition, etc., the MySQL index structure type is defined. MySQL supports the following index structures.

Table 11-2. *MySQL-supported index structures*

BTREE	This is the most used index structure, which enables queries for quick data lookup when using column comparisons like exact match, range, like, etc.
HASH	This index structure is used for queries fetching data using exact match comparison and doesn't support range. This is the default type for memory tables (tables created using the memory engine option).
RTREE	This index structure is exclusively used for tables storing spatial data like geographical, geometrical, shapes, etc.

Index Types

Considering the type of column data values like unique, duplicate, null or strings, query operations, etc., MySQL supports the following index types:

- **Non-unique (regular) index:** A non-unique index can be created on columns with duplicate values.

- **Unique index:** Unique index creation is allowed on columns with nonduplicate (unique) values, including null values.

- **Primary key index:** Primary key index is allowed on columns having unique values and doesn't allow null values in a column. This index will be created automatically when a primary key constraint is enabled on a table column.

- **Compound index:** The creation of an index on more than one table column is called a compound index. Having a compound index helps to avoid multiple indexes on the same columns.

- **Fulltext index:** A fulltext index is supported only on columns with Char, Varchar, and Text data types. The index stores the entire value of the column instead of partial or prefixed values.

- **Prefix index:** Prefix indexes can be created on string columns that use only the leading part of column values.

- **Spatial index:** A special index created on not null columns storing spatial data like geographical and geometrical values.

- **Functional index:** A functional index is an index that stores values after applying the function on column data as opposed to actual raw column data. This is helpful for the queries using functions in the where conditions.

- **Descending index:** By default, index data is stored in ascending order. With the DESC index, the key values are stored in descending order within the index, hence making the scan more efficient.

The following are some examples on the usage of non-unique, unique, primary key, compound, and hash indexes.

Note   Examples shown here are on existing tables in the database.

Before each scenario, previously created indexes are dropped for better explanation.

Non-unique (Regular) Index

Pre-Index creation SQL Execution plan and execution:
----

mysql> show indexes from my_emp;
Empty set (0.00 sec)

mysql> explain select * from my_emp where emp_no=12345;
*************************** 1. row ***************************
           id: 1
  select_type: SIMPLE
        table: my_emp
   partitions: NULL
         type: ALL
possible_keys: NULL
          key: NULL
      key_len: NULL
          ref: NULL
         rows: 299389
     filtered: 10.00
        Extra: Using where
row in set, 1 warning (0.03 sec)

>> In the explain plan 'type: ALL' indicates Full Table Scan

mysql> select * from my_emp where emp_no=12345;
+------+----------+----------+---------+------+----------+
|emp_no|birth_date|first_name|last_name|gender|hire_date |
+------+----------+----------+---------+------+----------+
| 12345|1954-04-29|Xuedong |Mellouli |F |1990-07-09|
+------+----------+----------+---------+------+----------+
1 row in set (0.91 sec)

Creating non-unique Index:

----

mysql> create index my_emp_ind_emp_no on my_emp (emp_no);
Query OK, 0 rows affected (4.25 sec)
Records: 0 Duplicates: 0 Warnings: 0

Post-Index creation SQL Execution plan and execution:

----

mysql> show indexes from my_emp\G
*************************** 1. row ***************************
          Table: my_emp
   Non_unique: 1
     Key_name: my_emp_ind_emp_no
 Seq_in_index: 1
  Column_name: emp_no
     Collation: A
   Cardinality: 299389
     Sub_part: NULL
       Packed: NULL
         Null:
   Index_type: BTREE
       Comment:
Index_comment:
       Visible: YES
   Expression: NULL
1 row in set (0.00 sec)

mysql> explain select * from my_emp where emp_no=12345;
*************************** 1. row ***************************
           id: 1
   select_type: SIMPLE
        table: my_emp
   partitions: NULL
         type: ref

```
    possible_keys: my_emp_ind_emp_no
              key: my_emp_ind_emp_no
          key_len: 4
              ref: const
             rows: 1
         filtered: 100.00
            Extra: NULL
row in set, 1 warning (0.00 sec)
```

>> In the explain plan 'type: ref' & 'ref: const' indicates compares a column value with a referre value (a const)
>>'possible_keys' & 'key' refers to the index

mysql> select * from my_emp where emp_no=12345;

```
+------+----------+----------+---------+------+----------+
|emp_no|birth_date|first_name|last_name|gender|hire_date |
+------+----------+----------+---------+------+----------+
| 12345|1954-04-29|Xuedong   |Mellouli |F     |1990-07-09|
+------+----------+----------+---------+------+----------+
```
1 row in set (0.00 sec)

Dropping Index:
----

mysql> drop index my_emp_ind_emp_no on my_emp;
Query OK, 0 rows affected (0.04 sec)
Records: 0 Duplicates: 0 Warnings: 0

Unique Index

Pre-Index creation SQL Execution plan and execution:
----

mysql> show indexes from my_emp;
Empty set (0.00 sec)

mysql> explain select * from my_emp where emp_no=23424\G
*************************** 1. row ***************************

```
          id: 1
 select_type: SIMPLE
       table: my_emp
  partitions: NULL
        type: ALL
possible_keys: NULL
         key: NULL
     key_len: NULL
         ref: NULL
        rows: 299389
    filtered: 10.00
       Extra: Using where
```
1 row in set, 1 warning (0.01 sec)

mysql> select * from my_emp where emp_no=23424;

emp_no	birth_date	first_name	last_name	gender	hire_date
23424	1962-10-17	Uriel	Hainaut	F	1987-02-24

1 row in set (0.81 sec)

mysql> explain select count(*) from my_emp where emp_no between 12345 and 23424\G
*************************** 1. row ***************************

```
          id: 1
 select_type: SIMPLE
       table: my_emp
  partitions: NULL
        type: ALL
possible_keys: NULL
         key: NULL
     key_len: NULL
         ref: NULL
        rows: 299540
```

```
    filtered: 11.11
       Extra: Using where
1 row in set, 1 warning (0.00 sec)
```

mysql> select count(*) from my_emp where emp_no between 12345 and 23424;

```
+----------+
| count(*) |
+----------+
|    11080 |
+----------+
```
1 row in set (0.67 sec)

Creating unique Index:

----

mysql> create unique index my_emp_uind_emp_no on my_emp (emp_no);
```
Query OK, 0 rows affected (8.26 sec)
Records: 0  Duplicates: 0  Warnings: 0
```

mysql> show indexes from my_emp\G
```
*************************** 1. row ***************************
        Table: my_emp
   Non_unique: 0
     Key_name: my_emp_uind_emp_no
 Seq_in_index: 1
  Column_name: emp_no
    Collation: A
  Cardinality: 299290
     Sub_part: NULL
       Packed: NULL
         Null:
   Index_type: BTREE
      Comment:
Index_comment:
      Visible: YES
   Expression: NULL
1 row in set (0.00 sec)
```

```
mysql> explain select * from my_emp where emp_no=23424\G
*************************** 1. row ***************************
           id: 1
  select_type: SIMPLE
        table: my_emp
   partitions: NULL
         type: const
possible_keys: my_emp_uind_emp_no
          key: my_emp_uind_emp_no
      key_len: 4
          ref: const
         rows: 1
     filtered: 100.00
        Extra: NULL
1 row in set, 1 warning (0.01 sec)

mysql> select * from my_emp where emp_no=23424;
+------+----------+----------+---------+------+----------+
|emp_no|birth_date|first_name|last_name|gender|hire_date |
+------+----------+----------+---------+------+----------+
|23424 |1962-10-17|Uriel     |Hainaut  |F     |1987-02-24|
+------+----------+----------+---------+------+----------+
1 row in set (0.00 sec)

mysql> explain select count(*) from my_emp where emp_no between 12345
and 23424\G
*************************** 1. row ***************************
           id: 1
  select_type: SIMPLE
        table: my_emp
   partitions: NULL
         type: range
possible_keys: my_emp_uind_emp_no
          key: my_emp_uind_emp_no
      key_len: 4
          ref: NULL
         rows: 21024
```

```
      filtered: 100.00
         Extra: Using where; Using index
1 row in set, 1 warning (0.00 sec)
```

mysql> select count(*) from my_emp where emp_no between 12345 and 23424;

```
+----------+
| count(*) |
+----------+
|    11080 |
+----------+
```

1 row in set (0.02 sec)

Primary Key Index

Checking constraint details:

**mysql> select * from INFORMATION_SCHEMA.KEY_COLUMN_USAGE where TABLE_
NAME='my_emp';**

```
Empty set (0.01 sec)
```

Adding Primary Key Constraint:

**mysql> ALTER TABLE my_emp ADD CONSTRAINT my_emp_pk_emp_no PRIMARY KEY
(emp_no);**

```
Query OK, 0 rows affected (7.76 sec)
Records: 0  Duplicates: 0  Warnings: 0
```

**mysql> select * from INFORMATION_SCHEMA.KEY_COLUMN_USAGE where TABLE_
NAME='my_emp'\G**

```
*************************** 1. row ***************************
         CONSTRAINT_CATALOG: def
          CONSTRAINT_SCHEMA: employees
            CONSTRAINT_NAME: PRIMARY
              TABLE_CATALOG: def
               TABLE_SCHEMA: employees
```

```
                    TABLE_NAME: my_emp
                   COLUMN_NAME: emp_no
              ORDINAL_POSITION: 1
POSITION_IN_UNIQUE_CONSTRAINT: NULL
      REFERENCED_TABLE_SCHEMA: NULL
        REFERENCED_TABLE_NAME: NULL
       REFERENCED_COLUMN_NAME: NULL
1 row in set (0.00 sec)
```

mysql> show indexes from my_emp\G
```
*************************** 1. row ***************************
        Table: my_emp
   Non_unique: 0
     Key_name: PRIMARY
 Seq_in_index: 1
  Column_name: emp_no
    Collation: A
  Cardinality: 299379
     Sub_part: NULL
       Packed: NULL
         Null:
   Index_type: BTREE
      Comment:
Index_comment:
      Visible: YES
   Expression: NULL
1 row in set (0.01 sec)
```

Sql Explain plan and execution with 2 indexes (primary & non-unique):

----

mysql> create index my_emp_ft_first_name on my_emp (first_name);
```
Query OK, 0 rows affected (6.20 sec)
Records: 0  Duplicates: 0  Warnings: 0
```

```
mysql> show indexes from my_emp\G
*************************** 1. row ***************************
        Table: my_emp
   Non_unique: 0
     Key_name: PRIMARY
 Seq_in_index: 1
  Column_name: emp_no
    Collation: A
  Cardinality: 299379
     Sub_part: NULL
       Packed: NULL
         Null:
   Index_type: BTREE
      Comment:
Index_comment:
      Visible: YES
   Expression: NULL
*************************** 2. row ***************************
        Table: my_emp
   Non_unique: 1
     Key_name: my_emp_ft_first_name
 Seq_in_index: 1
  Column_name: first_name
    Collation: A
  Cardinality: 1297
     Sub_part: NULL
       Packed: NULL
         Null:
   Index_type: BTREE
      Comment:
Index_comment:
      Visible: YES
   Expression: NULL
2 rows in set (0.01 sec)
```

```
mysql> explain select * from my_emp where emp_no=34567 or first_name like
'lill%'\G
*************************** 1. row ***************************
           id: 1
  select_type: SIMPLE
        table: my_emp
   partitions: NULL
         type: index_merge
possible_keys: PRIMARY,my_emp_ft_first_name
          key: my_emp_ft_first_name,PRIMARY
      key_len: 58,4
          ref: NULL
         rows: 244
     filtered: 100.00
        Extra: Using sort_union(my_emp_ft_first_name,PRIMARY); Using where
1 row in set, 1 warning (0.00 sec)

mysql> select * from my_emp where emp_no=34567 or first_name like 'lill%';
+------+----------+----------+----------+------+----------+
|emp_no|birth_date|first_name|last_name|gender|hire_date |
+------+----------+----------+----------+------+----------+
|10019|1953-01-23|Lillian    |Haddadi  |M      |1999-04-30|
<output truncated for better visibility>
|34567|1960-12-27|Zhaofang   |McClure  |F      |1992-10-13|
+------+----------+----------+----------+------+----------+
244 rows in set (0.00 sec)
```

Compound Index

```
mysql> show indexes from my_emp\G
*************************** 1. row ***************************
        Table: my_emp
   Non_unique: 0
     Key_name: PRIMARY
 Seq_in_index: 1
  Column_name: emp_no
```

```
       Collation: A
     Cardinality: 299246
        Sub_part: NULL
          Packed: NULL
            Null:
      Index_type: BTREE
         Comment:
   Index_comment:
         Visible: YES
      Expression: NULL
3 rows in set (0.01 sec)
```

Creating compound Index on 3 columns:

\-

mysql> create index my_emp_cind_emp_no on my_emp (emp_no,first_name,last_name);
```
Query OK, 0 rows affected (9.16 sec)
Records: 0  Duplicates: 0  Warnings: 0
```

mysql> show indexes from my_emp\G
```
*************************** 1. row ***************************
          Table: my_emp
     Non_unique: 0
       Key_name: PRIMARY
   Seq_in_index: 1
    Column_name: emp_no
      Collation: A
    Cardinality: 299246
       Sub_part: NULL
         Packed: NULL
           Null:
     Index_type: BTREE
        Comment:
  Index_comment:
        Visible: YES
     Expression: NULL
```

```
*************************** 2. row ***************************
        Table: my_emp
   Non_unique: 1
     Key_name: my_emp_cind_emp_no
 Seq_in_index: 1
  Column_name: emp_no
    Collation: A
  Cardinality: 299246
     Sub_part: NULL
       Packed: NULL
         Null:
   Index_type: BTREE
      Comment:
Index_comment:
      Visible: YES
   Expression: NULL
*************************** 3. row ***************************
        Table: my_emp
   Non_unique: 1
     Key_name: my_emp_cind_emp_no
 Seq_in_index: 2
  Column_name: first_name
    Collation: A
  Cardinality: 299246
     Sub_part: NULL
       Packed: NULL
         Null:
   Index_type: BTREE
      Comment:
Index_comment:
      Visible: YES
   Expression: NULL
*************************** 4. row ***************************
        Table: my_emp
   Non_unique: 1
     Key_name: my_emp_cind_emp_no
```

```
  Seq_in_index: 3
   Column_name: last_name
     Collation: A
   Cardinality: 299246
      Sub_part: NULL
        Packed: NULL
          Null:
    Index_type: BTREE
       Comment:
 Index_comment:
       Visible: YES
    Expression: NULL
4 rows in set (0.00 sec)
```

```
mysql> explain select * from my_emp where emp_no=215804;
*************************** 1. row ***************************
           id: 1
  select_type: SIMPLE
        table: my_emp
   partitions: NULL
         type: const
possible_keys: PRIMARY,my_emp_cind_emp_no
          key: PRIMARY
      key_len: 4
          ref: const
         rows: 1
     filtered: 100.00
        Extra: NULL
1 row in set, 1 warning (0.01 sec)
```

```
mysql> select * from my_emp where emp_no=215804;
+------+----------+----------+----------+------+----------+
|emp_no|birth_date|first_name|last_name |gender|hire_date |
+------+----------+----------+----------+------+----------+
|215804|1957-01-28|Mary      | Lorch    | F    |1994-03-09|
+------+----------+----------+----------+------+----------+
1 row in set (0.00 sec)
```

mysql> explain select * from my_emp where emp_no=32325 or last_name='Angel';
*************************** 1. row ***************************
```
            id: 1
   select_type: SIMPLE
         table: my_emp
    partitions: NULL
```
          type: ALL
possible_keys: PRIMARY,my_emp_cind_emp_no
```
           key: NULL
       key_len: NULL
           ref: NULL
```
          rows: 299246
      filtered: 10.00
```
         Extra: Using where
1 row in set, 1 warning (0.00 sec)
```

mysql> select * from my_emp where emp_no=32325 or last_name='Angel';

emp_no	birth_date	first_name	last_name	gender	hire_date
32325	1953-09-02	Magdalena	Taubenfeld	M	1993-11-26

emp_no	birth_date	first_name	last_name	gender	hire_date
499339	1961-02-21	Morris	Angel	M	1987-02-27

182 rows in set (0.64 sec)

mysql> explain select * from my_emp where last_name='Laurillard';
*************************** 1. row ***************************
```
            id: 1
   select_type: SIMPLE
         table: my_emp
    partitions: NULL
```
          type: ALL
possible_keys: NULL
          key: NULL

```
        key_len: NULL
            ref: NULL
           rows: 299246
       filtered: 10.00
          Extra: Using where
1 row in set, 1 warning (0.00 sec)
```

>> From the explain plan, it is seen that though the column used in the where condition is part of compound index, it is not used by the optimizer. >> Leading column must always be included in the where condition for the compound index to be used.

mysql> select * from my_emp where last_name='Laurillard';

```
+--------+------------+------------+------------+--------+------------+
|emp_no  | birth_date | first_name | last_name  | gender | hire_date  |
+--------+------------+------------+------------+--------+------------+
| 15920  | 1954-02-08 | Sanjit     | Laurillard | M      | 1988-10-04 |
<output truncated for better visibility>
|499109  | 1954-05-21 | Adel       | Laurillard | M      | 1991-04-23 |
+--------+------------+------------+------------+--------+------------+
```
175 rows in set (3.79 sec)

Hash Index

Creating a table with memory engine option:
----

mysql> create table my_empm engine = memory as select * from employees;
```
Query OK, 300024 rows affected (4.47 sec)
Records: 300024  Duplicates: 0  Warnings: 0
```

mysql> show create table my_empm\G
```
*************************** 1. row ***************************
       Table: my_empm
Create Table: CREATE TABLE `my_empm` (
  `emp_no` int NOT NULL,
  `birth_date` date NOT NULL,
```

```
  `first_name` varchar(14) NOT NULL,
  `last_name` varchar(16) NOT NULL,
  `gender` enum('M','F') NOT NULL,
  `hire_date` date NOT NULL
) ENGINE=MEMORY DEFAULT CHARSET=utf8mb4 COLLATE=utf8mb4_0900_ai_ci
1 row in set (0.00 sec)
```

```
mysql> show indexes from my_empm;
Empty set (0.01 sec)
```

Creating an index on memory table: By default,it gets created as hash:

```
mysql> create index my_empm_hi_fn on my_empm (first_name);
Query OK, 300024 rows affected (0.14 sec)
Records: 300024  Duplicates: 0  Warnings: 0
```

```
mysql> select TABLE_SCHEMA, TABLE_NAME, INDEX_SCHEMA, INDEX_NAME, COLUMN_
NAME, INDEX_TYPE, IS_VISIBLE from INFORMATION_SCHEMA.STATISTICS where
TABLE_SCHEMA='employees' and TABLE_NAME='my_emp';
*************************** 1. row ***************************
TABLE_SCHEMA: employees
  TABLE_NAME: my_empm
INDEX_SCHEMA: employees
  INDEX_NAME: my_empm_hi_fn
 COLUMN_NAME: first_name
  INDEX_TYPE: HASH
  IS_VISIBLE: YES
1 row in set (0.00 sec)
```

```
mysql> explain select * from my_empm where first_name='Troy' and last_
name='Radivojevic'\G
*************************** 1. row ***************************
          id: 1
  select_type: SIMPLE
       table: my_empm
  partitions: NULL
        type: ref
```

```
possible_keys: my_empm_hi_fn
          key: my_empm_hi_fn
      key_len: 58
          ref: const
         rows: 235
     filtered: 10.00
        Extra: Using where
1 row in set, 1 warning (0.00 sec)

mysql> select * from my_empm where first_name='Troy' and last_
name='Radivojevic';
+-------+----------+----------+-----------+------+----------+
|emp_no|birth_date|first_name|last_name  |gender|hire_date |
+-------+----------+----------+-----------+------+----------+
|499404|1963-01-30|Troy      |Radivojevic|F     |1990-07-09|
+-------+----------+----------+-----------+------+----------+
1 row in set (0.00 sec)
```

Invisible Indexes

MySQL optimizer may consider indexes available on a table during the generation of optimal execution plans. An invisible index is a feature that is helpful in evaluating the usage of an index and the performance of queries. This is an alternative to drop and re-create an index for testing its necessity on a table.

An index can be made invisible (not a primary key index) to make optimizers not consider it during the execution plan generation. Once the performance of an SQL is evaluated without an index in the execution plan, a decision can be made to make the index visible again or to drop.

The following is an example showing the difference with invisible indexes:

Creating an index and checking its visibility:
```
-------------------------------------------------
```

```
mysql> show indexes from my_emp;
Empty set (0.00 sec)
```

```
mysql> create index my_emp_ind_fn on my_emp (first_name);
Query OK, 0 rows affected (12.90 sec)
Records: 0  Duplicates: 0  Warnings: 0

mysql> select TABLE_SCHEMA, TABLE_NAME, INDEX_SCHEMA, INDEX_NAME, COLUMN_
NAME, INDEX_TYPE, IS_VISIBLE from INFORMATION_SCHEMA.STATISTICS where
TABLE_SCHEMA='employees' and TABLE_NAME='my_emp';
*************************** 1. row ***************************
TABLE_SCHEMA: employees
  TABLE_NAME: my_emp
INDEX_SCHEMA: employees
  INDEX_NAME: my_emp_ind_fn
 COLUMN_NAME: first_name
  INDEX_TYPE: BTREE
  IS_VISIBLE: YES
1 rows in set (0.00 sec)

mysql> explain select * from my_emp where first_name='Vivian' and last_
name='Barbanera';
*************************** 1. row ***************************
          id: 1
 select_type: SIMPLE
       table: my_emp
  partitions: NULL
        type: ref
possible_keys: my_emp_ind_fn
         key: my_emp_ind_fn
     key_len: 58
         ref: const
        rows: 245
    filtered: 10.00
       Extra: Using where
1 row in set, 1 warning (0.01 sec)
```

```
mysql> select * from my_emp where first_name='Vivian' and last_
name='Barbanera';
+------+----------+----------+----------+------+----------+
|emp_no|birth_date|first_name|last_name |gender|hire_date |
+------+----------+----------+----------+------+----------+
|499384|1956-06-03|Vivian    |Barbanera | M    |1990-11-19|
+------+----------+----------+----------+------+----------+
1 row in set (0.00 sec)
```

Making the index invisible:

```
mysql> alter table my_emp alter index my_emp_ind_fn invisible;
Query OK, 0 rows affected (0.06 sec)
Records: 0  Duplicates: 0  Warnings: 0
```

```
mysql> select TABLE_SCHEMA, TABLE_NAME, INDEX_SCHEMA, INDEX_NAME, COLUMN_
NAME, INDEX_TYPE, IS_VISIBLE from INFORMATION_SCHEMA.STATISTICS where
TABLE_SCHEMA='employees' and TABLE_NAME='my_emp';
*************************** 1. row ***************************
TABLE_SCHEMA: employees
  TABLE_NAME: my_emp
INDEX_SCHEMA: employees
  INDEX_NAME: my_emp_ind_fn
 COLUMN_NAME: first_name
  INDEX_TYPE: BTREE
  IS_VISIBLE: NO
1 rows in set (0.01 sec)
```

```
mysql> explain select * from my_emp where first_name='Sachin' and last_
name='Tsukuda'\G
*************************** 1. row ***************************
         id: 1
  select_type: SIMPLE
       table: my_emp
  partitions: NULL
        type: ALL
```

possible_keys: NULL
            key: NULL
        key_len: NULL
            ref: NULL
           rows: 299113
       filtered: 0.01
          Extra: Using where
1 row in set, 1 warning (0.00 sec)

mysql> select * from my_emp where first_name='Sachin' and last_name='Tsukuda';

```
+------+----------+----------+----------+------+----------+
|emp_no|birth_date|first_name|last_name |gender|hire_date |
+------+----------+----------+----------+------+----------+
|104454|1962-08-02|Sachin    |Tsukuda   | F    |1994-03-15|
|499999|1958-05-01|Sachin    |Tsukuda   | M    |1997-11-30|
+------+----------+----------+----------+------+----------+
```
2 rows in set (3.64 sec)

Forcing optimizer to use invisible index using variable option:
----

mysql> show variables like '%optimizer_switch%'\G
*************************** 1. row ***************************
Variable_name: optimizer_switch
         Value:**use_invisible_indexes=off**
1 row in set (0.01 sec)

mysql> set optimizer_switch = 'use_invisible_indexes=on';
Query OK, 0 rows affected (0.00 sec)

mysql> show variables like '%optimizer_switch%'\G
*************************** 1. row ***************************
Variable_name: optimizer_switch
         Value: use_invisible_indexes=on
1 row in set (0.00 sec)

```
mysql> select TABLE_SCHEMA, TABLE_NAME, INDEX_SCHEMA, INDEX_NAME, COLUMN_
NAME, INDEX_TYPE, IS_VISIBLE from INFORMATION_SCHEMA.STATISTICS where
TABLE_SCHEMA='employees' and TABLE_NAME='my_emp';
*************************** 1. row ***************************
TABLE_SCHEMA: employees
  TABLE_NAME: my_emp
INDEX_SCHEMA: employees
  INDEX_NAME: my_emp_ind_fn
 COLUMN_NAME: first_name
  INDEX_TYPE: BTREE
  IS_VISIBLE: NO
1 rows in set (0.01 sec)

mysql> explain select * from my_emp where first_name='Uri' and last_
name='Juneja';
*************************** 1. row ***************************
          id: 1
 select_type: SIMPLE
       table: my_emp
  partitions: NULL
        type: ref
possible_keys: my_emp_ind_fn
         key: my_emp_ind_fn
     key_len: 58
         ref: const
        rows: 225
    filtered: 10.00
       Extra: Using where
1 row in set, 1 warning (0.00 sec)

mysql> select * from my_emp where first_name='Uri' and last_name='Juneja';
+------+----------+----------+----------+------+----------+
|emp_no|birth_date|first_name|last_name |gender|hire_date |
+------+----------+----------+----------+------+----------+
|401478|1964-10-23|Uri       |Juneja    | M    |1994-12-16|
|499983|1955-08-29|Uri       |Juneja    | F    |1989-08-28|
+------+----------+----------+----------+------+----------+
```

621

2 rows in set (0.01 sec)

Forcing optimizer to use invisible index using hint option:
----

mysql> show variables like '%optimizer_switch%'\G
*************************** 1. row ***************************
Variable_name: optimizer_switch
        Value: use_invisible_indexes=on
1 row in set (0.00 sec)

mysql> set optimizer_switch = 'use_invisible_indexes=off';
Query OK, 0 rows affected (0.00 sec)

mysql> show variables like '%optimizer_switch%'\G
*************************** 1. row ***************************
Variable_name: optimizer_switch
        Value:use_invisible_indexes=off
1 row in set (0.01 sec)

**mysql> select TABLE_SCHEMA, TABLE_NAME, INDEX_SCHEMA, INDEX_NAME, COLUMN_
NAME, INDEX_TYPE, IS_VISIBLE from INFORMATION_SCHEMA.STATISTICS where
TABLE_SCHEMA='employees' and TABLE_NAME='my_emp';**
*************************** 1. row ***************************
TABLE_SCHEMA: employees
  TABLE_NAME: my_emp
INDEX_SCHEMA: employees
  INDEX_NAME: my_emp_ind_fn
 COLUMN_NAME: first_name
  INDEX_TYPE: BTREE
  IS_VISIBLE: NO
1 rows in set (0.00 sec)

**mysql> explain select /*+ SET_VAR(optimizer_switch = 'use_invisible_
indexes=on') */ * from my_emp
where first_name='Troy' and last_name='Radivojevic';**

```
*************************** 1. row ***************************
           id: 1
  select_type: SIMPLE
        table: my_emp
   partitions: NULL
         type: ref
possible_keys: my_emp_ind_fn
          key: my_emp_ind_fn
      key_len: 58
          ref: const
         rows: 223
     filtered: 10.00
        Extra: Using where
1 row in set, 1 warning (0.00 sec)
```

mysql> select /*+ SET_VAR(optimizer_switch = 'use_invisible_indexes=on') */
* from my_emp
where first_name='Troy' and last_name='Radivojevic';

```
+------+----------+----------+----------+------+----------+
|emp_no|birth_date|first_name|last_name |gender|hire_date |
+------+----------+----------+----------+------+----------+
|499404|1963-01-30|Troy      |Radivojevic| M   |1991-08-03|
+------+----------+----------+----------+------+----------+
1 row in set (0.00 sec)
```

Rebuild Indexes

An index can be rebuild using 'FORCE' option

mysql> select * from mysql.innodb_index_stats where database_
name='employees' and table_name='my_emp'\G
```
*************************** 1. row ***************************
   database_name: employees
      table_name: my_emp
      index_name: PRIMARY
```

```
          last_update: 2023-10-21 23:19:38
            stat_name: n_diff_pfx01
           stat_value: 299600
          sample_size: 20
     stat_description: emp_no
*************************** 2. row ***************************
        database_name: employees
           table_name: my_emp
           index_name: PRIMARY
          last_update: 2023-10-21 23:19:38
            stat_name: n_leaf_pages
           stat_value: 886
          sample_size: NULL
     stat_description: Number of leaf pages in the index
*************************** 3. row ***************************
        database_name: employees
           table_name: my_emp
           index_name: PRIMARY
          last_update: 2023-10-21 23:19:38
            stat_name: size
           stat_value: 929
          sample_size: NULL
     stat_description: Number of pages in the index
3 rows in set (0.00 sec)

mysql> alter table my_emp force;
Query OK, 0 rows affected (35.81 sec)
Records: 0  Duplicates: 0  Warnings: 0

mysql> select * from mysql.innodb_index_stats where database_
name='employees' and table_name='my_emp'\G
*************************** 1. row ***************************
        database_name: employees
           table_name: my_emp
           index_name: PRIMARY
          last_update: 2023-11-04 23:38:05
```

```
      stat_name: n_diff_pfx01
     stat_value: 299600
    sample_size: 20
stat_description: emp_no
*************************** 2. row ***************************
  database_name: employees
     table_name: my_emp
     index_name: PRIMARY
    last_update: 2023-11-04 23:38:05
      stat_name: n_leaf_pages
     stat_value: 886
    sample_size: NULL
stat_description: Number of leaf pages in the index
*************************** 3. row ***************************
  database_name: employees
     table_name: my_emp
     index_name: PRIMARY
    last_update: 2023-11-04 23:38:05
      stat_name: size
     stat_value: 1057
    sample_size: NULL
stat_description: Number of pages in the index
3 rows in set (0.01 sec)
```

Index Considerations and Syntax

- Index can be created during table creation or after the table is created.

- To add a non-unique index:

  ```
  ALTER TABLE <tablename> ADD INDEX (colname);
  CREATE INDEX <indexname> ON <tablename> (colname);
  ```

- To add a unique index:

  ```
  ALTER TABLE <tablename> ADD UNIQUE (colname);
  CREATE UNIQUE INDEX <indexname> ON <tablename> (colname);
  ```

- A primary key index cannot be created using the "CREATE INDEX" statement; instead, it can be created only by adding a primary key constraint on the table's column.

  ```
  ALTER TABLE <tablename> ADD PRIMARY KEY (col1, col2);
  ALTER TABLE <tablename> DROP PRIMARY KEY,ADD PRIMARY KEY
  (col1, col2);
  ALTER TABLE <tablename> DROP PRIMARY KEY;
  ```

- To add a functional index:

  ```
  ALTER TABLE <tablename> ADD INDEX ((func(colname)));
  CREATE INDEX <indexname> ON <tablename> ((func(colname)));
  ```

- To drop an index:

  ```
  ALTER TABLE <tablename> DROP INDEX <indexname>;
  DROP INDEX <indexname> ON <tablename>;
  ```

Summary

Performance tuning is a very critical function; in this chapter, we have discussed the better practices for designing databases for performance and understanding the performance bottlenecks and tools available to identify and improve the performance of databases. We have gone through the critical database parameters that affect the performance and how to approach and identify the challenges with the performance to perform the fix.

In the next chapter, we will discuss database enterprise monitoring and how to monitor the MySQL database with the MySQL Enterprise Monitor tool.

CHAPTER 12

MySQL Enterprise Monitor

Introduction

MySQL Enterprise Monitor (MEM) is an enterprise monitoring system for MySQL. MEM is a web-based application enabling you to monitor MySQL instances on your network or a cloud service. MEM is primarily used to read performance and configuration metrics. MEM continuously monitors MySQL servers and databases, sends notifications when potential issues and problems are detected, and provides recommended solutions to address the problem.

MEM gets its metrics from the MySQL server and the database's status variables and information tables. It uses a MySQL database in the back end to store all the metric data collected from all the servers and databases with the MEM agent installed and running. MEM has the following key features or capabilities:

- Advisors

- Continuous monitoring

- Automatic alerts

- Visual query analysis and graphs

- MySQL cluster monitoring

- Replication dashboard

- Backup management dashboard

- Security monitoring and audit

- Disk and OS monitoring

- Vulnerability scanning and reporting

© Y V Ravi Kumar, Arun Kumar Samayam, Naresh Kumar Miryala 2024
Y V Ravi Kumar et al., *Mastering MySQL Administration*, https://doi.org/10.1007/979-8-8688-0252-2_12

MEM has two major key components:

- MySQL Enterprise Monitor Agent

- MySQL Enterprise Service Manager

MySQL Enterprise Monitor Agent monitors the MySQL instances and hosts and collects data according to a defined schedule. It sends all the metric data collected to MySQL Enterprise Service Manager for analysis and presentation. The agent is installed on the same host as the monitored server. The agent also checks for server availability, configuration, and replication topology information if the server is set up for replication. The agent runs as a service on the monitored host and can be enabled or disabled.

MySQL Enterprise Service Manager is a web application on an Apache Tomcat server. The MEM service manager also has a monitoring agent that is automatically installed with the service manager to monitor the back-end repository and host. MySQL Service Manager receives and stores all the metric data received from the agents and stores it in the back-end repository database for analysis and reporting.

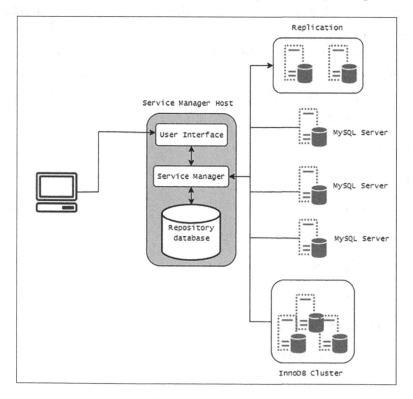

Figure 12-1. *MySQL Enterprise Monitor architecture*

MySQL Enterprise Monitor (MEM) is only available as part of the MySQL Enterprise Edition.

Installation Prerequisites for MySQL Enterprise Monitor (MEM)

1. Ensure all hosts where the service manager and agents will be installed are synchronized to the same time server.

2. Ensure all the hosts where the service manager and agents will be installed using different SSH host keys.

3. Ensure both *libaio* and *libnuma* libraries are installed if Linux hosts.

```
[root@mysql-a ~]# rpm -qa |grep libaio
libaio-0.3.109-13.el7.x86_64
[root@mysql-a ~]# rpm -qa |grep numactl*
numactl-libs-2.0.12-5.el7.x86_64
[root@mysql-a ~]#
[root@mysql-a ~]# sudo yum install libnuma*
Loaded plugins: fastestmirror
Loading mirror speeds from cached hostfile
 * base: tx-mirror.tier.net
 * epel: repos.eggycrew.com
 * extras: abqix.mm.fcix.net
 * updates: paducahix.mm.fcix.net
Package numactl-libs-2.0.12-5.el7.x86_64 already installed and
latest version
Nothing to do
```

4. Ensure Linux Standard Base (LSB) functions are installed.

```
[root@mysql-a ~]# rpm -qa |grep -i lsb
[root@mysql-a ~]# sudo yum install lsb*

  --Output truncated for better visibility
```

```
[root@mysql-a ~]# rpm -qa |grep -i lsb
redhat-lsb-core-4.1-27.el7.centos.1.x86_64
redhat-lsb-cxx-4.1-27.el7.centos.1.x86_64
redhat-lsb-printing-4.1-27.el7.centos.1.x86_64
redhat-lsb-desktop-4.1-27.el7.centos.1.x86_64
redhat-lsb-trialuse-4.1-27.el7.centos.1.x86_64
redhat-lsb-submod-multimedia-4.1-27.el7.centos.1.x86_64
redhat-lsb-submod-security-4.1-27.el7.centos.1.x86_64
redhat-lsb-languages-4.1-27.el7.centos.1.x86_64
redhat-lsb-4.1-27.el7.centos.1.x86_64
```

5. Ensure the following parameters are updated in the MySQL
    configuration file, **/etc/my.cnf**:

```
default-storage-engine=InnoDB
innodb_buffer_pool_size = 128M
innodb_file_per_table=1
innodb_flush_method=O_DIRECT
innodb_log_file_size=2048M
performance-schema-consumer-events-statements-history-long=ON
table_definition_cache=800
```

```
[root@mysql-a ~]# systemctl stop mysqld
```

BEFORE configuration changes
```
[root@mysql-a ~]# cat /etc/my.cnf
[mysqld]
```

```
datadir=/var/lib/mysql
socket=/var/lib/mysql/mysql.sock
log-error=/var/log/mysqld.log
pid-file=/var/run/mysqld/mysqld.pid
[root@mysql-a ~]#
```

AFTER configuration changes

```
[root@mysql-a ~]# cat /etc/my.cnf
[mysqld]
```

```
datadir=/var/lib/mysql
socket=/var/lib/mysql/mysql.sock
log-error=/var/log/mysqld.log
pid-file=/var/run/mysqld/mysqld.pid
```

 # MySQL Enterprise Monitor parameters

default-storage-engine=InnoDB
innodb_buffer_pool_size = 128M
innodb_file_per_table=1
innodb_flush_method=O_DIRECT
innodb_log_file_size=2048M
performance-schema-consumer-events-statements-history-long=ON
table_definition_cache=800
```
[root@mysql-a ~]#
[root@mysql-a ~]# systemctl start mysqld
```

6. Define a **service manager** user to enable MySQL Enterprise Manager to connect to, and modify, the repository and grant the required privileges:

   - **ALL** privileges on *mem%.** tables

   - **REPLICATION CLIENT, SUPER**, **PROCESS**, and **SELECT** on *all* databases in the repository

     ```
     [root@mysql-a ~]# su - mysql
     Last login: Wed Sep 13 22:23:01 CDT 2023 on pts/0
     -bash-4.2$
     -bash-4.2$ mysql -uroot -p
     Enter password:

     mysql> select user,host from mysql.user;
     +-------------------+-----------+
     | user              | host      |
     +-------------------+-----------+
     | mysql.infoschema  | localhost |
     | mysql.session     | localhost |
     | mysql.sys         | localhost |
     | root              | localhost |
     +-------------------+-----------+
     ```

4 rows in set (0.00 sec)

```
mysql> CREATE USER 'service_manager'@'localhost' IDENTIFIED BY
'WElcome_1234#';
Query OK, 0 rows affected (0.02 sec)

mysql> GRANT ALL PRIVILEGES ON `mem%`.* TO 'service_
manager'@'localhost';
Query OK, 0 rows affected (0.01 sec)

mysql> GRANT REPLICATION CLIENT, SUPER, PROCESS, SELECT ON *.*
TO 'service_manager'@'localhost';
Query OK, 0 rows affected, 1 warning (0.01 sec)

mysql> select user,host from mysql.user;
+-------------------+-----------+
| user              | host      |
+-------------------+-----------+
| mysql.infoschema  | localhost |
| mysql.session     | localhost |
| mysql.sys         | localhost |
| root              | localhost |
| service_manager   | localhost |
+-------------------+-----------+
5 rows in set (0.00 sec)
```

7. Ensure the MySQL daemon is up and running.

```
[root@mysql-a ~]# systemctl status mysqld
```

8. Update the /etc/hosts file to reflect the correct hostname.

BEFORE updates

```
[root@mysql-a ~]# cat /etc/hosts
127.0.0.1   localhost localhost.localdomain localhost4
localhost4.localdomain4
::1         localhost localhost.localdomain localhost6 localhost6.
localdomain6
192.168.2.15 mysql-s mysql-s
```

AFTER updates

```
[root@mysql-a ~]# cat /etc/hosts
127.0.0.1    localhost localhost.localdomain localhost4 localhost4.
localdomain4
::1          localhost localhost.localdomain localhost6 localhost6.
localdomain6
192.168.2.15 mysql-a mysql-a
```

Installing MySQL Enterprise Monitor

MySQL Enterprise Monitor will be available only on Oracle software delivery cloud or My Oracle support since it is a licensed feature. You can install MEM using a binary installer and will have to download both the MySQL agent software and the service manager software.

The service manager can use either an existing MySQL instance or a bundled instance that can run on its own port to store the metric data. Here are a few guidelines for the initial configuration based on your environment size:

- Small system (5 to 10 servers, 4GB of RAM)

- Medium system (up to 100 servers, 4 to 8GB of RAM)

- Large system (more than 100 servers, dedicated server, more than 8GB of RAM)

1. Log in to https://support.oracle.com/portal/. Go to *Patches & Updates*. Choose the following:

   Product as **MySQL Enterprise Monitor**.

   Release as **MySQL Enterprise Monitor 8.0**.

   Platform as **Linux x86-64**.

   Click **Search**.

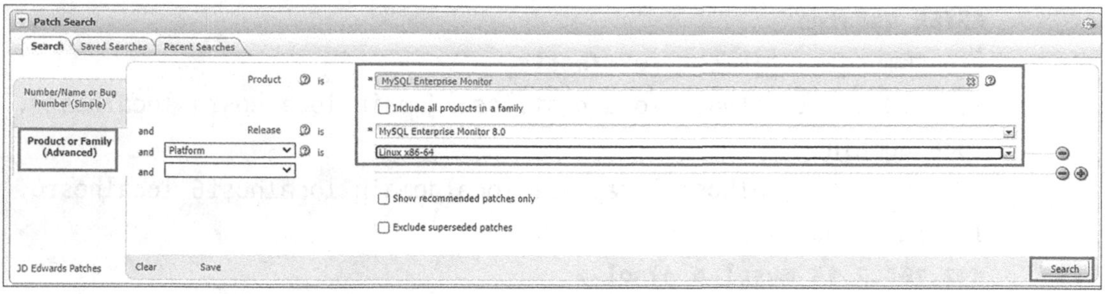

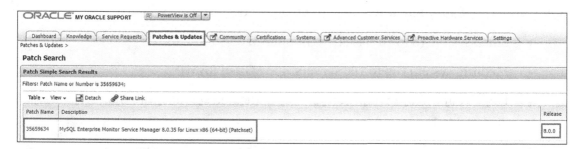

Figure 12-2. *MySQL Enterprise Monitor patch search*

2. Select and download the Service Manager and Monitor agent software patches.

- Patch *35659634*: MySQL Enterprise Monitor Service Manager 8.0.35 for Linux x86 (64-bit)

- Patch *35659637*: MySQL Enterprise Monitor Agent 8.0.35 for Linux x86 (64-bit)

Figure 12-3. *MySQL Enterprise Monitor Service Manager patch search*

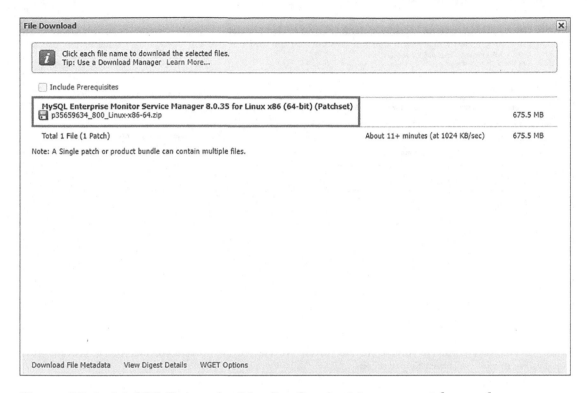

Figure 12-4. *MySQL Enterprise Monitor Service Manager patch search*

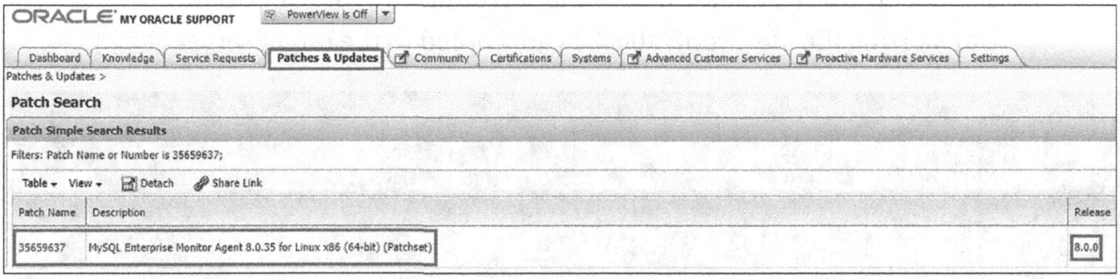

Figure 12-5. *MySQL Enterprise Monitor Agent patch search*

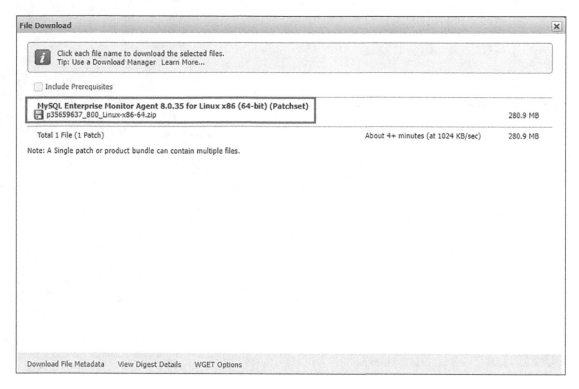

Figure 12-6. *MySQL Enterprise Monitor Agent patch search*

3. Transfer the downloaded files to the server using **WinSCP**. Upon
    transferring the files, verify the files are copied to the target server.

```
[root@mysql-a mysql_binaries]# pwd
/root/mysql_binaries
[root@mysql-a mysql_binaries]# ls -ltr
total 1986968
-rw-r--r-- 1 root root 1031792640 Sep 11 18:14 mysql-8.0.34-1.el7.x86_64.rpm-bundle.tar
-rw-r--r-- 1 root root  294504013 Sep 14 15:15 p35659637_800_Linux-x86-64.zip
-rw-r--r-- 1 root root  708352883 Sep 14 15:16 p35659634_800_Linux-x86-64.zip
[root@mysql-a mysql_binaries]#
```

Figure 12-7. *MySQL patch binary verification*

4. Unzip the downloaded software patches for MySQL EM Service
    Manager and the Agent.

    ```
    [root@mysql-a mysql_binaries]# pwd
    /root/mysql_binaries
    [root@mysql-a mysql_binaries]# ls -ltr
    total 1986968
    ```

```
-rw-r--r-- 1 root root 1031792640 Sep 11 18:14 mysql-8.0.34-1.el7.
x86_64.rpm-bundle.tar
-rw-r--r-- 1 root root  294504013 Sep 14 15:15 p35659637_800_
Linux-x86-64.zip
-rw-r--r-- 1 root root  708352883 Sep 14 15:16 p35659634_800_
Linux-x86-64.zip
[root@mysql-a mysql_binaries]#
[root@mysql-a mysql_binaries]# unzip p35659634_800_
Linux-x86-64.zip
Archive:  p35659634_800_Linux-x86-64.zip
  inflating: mysqlmonitor-8.0.35.1504-linux-x86_64-installer.bin
  inflating: mysqlmonitor-8.0.35.1504-linux-x86_64-update-
installer.bin
  inflating: README_en.txt
 extracting: mysql-monitor-html.zip
  inflating: mysql-monitor-html.tar.gz
  inflating: monitor.a4.pdf
  inflating: monitor.pdf
  inflating: LICENSES.pdf
  inflating: READ_ME_ja.txt
[root@mysql-a mysql_binaries]#
[root@mysql-a mysql_binaries]# unzip p35659637_800_
Linux-x86-64.zip
Archive:  p35659637_800_Linux-x86-64.zip
inflating: mysqlmonitoragent-8.0.35.1504-linux-x86-64bit-
installer.bin
inflating: mysqlmonitoragent-8.0.35.1504-linux-x86-64bit-
update-  installer.bin
replace README_en.txt?        [y]es,[n]o,[A]ll,[N]one,[r]ename: y
  inflating: README_en.txt
replace mysql-monitor-html.zip? [y]es,[n]o,[A]ll,[N]one,[r]ename: y
  extracting: mysql-monitor-html.zip
replace mysql-monitor-html.tar.gz?[y]es,[n]o,[A]ll,[N]one,
[r]ename: y
  inflating: mysql-monitor-html.tar.gz
```

```
replace monitor.a4.pdf?        [y]es,[n]o,[A]ll,[N]one,[r]ename: y
  inflating: monitor.a4.pdf
replace monitor.pdf?           [y]es,[n]o,[A]ll,[N]one,[r]ename: y
  inflating: monitor.pdf
replace LICENSES.pdf?          [y]es,[n]o,[A]ll,[N]one,[r]ename: y
  inflating: LICENSES.pdf
replace READ_ME_ja.txt?        [y]es,[n]o,[A]ll,[N]one,[r]ename: y
  inflating: READ_ME_ja.txt
[root@mysql-a mysql_binaries]#
[root@mysql-a mysql_binaries]# ls -ltr
total 2965784
-rw-r--r-- 1 root root     5283083 Jul 21 08:30 mysql-
monitor-html.zip
-rw-r--r-- 1 root root     6326928 Jul 21 08:32 monitor.pdf
-rw-r--r-- 1 root root     6317944 Jul 21 08:32 monitor.a4.pdf
-rw-r--r-- 1 root root      342413 Jul 26 14:58 LICENSES.pdf
-rwxr-xr-x 1 root root   349310626 Jul 27 14:56
mysqlmonitor-8.0.35.1504-linux-x86_64-installer.bin
-rwxr-xr-x 1 root root   349332557 Jul 27 14:59
mysqlmonitor-8.0.35.1504-linux-x86_64-update-installer.bin
-rwxr-xr-x 1 root root   140055129 Jul 27 15:03
mysqlmonitoragent-8.0.35.1504-linux-x86-64bit-installer.bin
-rwxr-xr-x 1 root root   140054542 Jul 27 15:04
mysqlmonitoragent-8.0.35.1504-linux-x86-64bit-update-installer.bin
-rw-r--r-- 1 root root         954 Jul 27 15:22 README_en.txt
-rw-r--r-- 1 root root     5258038 Jul 27 15:22 mysql-monitor-
html.tar.gz
-rw-r--r-- 1 root root         954 Jul 27 15:22 READ_ME_ja.txt
-rw-r--r-- 1 root root  1031792640 Sep 11 18:14 mysql-8.0.34-1.el7.
x86_64.rpm-bundle.tar
-rw-r--r-- 1 root root   294504013 Sep 14 15:15 p35659637_800_
Linux-x86-64.zip
-rw-r--r-- 1 root root   708352883 Sep 14 15:16 p35659634_800_
Linux-x86-64.zip
```

5. **Launch** the MySQL Enterprise Monitor installer from staging
    directory *mysql_binaries* like in the following and perform the
    installation:

```
[root@mysql-a mysql_binaries]# ls -ltr
total 2965784
-rw-r--r-- 1 root root     5283083 Jul 21 08:30 mysql-
monitor-html.zip
-rw-r--r-- 1 root root     6326928 Jul 21 08:32 monitor.pdf
-rw-r--r-- 1 root root     6317944 Jul 21 08:32 monitor.a4.pdf
-rw-r--r-- 1 root root      342413 Jul 26 14:58 LICENSES.pdf
-rwxr-xr-x 1 root root   349310626 Jul 27 14:56
mysqlmonitor-8.0.35.1504-linux-x86_64-installer.bin
-rwxr-xr-x 1 root root   349332557 Jul 27 14:59
mysqlmonitor-8.0.35.1504-linux-x86_64-update-installer.bin
-rwxr-xr-x 1 root root   140055129 Jul 27 15:03
mysqlmonitoragent-8.0.35.1504-linux-x86-64bit-installer.bin
-rwxr-xr-x 1 root root   140054542 Jul 27 15:04
mysqlmonitoragent-8.0.35.1504-linux-x86-64bit-update-installer.bin
-rw-r--r-- 1 root root         954 Jul 27 15:22 README_en.txt
-rw-r--r-- 1 root root     5258038 Jul 27 15:22 mysql-monitor-
html.tar.gz
-rw-r--r-- 1 root root         954 Jul 27 15:22 READ_ME_ja.txt
-rw-r--r-- 1 root root  1031792640 Sep 11 18:14 mysql-8.0.34-1.el7.
x86_64.rpm-bundle.tar
-rw-r--r-- 1 root root   294504013 Sep 14 15:15 p35659637_800_
Linux-x86-64.zip
-rw-r--r-- 1 root root   708352883 Sep 14 15:16 p35659634_800_
Linux-x86-64.zip
[root@mysql-a mysql_binaries]#
[root@mysql-a mysql_binaries]# ./mysqlmonitor-8.0.35.1504-linux-
x86_64-installer.bin
Language Selection
```

Please select the installation language
[1] English - English
[2] Japanese - 日本語
[3] Simplified Chinese - 简体中文
Please choose an option [1] : **1**
Info: During the installation process you will be asked to enter usernames and
passwords for various pieces of the Enterprise Monitor. Please be sure to make
note of these in a secure location so you can recover them in case they are
forgotten.
Press [Enter] to continue:

Welcome to the setup wizard for the MySQL Enterprise Monitor

Please specify the directory where the MySQL Enterprise Monitor will be installed

Installation directory **[/opt/mysql/enterprise/monitor]**:

Select Requirements

Please indicate the scope of monitoring this installation will initially encompass so we can configure memory usage accordingly. NOTE: This setting may have a big impact on overall performance. The manual contains instructions for updating the configuration later, if needed. This installation will monitor a:

System Size

[1] Small system: 1 to 5 MySQL Servers monitored from a laptop computer or low-end server with no more than 4 GB of RAM
[2] Medium system: Up to 100 MySQL Servers monitored from a medium-size but shared server with 4 GB to 8 GB of RAM

[3] Large system: More than 100 MySQL Servers monitored from a high-end server dedicated to MEM with more than 8 GB RAM
Please choose an option [2] : **1**

Tomcat Server Options

Please specify the following parameters for the bundled
Tomcat Server

Tomcat Server Port [18080]:

Tomcat SSL Port [18443]:

Service Manager User Account

You are installing as root, but it's not good practice for the Service Manager to run under the root user account. Please specify the name of a user account to use for the Service Manager below. Note that this user account will be created for you if it doesn't already exist.

User Account [mysqlmem]:

Database Installation

Please select which database configuration you wish to use

[1] I wish to use the bundled MySQL database
[2] I wish to use an existing MySQL database *
Please choose an option [1] : **1**

* We will validate the version of your existing MySQL database server during the installation. See documentation for minimum version requirements.

* Important: If your existing MySQL database server already has another MySQL Enterprise Monitor repository in it that you want to keep active, be sure to specify a unique name in the "MySQL Database Name" field on the next screen.

Visit the following URL for more information:

http://dev.mysql.com/doc/mysql-monitor/8.0/en/mem-install-server.html

----
Repository Configuration

Please specify the following parameters for the bundled MySQL server

Repository Username [service_manager]:

<<<<< Provide the password you created for service_manager user here from the prerequisites below >>>>>

Password :
Re-enter :
MySQL Database Port [13306]:

MySQL Database Name [mem]:

Setup is now ready to install MySQL Enterprise Monitor on your computer.

Do you want to continue? [Y/n]: **Y**

Please wait while Setup installs MySQL Enterprise Monitor on your computer.

Installing
0% _____ 50% _____ 100%
##

Completed installing files

Setup has completed installing the MySQL Enterprise Monitor files on your computer

Uninstalling the MySQL Enterprise Monitor files can be done by
invoking:
/opt/mysql/enterprise/monitor/uninstall

To complete the installation, launch the MySQL Enterprise Monitor
UI and complete the initial setup. Refer to the readme file for
additional information and a list of known issues.

Press [Enter] to continue:

Completed installing files

WARNING: To improve security, all communication with the Service
Manager uses SSL. Because only a basic self-signed security
certificate is included when the Service Manager is installed,
it is likely that your browser will display a warning about an
untrusted connection. Please either install your own certificate
or add a security exception for the Service Manager URL to your
browser. See the documentation for more information.

http://dev.mysql.com/doc/mysql-monitor/8.0/en/mem-ssl-
installation.html
Press [Enter] to continue:

Setup has finished installing MySQL Enterprise Monitor on your
computer.

View Readme File [Y/n]: Y

README
Copyright (c) 2005, 2023, Oracle and/or its affiliates.

This is a release of the MySQL Enterprise Monitor, version
8.0.35.1504.

License information can be found in the LICENSES.pdf file in the
licenses folder of the installation. This distribution may include
materials developed by third parties. For license and attribution
notices for these materials, please refer to the LICENSES.pdf file.

For more information on the MySQL Enterprise Monitor, visit
https://docs.oracle.com/cd/E17952_01/mysql-monitor-8.0-en/
index.html
or https://dev.mysql.com/doc/mysql-monitor/8.0/en/.
For additional downloads of MySQL Enterprise Monitor, visit
https://support.oracle.com/.

For further information about MySQL Enterprise Monitor or
additional
documentation, see:

  http://www.mysql.com
  http://www.mysql.com/products/enterprise
  http://www.mysql.com/products/enterprise/monitor.html

MySQL Enterprise Monitor is brought to you by the MySQL team
at Oracle.
Press [Enter] to continue:
Info: To configure the MySQL Enterprise Monitor please visit the
following page:
https://localhost:18443
Press [Enter] to continue:
[root@mysql-a mysql_binaries]#

6. Go to the MySQL Enterprise Monitor installation directory and
   check status.

```
[root@mysql-a mysql_binaries]# cd /opt/mysql/enterprise/monitor/
[root@mysql-a monitor]# pwd
/opt/mysql/enterprise/monitor
[root@mysql-a monitor]# ls -ltr
total 8076
-rw-r--r--  1 root root     954 Jul 27 14:54 README_ja.txt
-rw-r--r--  1 root root     954 Jul 27 14:54 README_en.txt
-r--r--r--  1 root root      45 Jul 27 14:54 version.txt
drwxr-xr-x  7 root root     224 Sep 14 15:45 java
drwxr-xr-x  6 root root      68 Sep 14 15:45 openssl
drwxr-xr-x 10 root root     234 Sep 14 15:45 apache-tomcat
```

```
drwxr-xr-x  3 root root        40 Sep 14 15:45 bin
drwxr-xr-x  2 root root        31 Sep 14 15:45 images
drwxr-xr-x  2 root root        26 Sep 14 15:45 licenses
drwxr-xr-x  2 root root       129 Sep 14 15:45 support-files
-rwxr--r--  1 root root     10184 Sep 14 15:45 mysqlmonitorctl.sh
-rw-------  1 root root       326 Sep 14 15:45 configuration_
report.txt
drwxr-xr-x  3 root root        22 Sep 14 15:45 etc
drwxr-xr-x 12 root mysql      279 Sep 14 15:45 mysql
-rwx------  1 root root   7165506 Sep 14 15:46 uninstall
-rw-------  1 root root    982491 Sep 14 15:46 install.log
-rw-------  1 root root      6730 Sep 14 15:46 uninstall.dat
[root@mysql-a monitor]#
[root@mysql-a monitor]# ./mysqlmonitorctl.sh status
MySQL Enterprise MySQL is running
MySQL Enterprise Tomcat is running
[root@mysql-a monitor]# cat configuration_report.txt
MySQL Enterprise Monitor (Version 8.0.35.1504 : 8.0.35.1504)

Here are the settings you specified:
Application hostname and port: https://127.0.0.1:18443
Tomcat Ports: 18080 - 18443 (SSL)
MySQL Port : 13306

Use the following command to login to the MySQL Enterprise Monitor
database:
mysql -u**** -p**** -P13306 -hlocalhost
```

7. Before launching the Enterprise Monitor URL (https://<host_
   name_of_service_manager>:18443), we need to enable the
   firewall rules on the server using the following steps:

```
[root@mysql-a monitor]# systemctl enable firewalld
Created symlink from /etc/systemd/system/dbus-org.fedoraproject.
FirewallD1.service to /usr/lib/systemd/system/firewalld.service.
Created symlink from /etc/systemd/system/multi-user.target.wants/
firewalld.service to /usr/lib/systemd/system/firewalld.service.
```

```
[root@mysql-a monitor]#
[root@mysql-a monitor]# systemctl start firewalld
[root@mysql-a monitor]# systemctl status firewalld
[root@mysql-a monitor]# firewall-cmd --zone=public
--add-port=18443/tcp --permanent
success
[root@mysql-a monitor]# firewall-cmd --zone=public
--add-port=13306/tcp --permanent
success
[root@mysql-a monitor]# firewall-cmd --zone=public
--add-port=3306/tcp --permanent
success
[root@mysql-a monitor]# firewall-cmd --permanent
--zone=public --add-service=http
success
[root@mysql-a monitor]# firewall-cmd --add-rich-rule='rule
protocol value="vrrp" accept' --permanent
success
[root@mysql-a monitor]# firewall-cmd --permanent
--zone=public --add-service=https
success
[root@mysql-a monitor]# firewall-cmd --reload
success
```

8. Launch the Enterprise Monitor URL using
   https://192.168.2.15:18443. In this URL, *192.168.2.15* is the
   host where Enterprise Monitor Service Manager is installed, and
   18443 is the port number.

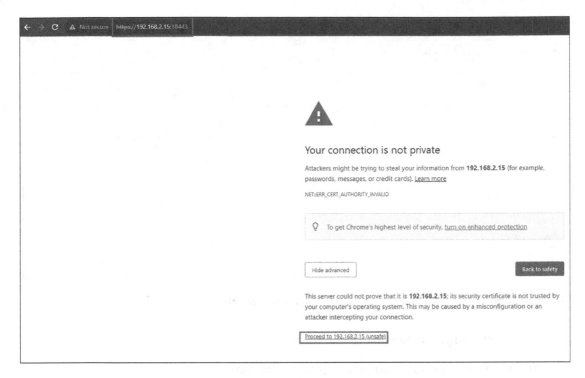

Figure 12-8. *MySQL Enterprise Monitor URL launch*

The Service Manager uses a self-signed certificate by default. In organizations where they have their in-house Certification Management System, this self-signed certificate can be replaced. If not, a security exception can always be added to the browser as an alternative.

9. Once launched, you will be taken to the MySQL Enterprise Monitor Welcome page to complete the setup. You will be asked to provide the *Manager* role (in our case, we set up the service_manager role already) and the *agent* role. In addition, you can choose your data retention settings for monitoring data.

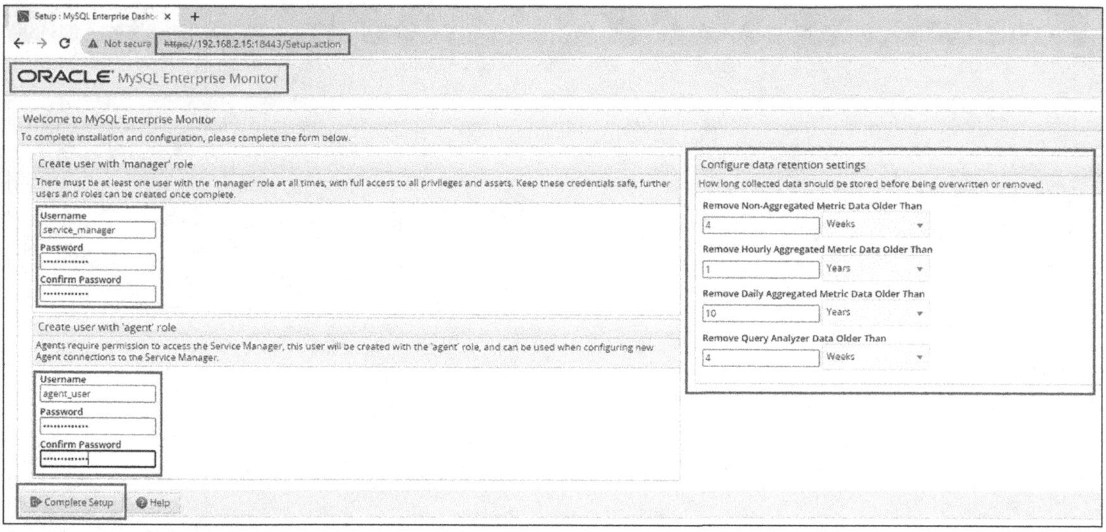

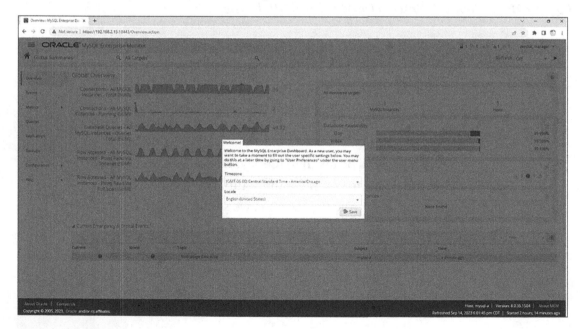

Figure 12-9. *MySQL Enterprise Monitor welcome page*

Click **Complete Setup** once configured.

10.   Choose your time zone settings and click **Save**.

Figure 12-10. *MySQL Enterprise Monitor welcome page*

11. Explore the MySQL Enterprise Monitor. Right now, you will see all monitoring data related to the current host you are on.

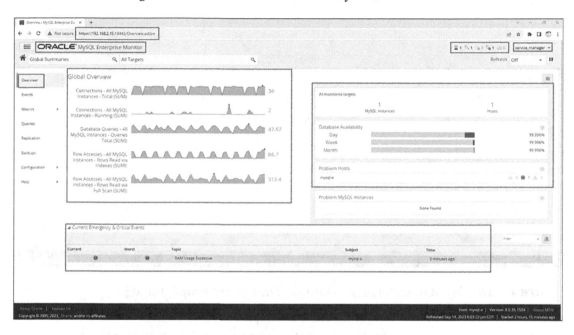

Figure 12-11. *MySQL Enterprise Monitor Overview page*

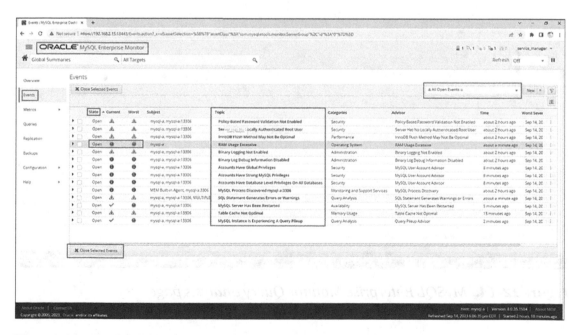

Figure 12-12. *MySQL Enterprise Monitor Overview page*

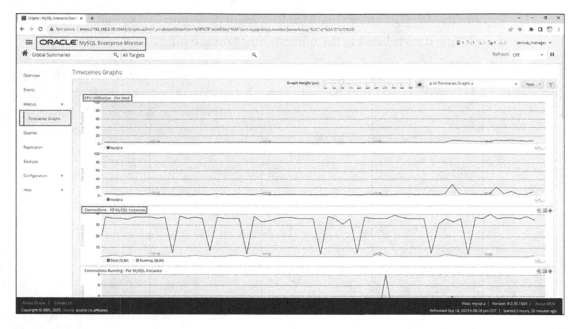

Figure 12-13. *MySQL Enterprise Monitor Timeseries graph page*

Figure 12-14. *MySQL Enterprise Monitor Query analysis page*

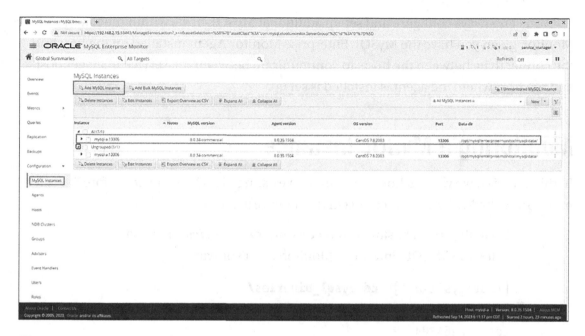

Figure 12-15. *MySQL Enterprise Monitor Instances page*

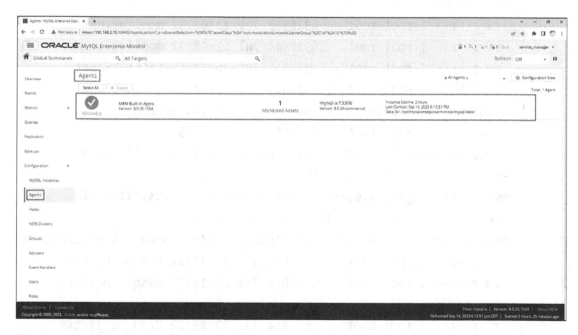

Figure 12-16. *MySQL Enterprise Monitor Agents page*

You can always configure and set up additional MySQL hosts within the Enterprise Monitor, given you have the MySQL Enterprise Monitor Agent installed on the host and the connectivity between the hosts to communicate between the service manager host and the host where the agent is installed is set up.

Monitoring a MySQL Instance

In this exercise, we will see how to monitor an existing MySQL instance. Before monitoring the MySQL instance, install the monitoring agent.

1. Go to the software staging directory *mysql_binaries* and install using the MySQL Enterprise Monitor agent software.

```
[root@mysql-a ~]# cd mysql_binaries/
[root@mysql-a mysql_binaries]# ls -ltr
total 2965784
-rw-r--r-- 1 root root     5283083 Jul 21 08:30 mysql-
monitor-html.zip
-rw-r--r-- 1 root root     6326928 Jul 21 08:32 monitor.pdf
-rw-r--r-- 1 root root     6317944 Jul 21 08:32 monitor.a4.pdf
-rw-r--r-- 1 root root      342413 Jul 26 14:58 LICENSES.pdf
-rwxr-xr-x 1 root root   349310626 Jul 27 14:56
mysqlmonitor-8.0.35.1504-linux-x86_64-installer.bin
-rwxr-xr-x 1 root root   349332557 Jul 27 14:59
mysqlmonitor-8.0.35.1504-linux-x86_64-update-installer.bin
-rwxr-xr-x 1 root root   140055129 Jul 27 15:03
mysqlmonitoragent-8.0.35.1504-linux-x86-64bit-installer.bin
-rwxr-xr-x 1 root root   140054542 Jul 27 15:04
mysqlmonitoragent-8.0.35.1504-linux-x86-64bit-update-installer.bin
-rw-r--r-- 1 root root         954 Jul 27 15:22 README_en.txt
-rw-r--r-- 1 root root     5258038 Jul 27 15:22 mysql-monitor-
html.tar.gz
-rw-r--r-- 1 root root         954 Jul 27 15:22 READ_ME_ja.txt
-rw-r--r-- 1 root root  1031792640 Sep 11 18:14 mysql-8.0.34-1.el7.
x86_64.rpm-bundle.tar
```

```
-rw-r--r-- 1 root root   294504013 Sep 14 15:15 p35659637_800_
Linux-x86-64.zip
-rw-r--r-- 1 root root   708352883 Sep 14 15:16 p35659634_800_
Linux-x86-64.zip
[root@mysql-a mysql_binaries]#
[root@mysql-a mysql_binaries]# ./mysqlmonitoragent-8.0.35.1504-
linux-x86-64bit-installer.bin
```

Language Selection

```
Please select the installation language
[1] English - English
[2] Japanese - 日本語
[3] Simplified Chinese - 简体中文
Please choose an option [1] : 1
```

Welcome to the MySQL Enterprise Monitor Agent Setup Wizard.

Installation directory
Please specify the directory where MySQL Enterprise Monitor Agent
will be installed

Installation directory [/opt/mysql/enterprise/agent]:

How will the agent connect to the database it is monitoring?

```
[1] TCP/IP
[2] Socket
```
Please choose an option [1] :

Monitoring Options

You can configure the Agent to monitor this host (file systems,
CPU, RAM, etc.) and then use the Monitor UI to furnish connection
parameters for all current and future running MySQL Instances.
This can be automated or done manually for each MySQL Instance
discovered by the Agent. (Note: scanning for running MySQL
processes is not available on Windows, but you can manually add
new connections and parameters from the Monitor UI as well.)

Visit the following URL for more information:
http://dev.mysql.com/doc/mysql-monitor/8.0/en/mem-qanal-using-feeding.html

Monitoring options:

[1] Host only: Configure the Agent to monitor this host and then use the Monitor UI to furnish connection parameters for current and future running MySQL Instances.
[2] Host and database: Configure the Agent to monitor this host and furnish connection parameters for a specific MySQL Instance now. This process may be scripted. Once installed, this Agent will also continuously look for new MySQL Instances to monitor as described above.
Please choose an option [2] :

Setup is now ready to begin installing MySQL Enterprise Monitor Agent on your computer.

Do you want to continue? [Y/n]: **Y**

Please wait while Setup installs MySQL Enterprise Monitor Agent on your computer.

Installing
0% _____ 50% _____ 100%
##

MySQL Enterprise Monitor Options

Hostname or IP address []: **192.168.2.15**

Tomcat SSL Port [18443]:

The following are the username and password that the Agent will use to connect to the Monitor. They were defined when you installed the Monitor. They can be modified under Settings, Manage Users. Their role is defined as "agent".

Agent Username [agent]:

Agent Password :
Re-enter :

Monitored Database Configuration Options

Validate hostname, port, and Admin account privileges [Y/n]: **Y**

Configure encryption settings for user accounts [y/N]: **N**

Configure less privileged user accounts [y/N]: **N**

Monitored Database Information

IMPORTANT: The Admin user account specified below requires special
MySQL privileges.

Visit the following URL for more information:
http://dev.mysql.com/doc/mysql-monitor/8.0/en/mem-agent-
rights.html

MySQL hostname or IP address [localhost]:
MySQL Port [3306]:
Admin User []: agent_user
Admin Password :
Re-enter Password :
Monitor Group []:

Configuration Report

MySQL Enterprise Monitor Agent (Version 8.0.35.1504)

The settings you specified are listed below.

Installation directory: /opt/mysql/enterprise/agent

MySQL Enterprise Monitor UI:

Hostname or IP address: 192.168.2.15
Tomcat Server Port: 18443

655

Use SSL: yes

Monitored MySQL Database:

Hostname or IP address: localhost
Port: 3306

Press [Enter] to continue:

Start MySQL Enterprise Monitor Agent

Info to start the MySQL Enterprise Monitor Agent

The MySQL Enterprise Monitor Agent was successfully installed. To start the Agent please invoke:
/etc/init.d/mysql-monitor-agent start
Press [Enter] to continue:

Setup has finished installing MySQL Enterprise Monitor Agent on your computer.

View Agent Readme File [Y/n]: Y

README
Copyright (c) 2005, 2023, Oracle and/or its affiliates.

This is a release of the MySQL Enterprise Monitor, version 8.0.35.1504.

License information can be found in the LICENSES.pdf file in the licenses folder of the installation. This distribution may include materials developed by third parties. For license and attribution notices for these materials, please refer to the LICENSES.
pdf file.

For more information on the MySQL Enterprise Monitor, visit
https://docs.oracle.com/cd/E17952_01/mysql-monitor-8.0-en/
index.html
or https://dev.mysql.com/doc/mysql-monitor/8.0/en/.
For additional downloads of MySQL Enterprise Monitor, visit

```
https://support.oracle.com/.
```

For further information about MySQL Enterprise Monitor or additional documentation, see:

```
http://www.mysql.com
http://www.mysql.com/products/enterprise
http://www.mysql.com/products/enterprise/monitor.html
```

MySQL Enterprise Monitor is brought to you by the MySQL team at Oracle.
Press [Enter] to continue:
[root@mysql-a mysql_binaries]# **/etc/init.d/mysql-monitor-agent start**
Starting MySQL Enterprise Agent service...   [OK]

2. To monitor a MySQL instance, go to the MySQL Enterprise Monitor home page. Under the **Configuration** tab, select **MySQL Instances**. Click the **Add MySQL Instance** button and proceed with providing the connection details and admin (agent_user) user details. See the following screenshots.

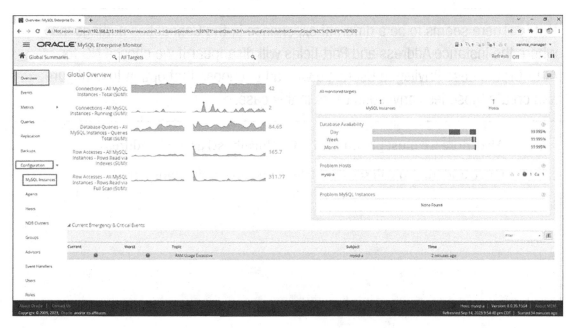

Figure 12-17. *MySQL Enterprise Monitor Instances page*

Since the agent is already installed, it will automatically discover unmonitored instances under the **Unmonitored MySQL Instances** section. Select the unmonitored instance and click the **Monitor Instances** button and proceed with the connection details.

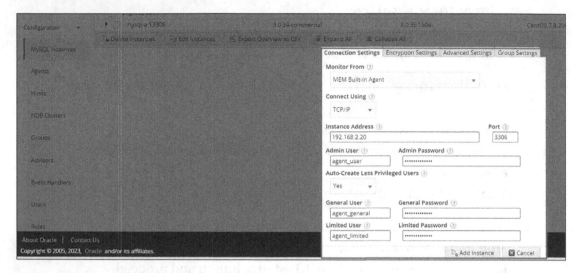

Figure 12-18. *MySQL Enterprise Monitor Instances page*

Note   There seems to be a different experience in the Connection settings tab where the Instance Address and Port fields will disappear if we choose NO for Auto-Create Less Privileged Users. So we had to choose that option to configure and create those less privileged users in this case.

Also, note we must provide 127.0.0.1 (localhost) as the IP address.

3.   Once added, you will see the MySQL instance being monitored.

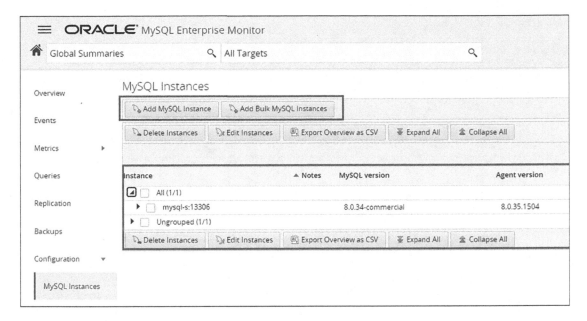

Figure 12-19. *MySQL Enterprise Monitor Instances page*

If you have multiple instances running on the same MySQL server, you can add them the same way as before.

Summary

Overall, MySQL Enterprise Monitor provides robust monitoring capabilities for MySQL servers and databases including valuable insights into query performance, backups, replication topologies, and security. It is highly recommended to configure MySQL Enterprise Monitor for optimal visibility into your MySQL environment. In the next chapter, we will discuss monitoring MySQL using Oracle Enterprise Manager Cloud Control 13c.

CHAPTER 13

Monitoring MySQL Using Oracle Enterprise Manager Cloud Control 13c

Introduction

One of the critical jobs of a database administrator is to monitor and manage the database systems for performance and other operations. This can be achieved through monitoring scripts or third-party tools installed on the systems that require additional maintenance.

MySQL database is no different from Oracle when it comes to monitoring and administration. MySQL server and MySQL NDB cluster can be monitored through MySQL Enterprise Monitor (MEM) and MySQL Plugin for Oracle Enterprise Manager (OEM).

This chapter describes the process involved in discovering MySQL server targets and monitoring them using plug-in installation in existing OEM Cloud Control 13c.

OEM is a management tool with comprehensive functionality and a centralized monitoring feature to monitor and administer key components like servers, databases, applications, storage, etc., in a database estate. OEM Cloud Control 13c has built-in management capabilities for a complete Oracle stack, including engineered systems. Still, with extended enhancements, features, and plug-ins, it also supports non-Oracle technologies.

OEM for MySQL Database plug-in extends monitoring of MySQL databases using OEM Cloud Control. It is considered one of the main advantages since monitoring of database estate is centralized if OEM is already being used in the environment.

OEM for MySQL Database is commercially licensed.

© Y V Ravi Kumar, Arun Kumar Samayam, Naresh Kumar Miryala 2024
Y V Ravi Kumar et al., *Mastering MySQL Administration*, https://doi.org/10.1007/979-8-8688-0252-2_13

The following are the high-level steps performed as part of this activity:

- Prerequisite checks

- Installing the MySQL Database Plug-in

- Adding MySQL targets

- Monitoring MySQL targets

The environment used for this activity are listed below:

Note   This chapter does not discuss OEM Cloud Control Installation/Configuration. Preexisting OEM Cloud Control 13c is used for demonstration.

Table 13-1. *Server names, IP address, and version information used in this chapter*

	Hostname	Host IP	Version	Name
OEM Cloud Control	-	-	13.5.0.0.0	-
Oracle Management Service Host	oel78-base	192.168.2.150	-	-
OEM Repository Database	oel78-base	192.168.2.150	19.17	EMREP
Management Agent Host	mysql-b	192.168.2.10	-	-
MySQL Database	mysql-b	192.168.2.10	8.0.34	-

Prerequisite Checks
Oracle Enterprise Manager Cloud Control Version

- Connect to the OEM repository database and validate that the existing OEM Cloud Control version is 13.5.0.0.0 or higher.

  ```
  [oracle@oel78-base ~]$ sqlplus / as sysdba
  Connected to:
  Oracle Database 19c Enterprise Edition Release 19.0.0.0.0 -
  Production
  ```

```
SQL> select name, open_mode from v$database;

NAME       OPEN_MODE
---------  --------------------
EMREP      READ WRITE

SQL> select version from sysman.mgmt_versions where
component_name = 'CORE';

VERSION
--------------------------------
13.5.0.0.0
```

EM Support for MySQL Version

- OEM supports MySQL 5.7 or higher.

- EM 13.2.4.0.0 or higher supports MySQL 8.0.x.

- Connect to the MySQL server and validate the version.

```
[root@mysql-b ~]# mysql -uroot -p
Enter password:
mysql> select version();
+-----------+
| version() |
+-----------+
| 8.0.34    |
+-----------+
1 row in set (0.01 sec)
```

Supported Platforms

- The plug-in can be deployed on the OEM Management Agent server running on Linux x86-64 (64-bit) and Microsoft Windows x86-64 (64-bit).

- Connect to the Management Agent host and validate the OS platform and version.

```
[root@mysql-b ~]# uname -a
Linux mysql-b 4.18.0-80.el8.x86_64 #1 SMP Thu May 30 02:01:36 GMT
2019 x86_64 x86_64 x86_64 GNU/Linux
[root@mysql-b ~]# cat /etc/os-release
NAME="Oracle Linux Server"
VERSION="8.0"
```

OS User for Management Agent

- Management Agent installing user must belong to the MySQL user group of monitoring database.

- The default user used for installing and monitoring agent is "mysql".

- Connect to the Management Agent host and validate the user and group.

```
[root@mysql-b ~]# id mysql
uid=969(mysql) gid=54331(mysql) groups=54331(mysql)
```

Monitoring User for MySQL Instance

- Create a new user (myoem) in the MySQL instance with the following privileges. This user is required during the promotion of targets for monitoring in OEM.

```
SELECT, REPLICATION CLIENT, SHOW DATABASES, PROCESS, EXECUTE
[mysql@mysql-b ~]$ mysql -uroot -p
Enter password:

mysql> create user 'myoem'@'localhost' identified by 'Welcome@123';
Query OK, 0 rows affected (0.03 sec)

mysql> grant select, replication client, show databases, process,
execute on *.* to 'myoem'@'localhost';
Query OK, 0 rows affected (0.01 sec)
```

```
mysql> select user, host from mysql. user where user like '%oem%';
+-------+-----------+
| user  | host      |
+-------+-----------+
| myoem | localhost |
+-------+-----------+
1 row in set (0.00 sec)
```

Update Hosts File

- Update /etc/hosts on both Agent Host and Oracle Management Server (OMS) Host to ensure the IP/hostnames are resolved from both sites.

  Connect to the Management Agent host and add IP and hostname of the OMS host in /etc/hosts.

  [root@mysql-b ~]# vi /etc/hosts

  ```
  >> Add below entry in this file
  192.168.2.150   oel78-base                oel78-base
  ```

  [root@mysql-b ~]# cat /etc/hosts

  ```
  127.0.0.1   localhost localhost.localdomain localhost4
  localhost4.localdomain4
  ::1         localhost localhost.localdomain localhost6
  localhost6.localdomain6
  ```
  192.168.2.10   mysql-b.localdomain   mysql-b
  192.168.2.150   oel78-base   oel78-base

  Connect to the OMS host and add IP and hostname of the Management Agent host in /etc/hosts.

  [root@oel78-base ~]# vi /etc/hosts

  ```
  >> Add below entry in this file
  192.168.2.10    mysql-b            mysql-b
  ```

```
[root@oel78-base ~]# cat /etc/hosts
127.0.0.1    localhost localhost.localdomain localhost4
localhost4.localdomain4
::1            localhost localhost.localdomain localhost6
localhost6.localdomain6
192.168.2.150   oel78-base      oel78-base
192.168.2.10    mysql-b         mysql-b
```

Open Firewall Ports

- Ensure the communication between the OMS host and Agent Server is successful through the following ports.

  Connect to the OMS host and validate the communication to the Management Agent server through ports - 3872 (agent) and 3306 (db).

```
[oracle@oel78-base ~]$ curl -vvv telnet://192.168.2.10:3872
* About to connect() to 192.168.2.10 port 3872 (#0)
*   Trying 192.168.2.10...
* Connected to 192.168.2.10 (192.168.2.10) port 3872 (#0)
^C
[oracle@oel78-base ~]$ curl -vvv telnet://mysql-b:3306
* About to connect() to mysql-b port 3306 (#0)
*   Trying 192.168.2.10...
* Connected to mysql-b (192.168.2.10) port 3306 (#0)
^C
```

  Connect to the Management Agent server and validate the communication to the OMS host through ports - 4903 (oms upload) and 7803 (EM console).

```
[mysql@mysql-b ~]$ curl -vvv telnet://192.168.2.150:4903
* Rebuilt URL to: telnet://192.168.2.150:4903/
*   Trying 192.168.2.150...
* TCP_NODELAY set
* Connected to 192.168.2.150 (192.168.2.150) port 4903 (#0)
^C
```

```
[mysql@mysql-b ~]$ curl -vvv telnet://192.168.2.150:7803
* Rebuilt URL to: telnet://192.168.2.150:7803/
*   Trying 192.168.2.150...
* TCP_NODELAY set
* Connected to 192.168.2.150 (192.168.2.150) port 7803 (#0)
^C
```

Agent Install Directory

- Connect to the Management Agent host and create a directory structure for Agent installation.

```
[mysql@mysql-b ~]$ pwd
/home/mysql
[mysql@mysql-b ~]$ mkdir agent
[mysql@mysql-b ~]$
[mysql@mysql-b ~]$ ls -ld /home/mysql/agent
drwxr-xr-x 5 mysql mysql 116 Sep 26 23:13 /home/mysql/agent
```

Installing the MySQL Database Plug-in

Checking the Availability of Plug-in in OEM Cloud Control 13c

- Log in to OEM Cloud Control 13c.

  - Navigate to Setup ➤ Extensibility ➤ Plug-ins.

Figure 13-1. *Navigation to the Plug-ins page*

- On the Plug-ins page, validate the existence of the "MySQL Database" plug-in and the latest available version.

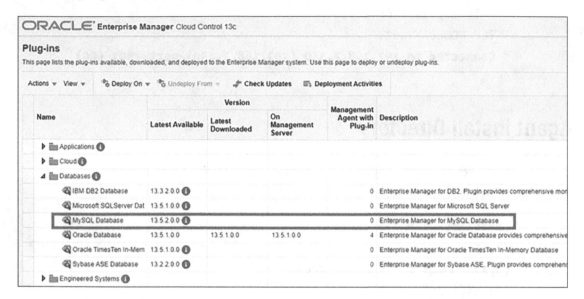

Figure 13-2. *MySQL Database Plug-in*

Viewing Information About Plug-in

- On the Plug-ins page:

  - Expand Databases

  - Click the "MySQL Database" plug-in to check the details like plug-in ID, latest available version, etc.

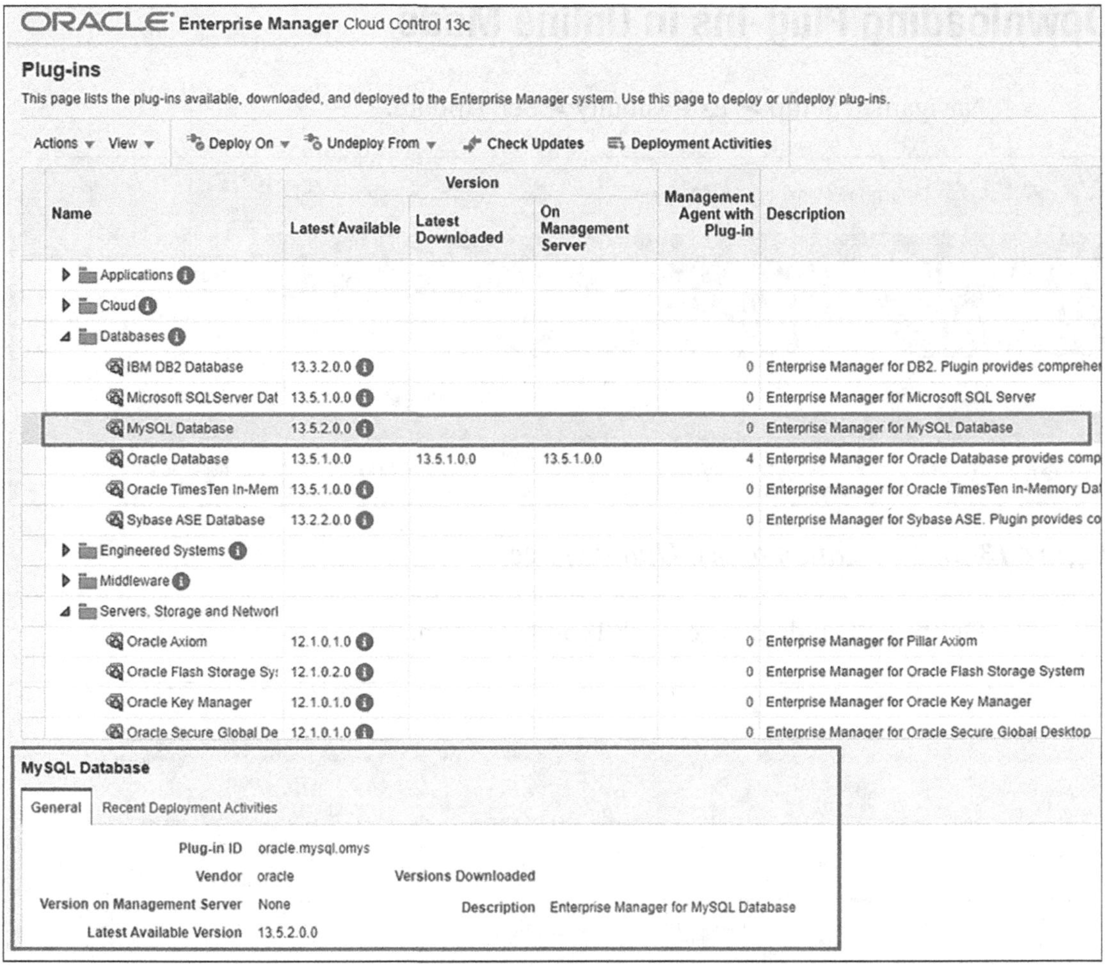

Figure 13-3. *MySQL Database Plug-in with version details*

Downloading Plug-ins in Online Mode

- Navigate to Setup ➤ Extensibility ➤ Self Update.

Figure 13-4. *Navigation to Self Update page*

- On the Self Update page, click Type ➤ Plug-in.

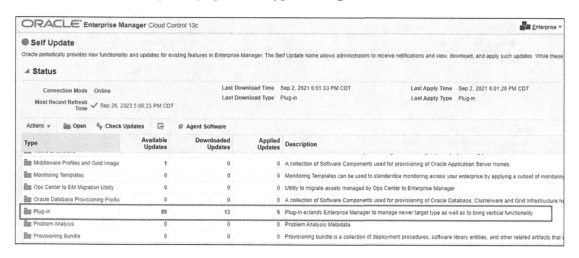

Figure 13-5. *Plug-in Type selection*

- On the Self Update - Plug-in Updates page:

  - Search for "mysql" in Search Description.

  - Select the "MySQL Database" plug-in latest version available for download.

  - Click Download.

Status	OS Platform	Plug-in Name	Revision	Version	Vendor	Size(MB)	Description
Available	Generic Platform	MySQL Database	0	13.5.2.0.0	ORACLE	138.098	Enterprise Manager for MySQL Database
Available	Generic Platform	MySQL Database	0	13.5.1.0.0	ORACLE	99.980	Enterprise Manager for MySQL Database
Available	Generic Platform	MySQL Database	0	13.2.4.0.0	ORACLE	91.551	Enterprise Manager for MySQL Database
Available	Generic Platform	MySQL Database	0	13.2.3.0.0	ORACLE	116.500	Enterprise Manager for MySQL Database

Figure 13-6. *MySQL Database Plug-in download*

- Check option "Immediately" in the Schedule Download dialog page and click Select.

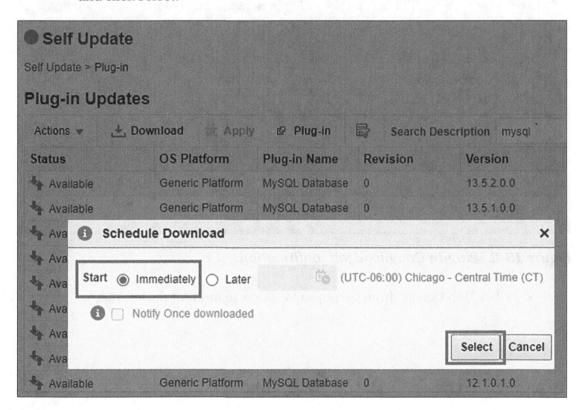

Figure 13-7. *Plug-in Download start option*

- A job will be submitted by OEM Cloud Control to download the selected plug-in from the Enterprise Manager Store to the Software Library.

- A confirmation dialog appears with job successful submission.

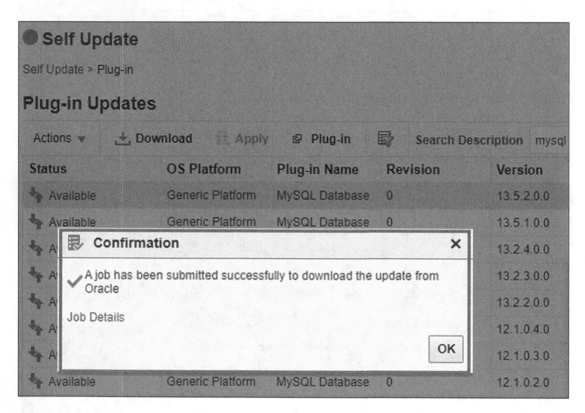

Figure 13-8. *Plug-in Download job confirmation*

- Click "Job Details" from the pop-up window to monitor the job status.

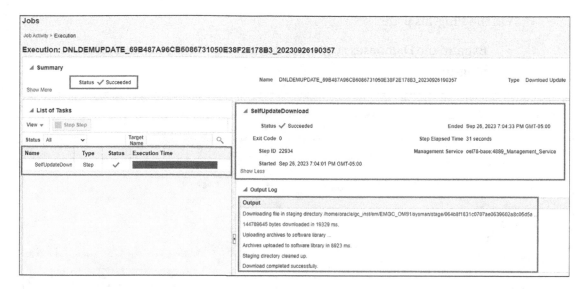

Figure 13-9. *Plug-in download completion*

Note   Once the plug-in is downloaded, it must be first deployed on the OMS, followed by deployment on Management Agents.

Deploying Plug-in on OMS

- Navigate to Setup ➤ Extensibility ➤ Plug-ins.

Figure 13-10. *Navigation to the Plug-ins page*

- On the Plug-ins page:

  - Expand the Databases section and select the "MySQL Database" plug-in.

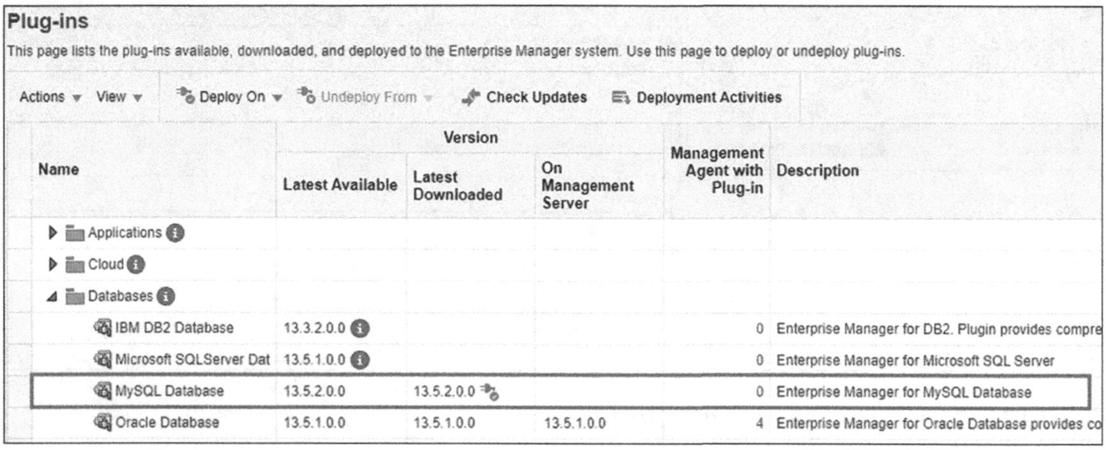

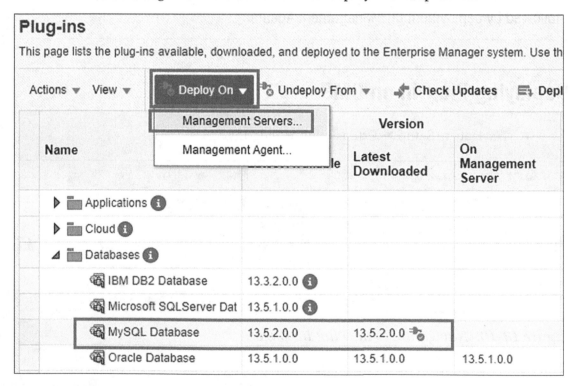

Figure 13-11. *Plug-in selection*

- Select "Management Servers" from the "Deploy On" drop-down.

Figure 13-12. *Plug-in deployment on the management server*

- Validate the plug-in name and version and click Next.

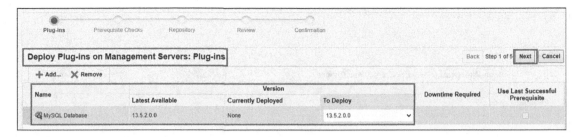

Figure 13-13. *Plug-in version validation*

- On the next page, it performs the prerequisite checks; validate the prerequisite status before proceeding further.

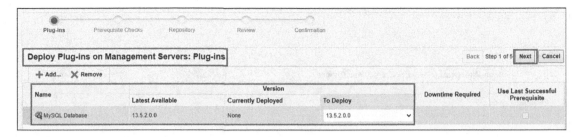

Figure 13-14. *Plug-in deployment prerequisite checks*

- Once the prerequisite checks are successful, click Next.

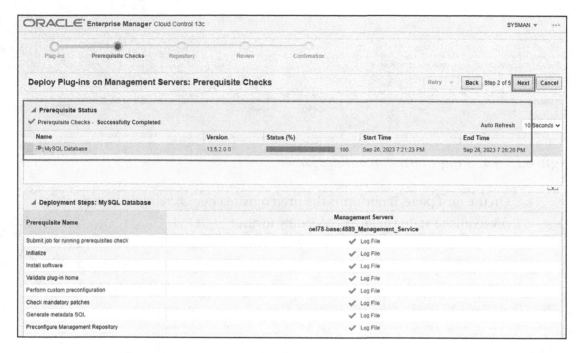

Figure 13-15. *Plug-in prerequisite status*

- On the next page, it prompts for SYS credentials; use existing named credentials; if not, create a new one by providing SYS user and password and click Next.

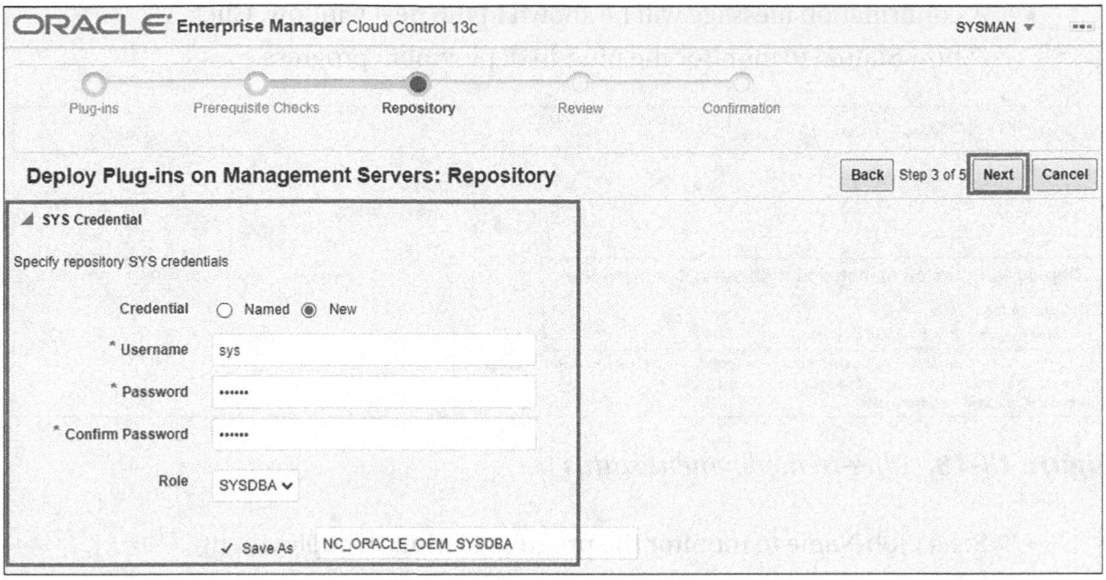

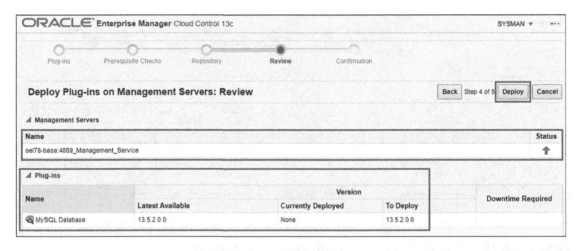

Figure 13-16. *Named credentials creation*

- Validate the OMS health status and continue with Deploy.

Figure 13-17. *Plug-in review for deployment*

- A confirmation message will be shown in the next window. Click "Show Status" to monitor the plug-in deployment progress.

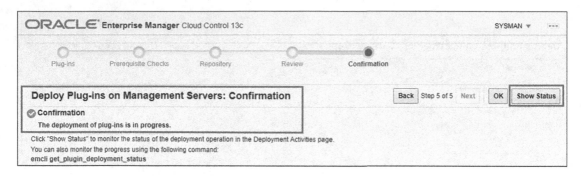

Figure 13-18. *Plug-in deployment status*

- Select Job Name to monitor the progress of plug-in deployment job tasks.

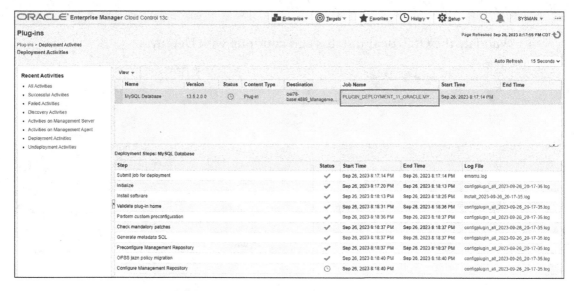

Figure 13-19. *Plug-in deployment status – continuation*

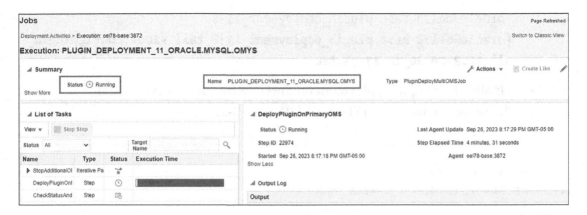

Figure 13-20. *Plug-in deployment job status*

- In parallel, the plug-in deployment job progress can be monitored from logs on the OMS server as follows:

[oracle@oel78-base ~]$ cd /home/oracle/middleware/cfgtoollogs/ pluginca/plugin_deployment_11/

[oracle@oel78-base plugin_deployment_11]$ ls -lrt
```
total 472
-rw-r-----. 1 oracle oinstall   1157 Sep 26 20:18 pre_custom_
cfg_2023-09-26_20-17-35.trc
-rw-r-----. 1 oracle oinstall   3879 Sep 26 20:18 pre_
mrs_2023-09-26_20-17-35.trc
-rw-r-----. 1 oracle oinstall   1867 Sep 26 20:18 configplugin_
all_2023-09-26_20-17-35.log
-rw-r-----. 1 oracle oinstall   1589 Sep 26 20:29 configplugin_
all_2023-09-26_20-17-35.out
-rw-r-----. 1 oracle oinstall 198701 Sep 26 20:29 configplugin_
all_2023-09-26_20-17-35.trc
-rw-r-----. 1 oracle oinstall   4866 Sep 26 20:29 post_
mrs_2023-09-26_20-17-35.trc
[oracle@oel78-base plugin_deployment_11]$
[oracle@oel78-base plugin_deployment_11]$
[oracle@oel78-base plugin_deployment_11]$ date
Tue Sep 26 20:29:21 CDT 2023
[oracle@oel78-base plugin_deployment_11]$
```

```
[oracle@oel78-base plugin_deployment_11]$
```

**[oracle@oel78-base plugin_deployment_11]$ tail -100f configplugin_
all_2023-09-26_20-17-35.trc**

- Finally, the plug-in deployment on the OMS host is successful, and
  the same can be seen in Figures 13-21 and 13-22.

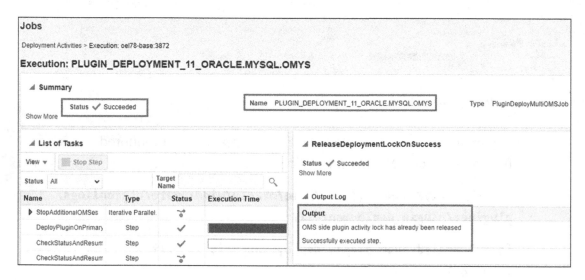

Figure 13-21. *Plug-in deployment successful*

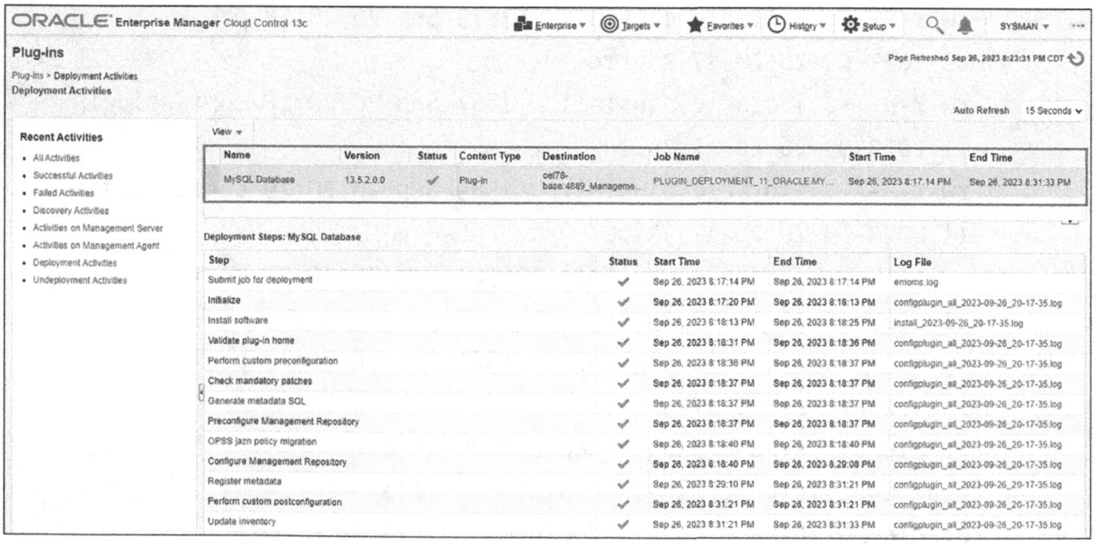

Figure 13-22. *Plug-in deployment job completion*

- Validate the deployed plug-ins on OMS from the OEM Cloud Control Console.

- Navigate to Setup ➤ Extensibility ➤ Plug-ins.

Figure 13-23. *Navigation to the Plug-ins page*

- On the Plug-ins page, we can now see that the "MySQL Database" plug-in is deployed on OMS.

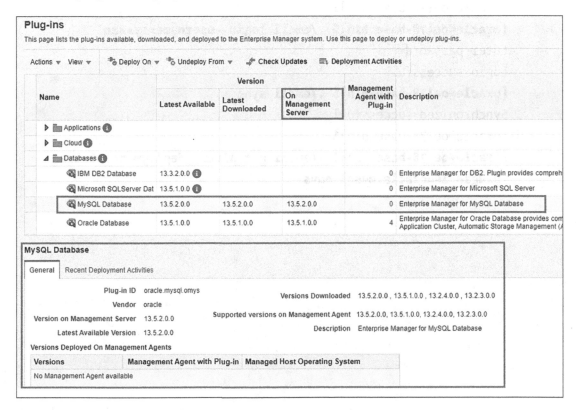

Figure 13-24. *MySQL Database plug-in additional details*

- Validate the deployed plug-in on OMS Physical Server using EMCLI.

  - Enterprise Manager Command Line Interface (EMCLI) is an interface that is used from hosts running OMS and helps to perform operations at command line as an alternative to operations performed from the OEM Cloud Control Console. EMCLI is enabled with functionality, security, and confidentiality same as the OEM Cloud Control Console.

    - Connect to the OMS host.

    - From the command prompt, log in to sysman user using emcli.

    - Perform sync.

    - Using emcli, get the plug-in deployment status.

```
[oracle@oel78-base ~]$ cd /home/oracle/middleware/bin
[oracle@oel78-base bin]$
[oracle@oel78-base bin]$ ./emcli login -username=sysman
Enter password
Login successful
[oracle@oel78-base bin]$ ./emcli sync
Synchronized successfully
[oracle@oel78-base bin]$
[oracle@oel78-base bin]$ ./emcli get_plugin_deployment_status
-plugin_id=oracle.mysql.omys
```

```
[oracle@oel78-base bin]$
[oracle@oel78-base bin]$ ./emcli get_plugin_deployment_status -plugin_id=oracle.mysql.omys
Displaying status for the latest deployment activity(deployment ID 11)
Plug-in Deployment/Undeployment Status

Destination        : Management Server - oel78-base:4889_Management_Service
Plug-in Name       : MySQL Database
Version            : 13.5.2.0.0
ID                 : oracle.mysql.omys
Content            : Plug-in
Action             : Deployment
Status             : Success
Steps Info:
------------------------------------------------------------------------------------------------
Step                           Start Time               End Time                 Status
------------------------------------------------------------------------------------------------
Submit job for deployment      9/26/23 8:17:14 PM CDT   9/26/23 8:17:14 PM CDT   Success

Initialize                     9/26/23 8:17:20 PM CDT   9/26/23 8:18:13 PM CDT   Success

Install software               9/26/23 8:18:13 PM CDT   9/26/23 8:18:25 PM CDT   Success

Validate plug-in home          9/26/23 8:18:31 PM CDT   9/26/23 8:18:36 PM CDT   Success

Perform custom preconfiguration 9/26/23 8:18:36 PM CDT  9/26/23 8:18:37 PM CDT   Success

Check mandatory patches        9/26/23 8:18:37 PM CDT   9/26/23 8:18:37 PM CDT   Success

Generate metadata SQL          9/26/23 8:18:37 PM CDT   9/26/23 8:18:37 PM CDT   Success

Preconfigure Management Repository 9/26/23 8:18:37 PM CDT 9/26/23 8:18:37 PM CDT Success

OPSS jazn policy migration     9/26/23 8:18:40 PM CDT   9/26/23 8:18:40 PM CDT   Success

Configure Management Repository 9/26/23 8:18:40 PM CDT  9/26/23 8:29:08 PM CDT   Success

Register metadata              9/26/23 8:29:10 PM CDT   9/26/23 8:31:21 PM CDT   Success

Perform custom postconfiguration 9/26/23 8:31:21 PM CDT 9/26/23 8:31:21 PM CDT  Success

Update inventory               9/26/23 8:31:21 PM CDT   9/26/23 8:31:33 PM CDT   Success

[oracle@oel78-base bin]$
```

Figure 13-25. MySQL plug-in on the OMS host

Deploying Plug-ins on Oracle Management Agent Host

Option 1: If EM Agent already exists on the Agent Server, then the plug-in that is deployed to OMS needs to be exclusively deployed on the Agent Server.

Option 2: If EM Agent does not exist on the Agent Server, then Management Agent needs to be installed manually using "Install Agent on Host" under the "Add Host Targets" wizard from the OEM Cloud Control 13c Console.

Option 2 automatically deploys all the plug-ins available in OMS to the Management Agent during installation.

In this example, Option 2 is shown as reference.

- On the OEM Cloud Control Console:

  - Navigate to Setup ➤ Add Target ➤ Add Targets Manually

Figure 13-26. *Navigation to add targets*

- On the Add Targets Manually page:

  - Select "Install Agent on Host" under the "Add Host Targets" section.

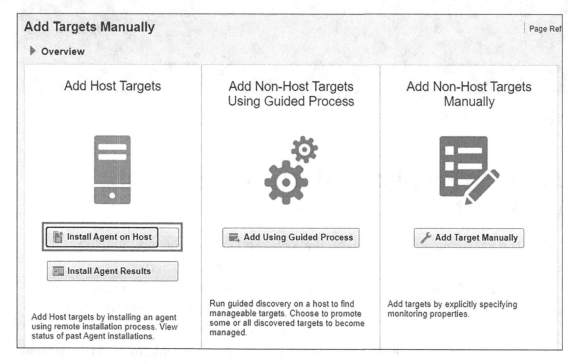

Figure 13-27. *Install Agent on Host selection*

- Click "+Add", enter agent hostname/IP, select the platform, and click Next.

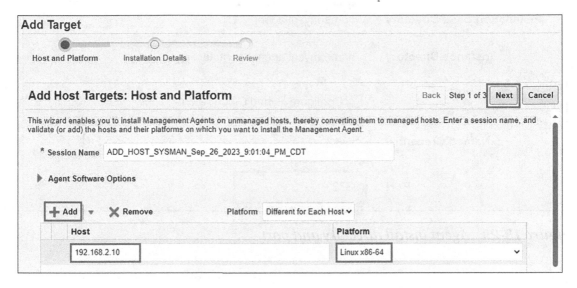

Figure 13-28. *Target host selection*

- On the next window, add values for the following:

    Installation Base Directory: /home/mysql/agent
    Port (agent): 3872
    For Named Credentials: Click "+" and create new credentials
    Named Credentials: Username – mysql; password – *****

- Once done, Click OK.

Linux x86-64: Agent Installation Details

* **Installation Base Directory**	/home/mysql/agent
* **Instance Directory**	/home/mysql/agent/agent_inst
	☐ Configure Hybrid Cloud Agent
Named Credential	Select ✓ ➕
Port	3872

Figure 13-29. *Agent install directory and port*

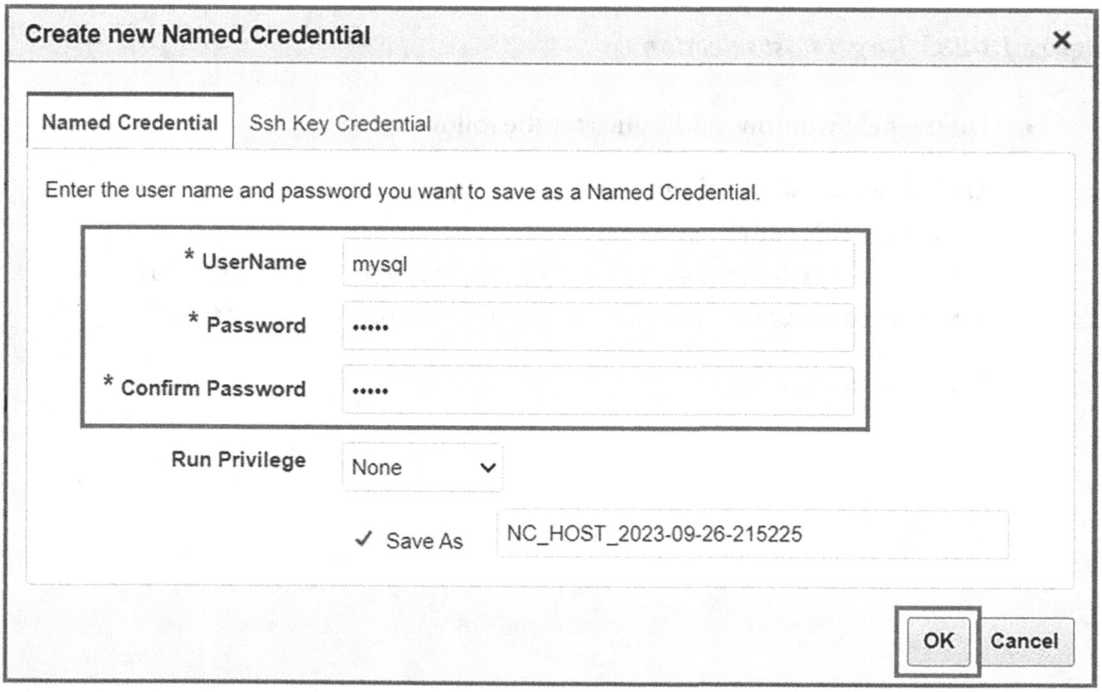

Create new Named Credential ✕

Named Credential	Ssh Key Credential

Enter the user name and password you want to save as a Named Credential.

* **UserName**	mysql
* **Password**	•••••
* **Confirm Password**	•••••
Run Privilege	None ✓
✓ Save As	NC_HOST_2023-09-26-215225

OK   Cancel

Figure 13-30. *Named credentials creation*

- On the next page, validate the details and click Next.

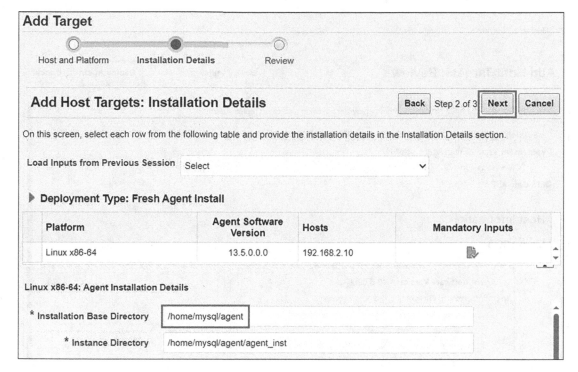

Figure 13-31. *Agent Installation directory and port details*

- On the next page, review the details and click Deploy Agent.

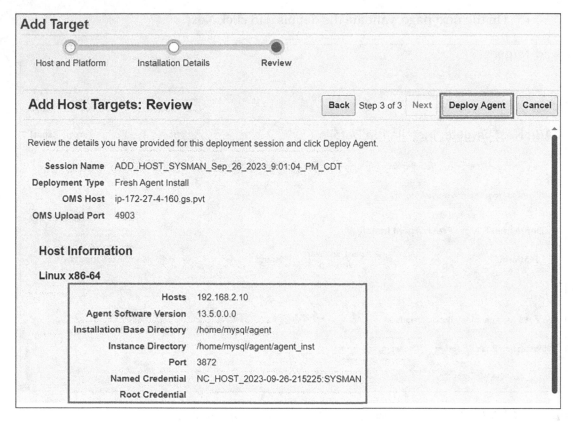

Figure 13-32. Installation inputs validation

- Agent deployment will run in three phases:

    - Initialization

    - Remote Prerequisite Check

    - Agent Deployment

Note   If any error is encountered in any of these phases, then the error needs to be corrected and the Agent Deployment can be re-run.

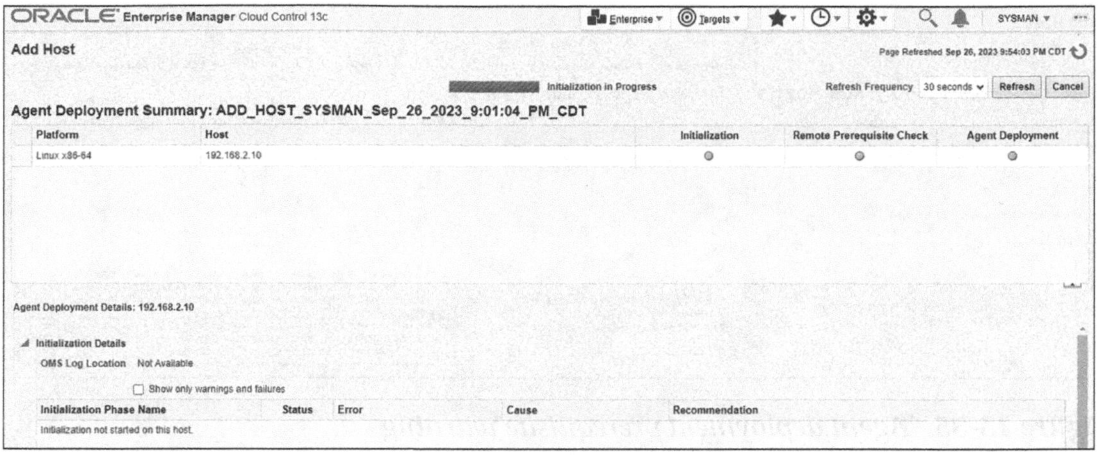

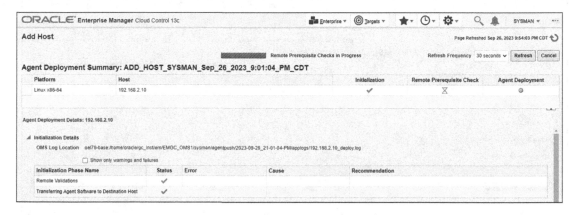

Figure 13-33. *Agent deployment initialization status*

Figure 13-34. *Agent deployment prerequisite check*

- Review the warning messages (if any) and act accordingly.

  - In this case, the warning message during "Remote Prerequisite Check" can be ignored since mysql user in named credentials is not given run privileges as root.

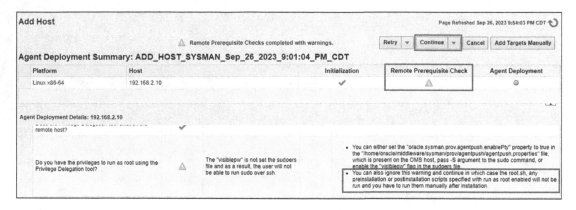

Figure 13-35. *Agent deployment prerequisite warning*

- Continue to monitor the agent deployment progress.

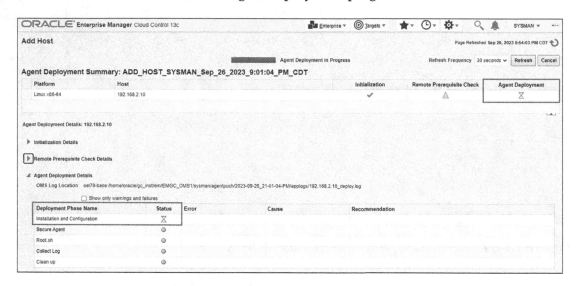

Figure 13-36. *Agent deployment progress*

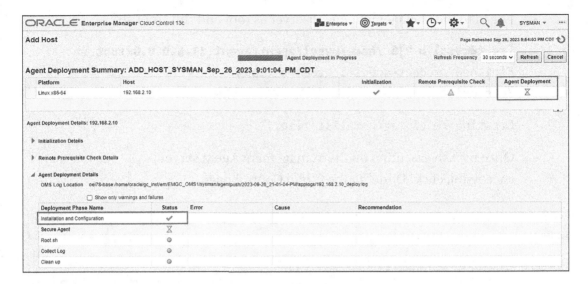

Figure 13-37. *Agent deployment progress – continuation*

- Finally, the agent deployment on the Management Agent server was successful with a recommendation to run root.sh on the agent server as root.

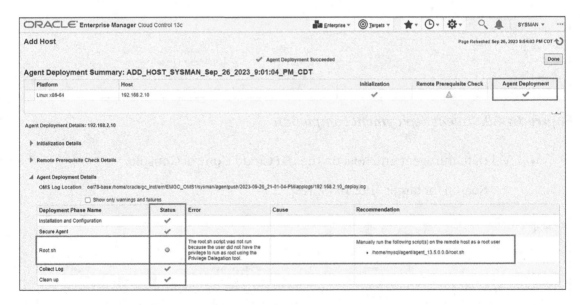

Figure 13-38. *Agent deployment successful*

- Log in to the Management Agent server as root and run "root.sh".

[root@mysql-b ~]# /home/mysql/agent/agent_13.5.0.0.0/root.sh
Finished product-specific root actions.
/etc exist

Creating /etc/oragchomelist file...

- Once root.sh execution on the Management Agent server is successful, click "Done" in the Cloud Control page.

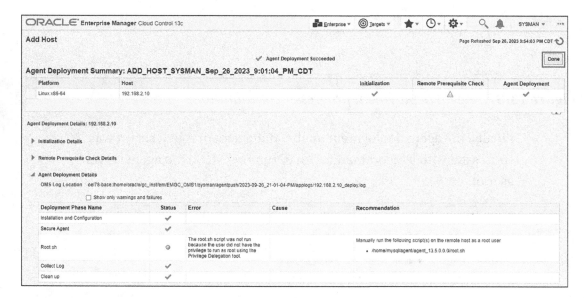

Figure 13-39. *Agent deployment completion*

- Validate the agent and host on the EM Cloud Control Console.

  - Search for target "192.168.2.10".

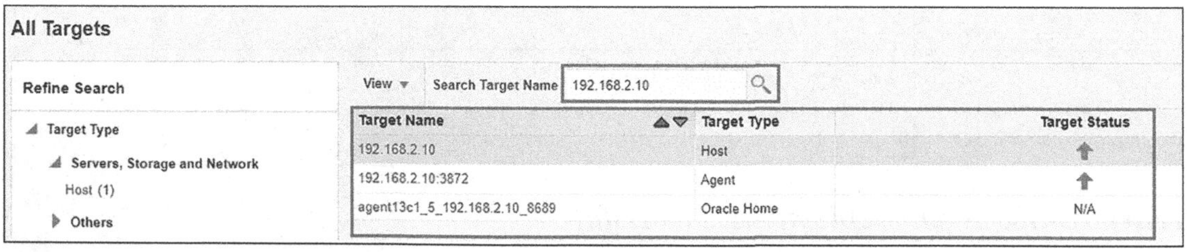

Figure 13-40. *Agent and Host target search output*

- Validate Agent Status on the Management Agent server.

  - Log in to the Management Agent host and check agent health.

```
[mysql@mysql-b ~]$
[mysql@mysql-b ~]$ cd /home/mysql/agent/agent_13.5.0.0.0/bin
[mysql@mysql-b bin]$
[mysql@mysql-b bin]$ ./emctl status agent
Oracle Enterprise Manager Cloud Control 13c Release 5
Copyright (c) 1996, 2021 Oracle Corporation.  All rights reserved.
---------------------------------------------------------------
Agent Version          : 13.5.0.0.0
OMS Version            : 13.5.0.0.0
Protocol Version       : 12.1.0.1.0
Agent Home             : /home/mysql/agent/agent_inst
Agent Log Directory    : /home/mysql/agent/agent_inst/sysman/log
Agent Binaries         : /home/mysql/agent/agent_13.5.0.0.0
Core JAR Location      : /home/mysql/agent/agent_13.5.0.0.0/jlib
Agent Process ID       : 6745
Parent Process ID      : 6716
Agent URL              : https://192.168.2.10:3872/emd/main/
Local Agent URL in NAT : https://192.168.2.10:3872/emd/main/
Repository URL         : https://oel78-base:4903/empbs/upload
Started at             : 2023-09-26 23:12:38
Started by user        : mysql
Operating System       : Linux version 4.18.0-80.el8.x86_64 (amd64)
Number of Targets      : (none)
Last Reload            : (none)
Last successful upload                       : (none)
Last attempted upload                        : (none)
Total Megabytes of XML files uploaded so far : 0
Number of XML files pending upload           : 0
Size of XML files pending upload(MB)         : 0
Available disk space on upload filesystem    : 89.43%
Collection Status                            : Collections enabled
Heartbeat Status                             : Ok
Last attempted heartbeat to OMS              : 2023-09-26 23:22:17
Last successful heartbeat to OMS             : 2023-09-26 23:22:17
Next scheduled heartbeat to OMS              : 2023-09-26 23:23:17

---------------------------------------------------------------
Agent is Running and Ready
[mysql@mysql-b bin]$
```

Figure 13-41. *Agent status on the host using emctl*

Adding MySQL Targets

Adding Targets Using Autodiscovery

- Navigate to Setup ➤ Add Target ➤ Configure Auto Discovery.

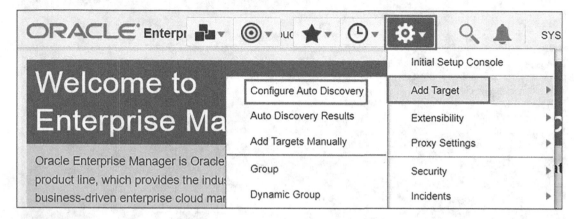

Figure 13-42. *Navigation to Configure Auto Discovery*

- On the Setup Discovery page, under the "Targets on Hosts" table:

  - Select the host and click "Discovery Modules".

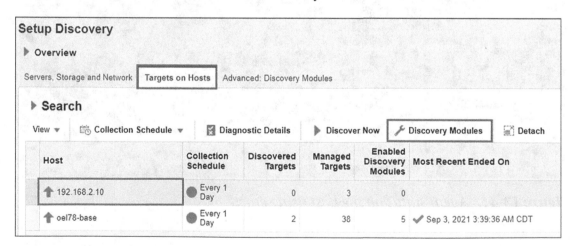

Figure 13-43. *Discovery modules in target host*

- On the next page (Discovery Modules: "Hostname/IP"):

  - Check the "Oracle MySQL Discovery" module and click OK.

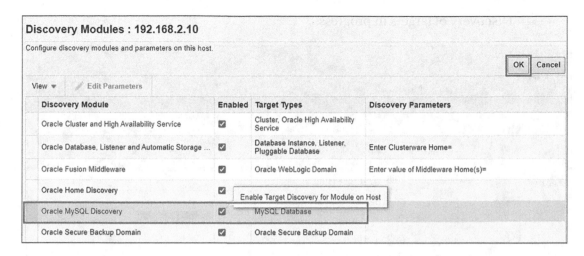

Figure 13-44. *Oracle MySQL Discovery selection*

- On the Setup Discovery page:

  - Select the host and click "Discover Now".

  - A dialog page is displayed to confirm the discovery run on target; click Yes.

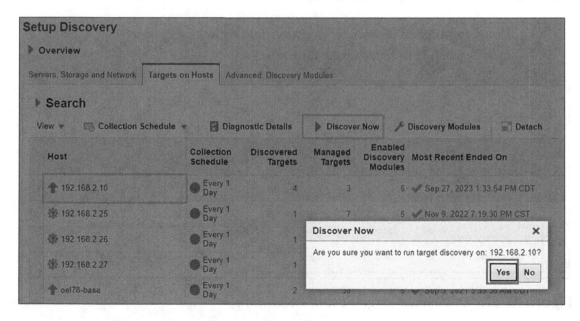

Figure 13-45. *Target discovery on selected host*

- Discovery of targets in progress.

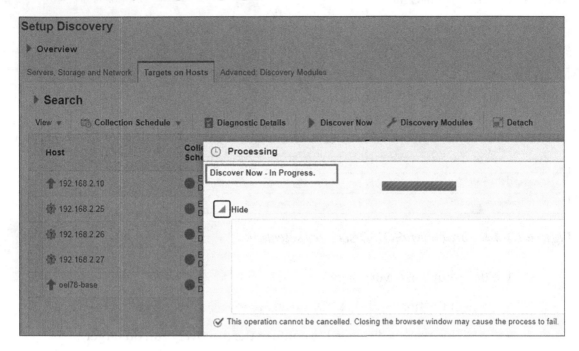

Figure 13-46. *Discovery progress status*

- Upon completion of discovery, appropriate count of discovered targets will be displayed against the host.

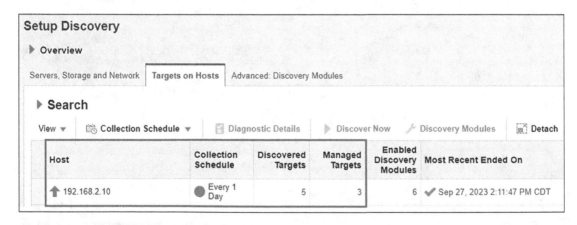

Figure 13-47. *Discovered targets count validation*

Promote the Discovered Targets

- Navigate to Setup ➤ Add Target ➤ Add Discovery Results.

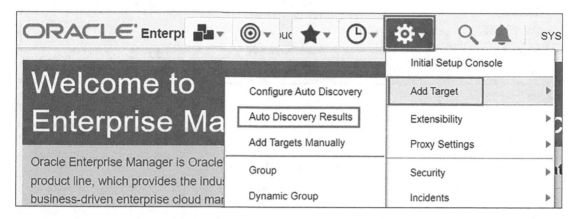

Figure 13-48. *Navigation to Auto Discovery Results*

- On the Auto Discovery Results page, under the "Targets on Hosts" table:

  - Select the target (in this case, mysql database) and click Promote.

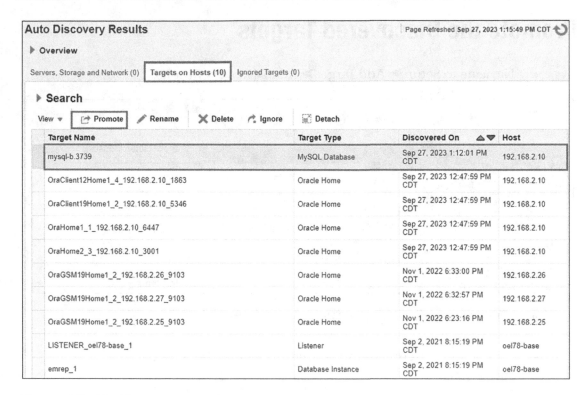

Figure 13-49. *Target promotion*

- On the next page, provide inputs for the following and click Promote:

  - **MySQL User:** myoem

  - **MySQL Password:** *****

  - **Confirm MySQL Password:** *****

  - **Port (mysql DB):** 3306

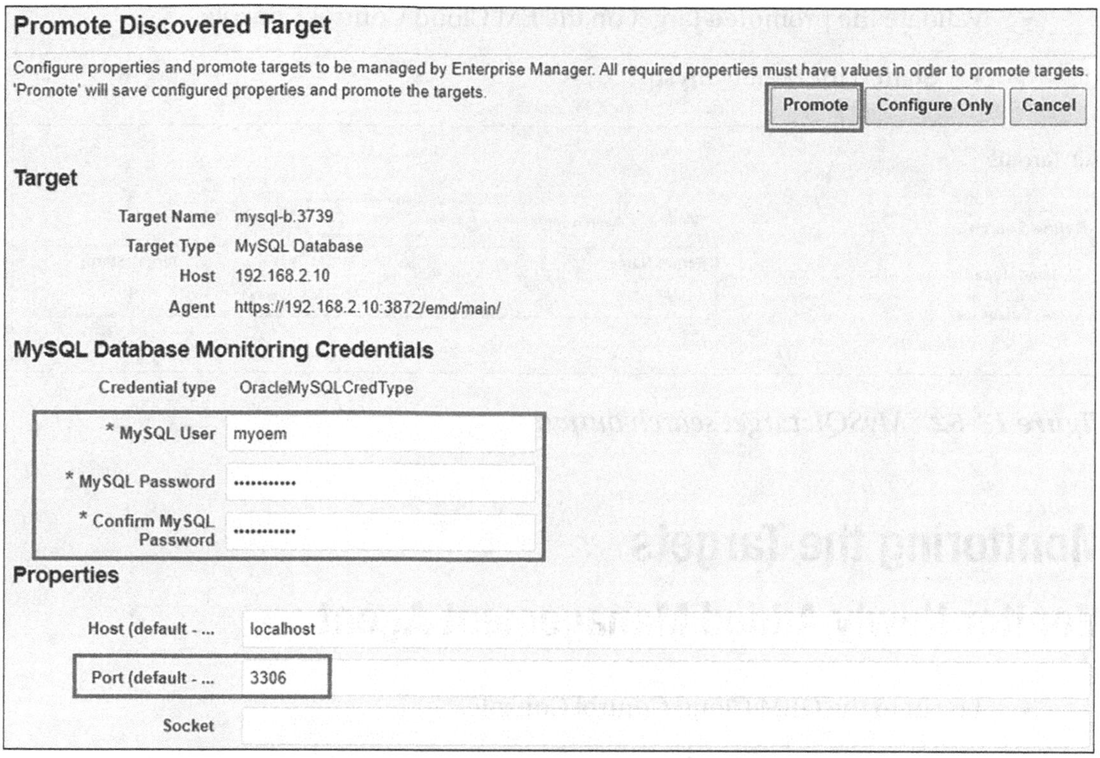

Promote Discovered Target

Configure properties and promote targets to be managed by Enterprise Manager. All required properties must have values in order to promote targets. 'Promote' will save configured properties and promote the targets.

[Promote] [Configure Only] [Cancel]

Target

Target Name	mysql-b.3739
Target Type	MySQL Database
Host	192.168.2.10
Agent	https://192.168.2.10:3872/emd/main/

MySQL Database Monitoring Credentials

Credential type   OracleMySQLCredType

* MySQL User	myoem
* MySQL Password	•••••••••••
* Confirm MySQL Password	•••••••••••

Properties

Host (default - ...	localhost
Port (default - ...	3306
Socket	

Figure 13-50. MySQL User/Password, port for promotion

- Target promotion completed successfully.

Confirmation

Promote Target - Completed Successfully

Hide

[Close]

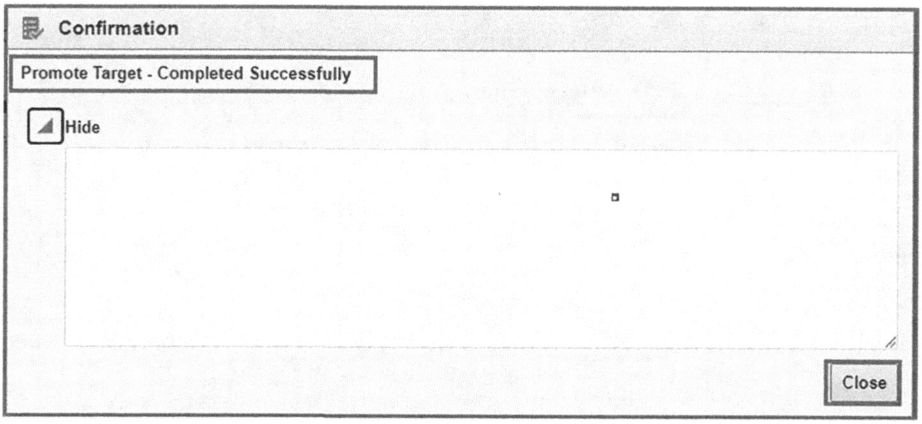

Figure 13-51. Target promotion successful

- Validate the promoted target on the EM Cloud Control Console.

  - Search for target "mysql".

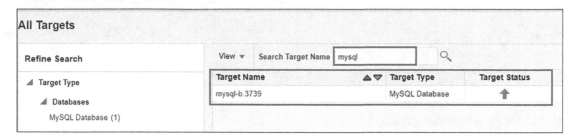

Figure 13-52. *MySQL target search output*

Monitoring the Targets
Monitor Newly Added Management Agent

- Log in to the OEM Cloud Control Console.

- Search for target "192.168.2.10".

- Click on agent target and monitor home page.

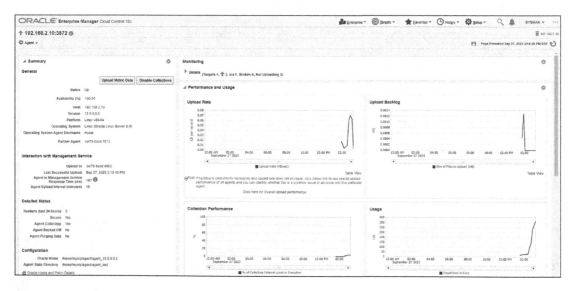

Figure 13-53. *Target Agent home page*

Monitor Newly Added Management Agent Host

- Log in to the OEM Cloud Control Console.

- Search for target "192.168.2.10".

- Click on host target and monitor home page.

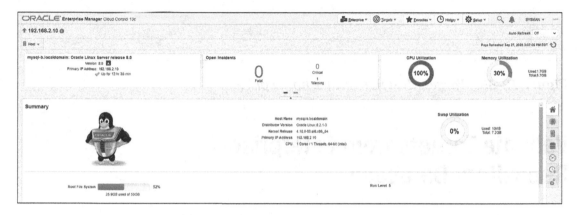

Figure 13-54. *Target Host home page*

Monitor Newly Added MySQL Target

- Log in to the OEM Cloud Control Console.

- Search for target "mysql".

- Click on target and monitor home page.

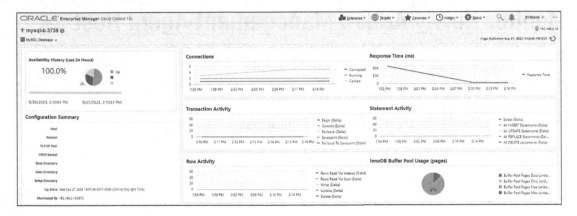

Figure 13-55. *Target MySQL instance home page*

Validate Targets from Enterprise Repository Database

- To verify the agent, host, and other targets from Enterprise Management Repository Database.

- Log in to EMREP database and run the query to find the target details.

```
SQL> select ENTITY_NAME, ENTITY_TYPE, MANAGE_STATUS, PROMOTE_STATUS, EMD_URL from sysman.EM_MANAGEABLE_ENTITIES
  2  where entity_name like '%192.168.2.10%' or entity_name like '%mysql%' order by entity_type;

ENTITY_NAME                                         ENTITY_TYPE              EMD_URL
-------------------------------------------------   --------------------     -------------------------------------
192.168.2.10                                        host                     https://192.168.2.10:3872/emd/main/
192.168.2.10:3872                                   oracle_emd               https://192.168.2.10:3872/emd/main/
192.168.2.10:3872_proxy                             oracle_emd_proxy         https://oel78-base:3872/emd/main/
OraHome1_1_192.168.2.10_6447                        oracle_home              https://192.168.2.10:3872/emd/main/
OraClient19Home1_2_192.168.2.10_5346                oracle_home              https://192.168.2.10:3872/emd/main/
OraClient12Home1_4_192.168.2.10_1863                oracle_home              https://192.168.2.10:3872/emd/main/
OraHome2_3_192.168.2.10_3001                        oracle_home              https://192.168.2.10:3872/emd/main/
agent13c1_5_192.168.2.10_8689                       oracle_home              https://192.168.2.10:3872/emd/main/
mysql-b.3739                                        oracle_omys_database     https://192.168.2.10:3872/emd/main/
```

Figure 13-56. *Target details from SYSMAN repository*

Summary

Oracle Enterprise Manager Cloud Control 13c is a comprehensive management tool to monitor, manage, and administer Oracle databases and non-Oracle environments with plug-ins. Using OEM for the MySQL database plug-in installed on OMS and Management Agents, MySQL systems are discovered as targets and monitored through OEM Cloud Control 13c.

In the next chapter, we will discuss a few critical MySQL errors and how to troubleshoot them.

Summary

CHAPTER 14

MySQL Troubleshooting

Introduction

MySQL database requires troubleshooting skills to manage the database. When working with the database, many challenges and issues are faced during regular support or maintenance activities performed on the database.

MySQL provides client-side error messages and server-side error messages. This chapter is focused on the server side's most common issues and how to troubleshoot them.

Scenario 1: Access denied for user root

MySQL requires a root password to log in to the database, and the root password is a random password generated during the installation.

We will get the following error if the password is lost or never set for root.

```
[root@mysqlhost01 ~]# mysql -uroot -p
Enter password:
ERROR 1045 (28000): Access denied for user 'root'@'localhost' (using password: YES)
```

Stop the MySQL database server.

```
[root@mysqlhost01 ~]# systemctl stop mysqld
```

Restart the MySQL server with the --skip-grant-tables option.

```
[root@mysqlhost01 ~]# mysqld_safe --skip-grant-tables &
[1] 3193217
```

© Y V Ravi Kumar, Arun Kumar Samayam, Naresh Kumar Miryala 2024
Y V Ravi Kumar et al., *Mastering MySQL Administration*, https://doi.org/10.1007/979-8-8688-0252-2_14

```
2023-10-15T09:54:26.925088Z mysqld_safe Logging to '/var/log/mysqld.log'.
2023-10-15T09:54:26.947153Z mysqld_safe Starting mysqld daemon with
databases from /var/lib/mysql
```

[root@mysqlhost ~]# ps -ef|grep -i mysql
```
root      3193217 3178042  0 02:54 pts/2     00:00:00 /bin/sh /usr/bin/
mysqld_safe --skip-grant-tables
mysql     3193363 3193217  0 02:54 pts/2     00:00:02 /usr/sbin/mysqld
--basedir=/usr --datadir=/var/lib/mysql --plugin-dir=/usr/lib64/mysql/
plugin --user=mysql --skip-grant-tables --log-error=/var/log/mysqld.log
--pid-file=/var/run/mysqld/mysqld.pid --socket=/var/lib/mysql/mysql.sock
```

Log in to MySQL as root user (no need to provide password) and reset the password.

[root@mysqlhost01 ~]# mysql -u root

mysql> use mysql;
```
Reading table information for completion of table and column names
You can turn off this feature to get a quicker startup with -A
```

```
Database changed
```

mysql> SET PASSWORD FOR 'root'@'localhost' = '<new password>';
```
Query OK, 0 rows affected (0.00 sec)
```

Bounce the MySQL server and connect using the new password.

[root@mysqlhost01 ~]# systemctl start mysqld

[root@mysqlhost01 ~]# mysql -uroot -p
```
Enter password:
mysql>
```

Scenario 2: MySQL too many connections

MySQL default connection limit is set to 151; this helps to avoid sudden connection bursts, but when there are more extensive connection requirements from the clients, we need to adjust the max_connections parameter; if not, clients will face the errors with too many connections..

```
mysql> SHOW VARIABLES LIKE 'max_connections';
+-----------------+-------+
| Variable_name   | Value |
+-----------------+-------+
| max_connections | 151   |
+-----------------+-------+
1 row in set (0.01 sec)
```

Set /etc/my.cnf to the value desired and restart mysqld.

```
[mysqld]
max_connections = 500
```

```
mysql> SHOW VARIABLES LIKE 'max_connections';
+-----------------+-------+
| Variable_name   | Value |
+-----------------+-------+
| max_connections | 500   |
+-----------------+-------+
1 row in set (0.01 sec)
```

Scenario 3: MySQL Host 'host_name' is blocked

When a mysql database receives too many connections from a host and when it is interrupted, we see the error message host is blocked; max_connect_errors defines the number of interrupted connections before the host is blocked.

The default value for max_connect_errors is 100; this issue is addressed in two folds, increasing the max_connect_errors and minimizing the errors from the host, so this can be minimized.

```
mysql> SHOW VARIABLES LIKE 'max_connect_errors';
+--------------------+-------+
| Variable_name      | Value |
+--------------------+-------+
| max_connect_errors | 100   |
+--------------------+-------+
1 row in set (0.00 sec)
```

Set max_connect_errors to 1000 and restart mysqld.

[mysqld]
max_connect_errors=1000

mysql> SHOW VARIABLES LIKE 'max_connect_errors';
```
+--------------------+-------+
| Variable_name      | Value |
+--------------------+-------+
| max_connect_errors | 1000  |
+--------------------+-------+
1 row in set (0.00 sec)
```

To resume the connections from the blocked host, perform the flush host command once the connection issue is fixed.

[root@mysqlhost01 ~]# mysqladmin   -uroot -p flush-hosts
Enter password:

Scenario 4: [InnoDB] Unable to lock ./ibdata1 error: 11

When we try to start mysqld, we see sometimes the following error message from the log file stating unable to lock.

From the log file /var/log/mysqld.log, an error message is found.

```
[ERROR] [MY-012574] [InnoDB] Unable to lock ./ibdata1 error: 11
```

Check if the data file is being accessed by any process.

[root@mysqlhost01 mysql]# lsof|grep /var/lib/mysql/ibdata1
```
mysqld    3445458                                 mysql    10uW
REG               253,0    12582912  100942068 /var/lib/mysql/ibdata1
mysqld    3445458 3445484 ib_io_ibu              mysql    10uW
REG               253,0    12582912  100942068 /var/lib/mysql/ibdata1
mysqld    3445458 3445485 ib_io_rd-              mysql    10uW
REG               253,0    12582912  100942068 /var/lib/mysql/ibdata1
mysqld    3445458 3445486 ib_io_rd-              mysql    10uW
```

```
REG                253,0    12582912   100942068 /var/lib/mysql/ibdata1
mysqld    3445458 3445487 ib_io_rd-            mysql   10uW
REG                253,0    12582912   100942068 /var/lib/mysql/ibdata1
mysqld    3445458 3445488 ib_io_rd-            mysql   10uW
REG                253,0    12582912   100942068 /var/lib/mysql/ibdata1
mysqld    3445458 3445489 ib_io_wr-            mysql   10uW
REG                253,0    12582912   100942068 /var/lib/mysql/ibdata1
mysqld    3445458 3445490 ib_io_wr-            mysql   10uW
REG                253,0    12582912   100942068 /var/lib/mysql/ibdata1
mysqld    3445458 3445491 ib_io_wr-            mysql   10uW
REG                253,0    12582912   100942068 /var/lib/mysql/ibdata1
```

Check if mysqld process is running.

[root@mysqlhost01 mysql]# ps -ef|grep mysql
```
mysql    3445458          1  0 17:32 ?          00:00:08 /usr/sbin/mysqld
root     3455476 3435542  0 18:49 pts/2        00:00:00 grep --color=auto mysql
```

Kill any mysqld process still running.

[root@mysqlhost01 mysql]# kill -9 3445458

Restart mysqld.

[root@mysqlhost01 mysql]# systemctl restart mysqld

Scenario 5: Fatal error: Please read "Security" section of the manual to find out how to run mysqld as <user>

When setting up replication or running, we might see this error where the user trying to start MySQL is not privileged, so setting up the user in the config file and restarting the database will solve the issue.

Stop mysqld.

[root@mysqlhost01 mysql]# systemctl stop mysqld

Set /etc/my.cnf with the following entry to allow the root user.

```
[mysqld]
user = root
```

Restart mysqld.

```
[root@mysqlhost01 mysql]# systemctl start mysqld
```

Scenario 6: MySQL packet too large

A MySQL packet is a single SQL statement or a row sent to the client or replication bin log; any of these network packets can be failed when the MySQL client or server receives a packet larger than the limit set in the MySQL config.

Default max_allowed_packet is 16M, and max can be set to 1GB.

```
mysql> SHOW VARIABLES LIKE 'max_allowed_packet';
+--------------------+----------+
| Variable_name      | Value    |
+--------------------+----------+
| max_allowed_packet | 16777216 |
+--------------------+----------+
1 row in set (0.01 sec)
```

Set max_allowed_packet to 128M and restart mysqld.

```
[mysqld]
max_allowed_packet=128M
```

```
mysql> SHOW VARIABLES LIKE 'max_allowed_packet';
+--------------------+-----------+
| Variable_name      | Value     |
+--------------------+-----------+
| max_allowed_packet | 134217728 |
+--------------------+-----------+
1 row in set (0.01 sec)
```

Scenario 7: MySQL standby replication stopped due to Error_code: 1032

MySQL replication error Error_code: 1032 is due to the standby server unable to find the row in the master server to replicate. This issue can happen due to many reasons as there is corruption on the row in the source or rows were deleted before standby could replicate the changes.

To fix this issue, please execute the following statements in the slave:

```
mysql> show slave status
*************************** 1. row ***************************
...
Last_SQL_Errno: 1032
Last_SQL_Error: Could not execute Delete_rows event on table inventory.
list; Can't find record in 't', Error_code: 1032; handler error HA_ERR_KEY_
NOT_FOUND; the event's master log mysql-bin.000042, end_log_pos 312
...
1 row in set (0.00 sec)

mysql_slave> STOP SLAVE;
Query OK, 0 rows affected (0.00 sec)

mysql> SET GLOBAL sql_slave_skip_counter = 1;
Query OK, 0 rows affected (0.00 sec)

mysql> START SLAVE;
Query OK, 0 rows affected (0.00 sec);

mysql> show slave status;
```

Note   Ensure replication is working fine; if not, check the details at Last_SQL_ Error: and take necessary action.

Scenario 8: [Repl] Replica I/O for channel: Error connecting to source 'replica_user@10.10.10.10:3306'

MySQL replication fails with the following error when the cluster is set up for the first time and replication is not working.

When using the caching_sha2_password in the replication with NDB cluster is erroring and the solution is to use the legacy authentication method mysql_native_password.

```
[ERROR] [MY-010584] [Repl] Replica I/O for channel '': Error connecting
to source 'replica_user@10.10.10.10:3306'. This was attempt 1/86400, with
a delay of 60 seconds between attempts. Message: Authentication plugin
'caching_sha2_password' reported error: Authentication requires secure
connection. Error_code: MY-002061
```

Set default_authentication_plugin in the /etc/my.cnf to mysql_native_password.

```
[mysqld]
default_authentication_plugin=mysql_native_password
```

[root@mysqlhost01 mysql]# systemctl restart mysqld

Scenario 9: MySQL Error: Out of memory

MySQL database during the startup allocated the buffer memory based on the setting in the my.cnf. When the database could not find the free memory on the server, an out of memory error would occur.

[ERROR] mysqld: Out of memory (Needed 10002030304 bytes)"

Increase the buffer pool size allocated to the database based on the requirement from the applications, while increasing the buffer pool, ensuring the server has required additional memory is available.

```
[mysqld]
Innodb_buffer_pool = 20G
```

Restart the server with new increased memory parameters.

[root@mysqlhost01 mysql]# systemctl restart mysqld

Scenario 10: MySQL Error: Unable to connect to database

When MySQL is enabled with TLS for the data transfer between client and server and when tried to connect, we might see the following error:

ERROR 2026 (HY000): SSL connection error: Unable to get private key.

The solution for this error is ensuring the user is enabled with X509 and the client private and public keys are copied from MySQL server to client machine.

```
[mysql@mysqlhost01~]$ cd  /var/lib/mysql/
[mysql@mysqlhost01~]$ scp -i /var/lib/mysql/client* mysql@<client
machine IP>
```

Scenario 11: MySQL Backup Error: MAIN: [ERROR] unknown variable 'defaults-file=/etc/my.cnf'

When issuing the MySQL Enterprise backup utility command, ensure the **--defaults-file** argument is the immediate argument.

```
[mysql@mysqlhost01~]$ /bin/mysqlbackup --user=mysqlbkpadmin --password
--host=127.0.0.1 --defaults-file=/etc/my.cnf --backup-image=/var/lib/
mysql-files/test_single_file_backup.mbi --backup-dir=/var/lib/mysql-files
backup-to-image
```

ERROR MAIN: [ERROR] unknown variable 'defaults-file=/etc/my.cnf'.

The solution for this error is to ensure the --defaults-file argument is the immediate argument when issuing the mysqlbackup command. For example:

```
[mysql@mysqlhost01~]$ /bin/mysqlbackup --defaults-file=/etc/my.cnf
--user=mysqlbkpadmin --password --host=127.0.0.1 --backup-image=/var/
lib/mysql-files/test_single_file_backup.mbi --backup-dir=/mysqlbkuptmp
backup-to-image
```

713

Scenario 12: MySQL Backup Error: MAIN ERROR: The backup directory does already exist and is not empty. Remove or clear it and retry.

When taking the backup, ensure the backup directory is always cleared and is empty.

ERROR: The backup directory does already exist and is not empty. Remove or clear it and retry.

The solution for this error is to ensure the backup directory is clean and no files exist; please perform the following steps to clean up the backup directory.

```
[mysql@mysqlhost01~]$ /bin/mysqlbackup --defaults-file=/etc/my.cnf
--user=mysqlbkpadmin --password --host=127.0.0.1 --backup-image=/var/
lib/mysql-files/test_single_file_backup.mbi --backup-dir=/mysqlbkuptmp
backup-to-image
```

```
[mysql@mysqlhost01~]$ cd /mysqlbkuptmp/
[mysql@mysqlhost01~]$ rm -rf *
```

Scenario 13: InnoDB Cluster Error: ERROR: New account(s) with proper source address specification to allow remote connection from all instances must be created to manage the cluster.

When performing admin operations on the InnoDB cluster, ensure you always log in as the cluster admin user that has all the necessary admin privileges to manage the InnoDB cluster.

ERROR: New account(s) with proper source address specification to allow remote connection from all instances must be created to manage the cluster.

Dba.checkInstanceConfiguration: User 'root' can only connect from 'localhost'. (RuntimeError)

The solution to this issue is to use the cluster admin user that was created to manage the DB cluster.

mysqlclusteradmin is the InnoDB cluster admin user created to manage the InnoDB cluster.

```
MySQL  localhost:33060+ ssl  JS > dba.checkInstanceConfiguration('mysqlclus
teradmin@localhost:3306')
```

Scenario 14: InnoDB Cluster Error: ERROR: The following tables do not have a Primary Key or equivalent column:

Ensure all tables have a primary key column or an equivalent column as MySQL Group Replication requires all tables to use InnoDB storage engine and have a primary key or an equivalent non-null unique key.

ERROR: The following tables do not have a Primary Key or equivalent column:

To solve this error validating all group replication requirements are met, you will notice the instance configuration is compatible with the InnoDB cluster like the following:

```
MySQL  localhost:33060+ ssl  JS > dba.checkInstanceConfiguration('mysqlclus
teradmin@localhost:3306')
Validating local MySQL instance listening at port 3306 for use in an InnoDB
cluster...

This instance reports its own address as mysql-c:3306
Clients and other cluster members will communicate with it through this
address by default. If this is not correct, the report_host MySQL system
variable should be changed.

Checking whether existing tables comply with Group Replication
requirements...
No incompatible tables detected

Checking instance configuration...
Instance configuration is compatible with InnoDB cluster

The instance 'mysql-c:3306' is valid to be used in an InnoDB cluster.
```

```
{
    "status": "ok"
}
 MySQL  localhost:33060+ ssl  JS >
```

Scenario 15: InnoDB Cluster Error: ERROR: RuntimeError: Cannot add an instance with the same server UUID

ERROR: RuntimeError: Cannot add an instance with the same server UUID (a52a1f b1-3272-11ee-9a0c-080027cf69cc) of an active member of the cluster 'mysql-a:3306'. Please change the server UUID of the instance to add, all members must have a unique server UUID.

Solution to this issue to ensure all servers within the cluster configuration have a unique server UUID

If auto.cnf does not exist, MySQL will automatically create a new file with a new UUID. So to resolve the issue:

- Stop MySQL process on the slave.

- Remove the auto.cnf file from the data directory.

- Start MySQL again on the slave.

```
[mysql@mysqlhost01~]$ systemctl stop mysqld
[mysql@mysqlhost01~]$ ls -ltr *auto*
-rw-r----- 1 mysql mysql  56 Aug  3 21:51 backup-auto.cnf
-rw-r----- 1 mysql mysql  56 Aug  3 21:57 auto.cnf
-rw-r----- 1 mysql mysql 468 Aug  8 22:23 mysqld-auto.cnf
[mysql@mysqlhost01~]$
[mysql@mysqlhost01~]$ mv auto.cnf /mysqlbkuptmp/.
[mysql@mysqlhost01~]$ systemctl start mysqld
[mysql@mysqlhost01~]$
[mysql@mysqlhost01~]$ ls -ltr *auto*
-rw-r----- 1 mysql mysql  56 Aug  3 21:51 backup-auto.cnf
-rw-r----- 1 mysql mysql 468 Aug  8 22:23 mysqld-auto.cnf
```

```
-rw-r----- 1 mysql mysql  56 Aug  9 21:15 auto.cnf
[mysql@mysqlhost01~]$
[mysql@mysqlhost01~]$ cat auto.cnf
[auto]
server-uuid=c89e42ed-3723-11ee-bfd3-080027cf69cc
[mysql@mysqlhost01~]$
```

Scenario 16: InnoDB Cluster Error: ERROR: The instance mysql-c:3306 does not belong to the cluster. ERROR: MYSQLSH 51104: Metadata for instance mysql-c:3306 not found

ERROR: The instance mysql-c:3306 does not belong to the cluster.

ERROR: MYSQLSH 51104: Metadata for instance mysql-c:3306 not found

Cluster.removeInstance: Metadata for instance mysql-c:3306 not found (MYSQLSH 51104)

Solution to this issue to ensure the corresponding metadata is cleaned up from the cluster configuration when removing or re-adding an instance upon failure.

On failed node (mysql-c in this case)

```
 MySQL  localhost:33060+ ssl  JS > \sql
Switching to SQL mode... Commands end with ;
Fetching global names for auto-completion... Press ^C to stop.
 MySQL  localhost:33060+ ssl  SQL > stop group_replication;
Query OK, 0 rows affected (0.0031 sec)
 MySQL  localhost:33060+ ssl  SQL > \js
Switching to JavaScript mode...
 MySQL  localhost:33060+ ssl  JS > dba.dropMetadataSchema();
```

On primary node (mysql-a in this case)

```
MySQL  localhost:33060+ ssl  JS > cluster.addInstance('mysqlclusteradmin@
mysql-c:3306',{recoveryMethod:'clone'});
```

Scenario 17: InnoDB Cluster Error: Dba.getCluster: This function is not available through a session to a standalone instance (metadata exists, instance belongs to that metadata, but GR is not active) (MYSQLSH 51314). Unable to get cluster status post reconnecting

When connecting to the cluster after an outage, we might get errors like the following:

Dba.getCluster: This function is not available through a session to a standalone instance (metadata exists, instance belongs to that metadata, but GR is not active) (MYSQLSH 51314)

To solve this issue, we need to perform a recovery to get the cluster back into a working configuration. Follow the steps listed in the following solution to get the cluster working again.

```
MySQL  localhost:33060+ ssl  JS > var cluster = dba.
rebootClusterFromCompleteOutage();
Restoring the Cluster 'myCluster' from complete outage...

  --output truncated for better visibility

The instance 'mysql-c:3306' was successfully rejoined to the cluster.

The Cluster was successfully rebooted.

MySQL  localhost:33060+ ssl  JS >
MySQL  localhost:33060+ ssl  JS > var cluster=dba.getCluster()
MySQL  localhost:33060+ ssl  JS > cluster.status()
```

Scenario 18: Binlog location is full

When binlog location is full, we can purge them ad hoc to free up the OS space using their purge command on MySQL.

The default expiry of the log file is determined by the binlog_expire_logs_seconds parameter, which is by default set to three days; we can change this to increase the expiry parameter.

To clean up when we run the purge command specifying the binlog to be deleted to free up the space.

```
mysql> SHOW BINARY LOGS;
+----------------+------------+-----------+
| Log_name       | File_size  | Encrypted |
+----------------+------------+-----------+
| binlog.000001  |        499 | No        |
| binlog.000002  |       3138 | No        |

    --output truncated for better visibility

| binlog.000042  |        180 | No        |
| binlog.000043  | 1209711404 | No        |
| binlog.000044  |        358 | No        |
| binlog.000045  |        180 | No        |
+----------------+------------+-----------+
52 rows in set (0.00 sec)

mysql> PURGE BINARY LOGS TO 'binlog.000040';
Query OK, 0 rows affected (0.00 sec)

mysql> SHOW BINARY LOGS;
+----------------+------------+-----------+
| Log_name       | File_size  | Encrypted |
+----------------+------------+-----------+
| binlog.000040  |        180 | No        |
| binlog.000041  |        387 | No        |
| binlog.000042  |        180 | No        |
| binlog.000043  | 1209711404 | No        |
| binlog.000044  |        358 | No        |
| binlog.000045  |        180 | No        |
+----------------+------------+-----------+
13 rows in set (0.00 sec)

mysql> SHOW VARIABLES LIKE 'binlog_expire_logs_seconds';
```

```
+----------------------------+----------+
| Variable_name              | Value    |
+----------------------------+----------+
| binlog_expire_logs_seconds | 2592000  |
+----------------------------+----------+
1 row in set (0.01 sec)
```

Summary

In this chapter, we have discussed some frequent issues and troubleshooting methods for the MySQL server management. There would be many different issues in MySQL database; we have outlined a few to provide context and understanding on how to troubleshoot MySQL database issues.

Index

A

ALTER TABLE statement, 152
Audit logging, 535

B

Backup security, 535
Binary log, 138, 229, 441
Binlog file, 134, 135, 241, 267
Binlog location, 718
Binlog replication, 229
    binary log coordinates, 235
    configuration file changes, 231–233
    databases and tables, 250–253
    data snapshot, 236
    logical backup, 236–238
    prerequisites, 231
    replication_user, 234
    sample reference, 234
    server-id, 231
    SKIP_NETWORKING variable, 234
    source configuration, 241, 243–245
    source/replicas, 231
    start replica statement, 246, 248–250
    UUID, 238, 240, 241
Built-in password, 534

C

Certification Management System, 647
Chain replication topology, 265

Client-side error messages, 705
Cloud storage, 525
cluster.setPrimaryInstance() method, 356
Cold backup, 484
COLUMNS partitioning, 218–220
Compound index, 600, 610–615
Connection error, 713

D

Data-at-rest encryption (DARE), 544
Database auditing, 535, 559
Database security
    audit logging, 535
    authentication, native, 565, 566
    backup, 535
    backup files, 554, 555
    benefits, 533
    changing port, 541, 542
    CLI, 539–541
    DARE/TDE, 544
    encrypting data, 535
    encryption
        enable, 547
        file-per-table tablespace, 548
        master key, 549
        post enable, 547
        pre-checks, 546
        redo log, 549
        SSL/TLS, 550–555
        tablespace, 548
        undo log, 549

© Y V Ravi Kumar, Arun Kumar Samayam, Naresh Kumar Miryala 2024
Y V Ravi Kumar et al., *Mastering MySQL Administration*, https://doi.org/10.1007/979-8-8688-0252-2

Printed in the United States
by Baker & Taylor Publisher Services

Printed in the United States
by Baker & Taylor Publisher Services